MW00782418

The Empathy Gap

The Empathy Gap

Male Disadvantages and the Mechanisms of Their Neglect

William Collins

lps publishing

Publisher's note: While every possible effort has been made to ensure that the information contained in this book is accurate, neither the publisher nor the author can accept responsibility for any errors or omissions, however caused. No responsibility for loss or damage occasioned to any person acting, or refraining from action, as a result of the material in this publication can be accepted by the publisher or the author.

This edition first published 2019

A catalogue record for this book is available from the British Library

ISBN: 9780957168886

Cover design by rawb

lpspublishing.wordpress.com

Contents

Preface

The disadvantages or inequalities suffered by men and boys are substantial and to be found across all aspects of life: education, accidents, health and longevity, domestic abuse, suicide, imprisonment, substance abuse, and as victims of crime, as parents and in respect of the impact of family breakdown. To some this may seem quixotic. "Inequality" is so often linked with women and girls, or with minorities, that it has become an unchallenged axiom that we need not be concerned about males *qua males*. Yet the evidence suggests this is misguided. The observation that senior positions are still occupied more by men than women – politicians, professors, consultants, high court judges – is not apposite. It is not these men who bring down the average male longevity or populate the prisons or swell the ranks of the under-educated. The intersection of men-plus-deprivation is a more virulent combination even than women-plus-deprivation, as the data to be presented herein will demonstrate.

The primary purpose of this book is to present the evidence of male disadvantages, with extensive referencing of sources, drawing on national statistics or data of comparable provenance as much as possible. This review will identify the broad factors that can negatively affect men and boys. Their impact on male health and well-being will be starkly clear across a range of metrics.

However, there is a further purpose. It is not only the evidence supporting claims of male disadvantage which needs to be expounded, but also the reasons for this compelling case being granted so little attention. Indeed, in some quarters, the notion that males may suffer disadvantage will be greeted with incredulity (Flood, 2004), even mockery (Phillips, 2015). The secondary purpose of the book is therefore to expose the mechanisms which distract attention from the male disadvantages, including outright denial. Regrettably, the problem of misinformation will loom large. The author has done his best not to add to it.

An explicatory theory is offered as a unifying principle for both the male disadvantages and their societal neglect. This will be a counter-narrative to the hegemonic paradigm which is usually invoked in the context of the male social position.

For the most part, quoted data will refer to the UK. In fact, most often this will be confined to England and Wales, which reflects how national statistics are collated. However, data from other countries, especially the USA, will also be deployed, either for comparison or when UK data is not available. Despite the predominant focus on the UK, it is likely that the qualitative features of the male disadvantages will be replicated to varying degrees in all other Western or Anglophone countries.

Style Issues

I confess my sin in using “male” and “female” as nouns, at least in the plural “males” and “females”. Blame the English language for having no alternative for the cumbersome “men and boys” and “women and girls”. I apologise to those whose grammatical sensibilities are offended. I use English spelling. However, in quotes from non-UK authors, their original spelling is retained without confusing the text with “(sic)”. Quotes use the single quote. Double quotes are used when making reference to a word or phrase, for example, when critiquing the use of the phrase “male privilege”. I may descend so far as to use scare quotes, for which I am only falsely apologetic. Acronyms are generally explained in each chapter in which they are used, but for readers’ convenience I gather them together after the main text.

Referencing

All references appear at the end of the book, in alphabetical order. The reference may by cited by author or by organisation, e.g., UK Government (listed under “u”). Authors may be cited only by surname, or using both forename and surname, but are always listed in the Refences in alphabetical order of the first author’s surname.

Acknowledgements

I take the usual cop-out that there are too many people to whom acknowledgement is due to attempt to name them all, which has the merit of being true. ‘It is easy to acknowledge, but almost impossible to realize for long, that we are mirrors whose brightness, if we are bright, is wholly derived from the sun that shines upon us’, (C.S.Lewis). Most happily I acknowledge all readers of this book, without whom it would have been pointless.

William Collins, June 2019.

1

The Differently Gendered Society

The last thing one knows in constructing a work is what to put first
Blaise Pascal (1623 - 1662)

1.1 Purpose of this Book

The primary purpose of this book is to present the evidence for men and boys being disadvantaged across a wide range of areas, including education, health, criminal justice, parenthood and safeguarding. Most data apply to the UK, so unless otherwise specified it is the UK to which I refer. Inferences from the situation in this country can then be drawn for other Western and Anglophone nations.

A secondary purpose is to examine why there is currently such a disconnect between what the evidence suggests and the popular and academic perception of the status of males. These two features - the male disadvantages together with the minimal societal concern which they provoke – constitute the Empathy Gap. Both women and men display this muted empathy towards males.

Detailed elucidation of the psychosocial, political, evolutionary, neuroscientific or ideological causes of the empathy gap is beyond the scope of this review. However, later in this introductory chapter I shall present a perspective on the origins of the empathy gap which will, I hope, both motivate and illuminate the chapters which follow.

I permit myself however to voice one opinion immediately: the empathy gap is a remnant of the old gendered mindset. This paradigm holds that men are strong, powerful, agentic, independent and responsible; whereas women are weak, vulnerable, passive, dependent and thus in need of protection, (Friedan, 1963) (Hughes, 2014). On the contrary, the evidence presented here suggests that it is not a person's sex which primarily determines these things, but other factors. Most men are not powerful, and some men are vulnerable, as this book serves to demonstrate. Moreover, women are as generically agentic and powerful as men. That being so, one purpose of this book is to ask, 'why should compassion be unevenly distributed?' From this perspective, the empathy gap may be seen as a major equality issue. However, one of the problems is that the concept of equality has itself become corrupted.

1.2 Equality?

It has become axiomatic that issues of gender equality deserve social and governmental attention. For this reason the UK's Equality Act 2010 was introduced, (UK Government, 2010). It recognises nine protected characteristics. The protected characteristics of greatest relevance in this book are sex and marital status. The other protected characteristics are sexuality, age, race, religion, disability, gender reassignment and pregnancy/maternity. The Act prohibits certain types of conduct relating to discrimination, harassment, victimisation or general disadvantage based on these protected characteristics.

The Act requires public bodies to ensure that people with protected characteristics are not unfairly discriminated against in the context of public service provision and employment. Public bodies are also subject to a general duty to promote equality, eliminate unlawful discrimination and promote good relations across all protected characteristics. Sex is a protected characteristic that applies to both men and women.

It is not appropriate to attempt here a complete account of this large and complex Act. However, an appreciation of some of its key aspects is pertinent because the focus of this book is upon one sex, itself a protected characteristic. Informally, the provisions of the Act are intended, at least ostensibly, to promote fairness. The provisions of the Act will be familiar to many as the basis of claims of discrimination against women or racial minorities. The manifold disadvantages suffered by males in the UK, to be made explicit in this book, raise an obvious question: are these disadvantages in violation of the Equality Act? Is society ignoring the issues associated with equality relating to the protected characteristic of being male? In examining these questions the reader may wish to bear in mind the following extracts from the Act.

Discrimination

Direct discrimination is prohibited: Quote, 'a person A discriminates against another person B if, because of a protected characteristic, A treats B less favourably than A treats or would treat others'. Thus, for example, discrimination on grounds of sex or marital status is prohibited. Exceptions may occur. For example, a man may not complain of being treated differently from a woman if the woman's different treatment resulted directly from her pregnancy or childbirth, which is also a protected characteristic.

Provision of services
'A person concerned with the provision of a service to the public must not discriminate against a person requiring the service by not providing the person with the service'.
Education
The responsible body of a school must not 'discriminate against a pupil (e.g., on grounds of sex, sexuality, religion or race) in the way it provides education for the pupil, in the way it affords the pupil access to a benefit, facility or service, or by excluding the pupil from the school'. This does not prohibit single sex schools.
Public sector equality duty
Quote: 'The need to advance equality of opportunity between persons who share a relevant protected characteristic and persons who do not share it involves having due regard to encouraging persons who share a relevant protected characteristic to participate in public life or in any other activity in which participation by such persons is disproportionately low'. Note how this clause confuses equality of opportunity with equality of outcome by asserting that "the need to advance equality of opportunity" involves encouraging the elimination of inequalities of outcome.
Positive action
Quote: 'If participation in an activity by persons who share a protected characteristic is disproportionately low, the Act does not prohibit taking any action which is a proportionate means of achieving the aim of enabling or encouraging persons who share the protected characteristic to overcome or minimise that disadvantage'. In effect, the Act enables policies aimed at producing equality of outcome.
Marital arrangements
The Act abolished a husband's duty to maintain his wife: Quote, 'The rule of common law that a husband must maintain his wife is abolished'.

The Government's Quick Start Guide to the 2010 Equality Act cautions against "treating everyone the same" in relation to the Public Sector Equality Duty, thus,

> 'The Equality Duty does not require public bodies to treat everyone the same. Rather, it requires public bodies to think about people's different needs and how these can be met. So the Equality Duty does not prevent public bodies providing women-only services - for example, for female victims of sexual violence or domestic violence. Indeed, such services may be necessary in order to ensure women have access to the services they need.' (UK Government Equalities Office, 2011).

In respect of the last issue, the alert reader may be concerned about a principle in which 'equality does not mean treating everyone the same'. This is justified in the legislation by the concept of "need". In the explicit case of provision of services to women due to a need resulting from pregnancy or childbirth, a need which men cannot share, the matter is clear. However, the reader may have a concern that the concept of "need" may permit inequality to be introduced unwittingly if the claimed "need" is not justifiable. This is especially a risk if there is a cultural norm which perceives "need" in a gendered manner. The example of domestic violence is a case in point, because men also suffer from domestic violence and the prevailing dearth of provision for male victims may be a result of a gender-biased perception of need being misaligned with the objective need (addressed further in Chapter 9). The same phenomenon presents a risk of unequal treatment in many areas, for example in respect of criminal justice, as discussed further below and in chapter 8.

There has been considerable focus on gender equality in relation to women and girls. There has been less focus in the past on equality issues for men and boys. This is exemplified by arrangements within the UK Parliament. The relevant All-Party Parliamentary Group is called the 'Women and Equalities Committee' (UK Parliament, 2018a), a title which reflects its focus of concern. The UK government has a 'Minister for Women and Equalities' (UK Government, 2018d) whose remit is policy on women, sexual orientation, transgender equality, and cross-government equality strategy and legislation. The focus on just a subset of the Equality Act's protected characteristics seems peculiarly at odds with the objective of equality. Similarly, the EHRC (Equality and Human Rights Commission) spends only a tiny proportion of its funds on men's issues. In 2010 to 2013 just 2.5% of EHRC grants went towards men's issues, compared with 26% to women, 28% to ethnic minorities, 18% to the disabled and 9% to LGBT (Collins W, 2016).

This skewed focus on some protected characteristics rather than others, particularly the male sex, stems from an implicit assumption about the prevailing direction of inequality. The purpose of this book is to demonstrate, with evidence, that this presumption is largely false.

One of the key issues, to be explored here, is that social disadvantage affects outcomes for males even more than it indubitably affects females. This is consistent with what is typically found in the social sciences: whatever attribute or characteristic is being discussed, the distribution for males will most often have a greater variance than that for females, (Stevens and Haidt, 2017). From this statistical vantage, it is to be expected that the extreme end of the distribution of deprivation will feature males disproportionately. It will be shown that the effects of this are evident in mortality data and other measures. It can be seen by all of us on the streets in the form of rough sleepers, who are predominantly men (Ministry of Housing, Communities and Local Government, 2018c).

This observation is sometimes obscured by a concentration on the other end of the same distribution: the relatively privileged. But the man who is under-educated, or unemployed, or socially isolated, or mentally or physically afflicted, hardly gains much succour from the thought that other men are quite the opposite: in high status employment and in rude good health. Unfortunately, the former are far more numerous, (The Equality Trust, 2016).

It will be seen that this conflict between public perception and factual evidence is played out across the whole range of male disadvantages. Consider, for example, the criminal justice system. Over 95% of prisoners in the UK are men, (Office for National Statistics, 2018a). The trend in the UK since the end of the second world war has been to incarcerate increasing numbers of men, both in absolute numbers and in terms of the percentage of the population. Yet the totality of crime has fallen dramatically since its peak in 1995, the number of crimes in England and Wales having reduced to about one-third of its peak by September 2017 (Office for National Statistics, 2018b). Moreover, the same source shows that violent crime has also been reducing since 1995 (despite the recent rise in knife crime). Why is the number, and the percentage, of men in prison increasing against a background of decreasing crime? And why does this odd anomaly not receive greater public attention?

It will be shown in Chapter 8 that men are more readily incarcerated, and for longer, than women, for the same offence category. In contrast, there is a strong lobby to imprison fewer women, exemplified by Baroness Jean Corston's 2007 Corston Report, whose dictum was 'equality does not mean treating everyone the same', (Corston, 2007). In the context of crime and punishment, one wonders why not. Is not the equality of all before the law a sacred principle? It seems no longer. The lobby against imprisonment of women has now succeeded in becoming a Government policy to treat the two sexes differently in respect of punishment, emphasising rehabilitation and compassion based on the disadvantages which lead women into crime to motivate a presumption against imprisonment of women. But, by omission, none of this applies to men.

Prisoners are not a representative cross-section of society. Overwhelmingly, prisoners, of either sex, are disadvantaged, often in multiple ways. Self-harm and suicide rates are horribly high in prisons. There is also a far larger number of older male prisoners, over 60, than there used to be. As a result, the non-self-inflicted death rate in men's prisons is also rising alarmingly. Moreover, these older male prisoners are particularly disadvantaged, often by limited mobility, or even dementia (Hill, 2017). The contrast between the way our society treats men and women is becoming greater, but this excites no societal concern. This is the empathy gap.

1.3 What is the Origin of the Empathy Gap?

This book will present an overview of the male disadvantages, or inequalities, in education, health and longevity, suicide, criminal justice, parental rights, homelessness, and as victims of violence. In tackling a subject of such enormous scope, it is not possible in a single work to be truly comprehensive. Nevertheless, the evidence of male disadvantage across this broad range of issues is voluminous and compelling. It is inevitable that the subject matter will place this work in antithesis with prevailing perceptions which may be represented, or perhaps caricatured, by terms and phrases such as "patriarchy", or "male privilege", or "hegemonic masculinity" – in other words, feminist theory. Such ideas will hardly seem an appropriate description of men and boys as presented here.

The attempt is sometimes made to resolve the conflict between the evidence of male disadvantages and these gender-theoretical ideas by appeal to explanations such as "patriarchy hurts men too" or "toxic masculinity". It is not the primary purpose of this book to discuss gender-theoretical ideas. But it would be disingenuous to pretend that the subject matter of the book is not an implicit challenge to these prevailing "explanations". In this context, it is important to note that these proffered explanations are always a variant on "it's men's own fault". Well, maybe it is, in part – but which men? And do women have no role in shaping society and society's impositions upon individuals, including upon men?

Underlying the insistence on the relevance of the above gender-theoretical terms is a mindset – or perhaps an argument of convenience - that men form an undifferentiated, monolithic section of humanity: that all men are the same. From such an improbable axiom, no sense can follow. If patriarchy does indeed hurt men too, which men constitute the patriarchy and which men are hurt? Not the same men, that is the salient fact. If the gender-political mantra were re-expressed as "men in power do no favours to disadvantaged men" then I think the two sides would find themselves much closer to agreement. That being so, is it not merely misleading to concentrate upon an identity group defined by being male?

This is a peculiar thing to assert in a book whose purpose is specifically *male* disadvantages. It is as well to expose the paradox that one faces in countering an invalid, but insistent, identity group based critical theory. One seems forced to adopt an equal and opposite identity group response, even though one knows it to be just as invalid. It is not "all men this" and "all women that". The only morally justifiable, and socially constructive, stance is to recognise that individuals are to be judged on their own merits as individuals, not defined by a tribal allegiance. Unfortunately, even that seemingly innocuous statement is now regarded as reprehensible by the dominant lobby on "identity" issues.

Some will see any discussion of male disadvantages as an attempt to gain a victimhood bonus, a mere play in the victimhood Olympics. This is not only wrong but it would be an act of folly for anyone to try to claim victimhood benefit for men as a class. The empathy gap itself precludes the possibility. Men as a class have been disenfranchised from the empathy needed to make victimology applicable.

This book does not set out to prove that all men are disadvantaged. The author himself has suffered none of the disadvantages he discusses. Rather, the implicit purpose of this book is to demonstrate a negative: that it is false to claim that all men are privileged. In that form the book aligns with an anti-identity-group perspective, not a pro-male-identity-group perspective. This is a crucial distinction which I would urge the reader to bear in mind.

The main purposes of the book are thus to provide empirical evidence of the many male disadvantages – albeit not all suffered by all men - and to provide examples of how these are neglected, minimised and hidden away, thus establishing the existence of an empathy gap. The inevitable question is: whence cometh this empathy gap?

On the one hand, to propose an explicit theory regarding the origin of the empathy gap is to risk prejudicing the main objective, namely to convince the reader that the empathy gap is real and pervasive. Any proffered theory regarding the origin of the empathy gap must be more tentative and less well established than the reality of the empathy gap itself, the latter being more closely tied to empirical evidence. There is a danger, then, of weaknesses in the explicatory theory being conflated with weaknesses in the case for the empathy gap itself.

However, it is of some importance to propose an explicatory set of ideas because a subsidiary purpose of the book is to examine the mechanisms by which the male disadvantages are tolerated and neglected. Consequently, I offer a set of perspectives on the issue with this end in mind. In so doing, I emphasise that the empirical support for the existence of the empathy gap remains valid even if the hypotheses prove unconvincing. The advantage of offering a theoretical perspective, however limited, is that it will form a conceptual backcloth to the tsunami of facts that will follow in the other chapters.

The first challenge I present to the reader is couched in a negative. It is often the case in science that, before progress can be made, the shortcomings of existing ideas must be accepted, (Kuhn, 2012). There is a negative to be demonstrated. The challenge to the reader is to critique currently dominant gender-theoretical ideas as explanations of the empathy gap. The reader may like to consider how well concepts like "patriarchy hurts men too", or "male privilege" or "traditional or hegemonic or toxic masculinity" perform as explanations of the disadvantages discussed, especially when confronted with the specific examples of how these inequalities are neglected. As observed above, all these ideas reduce to variants of "it's men's own fault".

Consider, then, whether "it's men's own fault" is itself a sentiment essentially based on the empathy gap. The dismissal of material disadvantage based on the victim-blaming stance that "he brought it on himself" is intrinsically lacking in empathy. This class of proffered explanations for the empathy gap is therefore a manifestation of the empathy gap. And it is logically invalid as an explanation of the empathy gap to appeal to ideas which implicitly assume the empathy gap. If there is an empathy gap, blaming men will not cut it as an explanation. Blaming men ***is*** the empathy gap.

As an example of how blaming men for their own disadvantage works in practice, consider male suicide. In the UK between 3 and 4 times more men than women kill themselves. This is now widely recognised and does receive some attention, for example in debates in Parliament on International Men's Day, (UK Parliament, 2017a). However, it is invariably the case that the reason for men's high suicide rate is blamed on some variant of pathological masculinity, or men not being in touch with their emotions, or men being reluctant to talk or to seek help, etc. All these explanations fall into the "it's men's own fault" category. And yet male suicide is known to peak after separation/divorce, especially if child contact is involved, as discussed further in Chapter 18. Is it these men's own fault that the Family Courts operate as they do? Would it be acceptable to blame a woman's suicide entirely on generic shortcomings in female behaviour? Or would it be a glaring admission of lack of compassion? In the context of female suicide we will suspect social and personal environment to be at least a contributory factor. Men do talk, but society does not listen. Society does not want men to talk, as the reaction to this book will no doubt testify.

Male suicide rates, longer prison sentences for men, shorter male life expectancy, men as rough sleepers, boys' failure in education, men's alienation from their children: I suggest it is unhelpful to "explain" these phenomena solely in terms which reduce to "it's men's own fault". In reality, men are impacted by the constraints and obligations imposed on them by society and the State. If you prick us, do we not bleed? But society requires men to be agentic, autonomous and self-reliant, and hence the societal prejudice is that any problems from which men suffer can only be self-induced. Such problems are a measure of a man's failure to perform; not a justification for assistance, but an indication that he needs to get his act together. It is not men upon whom society should be squandering resources to assist. This message is conveyed to men by the simple expedient of ensuring that resources which specifically preference men are a relative rarity, whilst those targeted at women and girls abound. The message is conveyed by the very evident empathy gap.

The readiness with which victim blaming has been adopted to rationalise male disadvantages is facilitated by the empathy gap. We are content with explanations which reduce to "it's men's own fault" only because of the empathy gap. Society has a deep-seated need to continue to believe in men's self-sufficiency, and the empathy gap is a psychological disposition, in both sexes, which facilitates it. This has always been the case. It formed a key psychological underpinning of the gendered society. The move away from the gendered society, had it been truly egalitarian, should have involved dissolution of this empathy gap every bit as much as it needed to involve women's greater independence and entry into the professions. Instead the changes have all concentrated upon the latter, whilst the empathy gap and the related male disadvantages have deepened. Indeed, it is the existence of the empathy gap which has encouraged this skewed approach.

1.3.1 The Nine Factors Underlying the Empathy Gap

I offer nine factors as an explanation of how the empathy gap arises and is then deepened. I make no claim for originality, except perhaps in manner of expression. Highly controversial to some, incomprehensible to others, to many the ideas set down here have in recent years become a familiar perspective.

I emphasise three things. Firstly, this view of gender relations is inevitably highly simplified and incomplete. Human behaviour is far more varied and nuanced than can be captured by such an overarching theory. Secondly, there is, of course, a more familiar and radically different perspective on gender, namely the feminist perspective. The ideas presented below are, in almost every respect, diametrically opposed to the feminist position. My contention is that the ideas below provide a far more coherent and convincing account of the male disadvantages, and their neglect, than feminist theories – but the reader shall decide. Nevertheless, no one having the monopoly on truth, and human affairs being so complex, it is likely that some aspects of the feminist view will be valid. Much of the dispute relates to human motivations, which can never be pinned down and put under the microscope as one might like. However, the uncontested and unfettered feminist perspective is, I insist, intellectually fraudulent, divisive and currently proving socially corrosive. A radically different alternative is a long overdue corrective. Both are in dire need of empirical dissection.

Lastly, and most importantly, the reality of the male disadvantages, and the empathy gap, do not depend upon the veracity of this perspective. The rest of the book will stand independently of this gender theory. I offer it mainly to provide a narrative thread through the rest of the book, and a possible explicative basis. This is offered in the spirit of hypothesis. The scientific method consists, after all, of conjecture and refutation. To all but the logical purists we may rephrase that as "conjecture and confirmation". Hence, these ideas are offered as conjecture. Unlike the rest of the book, which is heavy with source references, I offer little in the way of support. That is the nature of hypothesis. Its credibility, or otherwise, rests upon its success in providing an explicative basis for what follows: the male disadvantages and their neglect. That is not to say that these ideas, essentially those of the mainstream men's human rights movement (MHRM), could not be the subject of direct empirical investigation. They could, and should. It is long overdue. Initially I make just a brief statement introducing each of the nine factors. In the sections which follow I expand further upon some of these matters.

Matricentrism and Gynocentrism

Gynocentrism is the mindset which promotes a dominant focus on women. It is of ancient evolutionary lineage but has been culturally enhanced, both historically and recently. It is culturally transmitted and socially reinforced. Here I shall emphasise the distinction between the ancient gynocentrism which results from evolution, and its later cultural enhancements, by referring to the former as "matricentrism". This terminology is appropriate because the evolved condition relates to a preferencing, not of women *per se*, but of mothers as surrogates for their children. Matricentrism is an evolutionary adaptation which is positive in the sense that Homo sapiens would probably not exist without it. I shall reserve the term "gynocentrism" to mean the cultural intensifications of evolved matricentrism. The historical social benefit of this intensified gynocentrism is debatable and its current social effects are destructive.

Matricentrism/gynocentrism is a psychological asymmetry in the perception of the two sexes. Despite the huge societal changes over the last century, the psychologies of both men and women are still controlled by sentiments of female vulnerability, need of protection, and preferencing by society. This contrasts with assumed male independence, strength, autonomy and lack of neediness. This psychological orientation involves an attitude of deference by men towards women. It leads to a flow of resources, whether material or other forms of preferencing, from male to female. From the man's perspective, matricentrism is manifest by what Belinda Brown has referred to as "responsive masculinity", (Brown, 2019b): an emotionally based inclination towards a provider role as a precursor to nurturing and paternal investment. The relationship between this disposition and the human pair bond is obvious (and expounded further below). It leads to women's needs controlling men's efforts. What women say is good becomes men's definition of good – a ceding of moral authority to women. This is the most important feature of gender relations, but it goes unnoticed by feminists because they place patriarchy in its stead.

Matricentrism preferences women only as a surrogate for the child. The evolutionary function (I dare not say "purpose") of matricentrism is reproductive success. Evolution wastes no more sentiment on females than upon males. Evolution favours only genetic transmission, manifest in successful child raising. But the mechanism by which evolution enacts matricentrism is very much via sentiment. Indeed, a whole constellation of emotions are involved in attracting a man to a woman and keeping him there.

Whilst there have been enormous changes in the externalities in the last 50 years, for example women's entry into the professions, our underlying psychology has not kept pace. Society, which consists of both sexes, continues to police conformance with the gender scripts which promote matricentrism and its enhanced form, gynocentrism. The cultural intensification of gynocentrism, particularly that due to feminism, is (I contend) socially disbeneficial, divisive, and a contributory cause of male disadvantages and their neglect.

Critics sometimes misrepresent this perspective as "men's rights activists believe that women oppress men". This is actually a projection of the feminist theory of patriarchy: that men oppress women. But the idea of matricentrism/gynocentrism does not posit any conspiracy, only a set of psychosocial proclivities, in both sexes, which promote preferencing of women and hence, inevitably, the disadvantaging of men. It is a sociodynamic phenomenon, not a conspiracy, and the word "oppression" is not appropriate, though it could become so if this dynamic continues to amplify.

Male Utility / Male Disposability

"Be a man!" is an exhortation which carries a meaning which every man will understand. It is a reminder to a man that he has fallen short of expectations and that he needs to pull his socks up, pronto. Say to a woman "be a woman!" and she will merely look at you bemused. She may simply say, "I *am* a woman" and wonder what you were getting at. Absorb the lesson of those different reactions and you will understand what is meant by the aphorism 'women are human beings, men are human doings'. Women are valued in themselves, not for services they are required to perform. Male utility is Brown's "responsive masculinity", translated from the individual recipient to society as a whole, although it has its psychological origin in the biology of reproduction. Men's trivial biological investment in the process of creating, and nurturing, a baby puts them in a different category from women, whose investment is huge. Men achieve evolutionary worth by services rendered after birth. This imbues evolutionarily successful men with a psychology oriented towards being useful. Hence, men are human doings. This is male utility. Note how this is the flipside of matricentrism. Men's utility for the benefit of women is an expectation under evolved matricentrism: the inclination to give is matched by the expectation to receive. A man's right to be regarded by society as "a man" is dependent upon utility. To quote Geoff Dench (1996),

> 'A man who does not become a provider in one way or another fails to become a proper adult, and faces reduced life chances in almost every dimension. The community cares little about such men, because they make little input to it; and in turn this renders them prone to self-neglect.'

The hypothesis of male disposability is the extreme case of utility. Matricentrism gives us "women and children first", which is virtually explicit male disposability. War is the obvious example of male disposability. But "disposability" need not literally mean death. More generally it may refer to the potential harms arising from the relative disadvantage to men originating from matricentrism/gynocentrism. Hence, male disposability is essentially a corollary of gynocentrism rather than an entirely separate phenomenon. It is the inevitable adjunct of gynocentrism: preferencing women is the disfavouring of men. The institution of male disposability is facilitated by societal equanimity at male disadvantage, even at the risk of death. The empathy gap is precisely this equanimity. Just as gynocentrism is a psychological orientation of both men and women, so also is male disposability. Men willingly acquiesce to their own disposability.

Respect and Shame

Why would a man willingly collaborate with his own disposability? As always with altruistic proclivities, male disposability is motivated in the individual by an emotional reward, in this case the social emotion connected with the respect a man garners for fulfilling society's expectations. This is why, I presume, men are particularly sensitive to respect (or honour). Men's sensitivity to perceptions of honour is now mocked, but its function as a facilitator of disposability, and hence of gynocentrism, goes unremarked. This bears repetition: if men were not so concerned about respect (or honour) they would be less inclined to accept their disposability, for which respect is the reward, and as a result gynocentrism would flounder. The disrespect for men which feminism promulgates may therefore be the instrument of its demise.

Women are not required to be disposable and hence have less need to be motivated by respect or honour. But winning respect is a powerful motivator for men. Equally, the withdrawal of society's respect in the form of shaming is extremely psychologically harmful to men. This is why men accused of sexual misdemeanours frequently kill themselves, even if the accusation is entirely false. It is why men subject to being "white feathered" during World War 1 would inevitably remember the fact for the rest of their lives (sometimes to the surprise of women). It is also why the heresy being expressed in these pages may be in the heads of many but spoken by very few. To speak against feminism or gynocentrism is to invite severe social censure, which few wish to risk.

Lack of Male In-Group Preference

Men as a class have little, or no, in-group preference. This frustrates any gender-specific movements by men. In contrast, women do display in-group preference and readily form gender-specific groups to promote their interests. This is apparent in the uncountable number of charities and support groups specific to women and girls, but the relative rarity of such charities and support groups specific to men or boys. Even those which exist are generally run mostly by women. In part this reflects the skew in concern resulting from gynocentrism and male disposability.

Feminism

Matricentrism/gynocentrism, male disposability and lack of male in-group preference are all psychological characteristics. But when we turn to feminism we pass from the psychological to the political. I use the term "feminism" as an umbrella term for the highly influential lobby advocating for women and girls. There is no lobby advocating for men and boys which could currently be described as influential. The gynocentric psychological disposition lends great strength to the lobby for women and girls, but at the same time tends to delegitimise any similar claims for men and boys. In any case, the lack of male in-group preference frustrates a similar strong lobby for men and boys. As a result, the perception that women and girls deserve special assistance, stemming from gynocentrism, has been hugely amplified by successful lobbying and positioning. In turn, the relentless focus on claimed harms to, or needs of, females further enhances gynocentrism itself. Thus, gynocentrism and feminism are in a positive feedback loop, both reinforcing and amplifying each other. In contrast, men and boys do not deserve any particular consideration because male utility/disposability demotes such concern, and lack of in-group preference among men ensures there is no collective push-back. Feminism rationalises the absence of focus on males by claiming that they are already powerful and privileged. But the claim of male power and privilege is a delusion which provides spurious legitimacy to inclinations actually arising from gynocentrism and male disposability. That male power and privilege are delusions is evidenced by the male disadvantages: the subject of this book.

Patriarchy

Patriarchy is a central concept in feminist theory. Here I present, extremely briefly, the feminist idea of patriarchy. It exists in two forms, in the domestic world and in the external world of affairs, though the two are aspects of the same phenomenon. To feminists, patriarchy is a conspiracy amongst men to oppress women for their own advantage and satisfaction. Men oppress women domestically by lording it over them, by dominating them physically, sexually and financially. The traditional gendered world of affairs, business and politics, was a male world from which women were largely excluded. This was, to feminists, obviously a form of oppression of women, and its purpose was to maintain male control over finance. Power and control are the essence of man in feminist patriarchy theory. Under patriarchy theory, men's resource provision to the family – even if very hard won through endless back-breaking labour – is recast as financial oppression. Given such an opinion, it naturally follows that feminists' priority would be to make women financially independent of men. They would also want to make men unnecessary in raising a family. Both these objectives follow from the feminist assumption regarding the nature of the human pair bond, namely that it is simple outright oppression. Financial independence and ejection of men from the family home are the central objectives feminism has always pursued. The rather impressive constancy of these objectives, passed from generation to generation of feminists, arises because of their fundamental relationship with the principle credo of feminism: the oppressive patriarchy.

It is never explained why men should want to oppress women in this way. Even assuming all men are psychopaths is insufficient to explain it. Psychopaths are not noted for spending their lives in hard toil to provide hard-won resources to those whom they are supposed to be oppressing. They would surely be drummed out of the psychopaths' union for such behaviour. As feminists are generally hard-line social determinists, they can have no recourse to evolution to explain this behaviour. They regard patriarchal oppression as a learnt behaviour, passed from the current patriarchy to the next generation. That those young men who display the most reprehensible behaviour, most similar to the patriarchal caricature, are those raised with minimal exposure to adult male influence is one of the many embarrassing problems with feminist theory which we are not supposed to mention.

It is only possible to believe in patriarchy theory if you are profoundly ignorant of history, or wilfully distort history into the predetermined shape of this ideological conviction. It is also necessary to be able to distort the present into this shape, which appears to be achievable simply by the exercise of prejudice.

The views being presented here are sometimes accused of being a conspiracy theory. But I hypothesise no conspiracy, only a social dynamic with evolved elements. Feminist patriarchy theory is, on the other hand, explicitly a conspiracy theory. There *is* such a thing as patriarchy, but it is not what the feminists believe. I discuss an alternative view of patriarchy below.

Misandry

Misandry may be defined as dislike of, contempt for, or even hatred of, men, or ingrained prejudice against men. It is manifest by the bad-mouthing of men and the representation of men as stupid or vile. Misandry is both a psychological disposition which motivates certain feminists, and also a methodology which feminism deploys. By depicting men as villainous it renders men as undeserving, hence giving further succour to the gynocentric mindset, which, in turn, promotes feminism. Denigration is the handmaiden of discrimination.

Identity Politics

I have no intention of straying into general politics. The scope of this work is already great enough. However, the part which wider politics now plays in gender issues is too important to go completely unremarked. Identity politics places primacy on the identity group to which an individual belongs and makes subsidiary that individual's personal nature, biography or competence. Identity politics is ostensibly promoting social justice. But the approach taken in this philosophy is that entire identity groups are "owed" due to past oppressions, whilst other identity groups are to be suppressed due to their past guilt in being oppressors. It is identity politics which has made it acceptable to disparage, and discriminate against, white males, something which is now done openly in seats of power or influence. It is identity politics which has promoted the abusive and discriminatory expression "male, pale and stale". Identity politics is intrinsically divisive, though it wears the clothes of diversity. This truth is captured in the aphorism, "diversity is divisity".

There is nothing wrong with diversity *per se*. What is pernicious is giving primacy to identity group membership. At one time an attitude in which a person's sex or race was deemed unimportant, even unnoticed, was generally regarded as the morally correct orientation, avoiding sexism and racism. Under identity politics, this attitude is recast as sexism or racism. Under identity politics, not only are you obliged to notice a person's sex and race (and other identity characteristics), but you are obliged to treat people differently according to their identity group: "equality does not mean treating everyone the same". The two schools of thought therefore transpose sexism and the avoidance of sexism, ditto racism, etc. Identity politics is therefore a form of moral corruption.

To identity politicians, Martin Luther King's dictum that one should judge a man by the content of his character not by the colour of his skin is a racist opinion. The relationship of identity politics to gender is that gender (or sex) forms an identity characteristic, and feminism provides the archetype of an identity political stance. Their further relationship lies in both being connected to so-called left-wing politics, for example the Labour Party in the UK. An excellent exposition of the operation of identity politics in this context has been given by Ben Cobley (2018). The key feature of identity politics is not compassion for members of the identity groups apparently favoured, but a cynical exploitation of humans' capacity for envy and resentment in order to harvest political power via promoting division. This applies to feminism in particular and identity politics in general. The submerging of the individual, and the promotion of identity group membership to be of primary significance, results in conflict between different identity groups. Individual identity groups are also prone to schism ("I'm more oppressed than you") and escalating division. This can be seen in practice throughout the West. A catastrophic outcome of identity politics is inevitable, (Bradford R. , 2019).

Political Correctness

Politics is the pursuit of power. Power is the ability to impose your will on others. Power is achieved by maximising the number of your allies, or those who will vote for you. Human societies contain an in-built mechanism for promoting cooperation and harmony: a moral sense. By this means, almost everyone in a given, stable culture will agree on what behaviour is desirable and what is reprehensible. It follows that the shared moral sense is a very effective medium through which to attain influence, and hence political power. If a political opinion can be given the aura of a moral obligation, then a fast track to winning hearts and minds has been achieved. Once this has happened, it is no longer publicly acceptable to question the opinion, because it is no longer perceived as an opinion but as a moral imperative. This is political correctness. It is a form of propaganda and a form of social control. A society which has become infected with political correctness has already had some of its freedoms removed. An antidote to political correctness is freedom of speech. One of the symptoms of endemic political correctness is the erosion of freedom of speech. Political correctness is a tool deployed by all forms of identity politics. The claimed oppression of the favoured identity group is readily presented as a moral issue, which can then be used to lever political power. I will say no more about identity politics or political correctness, but both play a major part in feminism and the operation of the feminist State.

1.3.2 Discussion of the Factors Underlying the Empathy Gap

1.3.2.1 Matricentrism, Male Disposability and the Role of Emotions

"Matricentrism" may sound like a pejorative term. But the correct perspective on matricentrism – the original evolutionary form of gynocentrism - is that it is a psychological orientation, in both sexes, which facilitates the formation of pair bonds. The feminist insistence on patriarchy theory has blinded us to the obvious: the man's role in the pair bond is altruistic. Instead, feminists present the male inclination to pair bond as a wish to dominate and control women. It is understandable that some women might misunderstand a man's motivation. Matricentrism creates a profound asymmetry in the psychologies of the two sexes. This issue is of such central importance that a short digression is in order.

A discussion of what underlies human social behaviour would be too long a digression, even if the author were capable of writing it. One of its major features is the extremely large, cooperative, societies which humans form. It is particularly noteworthy that these large social structures do not depend upon kinship. Two phenomena contributing to human social behaviour can be distinguished: reciprocal altruism and genetic altruism. The first of these does not depend upon kinship. Instead Homo sapiens have the capacity to act in an apparently altruistic manner towards another human in the hope and expectation that he (or she) will be the recipient of similar largesse at some future date. Such behaviour requires sufficient cognitive capacity to be able to conceptualise the future, and to recognise individuals and remember their past behaviour. This type of social cooperation is essentially enlightened self-interest: it is based on the ability to conceive of reward integrated over time. It requires intelligence to exceed a certain minimum and the ability to delay gratification (accepting a cost now for a greater reward later). Some humans are more skilled at this behavioural practice than others. It is probably no coincidence that prisoners have IQs extremely skewed to low intelligence.

Reciprocal altruism can, at least in part, be modelled using game theory. However, a complete understanding necessarily involves appreciating the part played by the social emotions, such as shame and guilt, (Boyd and Richerson, 2009), as well as other forms of socially imposed retributions. These play a crucial role in controlling the prevalence of "free loaders" who might be inclined to take the benefits of a cooperative society without making the required contributions in turn. Thus, shame and social disgrace become powerful factors by which individuals are coerced to obey the diktats of society. Unfortunately, game theoretical modelling shows that any such diktats may be stabilised as long as the punishment of renegades is sufficiently severe, (Boyd and Richerson, 1992). Thus, a stable cooperative society need not be very nice: it might be a tyranny. Even tyrannous norms can be stabilised by shaming and social sanction. The success of a culture, defined as its support for extremely large numbers of people over very long periods of time, does not require it to be nice: it might be monstrous. The achievement of a decent culture which offers its people a reasonable degree of personal freedom requires features beyond what mere game theoretical modelling can address (and is also beyond my present ambition to elucidate).

But in addition to the form of enlightened self-interest known as reciprocal altruism, there is also what I am tempted to call "genuine altruism". This occurs when a mother or a father sacrifice themselves to save a child. Clearly this is not reciprocal altruism: the dead parent is no longer in a position to reap future benefit. Such behaviours are stabilised by evolutionary benefit. It is the gene line of the father which benefits from his proclivity to protect his child, even if it means his own death. It is a most intriguing phenomenon: the selfishness of genes leads to the ultimate lack of selfishness of the organism.

By what means is a father motivated to sacrifice himself to save his child? Does he think coolly to himself, as his child flounders, drowning, "I must maximise the chances of my gene line persisting by being willing to die"? No, the motivation is mediated entirely by emotion. The man's susceptibility to such an emotional pull has been inculcated in him by evolution. The genes of men who callously allowed their progeny to die due to their lack of care did not end up well represented in the gene pool. Evolution positively selects for parents who make the care of their children their paramount concern, even if it might mean self-sacrifice. This is not hard to understand. But the implications are profound as regards innate behaviours.

The purpose of this digression is to emphasise the central importance of innate emotional orientation. Such innate emotional proclivities are the means by which our genetic inheritance influences our individual behaviour. And we must allow that our genes can manipulate our behaviour, and hence influence our reproductive success, or else how would they have evolved? To feminists this is "biologism", and heresy. To me it is little more than common sense. The point I have been approaching, rather laboriously, is that matricentrism is an evolved trait. That, at least, is my hypothesis. Moreover, matricentrism is seated in the human emotional psyche.

In other words, the pair bond is mediated by emotion. Can this possibly be controversial? But emotions are, at least in part, the servants of genetic inheritance. The emotions surrounding sexuality are certainly an important part of this, though lust is not the only concomitant of sexual longing. More importantly, there is more to the emotional basis of the pair bond than just sex. The importance of sex diminishes significantly in marriages which persist long term. The man is emotionally bonded to the woman by more than sex. The keen desire in a man to be a resource provider and help-mate is emotionally situated. It is an altruistic proclivity, dreadfully maligned by the feminist theory of hegemonic patriarchy. Matricentrism subsumes a whole constellation of emotions underlying the pair bond, but their purpose is not "oppression".

Because matricentrism originates from the pair bond, whose evolutionary significance is (inevitably) successful reproduction, matricentrism can also be interpreted as a family-centric theory. This is extremely important. Nature has no particular interest in favouring females. Evolution is driven entirely by reproductive success. In that sense, nature cares about children. Whilst matricentrism directly favours females, this is only because females are a proxy for children. The woman, as mother, is a proxy for her children. This perspective may soften the apparently pejorative nature of the idea of matricentrism, which, in its original evolved form, is indirect infant-centricity.

It is appropriate that the word is gender-skewed because the pair bond is itself asymmetric (one sex gives, the other receives) and this asymmetry is ultimately based in biology (only one sex gives birth).

1.3.2.2 Gynocentrism

Gynocentrism is derived from matricentrism by processes of cultural intensification. But it is more than just intensification. Crucially it marks a corruption of matricentrism, whose "purpose" (evolutionary function) was to direct care and resources to children. Gynocentrism misappropriates the benefits intended for children. Whereas in matricentrism the woman is a surrogate for the child (actual or potential), in gynocentrism the child disappears from the picture. In gynocentrism, the directed flow of care and resources towards females has become divorced from its matricentric function. Under gynocentrism the preferencing of females is perceived as a good in itself, though it has become decoupled from its evolutionary "purpose".

Gynocentrism is culturally created by enhancement of natural matricentrism. In recent decades, feminism has been the mechanism by which gynocentrism has been enhanced (and *vice-versa*). But this is not the first time in history that this has occurred. Peter Wright (2014) refers to the intensification of naturally evolved matricentrism ("gynocentrism 1:0" in his terminology) which occurred in the Medieval period as "gynocentrism 2:0". Initially within the province of the court and the lordly classes, ladies became elevated to the pedestals upon which they still perch.

This cultural appropriation of the evolved trait was the start of gynocentrism drifting away from its original purpose of benefitting the offspring through the proxy of the mother, towards benefitting the woman *per se*. The extent to which this Medieval intensification of gynocentrism was socially beneficial or harmful is debatable. However, the trend has continued in recent decades with its further appropriation and intensification by feminism. These deflections of gynocentrism from its original matricentric purpose, namely to facilitate child rearing, is effectively an appropriation of benefit by women of benefit truly intended for the children. This distortion of intent is recognisable today in the lauding of abortion and in the manner in which divorce, child arrangements and the family courts are conducted (see chapters 10-14). These arrangements, and the associated social services, conflate the interests of the child with the interests of the mother. We can see the origin of this in the appropriation of evolved matricentrism as far back as the 12th century, but given much greater emphasis since the rise of twentieth century feminism: "gynocentrism 3:0" in Peter Wright's parlance. The persistence of these intensified forms of gynocentrism is now via cultural transmission and social conditioning.

However, we have seen that the psychological asymmetry of gynocentrism had its origin in biology. Women are the critical path in reproduction. In evolutionary terms, women's existence is fully justified by their ability to incubate and nurture babies. But one man could keep a large number of women permanently pregnant, so a man's existence is not fully justified by his role in conception. Moreover, he plays no part in gestation and no direct part in the nurturing of babies. Nevertheless, elementary arguments show why roughly equal numbers of males and females are born, (Fisher R. , 1930). Evolution hit upon a neat way of making use of what might otherwise have been a waste of human resource: a load of underemployed males. This is the pair bond, implemented via matricentric emotion, which directs male effort in the socially useful direction of benefitting the family. Its basis in evolution is not hard to understand given that such benefit can only increase the likelihood of the offsprings' survival to reproduce in their turn.

The psychosocial asymmetry of gynocentrism is consistent with the gendered society in which the two sexes had distinct roles. It is also consistent with the male function within the family being provisioning: the now-disparaged inclination of men to be the main breadwinner. This, in turn, is consistent with the inclination of women to feel entitled to receive such consideration and material support from their heterosexual partners. When a woman expects a man to pay on their first date, she is checking that his gynocentrism is still in place.

The working of the original matricentrism, as an evolved adaptation, was socially beneficial when confined to the domestic arena. However, as we have seen, this original evolutionary purpose has been hijacked by waves of cultural appropriations, latterly feminism. This has both intensified gynocentrism and also extended its sphere of applicability from the domestic to everything. The inevitable result is to focus concern on those perceived under gynocentrism as requiring concern, and that isn't men or boys. Worse, it can result in compassion being actively denied men and boys, of which we shall see many examples.

Furthermore, the operation of intensified gynocentrism, now virtually identified with feminism, has become destructive. Workplaces tend to involve hierarchies based broadly on merit. The sex-based preferencing arising from gynocentrism, and now being enacted by identity politics, does not sit well with this structure. The resulting conflicts are becoming increasingly evident. Even the general public are now aware of a rift opening between the sexes. The cause is gynocentric feminism.

A meaningful equality, what you might call egalitarianism, would have concentrated as much on the dismantling of gynocentrism as upon those issues normally listed under "women's equality". Instead, gynocentric impulses have been used to motivate only action to address "women's equality" issues but to exclude broader issues related to the male sex. The gynocentric basis of feminism precludes the possibility of an egalitarian perspective. The result is a feminism which thrives upon, and ever intensifies, gynocentrism. Feminism is explicitly sexist as it concerns itself only with the issues troubling one sex. But the response to anyone pointing out this readily apparent fact will be, "women cannot be sexist". The claim that women have suffered centuries of oppression at the hands of men conjures the impression that women have so much victimhood credit in the bank of grievance that whatever they say about men, or impose upon men, is justified. They write books filled with the most extreme anti-male bigotry and receive no public censure. Instead they obtain tenured positions in universities from which to spread their misandry.

I'll not regale the reader with quotes from feminist writings demonstrating their extreme anti-male position, there is no shortage of such material, see for example O'Pie (2012) or Purdy (2016). For a quarter of a century, people have been calling out feminism for its bigotry, dishonesty and intellectual incoherence. Many of those who have done so are women who call themselves feminists, e.g., Daphne Patai and Noretta Koertge (1994), Christina Hoff Sommers (1994), and Donna Laframboise (1996). But the gynocentric carapace around society's collective psyche remains intact.

Feminist protestations that feminism is for men too is dissembling. The universal cure they offer for men's ills is that men stop being masculine. Feminism tells us that we just need to be more like women and then we might be acceptable. Such prejudice would be palpable if translated to a race context. "The only thing wrong with black people is that they are not white. If only they could try to be whiter, they'd be so much better". But prejudice is not perceived as prejudice when it is the approved societal norm.

It may be tempting to think of the traditional world of affairs, business and politics, as it was years ago in the gendered society, to have been androcentric. On the face of it this would provide an appealingly balanced picture: the matricentric domestic environment balanced against the androcentric world of work. But the picture is false. One cannot invert one's psychology during the commute to work. An all-male space does not imply an androcentric psychology. Men at work may have many apparent motivations, including ambition, for example, and the desire for status. More prosaically, and universally, men are there to earn a crust. These disparate motivations can generally be traced back to a psychological origin in matricentrism: the desire to support wife and family, or to attain the status required to *have* a wife and family.

The view of the human pair bond presented above is very different from that of feminism which regards marriage as patriarchal dominance and control of women by men. Thus, the feminist view of traditional marriage is oppression of women by men. Indeed, feminists see the whole of our society as being oppression of women by men, even now, and in the West. This perspective sees marriage as being entirely for the benefit of men and the disbenefit of women. (Oddly, this has not stopped leading feminists getting married, sometimes more than once). The traditional perspective, in contrast, is of an emotionally mediated relationship which is perceived by the participants to be of mutual benefit and in which the two sexes have complementary but distinct roles.

It is quite chilling when one realises for the first time how firm a grip the gynocentric mindset has upon people who are basically decent. Many people will read, say, the Corston Report, and see in it nothing but good. They will see it only as arguing for a compassionate approach to female offenders. And compassion towards women is precisely what is promoted by gynocentrism. What's not to like? They will read,

> 'prison is disproportionably (sic) harsher for women because prisons and the practices within them have for the most part been designed for men'

and see in it nothing but an admirable call for a kinder treatment of women. Their gynocentric mindset blinds them to the corollary, the implied male disposability: that it is acceptable to treat one sex more harshly for no reason other than their sex. Yet the very same people would readily agree with the principle that everyone should be treated equally before the law!

If challenged as to why men should be treated more harshly than women in regard to prison sentencing, what will emerge, in one form or another, is a view that men should indeed be treated more harshly. Further challenging will reveal either an inchoate view of men as dangerous, so locking them up is the best thing to do, or an attempt to rationalise the different treatment of the sexes, for example by claiming that a greater proportion of male prisoners are violent. Pushing your antagonist yet further, by regaling them with the statistics on prisoners, will probably meet with a flat refusal to listen or believe you. The ultimate end point of this conversational cul-de-sac is the accusation that you are just a misogynistic old reactionary. But what such a conversation actually reveals is the impenetrable cognitive wall thrown up by the gynocentric mindset.

Note also how the above quote from the Corston Report demonstrates the verbal legerdemain which abounds in feminist expositions. The claim is made that prison is *harsher* for women because it's *the same* as it is for men. Let the illogic of that sink in. This is where society ends up when we adopt a philosophy that 'equality does not mean treating everyone the same'. This is the philosophy which tells us that inequality of treatment is the true equality. This is "some animals are more equal than others". So why is it that the less equal animals have for so long been content to tolerate this position? The answer is male disposability, that corollary of gynocentrism. Through the lens of gynocentrism and male disposability, the harsher treatment of males is right and proper. It aligns with male sacrifice. It aligns with male utility because, in being criminal, a man has violated his obligation to social utility – and hence deserves particular punishment. Simply put, under gynocentrism, women will always be preferenced.

The sentiment that 'equality does not mean treating everyone the same', when applied to the sexes, is an expression of gynocentrism. In feminism, this sentiment is rationalised by claiming historic female disadvantage. This is done quite explicitly within policy statements. For example, in the Istanbul Convention, (Council of Europe, 2011), we read,

> 'violence against women is a manifestation of historically unequal power relations between women and men, which have led to domination over, and discrimination against, women by men'

Staggeringly, no one whose voice will be heard ever objects that claiming present advantage based on disadvantage *to someone else in history* is morally illiterate and intellectually incoherent (even if the representation of history were accurate, which it is not). Such protestations would, in any case, fall on deaf ears because the purported historical justification is just a smokescreen for gynocentrism, which is emotionally based. Claims of present benefit based on historical oppression are an example of identity groups extending even to those long dead. It is morally fraudulent.

1.3.2.3 Lack of Male In-Group Preference

Many people may be surprised at the claim that men have little or no in-group preference. The presumption of traditional cultural dominance by men might suggest to some people that men must enjoy considerable in-group preference. This is a key ingredient of patriarchy theory. But a little reflection reveals that this assumption runs counter to what we know about typical male behaviour: men tend to be competitive and hierarchical. If you are competitive, you are more likely to succeed – but it's not because you have been assisted by those against whom you compete. What tends to be forgotten is that, in a competitive environment, there are more losers than winners. Once again we have fallen victim to the identity-group fallacy: perceiving "men" as an undifferentiated class.

What is regarded as "cultural dominance of men" is actually cultural dominance of a few men, those who have been successful in life's competition. These are not typically the men who are the educational failures, the imprisoned, the homeless, the prematurely dead or those most likely to have been fatherless. Yet even the men who are ultimately disadvantaged tend to be competitive; they merely fail. Roy Baumeister has argued that this competitive and hierarchical social style of men is key to the formation of very large scale human social structures (Baumeister, 2010). The more cooperative, intimate social style favoured by women works well in small groups, but is not conducive to large scale societal cohesion - so Baumeister argues. He is not alone. Vigil for example, concludes: 'Divergent social styles may reflect trade-offs between behaviors selected to maintain large, functional coalitions in men and intimate, secure relationships in women', (Vigil, 2007).

Men's strong sexual desire is also their weakness and provides another barrier to men forming sex-specific coalitions to promote their interests (and you will note the evolutionary relationship between the formation of male hierarchies and the sex drive). Quoting Dench (1996) again,

> 'The more powerful men's sexual impulses are, the stronger the bargaining position of women, and the smaller men's chances of coming together in a mutually regulatory system at the expense of women.'

In this we see the reason for women tending to be against porn and prostitution. It is because alternative outlets for the male sex drive diminish female power. It is also the reason why priests in many religions are required to be celibate. It is to avoid them having two masters: God and wife.

Hence, it is reasonable to argue that male hierarchies mitigate against strong in-group preference among men. Having in-group preference themselves, women naturally assume that the same must be true of men. This is a serious misunderstanding of men. It causes women to assume, for example, that the greater number of male than female MPs must mean that men's issues are disproportionately represented in Parliament. But this rests upon the presumption that men will preferentially represent men's issues. In fact, the operation of gynocentrism and the absence of male in-group preference ensures that this is not so. Men tend not to give preference to other men. There is approbation to be had in preferencing women and girls; there is only disapprobation to be had for any politician so brave – or so foolhardy – as to dare to claim equality for men or boys. Hence, it is *de rigueur* to support explicitly sexist policies such as those relating to violence against women and girls, but there is no political will to do anything about boys' increasingly serious educational failure. Thanks to the operation of gynocentrism, male disposability and lack of male in-group preference, "equality for males" is interpreted as reprehensibly reactionary. In truth it is radical and far more progressive than those who style themselves as progressive whilst clinging to their ancient gendered psychology. But it is too radical for men in power, who steadfastly turn away from addressing the issues of men and boys, with only a very few honourable exceptions.

1.3.2.4 Feminism

The gender revolution of the last 50 years was promoted as an attempt to overthrow the gendered society. But there was never any recognition by the feminists pursuing this project that the gendered society resulted from gynocentric psychology. The feminist revolution was presented to us as the pursuit of a more egalitarian society. But it is not so easy to overcome deep psychological proclivities as many would like to believe, especially when they remain unacknowledged and socially enforced. And the feminist project was tainted from the start as it drew its strength from the very thing it should really have been defeating: gynocentrism.

Feminism argues for preferencing of women and girls over men and boys and rationalises this by claiming that males are privileged. This insistence on male privilege then further reinforces society's tendency to view men through the masculine gender script, namely that men are agentic, powerful and independent. This inevitably renders incredible any claims of male disadvantage. How can the powerful and independent and privileged also be disadvantaged (Phillips, 2015)? By presenting men as privileged, the preferencing of women can be made to appear as a project for equality. In the gendered society, it was easy to present feminism as an equality project by shining a spotlight on areas of female disadvantage, which certainly then existed. As gender roles have converged, this disguise has become harder to maintain. Female disadvantages have markedly diminished whilst male disadvantages remain in their primitive state: lacking recognition or concern.

Claims of blanket male privilege are actually prejudice but are not perceived as such. The effect of feminism has been to disenfranchise men from empathy because men are presented as privileged, incapable of disadvantage and undeserving of concern. It is extremely dangerous to disenfranchise a group from empathy because of the opportunity it presents for escalating prejudice, free from the social brake of shame.

Feminism has been the main social and political force behind the attempt to overturn the gendered society, and this attempt has been female led. It has concentrated upon those areas where women were historically disadvantaged compared to men – primarily in the workplace. One of the main aims of that movement was to seek women's financial independence from men. In this they have been highly successful, both due to greater female penetration of higher paid work areas, including the professions, and due to the expansion of the welfare state. This has weakened women's need to ally with men domestically, a tendency enhanced by feminism's ideological emphasis on making men optional in a family. This has been accompanied by divorce and separation arrangements which distance men from their children, a new reality of which young people are now well aware.

The old marriage contract, crudely the exchange of resource provision for children, has been eroded. Women have less need of resource provisioning *directly* by men (though no less need *indirectly*), and men now have no secure means of attaining fatherhood. Being a father has become a temporary status conferred upon a man on sufferance by the mother. These are changes which have been deliberately wrought, purposefully to increase women's power. The result has been a steep decline in marriage and decline in birth rates. The average fertility in all Western and Anglophone countries has fallen well below replacement level.

Feminism was billed as a movement for equality of the sexes. But feminism has been driven by the ancient, and culturally enhanced, psychosocial biases of gynocentrism and male disposability and consequently was doomed to be inequitable because these tendencies are themselves skewed. This has led to a perversion of the very concept of equality which is evident in the mathematically nonsensical, but universally deployed, phrase "women's equality", the equality of one thing. It is enshrined in policy in the form of "equality does not mean treating everyone the same", which we have seen is implicit in the 2010 Equality Act (and is explicit in the formal guidance given to judges, as we shall see in chapter 8).

Feminism has never been about equality. The feminist project is about making women independent of men. First and foremost this means financial independence. But it also means domestic independence and making men optional within the family. In public discourse, feminists are less than frank about these objectives. But the policies they pursue have always been single-mindedly to these ends. This is the reason for the relentless focus on the so-called gender pay gap. The feminists, at least the better informed feminists, know very well what lies behind the pay gap: that it is not "less pay for the same work", though they will happily present it as such for public consumption. They know very well that, in order to achieve their objectives, they must get women working more hours, as well as in more senior positions – because that is the cause of the pay gap and that is the route to female financial independence.

This is a project which is divisive at its core. The rift opening between the sexes, of which the public are now becoming aware, is of long-term and deliberate feminist construction.

Feminism encourages a false perception of the past, as well as the present. The analogy that "the pendulum has swung too far" is misleading. The "pendulum" was never far over the other side, but used to be reasonably central, contrary to popular belief. The representation of history as centuries of men oppressing women is a distortion so egregious as to be merely a calumny. Yet it is now almost universally accepted without demur, despite the most cursory acquaintance with historical fact being sufficient to discredit the idea.

Feminism has moved us ever further away from equality. Some women perceive this and wonder why men do not form their own counter-movement. I have known women say, "we women have been active for a long time, it's time for men to do the same". But what such women fail to appreciate is that men in general are not psychologically capable of the gender-based coordinated movement of which women have proved so very adept. (Incidentally, that is why the concept of "patriarchy", as it is usually understood in feminism, is not only false but impossible).

Moreover, those few men who do attempt a pushback – men's rights activists – are very successfully neutralised by the dominant lobby which is now overwhelmingly politically and socially powerful and omnipresent. The reluctance by men, even those who quietly understand the problem, to actively promote men's interests and oppose the feminist hegemony results from gynocentrism which creates prohibitive public disapproval of men who attempt such a thing. Men are terrified of female disapproval. This is the power of moral authority. The fires of disapproval are further stoked by the feminist lobby whose interests are served by keeping gynocentrism firmly in place. This is done by public shaming and active opposition to any nascent men's groups (such as the many cases of NUS officers and activists opposing men's groups at universities).

Other women may perceive the absence of resistance from men as confirmation of continuing female disadvantage. So long as men do not push back, they may reason, the female army needs to continue to advance, just as an unresisting object subject to a force will continue to accelerate indefinitely.

Feminists will opine "women have come a long way, but we still have a long way to go". This sentiment ignores the entire raft of male disadvantage which is the subject matter of this book. Just as history can be misrepresented as men's oppression of women by selecting only the advantages to one sex and only the disadvantages to the other, so the present can be misrepresented in the same manner. But this is now wearing rather thin.

The key to understanding why a movement ostensibly about equality has gone so badly off the rails is to appreciate that it was always powered by gynocentrism, and hence carried the innate gender bias along with it. As a result, its every move for "equality" was actually a move for "women's equality": male disadvantages have always gone unnoticed or dismissed as "men's own fault". Thus, male disadvantages are never perceived as arising from society or imposed by the State. Male disadvantages are always recast as evidence of male brokenness: compassion unnecessary / blame appropriate.

The feminist depiction of men *en masse* as a villainous patriarchy, when coupled with gynocentrism and male disposability, produced a dynamical system with positive feedback. The feminist lobby keeps the fires of gynocentrism burning by promoting victimhood and demanding protection and preferencing. Virtually all men are inclined to oblige the feminists in their demands. And men in power are especially inclined to oblige them, including through legislation, even though their actions might disadvantage men as a class (men have no in-group preference).

The key to understanding male feminists is simplicity itself: it is gynocentrism combined with pandering to the prevailing power and fear of female disapproval. If women say they want feminism, then feminism is good and the good man is the man who helps deliver it. The decent man, keen to avoid the shaming that feminists will so readily pour upon his head, obliges them. He follows his natural inclination determined by gynocentrism and male utility. He knows that to be a good man, which is what he wishes to be, he must give women what they want – and they tell him they want feminism. So he becomes a male feminist. In doing so, he sets himself against those nasty men who oppose feminism, and he becomes the One Good Man who will protect women from these nasty men, (Tieman, 2011). The male feminist acolyte can comfort himself with the thought that the misandry does not apply to him. But it does. There is no escape. To quote Dench (1996) on how gynocentrism motivates the male feminist,

> 'Men are primed in all cultures to be responsive to women's needs and wishes, and to the values espoused by women. Feminism has confused this impulse considerably by introducing the notion that women would prefer to do for themselves many of the things which men were traditionally expected to do for them; and a half-hearted New Chivalry has consequently tried to articulate around the paradoxical project of helping women to be more independent of men.'

Since the 90s, the "half-hearted New Chivalry" has become a fully enthusiastic embracing of the doctrine of toxic masculinity by the male feminists. When men ceded moral authority to women, back in the mists of evolutionary time, no limits were placed on the direction women's moral power might take. This evolved matricentric proclivity can be deployed for whatever purposes women desire, including subverting its original purpose, and men are programmed to assist. It is a psychosocial pathology which has always been inherent in Homo sapiens, but lay dormant while social, economic and technological conditions kept women predominantly within the domestic sphere. Feminism – or gynocentrism:3.0 – is a disease of affluence.

Moral authority is the true hegemony, and it belongs to women. It always did. And this is the reason why feminism has been so successful and become so dominant within my lifetime without the need to win any elections. Women were always powerful, and much of their power was always expended on controlling men. Once one understands this, the feminist doctrine of a hegemonic patriarchy deploying power and control over women is seen to be a classic case of projection.

Instead of eradicating the gender bias explicit within gynocentrism, as is truly required, the gender revolution of the last 50 years has reinforced it. The feminist lobby – to the despair of many women themselves – has presented women as perpetual victims, and men as irredeemably toxic. This has come about because the feminists deployed what women have long known: that shaming is an effective weapon to use to coerce men into doing their bidding. Do note that shame can be deployed only by those who possess moral authority. Men's shame was easily created by presenting women as victims of men's bad behaviour, and thus a violation of men's duty of care inherent in male utility. This feminist power strategy has continually fed upon gynocentrism and male disposability *sans merci*.

Consequently, the old gendered society, rather than being rendered gender-equal, has given rise to a differently gendered society in which men may be freely denigrated with impunity and men's disadvantages no more recognised than ever, even though their extent has been deepened by feminism.

1.3.2.5 Patriarchy

In section 1.3.1 I gave an account of patriarchy as it is represented in feminism: men's oppression of women. Here I give my account of patriarchy, which is rather different. In the feminist view, the patriarchal pair bond is a result of men's desire to oppress women. In the evolutionary view, the pair bond is an adaptation which benefits gene line propagation. The psychological-emotional implementation of this adaptation is evolved matricentrism. However, this mechanism is personal: it acts on the individual. In contrast, patriarchy is a social phenomenon. A view of patriarchy which is consistent with the evolutionary view of the pair bond is that patriarchy is a sociological phenomenon which reinforces the pair bond by imbuing the arrangement with social respect and status. We have seen above that men are particularly influenced by respect and status, due to the association of these social rewards with male utility (which, in turn, is a reflection of evolved matricentrism, to which all these phenomena ultimately relate).

In reality, the pair bond implements men's provisioning to his female partner as a proxy for the children. But there is a danger that this would be seen, socially, as servitude (because, taking a narrow view, it is). The importance to men of respect and status would then act as a powerful disincentive against conforming to this arrangement. As a dynamical system, this is negative feedback which would weaken the pair bond. Patriarchy is the cultural adaptation which neutralises this negative feedback and hence reinforces the pair bond. Patriarchy consists of bestowing respect and status on men who fulfil their allotted role in entering into a pair bond. Patriarchy is essentially a piece of theatre, a con trick.

Whilst there are abusive men who do not conform to the norm, in the typical heterosexual relationship it is not the man who is the domestic power. This used to be perfectly well understood by all, though a man's blushes were spared by mutual agreement never to mention that it was his wife who was boss. In certain ceremonial matters, formal deference may have been paid to the man. But in everyday affairs, everyone knows who is the power in the home. Harmonious domestic life virtually demands that the man acquiesce to his partner's lead in a myriad of small matters, though no doubt there are exceptions and, occasionally, the need for resistance. Here's how Dench (1996) expressed it,

> 'Patriarchal exaggeration of men's importance obscures the deeper power of women, and behind the theatre of male dominion the palace holds many secrets.'
>
> 'It seems very likely that feminist promulgation of ideas that family life mainly serves men, and that women are "doing it all for men", is in part, at least, a reworking of traditional devices for exerting more leverage over men. The appearance of male control and benefit is a cover which permits women considerable moral power in practice. Hera, goddess of marriage and a jealous wife, is also the power behind the throne.'

One sees here the origins of the instinct towards victimhood. The patriarchal play-acting was itself a form of laying claim to victimhood by the wife. It has long been the case that such victimhood, or seeming subservience, worked as a source of women's moral leverage.

Dench used the fairy tale 'The Frog Prince' as an allegory for this view of patriarchy as a piece of cultural theatre, designed to tie men into socially useful provisioning. One could use 'Beauty and the Beast' in much the same way. The Frog, or the Beast, are socially disconnected. They have not yet fulfilled their role in the pair bond. Their transformation into a "prince" results from the acceptance by the "princess" of the Frog-Beast as an intimate partner. Her previous reluctance has been overcome by – what else – provisioning and evidence of gynocentric consideration. The status of "prince" is the allegorical analogue of the social respect bestowed upon a man as a reward for entering into a pair bond. Patriarchy is the bestowing of this status; a little respect is a cheap price to pay for the associated service. This is how Dench (1996) expressed the patriarchal con,

> 'The frog, knowing no dependents, is largely self-sufficient in his pool, and can find little reason to abandon freedom and precious playing time just to become a domestic help. To be tempted from the pleasures of the forest, men need to be flattered by an important sounding title, and by the hint – which becomes absurd as soon as it is examined closely – that all of this business of child rearing and reproducing society is in some way being done for them and takes place under their indispensable management. Want to be my helper? Well, maybe; I'll let you know. How about head of household, domestic monarch? Now that's more like it!'

Modern feminism thrives on misandry and the denigration of men, but this is not new. Dench opines that this has long been used to coerce men. Misandry is the stick, and the patriarchy illusion is the carrot. Both are required because men, ultimately, can always just walk away,

> 'What 'The Frog Prince' and its ilk have done in the past is to sell the path of matrimony and responsible fatherhood. Patriarchal cultures teach boys that their nature is evil and they must rebuild themselves around a sense of duty.'
>
> 'A man's pride and independence may be greater than his need for domestication. This underlines men's original power, very different from and far older than patriarchy, of being freer than women to walk away from relationships and situations that don't suit them….it is this raw power of men to care less than women which brings about patriarchy, rather than vice-versa. While one aspect of this cultural response to male offhandedness is to denigrate irresponsibility as childish, or a place of banishment and eventual failure – the forest – this probably will not be enough to convince all men. Some carrot is needed as well, some pull factors as well as push.' (Dench, 1996)

One of the intriguing things about 'The Frog Prince' and 'Beauty and the Beast' is that the Frog and the Beast were originally "princes" but had been under a spell which made them appear to be a Frog or a Beast. It was a wicked witch who made them appear thus. Here we have the analogue of misandry and shaming (the spell) and the compliance with gynocentric wishes being required to lift the spell and be rewarded with the illusion of patriarchal status. Dench writes,

> 'The whole plot existed first in the mind of the Witch. It was, I suspect, the mothers who conjured up the prince in their efforts to turn men into more reliable helpers; and it is the arrangements they invented which feminism now seeks to blame on men.'
>
> 'Patriarchy is a system that may well have been largely devised and promoted by primordial matriarchs in order to even out the burden on their children.'

Feminists want to "smash the patriarchy", but they have a false perception of what it is they are smashing. They no longer appreciate that the patriarchy delusion was a piece of theatre of their own making. Feminists are women who have lost contact with their own power. As patriarchy is an enchantment upon men, smashing the patriarchy potentially liberates men, not women. But it is a liberty men did not seek.

1.3.2.6 Misandry

Any discussion of the origins of the empathy gap is not complete without mention of misandry: the systemic vilification and shaming of males. Misandry is both a source and a consequence of the empathy gap. Misandry will not be addressed in this book, but only because the scope is already huge. Indeed, Paul Nathanson and Katherine Young have spent two decades compiling a four-volume epic on the subject: Spreading, Legalising, Sanctifying and Replacing Misandry, e.g., (Nathanson and Young, 2006).

Misandry appears in the unthinking acceptance without demur of sentiments like "men are violent". Misandry occurs in popular culture in the representation of men in comedies as bumbling fools, to the despair of their women folks' unfailing competence. In dramas, misandry is displayed in the relentless depiction of men as wife beaters, rapists and psychopaths. Perhaps more pernicious than misandry itself are the messages subliminally advising how a man may escape it. Good men are invariably portrayed by their service to women. Rescuing the damsel in distress is still a universal trope, even if it appears in disguised form. This is pernicious because it promulgates the message that men can only escape the blame and shame of misandry by continuing to be ruled by gynocentrism.

Once one is attuned to detecting misandry, it becomes clear that it is endemic in the output of TV and cinema, (Nathanson and Young, 2001). In current affairs, misandry is evident in a myriad of ways, not least the acceptability of portraying masculinity as intrinsically pathological, even in so august a place as Parliament. The invention of terms like mansplaining and manspreading is essentially a product of misandry.

Generic misandry has given way to targeted misandry. Social media is now used by women to advertise their mistreatment by men, often named men, making the shame as public as possible. No evidence is required, and the irreversible destruction of men's reputation is easily accomplished with no risk at all to the women themselves. This is the one-way operation of gynocentricity and male disposability in action. Many men – perhaps virtually all men, including myself – could claim similar infringements upon their person as are the subject of most women's complaints. But gynocentricity and male disposability ensures that no one cares about that. The ancient bias ensures that concern is only one-way, and this has been weaponised by feminism. In a culture which presents men in such a light, an empathy gap is hardly surprising.

Labelling an entire class of people as powerful and privileged causes individuals who are disadvantaged rather than privileged to be unjustly estranged from empathy or assistance. Based upon gynocentrism and male disposability, feminism has constructed a narrative of men as undeserving, dangerous, predatory, and undesirable, with associated social castigation. Individual men attempt to escape the blame and shame by distancing themselves as emphatically as possible from any alleged bad behaviour or contrary views. The result is a retreat from masculinity which is now presented to us as poisonous.

1.4 Aims and Limitations

To reiterate: the set of ideas outlined in section 1.3 is offered as hypothesis, not as established fact. This opening chapter differs from the rest of the book, which is about presenting empirical evidence on a range of topics relevant to sex/gender. My purpose in presenting the theoretical ideas of section 1.3 is to challenge the dominant narrative on gender, the feminist position, and to present an alternative conceptual framework within which to assimilate the empirical evidence which follows. All this theorising you may reject. What cannot be rejected however is the empirical evidence supporting the existence of an empathy gap. This stands quite independently of any theory about its origin. Reject my explanations if you will, but the evidence for the empathy gap remains. To this, the rest of this book now turns.

2

Education

This boy is Ignorance. This girl is Want. Beware them both, and all of their degree, but most of all beware this boy.
Charles Dickens (1812 – 1870), *A Christmas Carol*

A general State education is a mere contrivance for moulding people to be exactly like one another; and as the mould in which it casts them is that which pleases the dominant power in the government, whether this be a monarch, an aristocracy, or a majority of the existing generation; in proportion as it is efficient and successful, it establishes a despotism over the mind, leading by a natural tendency to one over the body.
John Stuart Mill (1806 – 1873), *On Liberty*

Few would doubt the importance of education. Historically, the masses were permanently disadvantaged by lack of education. Arguably, class, with all its concomitants of advantage or disadvantage, is defined at least as much by education as by wealth.

In view of this importance, educational attainment in the UK is reviewed in this chapter, at primary, secondary and tertiary levels. This overview of education in respect of the relative achievement of the two sexes reveals a shortfall in the attainment of boys which grows with age throughout formal education. It will be shown that male educational disadvantage in primary school becomes an even greater disadvantage at secondary school (age 16) and a greater disadvantage still at age 18 and university entrance.

The sex-ratio of teaching staff is also reviewed. Examples from the research literature illustrate the relevance of the gender of both staff and student, and their perceptions and expectations of each other.

The educational underperformance of boys and young men is widely recognised, but that does not mean there is any great concern about addressing it. Examples are given of how the extent of this male disadvantage is elided and minimised, both by government agencies and in the popular narrative.

The empathy gap is evident in the fact that the main concerns in education policy, despite clear male disadvantage, are "women in STEMM" (defined in Section 2.4), regional variations in educational attainment, and the gender pay gap – even though the latter is not an education issue. An issue that will not be tackled in any depth is the *quality* of education, past and present, except indirectly as it relates to exam grade inflation.

This chapter will refer to the following key stages in the UK education system,

Table 2.1: *Key Stages in the UK Education System*

Institution	Typical Ages	Final Exam or Award used here to gauge attainment
Primary School	5 - 11	Key Stage 2 SATS
Secondary School	11 - 16	GCSEs
"Sixth Form" or further education college	17 - 18	A Levels
University or other Higher Education Institution	18 - 22	First Degree (Bachelors or Masters)

Entry into universities or other higher education institutions is generally dependent on good performance at A Level.

2.1 Primary School Attainment

Primary school attainment can usefully be measured by the National Curriculum assessments carried out at Key Stage Two (colloquially known as the SATS, or standard attainment tests). These consist of both tests and teacher assessments and are taken in Year Six at age 10 or 11. In recent years, based on teachers' assessments, girls have outperformed boys on all subjects, in 2016 by the following percentages: reading (9%), writing (12%), science (4%) and mathematics (2%), (UK Government, 2016a). These percentages indicate the difference between the percentage of the female cohort reaching the expected standard and the percentage of the male cohort reaching the expected standard.

Based on testing, the gender gap in attainment is somewhat smaller. It is interesting that there is a consistent trend for the gender gap based on teachers' assessments to be larger than the gender gap based on tests. This is sometimes expressed as "girls underperform on tests". But if the tests are assumed to be an objective measure, whilst the teachers' assessments might potentially be prone to subjectivity, then the gender bias in teachers' assessments can be defined as (Ag – Tg) – (Ab – Tb), where A and T refer to the teachers' assessments and the test results respectively, and g and b refer to girls and boys. A positive bias indicates a relative favouring of girls; a negative bias indicates a relative favouring of boys. (For this purpose, the teachers' writing assessments have been paired with tests on "grammar, punctuation and spelling", which was the nearest equivalent). Figure 2.1 shows a persistent trend for teachers to mark girls up compared with boys, relative to tests, (UK Government, 2015b). A similar bias is apparent in mathematics, see (Collins W. , 2018e).

Figure 2.1: *Teacher Bias in Reading and Writing KS2 SATS (girls minus boys)*

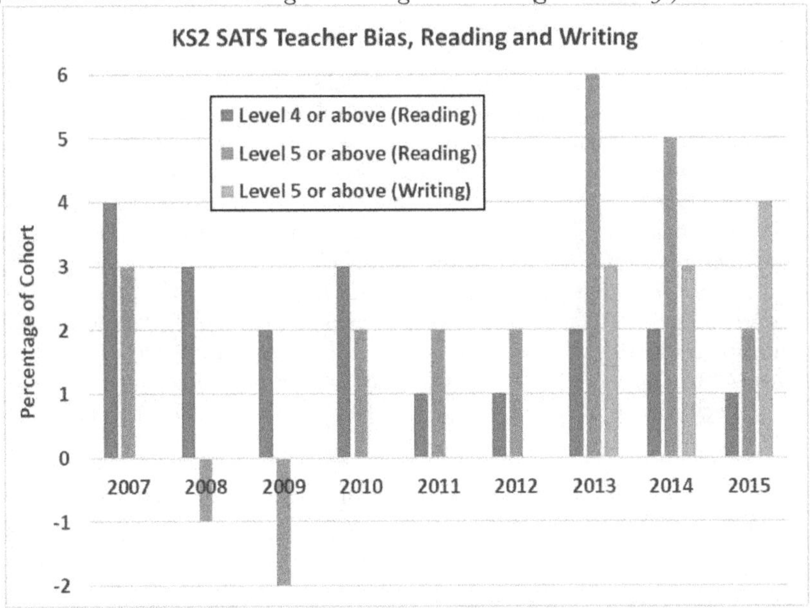

Christopher Cornwell and co-workers in the USA may have discovered the basis of this teacher bias. Their paper 'Non-Cognitive Skills and the Gender Disparities in Test Scores and Teacher Assessments: Evidence from Primary School' (Cornwell et al, 2013) identifies "non-cognitive skills" as the cause. This study found that, in every subject at primary school, boys are represented in teacher-specified grade distributions below where their test scores would predict. The Abstract of the paper reads as follows:

> 'Using data from the 1998–99 ECLS-K cohort, we show that the grades awarded by teachers are not aligned with test scores. Girls in every racial category outperform boys on reading tests, while boys score at least as well on math and science tests as girls. However, boys in all racial categories across all subject areas are not represented in grade distributions where their test scores would predict. Boys who perform equally as well as girls on reading, math, and science tests are graded less favourably by their teachers, but this less favourable treatment essentially vanishes when non-cognitive skills are taken into account. For some specifications there is evidence of a grade "bonus" for boys with test scores and behaviour like their girl counterparts.'

Cornwell *et al* attribute the marking-down of boys to the teachers awarding credit for "non-cognitive development". This is defined as attentiveness, task persistence, eagerness to learn, learning independence, flexibility and organisation. These phrases essentially mean "well behaved". Simply put, the gender disparity in this US study is largely due to boys being marked down for behavioural characteristics less common in girls. Cornwell commented on his research findings as follows (White, 2013),

> 'Eliminating the factor of "non-cognitive skills" almost eliminates the estimated gender gap in reading grades. He said he found it surprising that although boys out-perform girls on math and science test scores, girls out-perform boys on teacher-assigned grades. In science and general knowledge, as in math skills, the data showed that kindergarten and first grade white boys' grades "are lower by 0.11 and 0.06 standard deviations, even though their test scores are higher." This disparity continues and grows through to the fifth grade, with white boys and girls being graded similarly, "but the disparity between their test performance and teacher assessment grows." The disparity between the sexes in school achievement also far outstrips the disparity between ethnicities. "From kindergarten to fifth grade," he found, "the top half of the test-score distribution among whites is increasingly populated by boys, while the grade distribution provides no corresponding evidence that boys are out-performing girls".'

Notwithstanding any bias in the assessment, the test evidence in the UK clearly shows that boys genuinely underperform significantly in verbal skills compared with girls, both in the written and the spoken word. The persistence of boys' underperformance on verbal issues across most countries and cultures suggests a large part of this underperformance is likely to be innate sex differences, though researchers tend to ignore this possibility, e.g., (Moss and Washbrook, 2016). Any contribution to this male underperformance due to other, non-innate, factors becomes clearer at secondary school.

2.2 Secondary School Attainment Aged 16

At GCSE the gender gap in mathematics remains negligible, as it was at primary school. But the gender gap in English has increased, to as much as 19% (see Table 2.2). There are 7% more girls attaining pass grades in both English and Maths, and 5% more girls getting a pass at any science subject, (UK Government, 2018e).

It has been reported many times in the literature that teacher bias plays a part in boys' lower assessment grades at secondary school, as was seen for primary schools. The Programme for International Student Assessment (OECD, 2015) has reported that, 'teachers generally award girls higher marks than boys, given what would be expected after considering their performance in PISA (i.e., in tests)'. "PISA" is explained below.

In a comprehensive meta-analysis, Voyer and Voyer (2014) note that males outperform females in mathematics and science, quoting several references in support of this finding. In contrast they observe that, 'Although gender differences follow essentially stereotypical patterns on achievement tests, for whatever reasons, females generally have the advantage on teacher-assigned school marks regardless of the material. This gender difference has been known to exist for many years and has persisted in recent years, for both college students and primary school pupils.' (page 1174)

Table 2.2: *GCSE Gender Gap by Individual Subject, 2016/17 (Differences of percentages of cohort of same sex, girls minus boys)*

Subject	Grades 5 to 9	Grades 4 to 9
English language	19%	16%
English literature	17%	14%
Mathematics	0%	1%
Both English and Maths	6%	7%
Any science	-	5%

Whilst there may be a certain amount of discussion over boys' deteriorating educational performance, that there is no great political motive to tackle the issue is proved by a question raised by the political party 'Justice for Men & Boys' under the Freedom of Information Act in 2015. Addressed to the Department for Education (DfE), the question was 'does the DfE recognise boys' underachievement as a problem to be addressed, and if so, what initiatives are in place, and how much is budgeted for them in 2015/16?'. The Department for Education responded thus, 'The Department does not fund any initiatives that just focus on addressing boys' underachievement', (Buchanan M. , 2015).

An indication of how government discourse elides the underperformance of boys is provided by the report from Anne Longfield, the Children's Commissioner of England, 'Growing Up North – Look North: A generation of children await the powerhouse promise' (Longfield, 2018a). The report highlights the better educational attainment of children in London compared to elsewhere in England. It is perfectly valid to do so, as it would also be valid to point to the socioeconomic dependence of educational attainment. But it is strange not to mention the sex dependence of educational attainment because sex dependence is the dominant factor, as illustrated by Figure 2.2. It is in the intersection of demographic and being male where educational disadvantage is greatest. Yet the only mention of gender in the report is (on page 14),

> 'Differences between boys and girls: Throughout our work we encountered significant differences between boys and girls, both in terms of their career aspirations and what they believed their local area offered them. Within the context of regeneration we think this is important. We know girls outperform boys throughout school but are paid less as adults. This is a particular issue in many Northern areas where traditional industries have been very male-dominated. It is very important that regeneration strategies tackle this and speak to girls' aspirations, particularly if the regeneration is focused on industries which are perceived as male.'

This is odd for several reasons. Firstly, it confuses education with pay and employment, which betrays a political motivation beyond education. Secondly, it is very peculiar to refer to the decline of traditional industries, which impacts men particularly, in order to motivate a focus on "speaking to girls' aspirations". But oddest of all, this appears to be an attempt to deflect attention away from boys in a report which is specifically about education attainment gaps.

Figure 2.2: *Gender Gap in English KS2 SATS cf Regional Variations (girls minus boys)*

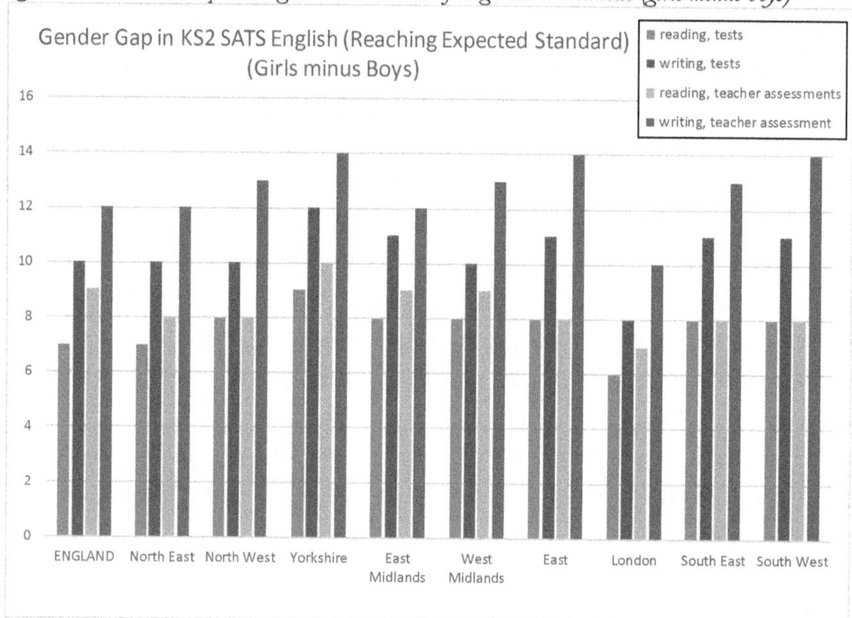

2.3 A Levels

The trend of worsening educational achievement by boys, compared with girls, persists at A Level (age 18). As an illustration of how this is obscured consider the newspaper headlines on A Level results day in England in 2017. The Guardian headline read, 'boys get more A*/A grades than girls for the first time in at least seven years', (Adams, Bengtsson and Weale, 2017), whilst in the Telegraph we could read, 'boys beat girls to top grades for first time in 17 years', (Turner and Kirk, 2017). Similar headlines were used in previous years.

These headlines are, however, grossly misleading. They refer only to the percentage of those of the same sex taking the exam who got top grades. To see how meaningless this statistic is, consider an extreme example. If 10 boys took the exam and all got the top A* grade, they would be considered as doing twice as well as a million girls getting A*s together with a million girls getting the lower A or B grades.

The issue is absolute numbers. There were 81,000 (22%) more female than male A Level candidates in 2017, and the trend in this gender gap has been upwards for decades, see Figure 2.3, (Stubbs, 2017). If we look at the top A*/A/B grades, the excess of girls over boys was 60,500 (32%) and 54,900 (29%) in 2016 and 2017 respectively. This is a very different picture from that provided by the news headlines. The gender gap in A Level attainment is larger even than the gaps at earlier stages of school education.

Figure 2.3: *Excess of Girls Over Boys as A Level Candidates*

2.4 University Entry

The gender gap in A Level performance is inevitably reflected in higher education entrance numbers. In 2016 and 2017 about 100,000 more women than men applied to UK universities and colleges (UCAS, 2017a). In terms of acceptances there were 71,100 (36%) more women than men approved to start at UK HE institutions in 2017. Entry rates were 27.8% and 37.7% for men and women respectively (UCAS, 2017b).

The gender gap to the disadvantage of males has thus gradually increased through their school career, being up to 12% in primary school, up to 19% by GCSE, 22%-29% by A Level and 36% in terms of university entrance.

Women have outnumbered men as undergraduates in the UK since 1993, a quarter of a century at the time of writing. 70% of subjects at UK universities are now dominated by women undergraduates. (Because the division into subjects may be arbitrary, a more precise statement is that 70% of undergraduates are studying subjects dominated by women students).

A clear distinction must be made between STEM and STEMM. The former refers to science, technology, engineering and mathematics. In STEMM the second M adds medicine and subjects allied to medicine. Contrary to popular belief, there are more women than men undergraduates in STEMM. This first occurred in 2015 and reached 6% excess women by 2017, see Figure 2.4 (UCAS, 2017b).

Figure 2.4: *Ratio of Women to Men Undergraduates in STEMM Subjects (Science, Technology, Engineering, Maths, Medicine and Subjects Allied to Medicine)*

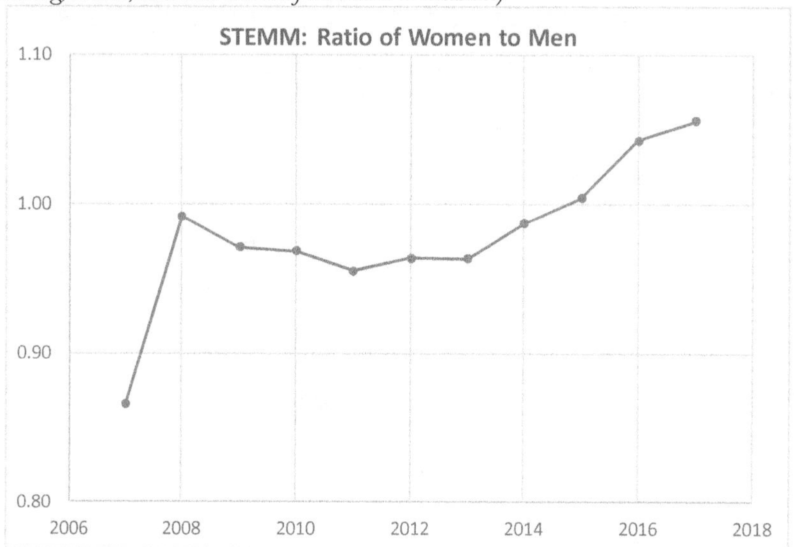

Those whose business it is to track equality issues know full well that women have become dominant in STEMM, despite being content to promote the opposite impression to the public. For example, the University of Bristol Annual Equality Monitoring Report (2014) whilst concentrating mostly on issues pertinent to that university, contains the statement,

> 'Across the sector as a whole, a slightly higher proportion of female students were studying STEMM subjects (51%)'

In fact, men dominate only in the "TEM" part of STEMM, since women also dominate in the pure sciences (due to their dominance in biological sciences outweighing men's dominance in physical sciences). Men's dominance in technology and engineering is well known, there being about five men to every woman undergraduate in these subjects. There are only two other subjects dominated by men: mathematics and architecture, where the ratio of women to men is about 0.6. Less well known is the emphatic extent of women's dominance in almost all other subjects, as follows,

- In medicine and dentistry women outnumber men by nearly 50%;
- In the social sciences women outnumber men by about 60%;
- In art and design women outnumber men by about 80%;
- In law there are twice as many women undergraduates as men;
- In languages and literature women are approaching three times more numerous than men;
- In veterinary science there are four times as many women, and women even outnumber men in agricultural sciences;
- In educational studies there are six times as many women as men;
- In "subjects allied to medicine" there are four and a half times more women than men, and the nursing component of this is in excess of nine times.

The subject area gender dominance aligns with great precision against the division into things (men) versus people or animals (women).

Despite the large and growing disadvantage to males in educational attainment at primary, secondary and tertiary level, the White Paper 'Education Excellence Everywhere' (Department for Education, 2016), which sets out Government policy on education, makes absolutely no mention of it. The Foreword to the report was provided by Nicky Morgan who was then both the Secretary of State for Education and also Minister for Women and Equalities. The only mention of gender in the White Paper was this (page 93),

> 'We will continue to address the gender gap in STEM subjects – supporting our ambition to narrow the gender pay gap – and are committed to increasing the proportion of entries by girls in science and maths subjects by 20% during this Parliament through our support for high quality teaching, the employer-led Your Life campaign and a wide range of STEM programmes in schools.'

Recall that women already dominate in the pure sciences at university. Once again there is a conflation of education with pay and employment. At best this is a confusion. Could it be an attempt to hide a politically inconvenient reality behind an approved political agenda item? (The pay gap is addressed in Chapter 7).

However, not everyone was content with the Government's policy position. Certainly not the Higher Education Policy Institute (HEPI), whose report 'Boys to Men: The underachievement of young men in higher education – and how to start tackling it' was highly critical of ignoring the plight of boys (Robinson, 2016). The former head of the Universities and Colleges Admissions Service (UCAS), Mary Curnock Cook, provided the Foreword to the HEPI report. The salient extract is this (page 3),

> 'The recent Department for Education white paper, "Education, Excellence, Everywhere" makes no mention of the chronic underperformance of boys in primary and secondary education. As the white paper title indicates, the Department is more exercised by geographical inequality in education outcomes and the document is peppered with maps to underline the point. There may be pockets of poor standards of education across the country, but the underperformance of boys is pervasive throughout social strata, geographies and phases. This (HEPI) report is compelling reading as it peels the onion of male underperformance in higher education, and it proposes some imaginative interventions. But its real value is in highlighting the sheer scale of the problem.'

While Curnock Cook was head of UCAS, the underperformance of boys was made explicit in their annual reports. For example, Figure 2.5 was taken from the UCAS, End of Cycle Report 2015 page 130 (Curnock Cook, 2015). This histogram gives the percentage of the population of each demographic who started at university between 2011 and 2015. The sample population comprised English 18 year old former state school pupils between 2011 and 2015 who live in POLAR3 quintile 3 areas. (This classification represents a geographical average participation rate in higher education). Twenty demographic classes are used in Figure 2.5, representing various combinations of sex, race and socioeconomic class. The poorer demographic is indicated by the receipt of free school meals (FSM). Salient features are,

- Eight of the top nine demographics in Figure 2.5 are female;
- The lowest ranked non-FSM demographic is white males at 14th position out of 20;
- Poor (FSM) white males are bottom of the list of 20 – though FSM white females are second to the bottom;

- An FSM black woman is *three times* more likely to go to university than an FSM white boy.

In terms of education, the intersectional disadvantage is white-plus-male, the opposite of public perception.

Figure 2.5: *Entry Rates for English 18 Year Old State School Pupils in POLAR3 quintile 3 by Ethnic Group, Sex and FSM Status at Age 15 (2011-2015), taken from (Curnock Cook, 2015) p.130*

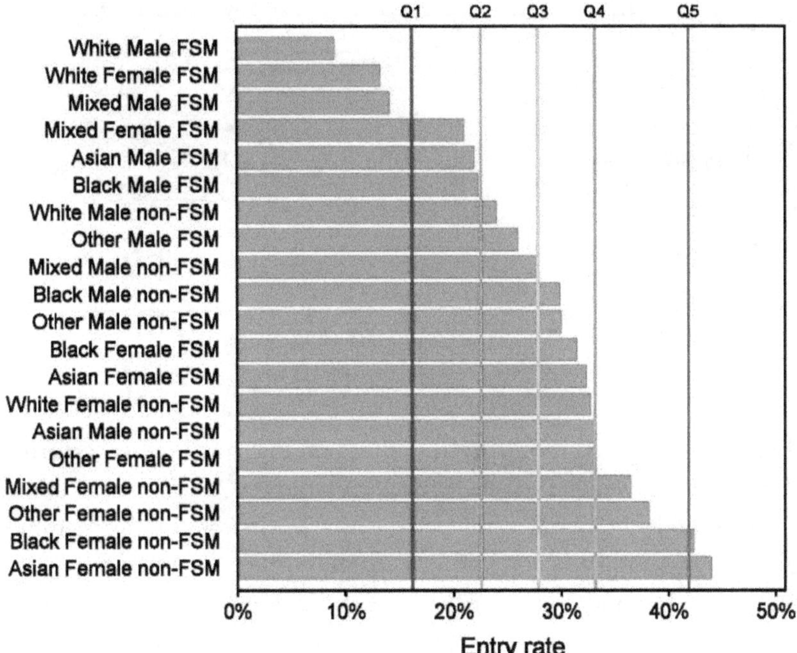

Since Curnock Cook left UCAS, they no longer report higher education entry in the form of Figure 2.5, which used to make male disadvantage clear. Instead a 'Multiple Equality Measure' (MEM) is used, which is claimed to 'facilitate more accurate identification of those individuals most and least likely to enter HE', (UCAS Analysis & Research, 2017), page 4. In my opinion it serves to obscure the dominant issue, i.e., gender.

2.5 Gender Gap and the Nature of the Award

No measure of educational attainment is perfect, and there are suggestions that part of the gender difference might be due to the nature of the awards. At age 16, the gender gap arose suddenly when the old O Levels were replaced by GCSEs, Figure 2.6, (Department for Education and Skills, 2007). Some have traced the ultimate under-representation of men in university to this poorer performance at GCSE, though its significance has been hotly debated.

Figure 2.6: *Percentage of School Leavers Achieving 5+ A-C (or Pass) O levels or A*-C GCSEs, by Gender (1962 – 2006) from (Department for Education and Skills, 2007)*

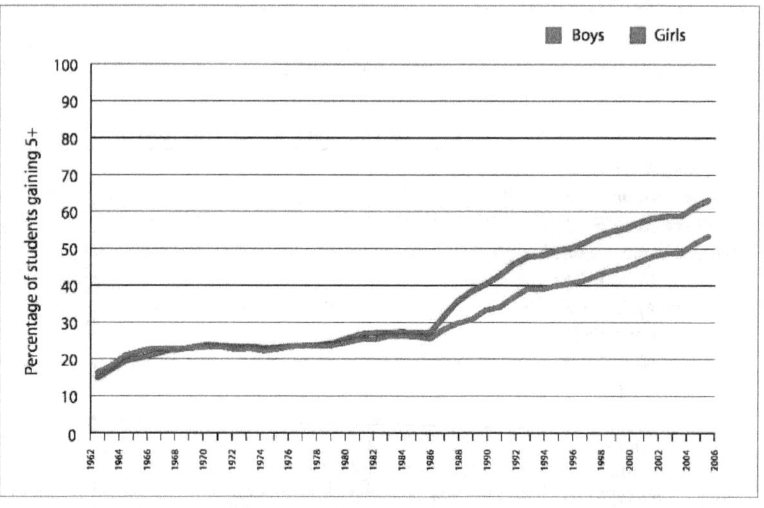

Source: Department for Education Statistics of Education

Further independent support for the contention that boys' underperformance at GCSE may be largely a result of the nature of these awards. is obtained by comparison with the OECD 2006 PISA study. PISA is the Programme for International Student Assessment organised by the OECD and, in the UK, by the National Foundation for Educational Research. The following account is based on the report by Bradshaw et al, (Achievement of 15-year-olds in England: PISA 2006 National Report, 2007).

The PISA involved assessment of 15 year olds in reading, mathematics and science via tests developed for the PISA exercise and intended to provide, amongst other things, a standard by which different nations can compare the effectiveness of their education arrangements. The UK component involved 502 schools and over 13,000 pupils.

In the science PISA males significantly outperformed females. In contrast with these PISA results, girls get more top grades (A*, A and B) in GCSE science than boys. In the maths PISA males also did significantly better than females. The difference of 17 scale points between females and males in maths was higher than the OECD average of 11 scale points difference. This was one of the highest differences within the 44 comparison countries with only three countries having a higher figure. The 2006 PISA report itself remarks on the contrast between this and the GCSE results in maths, thus:

> 'It is interesting to compare this pattern of male advantage (i.e., in the PISA tests) with that found in other assessments in England.... The GCSE mathematics qualification in 2007 showed no gender difference. 14 per cent of both males and females achieved grade A* or A... It seems then that results from measures that are used regularly in England do not tell the same story about gender differences as the PISA survey.'

These PISA results add to the suspicion that the gender gap in GCSE attainment may be at least partly an artefact of the nature of the award.

Similar observations have been made about A Levels. Kirkup et al (2008) have compared A level performance against the results of a Standard Attainment Test (SAT). It involved approximately 8000 students (46% male) in English schools and Further Education colleges, who took the SAT Reasoning Test in autumn 2005 during the final year of their two-year A Level courses. For most students this is the academic year in which their 18th birthday occurs. The SAT comprised three main components: Critical Reading, Mathematics and Writing.

Female students had higher total GCSE and A Level points scores and achieved significantly higher scores on the SAT Writing component than male students. There was no significant difference in the scores for male and female students on the SAT Reading component. Male students performed significantly better on the SAT Mathematics component and on the SAT as a whole.

That males performed better on the SAT as a whole is remarkable given that the three tests, Critical Reading, Mathematics and Writing, might have been supposed to consist of two playing to female strengths and just one playing to male strengths. The other main male strength, science, was not represented in the SAT.

Males did better on the SAT than expected based on their A Level attainment. In contrast, female students, some ethnic minorities, students with special educational needs (SEN) and students learning English as an additional language appeared to perform less well on the SAT than expected based on GCSE and A Level attainment.

As was the case for GCSEs, these results suggest that female dominance in A Levels may be partly to do with the nature of the UK award process itself rather than the candidates' merits. If true, this female dominance could be reduced, or even over-turned, by an alternative award or examination system. This could have substantial implications for the relative numbers of men and women attending universities in the UK. However, I doubt that this is the whole story. There are social and economic components to boys' relative educational failure which are beyond the direct influence of the education system itself, especially in respect of the lower socioeconomic classes.

However, that there is a deliberate feminisation of curricula and award systems in the UK is beyond doubt. The A Level physics syllabus and course structure has been altered explicitly in order to have greater appeal to girls, (Collins W. , 2015b).

One school of thought is that much, if not all, of the gender gap in attainment is a result of exams becoming easier. It is an hypothesis which is hard to deny when even the elite universities with the highest academic traditions are openly dumbing-down degrees explicitly to overturn a currently superior male performance. Oxford has been a major culprit.

In 2018 the Oxford Philosophy Faculty introduced "feminist philosophy" into their curriculum, (Turner, 2018). Am I the only one to whom "feminist philosophy" sounds ominously like "Aryan science"? Faculty guidance is now that 40% of recommended authors on philosophy reading lists should be women, and that first names must be included so that the sex of the author is clear. You might have thought that the content of the work was all that mattered, but it seems not. Students are being encouraged, by Faculty, to adopt an overtly sexist attitude by giving primacy to the sex of the author.

As of February 2019, the Faculty of Classics at Oxford is considering how their world-famous classics degree (known as Literae Humaniores or "Greats") might be modified, (Turner, 2019a). The motivation is consternation at the fact that, in 2018, 46.8% of men achieved a first in their finals compared to only 12.5% of their female peers. This might reasonably motivate some attention to female students of the subject, perhaps examining whether the same acceptance standard was being applied to both sexes. But dumbing-down the award itself has now become acceptable in the guise of being "female friendly". This is an insult to women, it fails to give the strongest candidates a chance to be recognised as such, and ultimately it will undermine Oxford's reputation for academic excellence.

In 2017, in response to men obtaining more first class history degrees than women, one of the final exams at Oxford was replaced by a take-home exam, again specifically with the intent of boosting the number of women getting firsts, (Turner, 2017). Prior to 2017, the percentage of men at Oxford achieving first class degrees in maths or computer science had been double that for women. It being axiomatic that this is a problem that must be fixed, students were given an extra 15 minutes in their exams, because (for reasons which escape me, other than outright misogyny) Faculty thought that 'female candidates might be more likely to be adversely affected by time pressure', (Diver, 2018).

Meanwhile, Cambridge University, at which the average gender gap in attainment in 2016 was nearly 9% in favour of men across all subjects, is also reviewing its exam system 'in order to understand fully any variations and how we can mitigate them effectively'. It is now an unchallenged axiom that any gender difference to women's disadvantage must be eliminated, by any means that may work, including the destruction of the subject itself.

Figure 2.7: *Trend in Percentage Achieving A/A* Grades at A Level*

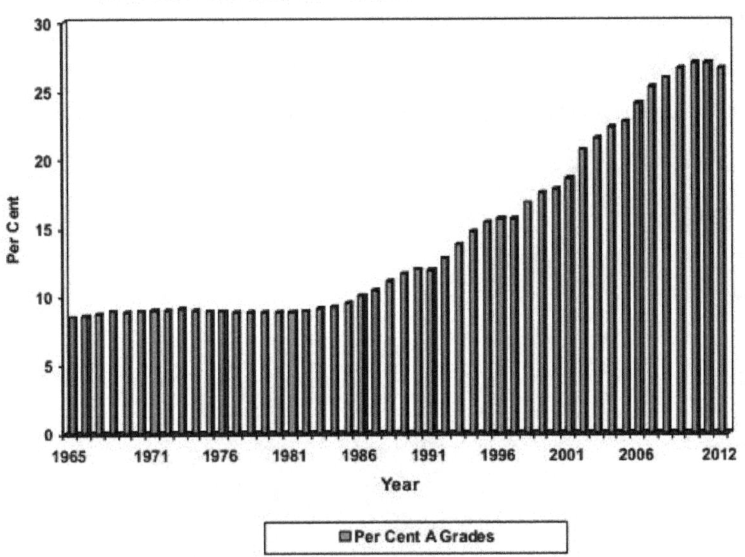

Evidence of a reduced standard in school exams comes from the marked grade inflation, evident at GCSE from Figure 2.6. A similar grade inflation has occurred at A Level. Before 1987, grade inflation was prevented by the requirement that not more than 10% of candidates would get an A, 15% a B, 10% a C, etc. This capping was abolished in 1987. Since then there has been a marked grade inflation as shown by Figure 2.7, (Full Fact, 2015). In 1982 the A grade was awarded to only 8.9% of entrants (there was no A* grade then, because there was no need for it). By 2012 26.6% of students were achieving A or A* grades. The result is that too many candidates now achieve straight-A/A* grades, thus failing to provide universities with sufficient discrimination. Some universities have instigated entrance exams to supplement A Levels, (Clark, 2008). There was evidence from a UK Clinical Aptitude test started for this purpose that men do relatively better than their performance at A Level would predict. However, such results may be reported instead as implying that the new test is biased in favour of men, (Devlin, 2010).

A remarkable observation by (Olson, 2014) is that, in the USA, there is a clear correlation between the average IQ of students studying a given subject and the gender ratio of that subject. Subjects dominated by men have high IQ averaged across all people studying the subject, whilst subjects dominated by women have relatively lower IQ averaged across all those studying the subject, see Figure 2.8. Note that "relatively lower" means closer to the national population average, but still above average (>100) because we are dealing with college students in all cases.

Figure 2.8: *Average IQ of USA Students by College Major Gender Ratio*

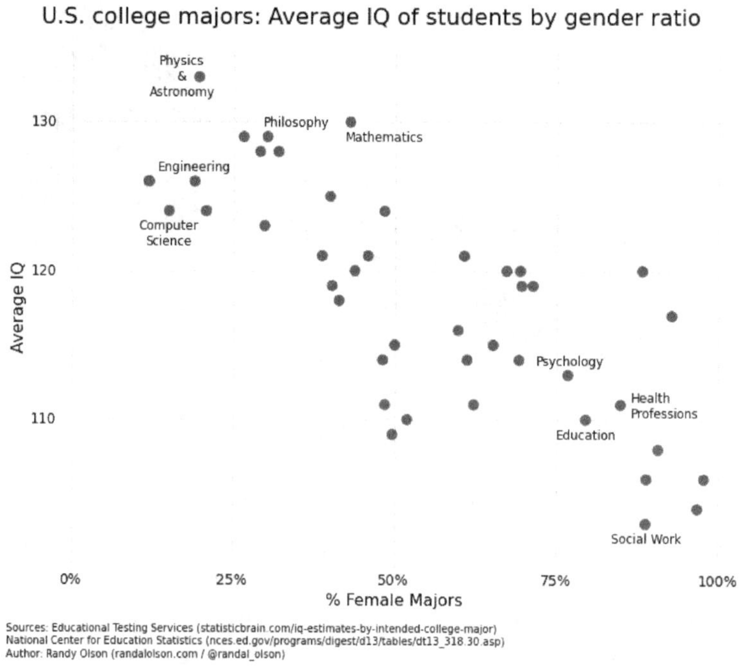

I cannot emphasise strongly enough that Figure 2.8 should not be taken to imply a difference in male and female average IQ. There is none. There are a number of possible explanations for how the correlation evident in Figure 2.8 arises. I refer you to the comment by Deborah Dixon in (Olson, 2014) for a good discussion of some of these factors. One issue is the possibility that men in the lower IQ bracket opt not to go to college but to learn a trade instead. This is perfectly possible, and Dixon also notes, in contrast, that those who might be considered the women who match these nascent tradesmen, women who are training to be nurses or teachers, *do* feature in the graph because these subjects have now been elevated to degree status. I could add, if only to be argumentative, that highly intelligent women might opt not to go to college, prioritising marriage and family instead. No, I have no data, but why should the hypothesis be automatically excluded?

A final caution to which Olson himself refers is that his data relate to students in their last year of undergraduate studies or to those who have already graduated. In the latter case the data refer to the subject chosen for postgraduate application. This creates scope for a Darwinian process in which the harder subjects retain only the brighter students. However, this does not explain the correlation with sex. A possible explanation for the gender effect is that it arises from the greater variance in male IQ, which leads to more men at the very high IQ end of the distribution, and hence more men in the harder subjects.

2.6 Innate Gender Difference? Adult Competencies

In the context of verbal competency at the primary school level, it was noted that boys' underachievement compared with girls may be innate, at least in part. However, this does not necessarily mean that such sex differences will persist. The innate difference might relate to different rates of cognitive maturation, for example. If so, the male underperformance compared with females might be expected to ameliorate with age. There is evidence in favour of this suggestion, i.e., that male underperformance at school in matters verbal does not persist as adults.

Figures 2.9 and 2.10 compare the gender gap in competencies at age 15 (y axes) with that at age 16 to 29 (x axes). The former is obtained from the 2012 Programme for International Student Assessment (PISA), whilst the latter is derived from the 2012 Programme for International Assessment of Adult Competencies (PIAAC). The graphics have been taken from Figure 4.16 of 'The ABC of Gender Equality in Education' (OECD, 2015). In these graphics the gender gap is defined as "b-g" (male minus female), so a negative value indicates female advantage. Both show results for a range of OECD countries.

Figure 2.9 shows the gender gap in reading attainment at age 15 versus the gender gap in literacy attainment in the adult age range 16-29. At age 15 the gender gap is emphatically in favour of girls across all countries. In contrast, the gender gap in literacy amongst young adults is insignificant for most of the countries plotted. In the case of 8 countries, the gender gap in adult literacy is in favour of young men, a reversal of the position at age 15 – and this includes the UK. The competency measures at the two ages are not the same. Nevertheless, one might expect attainment at reading to be strongly correlated with a meaningful measure of literacy. The turnaround therefore seems remarkable and noteworthy. One may speculate on the reasons for it. Possibly school pedagogy does not appeal to boys. Equally likely, perhaps, is that young men are better motivated when 'literacy' becomes relevant in the world of work, earning a living, and competitive financial success.

Figure 2.9: *Gender Differences (b-g) in Reading from the 2012 PISA for 15 year olds (y axis) Versus Gender Differences (b-g) in Literacy from the 2012 PIAAC for 16-29 year olds (x axis)*

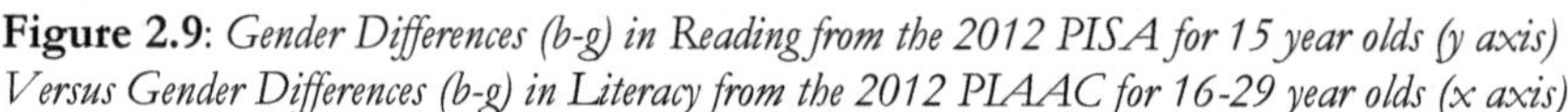

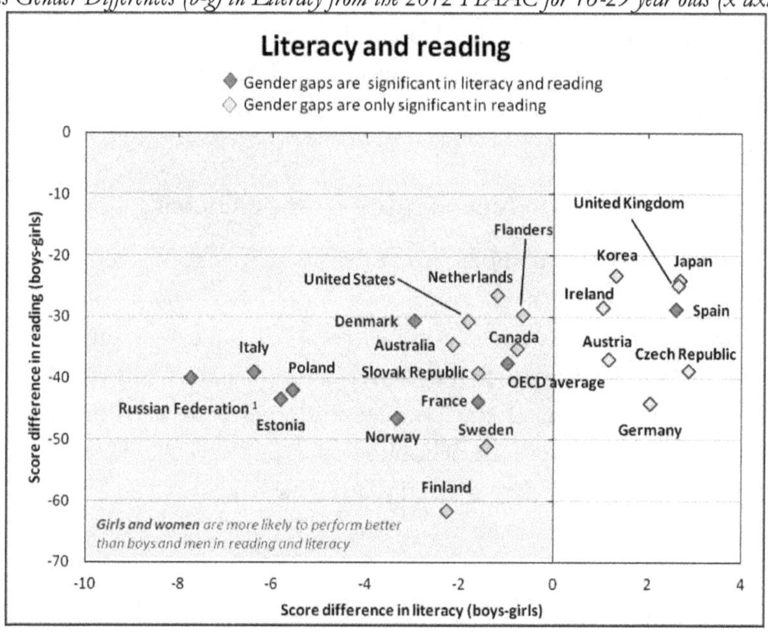

Figure 2.10 shows the gender gap in mathematics attainment at age 15 versus the gender gap in numeracy attainment in the adult age range 16-29. At age 15 the gender gap is either small or in favour of boys across all countries. This

remains the case for young adults, i.e., males maintain their advantage in numeracy, in contrast to Figure 2.9 for which men appear to catch up, or overtake, women in literacy.

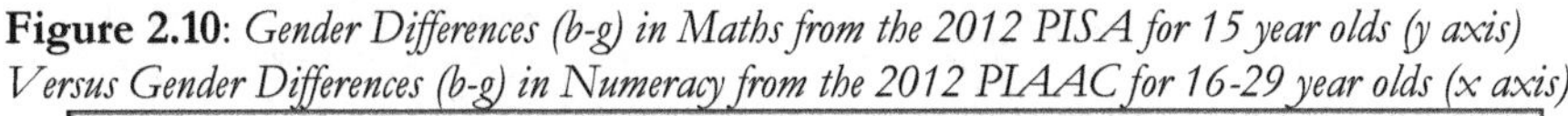

Figure 2.10: *Gender Differences (b-g) in Maths from the 2012 PISA for 15 year olds (y axis) Versus Gender Differences (b-g) in Numeracy from the 2012 PIAAC for 16-29 year olds (x axis)*

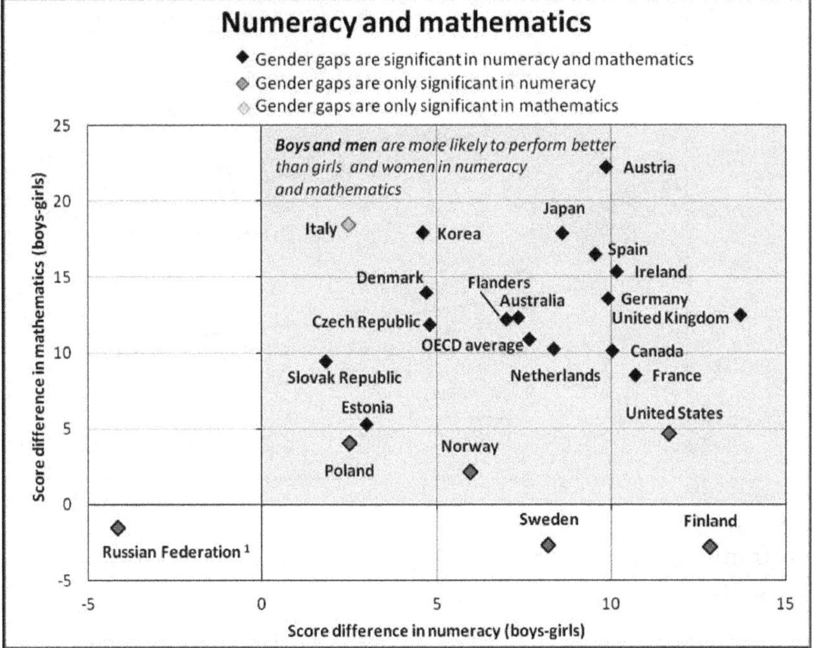

2.7 School Staff and Stereotyping

Over all grades and all schools, women teachers outnumber men three to one. Only one in eight primary classroom teachers is a man. In secondary schools, women classroom teachers outnumber men two to one. Women headteachers in primary schools outnumber men three to one. Headteachers in secondary schools are almost equally likely to be either sex. School teaching assistants are 93% female and other school support staff 54% female. The numbers of men in all categories of teaching have declined markedly over the last 50 years, Figure 2.11, (Department for Education and Skills, 2007), (UK Government, 2013), (UK Government, 2017b), (Department for Education, 2013).

A search conducted by Bradford (2015) failed to identify any concern by any of the teaching unions in the UK regarding the extent to which men are under-represented in teaching, nor any concern that this situation is becoming worse. In view of the importance attached to role models and the avoidance of stereotyping in other contexts, this seems peculiar.

Figure 2.11: *The Disappearing Male Teacher (England)*

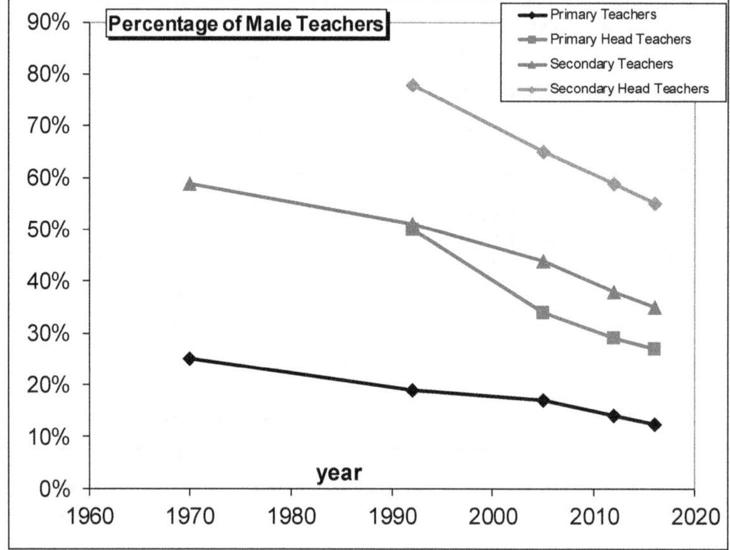

An example of the double standards which can be found is provided by this quote from 'Gender and Education: An NUT Policy Statement' (National Union of Teachers, 2001), page 1,

> 'At present, women are approximately four times less likely to become heads in primary schools than their male colleagues'.

The NUT claimed that this was indicative of disadvantage to women, an inequality which should be corrected by the appointment of more female heads. But this was written at a time when there were already twice as many female heads of primary schools as male heads. So to what does the claim that 'women are four times less likely to become heads in primary schools than their male colleagues' refer? It refers to the fact that there are eight times as many female classroom teachers as male classroom teachers in primary schools. The implicit argument is that, if all were fair, there should also be eight times as many female heads. This is where "women's equality" takes you.

Clearly, further exaggerating a large numerical inequality cannot be interpreted as a drive towards equality in any sense whatsoever. The contrast between this odd view from the NUT and the view in respect of, say, encouraging more women into STEM, is stark and unsettling. To explain the small numbers of male teachers, the NUT Policy Statement refers to low pay and men feeling 'unsure of their roles'. Graham Holley, the former Chief Executive of the Training and Development Agency for Schools, was more direct. In his 2008 letter 'The Quiet Conspiracy: men in primary schools', (Holley, 2008), he stated bluntly (pages 2/3),

> 'Men are deterred, partly because there is a prurient element of society that questions the motivation when men wish to work closely with young children. Recent NCH research supports this view. That is an immensely sad indictment of the way, in this so-called enlightened century, we can still be so uncritically suspicious of people who share the most selfless of motives: to help improve young lives. This fear of being labelled a paedophile is the single biggest deterrent to men who would otherwise consider teaching in our primary schools. Yet there is no evidence that our children are at widespread risk from men who want to teach.'

Holley was correct: there is indeed a widespread fear amongst men that a desire to work with children will expose them to accusations of paedophilia, what Anderson *et al* have called 'pedohysteria' (Anderson and Magrath, 2019).

2.8 University Staff, STEMM and Athena Swan

The staff in UK higher education (HE) institutions are reasonably close to gender parity overall. Women comprise 46% of academic staff and 63% of non-academic staff, or 53% of all staff. However, there are greater proportions of women who work part time, and smaller proportions who work full time – see Table 2.3 (Higher Education Statistics Authority, 2014/15).

Table 2.3: *Gender Breakdown of UK HE Staff, 2014/15 from HESA (Higher Education Statistics Authority, 2014/15)*

Employment Category	female	male	female as %
Academic staff, full time	53,120	79,745	40%
Academic staff, part time	36,105	29,365	55%
Academic staff, atypical	35,695	39,865	47%
Academic staff, total	124,920	148,975	46%
Non-academic staff, full time	76,095	63,285	55%
Non-academic staff, part time	52,705	13,410	80%
Non-academic staff, total	128,800	76,695	63%
All staff, full time/atypical	164,910	182,895	47%
All staff, part time	88,810	42,775	67%
All staff, total	**253,720**	**225,670**	**53%**

These headline figures provide no immediate motivation for concern regarding the numbers of women HE staff. The concern in some quarters focusses upon STEMM subjects and on the most senior staff. The drive to get more women into senior staff posts in STEMM is being headed by Athena SWAN, which is part of the charity Equality Challenge Unit (ECU).

The ECU is a private charity but is funded predominantly by the Higher Education Funding Councils and various Government departments. Consequently, despite its formal status as a private charity, the ECU is effectively an arm of Government. It also receives funding from various professional institutes and the universities themselves. Whilst making token mention of male HE staff in recent years, the true focus of attention for Athena SWAN remains as it was at its inception in 2005; namely, to 'encourage and recognise commitment to advancing the careers of women in science, technology, engineering, maths and medicine (STEMM) employment in higher education and research' (Athena SWAN Charter, 2018).

Athena SWAN operates a three-tier system of awards at institutional and departmental level (bronze, silver and gold standards). Achieving these awards requires more than promises or aspirations. It is necessary to provide evidence of increasing numbers of women in senior positions. This requirement may override the usual criterion of "the best person for the job". Recall that this form of affirmative action can be sanctioned by the 2010 Equalities Act, provided that a group defined by a protected characteristic is underrepresented.

Failure to achieve Athena SWAN awards may hit academics' funding streams. In 2011, the Chief Medical Officer for England, Professor Dame Sally Davies, stipulated that National Institute for Health Research funding of the Biomedical Research Centre and the Biomedical Research Unit would be dependent on their achieving at least a silver Athena SWAN award. In 2012 this ruling was extended to patient safety research funding. Not surprisingly, Athena SWAN then saw an increase in membership from medical and dental schools.

Although not yet obligatory for all research institutions, Research Councils UK (RCUK) have set out a Statement of Expectations (Research Councils UK, 2013) for equality and diversity for those receiving research council funding. RCUK expects the recipients to 'provide evidence of ways in which equality and diversity issues are managed at both an institutional and department level'. Moreover, the Statement recommends that, 'the evidence includes participation in schemes such as Athena SWAN, Project Juno, etc….to demonstrate departmental level action'. Bluntly put, meeting Athena SWAN expectations in terms of female staff ratios becomes essential if you wish RCUK funding to continue. This is a quota system enacted by financial blackmail in which the usual criteria of competence and contribution are ignored.

The next Research Excellence Framework, which will report in 2021, is likely to include a requirement not only that universities participate in Athena SWAN, but that individual departments have at least a bronze award. The implications of this in the longer term may be that it will be inadequate to have a staff gender balance across, say, all pure sciences, where an excess of women in biological sciences may balance with an excess of men in the physical sciences. Instead, a gender balance will be required in the physical sciences alone. Taking school teachers as our guide, it is unlikely that Athena SWAN, or anyone else, will exert pressure to gain more male staff in the biological sciences in order to maintain overall balance. At present, Athena SWAN is uninterested in those subjects where female staff predominate.

Women academics have been calling for some time for all research funding to be made conditional upon Athena SWAN accreditation, for example calls from Janet Beer, vice-chancellor of the University of Liverpool, (Beer, 2016), and from Professor Louise Morley, University of Sussex, (Morley, 2013).

Universities in the Republic of Ireland must achieve recognition by the end of 2019 to continue to be eligible for funding from the Science Foundation Ireland, the Irish Research Council and the Health Research Board (Times Higher Education, 2016).

Clearly there is some very effective lobbying to get more women HE staff in STEMM. The reader might reasonably assume that HE staff must currently be strongly dominated by men – in contrast to the broadly equitable position across all subjects as indicated by Table 2.3. But this is not so.

Athena SWAN have carried out their own survey, 'ASSET 2016: experiences of gender equality in STEMM academia and their intersections with ethnicity, sexual orientation, disability and age' (Athena SWAN, 2017). The survey covered only STEMM academic staff. The reader is referred to the report for a description of the pains taken to ensure the survey sampling was representative. The numbers of men and women in each post category are given in Table 5.1.1 of 'ASSET 2016'. The numbers of respondents to the question regarding their current post were 2821 women and 2050 men. However, to adjust for sampling bias the responses were re-weighted to an effective 2368 women and 2484 men. Results given in Table 5.1.1 of the report, and in Table 2.4 below, refer to the weight-adjusted results. (Note that without the weight adjustment the numbers of women would be greater, and the numbers of men fewer).

The results may be collated into three seniority bands. Junior posts are "teaching fellow" and below. Senior posts are "function head" and above, including professors. Middle ranking posts are lecturer, senior lecturer, reader, principal research fellow and their clinical equivalents. Table 2.4 gives the numbers of (weighted) survey respondents in each post band.

Table 2.4: *Athena SWAN's ASSET 2016 Survey Results of HE Staff in STEMM (Athena SWAN, 2017) Table 5.1.1*

Post Band	**Women**	**Men**
Junior Posts	826	476
Middle Rank Posts	1126	1173
Senior Posts	416	835
All Posts	2368	2484

Recall that these results apply only to STEMM subjects, which subsumes all subject areas dominated by male undergraduates other than architecture. All other subjects are dominated by women, at undergraduate level. Women are far more numerous at junior staff levels. At middle ranking staff level the numbers of men and women are essentially equal. Only at the senior level are there more men: twice as many as women. The senior ranks account for only 26% of the total. Moreover, if just 210 senior males (4.3% of the sample) were replaced by women, there would be equality at both senior and middle ranks, with women still dominant at the junior level.

The efforts of Athena SWAN, and all the funding and lobbying which surrounds the issue of "women academics in STEMM", is to achieve just a 4.3% sex rebalance at the senior level. Moreover, this is just in STEMM, which accounts for only about 30% of HE staff. One can reasonably question the value of the exercise, especially if it is at the expense of promotion on merit. Moreover, and of greater concern, is that the focus on the most senior staff levels in STEMM deflects attention from the overwhelming extent of male disadvantage as customers of the education system in all other subjects (bar architecture). Athena SWAN is focussing on a small island of remnant male dominance whilst ignoring the bigger picture in which women are very well represented and most often dominant.

There continues to be suggestions of hiring bias against women in STEMM academic posts. A rather emphatic refutation of this claim in the USA comes from the study of (Williams and Ceci, 2015). National randomized experiments were conducted on 873 tenure-track faculty (439 male, 434 female) from four different disciplines at 371 universities/colleges from 50 US states and the District of Columbia. Each faculty member assessed hypothetical applications to advise the lead candidate. The significance of the findings was reported thus,

> 'The underrepresentation of women in academic science is typically attributed, both in scientific literature and in the media, to sexist hiring. Here we report five hiring experiments in which faculty evaluated hypothetical female and male applicants, using systematically varied profiles disguising identical scholarship, for assistant professorships in biology, engineering, economics, and psychology. Contrary to prevailing assumptions, men and women faculty members from all four fields preferred female applicants 2:1 over identically qualified males with matching lifestyles (single, married, divorced), with the exception of male economists, who showed no gender preference. Comparing different lifestyles revealed that women preferred divorced mothers to married fathers and that men preferred mothers who took parental leaves to mothers who did not. Our findings, supported by real-world academic hiring data, suggest advantages for women launching academic science careers.'

These findings explode a whole cluster of shibboleths regarding academic hiring. The results in histogram form are shown in Figure 2.12. The women faculty members' bias in favour of women applicants was actually greater than a factor of two in all subjects, being a factor of three in the case of psychology. Inevitably, the study has come in for criticism and I link to one such for completeness, by LSE sociologist and social justice blogger Zuleyka Zevallos (2015).

A study in France has also indicated that women are favoured rather than the opposite in academic hiring in STEM fields. (Breda and Hillion, 2016) conclude as follows,

> 'Discrimination against women is seen as one of the possible causes behind their underrepresentation in certain STEM (science, technology, engineering, and mathematics) subjects. We show that this is not the case for the competitive exams used to recruit almost all French secondary and postsecondary teachers and professors. Comparisons of oral non–gender-blind tests with written gender-blind tests for about 100,000 individuals observed in 11 different fields over the period 2006–2013 reveal a bias in favor of women that is strongly increasing with the extent of a field's male-domination.'

Results like these cause a small ripple of interest when they are published, then the narrative reverts to the usual story: bias against women. Being myself a veteran job interviewer (though not in academia) I can understand how Figure 2.12 arises. If you need to reject a male applicant, no problem. No one will question whether the rejection is justified based on insufficient merit. Rejecting a female candidate, however, is something one tries to avoid, because one knows that a third-degree interrogation from HR may well result. You will need to be especially sure that all formal procedures have been followed to perfection and that no questions were asked which could be regarded as politically incorrect. There is inevitably a temptation to exercise positive discrimination in favour of a female candidate, simply to avoid the hassle.

Figure 2.12: *Percentage of Faculty Members Ranking the Applicant Number One, by Sex of Applicant and Sex of Assessing Faculty (Williams and Ceci, 2015)*

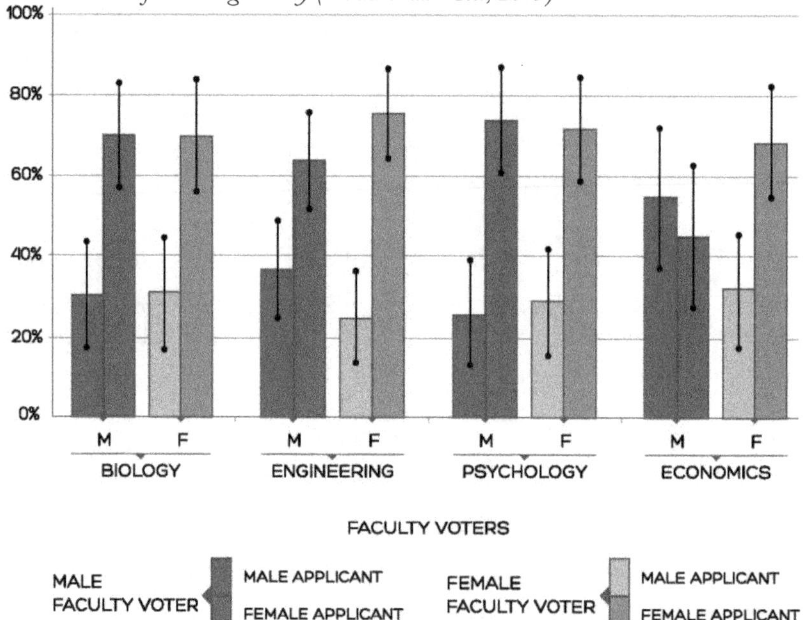

2.9 Gender Skew in Provision

Bradford (2015) reviewed initiatives to encourage women into mechanical engineering and physics. The review was confined to initiatives promoted by the professional bodies in these two subjects. An exhaustive list was prohibitively difficult to compile, due to the sheer volume of such initiatives. Had projects, support groups, etc., within universities and schools been included, it would have become quite unwieldy as virtually every university will have Women in Engineering and Women in Physics societies, for example. Even confining attention to the professional institutes there were many pages of female-specific awards, female-specific support groups, female-only bursaries, female-specific training, and many millions of pounds of funding to facilitate these activities.

The purpose of the review by Bradford (2015) was to contrast this with what is done for men in a discipline where *they* are under-represented: teaching. The answer in this case is far easier to summarise: nothing. Instead, the teaching unions are concerned only about "women's equality" issues and have no concern at all about their minority staff: men. The disappearance of the male teacher, as illustrated by Figure 2.11, excites not the slightest ripple of interest from the teaching unions. If men were treated with the same concern as women, here are some of things that would exist, as they do for women in engineering and physics,

- A campaign for "Men into Primary Teaching";
- Men-only bursaries to facilitate and encourage men into teaching;
- An annual award for the "Young Man Primary Teacher of the Year";
- A "Men First Award" to celebrate the achievements of ground-breaking men in primary teaching;
- A Male Primary Teachers Conference;
- A National Men in Teaching Day;
- An equivalent of the Juno Initiative for male teachers;
- An obligation on primary schools to acquire the equivalent of "Juno Champion" status in respect of male teachers;
- An equivalent of Athena Swan for male teachers;
- An obligation on schools to acquire the equivalent of Athena Swan accreditation in respect of male teachers;
- A calendar celebrating male primary school teachers, and reminding us that they are just 13% of primary teachers;
- An enquiry by a House of Commons Select Committee on gender equality in teaching;
- A requirement on teachers to submit evidence to such an inquiry, as has been the case in engineering.

As far as I am aware, none of the above exist. The drive to encourage more women into STEM often takes the form of financial assistance: scholarships, bursaries, etc. For example, in the USA, Tucker (2018) lists 36 scholarships exclusive to women in engineering, science, technology and business. Such sex-specific scholarships are being challenged on both sides of the Atlantic. In the USA, Kursat Pekgoz, a doctoral student in English literature at the University of Southern California, has filed complaints against three universities using the federal Title IX statute, which relates to gender equality in education. He is leading a coalition for the purposes of raising similar complaints at further universities. Under the lurid headline, 'Men's rights activists are attacking women's scholarships', Engelhart (2018) describes the complaint thus, 'a men's rights activist who has used federal complaints to target women-only scholarships and programs is now trying to start a national movement to end what he sees as discrimination against men'. But it is not "using" a law to raise a complaint for the authorities to consider, but simply expecting the law to be upheld, especially as there is a clear *prima facie* case.

Whilst there is no direct equivalent of Title IX in the UK, the 2010 Equality Act makes a general provision for equality on grounds of sex. This has already caused the university authorities at Oxford to open to male applicants a previously female-only scholarship. It seems inevitable that other female-only scholarships, and other universities, must follow suit or be open to legal challenge. As in the USA, there is a vociferous backlash from feminists who do not want to see their privileges removed, (Turner, 2019b).

This is happening as some universities in the UK are beginning to target recruiting white males as this demographic is being recognised as a minority group in universities. The report by Bodkin (2018) notes that, 'in 2016/17, only 27% of the UK undergraduate intake were white males.... on certain courses such as pharmacy, business and some science degrees, more than seven in 10 students is from an ethnic minority'. Across both sexes and all wealth classes, (UCAS Analysis & Research, 2017) gives the following participation rates at university entry in 2017 according to race, restricted to former state school pupils in the UK,

- Chinese 63.0%
- Asian 45.8%
- Black 40.4%
- "Any Other" 40.1%
- "Mixed" 34.0%
- White 29.3%

These may be compared with less than 10% for poor white males (Figure 2.5).

2.10 Perceptions and Expectations

The underperformance of boys and young men at all stages of education, primary, secondary and tertiary, is clear. However, there is little political will to address the matter; the focus of concern lies elsewhere, as illustrated by the preceding sections. This neglect is aided by minimising the visibility of male disadvantage. In some cases, this is achieved by the diversionary tactic of referencing the gender pay gap. At best this is a non sequitur. Another reaction is to focus solely on "women in STEMM", and associated arguments related to role models and stereotyping. Even in STEMM it is becoming harder to find female disadvantage as there is none as regards students and, as regards staff, it is confined to the professorial level (in the UK sense).

The proponents of stereotyping and role model arguments are often less willing to apply them in the context of the disappearing male teacher and boys' educational underperformance (Parson, 2016). Female primary school classroom teachers outnumber their male counterparts eight to one. But female heads of primary schools outnumber male heads of primary schools 'only' three to one. That the latter fact is interpreted as evidence of discrimination against women is bewildering. These are rather obvious examples of the empathy gap.

Harley and Sutton (2013) published a study on the role of stereotype threat in boys' underachievement, see also (Collins, N, 2013). The study presented 238 pupils aged four to ten with a series of statements such as "this child is really clever" and "this child always finishes their work" and asked them to link the words to pictures of boys or girls. The study found that girls think that girls are cleverer than boys. Girls at all ages said girls were cleverer. Boys aged between four and seven were evenly divided as to which gender was cleverer. But by the time boys reached seven or eight, they agreed with their female peers that girls were more likely to be cleverer and more successful.

There is a widespread claim that girls lack self-confidence (OECD, 2015). There is no evidence of it from this study. But this study does raise the question as to why the experience of school seems so decisively to dent boys' self-confidence. Researchers also found that the children believed adults shared the same opinion as them, meaning that boys felt they were not expected by their parents and teachers to do as well as girls and lost their motivation or confidence as a result.

In a separate experiment 140 of the children were divided into two groups, (Harley and Sutton, 2013). The academics told the first group that boys do not perform as well as girls. The second group were not told this. All the pupils were tested in maths, reading and writing. The academics found the boys in the first group performed significantly worse than boys in the second group, while girls' performance was similar in both groups. This appears to confirm that low expectations are a self-fulfilling prophecy.

The paper argues that teachers have lower expectations of boys than of girls and this belief fulfils itself throughout primary and secondary school. Girls' performance at school may be boosted by what they perceive to be their teachers' belief that they will achieve better results and be more conscientious than boys. Boys may underachieve because they pick up on teachers' assumptions that they will obtain poorer results than girls and have less drive.

In 'Students' Perceptions of Teacher Biases', Ouazad and Page (2012) present evidence of teacher gender bias. The study reports the results of an experiment that involved about 1,200 grade 8 pupils (aged 13) across 29 schools in London, Manchester, and Liverpool. Students were handed a sum of £4 which they could either keep or allocate part of the sum to bet on their own performance at a test where grading was partly discretionary. In a random half of the classrooms, grading was done anonymously by an external examiner. In the other random half, grading was done non-anonymously by the teacher. Thus, differences in students' betting behaviour across the anonymous and non-anonymous classrooms identified the effect of grading conditions on students' beliefs.

The study showed that pupils' perceptions were on average in line with teachers' actual behaviour. The experiment involved students and teachers of different ethnicity, gender, and socio-economic status. But gender was the only significant factor in the results. Male students tended to bet less when assessed by a female teacher than by an external examiner or by a male teacher. This was consistent with female teachers' grading practices; female teachers gave lower grades to male students. Female students bet more when assessed by a male teacher than when assessed by an external examiner or a female teacher. The study provided no evidence that students' beliefs depended on ethnicity or socio-economic status.

But the gender results showed that students' beliefs tend to increase the gender gap in investment and effort. A male teacher increases the effort and investment of a female student. A female teacher tends to lower the effort and investment of male students. These observations suggest that more male teachers would be beneficial to pupils of both sexes.

In 2012, a report commissioned by the All-Party Parliamentary Literacy Group, the "Boys' Reading Commission" (National Literacy Trust, 2012) observed (page 13),

> 'The predominantly female make-up of the school and children's workforce could mean that their knowledge of texts and reading materials could lead them to have a bias towards materials which suited girls' interests. So even though there is no evidence that the gender of the teacher impacts on the relative attainment of boys and girls in a class, it could well be that the teacher's gender could influence the extent to which they effectively promote books and reading materials that are attractive to boys and girls. Interestingly, one survey respondent who understood the need to promote reading materials that reflect the interests of boys at the same time made clear her discomfort with these interests: "We try to work from their interests no matter how banal, disgusting or undesirable"'.

That sentiment is very concerning. Children are remarkably sensitive to how adults perceive them, and "disgusting" is a highly corrosive attitude. The feminist novelist, Doris Lessing, became aware of the tendency by some teachers to demonise masculinity in 2001 when she visited a primary school. She remarked later, (Gibbons, 2001),

> 'Young boys were being weighed down with guilt about the crimes of their sex... I was in a class of nine- and 10-year-olds, girls and boys, and this young woman was telling these kids that the reason for wars was the innately violent nature of men. You could see the little girls, fat with complacency and conceit while the little boys sat there crumpled, apologising for their existence, thinking this was going to be the pattern of their lives.'

Lessing said the teacher 'tried to catch my eye, thinking I would approve of this rubbish'. She added: 'This kind of thing is happening in schools all over the place and no one says a thing.' This is what happens when gynocentrism and misandry run unchecked.

2.11 Worldwide

However badly boys and young men may be falling behind in education in the UK, at least we can be sure that in underdeveloped countries it truly is girls who are the educationally disadvantaged. We know this because all the great and the good have told us so. We know it because Boris Johnson and Prince Harry and Meghan Markle have told us so, (UK Government, 2018p). We know it because William Hague and Malala have told us so, (Jackson, 2012). We know it because rock star, Bono, has told us so, (Johnson, 2017). We know it because after Boko Haram kidnapped the girls from Chibok in Nigeria in 2014, Michelle Obama told us so. In May 2014, Barrack Obama yielded his weekly presidential address to his wife. She expressed her outrage and distress at the Chibok girls' kidnappings, driving home a message that Boko Haram is specifically attacking the education and emancipation of girls. From this she widened her concern to the worldwide disadvantage suffered by girls in education generally, (Obama White House, 2014).

But, in truth, Boko Haram were, and are, against western education for anyone, not just girls, as they are against western values generally. Their approach to boys in these schools had been rather more robust than kidnapping for some years prior to the Chibok event. Shooting, beheading or being burnt alive proved an efficacious cure for boys' tendencies towards seeking a western education. It might have been nice for Michelle Obama to recognise these facts. But perhaps she had a point. Kidnapping girls is news; killing boys is just business as usual. And there was little point, after all, in attempting to recommence the education of the boys in the picture shown in Figure 2.13.

Figure 2.13: *Nigerian Schoolboys Burnt Alive by Boko Haram*

The lack of any mention of boys in the above news links sends the clear message that it is girls in these underdeveloped countries who are uniquely disadvantaged compared with boys. The message is clear, but the message is false. The reason for the omission of any mention of boys is not because they are well educated, but because they don't matter.

To those who are inclined to be sceptical about the thesis of male disposability, please explain why Figure 2.13 - and dozens of similar incidents - did not merit a mention, and not only by Michelle Obama but by almost everyone. The West indulged in an orgy of virtue signalling over #BringBackOurGirls, but the mass killing of boys did not create a ripple of concern.

What is the factual position regarding the education of boys and girls across the world? Figure 2.14 shows United Nations literacy data for year 2015, (UNdata, 2015). The x-axis refers to different countries, plotting 159 of the world's 195 countries. The y-axis is the proportion of youths and young adults (ages 15 to 24) who are literate. The countries are ordered in descending percentage of male literacy. Hence the blue male line is a monotonically decreasing curve whilst the female line zig-zags around it. The key feature is that the female zig-zag pretty much follows the male curve. The correlation between male and female literacy rates is 0.96.

Figure 2.14: *Percentage Literacy by Country in Male Rank Order, 2015*

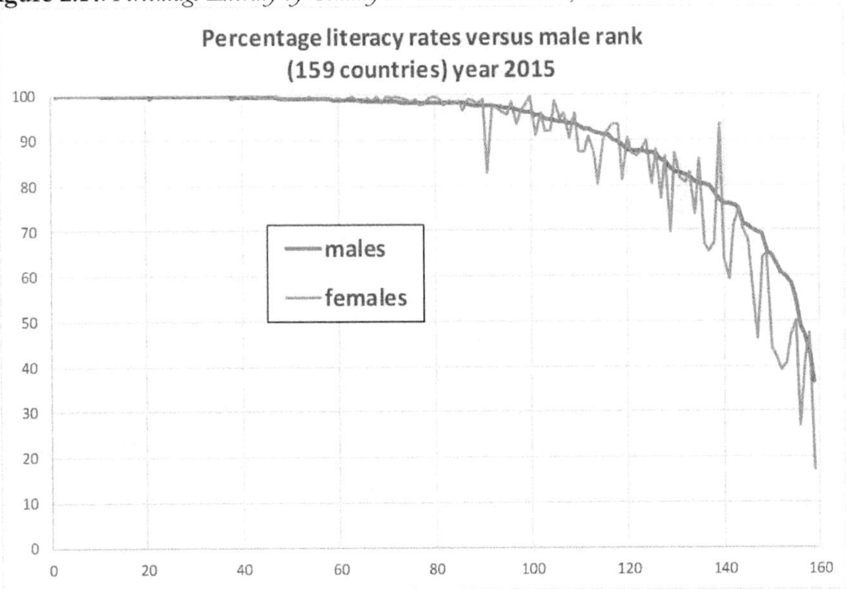

At the lowest levels of literacy the mean of the female zig-zag is a slightly lower than the male line. However, the difference between male and female literacy rates is not the dominant feature of the data. The dominant feature is that countries which educate their people to be literate do so for both sexes, whereas countries which educate only a proportion of their men to be literate also educate a comparable proportion of their women to be literate, the difference between the sexes being of second order of magnitude. This does not align terribly well with the picture of the matter being promulgated by politicians, royalty, celebrities, and the media generally.

Figure 2.15 shows in a similar format the average number of years of education received by the two sexes against country, (NationMaster, 2006). The data relates to around 2006 and 176 countries of the world's 195 are plotted. The data are again in rank order of male years of schooling, so the blue male line is a descending staircase. The female data again zig-zags around the male line with the same overall trend. The correlation between years of schooling of males and females is 0.93. Whilst there might be a tendency for a slightly smaller number of years of schooling for girls at the lowest end of the data, this is again hardly the dominant feature of the graph. The dominant feature is that countries which educate their children only to primary school level do so for both sexes, and if they educate to age 16 or to age 18, they do so for both sexes. This, again, does not align terribly well with the popular narrative.

Figure 2.15: *Years of Education by Country in Male Rank Order, 2006*

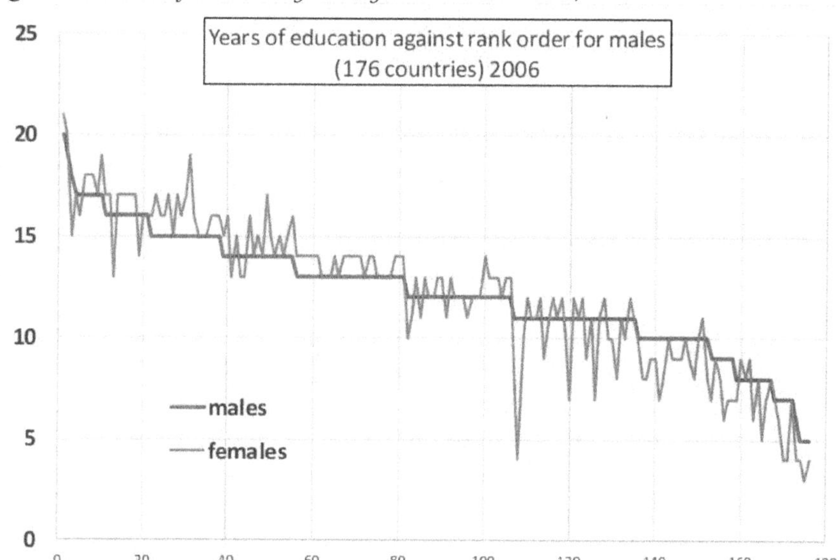

Figure 2.16 shows the ratio of the numbers of women to men enrolling in higher education, that is in university and college education, (NationMaster, 2005). There are more countries in which more women than men attend

university than the reverse. The top two countries, with in excess of three times more women than men going to university are Qatar and the United Arab Emirates. In Malala's Pakistan the ratio is 0.88, i.e., 0.88 women for every man going to university. In the UK the gender ratio, as we saw previously, is 1.37, with 1.37 women going to university for every man.

The issue in Pakistan, despite all the publicity and displays of Western concern over Malala, is not primarily the relative educational disadvantage of girls and young women, but the fact that both sexes are poorly educated in Pakistan. The average years of schooling in Pakistan are only 7 years for boys and 6 years for girls. Both sexes receive only primary level education on average, and only extremely small absolute numbers of either sex attend university.

The great and the good implicitly promulgate a false perspective by sins of omission. By never mentioning boys, they encourage the idea that, in underdeveloped countries, boys are being educated but girls are not. It's a false picture. But it is analogous to the same distorted picture of our own past in the UK. It's almost as if there are virtue signalling Brownie points to be had in wringing one's hands about girls' education, but none to be had for boys' education. It's almost as if there were an empathy gap.

Figure 2.16: *Ratio of Women to Men Enrolled in Tertiary Education by Country, 2005*

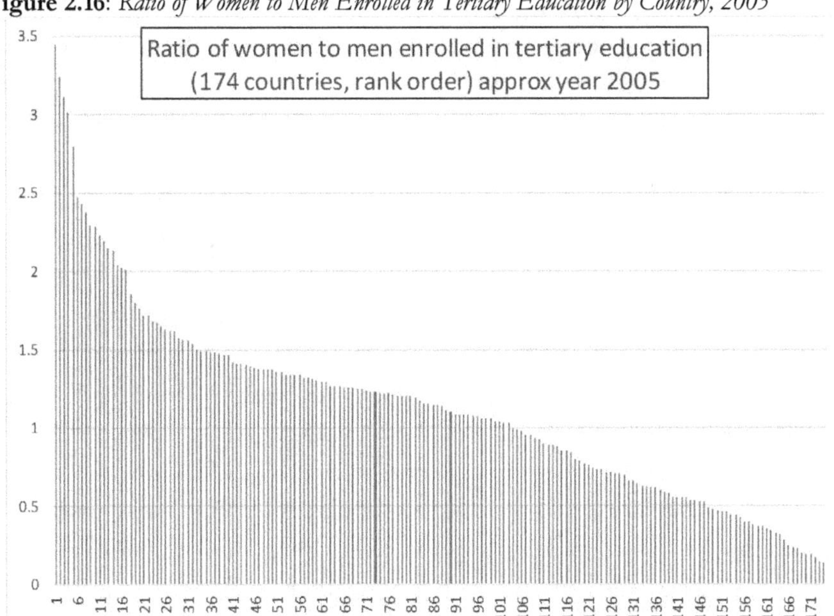

2.12 Summary: The Education Empathy Gap

In this chapter we have seen that boys do less well at school than girls in the UK. The gender gap in educational attainment is apparent from the earliest age and increases as boys and girls move from primary to secondary to tertiary education. The gender gap to the disadvantage of males gradually increases through their school career, being up to 12% in primary school, up to 19% by GCSE, about 22%-29% by A Level, and 36% in terms of university entrance. There is evidence from multiple sources that teacher bias contributes to the gender gap and that the nature of the award system in the UK also contributes to the gender gap. School teaching is strongly, and increasingly, dominated by women. But despite the emphasis placed on role models and stereotyping in other contexts, there is a reluctance to accept that these factors may be relevant to boys' underperformance. The large and increasing gender gap is well known, but Government policies display no political will to address it. Having Ministers for Education who are feminists does not help.

At universities, subject curricula and award processes are being redefined specifically to address any cases where men do better, reckless of the damage to the academic integrity of the subject. Women have outnumbered men as undergraduates in the UK for a quarter of a century. Women dominate in 70% of university subjects. Since 1900, a greater total number of degrees have been awarded to women than to men. Within a few years, women will have been awarded more degrees than men over the whole of UK history.

There is, of course, also a race and a class issue. But it is poor white people who are bottom of the heap in terms of university entrance, with poor white males the very bottom of all. A poor black woman is three times more likely to go to university in the UK than a poor white male. Across all economic classes, in 2016/17, only 27% of the UK undergraduate intake were white males.

Athena SWAN, indirectly funded by Government, is deploying financial coercion and moral blackmail to force universities to achieve higher proportions of women in senior staff positions in STEMM. It is noteworthy that women now dominate as undergraduates in STEMM. Women also dominate in junior staff positions in STEMM, whilst in middle ranking staff positions in STEMM there is gender parity. Athena SWAN is thus focussed on the most senior staff levels in STEMM, a small proportion of the total. This is typical of feminist activism which most often concentrates on the most senior positions, the objective being to place feminists in positions of power. And yet there is evidence from the USA and from France that academic hiring practices favour women over men in STEM fields.

There is enormous encouragement and support for women in STEM subjects or considering entering the STEM field. In the USA the determination to get more women in STEM has even given rise to classes in science and maths from which boys are excluded, (Peterson, 2015). In the UK, the male dominated professional institutes are heavily committed to promoting initiatives to encourage women into STEM. This has been the case for decades. In contrast, in areas where men are under-represented, such as teaching or nursing, there is no support for the minority men from the female dominated unions. In professions where women dominate, the focus remains just as emphatically on "women's equality" issues. This can only discourage men from applying to a hostile environment.

Some of the initiatives to encourage women into STEM include female-only scholarships or bursaries. These are now being legally challenged in the USA and the UK as violations of equality legislation. The outcome of these legal challenges remains to be seen.

In our society now, anti-male sentiment has become normalised (Nathanson and Young, 2001). "Laddishness" is a pejorative, especially in universities, (Phipps and Young, 2013), and teachers are trained in a culture in which masculinity is seen as a character flaw, something to be overcome or suppressed (Martino, 2018). In 2000, the philosopher Christina Hoff Sommers published a book drawing attention to the destructive effect of these attitudes on boys' education in the USA, 'The War Against Boys' (Hoff Sommers, 2000). Hoff Sommers challenged the divisive narrative that boys are intrinsically pathological. The challenge was not well received in some quarters.

The empathy gap can take a more subtle form. At the time of writing the Labour Shadow Minister for Education, and former Shadow Minister for Women and Equalities, is Angela Rayner. In January 2018 she was interviewed for an article in the Guardian, 'White working-class boys should be more aspirational' (Walker, 2018). Rayner said a focus in the educational system on women and minority ethnic groups had perhaps inadvertently had a negative impact on the attention paid to white working-class boys. 'They have not been able to adapt', she said, 'Culturally, we are not telling them that they need to learn and they need to aspire. They are under the impression that they don't need to push themselves, in the way that disadvantaged groups had to before.'

Rayner's diagnosis, that boys have not been able to adapt and need to try harder, is another variant of "it's their own fault". There is a deep issue lurking in the exhortation that "boys should be more aspirational". It lies in the word "should". What does the word "should" imply? It implies something necessary in order to achieve an objective or purpose. But that begs the question: towards what purpose does Ms Rayner assume boys *should* be striving? Towards a success which they have been taught is actually privilege and oppression of others? Why should they wish to aspire to be oppressors? And Angela Rayner's exhortation is strangely inconsistent with her complaint that universities are too male and pale, (Adams, 2019).

The age-old motivation of young males has always been to achieve sufficient financial success to be able to attract a mate and ultimately to support a family. There is nothing wrong with aspiring to this modest goal. It is presumptuous, and dare I say rather patrician, for a senior MP to demand that working class lads should wish to follow a "professional" route. It is rather fortunate that so many do not "aspire" in this way or tradesmen might become even harder to find, and we all depend a great deal more on them than we do upon lawyers or politicians or journalists. Perhaps Ms Rayner should, like them, "aspire" to be a more useful member of society, rather than yet another unnecessary politician.

It may seem like wild exaggeration to claim that, in education, we see male disposability in operation. But recall that "disposability" is to be interpreted in general as a lesser concern for males. The narrative of perennial female disadvantage, the unshakable conviction that males cannot be disadvantaged, except by their own nature, together with a strong women's lobby and the absence of such a lobby for males, lead to a focus on women and girls even in education, despite very clear statistical evidence that it is boys and young men who are predominantly disadvantaged in education. The empathy gap is the overarching psychological orientation which prevents any action being taken to redress male educational disadvantage, spuriously legitimised by variants of "it's their own fault". Not only do boys face a school system dominated by women, but Ministers and Shadow Ministers for Education seem all too frequently to hold, or have held, the "Women and Equalities" portfolio – yet another indication of what scant concern exists for boys' education.

3

Physical Health and Longevity

It is said that your life flashes before your eyes just before you die…it's called Life.
Terry Pratchett (1948 – 2018), *The Last Continent*

This chapter presents an overview of male longevity and the causes of men's early or premature death. The gender gap in longevity, and in the major causes of premature death, will be examined. It will be shown that the excess male over female death rate is not just a feature of the old but is the aggregated result of the greater death rate of males at all ages to 80.

I shall show that health and longevity are not determined solely by physical disease but also by a range of psychosocial factors. These non-physical factors will also be considered here, necessarily so for it will be found that disadvantages of psychosocial origin are often the chief cause of gender disparities in death rates to the disadvantage of males.

However, one must not lose sight of the fact that there are also biological differences between the sexes. In sex-specific ailments this hardly needs defending. However, even in diseases from which both sexes might be expected to suffer equally, there are sex differences in both incidence and mortality – generally to the disadvantage of males. In many cases it appears that males have impaired immune response compared with females. Testosterone has been implicated in this weakened immune response in males (Furman et al, 2014). The higher male than female death rate in babies and very young children is evidence of a purely physical component. Contrary to cultural assumptions, the male is more fragile than the female as regards health (Kraemer, 2000). Biology also matters.

The demographic dependence of health and longevity will also be considered. The extent of this demographic dependence will be seen to vary with gender, again to the disadvantage of men.

When it comes to disadvantage, being dead is indisputably a case in point. And when it comes to dying, male dominance remains unchallenged. And yet there are many areas in which health policy adds to the disadvantage of males, as will be shown.

3.1 Gender Disparity in Premature and Early Death

Longevity can be expressed in different ways. A common definition is "life expectancy at birth", which refers to the expected life of a baby born now if death rates at each age were assumed to remain constant. In England and Wales, based on years 2012-14, male life expectancy at birth ranged from 74.7 years to 83.3 years, with an average of 79.8 years. Female life expectancy at birth ranged from 79.8 years to 86.7 years, with an average of 83.4 years - data from (Office for National Statistics, 2015b). These ranges relate to local authority areas, so each is an average over a large population within that area.

Men can expect a shorter life than women. The gender gap in life expectancy ranges from 2.0 to 5.4 years depending upon local authority area.

Figure 3.1: *Gender Gap in Life Expectancy at Birth Versus Male Life Expectancy (2012-14 data from 346 local or unitary authorities in England and Wales)*

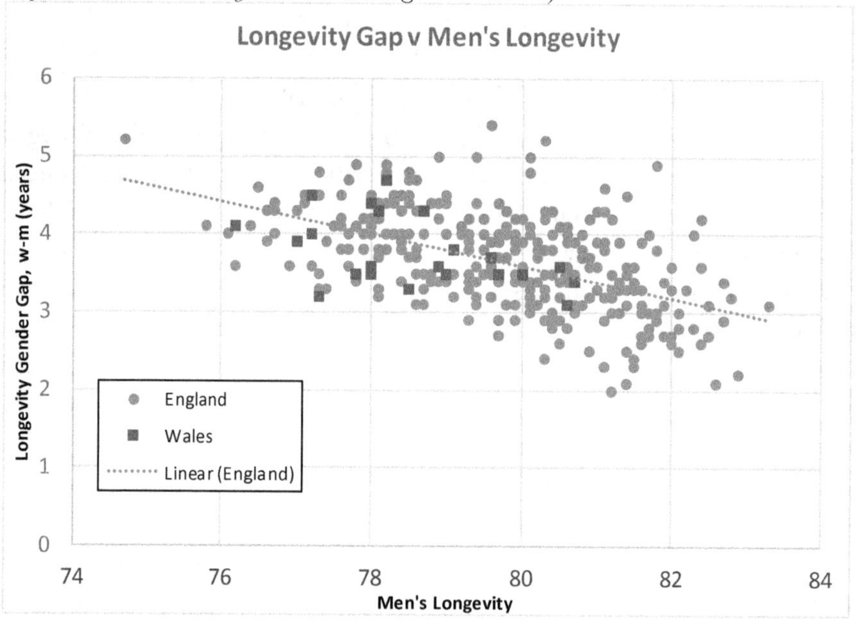

Men's life expectancy is impacted more than women's by economic disadvantage. In poorer regions for which the life expectancy is shorter, the gender gap in life expectancy is greater (Figure 3.1). Conversely, where life expectancy is longer, the gender gap in life expectancy is smaller. The longevity gender gap correlates quite strongly with male life expectancy (correlation coefficient -0.5) but only very weakly with female life expectancy (-0.1).

The review 'Inequalities matter: an investigation into the impact of deprivation on demographic inequalities in adults' by Mayhew et al (2018) notes that (page 21), 'It is particularly noticeable that men appear to be affected much more by extreme deprivation than women. Not only do women have a higher life expectancy than men but the range of difference between the most and least deprived percentiles is less by a couple of years'. Thus, for men, there is an intersectional effect of gender with socioeconomic disadvantage which increases the gender disparity in life expectancy.

Figure 3.2: *Percentage Gender Gap in Deaths by Age Range*

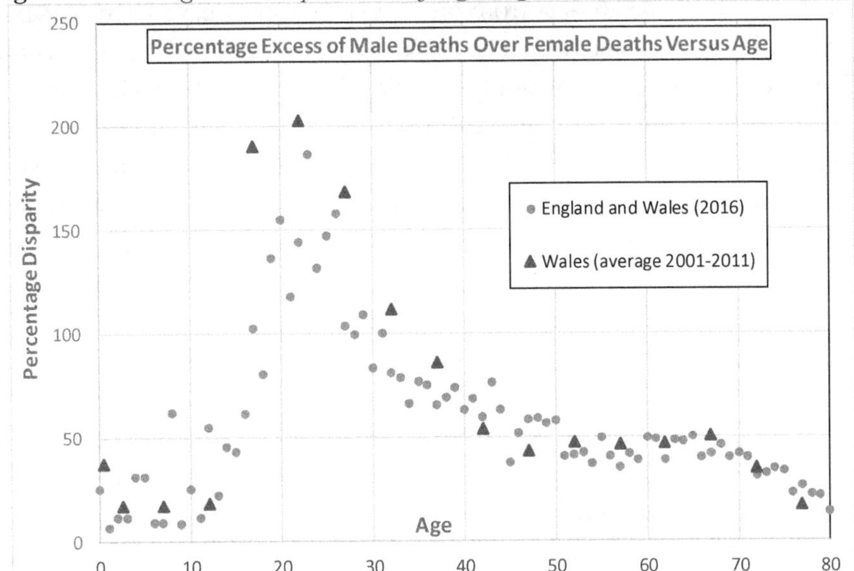

However, life expectancy does not provide a very sensitive measure of health disadvantage. What lies behind the gender gap in longevity is a huge percentage gender gap in premature death rates. For England and Wales jointly in year 2016 this is shown in Figure 3.2. Mortality data for England and Wales in 2016 at each age have been taken from (Office for National Statistics, 2017h) and mortality data for Wales at each age have been taken from (Stats Wales, 2011).

Young men between the ages of 18 and 30 have more than double the death rate of women of the same age (three times as great in their early twenties). Even mature men, between, say, 40 and 60 years old, still have death rates 40% to 70% greater than women of the same age. The number of male deaths exceeds the number of female deaths up to age 83. Even male babies have a significantly higher mortality than female babies.

Defining premature death as death before age 75, the number of premature deaths of males in England and Wales in 2016 was 105,808 compared to 73,794 females – an excess of male over female premature deaths of 43%. Figure 3.2 is an emphatic indicator of male health disadvantage, though it generally goes unremarked in favour of longevity measures.

3.2 The Leading Causes of Premature Death (<75)

Data for premature death (before age 75) in 2016 for England and Wales has been taken from (British Heart Foundation, 2018) and (Office for National Statistics, 2017e). Death data from other specific causes have been obtained from: (i) homicide data (Office for National Statistics, 2017j), (ii) alcohol related deaths (Office for National Statistics, 2017k), (iii) drug related deaths (Office for National Statistics, 2017m), and, (iv) suicide occurrences in England and Wales (Office for National Statistics, 2017n). All data quoted in this chapter have been derived from these sources unless otherwise stated. Perinatal deaths (prior to 28 days old) are excluded throughout.

Table 3.1 lists the numbers of premature deaths, by sex, together with the excess of male deaths for each cause of death. Note that more men die in almost all categories. The Table shows that in 2016 the top causes of premature death in England and Wales were cancers, cardiovascular diseases, respiratory diseases and digestive system diseases, in that order for both sexes, accounting in total for 74% of premature deaths of men, and 76% of premature deaths of women.

Across all causes there is a 43% excess of premature deaths of men over that of women in England and Wales. Cardiovascular diseases are by far the most significant cause of excess male over female premature deaths, with cancers in an easy second place. Digestive system diseases and suicide vie for third place. However, if drugs and alcohol were combined into one category, they would take third place. If suicide, drugs and alcohol were combined into one category they would account for a total of 6,055 excess male deaths over female, and hence would be the second most significant cause of excess male premature deaths. However, cardiovascular diseases remain overwhelmingly the dominant cause of excess male premature deaths.

A rather different picture emerges if the excess of male over female premature deaths is calculated as a ratio. Against this statistic, the most significant causes of excess male premature death are, in this order: transport accidents, suicide, homicide, poisoning by noxious substances other than drugs or alcohol, drugs, cardiovascular diseases, alcohol, undetermined causes, and the combined category of falls, drowning and fire. All these causes result in male premature death rates which are nearly double, or more than double, that of females. One of the most noteworthy features of the excess male premature deaths, when expressed in this way, is the prominence of the psychosocial causes: accidents, suicide, homicide, alcohol and drugs, over the physical diseases.

Table 3.1: *Gender Disparity in Premature Death (<75) in England and Wales (2016) (listed in order of excess male deaths)*

Cause of Death	Males	Females	Excess Male Deaths#
Cardiovascular diseases	24,842	11,755	13,087 (2.10)
Cancers	36,833	31,801	5,032 (1.16)
Digestive system diseases	6,931	4,479	2,452 (1.55)
Suicide	3,501	1,080	2,421 (3.24)
Respiratory diseases	9,935	7,747	2,188 (1.28)
Alcohol	4,416	2,232	2,184 (1.98)
Drugs	2,572	1,172	1,400 (2.19)
Transport accidents	1,182	310	872 (3.81)
Falls, Drowning, Fire	1,033	535	498 (1.93)
Endocrine diseases	1,681	1,240	441 (1.36)
Diseases of the Nervous System	3,528	3,117	411 (1.13)
Undetermined, including Sudden Infant Death	776	396	380 (1.96)
TB, HIV, Sepsis, Hepatitis, Meningitis	1,090	865	225 (1.26)
Homicide	371	156	215 (2.38)
Poisoning by noxious substances other than drugs or alcohol	316	141	175 (2.24)
Congenital & Chromosomal	614	502	112 (1.22)
Mental/behaviour disorders	1,391	1,279	112 (1.09)
Diseases of the blood or blood forming organs	274	187	87 (1.47)
Diseases of the skin, musculoskeletal system, or genitourinary system	1,305	1,466	-161 (0.89)
specific diseases contained in the above categories			
Alzheimer's disease	444	563	-119 (0.79)
Diabetes	975	621	354 (1.57)
ALL CAUSES	**105,808***	**73,794***	**32,014 (1.43)**

**Exceeds the sum of table entries since not all causes are listed*

#*Figure in parentheses is the ratio of male to female deaths*

However, one should not lose sight of the fact that, in terms of absolute numbers of excess male premature deaths, cardiovascular diseases are way out in front, with cancers an easy second. The prevalence of physical diseases in the gender death gap suggests that biology may be important as well as psychosocial factors. However, lifestyle issues will also impact on these physical diseases so the separation of causal factors is not easy.

Violence (by others) is sometimes claimed to be a major cause of death. This is untrue. Of the 21 causes of premature death listed in Table 3.1, homicide is 19th in terms of numbers of men's deaths caused, and 20th for women.

3.2.1 Cardiovascular Diseases

Since cardiovascular diseases are easily the most significant cause of excess male over female premature deaths they warrant more detailed attention. Cardiovascular disease (CVD) is the collective term for all diseases affecting the heart and blood vessels. This subsumes a large range of diseases including: coronary heart disease, myocardial infarction (heart attack), heart failure, and cerebrovascular diseases (including strokes), and many others. Coronary heart disease (CHD) is the collective term for diseases that occur when the walls of the coronary arteries become narrowed, usually due to a gradual build-up of fatty material called atheroma. Within the CVD categories, the biggest killers are CHD and stroke.

Despite the justified ongoing concern about CVD related deaths, it is worth pointing out that premature deaths by CVD have reduced dramatically over the decades, for both sexes, making a major contribution to increasing longevity in all the UK nations (see, for example, Figure 3.3 for Wales). Nevertheless, the ratio of male to female premature deaths by CVD has remained stubbornly persistent. Figure 3.4 illustrates how that ratio varies with age and with specific disease within the CVD group. For most CVD diseases the ratio of male to female deaths reaches a maximum in excess of two at about age 50. For CHD the peak male:female death rate ratio is in excess of four.

3.2.2 Cancers

Table 3.2 gives the number of premature deaths from cancers in 2016 for England and Wales. The number of premature male deaths from cancers exceeds the number of premature female deaths from cancers by 16%. The leading cancer causes of premature male mortality are lung cancer, colorectal cancer, oesophageal cancer and prostate cancer in that order. In women the top four causes of premature death by cancers are lung cancer, breast cancer, colorectal cancer and ovarian cancer, in that order. Lung cancer is easily the top cancer killer for both sexes, accounting for just under one-quarter of all cancer deaths for both sexes.

Figure 3.3: *Premature Death Rate from Cardiovascular Diseases in Wales, 1969 - 2016*

Figure 3.4: *Ratio of Male to Female Deaths from Cardiovascular Diseases Versus Age*

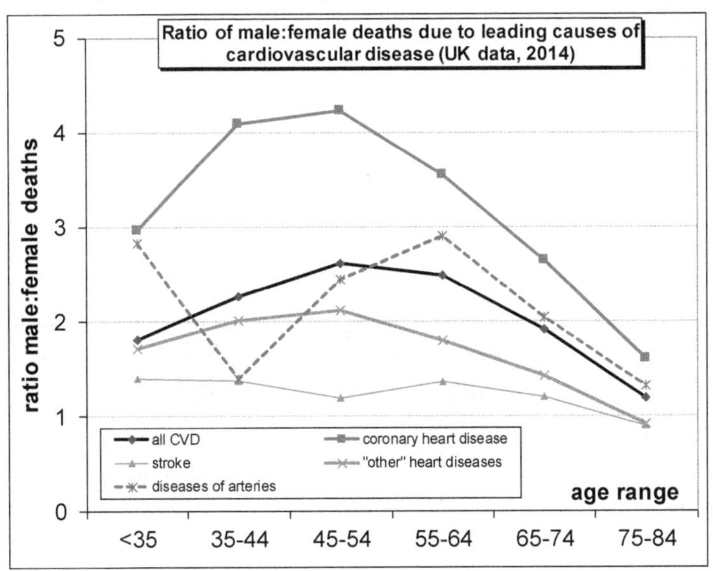

Table 3.2 shows that all types of cancer result in more premature deaths of men than of women, excluding only the female-specific cancers of breast,

cervix, ovary and uterus. The ratio of male to female cancer deaths, for all cancers except the female-specific cancers, are displayed in histogram form in Figure 3.5. Colorectal cancer is the second most important cancer for men, and the third most important for women after breast cancer, as regards premature deaths. Colorectal cancer has a national screening programme starting at age 60 for both sexes. It is the only national cancer screening programme applicable to men.

Table 3.2: *Premature Deaths from Cancers, 2016 (England and Wales)*

Cancer	England and Wales		
	Men	Women	Ratio, m:w
Lung, bronchus and trachea cancers	8,560	7,067	1.21
Colorectal Cancer	3,630	2,565	1.42
Oesophageal cancer	2,734	866	3.16
Prostate Cancer	2,588	-	-
Pancreatic cancer	2,355	1,745	1.35
Brain cancer	1,614	1,090	1.48
Liver cancer	1,526	831	1.84
Oropharyngeal cancer	1,242	466	2.67
Lymphomas	1,232	168	7.33
Kidney cancer	1,209	550	2.20
Stomach cancer	1,136	525	2.16
Leukaemia	1,079	689	1.57
Skin cancers	951	552	1.72
Bladder cancer	938	438	2.14
Mesothelioma	832	188	4.43
Multiple myloma	628	460	1.37
"Benign" neoplasms	568	406	1.40
Cancer of the larynx	327	80	4.09
Testicular cancer	45	-	-
Breast Cancer	42	5,340	-
Cervical cancer	-	499	-
Cancer of the uterus	-	1,034	-
Ovarian cancer	-	2,041	-
All Cancers	**36,833**	**31,801**	**1.16**

Oesophageal cancer is the third most important premature killer of men by cancer, and results in roughly three times as many premature deaths of men as women. Prostate cancer and pancreatic cancer are almost as significant as oesophageal cancer as regards premature deaths of men.

Figure 3.5: *Ratio of Male to Female Premature Deaths from Specific Cancers*

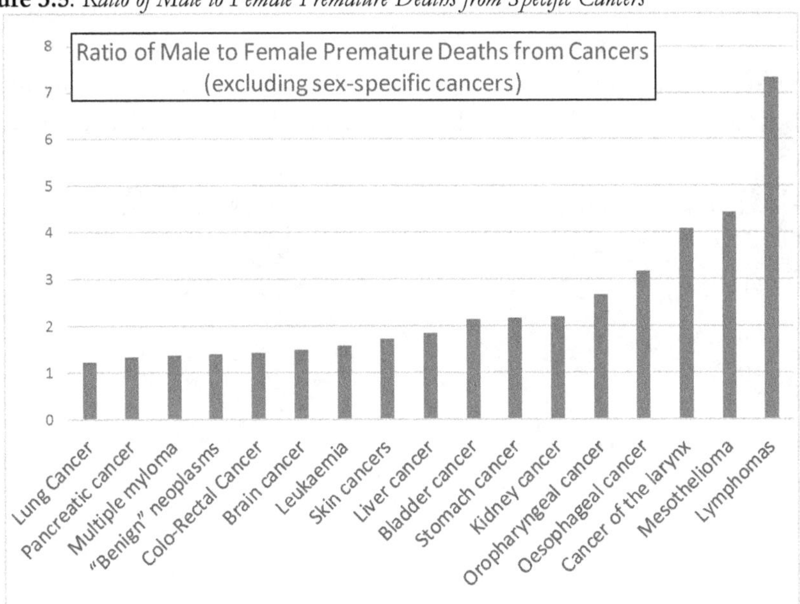

3.2.2.1 Lung Cancer

Data in this section are from 'lung cancer mortality statistics' (Cancer Research UK, 2014c). Lung cancer is by far the biggest cancer killer, for both sexes. It is also the cancer responsible for the largest number of premature deaths, in both sexes. Lung cancer causes more premature deaths of men than of women (by about 21%). A thorough review of lung cancer is beyond the scope of this book, but a few remarks regarding the influence of gender are pertinent.

By far the most important cause of lung cancer is smoking. Estimates are that between 80% and 90% of lung cancers are caused by smoking. At 2016, 17.7% of men and 14.1% of women in the UK were smokers, but the prevalence of smoking has been falling rapidly for both sexes. The difference in the prevalence of smoking between men and women in the UK has been slight, about 3 or 4 percentage points, for around 30 years (Office for National Statistics, 2017a), see also Figure 3.6. However, people who have never smoked can also get lung cancer.

Two other significant causes of lung cancer are exposure to carcinogenic substances, and natural radon. Implicated carcinogenic substances include diesel fumes, certain solvents, arsenic, some metals, asbestos, wood dust, 'second-hand' smoke, and a range of other chemicals. Exposure to these substances is often work related, with people such as painters, builders, plumbers, garage mechanics, truck drivers, and a whole range of manufacturing industries being potentially at risk. The gendered nature of employment in these areas leads to men being more at risk from these sources.

Figure 3.6: *Smoking Prevalence and Lung Cancer Incidence Rates, Great Britain, 1948-2013, taken from (Cancer Research UK, 2014b)*

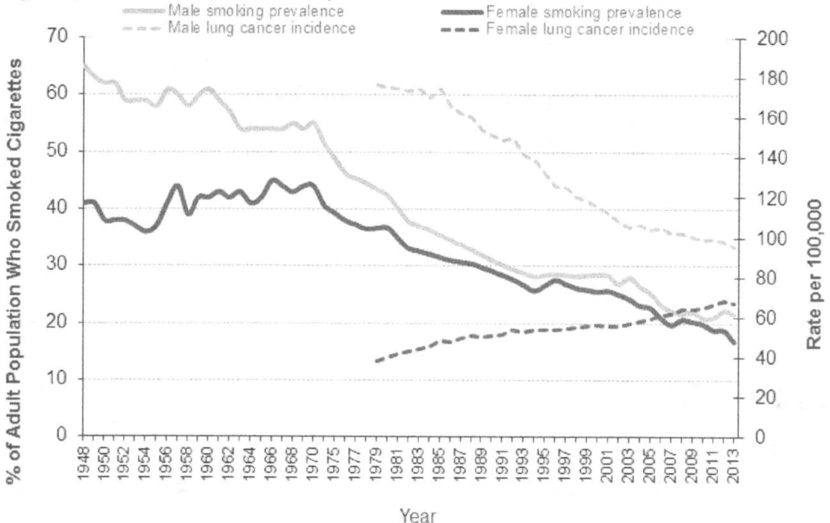

Naturally occurring radon is another cause of lung cancer. Though radon is thought to account for only about 4% of lung cancer deaths, in the UK this is over a thousand deaths. Radon concentrations vary with local geology.

The incidence of lung cancer in men exceeds that in women, as does the mortality. Survival rates in diagnosed men are poorer than those in women. It is beyond the scope of this review to examine the causes of this gendered effect. However, the male death rate by lung cancer has reduced markedly since the 1970s (Figure 3.7) as a result of the reduced prevalence of smoking. In 1948 some 65% of men in the UK smoked compared with 17.7% by 2016 (Office for National Statistics, 2017a), see also Figure 3.6. Male smoking prevalence has been reducing for 70 years.

In contrast, the death rate of women by lung cancer has increased since the 1970s, despite the prevalence of smoking amongst women having reduced from a peak of 44% in the mid-1960s to 14.1% by 2016. This is probably explained by the delayed effect of smoking, with women today paying the price for a habit indulged decades ago. What makes more obvious sense is that male and female mortality rates have tended towards convergence as smoking prevalence has also converged. An excess of male over female deaths due to lung cancer remains, probably due to a combination of men's greater smoking prevalence and poorer male survival rates but also due to the greater exposure of males to carcinogenic substances in the workplace.

Figure 3.7: *Lung Cancer Mortality Rates Versus Year, UK, 1971-2014, taken from (Cancer Research UK, 2014c)*

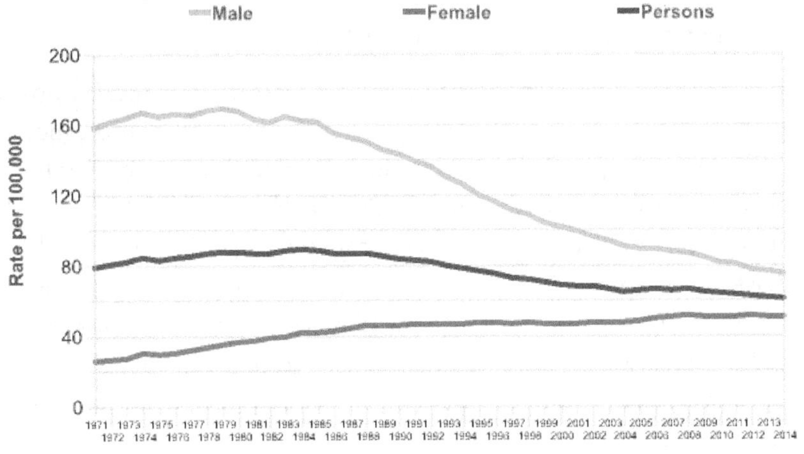

Figure 3.8: *Lung Cancer Mortality Rates by Deprivation Quintile, England 2007-11 taken from (Cancer Research UK, 2014d)*

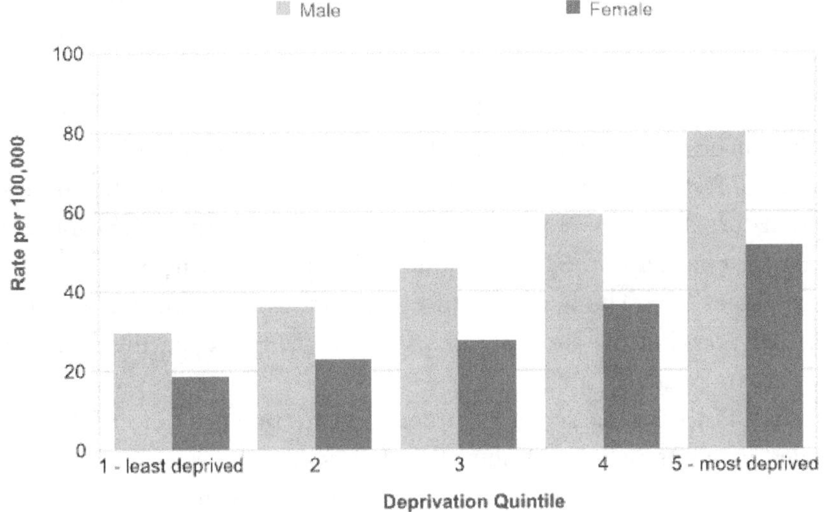

There is a strong socioeconomic dependence in the incidence of lung cancer. This is illustrated by Figure 3.8. The most deprived quintile is about 2.6 times more likely to die from lung cancer than the least deprived quintile. The most deprived quintile also has about a 3 times greater prevalence of smoking than the least deprived quintile (National Survey for Wales, 2016/17), suggesting that the demographical dependence simply reflects smoking prevalence, though occupational exposure to carcinogens is likely to be demographic dependent also.

3.2.2.2 Prostate, Testicular and Breast Cancer

Prostate cancer is frequently paired with breast cancer for purposes of comparison, because they are the most significant sex-specific cancers for men and women respectively, and by a large margin. Prostate cancer has now exceeded breast cancer as the larger killer. In England and Wales in 2016, 10,456 men died of prostate cancer compared with 10,178 women who died of breast cancer (plus 72 men). However, a larger proportion of these male deaths are post-75 than the female deaths. The number of *premature* male deaths from prostate cancer in 2016 was 2,588 compared with 5,340 *premature* deaths of women from breast cancer. Hence, prostate cancer accounts for roughly half as many *premature* male deaths as breast cancer does of women.

Nevertheless, even for deaths before age 75, prostate cancer is one of the leading cancer killers of men (4th in Table 3.2). Prostate cancer causes more premature deaths than ovarian cancer, and far more premature deaths than cervical cancer and uterine cancer combined. Across all ages, prostate cancer kills 60% more men than cervical cancer, uterine cancer and ovarian cancer combined kill women.

Men *can* get breast cancer. One of the most surprising facts in cancer death statistics is that more men in England and Wales die of breast cancer than die of testicular cancer, namely 72 and 50 respectively in 2016. In terms of premature deaths these figures were 42 and 45 respectively. The incidence of testicular cancer in the UK is about 2,400 cases per year, but the survival rate is about 98%. The incidence of breast cancer in UK men is about 390 cases per year, but the survival rate is very poor. However, these mortality numbers are relatively small.

There is no national screening programme for prostate cancer. This is not justified in terms of its mortality. Prostate cancer causes 5 times as many premature deaths as cervical cancer (and 14 times as many over all ages), yet there is a national screening programme for cervical cancer. Prostate cancer kills more men under the age of 75 than colorectal cancer kills women under 75, yet there is a national screening programme for colorectal cancer in women (and men).

The usual reason which is cited for this omission is the lack of a suitable, reliable diagnostic tool to form the basis of such a screening programme. The problem is exacerbated by the relative inaccessibility of the prostate (e.g., compared with a breast or testicle). A further exacerbation is that prostate cancer is often largely, or totally, asymptomatic until it reaches an advanced stage.

In the absence of a national screening programme, a man must be pro-active in seeking a diagnostic test for prostate cancer. This is usually a blood test, the so-called PSA (Prostate Specific Antigen) test. Men over 50 are entitled to a PSA test on the NHS, although this entitlement is described in NHS guidance with the proviso 'after discussing the pros and cons with your doctor' (UK Government, 2016b). The necessity to be pro-active, even in the absence of symptoms, is unfortunate. People are not generally pro-active when nothing seems wrong.

In practice, it is the experience of many men that GPs or practice nurses will be reticent about offering a PSA test (Prostate Cancer UK, 2016b). This reticence by GPs is largely due to the very high rate of both false positives and false negatives from the PSA test, though one suspects that practice costs also play a part. Nevertheless, the PSA test is the usual initial tool which may trigger further investigations. A digital-rectal examination can be a helpful additional check, a negative result of which can restore peace of mind. However, this, too, is unreliable. Emerging genetic testing may assist in assessing risk in the near future, (Spencer, 2019).

The usual follow-up to a suspicious PSA test or digital-rectal examination is a biopsy. Currently about 100,000 men in the UK are given prostate biopsies annually, and about 47,000 turn out to have prostate cancer (Cancer Research UK, 2015). It is most likely the desire to avoid unnecessary biopsies, which are both costly and uncomfortable for the patient, which motivates many doctors to discourage men from having a PSA test in the first place. Currently the NHS in England is trialling the use of an MRI technique as the follow-up to a suspicious PSA result as an alternative to an immediate biopsy, (NHS England, 2018).

The technique in question is mpMRI (multi-parametric magnetic resonance imaging). A study published in The Lancet has already provided evidence of its efficacy, (Ahmed et al, 2017). They found that use of mpMRI could avoid the need for biopsies in 27% of patients. If biopsies were required but were carried out using an earlier mpMRI as a guide, up to 18% more cases of clinically significant cancer might be detected. They concluded that mpMRI could also reduce over-diagnosis of clinically insignificant prostate cancer as well as improving detection of clinically significant cancer. The study has resulted in a recommended standard of mpMRI to be deployed, referred to as the PROMIS (PROstate Mri Imaging Study) standard.

Many health boards in England have now adopted mpMRI as part of their diagnostic pathway. Their experience with it has been very positive, (Prostate Cancer UK, 2018a). However, take-up in the other three UK nations lags behind. The following information was obtained via FOI, (Prostate Cancer UK, 2018b). As of 2018, in Northern Ireland mpMRI to PROMIS standard is not available at all. In Wales there are just two health boards which offer it on the NHS, namely the Cwm Taff and Aneurin Bevin Health Boards. In Scotland there are a few health boards that have adopted the technique, but most remain to be convinced of the benefits, which can be financial, not just diagnostic.

Angela Culhane, chief executive of the charity Prostate Cancer UK, has said that prostate cancer currently receives only half the funding and half the research that is devoted to breast cancer in the UK, adding that developing better diagnostic tests that could be used as part of a nationwide screening programme should be a priority, (Culhane, 2018). The current position in the UK is that 37% of prostate cancers are diagnosed only at an advanced stage (ORCHID, 2018). This compares with only 8% in the USA where there is screening, (Chinegwundoh, 2018).

One of the unfortunate aspects of the prostate cancer diagnostic problem is that the experts are openly in dispute about the merits of PSA testing. Some advise testing early, to obtain a baseline reading, and then repeat testing to identify changes. Others – and they are many – are sceptical about PSA testing at all. However, those who speak against PSA testing appear to offer nothing in its place (other than digital-rectal examination, which is no more reliable). This is disturbing. For men who have the urinary symptoms (frequent need to urinate, especially at night, slow to start urinating, weak stream) this can leave them with no means of putting their mind at rest. But prostate cancer is commonly asymptomatic until it reaches an advanced stage. The PSA nay-sayers would leave the asymptomatic man as a hostage to fortune. The author knows many men in their 50s or 60s whose prostate cancer was discovered following PSA testing (and subsequently successfully treated). Without the test, would these men's longevity have been compromised?

Amongst the PSA nay-sayers was an Editorial in New Scientist (Don't screen out the facts, 2018), which advised that, 'men should think twice about getting tested for prostate cancer, unless they have symptoms'. But the question remains: after thinking twice, what should the conclusion be? It gives one no comfort that this New Scientist Leader repeats a notorious example of the empathy gap, namely that 'men usually die with prostate cancer rather than of it'. This is male disposability as it manifests in practice. Indeed, it is true that, if a man lives long enough, it can be expected that he will eventually develop prostate cancer – and it might well be that something else kills him. But the prevalence of prostate cancer at the time of death has no bearing whatsoever on the death rate *due to* prostate cancer. The fact is that 10,456 men died *of* prostate cancer in England and Wales in 2016. It is completely irrelevant that an even greater number of men might have had prostate cancer but died of something else. It is hard to imagine the line taken by the PSA nay-sayers being applied to, say, the mammogram test for breast cancer, despite this being no more reliable than the PSA test (see below).

3.2.2.3 HPV Related Cancers

Human papilloma viruses (HPVs) are a group of more than 200 related viruses. More than 40 HPV types can be spread through direct sexual contact, from the skin and mucous membranes of infected people to the skin and mucous membranes of their partners. They can be spread by vaginal, anal, and oral sex. There are also HPVs which are not sexually transmitted and which cause non-genital warts. Around 90% of sexually active people will be infected with HPV at some time, though only around half with a high-risk variant (National Cancer Institute, 2015).

A range of HPVs are causally connected to various cancers. The most significant cancers caused by HPV are cervical cancer and oropharyngeal cancers. One HPV variant or another is responsible for virtually all cervical cancers. Hence, HPV caused 499 premature deaths of women by cervical cancer in England and Wales in 2016 (Table 3.2).

The proportion of oropharyngeal cancers which are caused by HPVs is uncertain, but substantial. Some sources put this at less than 50% (Cancer Research UK, 2016a). However, it is likely that this is based on old statistics prior to the incidence of HPV-related oropharyngeal cancers increasing steeply from the mid-1980s. The best estimate at present is that about 70% of oropharyngeal cancers are HPV induced (Chaturvedi et al, 2011).

Consequently, based on 70% of the data in Table 3.2, HPVs probably caused about 870 premature deaths of men and 326 premature deaths of women from oropharyngeal cancers in 2016 (England and Wales).

HPVs also cause about 95% of anal cancer (National Cancer Institute, 2015). There were around 140 anal cancer deaths of males in 2014, and about 220 of women (Cancer Research UK, 2014a). About half of these deaths occur after age 75, so the number of premature deaths due to anal cancer is about 70 and 110 for men and women respectively. There are other cancers associated with HPV, but they are relatively rare. In total, then, about 940 men and 935 women suffered premature deaths in 2016 due to HPV induced cancers in England and Wales.

Despite the number of premature deaths due to HPV cancers being virtually the same for the two sexes, over ten years ago the NHS introduced a free vaccination programme against HPV for girls, but with no such programme for boys. The NHS programme to vaccinate girls against the most high-risk variants of HPV was rolled out to Year 8 girls, i.e., from age 12, though it is available free up to age 18, (Public Health England, 2014). By 2012 the uptake of the complete course by girls in Wales was reported to be 87% (Public Health Wales Observatory, 2017). There was initially no NHS vaccination programme against HPV for boys. The usual reason cited (NHS, 2017) for this omission is that vaccinating girls 'helps to indirectly protect boys from these types of HPV through what's known as herd immunity because vaccinated girls won't pass HPV on to them'. The obvious flaw that this does not protect men who have sex with other men was ultimately recognised. In England, the government has recently confirmed that it will introduce a nationwide HPV vaccination programme for men aged 45 or younger who have sex with other men (UK Government, 2018f). This was made available at specialist sexual health clinics from April 2018 (so such men will need to be pro-active).

As well as the HPV vaccination for girls, cervical cancer in women is also routinely checked via a national screening programme (Public Health Wales Observatory, 2016). The so-called smear test is carried out every 3 or 5 years, depending upon age. There is no HPV infection screening for boys or men, nor any screening programme for oropharyngeal cancers which predominantly affect men. Thus, women enjoy a double protection, and men initially had none.

The initial absence of an NHS vaccination programme for heterosexual boys was highly controversial. The then-Secretary of State for Health and Social Care, Jeremy Hunt, reiterated in March 2018, ten years after the vaccination became routine for girls, that there was no intention to roll out the HPV vaccination for boys, on grounds of cost effectiveness, (Adams, 2018). Whilst vaccination at a private clinic might cost £300, it is believed that the cost to the NHS, due to economies of scale, is more like £30. Meanwhile, Australia, Austria, Croatia, and some provinces of Canada have state funded vaccination programmes for boys, with several more countries likely to recommend vaccination of boys, including many States of the USA.

The same argument based on "herd immunity" would apply equally if only boys but not girls were vaccinated. But would such an approach be regarded as acceptable, by anyone? Vigorous opposition from women's groups could be anticipated. It is unlikely that anyone would dare to vaccinate boys but not girls when both were equally at risk: such rationalisations as "herd immunity" would be immediately dismissed (rightly) as outrageous sexism.

Quite apart from issues of equality and ethics, even a lay person can see that the "herd immunity" argument was always seriously flawed. Many UK men will have sex with women from abroad at some time (and once is enough). One need only think of the large proportion of non-UK students at universities to be concerned. In a letter to the Secretary of State in June 2016, 13 HPV experts observed that 'approximately 15% of 25-34 year old males have had at least one sexual partner from outside the UK in the past five years', (Carlin, 2016). They added, 'the total burden of these diseases affects men and women about equally and we therefore believe that there is a strong ethical argument for the equal protection of both sexes'. They also noted that the costs of treating anogenital warts and oropharyngeal cancers was such that there was a cost-benefit case to be made for vaccinating boys. It would probably cost less than £20M per year to vaccinate all UK boys at the same age as girls.

Dentists are often the first to spot the signs of oropharyngeal cancer and so are particularly aware of its increasing incidence. British Dentists have been campaigning for years to get boys vaccinated (Oral Health Foundation, 2017). Senior doctors published their opinion on boys and the HPV vaccine in the

British Medical Journal in June 2016, including Elizabeth Carlin, president of the British Association for Sexual Health and HIV, and Saman Warnakulasuriya, emeritus professor of oral medicine and experimental pathology at King's College, London, (Gulland, 2016). They urged the then-Health Secretary, Jeremy Hunt, to extend the English national HPV vaccination programme to boys.

A campaign by the Men and Boys Coalition brought the EHRC into the fray, with an implied threat of legal action based on unlawful discrimination on grounds of sex, (Men and Boys Coalition, 2018). On 2 May 2018 the issue of vaccinating boys against HPV was debated in the House of Commons (UK Parliament, 2018b). There was impassioned support for vaccination of boys from Tory, Labour, Democratic Unionist and Scottish Nationalist MPs. News reports were bullish about a change of heart (Rose, 2018).

The Parliamentary Under-Secretary of State for Health and Social Care, Steve Brine, stated that he was awaiting advice from the NHS's Joint Committee on Vaccination and Immunisation (JCVI). The JCVI's interim advice in 2017 indicated that to vaccinate boys would be 'highly unlikely to be cost-effective in the UK, where uptake in adolescent girls is consistently high'. However, tellingly, the Minister also referred to 'a number of threats of judicial review related to equality and sex discrimination in relation to HPV vaccination'. Then on 24th July 2018 Steve Brine announced that boys aged 12 and 13 in England would be given the HPV vaccine, (UK Government, 2018q). Wales, Scotland and the Republic of Ireland made the same decision shortly after, though not Northern Ireland at the time of writing.

Brine's announcement followed a recommendation from the JCVI which said that a "gender-neutral" programme to protect against HPV would be cost-effective after all, (Roger, 2018). Whether the threat of legal action played a part in this turnaround I leave to the readers' judgment.

There is one outstanding issue. Virtually all women and girls under 25 in the UK are now protected against HPV. But the new Government recommendations will only vaccinate boys of age 12/13. Consequently the older cohort of boys and men will remain unprotected. It is inevitable that this cohort will have elevated rates of the associated cancers, particularly oropharyngeal cancer. This continues to be debated, not least in Parliament, Sharon Hodgson, Shadow Minister for Public Health, proposing a catch-up programme, (UK Parliament, 2019). Penny Mordaunt, then Minister for Women and Equalities, stated in reply that, 'it is the view of Public Health

England that a catch-up vaccination programme for boys is not necessary, as evidence suggests that they are already benefiting from the indirect protection known as herd protection', thus sticking to the line which has already been discredited. One suspects she placed the emphasis on the "Women" in her title rather than on the "Equalities". The statistics will eventually reveal how many men die prematurely as a result of this 10 year delay in HPV vaccination.

The disturbing aspect of the HPV vaccination saga is the amount of pressure, from a range of authoritative bodies - and ultimately the spectre of legal action - which was necessary to overturn a transparently sexist initial decision. Let those who are convinced about male privilege and incredulous at the idea of male disposability explain how vaccination for girls but not boys at equal risk was ever a policy regarded with equanimity. Let them contemplate how improbable it would be for anyone to have even contemplated vaccinating boys but not girls.

3.2.3 HIV-AIDS

Death from AIDS deserves a special mention because it affects men substantially more than women. The death rate from AIDS has now reduced markedly from its peak in 1994 when 1,537 men and 186 women died from AIDS in the UK. In 2017 there were 333 deaths of men from AIDS and 95 deaths of women. (These data relate to all ages). To date in the UK there have been five times more deaths of men than women from AIDS, (UK Government, 2018r).

3.3 The Leading Causes of Early Death (<45)

"Early" death may be defined as death before age 45. Data sources used here are the same as in section 3.2. Table 3.3 lists 17 causes of death and gives for each cause the numbers of male and female deaths before age 45, and their difference. There is an excess of early male deaths over early female deaths for all causes other than cancers. The probability of a man dying before age 45 is 78% greater than for a woman. In contrast to premature deaths, the two most significant causes of excess male early deaths are suicide and drugs, knocking cardiovascular diseases into third place. Table 3.3 confirms the frequently made claim that suicide is the biggest killer of men under 45.

Table 3.3 again confirms that the significance of inter-personal violence as a killer is exaggerated in popular discourse. Of the 17 causes of early death listed, homicide lies in 14th place in terms of the number of early deaths of men, and in 15th place for women.

As an example of how the significance of violence/homicide is exaggerated, consider the statement made in the Welsh Government's 'Measuring the health and well-being of a nation' (Public Health Wales, 2016b). It is stated under Item 43 that 'Suicide is one of the three leading causes of death in the most economically productive age group (15-44 years); the other two being road traffic injuries and inter-personal violence'. The statement is correct as regards suicide, but is inaccurate as regards transport accidents, and wildly wrong as regards inter-personal violence.

Table 3.3: *Gender Disparity in Early Death (<45) in England and Wales (2016)*

Cause of Death	Males	Females	Excess of Male Deaths#
Suicide	1,792	494	1,298 (3.63)
Drugs	1,300	376	924 (3.46)
Cardiovascular diseases	1,374	634	740 (2.17)
Transport accidents	710	164	546 (4.33)
Alcohol	685	368	317 (1.86)
Digestive system diseases	782	490	292 (1.60)
Falls, Drowning, Fire	251	64	187 (3.92)
Undetermined, including Sudden Infant Death	300	154	146 (1.95)
Homicide	240	94	146 (2.55)
Diseases of the Nervous System	450	329	121 (1.37)
Poisoning by noxious substances other than drugs or alcohol	140	41	99 (3.41)
Mental / behaviour disorders	150	71	79 (2.11)
Endocrine diseases	293	230	63 (1.27)
Respiratory diseases	447	387	60 (1.16)
TB, HIV, Sepsis, Hepatitis, Meningitis	179	140	39 (1.28)
Congenital & Chromosomal	252	229	23 (1.10)
Cancers	1,484	1,833	-349 (0.81)
ALL CAUSES	**10,829**	**6,098**	**4,731 (1.78)**

#*Figure in parentheses is the ratio of male to female deaths*

3.4 Occupational Health and Workplace Injuries and Deaths

3.4.1 Workplace Deaths in History

I confess, like many other people, I may have been inclined to complain from time to time about "health and safety gone mad". But we have reason to be grateful that modern standards of health and safety at work have improved beyond all recognition compared to, say, Victorian times. The Victorians were prodigious builders, but their many large civil works had a serious toll on men's lives. Building the Forth road bridge (opened 1890) took 78 men's lives for example, (The Scotsman, 2005).

And we *are* talking virtually exclusively of *men's* lives. During the industrial revolution, prior to 1830, some 4,000 miles of canals were dug by hand in Britain by men with picks and shovels (UK Parliament, 2018c). By 1914 men had also built 20,000 miles of railroad by hand, with some help from explosives, including many cuttings, embankments, viaducts and tunnels, (Encyclopaedia Britannica, 2018).

There are plenty of examples of high death counts constructing specific tunnels, viaducts or stretches of line. One such was the construction of the first Woodhead railway tunnel. At just over 3 miles, Woodhead 1 was one of the world's longest railway tunnels when it opened in 1845. At least 26 men died (other sources say 32) of the 400 men employed in the excavation and lining of the tunnel. The death rate among the men who built the tunnel (8%) was said to be higher than that of the soldiers who fought at the battle of Waterloo (Burns, 2017).

However, it has been estimated that around 200 men died constructing the Ribblehead viaduct, on which some 2,000 men were working at its height – which is a higher death rate still (10%) (Yorkshire Dales Trail, 2011). It is unlikely that the death rate was as high as these examples in all cases, but it is likely that of the million or so men who contributed to building Britain's canal and railway systems, the order of tens of thousands were killed on the job.

However, even that prodigious death toll is exceeded by coal mining. Between 1873 and 1953 some 85,000 men were killed in British coal mines, as many as 1800 in a single year, (Mining Institute, 2016). It is remarkable by today's standards that a single industry in a single country could cause over a thousand deaths per year, *on average*, for decade after decade, and yet be considered acceptable. This is what male disposability looks like.

Figure 3.9: *Annual Number of Fatal Injuries to Employees in Great Britain 1900-2016*

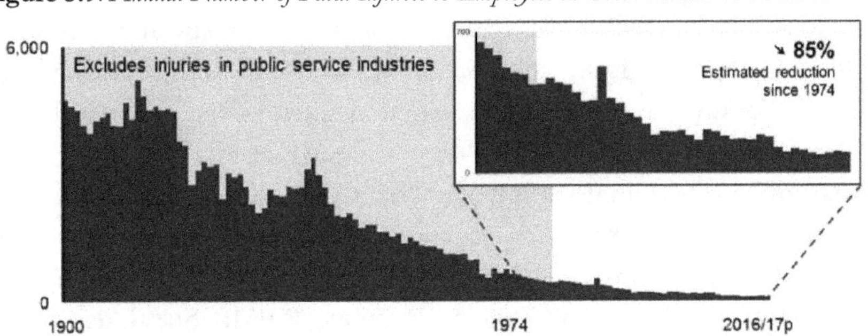

Source: ***RIDDOR and earlier reporting legislation***

Thankfully, the number of deaths at work has been falling steeply since the beginning of the 20th century, a trend which has continued over the last few decades, see Figure 3.9, (Health and Safety Executive, 2017f).

3.4.2 Workplace Deaths Now

Deaths at work are massively dominated by men. 97% of fatal injuries to workers in Great Britain in 2016/17 were men: 133 out of 137, (Health and Safety Executive, 2017m). In 2013/14 it was 98%: 122 out of 124, (Health and Safety Executive, 2014). However, the number of deaths at work has reduced substantially over the last 40 years. In the early 1980s there were typically around 500 deaths at work per year in Great Britain.

When judged by deaths per 100,000 employees, waste and recycling was clearly the dominant area in terms of worker death rate in 2016/17. Transport and manufacturing are the remaining significant sectors. Construction and agriculture are the main sectors resulting in deaths at work, between them accounting for 73% of such deaths. However, this is slightly misleading because of the large number of men employed in these sectors.

3.4.3 Non-Fatal Injuries at Work

Workers self-reported 609,000 non-fatal injuries in Great Britain in 2016/17, of which 62% were injuries to men and 38% to women (Health and Safety Executive, 2017d). The bulk of these will be minor injuries. A breakdown of the data by both injury severity and gender is not readily available (though the far greater male death rate at work suggests that severe injuries will also be skewed towards men).

3.4.4 Occupational Health Issues

Work-related ill health causes nearly five times more lost days of work than injuries at work, 25.7 million days and 5.5 million days respectively in Great Britain in 2016/17, (Health and Safety Executive, 2017g). The average number of working days lost per full time equivalent worker in 2016/17 was 0.84 (men) and 1.18 (women) (Health and Safety Executive, 2017b). Note that this contrasts with injuries at work, which are skewed towards men.

The number of new plus long-standing cases of work-related ill health in Great Britain in 2016/17 was 1.3 million. Men and women each comprised 50% of these cases, (Health and Safety Executive, 2017h). Stress, depression and anxiety account for 46% of these cases, and musculoskeletal disorders a further 31%, leaving only 23% for all other categories of ill health. Women account for the majority of the mental health cases, whereas men account for the majority of the physical health cases. The data given in the sections below refer to Great Britain.

3.4.4.1 Stress, Depression, Anxiety

526,000 workers suffered from work-related stress, depression or anxiety (new or long-standing) in 2016/17. In the three year period 2014/15 to 2016/17 the average incidence rate for work-related stress, depression or anxiety for males was 1,170 cases per 100,000 compared with 1,880 cases for females per 100,000. The three occupations with the highest rate of stress, depression or anxiety were: human health and social work, public administration and defence, and education, (Health and Safety Executive, 2017k). This is broadly consistent with the higher rate of mental disorders in women than in men in the general population (see chapter 17).

3.4.4.2 Musculoskeletal Disorders

507,000 workers suffered from work-related musculoskeletal disorders (new or long-standing) in 2016/17. The prevalence rate for males was statistically significantly higher than that for females, 1,730 and 1,560 cases per 100,000 workers respectively, averaged over the period 2014/15 to 2016/17. The four occupations with the highest rate of musculoskeletal disorders were construction, agriculture, forestry and fishing, transportation and storage, and human health and social work, (Health and Safety Executive, 2017j).

3.4.4.3 Hearing

20,000 workers in the UK are estimated to have work-related hearing problems. In the period 2007 to 2016 there were 1505 claims for work related deafness, of which 1495 were from men and just 10 were from women, (Health and Safety Executive, 2017c). Having myself spent some time in turbine halls with running 660MWe sets, I can understand why. These days, failing to wear ear protection is a disciplinary offence in any caring industry.

3.4.4.4 Vibration White Finger and Carpal Tunnel Syndrome

Carpal tunnel syndrome and so-called "white finger" are conditions caused by the prolonged use of vibrating hand-held tools. These are conditions which overwhelmingly affect men. Between 2007 and 2016 there were 10,990 new claims for these conditions, of which 10,670 were from men and just 320 from women, (Health and Safety Executive, 2017a).

3.4.4.5 Occupational Cancers

In 2015 there were about 8,000 cancer deaths, and 13,500 new cancer registrations, attributed to occupational exposure. The carcinogens responsible include asbestos, silica, diesel exhaust, mineral oils, and substances used by painters. Shift workers and welders are also vulnerable to occupation induced cancers, as are outdoor workers exposed to the sun. About half the occupational cancer deaths are attributable to asbestos. The construction industry accounts for nearly half the occupational cancer deaths, (Health and Safety Executive, 2017e). In view of the work areas and the nature of the offending substances, the majority of occupational cancers affect men. Of occupational cancer deaths, 79% were men (6366), and 21% women (1657). Of new occupational cancer registrations, 74% were men (10,074) and 26% women (3620), (Health and Safety Executive, 2010).

A major contributor to occupational cancer deaths is mesothelioma, which most commonly affects the lungs. 80% of mesotheliomas are caused by asbestos. In 2016 it killed 1,947 men and 366 women in England and Wales, (Office for National Statistics, 2017e). Figure 3.10 shows that the number of deaths from mesothelioma has been rising steadily since 1973, despite far greater precautions now being taken in respect of exposure to asbestos. This will be the legacy of past carelessness because of the disease's long latency of many decades.

Despite the decline in the British coal industry, there are still 200 to 300 new cases of coal dust induced pneumoconiosis annually, though the death rate is far smaller. This is virtually exclusively confined to men (Heath and Safety Executive, 2018).

Figure 3.10: *Annual mesothelioma deaths and cases in Great Britain, 1973 - 2016*

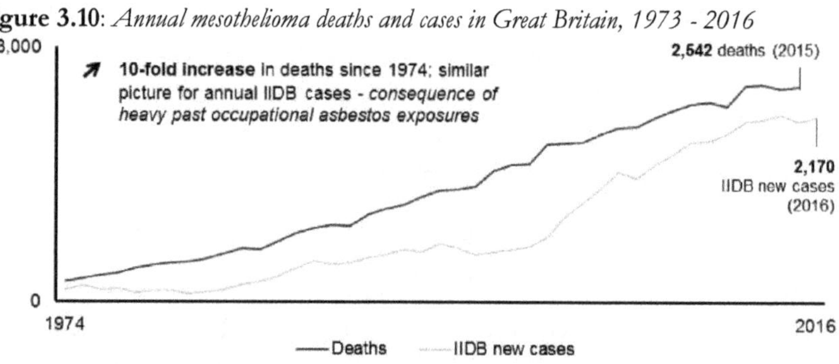

4

Men's Access to Healthcare and Health Spending by Sex

The only way to keep your health is to eat what you don't want, drink what you don't like, and do what you'd rather not.
Mark Twain, (1835 – 1910)

In the matter of health, the familiar signature of the empathy gap, "it's men's own fault", is manifest in claims that men do not look after themselves, that men do not see their doctor when they should, and that men delay too long in seeking medical help. In this chapter I review the evidence supporting or refuting these claims. I allude briefly to the global position which also indicates a relative subordination of men's health issues to those of women. I also review briefly the gender breakdown of spending on healthcare and medical research using the USA as an exemplar. The overall picture as regards the empathy gap in men's health is then summarised.

4.1 Men's Access to Healthcare

One of the explanations put forward to explain men's poorer longevity is that men "just don't look after themselves". Men, it is said, do not visit their GP or other health services when they should, and they delay consulting a doctor when they have a medical problem, thereby disadvantaging themselves. Is this true? Or is this just another instance of blaming men for their own disadvantage? Are poor health outcomes for men a product of a macho male gender script in which help-seeking is seen as weakness? Or is it a result of disadvantage imposed on men by society? Or is it biology?

It is certainly the case that men in the UK visit their GP less often than women. But this does not necessarily imply that men are gratuitously disadvantaging themselves. Women visit their doctor in association with contraception, pregnancy, neonatal and postnatal issues, as well as in the context of screening programmes. None of these apply to men, or apply to a much lesser extent, so less frequent visits by men to their GP is to be expected. In addition, it is known that people who work full time find it more difficult to attend GP appointments. This will affect more men than women, since more men work full time, see (White and Witty, 2009) and also chapter 7. So, are the less frequent visits by men to their GP a disadvantage imposed on them by their working patterns, rather than the fault of their self-destructive 'hegemonic masculinity'? In this section some of the academic publications are reviewed to shed light on the reasons for men accessing health services less often than women.

In 2008, the Men's Health Forum and the University of Bristol were commissioned by the Department of Health to examine the role of gender in accessing health services in the UK, (Wilkins et al, 2008). We have seen that the gender gap in premature death rate is dominated by cardiovascular diseases and cancers. This is what Wilkins *et al* (page 21) had to say about accessing health services by men and women in the context of cardiovascular problems – recalling that this is the top cause of the gender gap in premature death,

> 'There are a number of studies which look at the gap between the onset of symptoms related to heart attack/acute myocardial infarction (MI) and the decision to seek treatment. However, the evidence is not clear cut in terms of whether women or men are more likely to delay. In addition, although delays in help-seeking have important clinical implications - increasing the risk of mortality or subsequent morbidity - research does not tell us whether differences in delay between women and men are long enough to have clinical implications.'

> 'One review of over 100 studies of treatment-seeking delay in patients with heart attack and stroke reported that women had longer delays before seeking help when experiencing symptoms of heart attack, but there were no differences between women and men when experiencing symptoms of stroke. A 2004 meta-analysis of delays in treatment-seeking reported that larger-scale studies with greater statistical reliability were most likely to report longer delays in seeking treatment for women than men. In addition, one study suggested that, while men and women were equally likely to delay, the time elapsed before seeking treatment was longer for women than men, increasing their mortality risk.'

Similarly, in the context of cancers (the second most important cause of the gender gap in premature death), the relevant extracts from Wilkins *et al* are as follows, firstly on patient delays in seeking health care advice, (page 81),

> 'For 10 different groups of cancers combined, 13 studies showed greater delay in men (10 of the studies were rated as strong methodologically, 2 moderate and 1 insufficient), 11 studies showed greater delay in women (8 strong and 3 moderate), and 23 studies found that gender had no impact (11 strong and 12 moderate). There was only one cancer where research was decisive, but this was because there was only one study for that cancer, otherwise gender had no impact or the effect of gender was inconclusive.'

And on practitioner delay, Wilkins *et al* tell us, (page 82),

> 'The review by Macdonald et al (2004) of research on delay uses the term "practitioner delay" for the period between first consultation for symptoms and an appropriate referral. Overall, for the 10 different groups of cancers, four studies

> show greater delay when the patient was male (two strong methodologically and two moderate), six studies show greater delay for female patients (six strong), and four studies found that the gender of the patient had no impact (four strong). As with patient delay, there are conclusive results for individual cancers only when there has been a single study (on skin cancer, in which women had greater delay).'

In summary, (Wilkins et al, 2008) provide no support at all for the idea that men's delay in accessing health services is responsible for their adverse outcomes in the two key areas of cardiovascular diseases and cancers.

The study 'Do men consult less than women? An analysis of routinely collected UK general practice data' analysed GP consultation data from just under two million men and two million women, (Yingying Wang et al , 2013). The crude consultation rate was 32% lower in men than women. Accounting for reproductive-related consultations substantially diminished but did not eradicate the gender gap (Figure 4.1). However, consultation rates in men and women who had comparable underlying morbidities (as assessed by receipt of medication) were similar; men in receipt of antidepressant medication were only 8% less likely to consult than women in receipt of antidepressant medication, and men in receipt of medication to treat cardiovascular disease were just 5% less likely to consult than women receiving similar medication. These small gender differences diminished further, particularly for depression, after also taking account of reproductive consultations.

Wang *et al* were unable to control for the effect of full time working, due to limitations in the recorded data. However, as can be seen from Figure 4.1, the sex difference in consulting rates is confined to the working years and disappears below 16 and rapidly disappears above 60. It seems likely that if full-time working were accounted for, it might eradicate entirely any residual sex difference. Support for this contention is obtained from other studies, discussed below.

A by-product of the analysis of Wang et al is the significance of socioeconomic status. The gender gap in consultation rate becomes successively greater as one moves down the deprivation quintiles. This is in line with the general trend that socioeconomic disadvantage affects men even more than women. Women in the most deprived quintile consult their GP approximately 10% *more* often than women in the least deprived quintile. In contrast, men in the most deprived quintile consult their GP about 4% *less* often than men in the least deprived quintile.

Ian Banks and Peter Baker (2013) recognise the significance of full time working on men's accessing health care services, and the exacerbation of this problem for men in relative deprivation. They note (page 40), 'there are some specific groups of men who are likely to face additional barriers to accessing primary care. Low-income men in employment tend to have less flexible working hours and may lose pay if they take time off to attend an appointment....We now know that men will use primary care services that meet their needs. By providing a male-specific service that is also open in the evenings, the Camelon men's health centre in Scotland succeeded in attracting significant numbers of men, particularly from its target group: men in their 40s, living in deprived communities.'

Figure 4.1: *GP Consultation Rate per 1000 Person-Year by Gender and Age (5 years age bands) in 2010. From (Yingying Wang et al, 2013). This graph does not include the effects of full time working nor the dramatically reduced gender gap for diagnosed morbidities (see text).*

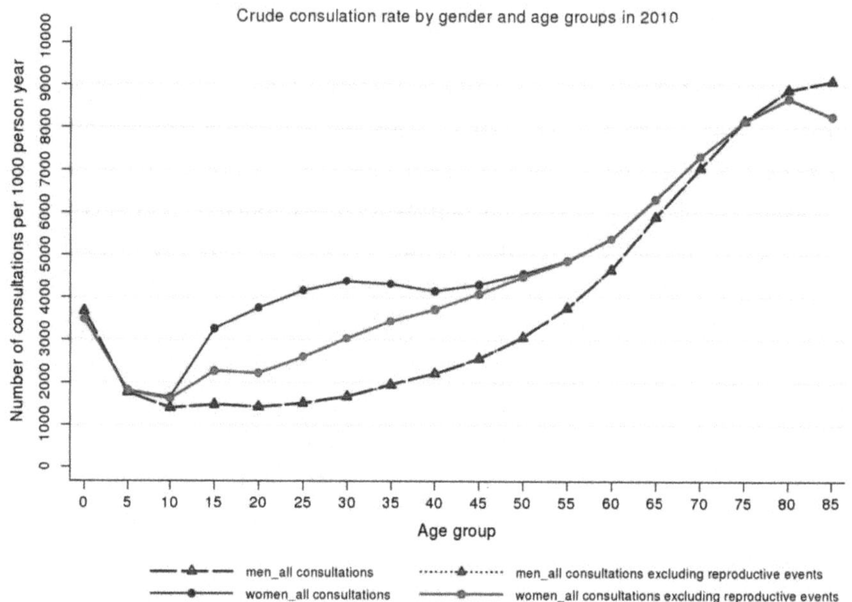

A report by the European Commission, 'Access to Healthcare and Long-Term Care: Equal for Men and Women?' observes,

> 'An additional cultural barrier that is worth mentioning mainly affects men and relates to the flexibility of services. An explanation given in the UK for men's lower use of primary care services is that the opening hours are incompatible with the long working hours that characterise the UK labour market. Men are unable or uninclined to access primary care services because they are more likely than women to work full-time and to work more than 45 hours per week.' (EGGSI coordinating team, 2009), page 105.

Similarly, Alan White and Karl Witty (2009), in their discussion of men's under use of health services, noted that, (i) 80% more men than women in the UK work full time, (ii) three times as many women work part-time, (iii) 50% more women who work full time have flexible working arrangements, and, (iv) three times as many men as women work more than 45 hours per week. They conclude that, for men 'attending for health checks during the working day is at best problematic, at worst impossible'. They go on to observe that the majority of community health promotion activities, such as weight loss groups, also take place during the working day. The relevance of working patterns in men's access to health services has also been raised by the National Pharmacy Association (Doward, 2012).

There are studies which, at least superficially, appear to blame men's under-utilisation of healthcare services on negative masculine behaviour traits. For example, in a review of the literature, Paul Galdas et al (2005) conclude in their Abstract that,

> 'the growing body of gender-specific studies highlights a trend of delayed help seeking when they (men) become ill. A prominent theme among white middle-class men implicates "traditional masculine behavior" as an explanation for delays in seeking help among men who experience illness.'

But a curious aspect of this conclusion is that it is based on a dismissal of gender-comparative studies. In respect of gender-comparative studies the paper includes this summary, (page 620),

> 'The review of key gender-comparative help seeking studies does not fully support the hypothesis that men are less likely than women to seek help when they experience ill health. Although many studies note the relative under use of health services and symptom reporting by men in comparison with women, conversely, many also find an increase in help seeking in men compared with women, or indeed, no significant difference in help-seeking behaviour between genders. The evidence suggests that occupational and socioeconomic status, among others, as more important variables than gender alone.'

Galdas et al leave one in the peculiar position of being asked to believe that men's and women's delay in seeking healthcare services are comparable, yet, at the same time, men's delay is to be blamed upon "traditional masculine behaviour". It rather begs the question: what causes women's similar delay, then? One cannot help but be suspicious that the "gender-specific" studies Galdas et al cite may have suffered from an over-willingness to make individual male behaviour culpable for a socially imposed disadvantage, namely working patterns.

A similar conflict between ostensible conclusions and research content is to be found in the American study by James Leone et al (2016). The Abstract states that 'results suggest gender norms and masculine ideals may play a primary role in how men access preventative health care'. But what we actually find within the paper is, (page 269),

> 'Using hegemonic masculinity theory we explored whether predictors of men not accessing health care would be due to a threat to perceived masculinity (macho/machismo), stigma, reactivity, and weakness/vulnerability. However, stigma and weakness/vulnerability did not play a role in the prediction model. This was somewhat of a surprise seeing that male gender norms and masculinity are closely related such that endorsement of male gender role norms often prompts some men to adopt a hypermasculine (i.e., hegemonic masculinity) ideal. We found less rigid gender role norms in our participants.'

And,

> 'We also assessed our conceptual model as to whether the TNC (theory of normative contentment) would align to men not accessing health care. Specifically, we were interested in fatalism, denial, low awareness of risks, and low knowledge; this was somewhat consistent. Fatalism and lack of knowledge did not achieve statistical significance in our model.'

Leone *et al* do not discuss the role of working patterns in men's health care access. A specific example where the role of work has been definitively established is 'Identifying Work as a Barrier to Men's Access to Chronic Illness (Arthritis) Self-Management Programs' by Lisa Gibbs (2007). She concluded in a Headnote,

> 'A qualitative study was conducted involving in-depth interviews with 17 men with arthritis. This paper discusses the role of work as one of the factors affecting men's access to arthritis self-management services. Work was found to be a significant conceptual, structural, and social barrier due to: its role in relation to men's concepts of health and fitness; practical difficulties in accessing services during business hours; and sociocultural influences resulting in prioritising of work commitments over health concerns. The structural, conceptual, and sociocultural work influences were more of a constraint for men in the middle stages of life when work and family obligations were greatest.'

In summary, the literature suggests that there is a smaller gender gap in accessing healthcare than is popularly believed, especially when the apparent gap is adjusted to allow for women's greater access for contraceptive, pregnancy, childcare and national screening purposes. The latter is a disadvantage imposed on men, not an aspect of male behaviour. The residual gender gap in access to primary healthcare, as displayed by Figure 4.1, is probably due in the main to men's working patterns, and the resulting difficulties of access to healthcare and community health programmes during the working day.

There is a willingness to attribute men's indisputable health disadvantages to men's lesser use of healthcare services, and to attribute this to men's destructive masculine characteristics. However, this hypothesis does not survive inspection. Not only is men's reduced access to healthcare not as marked as is often supposed, but the part of this reduced access which is not explained by valid sex differences in need may be explicable by working patterns. Whilst it might be argued that men's working patterns are an individual choice, it would be disingenuous not to concede a societal – and practical/financial - obligation which acts in this respect.

Finally, there are clear instances of poorer service provision for men, for example in respect of the dearth of national health screening programmes for men and the withholding of the HPV vaccination programme from boys for over 10 years. What has not been addressed here, but is badly needed, is a close examination of exactly what services for specific medical conditions are made available, and at what stage, under the NHS. In times of cost cutting, what services are pruned back? Is one sex more impacted than the other by such reducing provision? In passing I note just one: the availability of groin hernia (inguinal hernia) operations on the NHS.

In their lifetime, 27% of men will suffer from a groin hernia. Surgical treatment is relatively straightforward and takes only about 45 minutes. But in July 2018 it was revealed that over half of men seeking relief from their hernias are now being refused the operation on the NHS, (Spencer and Hargreaves, 2018). More than half the health boards in England refuse NHS funding for the 45-minute procedure unless patients are in enough agony to 'impede working life'. The criterion for surgery is now that the man is in too much pain to work. Those who doubt the hypothesis of male utility, take note: a man's pain is not sufficient reason for action unless his function may be compromised. The proportion of men being thus denied relief has doubled in four years. Surgeons have described the rationing rules as 'an absolute disgrace'.

There are signs here that male health disadvantage is more due to society-wide acceptance of such disadvantage than it is to destructive masculine traits. Adopting a stance that traditional male gender norms are responsible ("it's men's own fault") may be a subconscious means of avoiding acknowledging the implied empathy gap.

4.2 Global Health of Men

Although the focus of this review is on the UK, it is instructive also to consider briefly the international context, including under-developed countries. The 'Global Health 50/50 Report 2018' notes that, worldwide,

> 'Over the past 25 years, men have consistently suffered higher rates of ill-health (measured as Disability Adjusted Life Years, DALYs) than women…... in our sample of 40 NGOs, 14 stated that they focus exclusively on the health needs of women and girls….., no organisation in our NGO sample focuses exclusively on the health of men and boys, despite longstanding evidence of higher disease burden and lower life expectancy among men. This analysis of the focus of NGOs speaks to the need for organisations to truly adopt a gendered approach to programmes and strategies in realising the right to health for everyone.' (Hawkes et al, 2018), page 18.

This recognition of the dangers of conflating gender equality with women, and the importance of being driven by evidential data, is welcome. It is fully consistent with the World Health Organisations 'Gender Fact Sheet': 'Gender equality in health means that women and men, across the life-course and in all their diversity, have the same conditions and opportunities to realise their full rights and potential to be healthy, contribute to health development and benefit from the results'.

The Global Health 50/50 report also notes that the health organisations from which they obtained their data are still dominated, in terms of senior staff, by men: 'Global health is led by men: Sixty-nine percent (69%) of organisations are headed by men; Eighty percent (80%) of board chairs are men' (page 14). This further reinforces the danger, alluded to in chapter one, of conflating the fortunes at the top end of the male distribution with the misfortune at the bottom end of that distribution. There is a risk of holding the misguided belief that the preponderance of men in senior positions advantages the common run of men. It does not. Men in power do not favour other men over women. It is a lesson that many of our feminist MPs still need to learn.

4.3 Healthcare and Health Research Spending

In this section I use data from the USA, because quality data on healthcare and health research spending disaggregated by sex is less readily available for the UK. One needs to distinguish between spending on medical research and spending directly on the healthcare of individuals. Sex-specific data shows that both are biased towards women.

4.3.1 USA Healthcare Spending by Sex

Cylus et al (2011) have examined USA healthcare data for 2004. Table 4.1 gives their numerical results covering all ages and indicating that overall healthcare spending on women was 34% greater than that on men (or 32% when calculated per capita). Figure 4.2 gives their data in various age ranges. This shows that there is no sex difference up to age 18, but thereafter spending is greater on women than men. To quote,

> 'Per capita differences were most pronounced among the working-age population, largely because of spending for maternity care. Except for children, total spending for and by females was greater than that for and by males, for most services and payers. The gender difference in total spending was most pronounced in the elderly, as a result of the longer life expectancy of women.' (Cylus et al, 2011).

Table 4.1: *Personal Healthcare Spending in the USA Disaggregated by Sex, 2004, from (Cylus et al, 2011)*

Service	Women ($B)	Men ($B)	Women/Men
Hospital care	307.0	259.4	1.18
Physician and clinical services	230.8	162.8	1.42
Nursing home care	76.7	38.5	1.99
Prescription drugs	109.6	79.2	1.38
All other services	163.7	122.1	1.34
All personal health care	887.9	662.0	1.34

Figure 4.2: *Personal Healthcare Spending in the USA Disaggregated by Sex and Age Range, 2004, from (Cylus et al, 2011)*

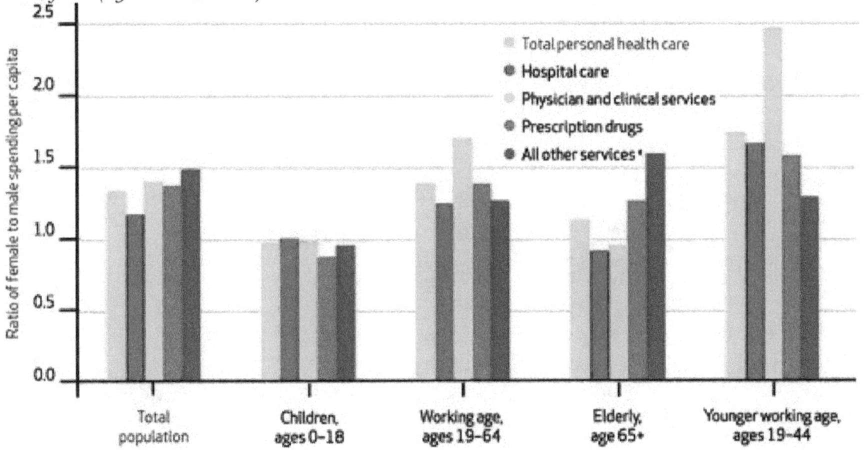

A more recent analysis of USA healthcare spending is that of Dieleman et al (2016). Their data for year 2013, disaggregated by sex and age, are displayed in Figure 4.3. This Figure tells essentially the same story as that of Cylus et al

(2011), except that, by year 2013, the cost implications of ADHD had become apparent in the data. They observe,

> 'Estimated spending differed the most between sexes at age 10 to 14 years, when males have health care spending associated with attention-deficit/hyperactivity disorder, and at age 20 to 44 years, when women have spending associated with pregnancy and postpartum care, family planning, and maternal conditions. Together these conditions were estimated to constitute 25.6% of all health care spending for women from age 20 through 44 years in 2013. Excluding this spending, females spent 24.6% more overall than males in 2013.'

It is rather alarming that the use of behaviour altering drugs on boys is now so extensive that its cost is evident in overall healthcare statistics (see also chapter 17). It is also worth emphasising Dieleman et al's last point: healthcare spending on women overall exceeds that on men by 24.6% even when spending on pregnancy, postpartum care, family planning, and maternal conditions are excluded.

Figure 4.3: *Personal Healthcare Spending in the USA Disaggregated by Sex and Age Range, 2013, from (Dieleman et al, 2016).*

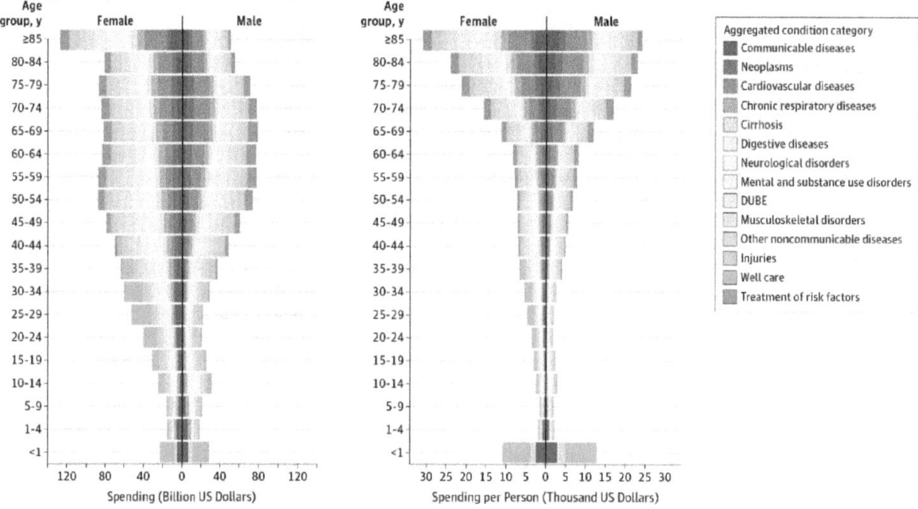

4.3.2 USA Health Research Spending by Sex

Data on USA health research spending is taken from the Office of Research on Women's Health 'Report of the Advisory Committee on Women's Health, Fiscal Years 2015/16', (National Institutes of Health, 2017). Table 2 of this 452 page report breaks down health research spending by disease, by sex, and for years 2015 and 2016. Table 4.2 reproduces the data for 2016, for the major headline disease categories only. The data relate to the research budgets of the U.S. Department of Health and Human Services (HHS) and the National Institutes of Health (NIH). Most research spending (80%) is not sex-specific. However, where it *is* sex specific, more is spent on women. Across all diseases, female-specific health research receives 2.32 times as much funding as male-specific research. There are only two categories where men's health research funding exceeds women's, namely substance abuse and environmentally induced diseases (and for these the spend is close to parity). Most odd is the spend on cancers, for which the female specific funding is 21.2 times the male-specific funding. Also surprising is the category "immune disorders". This would presumably include AIDS, which affects substantially more men than women, and yet the spend on women is 12.3 times that on men.

Table 4.2: *USA Health Research Budgets (HHS and NIH), 2016, by Sex*

Disease	Women $M	Men $M	Both $M	Ratio W/M
Cancers	1,251	59	4,326	21.2
Cardiovascular/Pulmonary	520	388	3,220	1.34
Reproductive	352	21	629	16.8
Ageing	695	399	953	1.74
Endocrine/Gastrointestinal	362	227	675	1.60
Substance abuse	327	342	780	0.96
Behavioural	51	24	1,298	2.13
Mental Health	106	46	1,266	2.30
Infectious diseases	354	209	3,677	1.69
Immune disorders	148	12	423	12.3
Neurological/Muscular/Bone	88	40	1,951	2.20
Kidney/Urological	36	18	559	2.00
Ophthalmic/Oral	37	12	1,315	3.08
Environmentally diseases	13	14	228	0.93
Service, training, miscellaneous	201	147	4,444	1.37
TOTAL	**$4.54B**	**$1.96B**	**$25.74B**	**2.32**

4.4 The Empathy Gap in Men's Health

To summarise chapters 3 and 4, we have seen that men in England and Wales are 43% more likely to die before age 75 than women, and 78% more likely to die before age 45. Men have a higher death rate from almost all causes. We have seen that psychosocial factors are certainly significant in this shorter male longevity, but that biological sex differences also play a part. The latter are evident in the fact that the death rate for male babies and young boys exceeds that of females of the same age by about 10% to 30%.

Suicide is the biggest killer of men under 45 (see chapter 18 for more on suicide).

Almost all fatal accidents at work are of men (97%). This is because of occupational polarisation (see chapter 7) which results in the at-risk occupations being overwhelmingly employers of men (construction, agriculture, waste, recycling, transport and manufacturing). Non-fatal accidents at work are also dominated by men.

The number of lost days of work per 100,000 employees due to occupational ill health is greater for women than men, though both sexes report the same number of incidents of ill health. Physical ill health due to occupation is more common in men, whilst occupational stress, depression and anxiety is more common in women. Fatal occupational health issues are dominated by men.

Both sexes suffer reduced longevity as a result of socioeconomic deprivation, but this demographic effect is significantly more marked for men. The intersection of deprivation and being male leads to the greatest health disadvantage.

Men suffer disadvantage in respect of cancers in several ways. Apart from the sex-specific cancers, more men die prematurely (<75) of every type of cancer. More men than women die from occupational cancers, especially mesothelioma. Prostate cancer now kills more men than breast cancer kills women, but there is no screening programme for prostate cancer whilst there is a screening programme for breast cancer. HPV infections are responsible for similar numbers of premature cancer deaths in both sexes, but it took ten years of lobbying by health bodies and others to persuade the Government to vaccinate boys as well as girls. Moreover, women have an NHS screening programme for the main HPV-induced cancer, cervical cancer, but there is no screening programme for oropharyngeal cancers which predominantly affect men and are mostly caused by HPV. Lung cancer, the biggest cancer killer, has a higher mortality in men. There is also a greater occupational exposure element to men's acquisition of lung cancer than is the case for women.

It is often claimed that men contribute to their own health disadvantage by their reluctance to seek medical advice in a timely fashion. However, a review of the evidence suggests this is less significant than is often supposed. Moreover, in as far as this may be a factor, men's lower GP consultation rates are probably largely a consequence of their difficulty in accessing health services due to working full time. The presumption that men create their own disadvantage by failing to look after themselves - perhaps due to hegemonic masculine norms - appears to be another instance of maintaining the appearance of agency with individual men themselves ("it's their own fault") rather than accepting any element of societal disadvantage.

The impact of inflexible working hours on GP consultation rates, and hence potentially on health outcomes, is more marked for socioeconomically disadvantaged men. The reverse is the case for women.

One issue which is sometimes cited as a health disadvantage for women is that trials of new drugs tend to be carried out on more men than women (Woodruff, 2010). Men and women are biologically different in a myriad of ways, and in particular they metabolise drugs differently. Consequently, the sex bias in testing may disadvantage women as regards the effectiveness of the drugs produced. However, test subjects in drug trials are volunteers. There is some risk in being such a volunteer. Sometimes a trial goes horribly wrong (Nelson, 2017). Where there is risk, you can expect there to be more men volunteering than women. The problem with under-representation of women in drug trials is that too few women volunteer (Westervelt, 2015).

Perhaps the most stark example of the empathy gap in the context of health is that, in December 2015, the Chief Medical Officer for England produced a report "The Health of the 51%: Women" (Davies, 2015) but she has refused to produce an equivalent for men (insideMAN, 2016). This is curious in view of the shorter life expectancy of men, and the fact that this is due primarily to cardiovascular diseases and cancers, causes which are firmly within the Chief Medical Officer's remit.

Caroline Dinenage, Minister of State in the Department of Health and Social Care, has seen fit to refer to the NHS as the National He Service, (Ley, 2018). She was speaking of the staff in the NHS. In similar vein, Health Secretary Matt Hancock has more recently opined that, 'we must build an NHS that works for women', (Blanchard, 2019). Perhaps these Ministers should concentrate more on the service users of the NHS, rather than viewing the NHS simply as a vehicle for female empowerment. But man-bashing is a popular sport amongst our political class, and men's myriad health disadvantages do nothing to ameliorate it in the context of the NHS.

In 2014, the then Health Secretary, Jeremy Hunt, called for 'more oestrogen to dilute the testosterone in NHS boardrooms', claiming that women make better leaders than men. He was of the view that there is a macho and bullying culture in the NHS which would be cured by promoting more women to senior positions, (Donnelly, 2014). No empirical evidence is necessary to support such assertions in our culture now; we have been conditioned to believe such statements without daring to demur. Even Ministers may now use the male hormone as a pejorative and attract only praise, not criticism. In the same article, the Chief Medical Officer, Sally Davies, complained that women who were already in senior positions were not using their positions to promote more women sufficiently often.

These sentiments, expressed by the most senior Government officials in health care, do not seem fully consistent with the ethos of equality. Whilst Dinenage and Hancock and Hunt and Davies were referring to senior NHS staff, it's worth noting that total NHS staff are 75% women (see chapter 7). Recall that Hunt was the same Health Secretary who withheld the HPV vaccine from boys. And Davies is the same Chief Medical Officer who saw fit to produce the report 'The Health of the 51%: Women', with no equivalent for men. So their views should not be assumed to have no impact on the health services they were charged with guiding.

An illustration of the operation of the gender empathy gap is provided by comparing screening women for breast cancer with the PSA test for prostate cancer. The reason always cited for not having a screening programme for prostate cancer is that the PSA test is unreliable. But 25% of men with a PSA over 4 ng/mL do turn out to have prostate cancer (National Cancer Institute, 2017), though this may simply be the prevalence in the general population over a certain age (U.S. Preventive Services, 2018). However, the use of screening in the USA has been claimed to result in a far smaller percentage of late diagnoses of prostate cancer. Contrast this with the breast cancer screening programme based on the mammogram, for which there are persistent reports that it saves no lives, or very few (Jaggar, 2018) (Health Impact News, 2018). In fact, there are claims it does more harm than good due to over-diagnosis and detection of tumours which precipitate traumatic treatments but which would never have grown to be life threatening. Up to 80% of positive mammogram results are said to be instances of such 'overdiagnoses'. Similar criticisms can, of course, be raised against PSA testing. Screening for prostate cancer based on PSA testing results in overdiagnosis in 20% to 50% of cases, (U.S. Preventive Services, 2018). It is not my purpose to argue in favour of PSA based screening for prostate cancer. It may well be that this would not be a net benefit to men, as argued by (Prostate Cancer UK, 2016a). My point is only that one could reasonably argue that the existing mammogram screening programme for breast cancer is no better motivated.

There was a top news story in May 2018 regarding nearly half a million UK women in the age range 68 to 71 having missed their routine mammogram. The Health Secretary and NHS chiefs were obliged to apologise publicly as stories circulated that 130 to 270 women may have died as a result (Parry and Tolhurst, 2018). The women in question will have had 5 or 6 previous mammograms since age 50, so they had not been neglected entirely. On the same basis, how many men might have died from not having a prostate cancer screening programme at all?

In view of the shortcomings of both the PSA and mammogram tests it is not clear which sex is better served by the current arrangements: to have, or not to have, a screening programme. But it seems that the different decisions for the two sexes can be related to the ancient perceptions of gender: vulnerable women, hardy men. In truth, both sexes are comparably vulnerable to cancer. The sentiment is inapplicable, but psychology is not so easily bypassed. The sentiment of female vulnerability is amplified by influential women's lobby groups and thus favours a decision to take action, and to be seen to take action, in implementing screening. In the case of men, in contrast, a decision based on cool logic and statistical evidence has proved more acceptable, unhampered by empathy. Decisions unhampered by empathy are sometimes the better ones. Despite my theme, empathy is not an unalloyed good in every case.

But whoever comes off best, the lack of a prostate cancer screening programme is not to be laid at the door of individual men as being "their own fault". And it would be unreasonable to blame individual men for choosing to work in occupations which have high death or disease rates. Women are not queuing up to work in these DAD (dirty and dangerous) jobs, and yet they are often the jobs that most need doing if society is to function. Nor is it men's own fault that testosterone is an immune suppressant, or that men's mortality from many diseases exceeds women's. The oft-repeated claim that men don't look after their health so well as women look after theirs, whilst it might be true to some degree, seems to have been exaggerated. It is a convenient rationalisation, though, behind which lurks the empathy gap.

5

Male Genital Mutilation: History and Harm

Not the violent conflict between parts of the truth, but the quiet suppression of half of it, is the formidable evil; there is always hope when people are forced to listen to both sides; it is when they attend to only one that errors harden into prejudices, and truth itself ceases to have the effect of truth, by being exaggerated into falsehood.
John Stuart Mill (1806 – 1873), *On Liberty*

The non-therapeutic removal of male minors' foreskins is arguably the starkest example of the empathy gap. There is immediately an issue of terminology. The non-therapeutic excision of the foreskin is generally called "circumcision" or "male circumcision" (MC) in popular discourse. However, the term "circumcision" is a euphemism. It literally means merely "a circular cut", and so is not specific to the penis. People opposed to the practice (sometimes called "intactivists") tend to refer to non-therapeutic MC as "male genital mutilation" (MGM). Given the dictionary definition of "mutilate" as 'to injure, disfigure, or make imperfect by removing or irreparably damaging parts', (Dictionary.com, 2018), the designation as MGM is reasonable. It is not necessary to make any analogy with female genital mutilation for this terminology to be applicable. However, it would be lacking in compassion to refer to a medically necessary circumcision as a mutilation. Similarly, one could reasonably argue that if an adult man willingly undergoes a non-therapeutic circumcision, referring to the resulting voluntary modification as a mutilation would not be appropriate. Consequently, I shall use the term MGM as a synonym for the non-therapeutic and non-consensual circumcision of males. For male infants or boys too young to give meaningful consent, their non-therapeutic circumcision is therefore MGM. Simply for variety I will use both the terms MGM and the long-form "non-therapeutic circumcision of male minors" synonymously.

Almost all MC is MGM. Therapeutic circumcision is a very small fraction of all circumcisions, and consensual but non-therapeutic MC of adult men quite rare (other than in African rites involving adolescents).

In the West there is no ambivalence regarding non-therapeutic interference with female genitalia. The practice of female genital mutilation (FGM) is prevalent in some countries, especially in central Africa and the Middle East. However, the practice is universally reviled in Western countries, and explicitly a criminal offence in most. Countries with a high incidence of

FGM also have a high incidence of MGM, usually associated with religious beliefs, especially Islam. In contrast, in Western and Anglophone countries, MGM can be prevalent despite FGM being illegal and of comparatively low incidence. Indeed, in the West, the practice of MGM arose within the white, "culturally Christian" demographic, whilst the incidence of FGM within this demographic has always been essentially zero. The Western practice of MGM, within the Christian-legacy demographic, arose without any religious motivation, in contrast to the overtly religiously motivated Judaic and Islamic practices. The question arises, therefore, whether there is a common psychological motivation for MGM between these disparate cultures which underlies the superficial motives. This is discussed in this chapter.

In this chapter the anatomy and function of the male foreskin are reviewed briefly. This is important because there is near universal ignorance about the foreskin. Staggeringly, even the mechanical function of the foreskin in normal sexual intercourse is unappreciated by most members of the public. This leads to embarrassingly ignorant descriptions of the foreskin as a "useless flap of skin".

The historical origins of MGM in various cultures are discussed. The various procedures adopted for foreskin removal are described, together with the practitioners who carry out the procedures, followed by a review of the prevalence and incidence of MGM in Western and Anglophone countries.

From experience I know that many people first become concerned about circumcision after viewing videos of the procedure being carried out, such as (Windisch, 2010) or the rather less graphic depictions in the film 'American Circumcision' (Marotta, 2018). If you do not fancy watching the genital cutting itself, the photos of boys' faces during the procedure may be an alternative, as shown by (Pleasance, 2017). Distressing to witness though these operations may be, in my opinion this alone does not constitute a valid objection to the procedure. Painful or distressing medical procedures are commonly accepted because of their benefits thereafter. The emotional reaction to a video of a baby's genitals being cut is understandable, but any case against MGM should not rest primarily upon that. Instead the case for or against MGM must rest primarily upon three issues,

- Whether there is long-term harm caused by MGM,
- Whether MGM confers significant long-term medical benefit, as is claimed by proponents, and,

- The right of the individual to protection from non-consensual violation of their bodily integrity.

The first of these key issues is addressed in this chapter, whilst the second and third are addressed in the next chapter. Male circumcision is discussed with two restrictions,

- Only the circumcision of minors is of concern here. If adult men opt to have their foreskin removed, that is entirely their own business. The issue is the removal of foreskins from babies or boys too young to make meaningful, uncoerced, decisions of their own.
- Only Western and Anglophone countries will be discussed. This will include both the "culturally Christian" demographic as well as other religious groups present within these societies and associated with MGM (Islam and Judaism).

In particular, I shall not address here those MC practices associated with "coming of age" rituals, common in sub-Saharan Africa. These involve physically mature young men (though they may be minors by Western standards). The rituals involved are invariably brutal. Their brutality is their point, the key requirement being for the young man to show no pain. Anyone seeking an illustration of societal suppression of male emotions need look no further than this. Many hundreds of these young men are permanently maimed annually in one district of South Africa alone, the Eastern Cape. Photographic evidence of what "maiming" means in this context can be found on the web site of Dingeman Rijken (2013a). Since 1995, over 1077 young men in Eastern Cape have died from these maimings (Rijken, 2013b). Nearly half a million young men have been hospitalised in the Eastern Cape and Limpopo districts alone in the period 2008 to 2014 (South African Health News Service, 2014). These indisputably destructive ritual circumcisions are now attracting Western tourists, (Fisher, 2016). What better illustration of the empathy gap do you want? It is inconceivable that female genital mutilation could ever be a tourist attraction. Such a thing would be utterly hateful, even to cultures which practice FGM.

Is it these young African men's own fault that such barbaric rites are expected of them? In many cases it is not voluntary, they are cut by force. In some cases the cutting-by-force in African countries occurs where traditional practices are being pursued under the cover of health programs, in which the West is deeply implicated, e.g., (Hudson, 2012), (Lagat, 2015). This has resulted in schoolboys being subjected to MGM at school without their consent or the consent of their parents. It has resulted in brutal circumcision mobs, where men are being obliged to unzip in the street to prove they have been circumcised and face forced circumcision where they stand if not.

No doubt some people will say that this is a phenomenon of the patriarchy, that mass manifestation of hegemonic masculinity. But such people will have to explain why it is that, in these cultures, it is just as often the women who insist that men are cut – so as to render them "fit to be our husbands". James Rush (2014) reports the following case,

> 'A dozen men are ambushed, stripped naked and forced to undergo circumcisions in Kenya after their wives complained that they were not as good in bed as circumcised men. One of the wives, Anne Njeri, who witnessed the incident, told the radio station: "We are happy with the move to have such men cut because uncircumcised men are dirty and do not perform well in bed and thus we are sure their wives will now enjoy their marriages."'

The men were from tribes which did not usually practice circumcision but were living amongst those who did. It is a matter of enforced "integration". MGM was carried out by force, on the filthy ground, by a mob. This was despite the men's best endeavours to hide and seek help, (BBC News, 2015). "This Is Africa" (2015) documents another case, with a video. A 39 year old man who had 11 children was exposed as uncircumcised by his ex-wife, thus precipitating a mob who carried out the cutting by force on the bare ground. This is MGM as a weapon of revenge, instigated by a woman.

Shovelling all blame for such things onto "the patriarchy" will not wash. Societies include women, and women have always exercised moral power in society. Women, too, are active participants in cultures, especially in matters pertaining to sex. However, I will say no more about circumcision practices outside the West or Anglophone countries.

5.1 Anatomy, Histology and Function of the Foreskin

Proponents of MGM often refer to the foreskin as 'an unnecessary piece of skin' or even 'a non-essential bacteria trap', (Kay, 2011), (Kay, 2016). My purpose here is to expose this opinion to critical appraisal.

In terms of anatomy, histology and function, the foreskin is a complex organ in its own right. Thanks to the prevalence of circumcision, many people will be unfamiliar with what a foreskin even looks like. The upper picture of Figure 5.1 shows the foreskin in place over the glans (the head of the penis), with the penis in the flaccid state. The lower picture of Figure 5.1 shows the erect penis with the foreskin fully retracted, exposing the glans. Figure 5.2 shows the frenulum, the connecting tissue between the foreskin and the glans. The frenulum forms an inverted V shape (on erection). The tissue between the frenulum and the bottom of the glans (the "corona") is known as the "frenulum delta". The frenulum, the frenulum delta and the glans are all normally covered by the foreskin and hence invisible in the flaccid penis.

Figure 5.1: *The Foreskin, Covering the Penis when Flaccid (upper picture) and Retracted when Erect (lower picture). Credit: 123GLGL - Own work, CC BY-SA 3.0, https://commons.wikimedia.org/w/index.php?curid=18107314*

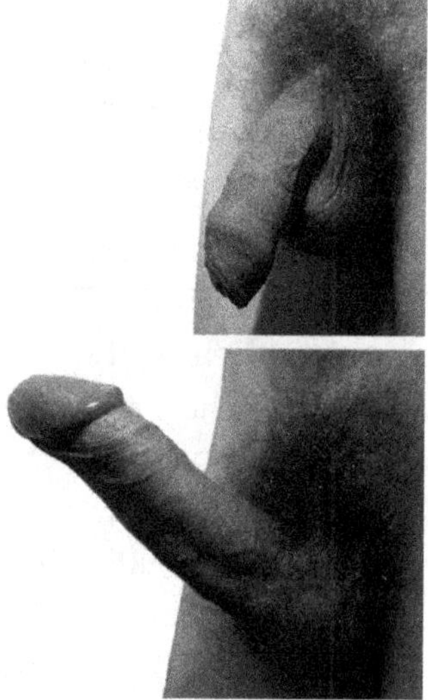

Figure 5.2: *The frenulum*

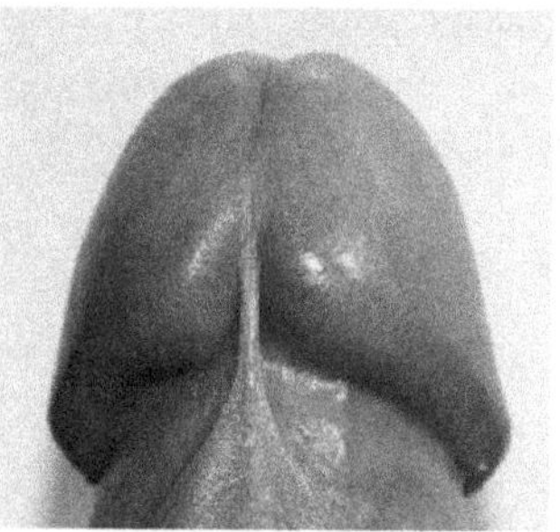

In my 64 years of life, I have never yet met a man who has a foreskin who regarded it as a "useless bit of skin". This is a view I have only ever heard expressed by people without a foreskin. Reasonably, one would expect the opinion of those who do have a foreskin to carry greater weight regarding its desirability than those who have never had a foreskin in their adult life. I have also never heard a man with a foreskin complain that it presented any hygiene difficulties. The penis, complete with foreskin, is extremely easy to wash: easier than a vagina or one's finger nails, for example. The myth common amongst the circumcised, that the intact foreskin is forever clogged with smegma, is just that – a myth.

There is a staggering degree of public ignorance about the function of the foreskin in heterosexual "penis in vagina" sexual intercourse. Those who incline to the "useless bit of skin" opinion are clearly unaware of it. The rolling action of the foreskin over the glans is a clever piece of natural engineering which reduces the relative sliding between the penis and the vaginal wall, thus reducing the need for lubrication. It forms a rolling bearing. For those who do not have a foreskin, you will probably need a video to convey what this means, see for example (Penis Project, 2016) or (Complete Man, 2018).

The same rolling action of the foreskin over the glans is deployed in masturbation by those males who have a foreskin. Masturbation by circumcised men is generally facilitated by lubrication. Thus, whilst lack of a foreskin does not prevent masturbation, it does frustrate its most convenient accomplishment.

Except during sexual arousal, when the penis becomes erect and extended, the glans is normally covered by the foreskin. The foreskin therefore acts as a protective covering for the glans which prevents the mucosal tissue of the glans from drying out. Without a foreskin, the glans is permanently dry. Over time, the glans of a circumcised penis becomes keratinized. One might expect this exposure and keratinization to lead to a loss of sensitivity in the glans of the circumcised penis. The evidence for and against this expectation is reviewed in section 5.5.1.

The detailed histological investigations by Taylor and Lockwood (1996) and by Cold and Taylor (1999) revealed, perhaps for the first time, the complexity of the foreskin and its density of nerves. These authors identified the 'ridged bands' emanating from the frenulum into the frenulum delta. They determined that this tissue contained more Meissner's corpuscles than the glans, these Meissner's corpuscles being nerve endings which are especially sensitive to light touch. In contrast they opined that the glans has quite low fine-touch discrimination. They concluded that 'the innervation difference between the protopathic sensitivity of the glans penis and the corpuscular receptor-rich ridged band of the prepuce is part of the normal complement of penile erogenous tissue' and that 'the prepuce is a specialized, specific erogenous tissue'. Since MC oblates this tissue, they recommended that 'surgical excision should be restricted to lesions that are unresponsive to medical therapy'. These authors were also the first to identify the significance of the dartos muscle, which is almost entirely contained within the prepuce and is therefore lost on circumcision. This renders the penis 'less able to make positional adjustments during erection' and may account for dispositional differences in a penis subject to MC.

More recently this perception of the sensitivity of the foreskin and its frenular structures has been argued by McGrath (2000) (2011). In McGrath's view, the frenulum is a junction for a nerve system which radiates out into the foreskin via the 'ridged bands'. The part of the foreskin immediately adjacent to the ridged bands and the frenulum vein forms the frenulum delta which is claimed by McGrath to be the most sensitive area of the penis. Note that the frenulum, the ridged bands and the frenulum delta would be invisible, on the underside of the foreskin, when the foreskin is in place covering the glans.

Older textbooks and papers refer to the source of penile sensation as being solely the glans and often justify the existence of the prepuce by stating that it merely protects the 'sensitive' glans. The work alluded to above suggests these statements are contrary to the neuro-anatomical and physiological facts, and that the prepuce is actually the primary sensory platform of the penis. McGrath claims that the human penis has a different nerve structure from other primates, and different also from female clitoral nerve structure. He claims that 'the foreskin is undoubtedly the main sensory unit of the penis' and has the 'highest concentration of sensory nerve endings anywhere on the body'. Clearly, if this perception is correct, the removal of the foreskin is a major loss to a man.

5.1.1 Foreskin Development: Retraction

A further example of the profound ignorance which surrounds the foreskin concerns its natural development in young boys. At birth the mucosa of the glans and the inside of the prepuce are fused together. Retraction of the foreskin is therefore prevented – and is not desirable. Staggeringly, until very recently, even doctors were unaware of the natural development of the foreskin, especially as regards retractability. In its natural development, the foreskin gradually becomes looser and more easily rolled back over a number of years. My own foreskin did not retract fully, to the extent illustrated in

Figure 5.1, until I was 10 years old, and that is within the normal range. Figures 5.3 and 5.4 plot data from (Oster, 1968) and (Hiroyuki Kayaba et al, 1996). To quote the latter, 'the incidence of a completely retractable prepuce gradually increased from 0 percent at age 6 months to 62.9 percent by 11 to 15 years'.

Medical ignorance of the normal development of the foreskin has led to widespread spurious diagnoses of phimosis, i.e., an interpretation that lack of full retractability in boys is pathological. Failure of the foreskin to fully retract in boys prior to physical maturity is rarely a condition requiring medical intervention, unless there are other complicating factors.

Figure 5.3: *Incidence of Preputial Adhesions in Various Age Groups. Data from (Oster, 1968) replotted by (Cold and Taylor, 1999)*

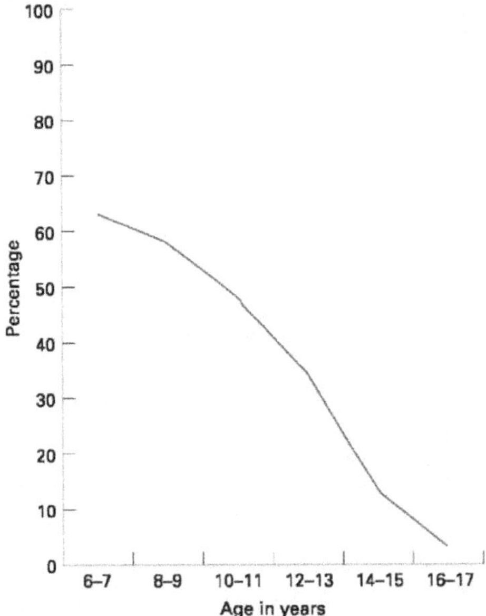

5.2 The History of MGM

Circumcision of males is required, or held to be desirable, within the major Abrahamic-Semitic religions, Judaism and Islam. Both worldwide and in Western countries, Muslims are far more numerous than Jews. Islam's holiest book, the Qur'an (Koran), does not mention circumcision. However, much of the teachings and practices of Mohammed are in the *hadith* (sayings or teachings) and this text is amongst those regarded by Muslims as sources of their religious lore. One of these *hadith* suggests that both male and female circumcision was recognized by the Prophet. Circumcision was said to be the

Prophet's way (*sunnat*) for men and ennobling (*makrumah*) for women, (al-Akiti, 1996). However, whilst most Muslims continue to be circumcised, there are some Muslims who question the practice, (Quranic Path, 2018).

Figure 5.4: *Retractability of the Prepuce in Various Age Groups. After (Hiroyuki Kayaba et al, 1996). Tight preputial ring is indicated in blue; retraction of the prepuce to at least the glans corona is indicated in red.*

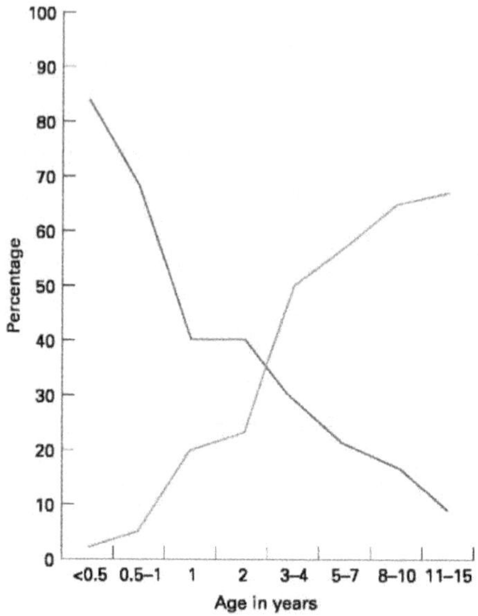

The book 'Marked in Your Flesh' by Leonard Glick (2005) provides a history of circumcision in the Judaic culture, in which MC is carried out in a ceremony called Brit Milah. Glick himself is against circumcision. As in Islam, there is also an anti-circumcision movement in Judaism which seeks to replace Brit Milah with Brit Shalom, which involves the ceremony without the genital cutting (Oryszczuk, 2018). The religious origin of the practice for Jews is Abraham's covenant with Jehovah, (Genesis 17, 10-14),

> 'This is my covenant, which ye shall keep, between me and you and thy seed after thee: every male among you shall be circumcised. And ye shall be circumcised in the flesh of your foreskin; and it shall be a token of a covenant betwixt me and you. And he that is eight days old shall be circumcised among you, every male throughout your generations, he that is born in the house, or bought with money of any foreigner that is not of thy seed. He that is born in thy house, and he that is bought with thy money, must needs be circumcised: and my covenant shall be in your flesh for an everlasting covenant. And the uncircumcised male who is not circumcised in the flesh of his foreskin, that soul shall be cut off from his people; he hath broken my covenant.'

This is clear, but people who are not inclined to believe that Abraham literally heard Jehovah's voice may look for what lies behind this mythologized account. Religious sacrifices were a common aspect of Old Testament cultures. The circumcision 'covenant' might be interpreted as such a sacrifice, specifically a type of child sacrifice which avoids the killing of the child. Abraham is, after all, the man who very nearly sacrificed his own son. Circumcision appears as a far preferable substitute. The relationship between circumcision and sacrifice is dealt with in some detail in (Glick, 2005)

People wishing to look beyond religious accounts to sociological reasons for the rise of circumcision in some cultures will be interested in the opinion of Moses Maimonides, the Jewish intellectual and physician, who expressed the following view as early as the twelfth century,

> 'With regard to circumcision, one of the reasons for it is, in my opinion, the wish to bring about a decrease in sexual intercourse and a weakening of the organ in question, so that this activity be diminished and the organ be in as quiet a state as possible. It has been thought that circumcision perfects what is defective congenitally…How can natural things be defective so that they need to be perfected from the outside, all the more because we know how useful the foreskin is to that member? In fact this commandment has not been prescribed with a view to perfecting what is defective congenitally, but to perfecting what is defective morally. The bodily pain caused to that member is the real purpose of circumcision. None of the activities necessary for the preservation of the individual is harmed thereby, nor is procreation rendered impossible, but violent concupiscence and lust that goes beyond what is needed are diminished. The fact that circumcision weakens the faculty of sexual excitement and sometimes perhaps diminishes the pleasure is indubitable. For if at birth this member has been made to bleed and has had its covering taken away from it, it must indubitably be weakened. In my opinion, this is the strongest of the reasons for circumcision. Jewish men, sexually subdued and readily controlled by their wives, don't stray into mischief. The power of his member has been diminished so that he has no strength to lie with many lewd women.' (Maimonides, translation 1963)

Maimonides is clear: the purpose of MC is to diminish male sexual function. But who benefits from a reduction in male sexuality? Moses Maimonides opines that it is a form of control which society exercises on men to encourage stable family units and discourage promiscuity. This explanation, in terms of diminished male sexual function, unites the Judaic and Western-medical traditions, to which I now turn.

The term "Western-medical tradition" will be used to describe the practice of MGM in Western countries, especially Anglophone countries, and amongst the majority, white, "culturally Christian", demographic. This is a relatively new cultural phenomenon, having arisen only in the 19th century.

Whilst Christianity is an Abrahamic religion, priority over the Old Testament is most often given to the New Testament, the testament of Christ and his disciples. St. Paul in (Galatians 5, 2-6) advises thus,

> 'Behold, I Paul say unto you, that if ye be circumcised, Christ shall profit you nothing. For I testify again to every man that is circumcised, that he is a debtor to do the whole law (i.e., the Judaic law). Christ is become of no effect unto you, whosoever of you are justified by the law; ye are fallen from grace. For we through the Spirit wait for the hope of righteousness by faith. For in Jesus Christ neither circumcision availeth anything, nor uncircumcision; but faith which worketh by love.'

This passage is to be interpreted as Paul warning that circumcision, as an outward sign of Judaism, carries the risk that the individual who opts for circumcision will revert to Judaism. In these early days of Christianity, Paul is attempting to delineate clearly between the old (Jewish) religion, and the new Christian religion. This passage makes clear that Paul regards circumcision as being a spiritual irrelevance, but a potential practical threat in terms of encouraging apostacy. In ruling that circumcision is not a requirement of Christianity, Paul is consistent with the Council of Jerusalem of a few years earlier (circa 50 AD). Circumcision has never been a requirement of any of the major branches of Christianity. For this reason I opt for the designation "Western-medical tradition" rather than "Christian tradition", which would be very misleading.

So, if the origin of the "Western-medical tradition" of circumcision does not lie in religion, what did cause it? The motive was overtly to diminish sexual function. We have already noted the role of MC in frustrating masturbation (though it does not prevent the determined). We shall see below that reduction of sensitivity is a defining characteristic of the circumcised penis. In 18th century Britain, circumcision was regarded as a rather embarrassing curiosity associated especially with Jews. We are informed by Robert Darby (2005) that 'between the mid 18th century and the late 19th century, the foreskin was transformed from an adornment which brought pleasure to its owner and his partners…to a useless bit of flesh and an enemy of the state'. Darby lays out clearly the origin of the Western medical tradition of MC in the obsession to stamp out masturbation and to impose what was seen as moral purity upon boys. A quote conveys the prevailing "wisdom",

> 'It (self abuse) lays the foundation for consumption, paralysis and heart disease. It weakens the memory, makes a boy careless, negligent and listless. It even makes many lose their minds; others, when grown, commit suicide…. Don't think it does no harm to your boy because he does not suffer now, for the effects of this vice

> come on so slowly that the victim is often very near death before you realize that he has done himself harm. It is worthy of note that many eminent physicians now advocate the custom of circumcision.' (Melendy, 1915)

It is not only in recent times that extraordinary claims have been made with no empirical basis whatsoever. John Harvey Kellogg (1888) informs us,

> 'A remedy for masturbation which is almost always successful in small boys is circumcision. The operation should be performed by a surgeon without administering an anaesthetic, as the brief pain attending the operation will have a salutary effect upon the mind, especially if it be connected with the idea of punishment. In females, the author has found the application of pure carbolic acid to the clitoris an excellent means of allaying the abnormal excitement.'

Many people opine that MGM and FGM are not to be compared because only FGM was carried out specifically for the purpose of diminishing sexuality (by the patriarchy, of course). Such an opinion is founded, as they so often are, simply on ignorance of history. It was not only masturbation which 19th century authors claimed could be cured by circumcision. There is hardly a disease known to man that has not at some time been claimed to be cured by MC, see for example, (Medicalization of Circumcision Timeline, 2014). The modern incarnation of such claims will be critiqued in chapter 6.

5.3 MGM Procedures, Practitioners and Risk

In the West, when MGM is motivated by religion or culture, it is carried out prior to physical maturity. The Western-medical tradition usually carries out MC on the new born infant. Similarly, the Judaic tradition circumcises at the eighth day after birth. The ceremony, known as Brit Milah, involves circumcision carried out by a specialist Rabbi, known as a Mohel. In Islam, circumcision is carried out on older boys, typically between 6 and 10 years old, though it can be younger in some cases. In the West, Muslim circumcisions may use the same surgical procedures as the Western-medical tradition, i.e., procedures carried out by doctors or qualified nurses, the main difference being the age of the child.

However, both Muslims and Jews may also opt, even in the West, for circumcisions carried out by persons without conventional medical training. Remarkably, anyone can set themselves up as a circumciser in the UK. Not only is the practice of circumcision tolerated, but it is not regulated either. Indeed, the lack of regulation is probably related to the fact that the procedure is actually illegal (see section 6.4) and any serious consideration of regulation would flounder on this simple fact. The refusal to acknowledge that MGM is assault therefore involves a double-whammy of disadvantage in which boys are also unprotected from brutally incompetent practitioners.

Unregulated circumcisers advertise their trade openly (Fogg, 2012). Even when the result is the baby's death, punishments are remarkably lenient, or non-existent. In 2010 the ironically named Goodluck Caubergs bled to death at 27 days old after suffering the ministrations of a nurse, Grace Adeyele. She carried out the procedure using ordinary scissors, forceps and olive oil, and without anaesthetic. Adeyele was subsequently convicted of homicide in 2013 but received only a suspended sentence, (Britton, 2013). She had previously carried out over 1000 circumcisions. In 2012, when one month old Angelo Ofori-Mintah died from massive blood loss two days after being circumcised at home by a Mohel, the Rabbi faced no charges. A verdict of accidental death was returned, (Brent & Kilburn Times, 2012). Had the Rabbi cut off any body part other than the baby's foreskin, with the same result, it is certain that he would have been found guilty of homicide. Taiwo Shittu was not quite so lucky as the Rabbi. But this bogus nurse got only 30 weeks in prison after the baby she circumcised in her home nearly bled to death (Rucki, 2014). The idea of male disposability is, you will no doubt recall, a theory entertained only by men's rights nutjobs.

Even surgical procedures carried out by qualified medical staff in hospitals make uncomfortable viewing. I recently attended a screening of the film 'American Circumcision', (Marotta, 2018), in which almost all the women, and many of the men, looked at their shoes during the footage of the procedure. I re-emphasise the point made previously that the procedure itself, however distressing, does not necessarily provide a valid motive for intactivism. However, the fact that the procedure involves significant trauma requires that any claims of subsequent benefit must be very clear indeed, and the benefit must be more than marginal.

There are a number of variants on the surgical procedure, depending upon the device used to clamp the foreskin or guide the cut. The following sources link to online videos. The first uses the Plastibell method, (Kumar, 2010). The next uses the Gomco clamp and is done by a nurse, her first circumcision, and she seems pleased with her performance, (Megan, 2014). The video has no sound, one wonders why not. This one does though, (Windisch, 2010). And finally this one uses a Mogen clamp (Duterte, 2018).

For older boys, or adult men, an alternative to surgery for foreskin removal is an ERCD (Elastic Radial Compression Device). These devices cause necrosis of the foreskin over a period of time by starving it of blood flow due to radial compression applied by an elastic ring. (World Health Organisation, 2012). These are the devices of choice for the mass circumcision programme in Africa (see chapter 6).

5.3.1 Risks of the Procedure

A review by Bollinger (2010) estimated that 117 circumcision-related deaths of infant boys occur in the USA annually. The study was based on claims that the extent of circumcision related deaths is not normally appreciated, as the formal cause of death is generally recorded as something else, e.g., surgical mishap, infection, haemorrhage, cardiac arrest, stroke, reaction to anaesthesia, or even parental neglect. Since there are over a million circumcisions annually in the USA, this is a fatality rate of roughly 0.01%. This puts the risk of death in perspective. However, if the procedure confers little or no benefit, and is actually harmful in other ways, then any deaths at all are unacceptable. But Bollinger's estimate has come in for severe criticism, (Circumcision News, 2010). Brian Earp et al (2018c) analysed a vast database of inpatient records over a ten year period in the USA and identified that just over 20 baby boys per million died following inpatient circumcision and before leaving the hospital. They caution that this should not be misinterpreted as the death rate *due to* circumcision,

> 'In the present analysis, we identified 1 early death for every 49,166 newborn inpatient circumcisions, or 10.2 early deaths per 500,000 newborn inpatient circumcisions. We stress that this figure refers to deaths that occurred subsequent to the circumcision but prior to discharge within the same hospital admission; it should not be taken to refer to the frequency of deaths caused by newborn circumcision, as the present data cannot directly support such an inference.'

When circumcision was more fashionable in the UK, (Gairdner, 1949) reviewed case histories of 90,000 circumcisions for boys under five years old from 1942 to 1947 in England and Wales, identifying 95 deaths attributable to circumcision, a fatality rate of about 0.1%, ten times worse than Bollinger's implied rate in the USA. This might be attributable to lower prevailing standards at that earlier date. However, complications short of death are far more common. The NHS tells us that the risk of circumcision carried out under proper medical conditions is as follows, (National Health Service, 2016),

> 'There's between a 1 in 10 and a 1 in 50 chance that you'll experience bleeding or infection. Other possible complications of circumcision can include permanent reduction in sensation in the head of the penis, particularly during sex.'

Note that the NHS in the UK has no financial interest in promoting MC, which may be why the NHS assessment of circumcision complications is more forthright than in cultures in which the practice is more widespread. In just one Birmingham hospital in one year, 105 boy babies were treated for complications arising from circumcision, about one per month being life threatening, (Poole, G, 2014a). Up to three baby boys per month are admitted to the Royal Manchester Children's Hospital because of bleeding after home-based circumcisions, (BBC News, 2012).

As well as the immediate risks of the procedure, MC can cause a large range of mutilations which are life-long. (CIRP, 2013) lists 292 references relating to complications of circumcision, to which I cannot hope to do justice here. They cover ablation of the penis, adhesions, amputations of the penis, anaesthesia problems, apnoea, bleeding, balanitis, botched circumcisions, concealed penis, cancer, circulatory complications, clamp complications, denudation of the penile shaft, emesis, infection, impotence, keloid formation, meatitis/stenosis, skin bridges, urethral fistula, urinary retention, urinary tract infection, and various other things.

5.4 Prevalence and Incidence of MGM

The "prevalence" of MC is the proportion of the male population who have been circumcised. "Incidence" refers to the proportion of a cohort being circumcised per year.

The official policy of the NHS since 1949 has been that they do not offer non-therapeutic circumcision for religious, cultural, social or personal reasons, because such circumcision is not a medical necessity. This 1949 decision led to a decline in the number of individuals undergoing circumcision in the United Kingdom. A number of NHS hospitals did re-start offering a free circumcision service locally to parents, especially during the 1980s, however this afterwards became rarer. Some Health Trusts take a view that offering non-therapeutic circumcision on the NHS is desirable to prevent the use of 'back street' circumcisers. The Baby Centre (2013) informs us,

> 'Not many NHS trusts fund circumcision for non-medical reasons, because the risks outweigh the potential health benefits. However, sometimes religious or cultural male circumcision is offered on the NHS, as it is safer than the circumcision being carried out elsewhere. In Scotland, it's recognised that circumcision in a safe, sterile environment, by a skilled surgeon, is better than the risks associated with unsafe, unregulated ritual practices.'

For example, prior to 2013, when MC was carried out free of charge by the NHS in Sheffield, about 200 non-therapeutic circumcisions were carried out for religious reasons there (BBC News, 2013). The incidence of MGM in the UK was about 35% in the 1930s, reducing to about 20% in the 1940s, and reducing further to around 6% by 1975, see sources cited by (CIRP, 2006). In the UK, Western-medical circumcision was almost exclusively confined to the upper and upper-middle classes. The prevalence of MC in the UK in 1970 has been reported to have been 24% (Public Health Agency of Canada, 2007), decreasing to around 15.8% in 2015 (Dave et al, 2003).

The 2011 census revealed that, in England and Wales, there were 162,000 male children of Muslim families not exceeding 4 years of age, and 9,000 male children of the same age designated as Jewish, (Office for National Statistics, 2011). Assuming all Muslim and Jewish boys are circumcised, and ignoring any other circumcisions, this suggests about 34,000 circumcisions per year. The number of Muslims in the UK has increased further, by about 15%, between 2011 and 2018, but the estimate of 34,000 circumcisions per year in the UK will be accurate if the percentage of Muslim and Jewish baby boys being circumcised is actually 85% and the number of circumcisions amongst the rest of the population is negligible. This suggests a current incidence of at least 8%.

Figure 5.5: *Prevalence of MC in Australia, from (Circinfo, 2013)*

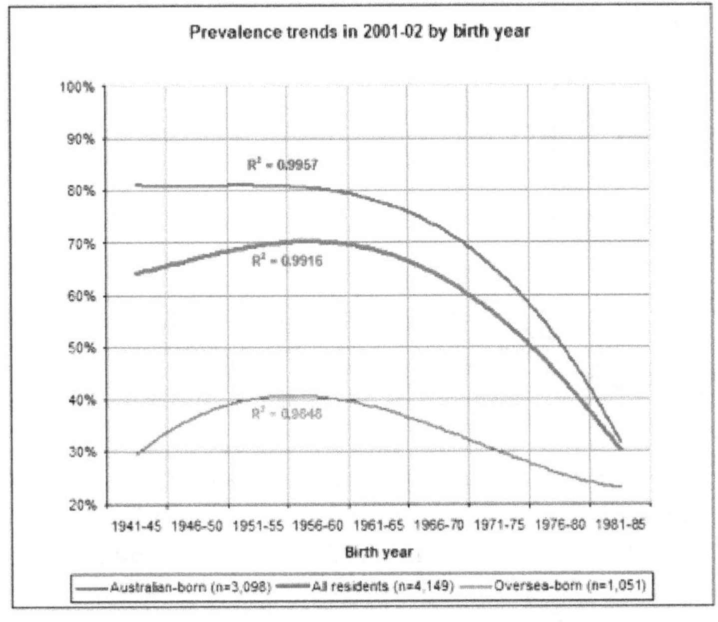

Neonatal circumcision was routine in Australia until the 1970s. Based on 7,060 men aged 16-59 responding to a survey in Australia in 2001/2, 59% were circumcised. Restricting to the Australian-born the prevalence was even greater, 69%. In young men aged 16-19 the prevalence was lower, but still substantial, at 32%, (Richters et al, 2006). Figure 5.5 shows the rapidly falling prevalence of MC in Australia, though it remains high in absolute terms.

Within the USA, the incidence of neonatal MGM carried out in hospitals immediately after birth is plotted against year in Figure 5.6. This excludes circumcisions not carried out in hospitals and also MC carried out at a later date. The incidence has fallen from 64.5% in 1979 to 58.3% in 2010, (Owings and Williams, 2010). In the west of the USA the incidence in 2010 was 40% whereas in the midwest it was 70%. Between 1930 and 1965 the US incidence increased from 31% to a peak of 85% (Circumcision Reference Library, 2012). In the period 2005 to 2010, the prevalence of MC amongst American males aged 14 to 59 was 80.5%, and 90.8 % for non-Hispanic white males.

Figure 5.6: *Incidence of MGM in the USA, from (Owings and Williams, 2010).*

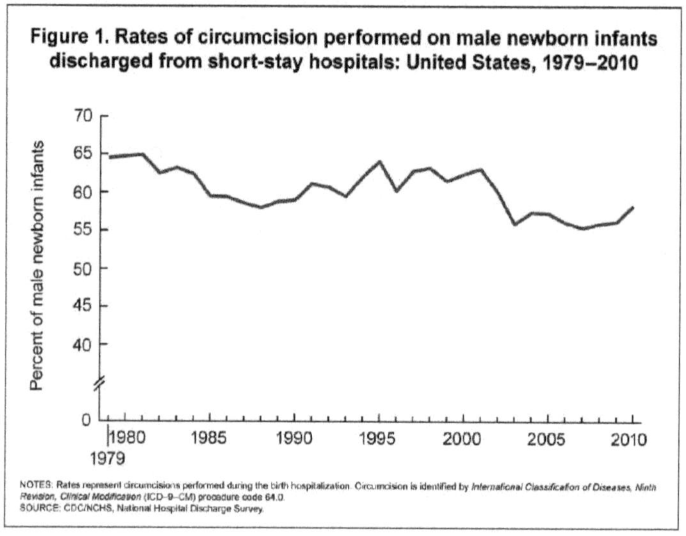

In 1970 the prevalence of MC in Canada was 48% (Canadian Medical Association, 1996). In 2007 the incidence of neonatal MC in Canada was 32% (Public Health Agency of Canada, 2007). 44% of mothers stated their decision to circumcise was based on health or hygiene, 36% was to be like their father, and 17% was religious.

The very high prevalence of MC in the USA (about 80%) compares with just 2.7% of the US population being Jewish or Muslim. In Canada, only about 4% of the population is Jewish or Muslim, and in Australia 2.2%. These figures contrast with MC prevalence in the recent past of around 30%. Hence the overwhelming majority of circumcised men in these Anglophone countries are not circumcised for religious reasons. This used to be true also in the UK, in the 20th century. But now, the relative rarity of Western-medical circumcisions in the UK, together with the steep increase in the UK Muslim population, means that the current incidence of MC in the UK is overwhelmingly Muslim. Worldwide, Islam also accounts for the overwhelming majority of circumcisions.

5.5 The Harmful Effects of MGM

In this section I address the potential long-term harm of MGM. The risk of the procedure itself has been dealt with in section 5.3.

5.5.1 Studies of Sensitivity

According to McGrath (2011), circumcision removes around 50 cm^2 of skin. All the ridged banding is lost. The frenulum may or may not be ablated but is usually adversely affected. More than half the sensory nerve endings of the penis are lost. The expectation that neonatal foreskin removal will result in sensitivity loss in the glans has been reported to be measurable by some authors. For example, the conclusion of Sorrells et al (2007) was,

> 'The glans of the circumcised penis is less sensitive to fine touch than the glans of the uncircumcised penis. The transitional region from the external to the internal prepuce is the most sensitive region of the uncircumcised penis and more sensitive than the most sensitive region of the circumcised penis. Circumcision ablates the most sensitive parts of the penis.'

The "transition region" to which Sorrells et al refer is the frenulum delta, and can be seen on Figure 5.1 (lower) as the more pink region lying between the glans corona and the exterior of the foreskin. However, the conclusion of Sorrells et al is by no means uncontentious. For example, Kimberley Payne et al (2007) measured penile sensitivity in sexually aroused men, on both the shaft and the glans of the penis. They concluded that their results 'do not support the hypothesized penile sensory differences associated with circumcision'. A similar negative result from Clifford Bleustein et al (2005) was that, in a study of neonatally circumcised men, 'circumcision status does not significantly alter the quantitative somatosensory testing results at the glans penis'.

Consequently, the effect of neonatal foreskin removal on the subsequent sensitivity of the glans remains contentious. One of the problems in this area is that there is no unique measure of "sensitivity". The apparent sensitivity depends upon what sort of stimulus is deployed. Nor is there any guarantee that any given method of measuring sensitivity will correlate with sexual performance. Most importantly, though, the studies of Payne et al and Bleustein et al did not address foreskin sensitivity, which is actually the key issue.

In that respect, the paper by Jennifer Bossio, Caroline Pukall and Stephen Steele (2016) is of greater potential significance because it included sensitivity tests on the foreskin. The results and conclusions from the paper are,

> 'Results: Penile sensitivity did not differ across circumcision status for any stimulus type or penile site. The foreskin of intact men was more sensitive to tactile stimulation than the other penile sites, but this finding did not extend to any other stimuli (where foreskin sensitivity was comparable to the other sites tested).'
>
> 'Conclusions: Findings suggest that minimal long-term implications for penile sensitivity exist as a result of the surgical excision of the foreskin during neonatal circumcision. Additionally, this study challenges past research suggesting that the foreskin is the most sensitive part of the adult penis. Future research should consider the direct link between penile sensitivity and the perception of pleasure/sensation. Results are relevant to policy makers, parents of male children and the general public.'

This paper garnered some public attention and provides the most significant recent counter-narrative to intactivists, (Craig A. , 2016) (Bakalar, 2016). One of the authors, Caroline Pukall, a professor of psychology, was quoted in the latter article thus, 'Neonatal circumcision doesn't make the penis less sensitive. We can conclude that there are no significant differences in sensitivity between the circumcised and uncircumcised groups'.

However, there is rather a mismatch between the results and the conclusions of Bossio et al. Their results indicate that the foreskin is no less sensitive than other parts of the penis. In fact, their results indicate that the foreskin is *more* sensitive, but let that pass for now. Assume, for sake of argument, that the foreskin had the same sensitivity as the glans. The foreskin is large – typically around 50 cm^2 in the adult male. Its removal is therefore an indisputable loss of sensory tissue. Bossio et al make no allowance for the extent, or quantity, of sensory tissue. They implicitly assume that if any tissue remains which has unchanged sensitivity, then 'circumcision doesn't make the penis less sensitive'. On that basis one could claim that one's hand would be no less sensitive if three fingers became completely numb (or, equivalently, were removed). It is spurious to claim that 'there are no significant differences in sensitivity between the circumcised and uncircumcised groups' when the former has had a large proportion of tissue removed and this tissue was, even according to Bossio et al, at least equally sensitive as the remaining tissue.

There are further difficulties with the paper of Bossio et al, as identified by Earp (2016). The statistics are low, just 30 circumcised and 32 intact men contributed to the study. More importantly, the maximum age of men taking part was 37. This is a serious criticism because anecdotal evidence is that serious loss of sensitivity in men subject to neonatal or boyhood MGM becomes far greater in middle age. (Consider how useful would be a study of the link between smoking and lung cancer if confined to people no older than 37). Moreover, participants with a past or present sexual dysfunction were screened-out. To quote Earp (2016), 'it is simply not possible to draw meaningful conclusions about the effects of infant circumcision on sexual dysfunction in adulthood by first excluding men with sexual dysfunction from the study sample'. It's hard to disagree. Other methodological difficulties with Bossio et al include testing the foreskin sensitivity only on its outer surface, where it is likely to be less sensitive. The underside of the foreskin, the 'ridged band' region, the frenulum, and the frenulum delta, were not tested, but these are the areas identified by McGrath and others as the most sensitive areas of the foreskin. Also, Bossio et al appear to have tested the penis in the flaccid condition, which may not be indicative of typical sexual experience.

But most peculiarly, Bossio et al's own findings do show that the foreskin is more sensitive than all other areas of the penis to tactile stimulation and to warmth – despite all the above shortcomings. This is illustrated by Figure 5.7, taken from Figure 2 of (Bossio et al, 2016) as replotted by (Earp, 2016). These histograms plot detection thresholds to punctuate stimuli and thermal stimuli (smaller values indicate greater sensitivity). The foreskin is the most sensitive of the penile regions tested to both types of stimulus. Bossio et al also gave results for pain thresholds. The foreskin was the most sensitive to heat-induced pain, whilst for punctuate pain the foreskin was comparable to other regions of the penis. However, the detection threshold is the better measure of sensitivity (pain, after all, is unpleasant).

Figure 5.7: *Penile Sensitivity Results of (Bossio et al, 2016) as replotted by (Earp, 2016). Note that the lower the detection threshold, as plotted below, the more sensitive the region in question. Hence, these histograms indicate the greater sensitivity of the foreskin.*

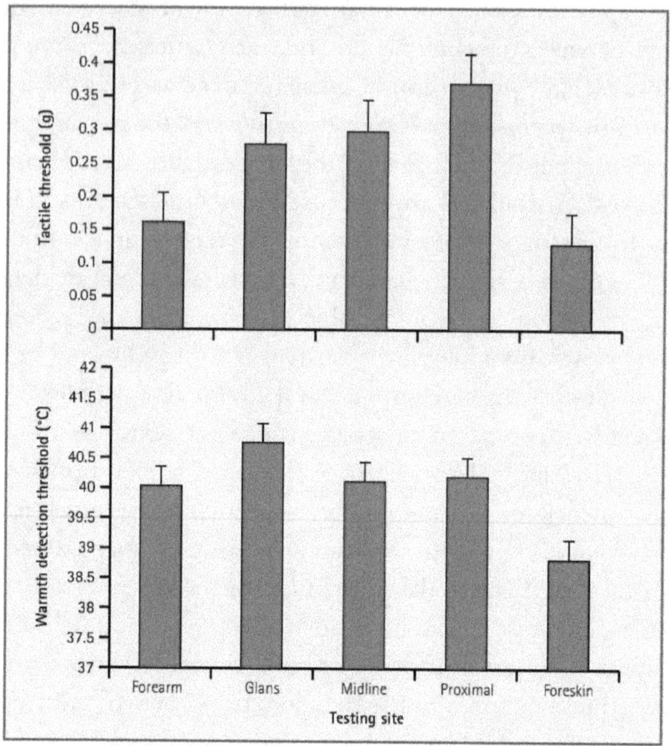

5.5.2 Studies of Men's Sexual Experience after Circumcision

5.5.2.1 After Neonatal MGM

The direct tests of penile sensitivity discussed in section 5.5.1 may not necessarily be a good indicator of sexual function and satisfaction in practice. This section addresses the results of comparative studies of circumcised and intact men's sexual function and experiences. The Abstract from Bensley and Boyle (2001) reads,

> 'Circumcised and genitally intact men, as well as female and gay partners having sexual experience with both circumcised and intact men, were surveyed in order to investigate the long-term effects of infant circumcision. Both circumcised men and the sexual partners of circumcised men reported a number of adverse physical, sexual, and psychological sequelae. Logistic regression analysis revealed that circumcised men could be reliably classified as having penile scarring, need for use of lubrication when undertaking sexual activity, reluctance to use condoms, progressive decline in sexual sensitivity, as well as unhappiness with and reluctance to think about their circumcision status. Female and gay sexual partners reported

that their circumcised partners were more likely to experience reduced sexual sensation as compared with their intact partners, as well as dissatisfaction with their orgasms and a wide range of negative emotions associated with being circumcised. Evidently, there are many adverse physical, sexual and psychological effects from infant circumcision, which need to be acknowledged in any discussions pertaining to informed consent in relation to circumcision surgery.'

Not only circumcised men but also their female partners report less sexual satisfaction. For example, Frisch et al (2011) observed that (omitting the detailed statistics),

> 'Circumcised men reported more partners and were more likely to report frequent orgasm difficulties after adjustment for potential confounding factors, and women with circumcised spouses more often reported incomplete sexual needs fulfilment and frequent sexual function difficulties overall, notably orgasm difficulties and dyspareunia (painful intercourse). Findings were stable in several robustness analyses, including one restricted to non-Jews and non-Moslems.'

Since the perception of sexual capacity is necessarily psychological, it is relevant also to enquire into how men subject to MC regard their status *vis- a-vis* intact men. The Abstract from Earp, Sardi and Jellison (2018) tells us,

> 'Critics of non-therapeutic male and female childhood genital cutting claim that such cutting is harmful. It is therefore puzzling that 'circumcised' women and men do not typically regard themselves as having been harmed by the cutting, notwithstanding the loss of sensitive, prima facie valuable tissue. For female genital cutting (FGC), a commonly proposed solution to this puzzle is that women who had part(s) of their vulvae removed before sexual debut 'do not know what they are missing' and may 'justify' their genitally-altered state by adopting false beliefs about the benefits of FGC, while simultaneously stigmatising unmodified genitalia as unattractive or unclean. Might a similar phenomenon apply to neonatally circumcised men? In this survey of 999 US American men, greater endorsement of false beliefs concerning circumcision and penile anatomy predicted greater satisfaction with being circumcised, while among genitally intact men, the opposite trend occurred: greater endorsement of false beliefs predicted less satisfaction with being genitally intact. These findings provide tentative support for the hypothesis that the lack-of-harm reported by many circumcised men, like the lack-of-harm reported by their female counterparts in societies that practice FGC, may be related to holding inaccurate beliefs concerning unaltered genitalia and the consequences of childhood genital modification.'

Consistent with this, my personal experience has been that circumcised men generally believe that having a foreskin is unhygienic; that the foreskin is dirty and difficult to clean, though this is untrue. In criticising the pro-circumcision paper by Tobian and Gray (2011), Boyle and Hill (2012) make some very hard-hitting observations,

> 'Most doctors favouring MC are circumcised themselves. Circumcision status 'plays a huge role in whether doctors are in support of circumcisions or not'. Circumcised doctors often defend circumcision by producing flawed papers that minimise or dismiss the harm and exaggerate alleged benefits. Tobian and Gray are products of circumcising cultures. Their article exudes Freudian defences of denial and rationalisation. The authors seem blinded by their own circumcision-generated emotional needs. The readers of such articles must be aware of the culture-of-origin and circumcision status of the authors, in order to properly evaluate assertions about MC. Invariably, when biased opinions promoting MC are published by doctors trying to justify their own psychosexual wounding, uncircumcised doctors (who mostly see no need for amputating anatomically normal healthy erogenous tissue) are quick to refute such overstated claims. We fully expect that this distortion of the medical literature will continue until non-therapeutic male circumcision is prohibited by law and most circumcised male doctors have passed from the scene.'

There is now a large number of publicly available video recordings providing men's personal testimonies regarding their experience of the long-term harm of MGM. I give just a few here, all of them doctors or professors. Gregory Boyle was the professor of psychology at Bond University in Australia from 1993 to 2013. He gives a passionate account of the harm he has suffered from MGM, (Gregory Boyle, 2014). John Warren (2011), a UK doctor and the founder of NORM-UK, talks here about his intactivism and how he realised in middle age that his diminishing sensitivity was due to circumcision, after which he uncovered the whole unfortunate story. George Denniston (2017) of Doctors Opposing Circumcision reminds us that there is no national medical society in the world that recommends routine infant circumcision. He describes MGM as an atrocity. Ken McGrath (2011) describes his work on the histology of the foreskin and the neurological evidence for its high sensitivity. Morten Frisch, a doctor and professor of sexual health epidemiology at Statens Serum Institut in Copenhagen and at Aalborg University in Denmark, discusses his 2011 study on sexual function difficulties in circumcised men and their female partners, (Frisch, 2012). In particular, he tells us of his difficulty getting the work published in the face of hostile referees.

5.5.2.2 Before and After Adult Circumcision

The overwhelming majority of circumcisions are carried out prior to physical maturity, and hence prior to sexual experience. In principle, one might expect the best evidence for the effects of MC on sexual function to come from the minority of cases where the procedure is carried out on men with prior sexual experience, thus providing a "before & after" comparison. There are such studies, but unfortunately they are mostly seriously marred by one factor: men who elect to be circumcised as adults almost always do so because they have a medical problem which circumcision is intended to ameliorate. This is a rather serious skew in such evidence because an improvement in function is obviously far more probable in cases where there was a prior medical condition (as contrasted with the case for the overwhelming majority of MGM).

Cases in point are Fink, Carson and DeVellis (2002) and Patel, Palmer and Sheriff (2005). In the first of these, 123 men were identified who were circumcised when aged 18 or older. However, 93% of these men were circumcised to correct medical problems, only 7% were described as "elective". 44% of the men responded to the survey, with a mean age of 46 (42 at circumcision). The survey results showed,

> 'Adult circumcision appears to result in worsened erectile function, decreased penile sensitivity, no change in sexual activity and improved satisfaction. Of the men 50% reported benefits and 38% reported harm. Overall, 62% of men were satisfied with having been circumcised.'

Given that 97% of these men had the surgery to correct problems, an overall perception of benefit of only 50% - with 38% reporting harm – is not impressive. The findings of Fink, Carson and DeVellis (2002) certainly do not indicate any benefit of MC for men without medical conditions, and actually indicate harm (worsened erectile function and decreased penile sensitivity).

Patel et al (2005) identified 'one hundred and fifty men between the ages of 18 and 60 years as being circumcised for benign disease between 1999 and 2002'. 59% of these responded to a questionnaire, which led to the following conclusion: 'Penile sensitivity had variable outcomes after circumcision. The poor outcome of circumcision considered by overall satisfaction rates (61%) suggests that when we circumcise men, these outcome data should be discussed during the informed consent process'. A shortcoming of both these studies is that the surveys were carried out only a few years after circumcision, whereas sensitivity loss is known to accumulate over time.

Not all studies report diminished sexual function due to MC. The study of Temucin Senkul et al (2004) concerned men circumcised when adult, but not predominantly for medical reasons. Of the 42 men in the study, 39 desired circumcision for religious reasons. Their median age was 22.3 years. Their sexual performance before and after MC was evaluated using the Brief Male Sexual Function Inventory. Senkul et al concluded that 'adult circumcision does not adversely affect sexual function' but that 'the mean ejaculatory latency time was significantly longer after circumcision'. The term "ejaculatory latency time" refers to the time for a man to reach orgasm from first vaginal penetration. Whilst a longer ejaculatory latency time can be regarded as beneficial (perhaps especially for the female partner) it can also be regarded as symptomatic of reduced sensitivity. Longer times to climax in circumcised men have also been reported by other investigators, e.g., (Frisch, 2012). More seriously, the "after" survey was conducted shortly after recovery from MC, and the men in question were very young. Indications from other studies and surveys are that sexual function becomes more seriously degraded later in life, especially in middle age and after.

In summary, before/after studies of the effect of MC on sexual function are inconclusive and marred by serious skews or limitations in the samples surveyed.

5.5.3 Survey Evidence: Men's Subjective Experience of Circumcision

The majority of circumcised men do not report being unhappy with their condition. However, one should bear in mind that the overwhelming majority of circumcised men have known no other condition as a sexually mature adult. Nevertheless, American and Australian Surveys cited by Tim Hammond and Adrienne Carmack (2017) suggest between 20% and 50% of circumcised men are dissatisfied with their condition.

The PhD thesis of Bossio (2015) reports an online study of 657 men (367 neonatally circumcised, 290 intact). She reports that, 'intact men almost unanimously rated that they were highly satisfied with the amount of foreskin they have'. Hence, whilst a substantial proportion of circumcised men are dissatisfied with their condition, intact men are virtually never dissatisfied. This simple observation is telling but generally passes unnoticed in debates on MGM. Bossio (2015) indicates that circumcision dissatisfaction can be a serious issue: 'the largest proportion of circumcised men reported feeling extremely dissatisfied with being circumcised, while the largest proportion of intact men reported feeling extremely satisfied with being intact. The more foreskin a participant reported having, the greater their self-reported satisfaction with their circumcision status.'

The Global Survey of Circumcision Harm has been reported in (Hammond and Carmack, 2017) and a video presentation of the results given in (Hammond, 2015). It is important to note the goal of this survey was not to seek a representative sample of all circumcised men, but to qualitatively explore experiences of only those who already consider themselves harmed by involuntary non-therapeutic circumcision. Moreover, the focus was not on botched procedures, but on surgeries that respondents believed were ordinary. Most respondents (60%) reported becoming aware of their circumcision harm before age 19, including 25% reaching this awareness before age 13.

The physical damage or deformities reported were as follows (noting that the percentages refer to respondents to a survey focused on harm, not to a representative sample of circumcised men).

- Partial/total loss of the frenulum 72%
- Prominent circumcision scar(s) 63%
- Little/no shaft skin mobility when erect; tight cut 56%
- Drastic skin tone variance on either side of scar 46%
- Distal shaft hair (causes friction during sex) 45%
- Twist/bend in penis when flaccid or erect 25%
- Meatal stenosis 24%
- Skin tag(s) 20%
- Skin bridge(s) 10%
- Partial/total loss of penile body/shaft 10%
- Gouges/surgical deformities of the glans 8%

The most frequent physical problems which resulted were,

- Insensitive glans 67%
- Dry, keratinized glans, needs lubricants before sex 75%
- Excess stimulation needed to achieve orgasm 59%

The resulting psychological or emotional problems reported included,

- Anger 71%
- Frustration 72%
- Betrayed by mother/father/doctor for lack of protection 55% / 50% / 58%
- Dissatisfied with my condition 77%
- Feel mutilated 61%
- Violated / raped 55%
- My human rights were violated 73%
- Feel inferior to intact men 66%
- Causes distrust of medical profession 65%

The detailed results of the Global Survey of Circumcision Harm as they stood in 2012 recorded hundreds of subjective comments by respondents, of which a few are given below, (Hammond, 2012),

- Frequent ripping of what is left of my frenulum;
- Wooden stick feeling during sex;
- Loss of feeling in glans (this many times in various words)
- Scar is too tight to accommodate a full erection comfortably;
- Glans is sensitive but in a sandpaper sort of way, not pleasurable;
- Complete sexual dysfunction with no feeling whatever;
- No pleasure and feeling of envy towards intact boys;
- Cut into urethra causing fluid filled cysts;
- Penis bent on erection, will not straighten;
- Pain when erect;
- If I wear a condom I feel absolutely nothing;
- Pubic hair growing at scar / discomfort to partner prohibits sex

This survey provides many men's personal testimonies. There is a book consisting of nothing but men's personal testimonies about their circumcision status and how it has affected their lives 'Unspeakable Mutilations: Circumcised Men Speak Out', (Watson, 2014). Further sources may be found in (Circumcision Resource Centre, 2018).

The preceding discussion has concentrated upon physical forms of harm, or psychological problems stemming directly from the physical harm. However, there is some evidence that the trauma of the circumcision procedure itself may cause lasting psychological damage. For example, Bollinger and van Howe have presented evidence that circumcised men exhibit elevated alexithymia (the reduced ability to identify, describe or recognise one's own emotions) compared to intact men, (Bollinger and van Howe, 2011).

A summary of this chapter is included at the end of the next chapter where we shall turn our attention to the veracity, or otherwise, of the claimed benefits of circumcision and its legal status in various countries, including the UK.

6

MGM: Claimed Benefits and Legality

The only purpose for which power can be rightfully exercised over any member of a civilized community, against his will, is to prevent harm to others. His own good, either physical or moral, is not sufficient warrant.
John Stuart Mill (1806 – 1873), *On Liberty*

In chapter 5 I reviewed the anatomy of the foreskin, the history of practices to remove it, and the harm that can accrue as a result of male circumcision (MC). In this chapter I look at the other side of the argument: the claims that non-therapeutic circumcision of male minors, or male genital mutilation (MGM), is medically beneficial. The issue of legality in the UK and elsewhere is also briefly considered. Whilst harms and benefits are relevant to this, there is also a matter of principle: the right of children to have their bodily integrity protected. Finally, both chapters 5 and 6 are summarised.

The claim of medical benefit is the key issue in the defence of MGM. It is therefore necessary to provide a review and critique of the evidence. It is unavoidable that some medical detail will be necessary. However, the literature on the subject is huge. A thorough literature review is impractical in this book, and excessive medical detail is inappropriate. To give focus to the discussion, therefore, I shall concentrate upon critiquing a recent review of medical evidence by leading proponents of MGM, Brian Morris et al (2017). Some observations are made about this paper before proceeding to the review of medical evidence.

6.1 Background to the 2017 review of Morris et al

Brian Morris is a prolific author of journal articles presenting the case for medical benefits of MGM, (Morris, 2018). Morris is a founding member of the Circumcision Foundation of Australia which changed its name to the Circumcision Academy of Australia in 2014. The paper (Morris et al, 2017) includes eight co-authors. The conflict-of-interest statement in the paper states, 'Authors are members of the Circumcision Academy of Australia', and that the organisation's purpose includes the provision of 'contact details of doctors who perform the procedure'. It is reasonable to conclude that this indicates a favourable bias towards MGM. In a letter to the editor of the Canadian Journal of Urology, Joan Robinson, Ann Jefferies and Thierry

Lacaze (2017) noted that the two Canadian co-authors of (Morris et al, 2017) operate circumcision clinics, which represents an obvious conflict of interest.

Morris et al (2017) represented the policy statement of the American Academy of Pediatrics (AAP) in a light more favourable to circumcision than strictly justified, referring to the AAP's 'formulation and release of a new affirmative early infant MC policy statement in 2012'. The actual view of the AAP is discussed in section 6.3 and includes the statement, 'health benefits are not great enough to recommend routine circumcision for all male newborns'. Morris et al's claim that 'Australia is the only non-United States country in which an evidence-based policy statement has been produced' is rather odd given the statements made by authoritative medical establishments in New Zealand, Canada, Finland, the Netherlands and Great Britain, to name just a few, as summarised in section 6.3.

Morris and other co-authors have previously been taken to task by an authoritative medical body for misrepresenting their position in published work. The paper by Morris et al (2016), 'Canadian Paediatrics Society (CPS) position statement on new-born circumcision: a risk-benefit analysis revisited' so upset the CPS that three members of the CPS wrote a detailed rebuttal in a letter to the editor of the Canadian Journal of Urology, (Robinson, Jefferies and Lacaze, 2017). Noting that neonatal circumcision is an operation with lifelong consequences performed without patient consent, and further noting deaths from surgical circumcisions in Canada as elsewhere, the CPS authors conclude that the existing evidence fails to provide a case for the CPS to recommend routine circumcision. They also note that 'no country outside of Africa has adopted a national policy promoting routine circumcision'.

Morris et al (2017) garnered media attention, e.g., the Australian news report in (Wiedersehn, 2017) which re-iterated the claim in the journal paper that 'uncircumcised males face an 80 percent risk of developing a foreskin-related condition requiring medical attention'. The claim is extraordinary. Living in a culture in which the large majority of men are intact, I might have expected to be aware of instances of such medical problems in men of my acquaintance. I can think of none. Whilst men may be reticent about talking of such matters, a prevalence as high as 80% seems startlingly inconsistent with personal experience.

6.2 Critique of the claims of Morris et al, 2017.

The claims of (Morris et al, 2017) are critiqued below as a convenient device to examine the claims typically made for the medical benefits of MGM. I address the different diseases for which benefit is claimed in turn.

6.2.1 Urinary Tract Infections

Morris et al (2017) claim as follows,

> 'Of any year of life, urinary tract infection (UTI) in males is most common in the first year, affecting 1%-2% of uncircumcised boys compared to 0.1%-0.2% of boys who are circumcised. Risk reduction continues, however, beyond infancy. The most recent meta-analysis (in 2013) noted that over lifetime 1 in 12 circumcised males experience a UTI compared with 1 in 3 uncircumcised males.' (Morris et al, 2017)

The effect of MGM on prevalence alone is insufficient to justify its use as a preventative (even assuming the claim were valid). Whether or not the condition is serious, and the availability of treatments less invasive than circumcision, are also important. According to the NHS the prevalence of UTIs in children in the UK is as follows, (NHS, 2016),

- Boys have a higher incidence of UTI up to the age of 6 months, after which it is more common in girls;
- Girls have a higher incidence of recurrent UTI;
- 3% of girls and 1% of boys will have an upper UTI by the age of 7;
- 1 in 10 girls and 1 in 30 boys will have a UTI by the age of 16.

Prevalence at later ages is indicated by German data taken from (Guido Schmiemann et al, 2010) and reproduced as Figure 6.1. The prevalence of UTIs in young men is extremely low. Its prevalence in young women is far higher. Note that UK and German data refer to societies in which the incidence of MC is modest or low (16% or less). If one hypothesises that the foreskin is causally related to UTIs in men, why is this not apparent in young men? Figure 6.1 indicates a far lower prevalence of UTIs in adult men than claimed by Morris et al. Increased prevalence of UTIs in older people is often related to catheterisation.

UTIs are generally successfully treated with antibiotics. In the case of females, where the incidence of UTIs is far greater after early infancy, no other treatment is being sought. Even if one takes at face value Morris et al's claimed benefits of MGM on UTI incidence, the number of circumcisions needed to prevent one UTI is at least 73, and perhaps over 100 (Robinson, Jefferies and Lacaze, 2017). Since treatments with antibiotics are generally successful, this means 73 surgical operations would be required to avoid one course of antibiotics.

Figure 6.1: *Prevalence of UTIs per 1000 from (Guido Schmiemann et al, 2010)*

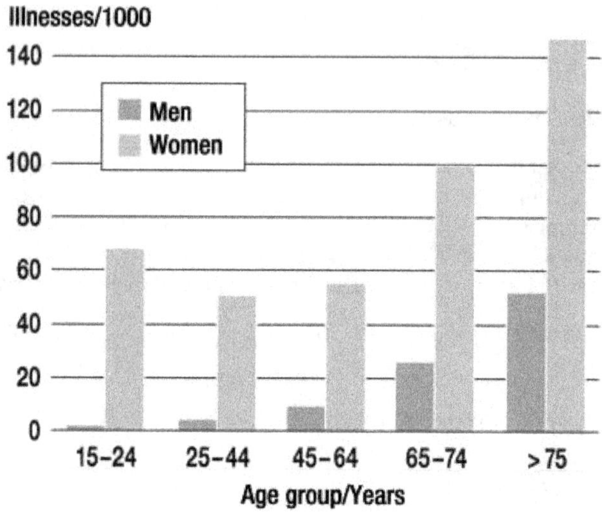

However, Morris et al's claims on the effect of MGM in reducing UTI incidence are not secure. To quote (Robinson, Jefferies and Lacaze, 2017), 'The literature in this area is difficult to interpret because urines obtained via a midstream or catheter specimen from an uncircumcised male are commonly contaminated by organisms under the foreskin. Evidence for this is that 9% of uncircumcised and 0.5% of circumcised asymptomatic males had bacteriuria later verified by suprapubic urine collection to be falsely positive.' Here, "suprapubic urine collection" refers to urine extracted from the bladder directly by inserting a needle through the abdominal wall. By this means, contamination of the urine as it passes out of the urethra is avoided. This observation implies that specimens collected in the usual manner will seriously over-estimate the incidence of infection in intact males.

Moreover, a close examination of the data sources reveals that there is a dearth of data for adult men, (Collins, W, 2017f). Robinson et al therefore conclude that, 'there is only very low quality evidence that circumcision prevents UTIs beyond infancy'. More importantly, it makes no sense to carry out 73 surgical operations to avoid one course of antibiotics, especially as antibiotics are regarded as adequate to treat females, who are the overwhelming majority of sufferers from UTIs. UTI prevention does not provide a motivation for MGM.

6.2.2 Phimosis

Phimosis is the term given to an inability to fully retract the foreskin (the lower picture of Figure 5.1 shows full retraction). Morris et al claim that phimosis 'affects approximately 10% of uncircumcised adolescent and adult males'. In contrast, the University of California Department of Urology (2018) advises that the 'current incidence of phimosis is about 1% in 7th grade boys' whilst Robert van Howe (2006) states that 'the incidence of true phimosis is less than 2%'. In India, Shahid (2005) distinguishes between physiologic and pathologic phimosis. He notes that '2% of normal males continue to have non-retractability throughout life even though they are otherwise normal' and that 'the incidence of pathological phimosis is 0.4 per 1000 boys per year or 0.6% of boys are affected by their 15th birthday.'

Phimosis is a common reason for medically-advised circumcision, but this appears to have been due to widespread ignorance in the medical community regarding the natural development of the foreskin. As explained in section 5.1.1, full retraction is commonly not possible before physical maturity, or even a few years thereafter (see Figures 5.3 and 5.4). Whilst removal of a foreskin is clearly a cure for phimosis, in boys and young men a tight foreskin is not necessarily phimosis, i.e., it is not necessarily a pathological condition. Prior to physical maturity it is most likely to be a condition which will rectify itself. If persistent post-puberty, steroid creams can be effective. Physically mature young men who still cannot fully retract their foreskin might be best advised in the first instance to masturbate more often, perhaps modifying their technique, (Beaugé, 2005).

Even when the phimosis appears genuine, and doctors refer the patient for circumcision, (Kumar, Deb and Das, 2009) record that, out of 100 such referrals, only 12 were actually genuine phimosis for which circumcision was ultimately indicated. This aligns well with other sources which indicate that circumcision can be avoided, even when phimosis is genuine, in about 87% of cases, (Circinfo.org, 2014). In summary, in severe and genuine phimosis, circumcision may ultimately be indicated, but not before other treatments are tried as these are likely to be successful. Circumcision is genuinely indicated at an incidence of only about 0.1%. Phimosis prevention does not provide a motivation for routine MGM.

6.2.3 Balanitis / Candidiasis

Balanitis is redness, swelling, soreness or rash around the glans (the head of the penis) or the foreskin. The cause of balanitis is generally poor hygiene. The incidence of balanitis is almost an irrelevance since effective treatment generally requires merely better hygiene. Cleaning the uncircumcised penis presents no problems. Soap and water, chaps – and if that doesn't work, then just warm water (the soap may be the problem). For persistent cases, antibacterial, or antifungal, or possibly steroidal, creams will be effective almost always. If re-infection occurs repeatedly after successful treatments, it is likely to be either thrush (candida) or streptococcal bacteria. In both cases the most probable source of infection is the man's female partner: the vagina tends to harbour these infectious agents (Men's Health Forum, 2014). Incidence rates of balanitis are high, perhaps 3% - 11% (Medscape, 2017), though sources are very variable. Morris et al's claim in regard to the incidence of balanitis amongst intact men and boys is reasonable, but the effectiveness of MGM in reducing it is less clear. Some studies suggest that circumcised men actually suffer greater rates of balanitis, (van Howe, 1997). In the case of balanitis, though, the incidence of the condition is relatively unimportant since it is so easily treated. The use of surgery to treat such a minor condition which is so easily treated by improved hygiene is clearly disproportionate.

6.2.4 Human Papilloma Virus (HPV)

Of all Morris et al's claims, that relating to HPV is most baffling. The HPV threat to males is principally oropharyngeal cancer from HPV infection acquired through oral sex. Obviously this cannot be influenced by the status of the man's penis. Nevertheless, Morris et al claim that MGM reduces the risk of HPV infection by 40% to 65%. This is not credible. Now the decision has been taken to offer the HPV vaccine to boys on the NHS, the rate of HPV infection in men and the incidence of oropharyngeal cancers can be anticipated to reduce in the UK. HPV does not motivate MGM.

6.2.5 Human Immunodeficiency Virus (HIV)

Perhaps the most important health claim for MC is that it reduces the likelihood of becoming infected with HIV, especially as regards health policies in Africa. Morris et al claim a 60% reduction in female-to-male heterosexual HIV infection probability consequent upon being circumcised. I examine the provenance and reliability of this claim in this section. However, the claim runs counter to elementary observations. For example, compare the prevalence of HIV in the UK and the USA. The UK annual data tables for HIV, (UK Government, 2017d), give the following data for total cases by the end of 2016,

- Persons seen for HIV care in the UK: 91,987
- Total UK HIV diagnoses minus deaths, 150,726 – 23,374 = 127,352

Dividing these figures by the UK population gives a prevalence of 0.14% to 0.19%. In contrast, the Centers for Disease Control and Prevention (2018) state, 'At the end of 2015, an estimated 1.1 million persons aged 13 and older were living with HIV infection in the United States, including an estimated 162,500 (15%) persons whose infections had not been diagnosed'. Dividing by the USA population at that time gives a prevalence of 0.34%.

Hence the prevalence of HIV in the USA is about double that in the UK, whereas the prevalence of MC in the USA is around 80% compared with about 15% in the UK. This runs contrary to expectation if MC was protective and also the only factor involved. In reality, of course, there are other factors involved – race, for example. The prevalence of HIV is greater amongst blacks than whites, and the USA has a higher proportion of blacks than the UK.

However, even within the USA there is no correlation between circumcision and the prevalence of HIV, and this remains the case if only black men or black men who have sex with other men are included, (Fox, 2007).

An even more emphatic example is provided by those African countries with very high prevalence of MC. The following countries have a circumcision prevalence greater than 80%: Gabon, Djibouti, Eritrea, Kenya, Somalia, Benin, Burkina Faso, Cameroon, Equatorial Guinea, Gambia, Ghana, Guinea, Guinea-Bissau, Ivory Coast, Mali, Niger Nigeria, Senegal, Sierra Leone and Togo. The average prevalence of MC in these 19 countries is 90%, but the average prevalence of HIV is very high by Western standards, namely 2.1% in 2017 (down from 2.4% ten years earlier). Admittedly the HIV prevalence in these 19 countries is modest by African standards. Botswana, Lesotho, Malawi, Mozambique, Namibia, South Africa, Swaziland, Zambia and Zimbabwe all have horribly high HIV prevalence between 10% and 26%. Nevertheless, an HIV prevalence some 11 times higher than in the UK in 19 African countries with an average MC prevalence of 90% hardly invites an hypothesis of protection by MC.

On the other hand, those African countries with extremely high HIV prevalence do have lower prevalence of MC. All these observations are confused by other variables, of course. In the case of MC prevalence in Africa, the obviously correlated variable is religion (Islam versus Christianity especially), with all the cultural differences that implies, e.g., alcohol consumption, women's free association, etc. Then there are countries like Rwanda, which has an MC prevalence of only 10% but also (for Africa) a low HIV prevalence of 2.7%, comparable with African countries with around 90% MC prevalence. One can reasonably question the likelihood of mass circumcision programmes being beneficial in Rwanda. [African data for HIV has been taken from (World Health Organisation, 2018b), and for MC from (Williams et al, 2006)].

The three African randomised controlled trials (RCTs) on which Morris et al's claims depend are the same studies upon which the World Health Organisation (WHO) based their recommendation for circumcision as an effective HIV preventative in 2007. On the strength of these studies, the WHO and the Joint United Nations Programme on HIV/AIDS (UNAIDS) have rolled out a programme to circumcise over 20 million African men. As of 2017, a total of 14.5 million African men had been circumcised under this programme, across 14 sub-Saharan African nations, and the rate of circumcising has been increasing (World Health Organisation, 2017). The claim is that this programme will avert over half a million new HIV infections by 2030. It has been funded in part by the Gates Foundation.

Irrespective of how efficacious MC might be as an HIV preventative, I have some unease that this WHO/UNAIDS programme represents a new form of medicalised neo-colonialism. Daniel J Ncayiyana, editor of the South African Medical Journal, has observed that, 'it is curious and even worrisome that the campaign to circumcise African men seems to be driven by donor funding and researchers from the North', (Ncayiyana, 2011). He was being diplomatic. He meant, I think, 'white men telling black men what to do with their bodies'. He has a point.

Consequently I now concentrate on these three African RCT studies, thus addressing both Morris et al and the basis of the WHO/UNAIDS mass circumcisions of African men at the same time. The studies in question are (Auvert et al, 2005), (Bailey et al, 2007) and (Gray et al, 2007). These three studies concluded that circumcision reduces female-to-male HIV transmission rates by 60%, 53% and 51% respectively. There is no claim that the rate of transmission of HIV to women will be affected.

Two issues arise: firstly, how reliable are these studies as indicators of long-term HIV reduction in circumcised men? Secondly, is a 50% to 60% reduction in HIV infection a sufficient benefit against the requirement to circumcise several tens of millions of men?

Before critiquing the underlying studies, it is worth noting that latex condoms, used consistently and correctly, are 87%-95% effective in preventing HIV transmission, (Pinkerton and Abramson, 1997), (Davis and Weller, 1999). Hence, the effectiveness of consistent condom usage in preventing HIV transmission is comparable to its effectiveness at preventing conception. Studies that do not isolate consistent condom usage suggest that intermittent usage is 60% - 70% effective against HIV transmission. A concern might be that the reduced sensitivity of the circumcised penis might discourage condom usage, and thus ultimately have an adverse effect on HIV transmission rates.

The three RCT studies have come in for substantial criticism on methodological grounds. The key criticisms are summarised below and expanded upon in, for example, (Boyle and Hill, 2011) and (Earp, 2012), in particular the note dated 4/3/14 in the latter referring to various counter-arguments.

- The studies were stopped early, based on early positive findings (termination bias);
- No account was taken of the fact that circumcised men would be sexually inactive for a couple of months while their wounds healed – so inevitably they had less sex than the control group;
- Participants in the circumcised group received two year's free healthcare and safe sex counselling;
- Significant numbers of men who became infected reported never having sexual activity or reported having always used condoms, suggesting non-sexual routes to infection which have not been allowed for when interpreting the data;
- Parallel studies showed an increase in HIV transmission, but these have been side-lined;
- The claim that the observed reduced HIV transmission would apply for life is unproved, none of the tests extending for longer than 2 years;
- Anomalous results which cast doubt on the veracity of subjects' self-reporting, (Ncayiyana, 2011);

- That the studies considered female-to-male HIV transmission only, not male-to-female or male-to-male.

A follow-up study to the Ugandan trials of Gray et al was carried out, in which MC was offered to the uncircumcised control group from the earlier trial, (Gray et al, 2012). Surveillance was then maintained for 4.79 years. The conclusion was, 'Post-trial HIV incidence was 0.54/100 py in circumcised and 1.71/100 py in uncircumcised control arm men (adjusted effectiveness 67%). There were no significant differences in sociodemographic characteristics and sexual behaviors between controls accepting MC and those remaining uncircumcised.' A rather obvious problem with this study is that the men who were circumcised were self-selected. The danger, then, is that men accepting circumcision might be those who are more inclined to safe sex practices, e.g., condom use, which would badly skew the findings. Gray et al did attempt to control for this via statistical tests, but it is not clear if this is sufficient to eradicate the bias in the data.

There is a substantial literature commenting adversely on the three RCT trials, some quite excoriating. Some of these have been summarised in the Appendix of (Collins W. , 2017g). It may never become clear if the mass circumcisions being carried out on African men have had the desired beneficial effect because the prevalence of HIV is already falling across Africa as a whole.

Reports from Malawi indicate that 'circumcision does not help in the reduction of HIV but exacerbates it', (Malawi24, 2015). They write, 'HIV infection rate in Malawi has doubled in recent years despite a range of interventions put in place to tackle the spread of the virus that have included relentless campaigning on condomisation and circumcision'.

In summary, despite the massive WHO/UNAIDS programme to mass circumcise African men as an AIDS preventative, the evidence that this will prove efficacious is fragile and a weight of counter-evidence exists. Moreover, as an AIDS preventative in Western countries, as claimed by Morris et al, there is no evidence to support it at all but there is evidence to the contrary.

6.2.6 Other Diseases

Morris et al claim benefits of MGM for a whole range of sexually transmitted infections (STIs). It is inappropriate to reproduce the details here. An accessible review can be found in (Collins W. , 2017g), and a thorough analysis in 'Sexually Transmitted Infections and Male Circumcision: A Systematic

Review and Meta-Analysis', by (van Howe, 2013). The Abstract from that paper serves to summarise the position for STIs,

> 'The claim that circumcision reduces the risk of sexually transmitted infections has been repeated so frequently that many believe it is true. A systematic review and meta-analyses were performed on studies of genital discharge syndrome versus genital ulcerative disease, nonspecific urethritis, gonorrhea, chlamydia, genital ulcerative disease, chancroid, syphilis, herpes simplex virus, human papilloma virus, and contracting a sexually transmitted infection of any type. Chlamydia, gonorrhea, genital herpes, and human papillomavirus are not significantly impacted by circumcision. Syphilis showed mixed results with studies of prevalence suggesting intact men were at greater risk and studies of incidence suggesting the opposite. Intact men appear to be of greater risk for genital ulcerative disease while at lower risk for genital discharge syndrome, nonspecific urethritis, genital warts, and the overall risk of any sexually transmitted infection. In studies of general populations, there is no clear or consistent positive impact of circumcision on the risk of individual sexually transmitted infections. Consequently, the prevention of sexually transmitted infections cannot rationally be interpreted as a benefit of circumcision, and any policy of circumcision for the general population to prevent sexually transmitted infections is not supported by the evidence in the medical literature.'

Morris et al claim benefits of MGM for two final diseases: penile cancer and prostate cancer. The main source on which Morris et al's claims rest as regards penile cancer is the meta-analysis of (Larke et al, 2011). The wording of these authors' conclusions does indeed suggest a beneficial effect of childhood circumcision. However, examination of the paper's Figures 2 and 3 is unconvincing since results from 11 of the 14 studies plotted in these Figures are consistent with there being no effect (i.e., the 95% confidence interval encompasses an odds ratio of one). See (Collins W. , 2017g) for further discussion.

Finally, Morris et al claim a benefit of MGM in respect of prostate cancer, their quoted source being (Pabalan et al, 2015). However, the studies compiled by Pabalan et al, when combined, show no statistically significant effect. When outliers are removed the results are as shown in Figure 6.2, i.e., negligible effect. A far more reliable, and far more pleasurable, means of protecting the health of your prostate is to have regular sex – alone if necessary.

The position on claimed health benefits of MGM has been summarised by Morten Frisch et al (2013). They conclude that whilst there is a possible protection against urinary tract infections in infant boys, which can easily be treated with antibiotics without tissue loss, 'the other claimed health benefits, including protection against HIV/AIDS, genital herpes, genital warts, and penile cancer, are questionable, weak, and likely to have little public health relevance in a Western context, and they do not represent compelling reasons for surgery before boys are old enough to decide for themselves.'

Figure 6.2: *Effect of MC on Prostate Cancer, data after removal of outliers. From (Pabalan et al, 2015). Odds ratio of 1 means no effect.*

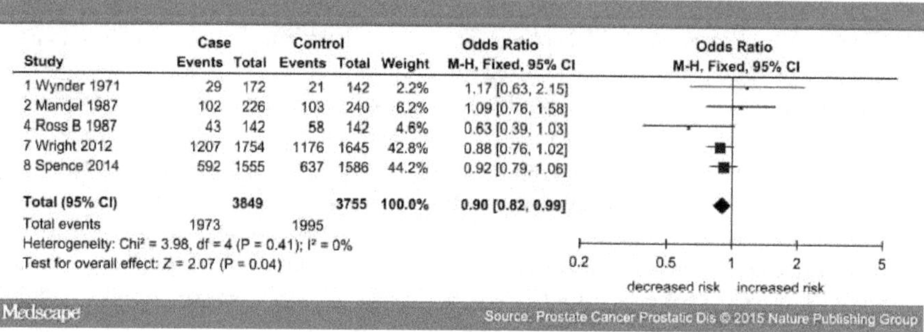

6.3 The Opinion of Medical Bodies Worldwide

No authoritative medical body in any country in the world has recommended routine circumcision of males outside of Africa. The most positive statements on infant MGM have been made by the American Academy of Pediatrics (AAP) and the US Centers for Disease Control (CDC). The AAP caused some controversy when they released a revised statement on MGM in 2012, having previously been unambiguously negative. Extracts from the 2012 AAP statement are,

> 'Evaluation of current evidence indicates that the health benefits of newborn male circumcision outweigh the risks.'
>
> 'Although health benefits are not great enough to recommend routine circumcision for all male newborns, the benefits of circumcision are sufficient to justify access to this procedure for families choosing it and to warrant third-party payment for circumcision of male newborns. It is important that clinicians routinely inform parents of the health benefits and risks of male newborn circumcision in an unbiased and accurate manner.'
>
> 'Parents ultimately should decide whether circumcision is in the best interests of their male child.....The medical benefits alone may not outweigh these other considerations for individual families.' (American Academy of Pediatrics, 2012)

The cynic may focus on the above approval of 'third-party payment', noting that the membership of the AAP comprises those who would financially benefit. The careful wording of the advice throws the actual decision regarding risk versus benefit upon the parents.

The AAP's stance that circumcision carries a net benefit over its risks has been echoed by the CDC who reiterate the claims of medical benefit in respect of UTIs, STIs, balanitis, penile (and 'possibly' prostate) cancer and HIV, (Centers for Disease Control and Prevention, 2014). However, these two American medical bodies appear to be out of step with the rest of the world, and one should recall that the USA is a circumcising culture.

In 1996 the Canadian Paediatric Society stated their view that, 'the overall evidence of the benefits and harms of circumcision is so evenly balanced that it does not support recommending circumcision as a routine procedure for newborns'. This advice was reviewed in 2015, their updated position being,

> 'Recent evidence suggesting the potential benefit of circumcision in preventing urinary tract infection and some sexually transmitted infections, including HIV, has prompted the Canadian Paediatric Society to review the current medical literature in this regard. While there may be a benefit for some boys in high-risk populations and circumstances where the procedure could be considered for disease reduction or treatment, the Canadian Paediatric Society does not recommend the routine circumcision of every newborn male.'

The Central Union for Child Welfare, Finland, gave the following opinion in 2003,

> 'Circumcision of boys that violates the personal integrity of the boys is not acceptable unless it is done for medical reasons to treat an illness. The basis for the measures of a society must be an unconditional respect for the bodily integrity of an under-aged person. Circumcision intervenes in the sexual integrity of a male child causing a permanent change in organs and has consequences pertaining to both health and quality of life. The circumcision of girls is rightly considered as inhuman mutilation of the genitals and is punished abuse. Also boys must be guaranteed a similar protection by law. According to the opinion of the Central Union for Child Welfare in Finland nobody has the right, on behalf of the child, to consent to the operation, violating the bodily integrity of the child, if it is not done to treat an illness.'

In one legal case in Finland, the circumcision of a four year old boy was ruled illegal. The court noted that 'not even a long religious tradition justifies protecting the bodily inviolability of boys to a lesser degree than that of girls', (Sanomat, 2006). A commentary on the web site of the Finnish Central Union for Child Welfare by a special adviser expressed the following view. 'There is no rational doubt about the harmfulness and suffering of circumcision. It is a question of daring to finally make a decisive political action to outlaw it unequivocally in a criminalising law' (Sariola, 2012), translated from the Finnish.

The Royal Dutch Medical Society (2010) issued the following position statement (extracts only),

> 'There is no convincing evidence that circumcision is useful or necessary in terms of prevention or hygiene. Partly in the light of the complications which can arise during or after circumcision, circumcision is not justifiable except on medical/therapeutic grounds.....Non-therapeutic circumcision of male minors is contrary to the rule that minors may only be exposed to medical treatments if illness or abnormalities are present, or if it can be convincingly demonstrated that the medical intervention is in the interest of the child, as in the case of vaccinations. Non-therapeutic circumcision of male minors conflicts with the child's right to autonomy and physical integrity..... There are good reasons for a legal prohibition of non-therapeutic circumcision of male minors, as exists for female genital mutilation.'

This strong statement ended, 'However, the KNMG (i.e., the Royal Dutch Medical Society) fears that a legal prohibition would result in the intervention being performed by non-medically qualified individuals in circumstances in which the quality of the intervention could not be sufficiently guaranteed. This could lead to more serious complications than is currently the case.' The British Medical Association (2006) published advice which is still linked on their web page as updated on 26 February 2018. They write,

> 'In the past, circumcision of boys has been considered to be either medically or socially beneficial or, at least, neutral. The general perception has been that no significant harm was caused to the child and therefore with appropriate consent it could be carried out. The medical benefits previously claimed, however, have not been convincingly proven, and it is now widely accepted, including by the BMA, that this surgical procedure has medical and psychological risks. It is essential that doctors perform male circumcision only where this is demonstrably in the best interests of the child.'

The BMA then duck the issue by adding, 'the responsibility to demonstrate that non-therapeutic circumcision is in a particular child's best interests falls to his parents'. This is an abdication of responsibility. The key issues in making this decision relate to claimed medical benefits and the potential risk or harm of MGM. If the BMA are not confident to advise on these matters, then parents clearly cannot do so in any meaningful way.

The Royal Australasian College of Physicians (2010) published a review in which they concluded,

> 'After reviewing the currently available evidence, the RACP believes that the frequency of diseases modifiable by circumcision, the level of protection offered by circumcision and the complication rates of circumcision, do not warrant routine infant circumcision in Australia and New Zealand.'

This policy position was reiterated by an RACP spokesperson in 2017, (Wiedersehn, 2017). The London Safeguarding Children Board (LSCB) have issued guidance on male circumcision, thus recognising that MGM is potentially a child safeguarding issue. The guidance quotes the British Association of Paediatric Surgeons advice that 'there is rarely a clinical indication for circumcision'. Extracts from LSCB guidance are,

> 'Doctors / health professionals should ensure that any parents seeking circumcision for their son in the belief that it confers health benefits are fully informed that there is a lack of professional consensus as to current evidence demonstrating any benefits. The risks / benefits to the child must be fully explained to the parents and to the young man himself, if Fraser competent. The medical harms or benefits have not been unequivocally proven except to the extent that there are clear risks of harm if the procedure is done inexpertly. The legal position on male circumcision is untested and therefore remains unclear.' (London Safeguarding Children Board, 2017a).

A more comprehensive collection of statements on non-therapeutic MC has been collected by (CIRP, 2016).

6.4 Legal Issues

6.4.1 The Illegality of MGM in the UK

The UK public can be forgiven for believing that non-therapeutic circumcision of male minors, subject to parental consent, is legal in the UK. After all, such circumcisions are carried out openly. Circumcision clinics advertise their services and the NHS is involved in the practice on some occasions. But this conflates legality with tolerance. MGM is tolerated, in part, because of its association with religions, and because there is a reluctance to face down the accusations of antisemitism. (The term "antisemitism" incorporates both anti-Jewish and also anti-Arabic opinions, most Arabs being Muslim). Toleration is reinforced by claims of medical benefit, and the general belief that MGM does no harm. Circumcision then becomes conflated with other medical procedures which confer indubitable benefits. Where there are genuine medical reasons for surgery, it is accepted that parents can consent on behalf of the child.

However, parents have an obligation to protect their children, not a right to consent to procedures which do not provide indisputable benefit. For example, in the UK, parents cannot consent to having a child tattooed. The legality of infant or childhood MGM therefore hinges upon the claimed benefits, and lack of harm, i.e., the net benefit. Even if this test were passed, there is also the separate issue of principle: the child's right to bodily integrity. In the foregoing sections I have argued that the claimed medical benefits are spurious or very minor at best, whilst the long-term damage can often be substantial, albeit not in every case. The most favourable summary is that a clear demonstration of net benefit has not been demonstrated. A more accurate summary is probably that MGM is likely to be a net harm.

Under these conditions, non-therapeutic circumcision of male minors, too young to give meaningful consent themselves, is illegal under the assault laws. To be legal there would need to be legislation making MGM specifically exempt from the assault laws. There has been no such legal over-ride in the UK. In a submission to the Law Commission for England and Wales, Christopher Price (1996) concluded the following,

> 'Non-therapeutic circumcision is painful, risky and disabling; as such it is unlawful and offends against domestic and international laws: it gives rise to criminal and civil liability. It raises issues of individual human rights, moral issues, issues of discrimination, physical and psychological damage: it is an abuse (sexual, physical and emotional) of the child.'

> 'Although existing laws are sufficient to sustain a prosecution and a civil claim arising from circumcision, for the avoidance of any doubt (for the same reasons that the Prohibition of Female Circumcision Act 1985 was passed) and to avoid discrimination as between the sexes and/or between groups of male children, male non-therapeutic circumcision should be accorded the same legislative prohibition as female circumcision.'

> 'Circumcision done as a non-therapeutic procedure to an unconsenting child is abhorrent, destructive and a legal, ethical and moral affront which has no place in any society which wishes to call itself civilised.'

My argument that MGM is illegal is, of course, the opinion of a lay-person. A more legally cautious exposition of the situation has been given by barrister James Chegwidden in a presentation to the group Men Do Complain, as can be seen in the video here, (Duncker, 2017). Chegwidden makes reference to a ruling by Sir James Munby, then President of the Family Division, in a case known as "In the matter of B and G (Children)", (Royal Courts of Justice, 2015). In it Munby repeats an observation made originally by the Applicant's counsel, Mr Hayes, who quotes Baroness Hale, who was then a Justice within the Supreme Court and is now its President, as follows,

> 'Baroness Hale of Richmond said in Re B (Care Proceedings: Appeal) [2013] UKSC 33, [2013] 2 FLR 1075, para 185, that any form of FGM, including FGM WHO Type IV, amounts to "significant harm". To use Lady Hale's language, no form of FGM can, Mr Hayes says, be characterised as trivial or unimportant, having regard

not merely to its purely physical characteristics but also to its associated trauma and potential emotional or psychological consequences.'

Nothing could have been further from Baroness Hale's mind in making the above remarks than bolstering a case against MGM. But that may be their import. It has to be conceded (and Munby does concede) that MGM is far more invasive than Type IV FGM, which is the slightest nick or puncture of the clitoral hood. Munby writes (para 69),

> 'Given the comparison between what is involved in male circumcision and FGM WHO Type IV, to dispute that the more invasive procedure involves the significant harm involved in the less invasive procedure would seem almost irrational. In my judgment, if FGM Type IV amounts to significant harm, as in my judgment it does, then the same must be so of male circumcision.'

One might think that this is virtually a slam-dunk for ruling MGM illegal. Unfortunately Munby manages to rule in favour of the status quo, despite his own compelling logic – see (Royal Courts of Justice, 2015) or (Duncker, 2017). His "argument" is revealing as he bases his ruling on existing societal norms and prejudices, and rules the harm of genital cutting, that he himself has identified, as being of lesser significance – but only for males. He writes (paras 72, 73),

> 'Whereas it can never be reasonable parenting to inflict any form of FGM on a child, the position is quite different with male circumcision. Society and the law, including family law, are prepared to tolerate nontherapeutic male circumcision performed for religious or even for purely cultural or conventional reasons, while no longer being willing to tolerate FGM in any of its forms. There are, after all, at least two important distinctions between the two. FGM has no basis in any religion; male circumcision is often performed for religious reasons. FGM has no medical justification and confers no health benefits; male circumcision is seen by some (although opinions are divided) as providing hygienic or prophylactic benefits. Be that as it may, "reasonable" parenting is treated as permitting male circumcision.
>
> I conclude therefore that although both involve significant harm, there is a very clear distinction in family law between FGM and male circumcision.'

Munby has here capitulated to the status quo. He has concluded that "reasonable" parenting can include the inflicting of harm, but only if the child is male. This is male disposability. It is so firmly psychologically embedded that it resists attack by logic and law.

As regards the "two important distinctions" to which Munby appeals, we have seen that the medical benefit claim is spurious – and that this is underwritten by a wide range of authoritative medical bodies worldwide. But the religious distinction is also spurious, as emphasised by (Earp, 2018a).

Whilst female cutting is not mentioned in the Qur'an, neither is male cutting, both are mentioned only in the *hadith*. (Judaism has the stronger case here, as the Old Testament refers only to male cutting). In any case, there is more to religious tradition than is necessarily to be found in their holy scriptures. So Munby's argument fails even on its own merits. In truth, he was rationalising a conclusion he felt socially constrained to reach.

6.4.2 Attempts to Make MGM Illegal in Other Countries

There have been attempts in a number of European countries to make non-therapeutic circumcision of male minors explicitly illegal.

6.4.2.1 Germany

The Germans got close to banning non-therapeutic circumcision of male minors in 2012, but then backed off. In 2012 a Higher Regional Court in Cologne decided that religious circumcision of boys constituted bodily harm, (Spiegel Online, 2013). This sparked intense opposition, especially from Jewish groups, the outcome of which was a Bill to clarify that non-therapeutic circumcision of male minors was, in fact, legal. This was passed in the Bundestag in December 2012, (Scholz, 2012). Subsequently, in 2013, the Higher Regional Court of Hamm, a city in western Germany, prohibited a mother from having her 6 year old son circumcised and ruled that parents and doctors are obliged to inform the child 'in a manner appropriate to his age and development' about the procedure and be mindful of his wishes. In my opinion, this is passing the buck. Every time a court resorts to "the voice of the child" they are abdicating their responsibility. The procedure remains legal in Germany, but either parents or doctors might (in principle) fall foul of consent requirements.

6.4.2.2 Sweden

There was a motion to ban non-therapeutic circumcision of male minors in Sweden in 2013. The claim by its proposers was that,

> 'boys should have the same right to avoid both complications of reduced sensitivity in the genitals, painful erections, increased risk of kidney damage and psychological distress by permanent removal, and the tremendous violation of privacy that circumcision actually means.'(Canadian Jewish News, 2013)

The initiative failed, as such initiatives have failed elsewhere. The article repeats a falsity about the motivation of intactivists: 'ritual circumcision of underage boys increasingly has come under attack in Scandinavia, both by left-wing secularists as well as right-wingers who fear the influence of immigration from Muslim countries'. The motivation of intactivists is not political, and certainly not an attack on any religion. The motivation is that MGM is a non-consensual violation of bodily integrity, coupled with potential harm and lack of commensurate benefit. The motivation is compassionate, and that many parties see only political, or antisemitic, motivations is indicative of their own incredulity that compassion might be the motive. It is indicative of their empathy gap.

6.4.2.3 Iceland

In 2018 there was a renewed flurry of activity. Silja Dögg Gunnarsdóttir of the Icelandic Progressive Party proposed a Bill based on the argument that 'if we have laws banning circumcision for girls, then we should do so for boys'. The Bill came in for the usual vigorous opposition from religious groups, (Sherwood, 2018), and was projected to fail, (Demurtas, 2018), despite strong support from the Icelandic medical community, (Harretz, 2018). In the event, the Bill was not heard. The status quo – the empathy gap – wins again, despite all sound arguments to the contrary.

6.4.2.4 Denmark

The issue of explicitly banning non-therapeutic circumcision of male minors arose again later in 2018, this time in Denmark following a people's petition which reached the requirement of 50,000 votes to trigger parliamentary debate, (Mattha Busby agency, 2018). Once again, though, politicians lacked the courage to enact a ban, though intactivist campaigners in Denmark remain hopeful.

6.4.2.5 The USA

A recent legal issue arose in the USA, not in the context of attempting to ban non-therapeutic male circumcision, but in the context of a case brought to prosecute on FMG charges. Antony Lempert (2018) has observed that the repeated failure of attempts, worldwide, to criminalise MGM is increasingly throwing a spotlight on the inconsistencies in the legal treatment of males and females. This is bringing forcibly to the attention of the public and politicians alike the failure to abide by the precepts of equality legislation. The unintended consequence of failing to protect male minors might be that the existing statutes to protect females from FGM are judged unlawful. This has now happened in the USA. (Earp, 2018a) has summarised the situation, emphasising that awareness of the legal inconsistency is only getting more insistent. He gives illustrations of how some pro-FGM groups are using this inconsistency as an argument for making some of the less invasive forms of FGM legal. He also points out the problem of intersex children. At what point does a small penis become a large clitoris? Hence at what point is surgical modification of such genitalia legal and when will it attract many years in prison?

In a separate video, Brian Earp (2018b) has explained a ruling made in a US District Court in Michigan in November 2018. The judge's ruling in that court was that the US federal law, Title 18 Code 116, which purports to make FGM illegal throughout the USA, is unconstitutional. As Earp notes, the Michigan judge's ruling does not mean that FGM has suddenly become legal in the USA. In fact, the statutes prohibiting sexual assault, common assault or child abuse made FGM illegal prior to the explicit Code 116 – just as was also true in the UK. The Michigan judge's ruling was based on his view that the US Government had exceeded their powers in enacting a federal level law, and that such legislation should properly rest at the State level. On these grounds he considered he had the legal power to strike it down as regards local (State) application. However, his reason for wishing to do so was precisely that the statute is explicitly discriminatory based on sex, i.e., that it fails to provide the same protection to both sexes. It was due to this – the glaring inconsistency that is not going to remain hidden any longer – that he declared the federal statute unconstitutional. This is a remarkable state of affairs.

6.4.2.6 Religious Objections

In summary, no country has passed a law making non-therapeutic circumcision of male minors explicitly illegal. Though many countries have assault laws, or other laws, under which the practice could be legally challenged, the *de facto* position at present is tolerance of the practice. As far as I am aware, only two countries (Norway and Sweden) have even stipulated that the procedure must deploy anaesthesia.

The deference given to the opposition from Jewish groups contrasts with the simple observation that the number of men who have been circumcised in one country alone (the USA) is about 17 times larger than the total number of male Jews worldwide.

Interestingly, Israel only regards male circumcision to be a religious act, and as such can legally be carried out by a person without formal medical training, up to the age of six months. After this age, circumcision in Israel must be carried out as a surgical procedure by surgically qualified persons, (UNAIDS, 2010). It is not clear whether this imposes a restriction on non-therapeutic circumcisions beyond the six month age limit. This does not affect Jews, as the Jewish custom is to circumcise at 8 days old. However, the Moslem practice is to circumcise boys well past the infant stage. Jews are very active in opposing moves to outlaw non-therapeutic male circumcision in other countries, claiming it would be antisemitic. It would be hypocritical if they had, in practice, imposed such restrictions in Israel, though this is not entirely clear.

In order to avoid the religious objection, some people have argued there should be a specifically religious exemption from a law that would otherwise ban non-therapeutic circumcision of male minors. There are several serious objections to such a proposal. One is that it opens the door to making FGM legal if groups argue that their religion calls for it. (And despite the oft-repeated fact that the Qur'an does not require female cutting, there are other Moslem texts which do mention it and a case for FGM being a religious practice could be made by determined proponents). A second objection is that it opens the door to other religious exemptions, with very unfortunate consequences. There have been a number of cases in the UK of severe child abuse, sometimes leading to death, as a result of traditional African practices. While we would dismiss these as "witchcraft", a case could be made for one person's witchcraft being another person's religion. Making exemptions from laws for certain classes of people, however such classes be defined, would be terribly retrograde. All groups should be content to live within the law of the land. A third reason that a religious exemption to the illegality of non-therapeutic circumcision of minors should be avoided is simply that it is discriminatory. Making it illegal to cut a nice Christian boy, but saying it is perfectly fine to cut those Jewish or Moslem boys – how could that be acceptable?

6.5 The Male Genital Mutilation Empathy Gap

The wildly different perceptions of FGM and MGM by many members of the public, and by the criminal justice system, is a particularly stark example of the empathy gap. We have seen that Lord Justice Munby was obliged to conclude that if FGM always constitutes harm, as Lady Justice Hale asserted before him, then MGM must also be considered a harm. The medical evidence concurs. It is remarkable, then, that a non-consensual violation of the bodily integrity of a child, which has been judicially ruled to constitute a harm, nevertheless is still to be treated as legal. This position is arrived at by rationalisations which do not bear scrutiny and which are actually for the purpose of protecting the status quo rather than the child.

In no cultural tradition was medical benefit the original motivation for circumcision. In the "Western-medical" tradition, the original motivation was indisputably to diminish male sexual function, especially as regards discouraging masturbation. Claims of medical benefit arose later as a *post-hoc* rationalisation. But the claims of medical benefit are dubious, and marginal at best, whilst the harm done by MGM can be substantial for a significant proportion of circumcised men. The net effect cannot be asserted to be a benefit with any confidence, and is, on average, likely to be a disbenefit. The trauma of the procedure further tips the scales in the negative direction. However, the invasion of the bodily integrity of the child is the decisive factor.

The illegality of MGM has yet to be tested in the UK by bringing a case to court. However, the CPS are unlikely to allow this to happen. Even cases where there has been a failure to obtain parental consent, a clear breach of law, tend not to be prosecuted. It is an unfortunate characteristic of human societies that the public can be inveigled into accepting anything, so long as everyone else goes along with it – even cutting body parts off babies.

It is not only religious groups who will oppose moves to outlaw MGM. Women's groups have in the past actively opposed such moves. For example, following the initial ruling in Germany in 2012 to make MGM illegal, we read,

> 'Women's rights groups and social policy makers also condemned the decision, but for the reason that it would have the effect of putting male and female circumcision on the same footing, when they were "in no way comparable", said Katrin Altpeter, social minister in the state of Baden-Württemberg. Female circumcision she said, was a far more drastic act. It is already outlawed in Germany.' (Connolly, 2012)

But it is not really the relative severity of MGM versus FGM which lies behind this view. Anyone who has campaigned, or spoken out publicly, in opposition to MGM will probably have met with an angry retort from some people. They react with passionate hostility towards you. If one were to campaign in *favour* of cutting body parts off babies, I can readily understand why people would react with passionate hostility. But why should people react with such venom to campaigning *against* doing so? This reaction is revealing. To disagree is one thing, but it is the anger which is illuminating. The retort is likely to be, "FGM is *far* worse". But it will not placate your interlocutor to stress that you are equally opposed to FGM. I have never come across any intactivist who is not equally opposed to FGM. "Equally", you see, is not sufficient. My interpretation of the psychology at work here is that the anger comes from a deep prejudice that the spotlight of concern should never be shone upon males. Males are not the proper recipients of concern. Females must retain their monopoly on victimhood and its attendant benefits. This is feminist intensified gynocentrism and its correlate, male disposability: the empathy gap. This is unfortunate because the peculiar characteristic of compassion is that it is not diminished by being bestowed more widely: the quality of mercy is not strained.

7

Work, Pay, Tax, Spending and Pensions

State providing as a matter of routine soon creates a victim culture in which all but the richest people feel that far from owing the community anything, they deserve more from it. This deprives the mass of citizens of the elementary self-respect which they need to have in order for a moral economy to operate.
Geoff Dench (1940 - 2018), *Transforming Men*

The fundamental public duty of any able-bodied citizen is to minimise calls on community resources both by being self-reliant where he or she can, and through helping out family members too, in order to limit the use made of state help. Communities would soon get overdrawn without families.
Geoff Dench (1940 - 2018), *Transforming Men*

In this long chapter I examine UK employment, pay, working hours, tax, pensions and spending and how these vary with sex. This includes data on unemployment and economic inactivity for men and women. The polarization of employment by gender is considered, and examples given of occupations dominated by women, including the significance of the public sector in this respect. I then consider one of the most contentious subjects in the context of gender: the pay gap, including how it varies with age and with full time or part time working. ONS data for the gender pay gap are compared with data from individual company submissions under the 2017 legislation which has made gender pay gap reporting obligatory in the UK. The latter data is examined to determine the proportion of companies which pay women significantly more than men, as well as vice-versa. Based on ONS data I also consider examples of occupations for which the pay gap is in favour of women, to balance the usual narrative.

I then examine total paid working hours by sex, and the greater prevalence of part time working amongst women. This provides a complementary picture to pay: men earn more and also work more paid hours. Evidence from British Social Attitudes Surveys is reviewed to discern whether there is general public contentment, or discontent, as regards the prevailing gendered working patterns. Next, I consider who spends the household money, irrespective of who may earn it. There is a long section on pensions, concentrating upon the UK, and drawing out inequality issues. Finally, I discuss the contribution to unpaid housework by the two sexes, including caring responsibilities.

The picture which emerges from this broad sweep of issues related to work and financial matters is far from being the one which is usually presented.

7.1 UK Unemployment Data

The "unemployed" are defined as those without a job but who have been actively seeking work in the last four weeks and are able to start work in the next two weeks. The "labour force" consists of those people in the nominal working age range (16 to 64) who are employed, plus those who are unemployed in the above sense. People who are of nominal working age who are not within the labour force are said to be "economically inactive". This includes full time students and all people who do not wish to be in paid work, e.g., full time home-makers, those who are retired prior to age 65, or simply people who do not wish to work.

The unemployment rate is the number of unemployed as a percentage of the labour force. Note that the unemployment rate is not usually defined as a percentage of the whole population or even the whole population of working age. The economic inactivity rate is the number of economically inactive people as a percentage of the working age population. The labour force participation rate is the number of people in the labour force as a percentage of the working age population. The economic inactivity rate and the labour force participation rate are thus complementary measures; they add to 100%.

Figure 7.1 shows the unemployment rate in the UK from 1971 to the end of 2017, (Office for National Statistics, 2018k). In April 2018, the UK unemployment rate (4.2%) was at a 42-year low and was essentially equal for men and women. However, historically, the unemployment rate for men has been higher than that for women since 1981. The peaks in the unemployment rate evident in Figure 7.1 demonstrate how recessions affect men's employment more than women's (e.g., those in the early 1980s, early 1990s and post-2008). At the end of 2017 there were 782,000 unemployed men and 689,000 unemployed women. However, it is important to recall that the 'unemployment rate' only measures those actively seeking and able to work. It does not measure those who have dropped out of being recognised as economically active.

Young people who leave education at age 16 have very high rates of unemployment. In 2018 the unemployment rate for 16 to 17 year olds in the UK was about 30%, a decrease from about 40% a few years earlier. This is the demographic within which much future disadvantage will be focused. Young people who are not in education, employment or training ("NEETs") are of particular interest. Figure 7.2 shows the number of NEETs in England in the age range 16 to 24 as a percentage of people of the same age and sex versus year, (Office for National Statistics, 2018g). There used to be more female NEETs, but in recent years the prevalence of NEETs has converged for the two sexes.

Figure 7.1: *UK Unemployment Rate by Sex versus Year (Percent)*

Figure 7.2: *NEETs in England by Sex versus Year*

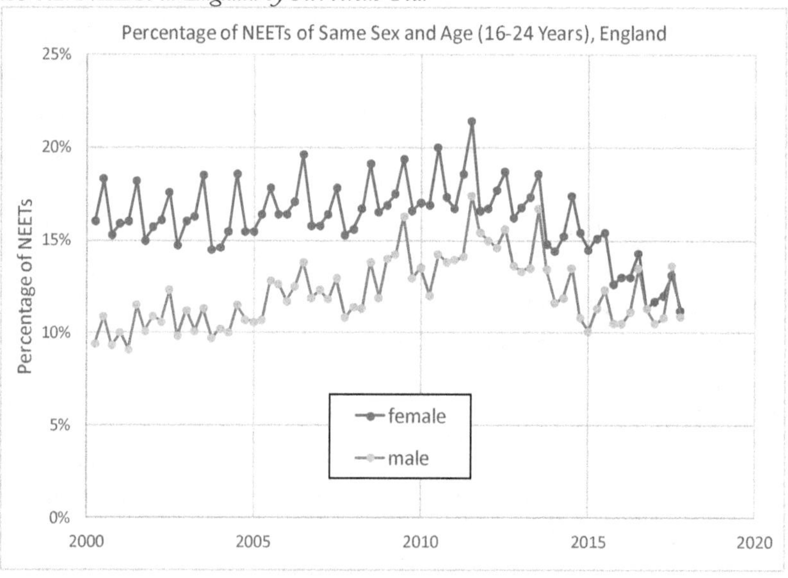

7.2 UK Economic Inactivity

People between 16 and 64 who do not feature as either employed or unemployed are the economically inactive. One of the most significant features of the huge social changes over the last half-century is the increasing participation of women in the labour force. Figure 7.3 shows how the percentage of women who are economically inactive has reduced from 45% in 1971 to an all-time low of 26% by 2017, (Office for National Statistics, 2018j). What is less widely appreciated is the huge increase in men's economic inactivity. In 1971 only 5% of men were economically inactive, i.e., 95% of working age men were participating in the labour force. Now some 17% of working age men are economically inactive.

Figure 7.3: *UK Economic Inactivity Rates by Sex (Percent)*

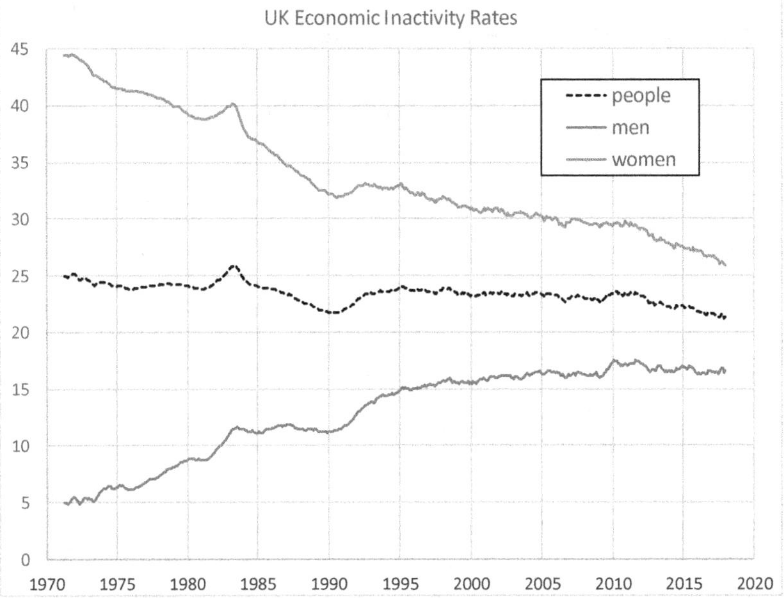

The obvious feature of Figure 7.3 which tends to be elided in popular discourse is that the increasing economic participation of women has been largely mirrored by a decreasing economic participation of men. Overall, economic inactivity has reduced only marginally, from 25% (1971) to 21% (2017). The main reason for this is more women in the workplace (fewer women as full time home-keepers). But this is offset by substantial increases in the number of full time students and also increases in the number of long term sick. The dominant reason for men being economically inactive is being in full time education, closely followed by long term sickness. The dominant reason for women being economically inactive is being a full time home-keeper followed by being in full time education and long term sickness.

Over the period 1971 to 2017 the working age male population of the UK increased from 16.5 million to 20.5 million. Hence, in 1971 there were 0.8 million economically inactive men in the UK, but by 2017 this had increased to 3.4 million. There are more than four times more economically inactive men of working age than there used to be in 1971.

The bulk of the sex disparity in the economically inactive is due to the difference in full time home-keeping. In the last 25 years, the number of men in a full time home-keeping role has increased substantially from about 100,000 to about a quarter of a million, see Figure 7.4. Over the same period the number of economically inactive women in that role has reduced from just under 3 million to just under 2 million.

Figure 7.4: *Numbers of UK Home-keepers by Sex versus Year (note the different scales for the two sexes)*

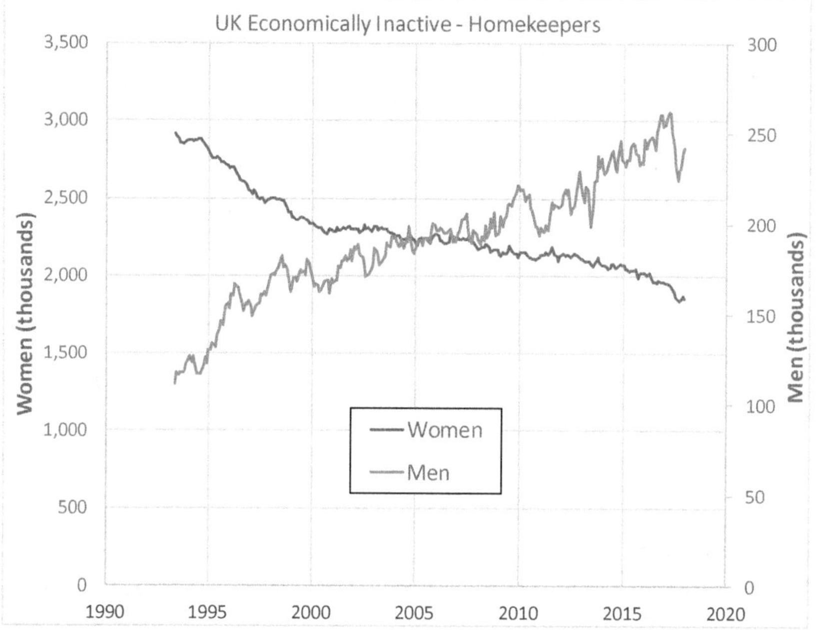

There are still more women than men under 65 who are retired, but these numbers are converging due to the raising of the retirement age for women.

At the end of 2017, 25% of men and 22% of women who were economically inactive did, in fact, want a job (850,000 men and 1.16 million women respectively). These figures are larger than the numbers classed as unemployed, illustrating how the unemployment figures under-state the number of people who want a job. The sum of the unemployed and the economically inactive who wished to work at December 2017 was 1.63 million men and 1.85 million women.

Finally, there is a sizeable number of the economically inactive classed either as "discouraged workers" or simply as "other" (440,000 men and 538,000 women). We might expect to find particular disadvantage in these categories.

7.3 Gendered Occupations

Employment tends to be polarised by sex. This is often referred to as "occupational segregation". However, the term "segregation" is loaded, redolent as it is of racially segregated societies and hence a separation enforced by hegemony. But it is personal preference which drives most employment areas to deviate substantially and consistently from a random distribution of the sexes.

The number of employees in the UK by occupation category may be obtained from the Government dataset dated April-June 2017, (Office for National Statistics, 2017f). 331 listed employment areas included data sufficient to deduce a ratio of male to female employees. 142 of these (43%) employed more women than men; 189 (57%) employed more men than women. Just 73 occupations (22%) had employee numbers within plus or minus 30% of equality. 151 (46%) had an excess of male employees over female employees exceeding 30%. 107 (32%) had an excess of female employees over male employees exceeding 30%. This is employment polarisation. We hear a great deal about employment segregation – but generally only in respect of a small subset of jobs, namely certain desirable professions in which men dominate but feminist women covet.

A thorough review of employment by gender across all occupations is beyond the scope of this book. However, since the subject at hand is male inequality, it is appropriate to consider briefly some of the sectors and occupations in which men are underrepresented. A sample of the 142 occupations which employ more women is provided in Table 7.1 together with the percentage by which women outnumber men, (Office for National Statistics, 2017f). The list is not exhaustive, merely some illustrations. They are overwhelmingly dominated by jobs that involve working with people or animals. In contrast, the occupations in which men are most emphatically dominant are the skilled trades, which primarily involve the manipulation of inanimate matter.

Table 7.1: *Examples of occupations in which women outnumber men (UK).*

Standard Occupational Classification	% Excess of Women
Dental nurses	(49,138)*
Childcare and Related Personal Services	1352
Nursing and Midwifery Professionals	541
Senior care workers	503
Social workers	391
Houseparents and residential wardens	378
Therapy Professionals	376
Care workers and home carers	372
Child and early years officers	350
Special needs education teaching professionals	343
Finance officers	332
Nursing auxiliaries and assistants	323
Health associate professionals	312
Pharmaceutical technicians	300
Education advisers and school inspectors	201
Office Managers and Supervisors	185
Pharmacists	164
Careers advisers and vocational guidance specialists	162
Youth and community workers	161
Counsellors	158
Health Associate Professionals	153
Other Financial administrative occupations	152
Travel agents	150
Social services managers and directors	141
Local government administrative occupations	139
Other welfare and housing associate professionals	130
Physiotherapists	128
Senior professionals of educational establishments	115
Housing officers	111
Medical radiographers	106
Public relations professionals	102
Conference and exhibition managers and organisers	97
Legal associate professionals	97
Public services associate professionals	89
Credit controllers	80
Veterinarians	71
Authors, writers and translators	58
Human resources and industrial relations officers	56
Buyers and procurement officers	49
Health services and public health managers and directors	37
Marketing associate professionals	37
Medical and dental technicians, Ophthalmic opticians	34

**no male dental nurses listed, this is the actual number of female dental nurses*

Even those professions in which men are most dominant tend to be associated with the inanimate rather than the animate, e.g., engineering and IT. This is hardly news but bears repeating, as does the fact that this division into people versus things is reflected also in subject choice at university (see chapter 2).

7.3.1 The Public Sector

In 2017/18 total public spending was £802 billion (UK Government, 2018b). This £802 billion public spending compares with the UK's total GDP which is about £2 trillion (Trading Economics, 2018). In December 2018, some 5.37 million people were employed in the public sector, and 27.34 million in the private sector, (Office for National Statistics, 2018h). Hence, the public sector accounts for roughly 40% of GDP, but only 16.5% of employment.

Across all areas, women are 46% of those employed, men 54% (this includes part-time workers). But in the public sector, women comprise about two-thirds of employees, twice as many as men. In contrast, women account for only about 42% of private sector employees (NCVO UK Civil Society Almanac, 2017). Staff in the voluntary sector, totalling 853,000 people in 2016, are about 65% women (NCVO UK Civil Society Almanac, 2017).

Health and education together account for significantly more than half of public employees, and both these areas are strongly dominated by women. About 1.1 million people are employed in schools in England alone, (UK Government, 2018s). Across the whole of the UK education sector there are 1.51 million public employees, (Office for National Statistics, 2015g). The sex ratio of school employees is as follows, (Higher Education Statistics Authority, 2016),

- Of all teaching staff, across all schools, 24.2% are men and 75.8% are women;
- Auxiliary staff across all schools are 20.4% men and 79.6% women;
- Across all schools and all staff, 22.1% are men and 77.9% are women.

At March 2018 the NHS employed 1.64 million people, UK wide (Office for National Statistics, 2018h). This comprises 1.33 million in England and about 161,000, 84,000 and 66,000 in Scotland, Wales and N.Ireland respectively (NHS Choices, 2016). Of these, roughly half are clinically qualified (doctors, nurses, midwives, dental staff, health service staff, radiologists, paramedics, etc). Overall, NHS employees are roughly 75% women (90% of nurses/midwives, 80% of non-professional staff, and about half of the rest (The King's Fund, 2018)).

Hence, education and healthcare account for about 3.15 million of the 5.35 million public sector workers (59%). Of this 3.15 million, about 2.4

million (76%) are women. Of the remaining 2.2 million public sector employees, excluding health and education, more than half (53%) are women.

7.3.2 Armed Forces

Between 9% and 14% of UK armed service personnel are women. Women account for a larger percentage of officers than other ranks across all three main services, Table 7.2, (House of Commons Library, 2017). The proportion of deaths accounted for by women in recent military campaigns was substantially smaller than their proportion in the forces. In the campaign that followed the invasion of Iraq on 20 March 2003 and came to an end in April 2009, the UK war deaths were 173 men and 6 women (3% women), (BBC News, 2016). In the 14 years starting in October 2001, the number of UK war deaths in Afghanistan were 453 men and 3 women (0.7% women), (BBC News, 2015).

Table 7.2: *Percentage of UK Armed Service Personnel who are Women*

Service	Officers	Other Ranks
Army	11.8%	8.6%
Navy	9.3%	8.9%
RAF	16.9%	13.2%

Figure 7.5: *The Number of UK Apprentices by Sex and Year*

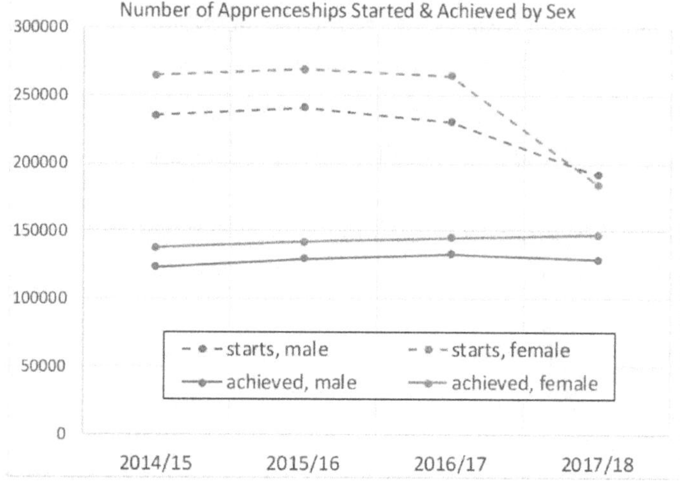

7.3.3 Apprenticeships

With one exception (which looks anomalous) more young women than young men start, and complete, apprenticeships, see Figure 7.5, (Department for Education, 2019). Nevertheless, Unionlearn, the learning and skills organisation of the TUC, together with the National Apprenticeship Service and the Skills Funding Agency, have published research which gives the opposite impression. They write in their report,

> 'recommendations are made for how the range of stakeholders in the Apprenticeship system can take action to increase interest in Apprenticeships and reduce barriers to access generally, as well as specifically act to promote the greater inclusion of young women and ethnic minority groups.' (Becci Newton and Joy Williams, 2013)

It is easy to see why well-meaning people will get entirely the wrong impression when such misleading material is so common. There is a mindset so intent on seeing female disadvantage everywhere that evidence to the contrary becomes invisible to them.

7.3.4 The Gender Equality "Paradox"

A perennial theme amongst feminists is the underrepresentation of women in STEM subjects at university and in STEM employment. The so-called "paradox" is that data from many countries shows that the more "gender-equal" the society, the greater is the degree of occupational gender segregation. For example, the greater the gender equality, the smaller the proportion of women in STEM occupations. Stoet and Geary (2018) have presented a particularly thorough analysis and their main results are shown in Figure 7.6. The y-axis in these graphs is a measure of how gender-equal is the country in question. Both graphs plot points representing a range of countries. Graph (b) shows that the more gender-equal the society, the smaller the proportion of women in STEM (correlation -0.47). Conversely, the countries with the largest proportion of women in STEM are countries which are not noted for their equitable treatment of women.

The so-called "paradox" is only paradoxical if one insists on maintaining that there are no innate differences between the sexes. Actually, the "paradox" is evidence that there *are* innate sex differences. If one is happy to acknowledge innate sex differences, then there is no paradox. The differences in question need not be differences in ability. They may be differences in preference, and probably are. One of the things which exercises women's advocates is that women's underrepresentation in STEM appears incommensurate with their ability in science at school level.

Figure 7.6: *A Measure of a Country's Gender Equality (GGGI) versus, (a) Gender Gap in Intraindividual Science Performance, and, (b) Percentage of Women in STEM Graduates, from (Stoet and Geary, 2018)*

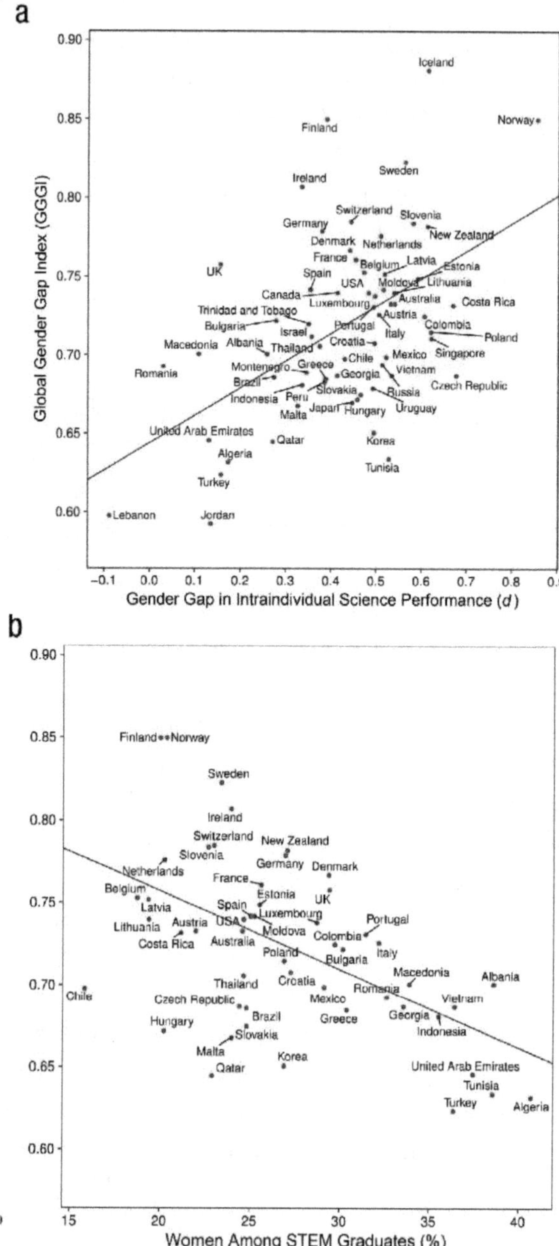

Graph (a) in Figure 7.6 is particularly interesting in this regard. It uses an x-axis defined by the gender gap in an intraindividual science performance measure. This measure depends, not just upon performance in science, but also on performance in maths and reading. The intraindividual science score for a given individual is the difference between that individual's performance in science and his (or her) average performance across science, maths and reading. Thus, an intraindividual science score may be boosted by being poor at reading, say. A girl may have a science score equal to that of a boy, but girls who are good at science tend also to be good at the other subjects, and perhaps even better at reading. A boy who is good at science, however, is often poor at reading. The gender gap in their intraindividual science performance measures may therefore be large, not because the boy is better at science but because he is poor at reading (though the measure would also register a boy's particularly strong science performance, of course).

Graph (a) shows that the more gender equal the country, the greater is the gender gap in the average intraindividual science performance measure (correlation 0.42). From this perspective the dominance of men in STEM may be as much to do with women who are verbally gifted compared to men as it is to do with men who are scientifically strong. Even women who are scientifically capable may opt for non-scientific subjects because they are just as capable in those alternative subjects, and perhaps prefer them.

I have long maintained that boys opt for maths, physics and IT at A Level partly to get away from the dreaded *word*, lack of facility with which has plagued them throughout their school career up to that point. Graph (a) may be a manifestation of that, in part.

The bottom line is that UK women dominate in every subject apart from TEM and architecture (recalling that women dominate in the pure sciences in the UK). People who agonise over "women in STEM" never seem concerned that, other things being unchanged, more "women in STEM" would mean that women's overall dominance at university would increase above its current 37%. The lesson of Graph (a) may be – and this is the true paradox – that achieving a greater proportion of women in STEM may be best accomplished by improving boys' reading and writing.

If the innate sex differences which lie behind Figure 7.6 relate to preference, then this might be expected to manifest also in non-academic measures. Giolla and Kajonius (2018) have shown that sex differences in personality are larger in more gender equal countries, Figure 7.7 (correlation 0.69). Sex difference in personality was defined by measuring the "big five" personality traits (neuroticism, extraversion, openness, agreeableness and conscientiousness) and defining a "distance" measure, essentially as the

Euclidean distance between the two points in this 5-dimensional space. The Scandinavian countries are most gender-equal and also have the largest sex difference in personality. Does a more equal culture cause the personalities of the two sexes to diverge? Or does a more equal culture merely provide the opportunity for innate personality differences to be manifest?

Figure 7.7: *Gender Equality Index versus Sex Difference in Personality, from (Giolla and Kajonius, 2018)*

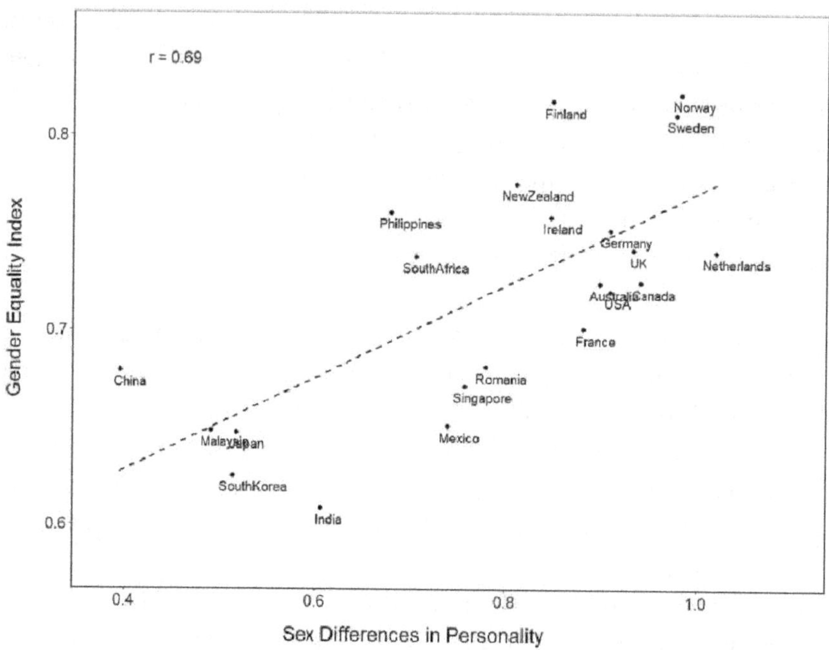

Giolla and Kajonius (2018) also show how each of the big five personality traits vary with the countries' gender equality, disaggregated by sex. Where increased gender equality has a beneficial effect, the benefit is greater for women than for men (improved openness and agreeableness). Greater gender equality leads to decreased conscientiousness in both sexes, but the effect is more marked for men. Greater gender equality leads to greater introversion in men, but not in women. In short, greater gender equality is beneficial for women (except as regards diminished conscientiousness). But the same cannot be said for men, the benefits being more muted and there being as many disbenefits. This may be because the standard measure of "gender equality" is actually a measure of "women's equality", not a measure of equality at all. If more (of this type of) gender equality results in divergence of personality between the sexes, is this related to increasing inter-sex conflict? (I note in passing that measuring only the "big five" personality traits probably underestimates sex differences, which might be greater in the associated sub-traits).

7.3.5 Diversity?

There is now a very strong initiative across most large corporations, driven by Government, to achieve "balance" or "diversity", generally defined as a workforce whose demographic composition mimics that of the population as a whole – but only in a limited sense. The demographic characteristics which are subject to this equalisation initiative vary but generally include sex, ethnicity, disability status and sexuality. (At what point did it become acceptable to make revealing one's sexuality obligatory?).

For example, the BBC has declared their targets, both on and off screen, to be 50% women, 15% BAME, 8% with disabilities, and 8% LBGT, (BBC, 2016). There is no requirement to employ straight white men in the same proportion as in the general public. The over-constrained nature of these quotas means that it is inevitable, if the quotas are met, that the number of straight white men employed will be substantially less than in the general public. Do not imagine this is an oversight. It is a deliberate plan to de-power white men. One hopes they will find a good number of talented disabled, black lesbians otherwise the quotas will leave just 19% for heterosexual white men. This drive to "equalise" across the demographic spectrum (apart from heterosexual white men) is, in some cases, being insisted upon at all levels in the organisation. This is to prevent those nasty old white patriarchs filling up their quota of women and ethnic minorities with cleaners and junior clerks, of course.

This is not a joke. It is overt discrimination and it is going to happen. Disabled BAME women really will be able to name their price, even if they have absolutely nothing to offer the company, especially if they are also willing to identify as lesbian or bisexual. Such people will be gold dust in order to meet the quotas whilst allowing straight white men in senior positions to hang onto their jobs. There will be a disabled BAME lesbian on every Board of any company with quotas – or, at least, every Board that can find one.

Anecdotally, it is already beginning to be noticed by the unwanted heterosexual white men that they are being passed over for promotions on the sole grounds of being the white, male and straight. One does not need to be a genius to foretell the inevitable resentment that will follow. Unfair, enforced diversity is divisity. The disgruntled men will be told that this is what loss of their male privilege feels like. No, it's what prejudice feels like. But companies will still be reliant on the dedication of these same men – more so than before as senior roles become filled with sub-standard people who merely meet a demographic requirement. Becoming increasingly dependent upon a section of staff whom you are disadvantaging and alienating is not a good business model. It is not hard to foresee companies collapsing as a result, but the cause will never be admitted. It is also easy to guess that competent men suffering this treatment will form new companies with predominantly white male staff, putting up two fingers to both the law and social disapprobation.

But I feel confident that this draconian drive for equalisation will leave the public sector, with its two-thirds female workforce, untouched. The areas where there would be real social benefit in greater gender balance is in teaching, nursing, psychology, counselling and social work. But I doubt that these occupations will come under any pressure at all to employ more men in their grossly female skewed professions. Nor will anyone express concern that the blue-collar skilled trades will continue to be a male monopoly. The drive for more women in professional areas where they are currently underrepresented is not about fairness or equality; it's about power. "Diversity" is a strategy to de-power white men and hence to facilitate socialist State control.

Table 7.3: *Percentage of Female Applicants for Tenure-Track Positions Invited for Interview and Offered Positions at 89 Research Universities in the USA, 2010, from (Ceci et al, 2014)*

Field	Mean percentage of female applicants	Mean percentage of women invited to interview	Mean percentage of women offered position
Physics	12%	19%	20%
Biology	26%	28%	34%
Chemistry	18%	25%	29%
Civil engineering	16%	30%	32%
Electrical engineering	11%	19%	32%
Mathematics	20%	28%	32%

There is already evidence that female candidates are preferred for academic posts in STEM. In chapter two I discussed the 2015 findings of Wendy Williams and Stephen Ceci, based on fictional applicants to academic posts, which indicated a preference for female candidates over male candidates by a factor of between two and three in biology, engineering and psychology (and also in economics as regards female faculty preference). A long and detailed paper the previous year, (Ceci et al, 2014), indicates an emphatic preference for female candidates across STEM subjects (Table 7.3). These data suggest that female candidates for STEM tenure-track academic positions in the USA have on average an 85% greater chance of being hired than their male counterparts.

7.4 The UK Gender Pay Gap

With the possible exception of sexual assault, the gender pay gap is the issue which most exercises people advocating for "women's equality". The controversy has been exacerbated by the legal requirement on UK companies with more than 250 staff to report their gender pay gap data annually. The first deadline was April 2018, (UK Government, 2017a). Data submitted by individual companies provide ample opportunity for those wishing to play the politician and "cherry pick" data which suit their purpose. I take a look at the data submitted in section 7.5 below. Firstly, I review the pay data from the ONS's Annual Survey of Hours and Earnings (ASHE), which is available for several years the latest being 2017 (Office for National Statistics, 2017d). It should be noted that ASHE, which is the source usually quoted in discussions about pay, relates to surveys of employees only. The self-employed do not feature in this dataset. It should not be assumed that this excludes only high-earning business people. Many of the self-employed are tradesmen, for example, whose earnings may be precarious. Recall it is the self-employed who may legally pay themselves less than the minimum wage, and frequently do.

These surveys take a 1% sample of data from HMRC PAYE (tax office pay-as-you-earn) returns. The data refer to the UK as a whole. It is important to distinguish between earnings and pay rate. One person will earn more than another if he works more hours but their pay rates are the same. Overtime often attracts a higher pay rate. Thus, a person working the same number of hours as another, with the same nominal pay rate, will nevertheless earn more if a larger proportion of his working hours are overtime (antisocial) hours. Finally, one person may earn more than another due to receiving a performance related bonus. All these things would complicate comparisons if included. Consequently, it is appropriate to concentrate upon hourly rates of pay excluding overtime and bonus payments.

Two further factors are of importance. Firstly, the distinction between part-time and full-time working is important. Full-time working is defined as employees working more than 30 paid hours per week (for the teaching professions, 25 or more hours). Secondly, the age-dependence of the gender pay gap is also very important.

It is usual to concentrate upon the median value of the pay gap, rather than the mean, since the latter can be sensitive to a small number of outliers. The pay gap is defined as the difference between men's and women's hourly pay rates expressed as a percentage of men's pay rate (excluding overtime and bonuses). Table 7.4 shows that the median pay gap for part time workers in 2017 was in favour of women by 5.1%. For full time workers, the median pay gap was in favour of men by 9.1%. The figures of Table 7.4 apply before tax. After income tax, the median pay gap for full time workers is about 7% (Collins W. , 2017a). These figures relate to all ages combined. Figure 7.8 shows the full time gender pay gap as a histogram against age range. This reveals an important feature: the gender pay gap is almost zero, within about 2%, between the typical graduate age (22) and 39.

Table 7.4: *All-Ages Median Gender Pay Rate Gap Excluding Overtime (UK). 2015 data from (Office for National Statistics, 2015a); 2017 data from (Office for National Statistics, 2017b). Negative values mean a pay rate gap in favour of women.*

Employment	2015	2017
Full Time	9.4%	9.1%
Part Time	-6.5%	-5.1%

Figure 7.8: *Full-time UK Median Gender Pay Gap as Histogram against Age*

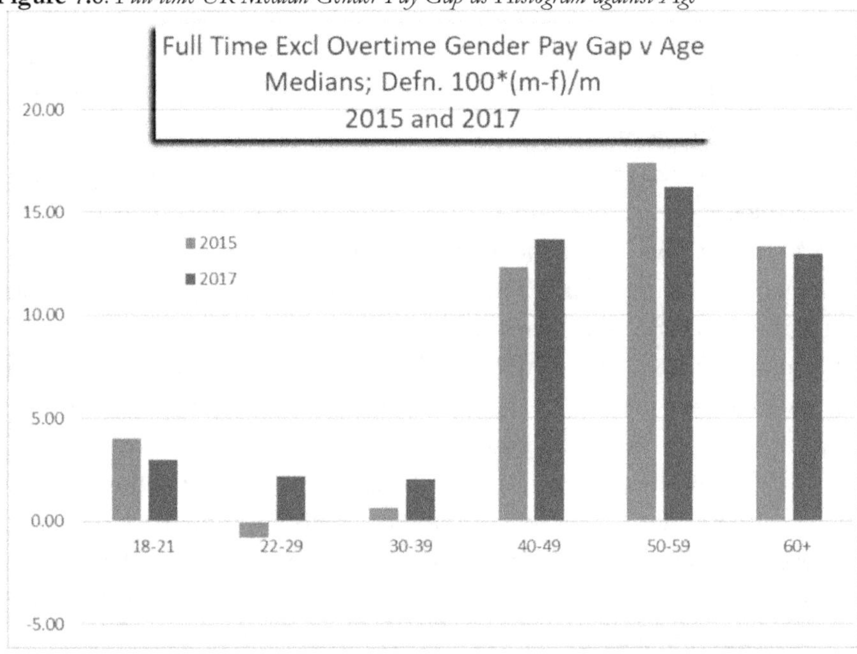

Another important feature of the data, which is rarely brought out in discussions of only median or mean values, is the huge spread of pay rates. Figure 7.9 shows, for people in the age range 22 to 39, the distribution of full time pay rates, from the lowest to the highest decile. This Figure also illustrates how tiny is the gender pay gap in this age range.

Figure 7.10 is a similar graph for the age ranges 40-49 and 50-59. In the latter age range, for which the gender pay gap is greatest, the pay rate for men varies from £9.00/hr to £35.68/hr (lower and upper deciles). For women the range is from £8.18/hr to £27.01/hr. Hence, the gender gap is small compared with the huge range of pay rates. The overlap of the distributions is more significant than the difference of their medians.

Figure 7.9: *Full Time UK Pay Rate Distributions for Men and Women, Ages 21 to 39*

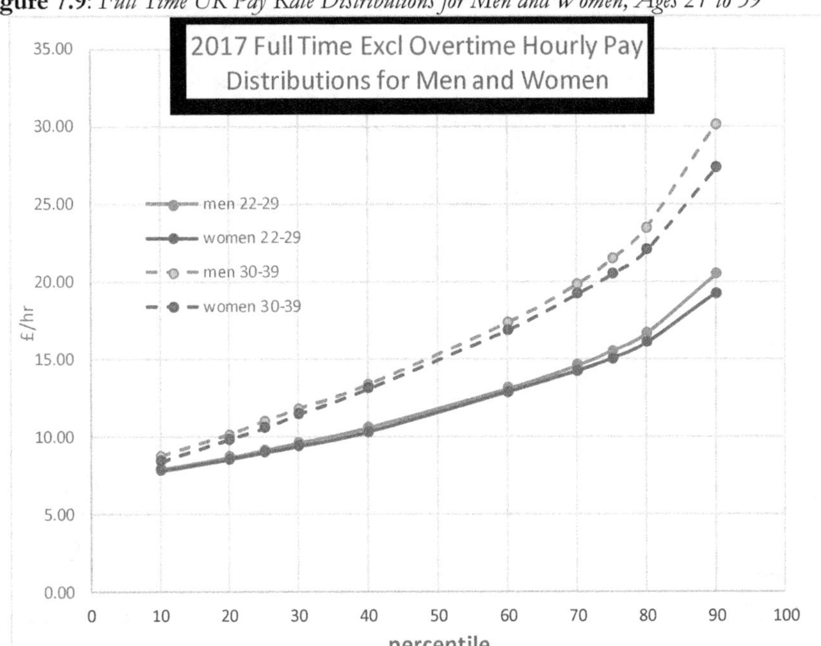

More women than men work part time and the pay gap is in women's favour for part time working. More men than women work full time and the pay gap is in men's favour for full time working. Full time working attracts substantially higher hourly pay rates, on average, than part time working. The pay rate penalty for working part time is far larger than the gender pay gap, as illustrated by Table 7.5 below.

Some sources combine all workers to produce a "gender pay gap" which covers both full time and part time working. Because far more women than men work part time, and more men than women work full time, and because of the very different pay rates for full time and part time working, this produces a much larger apparent "gender pay gap", namely 18.4% in 2017. But this is merely statistical legerdemain. This figure reflects the pay rate penalty for part time working, not really a gender gap at all.

Figure 7.10: *Full Time UK Pay Rate Distributions for Men and Women, Ages 40 to 59*

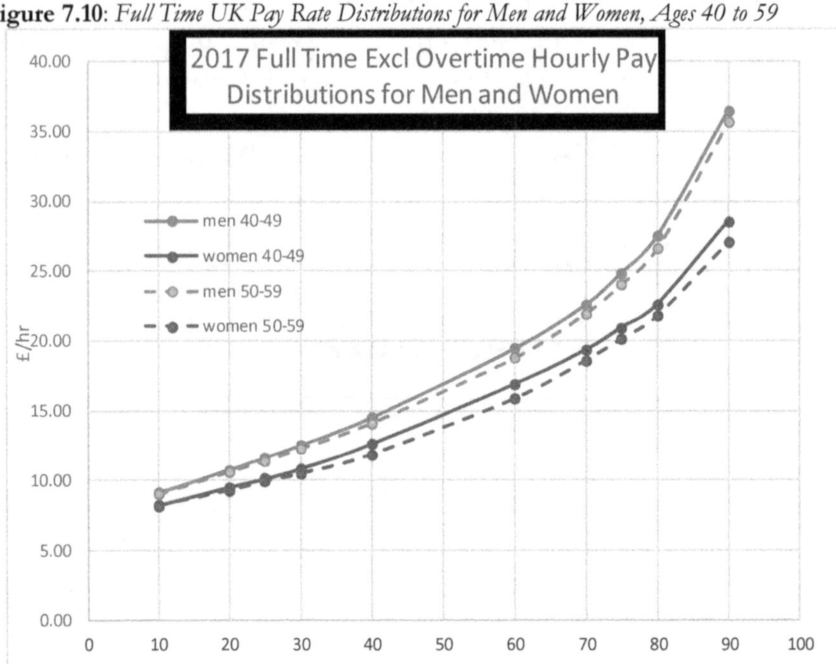

Table 7.5: *Full Time and Part Time UK Median Pay Rates Compared, £/hour, 2017*

Employment	Men	Women	Gender pay gap
Full time	14.48	13.16	9.1%
Part time	8.76	9.21	-5.1%

In an excellent short summary of pay gap data, Kate Andrews of the Institute of Economic Affairs has decried the use of misleading measures which purport to be, but are not, a "gender pay gap", (Andrews, 2017).

So far in this section, all data has applied to the UK as a whole. However there are substantial differences between the four nations of the UK. The disaggregated median full time gender pay gaps for the four nations in 2017, taken from Figure 14 of (Office for National Statistics, 2017c), were England 10%, Wales 6.3%, Scotland 6.6% and Northern Ireland -3.4%. When the Prime Minister refers to the 'burning injustice of the gender pay gap',

(Casalicchio, 2018), she, like others of the same view, never mentions that men in Northern Ireland must, by the same reasoning, also be considered as suffering a burning injustice. But a more measured perspective is that these gender pay gaps are tiny in comparison with the gap between the lowest paid and the highest paid quintiles, as shown by Figures 7.9 and 7.10. The concentration of the popular narrative on the gender pay gap does not reflect a concern over social injustice, as its proponents assert. Actually, it deflects attention from the greater pay gap. This skewed focus reflects the interests of the dominant voices, middle class feminist women, and their quest for power.

The assertion that the gender pay gap represents "less pay for the same work" is mere propaganda, which even those who assert it know to be untrue. The predominant reason for a full time pay gap in favour of men relates to working hours and years (section 7.6). The absence of any significant pay gap below the age of 40 does not support the idea of endemic sexism in pay. (Why would the patriarchy apply their vile misogyny only to women over 40?). Nor does it support the idea that men on average work in higher paid occupations. For every highly paid IT professional there is a very badly paid manual worker. Far from women being disadvantaged when like is compared with like, the increasing education gap in favour of women is likely to drive the opposite disadvantage. For example, in the USA, it has been the case for a decade now that unmarried, childless women under 30 living in cities are paid more than men in the same position, by up to 20% (Luscombe, 2010).

7.5 Gender Pay Gap Reporting: Company Submissions

As of 18th June 2018, 10,522 companies had uploaded their 2017/18 pay gap data, as per Government requirements. The data can be obtained from (UK Government, 2018c). Like ASHE, the company reporting data relates only to employees (agency staff are also included, but not the self-employed). Also included are data on bonus payments.

The median of the 10,522 submitted median pay gaps is 9.2%. This is in excellent agreement with the 9.1% median pay gap derived from the ASHE (see Table 7.2). (In passing I note that the mean of the 10,522 submitted mean pay gaps is 14.3%, which is also in excellent agreement with the mean pay gap reported by ASHE in 2017, i.e., 14.1%).

The median bonus payment received by men was 19.5%, compared with 17.2% for women. The median gender gap in bonus payment was 5.0%, substantially less than the gender gap in normal full time pay rates.

In terms of the overall picture, the pay gap submissions under the new legislation do not alter what was already known via the ASHE. However, unlike the ASHE, the new legislation provides published data for each company separately. This provides an opportunity for people to 'cherry pick' companies according to their reported pay gaps. The press was full of examples of this in April 2018, the deadline for submissions. For example, the Independent informed us that, 'Ryanair pays women 67 per cent less than men, on average….The figures mean that for every £1 men are paid at Ryanair, a woman is paid just 33p', (Chapman, 2018). They did not mention that whilst men at Ryanair got an average bonus of 27.8%, women received an average bonus of 82.8%. Moreover, the pay gap has an obvious origin in the case of an airline company: most men are pilots, whereas most women are cabin crew.

Of the 10,522 companies which had submitted data as of 18th June 2018, 1,932 reported pay gaps in favour of women on either a mean or median basis. 15 companies reported median pay gaps in favour of women exceeding 60%. Four of these were sizeable companies in the 1000 to 5000 staff range. Median pay gaps ranged up to 197% in favour of women. I note this only to illustrate that the Ryanair example could be done in reverse, if one were so inclined.

The ONS has a very useful on-line service which provides pay gaps disaggregated by employment category and based on the 2016 ASHE (Office for National Statistics, 2016a). The data is based on medians. Most occupations return a positive pay gap, i.e., in favour of men, because the overall pay gap is in favour of men. However, there are many employment categories in which men are paid less (negative pay gap). Some of the employment categories where the pay gap is negative may surprise. They include, in order of increasing pay gap in favour of women,

- Primary and nursery education teaching professionals;
- Chartered surveyors;
- Human resources & industrial relations officers;
- Child & early years officers;
- Civil engineers;
- Receptionists;
- Electrical engineers;
- Therapists;
- Musicians;

- Veterinarians;
- Psychologists;
- Security guards & related occupations;
- Physical scientists;
- Medical radiographers;
- Counsellors;
- Physiotherapists;
- Fitness instructors;
- Probation officers;
- Midwives

This is just a small sample, and is based on 'all' working, both part time and full time. The pay gap for midwives is an enormous 62% in favour of women. This may help explain why only about 100 of the UK's roughly 31,000 midwives are men (0.3%), though men also face discrimination in that role quite apart from the pay (Mertz, 2014). The Sex Discrimination Act was passed in 1975, but midwifery was made an exception due to firm opposition to male midwives from the Royal College of Midwives. This was not overturned until 1983. One of the first men to qualify and practice as a midwife, Richard Mountford, finally brought a sex discrimination case, due mostly to the attitude of GPs rather than the expectant mothers, (Mertz, 2014).

7.6 Working Hours: The Gender Pay Gap is a Work Gap

Those advocating for women will cite the gender pay gap (for full time workers) as an instance of women's disadvantage. However, it is clear from the data that the 9.1% median pay rate gender gap for full time workers in the UK (in 2017) is related to men's longer working hours and greater number of continuous years in their jobs.

The popular narrative regarding women's historical working hours is at variance with reality. It is worth a brief digression to understand how this false perception has arisen. With the industrial revolution came the rise of the middle class, or bourgeoisie. In gender politics this is crucial, because it is in respect of women that class distinctions became most emphatic amongst the resulting *nouveau riche*. Whilst the mill owner could hardly be compared with his workers, he was, at least, involved in running his business. The hallmark of the middle-class wife, on the other hand, was complete disassociation from the world of work. At this point one might be tempted to refer to "the male world of work", but, of course, it wasn't. The mills were full of women. Women had, in truth, been closely involved in remunerated work throughout history. From the feudal system and the era of domestic trades through to the industrial period, women (and children) had worked alongside men. Sure, women's working years, and hours, were constrained by childbirth and childcare, and also limited to areas not requiring great physical strength. Nevertheless, in 1850 to 1900, at least 30% of the workforce were women (the largest number being in domestic service). To quote Catherine Hakim (2011),

> 'Women's full-time employment rate has remained constant, hovering between 30% and 40%, about one-third of the age group since at least 1850 in Britain, similar to many other European countries.'

The perception that "men did paid work, women did not" was never the correct story for the working class. The perception that "men went to work, women stayed at home" was only the norm for middle class woman, the bourgeoisie. The vague impression amongst the public that the non-working wife was the historical norm is a result of the dominance of the feminist narrative and the fact that feminism is a movement of middle-class women. What has changed over the last 50 years is the large-scale entry of women into the professions (i.e., middle class jobs). What has *not* changed greatly is women's proportion of total paid working hours.

Averaged over the year April 2017 to March 2018, the totality of men in the UK worked 620.1 million paid hours per week compared with women's 409.1 million hours (Office for National Statistics, 2018e). Thus, men do 52% more paid hours work than women. The average number of hours worked by part-time workers was very similar for men and women (16.1 and 16.3 hours respectively). But for full-time workers, men worked on average 39.1 hours compared to women's 34.1 hours in their main job.

In December 2018 there were 17.7 million men and 15.0 million women employed in the UK, (Office for National Statistics, 2018h). Women's employment is strongly skewed towards part-time working, with 42% of employed women working part-time compared to only 13% of men (House of Commons Briefing Paper, 2018). Hence, the number of workers in the UK in 2017/18, disaggregated by part time or full time working is as given in Table 7.6. Three times as many men as women work more than 45 hours per week (White and Witty, 2009).

Table 7.6: *Number of Workers in UK*

millions	Full Time	Part Time
Men	15.4	2.3
Women	8.7	6.3

Rates of pay increase with seniority and experience, which in turn result from working more hours and accumulating more continuous years in the job. The percentage differences between men's and women's working hours are very substantial, far greater than the gender pay gap. The former is therefore the most likely cause of the latter. Consequently, even people (ostensibly) advocating for women tend to concentrate upon increasing women's paid working hours, arguing that this should be facilitated by state-subsidised child care and by encouraging men to 'lean out', i.e., to work fewer hours and do more child care.

Whilst this may be the opinion of certain women's advocates, it is not necessarily the opinion of the majority of women themselves. It is worth considering briefly women's wishes in respect of employment. This is pertinent because, if women are being constrained from partaking in paid work as much as they would wish, then 'work and pay' is indeed an area of disadvantage for women. On the other hand, if women's working patterns predominantly reflect their unconstrained wishes, then men's substantially larger number of working hours represent men's positive contribution to family life, and society generally, rather than being an aspect of "patriarchal dominance".

The opinion of both men and women in the UK on these issues is revealed by the British Social Attitudes Survey (2012). The data summarised below refers to both male and female respondents, but, interestingly, there was generally little difference between the responses of men and women to these questions.

As is common with surveys, similar questions can elicit very different answers depending on how the question is phrased. For example, responding to the question 'a man's job is to earn money; a woman's job is to look after home and family', Figure 5.2 of the British Social Attitudes Survey (2012) records that only 13% agreed. This is not surprising because the phrasing of the question makes it sound like a vote for patriarchal oppression. People have been primed by the popular narrative to react to, and resist, suggestions which sound like "a woman's place is in the home".

But other questions reveal that, in truth, this sentiment does continue to colour what most people think - or, at least, a man's place is definitely not in the home. For example, Table 5.3 of the survey gives the responses to the question 'what is the best and least desirable way for a family with a child under school age to organise family and work life by sex'. This is how Glen Poole (2014b) summarised the responses,

- 69% of us think dad should be the primary earner;
- 9% of us think mum and dad should share the earning responsibility equally;
- Zero percent think mum should be the primary earner;
- 73% of us think dads should work full time;
- 5% of us think dads should work part time;
- Zero percent of us think dads should stay at home full time.

No one (within rounding) approves of a man being a full-time stay-at-home dad, and no one wants to see a woman as the primary earner. Table 5.1 of the survey reveals that only 5% of respondents think mums should work full time before the children start school.

Overwhelmingly, people (of both sexes) expect men to be the primary resource provider. One of the disadvantageous aspects of this for men is that they have no choice. Provision of resource is a man's only "permitted" role (in the sense of being the only role which the majority of society sanctions as desirable). In contrast, according to Table 5.1 of the survey, women have a range of options (not working or working part time or working full time) which society regards as roughly equally acceptable,

- 33% think mums should stay at home until the children start school;
- 43% think mums should work part time until the children start school;
- 28% think mums should work full time once the kids start school;
- 52% think mums should work part time after the kids are at school.

Those who advocate for increasing women's working hours and getting more women working full time do not reflect the majority opinion of women themselves (nor men's opinion, not that anyone is interested in that). Dench (2010) summarises the choice of many women to work part-time, and the disconnect between women's wishes and the lobbying by women's advocacy groups, as follows.

> (page 28) 'What is very significant here is that women working part-time are not only happier in themselves and their family lives than those working full time, but *also* than housewives not working at all. Unfortunately, many analysts and commentators in this field have been reluctant to acknowledge this; and those like Catherine Hakim who have recognised women's attachment to domestic life – including the

> preference of many to look after their children themselves – have come under heavy attack.'

Referring to these critics, Dench writes,

> (page 29/30) 'The reason for this hostility seems to be that, in the eyes of commentators such as these, traditional family practices, even or especially *modified* traditional practices, are not connected to women's own desires, but are cultural inventions which constrain women into particular roles that are against their better interests. Crompton and most other academic commentators in this area do not seem to believe that any woman really wants to play a central part in family life – which they tend to dismiss as unwelcome "conventionally assigned family responsibilities", which get thrust upon women from the outside. These would not be chosen by free women who were allowed to exercise their own wills.'

7.7 Spending and Wealth by Sex

A generation or two ago, working class men were generally paid weekly in cash. Each man received his wages in a brown paper envelope every Friday. For most of these men, a small domestic ritual followed. On returning home, the man would present said brown paper envelope of cash to his wife, proudly confirming he had done his duty. The wife would then return a small amount to the man for his 'spending money', keeping the rest for the housekeeping of which she was in charge, (Scruton, 1999). It was accepted that the wife's role was to manage the household finances. This was not an enviable task when a small sum had to be stretched over the many necessary expenses of a family with several children. No doubt there were some men who kept their wives short of money, for selfish reasons, but the above vignette illustrates the approved social norm at the time.

How much have things changed? Men still earn more than women. In the tax year 2015/16, men in the UK earnt 91% more than women: £680 billion to women's £356 billion, mainly due to working more hours (UK Government, 2018a). Men may earn more, but who actually spends the household money? It is rather hard to obtain quality data on spending by sex, surprisingly. The UK Government conducts regular surveys of household spending in the UK, but in recent years the data has not been disaggregated by sex, e.g., (Office for National Statistics, 2018d). One must distinguish between two things,

- Direct spending: that is cash personally handed over by the individual, or card purchases or electronic purchases authorised by the individual;

- Indirect spending: in which the individual exercises influence or control over a spending decision, to an equal or dominant degree, even if the direct spending is by another person, usually a partner.

There are two means of obtaining data on spending; by survey or by detailed diary keeping. Most reported data are obtained by survey. However, this is an imprecise measure because it relies on memory and interpretation of the questions asked. Indirect spending can only be gauged from surveys. For direct spending, however, the better method is to arrange for a group of people to log everything they spend over a given period, down to the tiniest level. Such studies are scarce. In the next section I use the results of a UK study using spending diaries from year 1993/4. However, these data are a quarter century old as I write, and over that period women have become dominant in educational attainment and entered the professions in greater numbers. I include this older study because of the detailed breakdown by sex, but also because it provides an historical marker. In the section that follows I look at more recent data, for both the UK and the USA, which confirms that women have now become dominant in spending.

7.7.1 UK in Year 1993/4

The data from the 1993/4 spending diary study has been used by Pahl (2000) to identify the proportion of spending in various categories according to sex, see Table 7.7. Recall that this is historical data – the picture is rather different now.

Table 7.7: *Breakdown of Household Direct Spending by Sex (Pahl, 2000)*

Items	% of total spent by women
Women's clothes	90%
Children's clothes	85%
Food	80%
Educational courses	79%
Child care/school expenses	78%
Medical/dental	59%
Household goods	51%
Tobacco	43%
Recreation	42%
Men's clothes	40%
Holidays	36%
Gambling	35%
Meals out	34%
Repairs to house	33%
Motor vehicles	31%
Alcohol	27%

The percentages of spend by women given in Table 7.7 can be used together with the spend by category given in (Office for National Statistics, 2018d) to deduce the weekly spend in pounds by women, and hence the total weekly spend by women, Table 7.8. The result is that I estimate that UK women in 1993/4 directly spent about 51% of the household monies.

Table 7.8: *Average Weekly Household Direct Spending by Category and Sex (Disaggregation by sex based on 1993/4 data, but spend in 2017 pounds)*

Item of Expenditure	Total Weekly Spend, £	% Spent by Women	Weekly Spend by Women
Food and non-alcoholic drinks	58.00	80%	46.40
Alcoholic drink, tobacco and narcotics (1)	11.90	35%	4.17
total clothing for women	12.90	90%	11.59
total clothing for men	8.20	40%	3.27
total clothing for children	4.10	85%	3.47
Housing, fuel and power (2)	72.60	50%	36.30
Household goods and services	39.30	51%	20.04
Health	7.30	59%	4.31
Transport (3)	79.70	31%	24.71
Communication (2)	17.20	50%	8.60
Recreation and culture	73.50	42%	30.87
Education	5.70	79%	4.50
Restaurants and hotels (4)	50.10	35%	17.54
Miscellaneous goods and services (5)	41.80	74%	30.93
All expenditure groups	**482.20**	**51%**	**247**

(1) *average of 43% for tobacco and 27% for alcohol*

(2) *assumed 50/50*

(3) *taken as that for "motor vehicles"*

(4) *average of 36% for holidays and 34% for eating out*

(5) *estimated, includes items such as hairdressing, toiletries, jewellery*

Some care is necessary in the interpretation of this result. The ONS survey data on which it is based samples households of all types. (A total of 5,040 households were surveyed in the 2017 dataset). This includes people living on their own, single-parent households, childless adults living with parents, and gay and lesbian couples. Consequently, whilst it is tempting to interpret Table 7.8 in the context of two heterosexual adult households, the data can only be a rough guide to this. Women outnumber men in the UK population by around one million. Some 28% of households (7.7 million) now comprise a lone adult, and lone women outnumber lone men by 585,000. In addition,

10% of households (2.7 million) consist of a single-parent with child(ren), of which 92% are women (Office for National Statistics, 2017g). Only about 61% of households consist of two adults, with or without children.

Pahl (2000) also includes data on how many items were purchased by cost. Women directly bought substantially more items than men (69%), but these were mostly low costs items, see Table 7.9. Assuming prices at the mid-range shown in Table 7.9, and ignoring the small number of items over £1000, this Table suggests that women account for 54% of household spending (£2,401,000 out of £4,423,000 below £1000, noting that the data relate to spending over a two week period by the respondents to the survey only). This is quite close to the estimate based on Table 7.8. However, the data in this section, as well as being historical, relates to direct spending. It fails to account for a woman's influence over spending decisions which are directly made by her male partner (and vice-versa).

Table 7.9: *Direct Spending by Women by Cost of Item, 1993/4, (Pahl, 2000). The data relate to spending over a two week period by the respondents to the survey.*

	Cost of Individual Items			
	Under £10	**£10-100**	**£100-1000**	**Over £1000**
% of all items bought by women	71	52	39	38
Total number of items bought	281,811	31,492	2,330	105
Total cost, £	1,409,000	1,732,000	1,282,000	?
Spent by women, £	1,000,000	901,000	500,000	?

7.7.2 Wealth and Spending, UK and USA, 2008 to 2018

Pay and earnings are not the best indicators of financial privilege. Earnings, after all, are just that – earned. The better measures of privilege are wealth and spending. Wealth is cash and assets held personally in the name of the individual. And spending may be direct or indirect, an important distinction which many sources fail to make clear. In this section I have recourse to sources which are neither national statistics nor academic. It is with some reticence that I use these sources because I am uncertain of the provenance of their data. Please treat the data in this section with caution. Had I better sources to quote I would have done so. The data relates to years from 2008 to 2018.

Worldwide, men are on average wealthier than women. However, in the UK and USA, women now own more wealth than men on average. As early as 2005 women in the UK already owned 48% of Britain's assets, and this will be well over 50% by now, (Carvel, 2005). The Bank of Montreal's Wealth Institute concluded that by 2015 women in the USA 'controlled 51% of personal wealth', (Gorman, 2015). They also advised that, by 2015, women held the majority (52%) of management, professional and related positions in the USA. Other sources indicate that women held the majority of private/personal wealth in the USA as early as 2012, and also by that date the majority of stocks, (Krasny, 2012), (Walter, 2012).

By 2016, 46% of the UK's 376,000 millionaires were women, (Gotts, 2017). The same source quotes leading gender analysts, Catalyst.Org, as estimating that, by 2017, 'on average, 67% of all UK household consumption is controlled or influenced by women. And it is much greater in many key household areas'. The same source, as well as research by Gloria Moss, reader in management and marketing at Buckinghamshire New University, (Bignell, 2013), indicate that women in the UK buy 93% of food, 83% of all "shopping" purchases, and 'make the decision or influence the purchase of 92% of holidays'. These findings do not surprise, but more surprising is that UK women buy 60%-65% of cars and 55%-61% of home computers, though the sources may be guilty of blurring the distinction between "buying" and "influencing the purchase".

A survey of 1,260 respondents living as (heterosexual) couples was reported by (Pew Research, 2008) and confirmed that it is women who dominate in financial decision making. In respect of major household purchases, their result was 'a large plurality of couples (46%) jointly make decisions about buying major items for the home. But, in families in which one person makes most of these decisions, it's the woman and not the man who has the last word when purchasing big-ticket items for the home (30% vs. 19%)'. Qualitatively the same result was found in answer to the question 'who mostly manages the household finances?'. More men answered that their female partner generally managed the finances than vice-versa (30% vs. 23%). And more women than men answered that they tended to manage the finances themselves (45% vs. 37%).

In 2009, the Harvard Business Review indicated that women controlled two-thirds of consumer spending in the UK, and nearly three-quarters in the USA, (Silverstein and Sayre, 2009). Other sources say that women in the USA 'account for 85% of all consumer purchases', (girlpowermarketing, 2018), (she-conomy, 2013). The sources cited in this section indicate that women in the USA purchase the following percentages of specific items (but noting again that the sources may blur the distinction between "buying" and "influencing the purchase"),

- 93% of food;
- 91% of houses;
- 92% of holidays;
- 89% of bank accounts;
- 80% of healthcare products and services;
- 60% to 68% of new cars;
- 51% to 61% of home electronics
- 66% of PCs
- 58% of all online purchases.

Half of products typically marketed to men are actually purchased by women. Recall that women earn substantially less than men. It seems clear, therefore, that the tradition represented by the handing-over of the brown paper pay packet still lives on, albeit in mutated form. Men earn more, but women spend more, ergo there is a transfer of money from men to women. Is this male hegemony?

7.8 Income Taxes

In this section I address only income tax, not National Insurance or any other form of taxation. Income tax data is taken from (UK Government, 2019a) and working hours data from (Office for National Statistics, 2019a). Women comprise 47% of the UK workforce, and yet men pay vastly more income tax. In 2016/17 men paid a total of £127.0 billion in income tax compared to women's £47.6 billion. So women pay 27% of the total income tax to men's 73%, i.e., men are paying 167% more tax than women despite being only 13% more of the workforce. Similar figures apply in the years since 2013/14 (see Table 7.10). Clearly a 167% greater tax bill does not arise due to a median 9.1% greater hourly pay rate. The reason men pay more tax is because they earn more, and they earn more primarily because they work longer hours. In 2016/17, the totality of men in the UK worked on average 620 million hours per week, compared to women's 403 million hours, i.e., men work 54% more hours.

Far more women than men work part time. And even women who work full time work shorter hours than men on average (34.4 hours per week versus 39.4 hours per week, 2016/17). Because of the way the tax system works, with increasing tax rates as earnings increase, men's 54% greater number of working hours becomes a 167% greater tax bill. (There is also a contribution from higher average pay rates and a larger number of men who are very high earners). In effect, the taxation bands are set to clobber men and spare women. This is illustrated by calculating the income tax per hour worked (Table 7.11). Men pay tax at a rate which is 74% greater than women's tax rate (£3.94 per hour versus £2.27 per hour in 2016/17).

Table 7.10: *Total Income Tax by Sex (UK)*

Year	Men (£M)	Women (£M)	Excess of Men over Women
2013/14	120,051	44,650	169%
2014/15	121,119	45,489	166%
2015/16	130,000	48,300	169%
2016/17	127,000	47,600	167%

Table 7.11: *Income Tax Rate by Sex (UK)*

Year	Men £/hr	Women £/hr	Excess of Men over Women
2013/14	3.91	2.26	73%
2014/15	3.86	2.24	72%
2015/16	4.09	2.35	74%
2016/17	3.94	2.27	74%

This, incidentally, is why the Government (and globalists like the World Economic Forum) are very keen to get more women working full time. They have their eye on the huge disparity between the male tax contribution into the Exchequer, £127 billion, and the relatively small female contribution of £47.6 billion. They see considerable scope for pushing the latter closer to the former, and the key is women's working hours. This is why Governments, the EU, the UN, the WEF, etc., are more than happy to go along with the feminist agenda on women's pay. The feminist narrative plays right into their hands. If the Government were to tell women to stop doing frivolous things like childcare and get out of the house and work longer hours, it would not go down too well. But along come the feminists who tell women to make themselves financially independent of the evil patriarchy by being career minded and keen to work full time. Don't do childcare, ladies, that's just a patriarchal con – displace those nasty men from their cushy satisfying careers. Tell women that those darned men are oppressing them by keeping them from working full time, and they might be more likely to fall for it. It isn't working, but you have to admit it's a cunning plan.

7.9 Pensions

Pensions are a very involved topic. Here I attempt only the crudest guide to this arcane subject. It is important to do so because there are large sex differences in pension statistics. In fact, despite the popular focus on the gender pay gap, it is for pensions that the numerical gap between the sexes is larger.

7.9.1 Occupational and Personal Pensions; the Private and Public Sectors

In the UK there are three broad classes of pension: the State pension, private (or personal) pensions, and occupational pensions. Occupational, or workplace, pensions may relate to the private or public sectors. Personal pensions are essentially a form of investment saving. Neither the Government nor your employer is involved in a personal pension. It is an arrangement between you and the financial institution offering the investment service (usually an insurance company).

Almost everyone who is a long-term UK resident will be entitled to a State pension, once they reach State Pension Age (SPA), though the amount of the pension will vary (see section 7.9.2). Many people have a personal or occupational pension in addition to their State pension, especially those who are, or were, more highly paid. Unlike the State pension, which is payable only after SPA, personal and occupational pensions may be payable earlier, depending upon the scheme conditions, but benefits will be reduced if paid before the scheme's full pension age.

A major advantage of occupational pensions over personal pensions is that the employer invariably makes a contribution to your pension pot in addition to your own contribution. The employer's contribution is usually substantially greater than your own, boosting your savings considerably. The self-employed do not have this option, nor do employees of small companies which have no company pension scheme. There was a vogue for opting for personal pensions in the 1990s, even when an occupational scheme was available, but it never made financial sense.

In the UK, payments into a pension scheme can attract tax relief. I will spare you any further discussion of that except to note that such tax relief can be a substantial benefit to higher rate income tax payers, though availing oneself of it means reducing current disposable income in favour of net benefit on retirement.

Pensions may be of two broad types: defined contributions or defined benefits. In defined contribution schemes, the benefits to which you are entitled on retirement (e.g., a monthly pension payment or a lump sum payment) relate to the amount of money that has accumulated in your 'pension pot'. Personal pensions are invariably defined contribution schemes.

Defined benefit schemes, in contrast, entitle the pensioner to payments calculated according to a fixed formula depending upon salary history and years of service. The gold standard is a "final salary" scheme in which an annual pension is calculated as some fraction of the member's final salary, e.g., 1/80'th of the final salary for every year's service. Pensions under defined benefit schemes are usually guaranteed to rise annually according to some fixed formula linked to inflation. Defined benefit schemes usually also contain provisions for a deceased member's spouse. If the deceased was drawing a pension, a common entitlement was a widow's (or widower's) pension at half rate. If the deceased was still working and contributing pension payments, the widow's terms were often very generous. My father used to say he was worth more dead than alive, which was also true of myself when I was still working full time.

Defined benefit schemes are advantageous for the scheme member, providing both greater security and more generous pay-outs than defined contribution schemes. However, they present a risk to the scheme fund which is difficult to manage because the obligations to pensioners are not directly linked to the funds' ability to pay.

It used to be common for large companies to offer defined benefit schemes. However, the financial cost and risk has led to almost all such schemes in the UK private sector being closed to new members. Private sector defined benefit schemes are almost extinct as regards new members. The largest private defined benefit scheme still open in the UK is the Universities Superannuation Scheme, but the scheme is actively attempting to close to new members and switch to defined contributions, as other schemes have done already, (Fox, 2018). In contrast, most public sector occupational pension schemes were – and remain – defined benefit schemes. Since private sector defined benefit schemes have been obliged to close for fear of becoming insolvent, why have public sector pensions been able to sail blithely on as defined benefit schemes, to the considerable advantage of their members? The answer lies in the different funding arrangements for private and public sector pensions.

Private sector pensions, whether defined benefit or defined contribution schemes, involve payments being invested, usually in stocks and shares. At any time, the scheme fund has a definite value: the total value of all its assets, mostly said stocks and shares. This is just like the investment savings of a private individual, but on a larger scale. Such schemes are said to be "funded".

Public sector schemes, however, are not funded. In public sector schemes, pension payments docked from an active member's monthly pay go to the Treasury. The Treasury spends the money. There is no pension pot corresponding to public sector pensions. Public sector pensions are unfunded. Instead the Government undertakes to honour the pension entitlements of public sector scheme members, assuming it will be able to do so – and this means assuming that future tax revenues (plus pension payments) will cover the bill. The reader may think this sounds rather like a Ponzi scheme. I couldn't possibly comment.

There is no such thing as pension security. Private sector pensions are subject to stock market performance. Public sector pensions are subject to the whims of Government, and the economy of the country. But at least funded schemes are subject to the rigours of actuarial accounting. It is because of this that the private sector has managed its way out of defined benefit schemes, which accounting has identified as representing future commitments that may be unmeetable. Public sector schemes have been slower to accept that defined benefit schemes are an obligation which they may not be able to honour.

But the most pernicious thing about the unfunded public sector is that it places the burden of funding pensioners on younger people. It is effectively a way of passing on debt to the next generation. In funded schemes, in contrast, one effectively saves for one's own retirement.

To make this worse, most public sector schemes, including those for teachers and NHS staff, are of defined benefit type. The difference in pension benefits between a member of these public sector schemes and a member of a private sector "defined contribution" scheme, assuming they both contribute exactly the same payments, is now so great that it has been dubbed "pensions apartheid", (Morley, 2016). Morley gives the following numerical example (using figures which prevailed in 2016),

> 'A fully qualified nurse aged 25, earning £21,692 and joining the pension scheme today, will typically contribute 7.1% of salary each year to fund their retirement. If they work for 40 years, stay in the same band of earnings throughout and attain 4% annual increases in pay, they could retire on an annual pension of £30,700 in today's

money. This income is guaranteed by the state and will also increase each year in line with inflation, protecting its value over time.'

Morley contrasts this with someone in the private sector,

> 'Taking into account current annuity rates, if someone wanted to purchase the same level of income for life at the age of 65.... This would involve the nurse contributing 43% of her gross salary into a pension, assuming her fund grows by 5% a year excluding charges.'

One needs to be careful, however. Does the 43% figure quoted refer to a private pension, as opposed from a typical private sector pension scheme? The difference is the contribution to the member's pension pot made by the employer, which is substantial. Not so substantial as to make up the difference between 7.1% and 43%, however, so the illustration still stands as an indication of the greater benefit of the public sector scheme, though not quite as marked as those numbers suggest. However, it may not be far off as the median employers' contribution to private sector defined contribution pensions is now very small (only 2.1%, see below).

Figure 7.11: *Median Contribution Rates to Workplace Pensions by Sector, to 2014, taken from (Taxpayers' Alliance, 2018)*

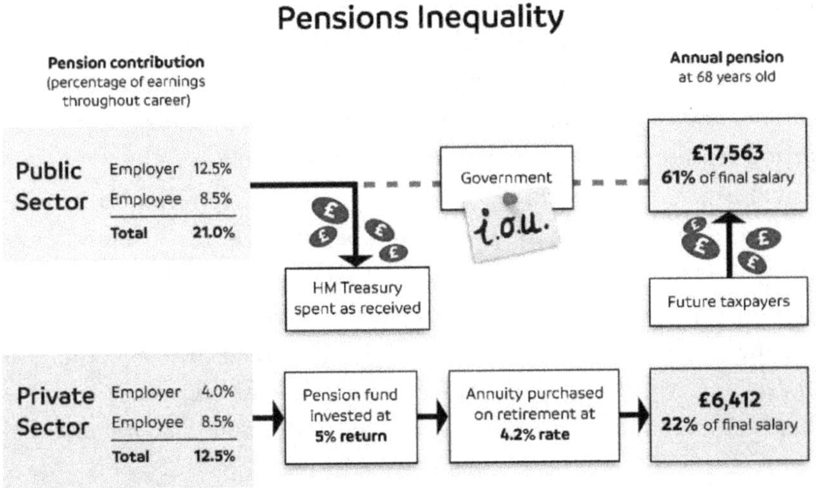

A similar but more recent numerical example has been given by the Taxpayers Alliance (2018), as follows. Making contributions of 8.5% of the average national wage of £28,600, they report that a 25 year old starting in a private sector job can expect to save a lump sum capable of buying an annuity of £6,412. In the public sector the same contributions on the same wage would earn an annual income of £17,563. They claim that the private sector worker would have to save 30% of their salary to retire with a pension as large as the public sector worker's pension. These calculations are based on the assumption that the public sector employer contributes to the pension at 12.5%, whereas the private sector employer contributes only 4%, which is reasonably indicative of the difference in median rates. The comparison between private and public sector pensions is illustrated by Figure 7.11.

The median contributions to occupational pensions by both employers and employees, disaggregated by sector, are given by (Office for National Statistics, 2015h). These data include both defined contribution and defined benefit schemes. The averages over age bands are plotted against year, up to 2014, in Figure 7.12. Since 2014 the weighted-average contribution rates for occupational defined contribution schemes have fallen further, reaching just 1.2% for employees and just 2.1% for employers by 2017, see Figure 7 of (Office for National Statistics, 2018v). The reason for this is partly the obligation on employers for automatic enrolment of new employees, and the resulting substantial increase in the number of people with workplace pensions. However, it also reflects the closing of defined benefit schemes in the private sector. By 2017, those defined benefit schemes which still existed in the private sector had radically higher contribution rates (6.0% for employees and 19.2% for employers). However, the very low contribution rates in defined contribution schemes will now increase. As from April 2019, legislation requires the minimum employer's contribution to be 3% and the minimum employee's contribution to be 5%, (The Pensions Regulator, 2019).

The difference in contribution rates between the private and public sectors is stark and does seem to justify the claims of "pension apartheid". It arises primarily from the persistence of defined benefit schemes in the public sector, the closure of such schemes in the private sector, and the larger employers' (i.e., the public's) contribution in the public sector.

And yet the public sector is entirely funded by taxes originating from the private sector. (Yes, I know people employed in the public sector also pay tax, but let's not pretend that one can pick oneself up by one's own shoelaces). Moreover, two-thirds of public sector employees are women, but men pay 73% of the income tax and men are the majority of private sector employees. Thus, it is predominantly women who are the beneficiaries of employment funded predominantly by men, and it is predominantly women who benefit from the highly advantageous public sector pensions whilst their funders, predominantly men, have far less favourable pension terms.

Figure 7.12: *Occupational Pension Contribution Rates by Sector*

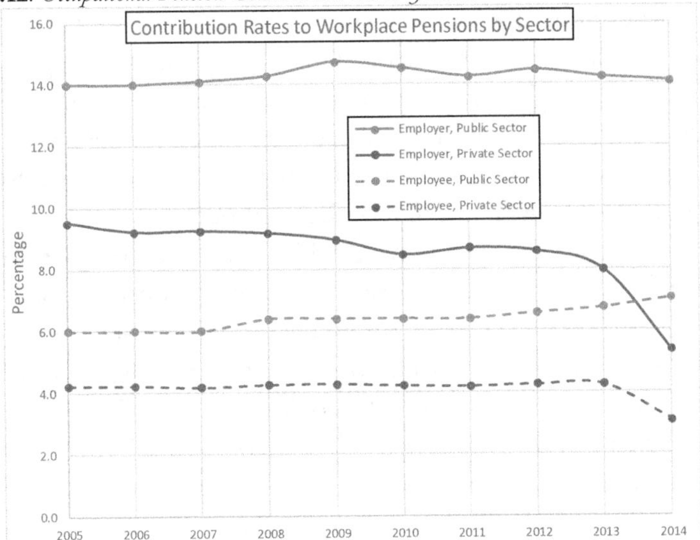

7.9.2 The State Pension

Most UK residents will qualify for a basic State pension when they reach their State Pension Age (SPA). Before 2010, the SPA was 60 for women and 65 for men. Between 2010 and 2018 the SPA for women was increased to that of men, i.e., 65. The SPA for both sexes was then raised to 66, 67 or 68, according to birth date, keeping the sexes equal. There are plans to increase the SPA further.

For people reaching their SPA prior to April 2016 there were two distinct State pensions: the basic State pension (BSP) and the State Earnings Related Pension Scheme (SERPS). As the name implies, the latter was related to earnings, whereas the former was not. Many members of an occupational pension scheme would be "contracted out" of SERPS, and hence this second State pension would not be applicable to them. For people reaching their SPA since April 2016 SERPS no longer applies.

People do not directly pay into the State pension. Instead, eligibility depends upon National Insurance (NI) payments or credits. The complete rules on NI are complicated. For people who are working, the payments increase with salary. For those on low pay the rate is zero but NI credits are received. People who are unemployed but registered as Jobseekers can still get NI credits. Similarly, the disabled and people on sick leave or maternity leave can gain NI credits, as can people on a range of benefits (working tax credit / universal credit). The amount of State pension you will eventually receive depends upon the number of years you have paid the required NI, or received credits, but it does not depend upon the amount paid. Thus, people on high salaries will pay more NI contributions than those on low pay, but receive the same pension for the same number of years paid. People on higher salaries will generally also pay into a separate personal or occupational pension rather than relying entirely on the State pension.

Before 2010, men needed to have paid 5 years more NI than women to qualify for the full State pension. Since 2016 this has been equalised to 35 years for both sexes. The pension payable reduces pro-rata with years of contribution, but requires at least 10 years NI to receive any pension.

For married (or formerly married) people reaching their SPA before April 2016, but with an incomplete NI record, they could claim NI credit based on their spouse's NI record, and hence receive a pension up to 60% of their spouse's (or ex-spouse's) BSP. For divorcees, the ex-spouse need not know about this claim. Overwhelmingly, this would be wives, or ex-wives, claiming credit for their husband's, or ex-husband's, NI record. However, this is no longer applicable for new retirees.

People claiming child benefit for a child under 12 also receive NI credits and hence will ultimately benefit in terms of their BSP. Again, this will overwhelmingly be women. Many people will see such provision as reasonable to avoid penalising via their pension those who opt for full-time childcare. At the present time, the role of stay-at-home-parent needs encouragement rather than penalising.

The changes to the BSP have removed the earlier, explicitly gender based, inequalities. However, not everyone sees it that way. The campaign group Women Against State Pension Inequality (WASPI) has claimed – as their name suggests – that this equalisation is actually inequality. In particular, they claim that many women were unaware of the changes, which came as a shock when they realised they would have to work 5 or 6 years longer before receiving a pension. But the law to change the pension age for women was passed in 1995, and the changes were phased in between 2010 and 2018, so they had plenty of time to accommodate the changes. Their campaign, though extremely vociferous, has failed to gain much sympathy, commentary being along the lines 'The WASPI campaign's unreasonable demand', (Coppola,

2016), and 'WASPI's is (Mostly) a Campaign for Inequality', (Pemberton, 2017). The fact that it is entirely unambiguous that the change in women's SPA to equal that of men is a change from inequality to equality does not prevent a campaign claiming the opposite. The granting of an unjustified judicial review to this campaign is characteristic of how society is always ready to capitulate to women claiming unfairness, regardless of merit (Peachey, 2018).

7.9.3 Numbers of Payees and Recipients

Official sources can mislead the unwary with jargon. "Members" of a pension scheme include three different classes of people: those who are "active", those who have frozen benefits within the scheme but are not active, and those who are currently receiving a pension from the scheme. The active members of a scheme are those who are contributing payment into the scheme, or having contributions made on their behalf. People who have moved from one scheme to another, often because they have changed jobs, will have frozen benefits in one or more schemes, as well as being active in another scheme.

Figure 7.13 shows the number of people drawing a State pension against year, a total of 12.8 million in 2018. The number of men drawing a State pension has increased steadily as the number of men aged 65 and over has increased. However, the number of women drawing a State pension has reduced since 2011 as the effect of women's SPA increasing from 60 to 65 has taken effect. There will always be more women pensioners, however, due to men's shorter average lifespan. For the same reason, despite the equalisation of pension age, women will, on average, draw a pension for longer than men (currently by about 4 years).

The disparity between the sexes in this respect used to be far worse. In 1951 the mean life expectancy at birth was only 66 for men and 72 for women, i.e., one year and 12 years longer than their respective State retirement ages at the time. Most men before 1951 would not live to draw a pension (not only because they might die before 65, but also because the State pension age prior to 1940 was 70). A man who lived to 65 to start drawing his State pension in 1970 could expect to live another 12 years, (Office for National Statistics, 2015j). A woman who lived to 60 to start drawing her State pension in 1970 could expect to live another 21 years, hence drawing her pension some 9 years longer than the man.

Figure 7.14 shows the number of men and women who are paying into personal pensions in the UK, from (UK Government, 2018t). As of 2016/17 this was 6.0 million men and 4.2 million women. This compares with the number of men aged 16 to 64 of 20.5 million and the number of women aged 16 to 64 of 20.7 million.

Figure 7.13: *Numbers of Men and Women Drawing a State Pension*

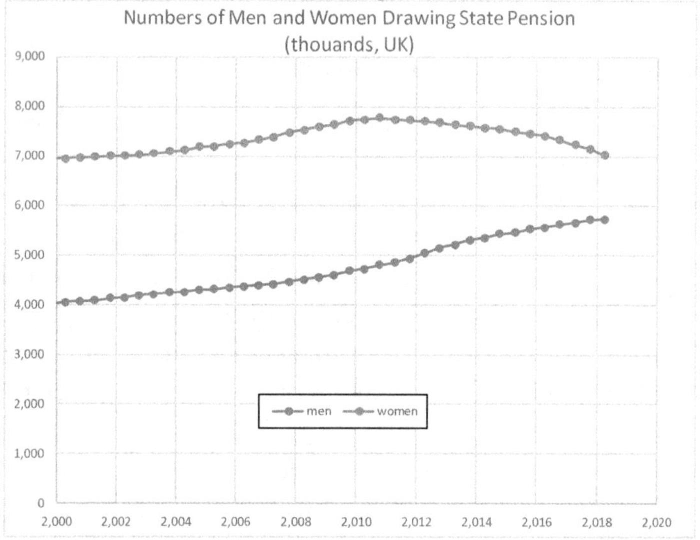

Figure 7.14: *Numbers of Men and Women Paying into Personal Pension Schemes*

Figure 7.15 shows the numbers of people paying into occupational pension schemes by sector, from (Office for National Statistics, 2018v). Membership

of private sector occupational pension schemes has tripled since 2013, due to the introduction of a legal obligation on companies to automatically enrol new employees. Active membership of occupational pension schemes was 15.1 million in 2017, split between the private sector (8.8 million) and the public sector (6.3 million). From the same source, Figure 7.16 shows the number of people in receipt of pensions from occupational schemes: 5.2 million in the private sector, and 5.0 million in the public sector.

Figure 7.15: *Number of People Paying Into Occupational Pension Schemes by Sector*

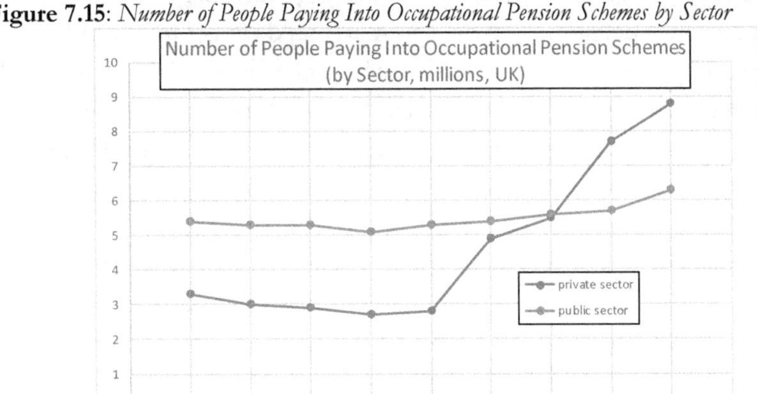

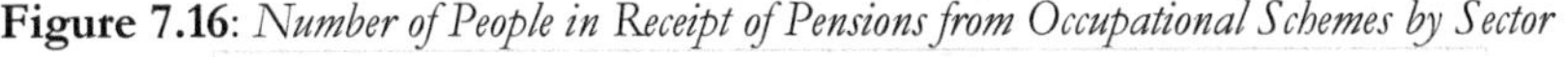

Figure 7.16: *Number of People in Receipt of Pensions from Occupational Schemes by Sector*

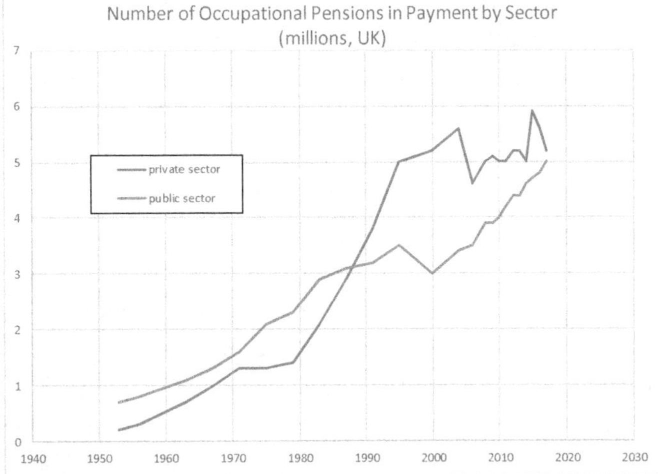

Recall that the public sector accounts for just 16.5% of employment in the UK, and in the past this would have been a smaller percentage. And yet the number of public sector pensioners is essentially the same as the number of private sector occupational pensioners. This is another aspect of the advantageous pension provisions for public sector workers (two-thirds of whom are women).

7.9.4 Gender Pension Inequality?

In the recent past there was explicit discrimination against men compared with women in State pension provision, men receiving their basic State pension five years later than women and requiring five years more NI contributions to get the full pension. 70 years ago, most men did not live long enough to receive a pension. 50 years ago men could expect to live little more than half as long after retirement as women. State pension reforms, finally enacted only in 2018, have removed the explicit gender discrimination in State pension age, but men can still expect to draw their State pension for around four fewer years than women.

On average, women receive smaller pensions than men, but the gap is closing. In the case of State pensions the gap is reducing partly because of the equalisation of the State pension age: 'while in February 2018, the average weekly amount of State pension received by women was 82% of that for men, for those in the new system it was 95%.', (Thurley and McInnes, 2018). The gender gap in State pension would be larger were it not for the NI credits awarded to those eligible for child care benefit for children under 12. Most people will consider that provision to be reasonable to avoid penalising stay-at-home mothers (or fathers) years later via their pensions.

The average man's total pension, including occupational or personal pensions, is larger than the average woman's – and for the usual reason: the years women leave full time work for childcare (or opt for part time work by preference). For funded schemes in the private sector this is unavoidable since such schemes are necessarily geared to contributions.

The persistent inequalities of outcome for the two sexes do not result from explicit discrimination but from differing contributions, resulting, as usual, mostly from childcare. However, the greatest inequality is not that between the sexes but between the public and private sectors. The retention of defined benefit schemes by the public sector, which the private sector cannot afford, together with the generous employers' contributions in the public sector, make a public sector pension worth two or three times as much as a private sector pension for the same cost to the employee. This is an indirect discrimination against men as the public sector is two-thirds women and is funded by taxes, 73% of which are paid by men predominantly working in the private sector with inferior pension arrangements.

The equalisation of SPA does not mean its effects have immediately ceased. My own occupational pension would be 4% larger if I were female, other things being equal.

It is probably still the case that many married women pay scant attention to pensions. If I may indulge in personal anecdote. During my working life I frequently considered moving jobs but was constrained by the potential loss of an existing beneficial pension scheme and uncertain transfer terms. In effect, a large swathe of my life ended up being controlled by pension constraints. In contrast, my wife had negligible pension provision, despite being a self-employed professional (but working only part-time). She never gave her pension any thought, just relied upon me (hence making my own prudence that much more necessary). I eventually made separate pension arrangements for my wife, in addition to my own, providing her with a personal pension largely at my own expense. I expect I shall be drummed out of the Patriarch's Union if they find out.

7.10 Housework and Unpaid Caring

7.10.1 Men and Housework

Who does more housework, men or women? There are many informal surveys and also a large academic literature on the subject. Care is needed because many informal surveys are clearly skewed. For example, that carried out by (Mumsnet, 2014) surveyed only women. Moreover, it included 54 chores of which almost all were traditional "housewife tasks" and just one was "DIY". It would be possible to survey against a list of many different categories of DIY task, and just one task called "housework" – and to ask only men (though I'm not aware of anyone having done so). Such surveys are not helpful.

The survey of 1001 British adults, commissioned by BBC Radio's *Woman's Hour* and carried out by (ComRes, 2015) indicated that, on average, women do 11.5 hours of housework per week compared with men's 6.1 hours, a difference of 5.4 hours. Averaging results for both sexes indicated that single people did the least amount of housework (7.2 hours per week) and that divorced people did most (11.6 hours). Averaging over both sexes, people working full time did 7.0 hours of housework per week, compared with 10.6 hours for people working part time. The latter observation, together with the greater proportion of women working part time, suggests that the bulk of the gender difference in housework effort may be mostly a reflection of who is working part time rather than full time.

Section 7.6 identified that men do 620.1 million hours of paid work per week compared with women's 409.1 million hours, a difference of 211 million hours. Dividing by the 17.7 million working men, this suggests an average of 12 hours per week additional paid work being done by each working man. (Alternatively, dividing by the number of men of working age, 20.5 million, gives an average of 10.3 hours per week excess paid work by men). This is substantially larger than the 5.4 extra hours of housework identified by (ComRes, 2015) as being done by women, or even the 8.3 hours extra identified by (Kan and Laurie, 2016). This suggests that when both paid work and unpaid housework are considered, men do more work than women in total rather than less.

However, surveys may be unreliable because they depend on people's memory and their accurate estimation of the time taken over tasks. Academic work tends to be based on studies in which participants are asked to keep detailed time diaries. A sample of the results of these studies are as follows. Burda, Hamermesh and Weil (2013) conclude in their Abstract,

> 'Time-diary data from 27 countries show a negative relationship between GDP per-capita and gender differences in total work - for pay and at home. In rich non-Catholic countries, men and women average about the same amount of total work. Survey results show scholars and the general public believe that women work more.'

The Abstract of Bianchi, Milkie, Sayer and Robinson (2000) reads,

> 'Time-diary data from representative samples of American adults show that the number of overall hours of domestic labor (excluding child care and shopping) has continued to decline steadily and predictably since 1965. This finding is mainly due to dramatic declines among women (both in and out of the paid labor market), who have cut their housework hours almost in half since the 1960s: about half of women's 12-hour-per-week decline can be accounted for by compositional shifts - such as increased labor force participation, later marriage, and fewer children. In contrast, men's housework time has almost doubled during this period (to the point where men were responsible for a third of housework in the 1990s), and only about 15% of their five-hour-per-week increase can be attributed to compositional factors. Parallel results on gender differences in housework were obtained from the National Survey of Families and Households estimate data, even though these produce figures 50% higher than diary data. Regression results examining factors related to wives' and husbands' housework hours show more support for the time-availability and relative-resource models of household production than for the gender perspective, although there is some support for the latter perspective as well.'

Catherine Hakim (2007) summarised the position thus,

> 'The key finding is that when all forms of work are added together, men and women do exactly the same total hours of productive activity: just under eight hours a day. As expected, men do substantially more hours of paid work, while women's time is divided fairly evenly between paid and unpaid work. Men and women do roughly equal amounts of voluntary work—contrary to the popular myth that women do vastly more than men.'

7.10.2 Men as Unpaid Carers

Most people have the impression that almost all unpaid caring is done by women, for example see (Thomson, 2017). But the evidence contradicts this impression. A report from (Men's Health Forum, 2014) showed that, over all age ranges, men are 42% of unpaid carers,

> 'More than four in ten (42%) of the UK's unpaid carers are male, dispelling the stereotype that caring is a female issue, according to a new report from the Men's Health Forum and Carers Trust. The report 'Husband, Partner, Dad, Son, Carer?' was commissioned to look into the experiences and needs of male carers and to help raise awareness of the fact that male carers may not be getting the support they need. Martin Tod, chief executive of the Men's Health Forum said: "The UK's 2.5 million male carers have been ignored for too long. They make a vital contribution, but face real extra health and work challenges that aren't always properly addressed".'

Men's contribution to unpaid caring takes on a rather different perspective when combined with full time working. The (Office for National Statistics, 2013) provides data on unpaid caring in England and Wales. For example,

> (page 14) 'In 2011 in England, 116,801 men and 81,812 women were in full-time employment while providing 50 hours or more unpaid care (per week); in Wales the equivalent numbers were 9,320 and 5,068 respectively.'

Men make a greater contribution to unpaid caring than women when over 65. (Office for National Statistics, 2013) provides the following information,

> 'In the age category 65 and above, the disparity reversed, with the percentage of men in both England and in Wales providing unpaid care exceeding the percentage of women.'

In fact, a greater percentage of men over 50 than women under 50 perform caring roles. It is particularly noteworthy that men do more of the caring in the retired age range, in view of men's shorter life expectancy.

7.11 The Empathy Gap in Work, Pay, Wealth, Spending and Taxes

The empathy gap in the context of work and pay is manifest in the perception that "women work more but are paid less", together with men's greater earnings being presented as a key aspect of patriarchal power. This has the perverse effect of portraying men's positive contribution to family life, and society generally, as oppression. The evidence is that the situation is rather more nuanced, and considerably less one-sided.

Since 1971 women's economic inactivity has reduced from 45% to an all-time low of 26%. In contrast, men's economic inactivity has increased from 5% to 17%. The dominant reasons for the increase in men's economic inactivity are full time education and long-term sickness. A further contribution is the increase in the number of men in a full-time home-keeping role, now about a quarter of a million in the UK. For women this is just under 2 million.

The unemployment rate is currently the same for men and women, and is at a four-decade low. Prior to 2018, men's unemployment rate had been greater than women's for 37 years. Recessions affect men's employment more than women's.

Employment is gender-polarised: most occupations have significantly different numbers of male and female employees. Of 331 employment areas just 73 occupations (22%) have employee numbers within plus or minus 30% of equality. 151 (46%) have an excess of male employees over female employees exceeding 30%. 107 (32%) have an excess of female employees over male employees exceeding 30%.

Across all areas, women are 46% of those employed, men 54%. But in the public sector, women comprise about two-thirds of employees, twice as many as men. The education sector is roughly 78% female. NHS employees are roughly 75% women.

At present there are pressures to increase diversity within companies. This is interpreted to mean reproducing the nation's demographic distribution within each company. It is beyond the scope of this book to critique this initiative. However, the extent of polarisation in employment at present indicates the scale of the redistribution of workers which would be required to achieve such an objective. The requirement to reproduce the macro-demographics within, not just every company, but at every level of seniority within each company, represents a massively over-constrained problem. So far the drive for increasing diversity has been confined to areas where women or minorities are underrepresented, and also in occupations which might be deemed desirable. There is less appetite for rebalancing in areas where men are underrepresented, as we saw in the case of education (see sections 2.6 and 2.7). Nor is the idea so popular in those occupations which currently result in the majority of fatal workplace accidents or fatal occupational illnesses, which society and feminists are content to remain a male preserve (see section 3.4).

The median gender pay gap for full time employees across the whole UK was 9.1% in favour of men in 2017. However, the full time pay gap is negligible below the age of 40. The pay gap varies significantly across the four nations of the UK. In Northern Ireland the median full time pay gap is in favour of women (-3.4%). The part-time median pay gap, UK wide, is in favour of women (-5.1%).

Legislation to force UK companies with more than 250 employees to report their gender pay gap data resulted in 10,522 companies submitting data for 2017/18 by 18th June 2018. Of the 10,522 companies, 1,932 reported pay gaps in favour of women on either a mean or median basis. Women's employment is strongly skewed towards part-time working, with 42% of employed women working part-time compared to only 13% of employed men.

The 2012 British Social Attitudes Survey revealed that 69% of people believe that fathers should be the primary earner for the family, and 73% believe that fathers should work full time. No respondents (to within rounding) thought the mother should be the primary earner, and only 9% thought that mum and dad should share the earning responsibility equally. Based on this survey, those people who advocate for increasing women's working hours and getting more women working full time – and more men working part time in favour of childcare - do not reflect the majority opinion of women themselves (nor men's opinion). The British Social Attitudes Survey appears to suggest that women's preference for part time working reflects their unconstrained wishes, as does men's preference for full time working.

Over the UK as a whole, men work 52% more paid hours than women and earn about 91% more. But women now spend more money – or influence the spending of more money – than men, so there is a net flow of money from men to women for the purposes of spending.

Men pay 73% of the income tax into the Exchequer. This funds the public sector, two-thirds of whose employees are women. The public sector enjoys far more lucrative pension provisions than the private sector, similar provisions having almost disappeared from the private sector due to unsustainable costs. The previous explicitly sexist State pension rules have now been equalised, but not without cries of "inequality" from adherents of the "equality is inequality" school of thought. Women do have smaller pensions on retirement than men, due to lesser contributions, despite provision for NI credits associated with child benefit and similar arrangements for other benefits. However the gap is reducing. And women receive a pension for longer on average than men. There are a million more women than men in receipt of a State pensions, and it used to be far more.

Over the last 40-50 years, the time spent by women on housework has reduced substantially, whilst the time men spend on housework has increased substantially. Nevertheless, men still do less unpaid housework than women, though the bulk of the difference can be attributed to who is more likely to be working part-time, or not at all. Combining paid working hours and unpaid household work, men and women work either about the same number of hours on average, or men work rather more.

Men and women do about the same amount of unpaid voluntary work. Contrary to popular belief, men carry out a substantial proportion of unpaid caring (42%), and a larger proportion of men than women are unpaid carers in the over 65 age range. Substantially more men than women do 50 or more hours of unpaid caring weekly as well as working full time.

All these observations together imply that men's substantially larger number of paid working hours, and hence greater earnings, represent a positive contribution that men make to family life, and society generally. Men's longer paid working hours lead to men's far larger payments into the Exchequer in tax which funds the welfare state and the public sector, from which women benefit more than men. In short, the economy is "gendered" in the sense that money flows from men to women. The presentation of this male contribution as 'patriarchal dominance' is a calumny. The acceptance by the public of the feminist narrative on the pay gap to the neglect of all the other factors addressed in this chapter is an aspect of the empathy gap.

8

Imprisonment

The quality of mercy is not strained.
William Shakespeare (1564 – 1616), *The Merchant of Venice*

The claims of an opinion to be protected from public attack are rested not so much on its truth, as on its importance to society.
John Stuart Mill (1806 – 1873) *On Liberty*

At the time of writing there are 21 times more men than women in prison in England and Wales. The reasons for this extremely large sex ratio are examined in this chapter. The statistics on deaths and self-harming in prison are reviewed, and the sexes compared. The personal characteristics of prisoners are also considered. They are far from a random cross-section of the population. Prisoners do not naturally attract public compassion; many have committed heinous acts. Yet compassion may be appropriate, if only from the utilitarian perspective that understanding may be a necessary precursor to effective rehabilitation. An issue to be exposed is whether such compassion is distributed equally between the sexes.

8.1 Harsher Treatment for Men

8.1.1 Harsher Treatment Over Time

Men are convicted of more crimes than women. It is not surprising, then, that there are more men in prison. In England and Wales at 29th June 2018 there were 79,142 men and 3,819 women in prison (UK Government, 2018g), i.e., 95.4% men and 4.6% women, or nearly 21 times more men. The number of prisoners was down slightly from a year earlier, 81,856 men and 4,007 women (UK Government, 2017c), but the longer-term trend has been for an increasing population of male prisoners.

The following historic data is taken from House of Commons Briefing Paper 'UK Prison Population Statistics' (House of Commons, 2017). The percentage of prisoners in England and Wales who are women has remained in the range 3% to 5.5% since the end of the second world war (1946). At that time the number of women prisoners was about 1,000, and reached a peak of 4,467 in 2005, but has been reducing since.

Figure 8.1 shows that the prison population is five times greater now than it was in 1946. Because men have comprised ~95% of prisoners throughout this period, Figure 8.1 can be taken as roughly indicative for male prisoners alone. Whilst the population of the country has increased since 1946, this does not explain the massive increase in prison population. Figure 8.2 shows the prison rate, i.e., the number of prisoners per 100,000 of the population. This has also increase massively, by more than 3.6 times, from below 50 in 1946 to about 180 in 2016.

Figure 8.1: *Increase in Number of Prisoners with respect to 1900 (House of Commons, 2017)*

Percentage change in prison population, England & Wales and Scotland
+400%
+300%
+200%
+100%
0%
-100%
England & Wales
Scotland
1900
1920
1940
1960
1980
2000
2020

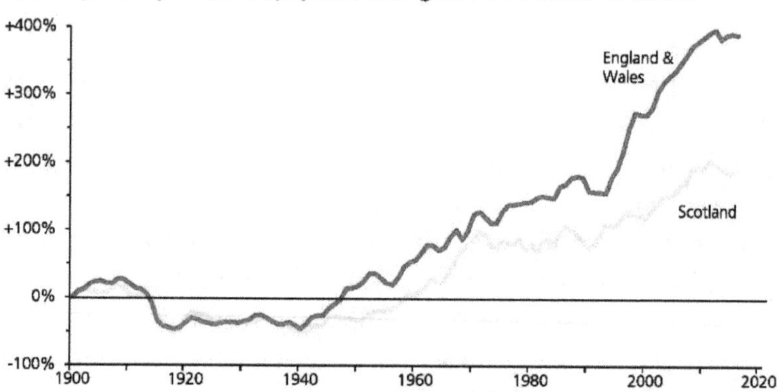

Figure 8.2: *Increase in Prisoners per 100,000 of the Population (House of Commons, 2017)*

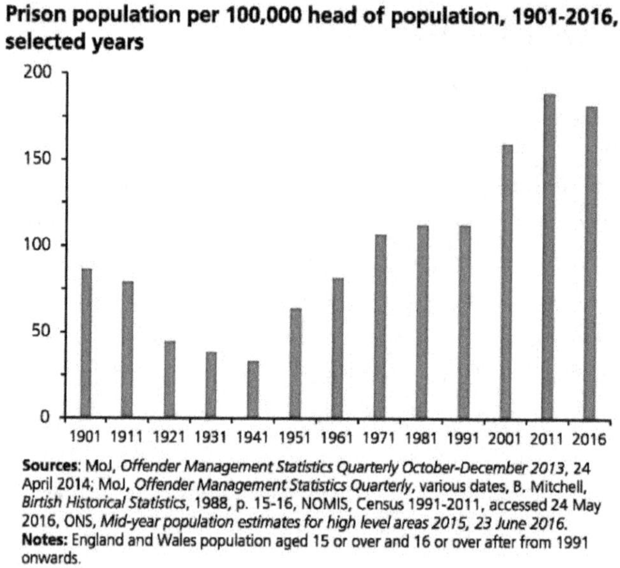

Prison population per 100,000 head of population, 1901-2016, selected years
200
150
100
50
0
1901 1911 1921 1931 1941 1951 1961 1971 1981 1991 2001 2011 2016
Sources: MoJ, Offender Management Statistics Quarterly October-December 2013, 24 April 2014; MoJ, Offender Management Statistics Quarterly, various dates, B. Mitchell, Birtish Historical Statistics, 1988, p. 15-16, NOMIS, Census 1991-2011, accessed 24 May 2016, ONS, Mid-year population estimates for high level areas 2015, 23 June 2016.
Notes: England and Wales population aged 15 or over and 16 or over after from 1991 onwards.

It is worth noting how anomalous this increasing prison population appears when compared to the crime data, taken from the Crime Survey for England and Wales (Office for National Statistics, 2018n). Figure 8.3 shows how the volume of crimes in England and Wales has fallen precipitously since 1995, now standing at one-third of its peak level (based on like-for-like counting, see Figure 8.3). This includes *all* crimes, most of which are minor in nature and would not result in a prison sentence. However, we shall see that serious crimes, such as violent crimes and homicides, have also reduced steeply over the last couple of decades.

The reasons for this gross mismatch between plummeting crime rates and the rising prison population are beyond the scope of this review to elucidate fully. However, clarification of the reasons is clearly called for, especially in view of the concentration of disadvantage in this demographic, as we shall see. At least part of the reason is a trend for longer sentences (for men), which we shall also see below. Another reason is the increasing numbers of men imprisoned for sexual offences.

Figure 8.3: *Decline in All Crime from the Crime Survey for England and Wales (CSEW). (Office for National Statistics, 2018n)*

8.1.2 Harsher Treatment by Sex

The huge preponderance of male over female prisoners (21 to 1) is only partly, but not entirely, due to men's greater criminality. In round numbers men are convicted of rather fewer than 3 times more crimes than women. However, this includes the more minor "summary" offences, for which a prison sentence is unlikely, and, if so, would only be a very short sentence. Men are convicted of about 6 times more serious (indictable) offences than women, and these will account for the majority of prisoners. There is therefore a mismatch between the ratio of the number of serious crimes for which men and women are convicted (i.e., the factor of 6) and the fact that there are 21 times more men in prison. The conviction data for England and Wales in 2017 is summarised in Table 8.1, (Ministry of Justice, 2018a).

Table 8.1: *Convictions in England and Wales, 2017 (Ministry of Justice, 2018a). Includes trials at all courts, and offenders of all ages, ethnicity, etc,*

Offence Type	Number Convicted in 2017		Ratio Men/Women
	Men	Women	
Indictable or Triable Either Way	190,966	32,423	5.9
Summary	617,624	260,114	2.4
Total	808,590	292,537	2.8

In fact this mismatch appears to be gender bias (a gender disparity factor of 21/6 = 3.5). There is a popular mythology that women are treated more harshly in the criminal justice system (see section 8.2), but the evidence is very much in the opposite direction.

Of course, it does not follow immediately that this factor of 3.5 represents unfair treatment of men compared with women. The most obvious hypothesis would be that men's crimes are more serious on average. However, this easy assumption is challenged, if not discredited entirely, by two observations which are detailed below: firstly, a disparity to men's disadvantage is evident across all major offence categories, and secondly, the pattern of men's and women's offending is quite similar, with the exception of sexual offences.

8.1.2.1 Gender Disparity by Offence Category

8.1.2.1.1 Gender Disparity in Sentencing to Immediate Custody

The sentencing data tool from (Ministry of Justice, 2018a) can be used to extract the numbers of men and women sentenced (in any way) across 12 offence categories, as well as how many were sentenced to immediate custody. Hence, the percentage of convicted men who were sentenced to prison can be found for each of these 12 offence categories, as can the corresponding percentages for convicted women. For example, 24,754 men were convicted of violence against the person (VAP) in 2017, of whom 11,031 were sent to prison (45%). In the same year, 3088 women were convicted of VAP, of whom 658 were sent to prison (21%). The gender disparity in VAP was thus 45%/21% = 2.1 in 2017.

Table 8.2 gives the percentage of convicted offenders who were sentenced to prison for each of the 12 offence categories, and hence a disparity factor for each, in year 2017. The gender disparity is greater than 1, indicating that a convicted man is more likely to be imprisoned than a woman convicted of the same offence, and this is true for all offence categories.

Table 8.2: *Gender Disparities on Sentencing for Various Offence Categories, 2017. Data from (Ministry of Justice, 2018a). See text for definition of this disparity.*

Offence Category	Percentage of convicted men sent to prison	Percentage of convicted women sent to prison	Disparity on imprisonment
Violence against the person (VAP)	45%	21%	2.1
Sexual offences	60%	53%	1.12
Robbery	70%	68%	1.04
Theft	33%	20%	1.63
Criminal damage or arson	33%	24%	1.34
Drug offences	23%	15%	1.51
Possession of weapon	36%	23%	1.56
Public order offences	31%	20%	1.57
Miscellaneous crimes against society	32%	19%	1.75
Fraud	27%	11%	2.48
Summary Offences (Non-Motoring)	4.5%	0.5%	8.7
Summary Offences (Motoring)	0.8%	0.1%	6.7
All offences	**9.7%**	**2.5%**	**3.9**
All indictable offences	**34.2%**	**19.5%**	**1.75**

This is not new, and 2017 is not an uncharacteristic year. Figure 8.4a plots the gender disparity on imprisonment for indictable offences, calculated in the same manner, for years 2006 to 2016, (Office for National Statistics, 2018w). Figure 8.4b is the equivalent for summary offences, and shows very large disparity factors, up to a factor of 10. Similar data for years 1999 to 2009 can be obtained from (Ministry of Justice, 2012). Based on all offences (summary offences and indictable offences) the disparity on imprisonment has increased from 2.4 in 1999, to 3.4 in 2009 and to 3.9 in 2017, the latter from Table 8.2. Based on indictable offences only, the gender disparity based on Table 8.2 for 2017 is 1.75.

Figure 8.4a: *Gender Disparity on Sentencing to Immediate Custody, 2006-2016 (Indictable Offences)*

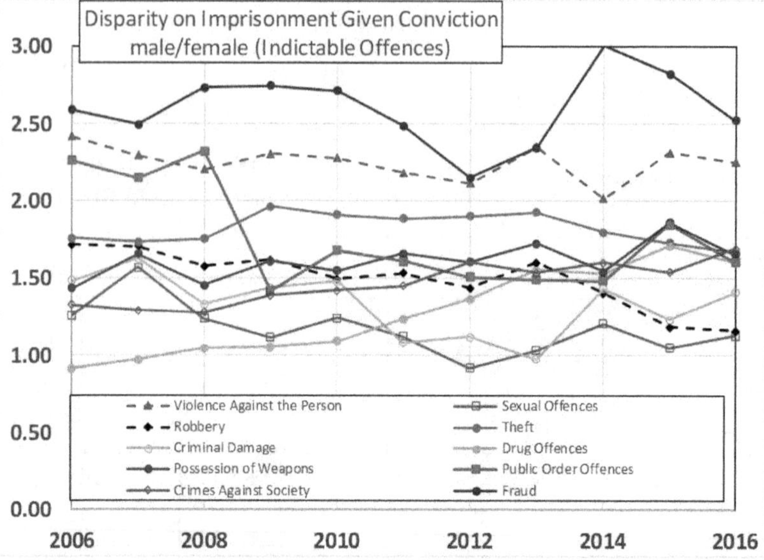

Figure 8.4b: *Gender Disparity on Sentencing to Immediate Custody, 2006-2016 (Summary Offences)*

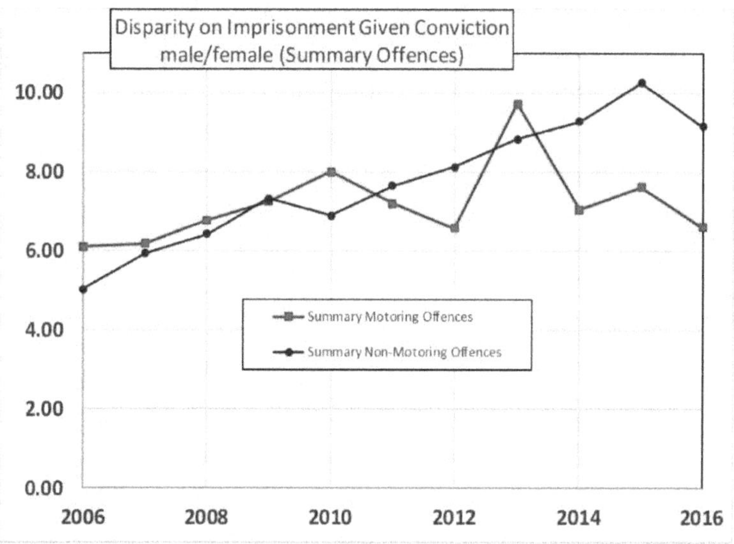

In 2016 the Ministry of Justice published a report 'Associations between being male or female and being sentenced to prison in England and Wales in 2015' (Hopkins, Uhrig, and Colahan, 2016). This MoJ analysis was based on multivariate logistic regression models to account for possible dependences of imprisonment on not only sex and offence category but also ethnicity, age and previous criminal history. This allowed the associations between sex and imprisonment to be examined under similar criminal circumstances. Moreover, the MOJ used 20 offence categories, more than the 12 categories in Table 8.2. The MoJ's headline finding was that under similar criminal circumstances the odds of imprisonment for males were 88% higher than for females, i.e., an imprisonment disparity factor of 1.88 in 2015. This is quite close to the disparity of 1.75 for indictable offences in 2017 from Table 8.2 even though based on a different methodology.

The MoJ rightly note this disparity might not be gender bias but rather that there could be systematic differences between the sexes in offending severity even within the same offence category. Essentially this is a recognition that even 20 offence categories may provide insufficient granularity. This does need further investigation, though it is worth noting that analyses of USA data, e.g., that by Sonya Starr of the University of Michigan in 2012 (see section 8.1.2.7), indicate a similar gender sentencing disparity based on far greater granularity. Some of the findings of the MoJ report for year 2015 were as follows (pages 3 and 4),

- Females were less likely to be imprisoned than males, 8% of those sentenced versus 18% of men.
- The most common offence for both sexes was Violence Against the Person (VAP)*, accounting for 22% of women convicted and the same percentage of men convicted. However, whilst 20% of men convicted for VAP were imprisoned, only 7% of women convicted for VAP were imprisoned. (*For women, theft also accounted for 22% of convictions).
- The second most common offence for both men and women was drink-driving, accounting for 15% of women's convictions and 12% of men's. However, whilst about 700 men were imprisoned for drink-driving, seemingly no women were (though "0%" may be rounded).
- 31% of men convicted of fraud or forgery were imprisoned, compared with 18% of women.
- 23% of men convicted for handling stolen goods were imprisoned compared with 10% of women.
- 63% of men convicted for domestic burglary were imprisoned compared with 35% of women
- 13% of men convicted of public order or harassment offences were imprisoned compared with 4% of women.

- 20% of men convicted for vehicle-related theft were imprisoned compared with 6% of women.
- 4% of men convicted of welfare fraud were imprisoned compared with 2% of women. (This was a rare instance of the absolute number of women offenders exceeding that of men).
- 11% of men convicted of absconding/jumping bail were imprisoned compared to 7% of women.

Women are systematically less likely to be imprisoned in every offence category. It is rather hard to understand why women's offending should be less serious in every category, including such things as fraud, forgery, handling stolen goods, vehicle related theft and jumping bail. A harsh penalty, such as imprisonment, for drink-driving is because of the danger this represents to the public. In what way is the danger less if the drink-driver is female? Yet no women were imprisoned for drink-driving to men's 700, despite drink-driving accounting for 15% of women's convictions.

8.1.2.1.2 Gender Disparity in Sentence Length

It is not only in the probability of being sentenced to immediate custody (assuming conviction) in which there is a gender disparity. Assuming a man and a woman are both convicted within the same offence category, and further assuming that both are sentenced to prison, the man can expect a longer sentence. The gender disparity in this case is defined as the ratio of the sentence lengths. These disparities on sentence length are plotted in Figure 8.5a for years 1999-2009 based on the same 12 offence categories as Figure 8.4 (Ministry of Justice, 2012). Figure 8.5b plots similar data for years 2006-2016 and for indictable offences. For all but one or two offences, the disparity is greater than one, i.e., men receive longer prison sentences even when a woman is convicted and sentenced to prison for the same offence category. Across all offences in 2009, the disparity in sentence length was about 1.4. But the average custodial sentence for men has been increasing over the last 11 years, as shown by Figure 8.6. That for women has not increased. The gender disparity in sentence length has therefore been increasing: in 2015, averaged over all offences, it reached 1.78 (Ministry of Justice, 2016a).

In 2016, Baroness Corston wrote an article in the Guardian attempting to refute claims that it is men, not women, who are treated more harshly in prison sentencing, (Corston, 2016). The article was sub-titled 'Labour peer Jean Corston says there is indisputable evidence that the justice system treats women harshly'. In the article Corston noted that, in 2009, 'women were sentenced to an average of 17.9 months in prison for violence against the person, compared with 17.7 months for men'. These figures are correct and correspond to a disparity on sentence length of 0.99. The data point in question is indicated by the black arrow on Figure 8.5a. Readers will come to their own view as to whether the point picked fairly represents the totality of the data in Figures 8.5a and 8.5b. Moreover, the Baroness was unmoved by the fact that the disparity on imprisonment for VAP in 2009 was over 2.

Figure 8.5a: *Gender Disparity on Sentence Length, 1999-2009 (assuming a prison sentence has been awarded), data from (Ministry of Justice, 2012)*

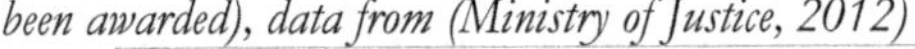

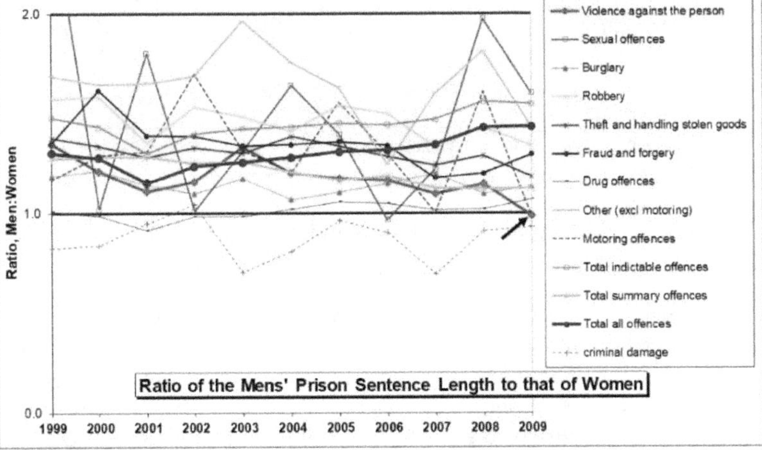

Figure 8.5b: *Gender Disparity on Sentence Length, 2006-2016 (assuming a prison sentence has been awarded), data from (Office for National Statistics, 2018w).*

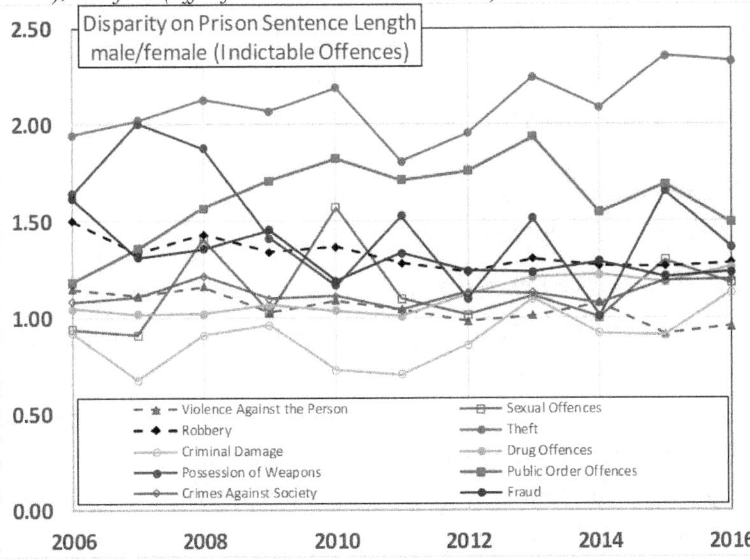

Figure 8.6: *Average Custodial Sentence Length for Offenders Sentenced to Immediate Custody, by Sex, 2005 to 2015. From (Ministry of Justice, 2016a).*

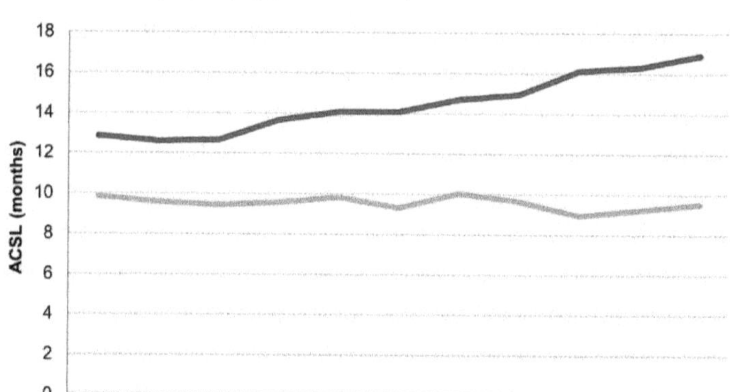

The (Ministry of Justice, 2016a) have provided an opinion on the reason for the increasing average custodial sentence length (ACSL) for men,

> 'The overall increase in male ACSL is in part caused by changes in legislation and in part by the impact of sexual offences. More male offenders are being sentenced for sexual offences, and these sentences are getting longer (with the ACSL increasing by 20 months), which is driving up the overall average. The largest increase in ACSL within this offence group was for rape of a female child under 13 by a male, for which ACSL has more than doubled and the number sentenced to immediate custody is four times higher than in 2005.
>
> The total number of males sentenced to immediate custody for sexual offences in 2015 was around 4,000, up from 2,700 in 2005; this change could be related to improved reporting and recording of sexual offences, as well as an increased public focus. The number of females sentenced to immediate custody for sexual offences was much smaller - 57 in 2015, up from 23 in 2005.'

A number of concerns arise in the context of sexual offences. These issues will be addressed in chapters 19 and 20.

8.1.2.2 Gender Parole Disparity

Prisoners on determinate sentences do not usually serve their full sentence. The parole system usually permits prisoners to be released early. The proportion of sentence served differs systematically for men and women. In 2015, 2016 and 2017 the median release for male prisoners was 53%, 58% and 59% of their full sentence respectively (Ministry of Justice, 2018b). For women prisoners the median sentence actually served was 46%, 46% and 47% of their full sentence respectively. Consequently, there is a gender disparity in the proportion of time served, over and above the awarded sentence length, of between 1.15 and 1.26. Figure 8.7 shows how the actual prison time served by male and female prisoners has changed since 2002. That for women has decreased slightly. But for men, the mean time served has increased substantially (by more than 50%).

Figure 8.7: *Actual Time Served in Prison by Sex. Data from (Ministry of Justice, 2018b). Note the large difference between mean and median terms.*

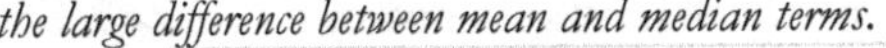

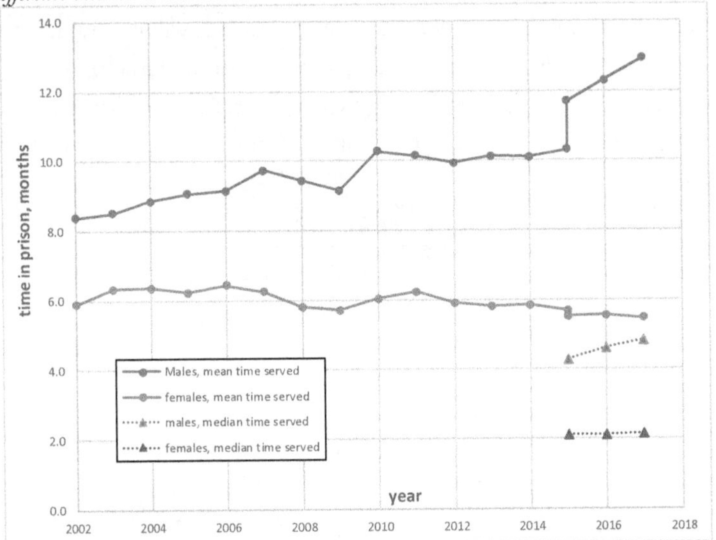

The difference in early release between the sexes is not due to better behaviour in prison by women. In fact, the number of disciplinary offences per 100 prisoners is similar in men's and women's prisons, perhaps with somewhat more in women's prisons, see Table 8.3.

Table 8.3: *Disciplinary Offences within Men's and Women's Prisons. Data for 2005 to 2009 from (Ministry of Justice, 2010b), data for 2010 and 2015 from (Ministry of Justice, 2016b). Incidents per 100 prisoners.*

Sex	2005	2006	2007	2008	2009	2010	2015
All Offences / Adjudications							
Men	143	131	133	133	124	210	170
Women	193	204	189	180	150	160	210
Violent Offences / Assaults							
Men	23	22	22	22	21	-	24
Women	33	33	30	31	24	-	20

8.1.2.3 Other Known Disparities

Women who are convicted are more likely than convicted men to receive a conditional discharge or unconditional discharge, more likely to be given a suspended sentence, and more likely to be given a community sentence. These disparities have been quantified by Collins (2018a). The likelihood of a prosecution resulting in a conviction is subject to less disparity, but where there is disparity it is men who are more likely to be convicted.

An issue which receives less attention is the use of cautions. Following an arrest, the police have an alternative to pressing for a prosecution. They may instead offer the arrestee a caution. If the arrestee accepts the caution, prosecution, and any further action, is avoided. However, by accepting the caution the arrestee is admitting guilt, and will then have a record to that effect. Where the arrestee is indeed guilty, to accept a caution is to be let off lightly compared with the possible consequences of being prosecuted and convicted.

Figure 8.8: *Gender Disparity on Cautions, 2006-2016*

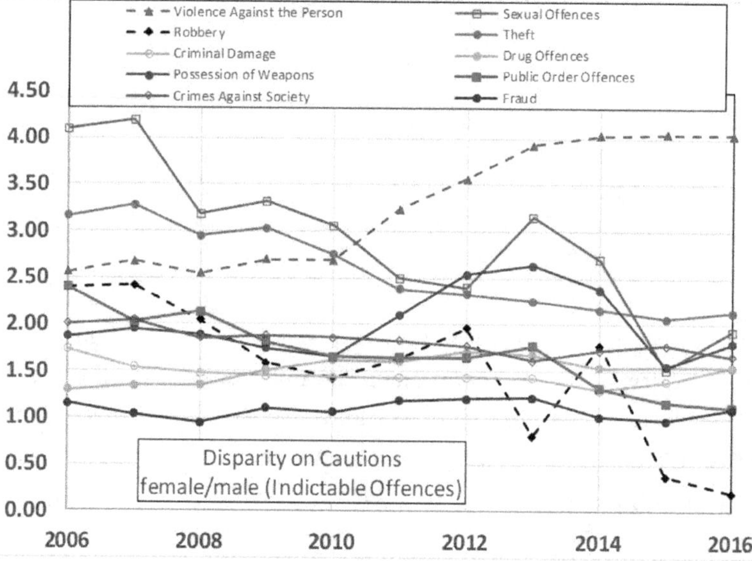

To evaluate a gender disparity on cautions, the number of cautions per 100 prosecutions for the same offence is first calculated. The caution disparity is then defined as the number of cautions accepted by women per 100 prosecutions of women divided by the number of cautions accepted by men per 100 prosecutions of men for the same offence. The resulting caution disparities are plotted in Figure 8.8 for 2006 to 2016 and for ten indictable offences. The caution disparity is almost always larger than 1, i.e., more women than men escape prosecution by accepting a caution. The caution disparity is particularly large for VAP offences in recent years (about 4).

Consequently, claims about the relative number of violent offences committed by men and women based on conviction data alone will be misleading, as more women than men who are arrested for violence will avoid prosecution via a caution (quantified in section 9.1.2).

8.1.2.4 Pattern of Offending by Gender

To rationalise the disparities observed above, the argument is sometimes made that women's pattern of offending is different from men's, implying that it is generally less serious even in the same offence category. But actually women's and men's patterns of offending are very similar, as shown by Figure 8.9 (arrests) and Figure 8.10 (prisoners). Note that these Figures do not show absolute numbers, but the proportions of offenders of the same sex. The volume of offending (at least as indicated by convictions) would be far greater for men than for women. However, Figures 8.9 and 8.10 do faithfully depict the pattern of offending by sex, i.e., which types of offences are most common. The only major difference in pattern of offending is for sexual offences and there are particular issues associated with that (see chapters 19 and 20). Further evidence for similar patterns of offending by the two sexes is the closely comparable distribution of legal aid amongst crime categories (Figure 8.11). The commonest reason for a man to be arrested is for violence. Some people might be surprised to learn that the same is true for women (Figure 8.9). Similarly, the largest proportion of male prisoners were sentenced for violence against the person (VAP). It may surprise some people that the same is again true for women (Figure 8.10). This point is brought out clearly in the report 'Statistics on Women and the Criminal Justice System 2015', (Ministry of Justice, 2016a), which states,

> (page 118), 'For both male and female prisoners, the most common offence group for which they were convicted at 30 June 2015 was violence against the person (25% and 27% respectively).'

The exception to the generally similar pattern of offending between the sexes is sex offending. Sex offences accounted for about 5% of men sent to prison in 2017, (Ministry of Justice, 2018a), but about 16% of male prisoners are inside for sex offences, see Figure 8.10. The distinction arises from the long sentences awarded for sex offences. Sex offences are perhaps the most extreme example of gender disparity. Sex offences committed by women are regarded as less serious than those committed by men, even when perpetrated against children. And female sex offending against adult males is popularly regarded as a virtual impossibility. These matters are taken up in chapter 20.

8.1.2.5 Overall Gender Disparity in Criminal Justice

The criminal justice process consists broadly of four sequential processes, (i) Arrest, (ii) Decision to Prosecute, (iii) Conviction, and, (iv) Sentencing. In the foregoing sections I have addressed quantitatively only gender disparity in sentencing, assuming all is fair up to and including conviction. Given the strong case for gender bias in sentencing, it is natural to be concerned that

Figure 8.9: *Proportion of Arrests within each Offence Group by Sex, 2015/16. From (Ministry of Justice, 2016a) Figure 4.05.*

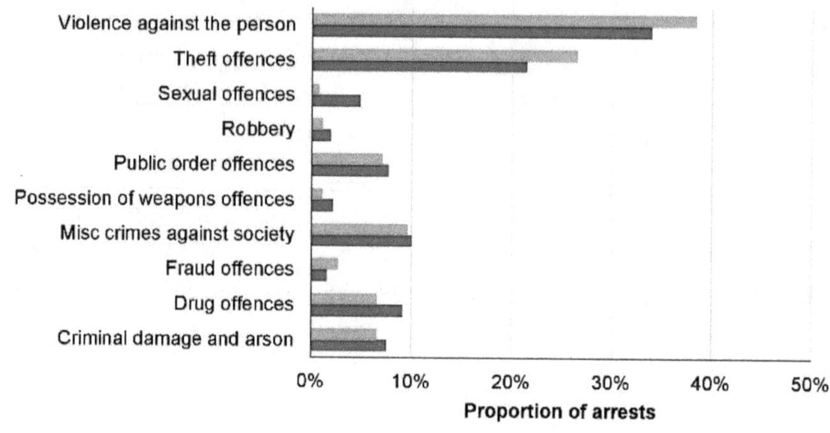

Figure 8.10: *Proportion of Sentenced Prisoners by Offence Group and Sex, June 2015. From (Ministry of Justice, 2016a) Figure 7.08.*

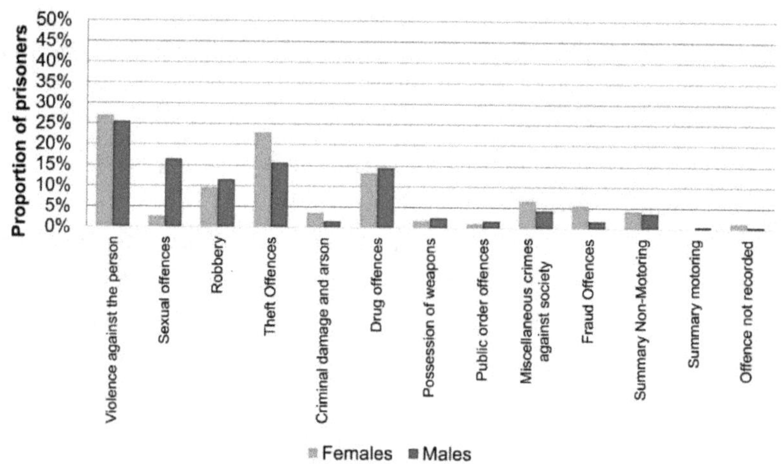

Figure 8.11: *Proportion of Legal Aid Workload in Magistrates' Courts by Offence Group and Sex, 2015. From (Ministry of Justice, 2016a) Figure 5.10.*

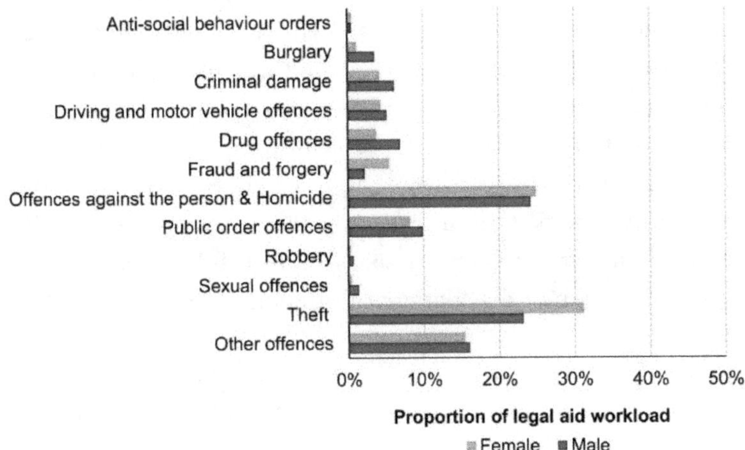

there might also be gender bias in the earlier three steps in the criminal justice process. Obtaining data on these earlier steps is not so easy. In particular, if the police do not arrest a person, then that person and their potential misdemeanour never appear in any statistics. Consequently, the disparity in sentencing must be interpreted as a lower bound to the overall disparity in the criminal justice process. I have noted above that there is a small disparity in conviction rate and a large disparity in the use of cautions (Figure 8.8), both to men's disadvantage.

Given conviction, the overall disparity on imprisonment comprises: disparity in being sentenced to immediate custody for the same crime category; disparity in sentence length awarded for the same crime category; and disparity in the proportion of time actually served (parole). For the most recent years for which data has been obtained (2015 to 2017) these disparity factors have been estimated, above, to be 1.88, 1.78 and about 1.2 respectively. The product of these provides the overall prison-time disparity of 1.88 x 1.78 x 1.2 = 4.0.

This overall disparity is more than enough to account for there being 21 times more men in prison despite the number of indictable offences committed by men exceeding that committed by women only by a much smaller factor (about 6).

It has not been conclusively proved that this disparity is gender bias, rather than a pervasive tendency for men's offending to be more serious across all offence categories. However, that assumption is seriously challenged by the similarity of men's and women's patterns of offending, as well as the occurrence of gender disparity across all offence categories. If you run over someone due to driving drunk, why should you be more culpable if male? Similar remarks apply for fraud or theft or any of the majority of offences which do not involve violence or a sexual offence. Even that proviso about violent offences appears to be only popular prejudice. Lightowlers (2018) has provided a breakdown of VAP offences into six sub-offences of varying severity. The pattern of offending across these six VAP sub-offences is again very similar for the two sexes (Figure 8.12). This seems to be a convincing refutation of the "pattern of offending" explanation of the gender disparities.

Any residual doubt that the criminal justice process is systemically sex biased is unlikely to survive consideration of the policies that are in operation, as we shall see next.

Figure 8.12: *Pattern of Offending by Sex across Six VAP Sub-Offences*

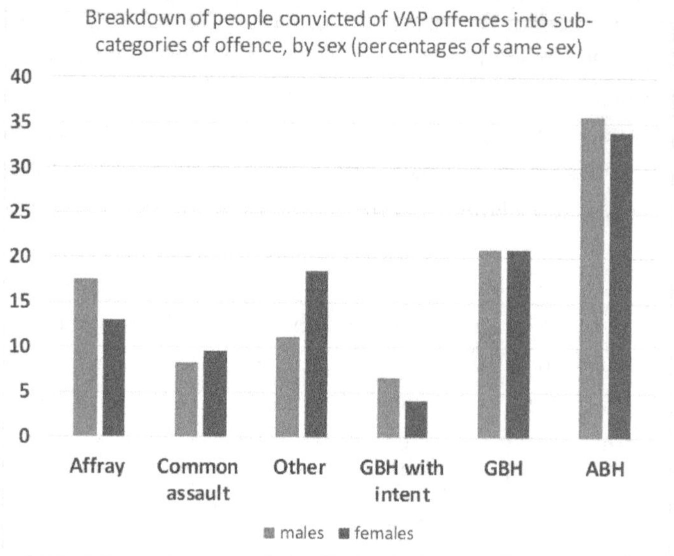

8.1.2.6 Sex Bias by Policy?

The different treatment of men and women in the criminal justice process is driven by policy as well as by sentiment. This is illustrated here by two documents and also a Government announcement in June 2018. The documents are the Corston Report (Corston, 2007) and the Equal Treatment Bench Book (Judicial College, 2018). The latter is the formal guidance to judges on "equality", covering issues relating to race, religion, sexuality and gender, as well as specific issues like modern slavery, the treatment of children, etc. The Corston Report, authored by former Labour MP Jean Corston, now in the House of Lords, concerned women in prison. The report effectively formed an agenda which was later taken up in policies and embodied in the Equal Treatment Bench Book. The line of argument within the Corston Report is clear from a few quotes,

> (page 23) 'Equality does not mean treating everyone the same'

This is the most succinct expression of one perspective regarding what constitutes "equality". The most benign view is that this is a view focused on outcomes. But more bluntly, it is an identity political credo in which some identity groups are more deserving than others. We will see below that this perspective is enshrined in the Equal Treatment Bench Book and hence is being used to legitimise different treatment of men and women in criminal justice. One may object to it on principle, if one believes that equality *does* mean treating everyone the same, as I do. But, even if one does not object on principle, there are major problems with this view in practice due to the ambiguity in what the outcomes might be.

> (page 3) 'Prison is disproportionably (sic) harsher for women because prisons and the practices within them have for the most part been designed for men'

This asserts that the outcome of imprisonment is *harsher* for women because the practices of imprisonment are *the same* as they are for men. The outcome is different, because the treatment is the same - it is claimed. Why should the outcome be different for women, unless they are intrinsically more vulnerable? In other words, the Baroness's view is based on the traditional gender scripts. It is actually an appeal to gynocentricity: women must be treated better than men. But why should we be unconcerned about imposing treatments upon men which are deemed too harsh for women unless there is an empathy gap? Here we see "outcomes" as a subterfuge for the unequal allocation of compassion. Much of the rest of the Corston Report betrays this disconcerting lack of concern for men - a rich source of illustrations of the empathy gap - as the following extracts illustrate.

> (page 18) 'Women commit a different range of offences from men. They commit more acquisitive crime and have a lower involvement in serious violence, criminal damage and professional crime'

Women do commit a smaller volume of crime, but, as we have seen, their pattern of offending - including violence - is similar to men's (Figures 8.9-12).

> (page 19) 'Drug addiction plays a huge part in all offending and is disproportionately the case with women'

Drug addiction does indeed account for a large part of offending, for both men and women. But a larger proportion of men than women are arrested and imprisoned for drug offences (Figures 8.8-10). In 2017, 19 times more men were sent to prison for drug offences. So Corston's claim that women are disproportionately affected is false. Drugs cause more than double the number of premature deaths in men than women (Table 3.1).

> (page 19) 'Outside prison men are more likely to commit suicide than women but the position is reversed inside prison'

Of all the examples of the empathy gap this is perhaps the most egregious, as well as being untrue. Prison suicide is considered in section 8.6.1. Averaged over the last 10 years, the rate of suicide in men's prisons, per 1000 prisoners, is comparable with, but slightly greater than, that in women's prisons. The actual number of men killing themselves in prison was 22 times the number of women prisoners killing themselves over the same period.

> (page 20) 'Self-harm in prison is a huge problem and more prevalent in the women's estate'

It is true that the rate of self-harming by female prisoners, say per 1000 prisoners, is greater than the rate for male prisoners. Nevertheless, in year 2015/16 about 8 times more male prisoners self-harmed (section 8.5). Ask yourself, why is Baroness Corston unconcerned about that?

> (page 58) 'Women must never be sent to prison…to teach them a lesson'

Whilst I am not against a focus on rehabilitation, for both sexes, this is an extraordinary recommendation. Punishment has always been seen as a valid aspect of justice, and one which victims, and the public generally, have a right to expect. Yet this policy appears to have been adopted, as of June 2018 (see below) – but only for women. Turning now to the Equal Treatment Bench Book (Judicial College, 2018), some extracts are as follows.

> (page 3) 'True equal treatment may not, however, always mean treating everyone in the same way. As Justice Blackmun of the US Supreme Court commented: "In order to get beyond racism, we must first take account of race. There is no other way. And in order to treat some persons equally, we must treat them differently."'

> (page 6-16, in the context of gender) 'true equal treatment may not always mean treating everyone in the same way'

This is the same perspective on "equality" as espoused by the Cortson Report, and informs the tenor of both. Here it is less carefully phrased: it claims that different treatment may be 'true equal treatment'. It begs the question, just how differently must people be treated in order to be "equal"? And which groups are to be favoured with "more equal" treatment? One presumes the latter question is answered thus: the favoured groups are those explicitly mentioned in the Equal Treatment Bench Book. So, we see that this judicial guidance is actually a manual for identity politics. The Equal Treatment Bench Book quotes Baroness Hale from her 2005 Longford Trust Lecture (Hale, 2005)

> (page 6-16) 'It is now well recognised that a misplaced conception of equality has resulted in some very unequal treatment for the women and girls who appear before the criminal justice system. Simply put, a male-ordered world has applied to them its perceptions of the appropriate treatment for male offenders.... The criminal justice system could ... ask itself whether it is indeed unjust to women.'

Baroness Hale is now President of the Supreme Court and the most senior judge in the land. This quote states that, in the Baroness's opinion, treating women in the same way that men are treated is a 'misplaced conception of equality'. This is the same sentiment again. Women should be treated differently from men, and this can only mean more leniently than men. Hence, for women to be treated equally (i.e., justly), they must be treated preferentially. This is what gynocentrism looks like. For this to be justified, even by the standards of this identity-group perspective, it has to be established that women are endemically socially disadvantaged compared with men. This book challenges that presumption, but the Equal Treatment Bench Book is nevertheless predicated upon that position. The direction of argument of its 24 pages is faithfully captured by the following few extracts.

> (page 6-2) 'Women remain disadvantaged in many public and private areas of their life; they are under-represented in the judiciary, in parliament and in senior positions across a range of jobs; and there is still a substantial pay gap between men and women.'

A more balanced perspective on pay, employment and associated issues has been given in chapter 7. Claims of endemic female disadvantage are an article of faith rather than an empirical truth. Regardless of that, what are these matters doing in a document which is supposed to guide the treatment of criminals?

> (page 6-2) 'Women are still the primary carers of children. Overall, 73% of women with children work, including 53% of women with children under five, but they still

> spend three times as much time as men on caring for children. Many women also provide unpaid care by looking after an ill, older or disabled family member, friend or partner.'

A more balanced perspective on caring and total working hours has been given in chapter 7.

> (page 6-3) 'Sexual harassment remains a problem for women both in and outside work. According to a survey, 85% of women aged 18–24 have experienced unwanted sexual attention in public places and 45% have experienced unwanted sexual touching. 52% of women in a 2016 TUC poll had experienced some form of sexual harassment at work.'

How low has our criminal justice process sunk that these wild feminist statistics are included in a document with such serious implications? Sexual offending against men and boys is addressed in chapter 20. It fails to have the same sociopolitical impact as offending against women and girls.

> (page 6-3) 'Women can be subject to domestic and gender based violence, some of which is evident and overt; some which is less so, such as coercive control, which has a profound and pervasive impact on a woman's autonomy and well-being. On average, two women in England and Wales are killed every week by a current or former male partner.'

The reader will have got the measure of this discourse. The emphasis on pay, domestic work, sexual assault and violence clearly establishes its feminist origins. Note the loaded language "gender based violence". Academic research repudiates the bulk of domestic violence being classed as "gender based", as discussed in chapter 9 along with men and boys as victims of violence. But again, violence against men and boys fails to have the same sociopolitical impact as such offences against women and girls. Finally, this quote,

> (page 6-2) 'Of course, men can suffer from gender discrimination too. This chapter reflects the reality that this is rarer.'

No, it does not. It reflects the reality of gynocentrism. It reflects the reality of the grip that gynocentric feminism now has on all aspects of our society, including criminal justice.

One may object to the line taken by the Equal Treatment Bench Book in two ways: empirically or on principle. One may object based on the principle that social disadvantage should not justify preferential treatment in criminal justice. The dictum "equality does not mean treating everyone the same" repudiates that principle (wrongly, in my opinion). But once that dictum is accepted, if it can be argued that women suffer substantially more social disadvantage than men, then preferential treatment of women will be the result. This is the purpose of the discourse alluded to above. An equal, or greater, social disadvantage of men cannot be acknowledged without undermining that position. The empirical challenge to the position adopted by the Equal Treatment Bench Book is that men are indeed at an equal or greater social disadvantage. The objective of this book is to demonstrate that discrimination against men is not rarer, but endemic and ignored.

The latest development in the different treatment of male and female offenders is an explicitly declared change in Government policy. Following the closure in 2016 of Holloway, at one time western Europe's largest women's prison, it had been the intention to build five new community prisons for women. In June 2018 these plans were cancelled. Lord Chancellor and Justice Secretary, David Gauke, announced a new policy to 'divert the most vulnerable women in the criminal justice system away from custody' (UK Government, 2018h). The new strategy is intended to 'break the cycle of female offending' and will involve only sending women to prison in the last resort, more often putting the emphasis on rehabilitation. In contrast, it is still planned to build up to six more prisons for men, with the potential to expand the current male prison population by a further 10,000 (Ford, 2018). Here we see the two strands of policy made explicit: compassion for women, punishment for men.

8.1.2.7 Evidence of Gender Disparity from the USA

There have been a number of studies on gender disparity in sentencing in the USA. Perhaps the most thorough is that of (Starr, 2012). Its headline conclusions are,

- This study finds dramatic unexplained gender gaps in federal criminal cases. Conditional on arrest offense, criminal history, and other pre-charge observables, men receive 63% longer sentences on average than women do.
- Women are also significantly likelier to avoid charges and convictions, and twice as likely to avoid incarceration if convicted.

These conclusions are broadly consistent with my findings, above, for the UK.

8.2 Pop Goes the Woozle

The subject of women prisoners is replete with woozles.

Woozle (noun, idiomatic): A widely quoted claim which has gained acceptance through repetition but which has no, or insufficient, basis in fact.

Sometimes a claim about women prisoners is made which the listener is implicitly invited to assume must be different for men, but actually is not. These are not quite woozles but I will classify them as such because they have the same misleading effect. Examples of woozles and are as follows.

Woozle: Eighty-four per cent of women's prison sentences are for non-violent offences

It is important to distinguish between the proportion of people sentenced to prison per year for a given offence, and the proportion of people currently in prison for a given offence. It is correct that 84% is a typical figure for the proportion of women sentenced to prison for non-violent offences in a given year, but so it is also for men (Ministry of Justice, 2018a). As for people in prison for violence, the report (Ministry of Justice, 2016a) states (page 118), 'For both male and female prisoners, the most common offence group for which they were convicted at 30 June 2015 was violence against the person (25% and 27% respectively).'

Woozle: Women are more likely than men to be imprisoned for a first offence

False. This is perhaps the most frequently repeated woozle in the context of criminal justice. The report (Ministry of Justice, 2016a) states (page 98), 'In 2015, the most common disposal for offenders convicted of an indictable offence with no previous sanctions was a community sentence for both males (33%) and females (29%). However, males were much more likely to receive an immediate custodial sentence (25%) than females (14%). In comparison, a higher proportion of females received suspended sentences and conditional discharges compared with males', see Figure 8.13.

Woozle: Women are more likely than men to be imprisoned for minor offences like shoplifting

False. The report (Ministry of Justice, 2016a) states (page 152), 'The custody rate in 2015 for females sentenced for shoplifting was 15%, and for males was 22%'. It also states that, 'For both sexes, 89% of offenders sentenced (for shoplifting) had a previous caution or conviction for shoplifting.'

Woozle: Men's harsher sentencing is due to their offending history

The degree of recidivism is not markedly different between men and women and does not appear to account for different sentencing. Quotes from (Ministry of Justice, 2016a) are, (page 11) 'Males were more likely to be sentenced to immediate custody and to receive custodial sentences of 6 months or longer than females with a similar criminal history.'

(page 11) 'Although males were more likely to reoffend, females had a higher number of proven reoffences on average per reoffender.'

Figure 8.13: *Proportion of Offenders Sentenced for an Indictable Offence who have No Previous Sanctions, by Sentencing Outcome and Sex, 2015*

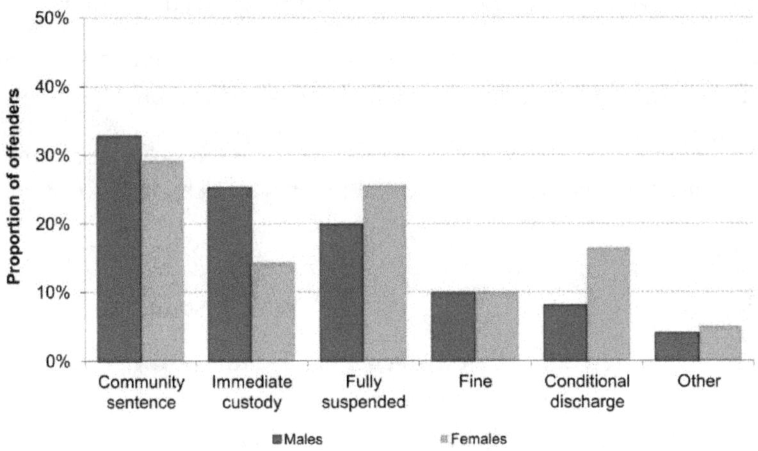

Woozle: Most women in prison had been caring for dependent children
False. Page 2 of the report (Ministry of Justice, 2015) identified that, 'Between 24% and 31% of all female offenders were estimated to have one or more child dependents. Among the different disposal types, women receiving immediate custody were significantly less likely to have child dependents (between 13% and 19%).'

8.3 Characteristics of Prisoners

Prisoners, and ex-prisoners, are not a representative cross-section of society. They are a separate demographic, strongly skewed to multiple disadvantages. The report 'Prisoners' childhood and family backgrounds', (Williams, Papadopoulou and Booth, 2012) provided the following results, based primarily on a survey of 1,435 prisoners serving sentences between 1 month and 4 years. The survey involved both sexes but the results were weighted to match the prison population, i.e., 95% men, so the results can be taken as applicable to male prisoners to a good approximation.

- 24% had been in care as a child (page ii);
- 29% had been abused as a child (page ii);
- 41% had observed violence in the home as a child (page ii);
- 31% had a family member who had been imprisoned (page ii, 84% of 37%);
- 27% had a family member with a drug or alcohol problem (page 13);
- 59% had regularly played truant from school, 63% had been suspended, and 42% had been permanently excluded or expelled (page ii);

The following responses relate to prisoners' living arrangements as children and refer to arrangements which applied "most of the time until age 17". Other arrangements might prevail at other times. From page 8,

- 53% had not lived with both natural parents as a child;
- 34% lived with one natural parent only;
- 6% lived with one natural and one step parent as a child;
- 13% lived with grandparents, foster parents, in institutions, etc.

Williams et al quote a 2004 survey which indicated that 43% of male prisoners who reported having dependent children had been living with their children prior to imprisonment, compared to 58% for female prisoners. The 2014 report 'A Presumption Against Imprisonment' (British Academy, 2014) tells us that,

- 68% of prisoners were not in paid employment prior to being imprisoned (page 42)
- 59% of young offenders have learning difficulties or borderline learning difficulties (page 43)
- 47% of prisoners have no educational qualifications (page 42)
- 15% of male prisoners were homeless prior to being imprisoned (page 42)

Risk factors for future offending and antisocial behaviour include low family income, delinquent or convicted family members, histories of violence, parental mental illness, parental substance abuse, poor relationships with parents, low IQ and low school attainment. That these factors are also disproportionately present in child offenders can be seen in the next Section.

8.3.1 Children in Prison

The secure estate for children consists of secure children's homes (for age range 12 – 16), secure training centres (up to age 17), and young offender institutions (15 – 18). In 2002 the total number of children under 18 in custody, including both sentenced and remanded children, peaked at 3,145. This has reduced dramatically since then, due to adopting policies based on prevention and more flexible community sentencing. As of April 2018 there were 940 under 18s in custody, of which 913 are boys and just 27 were girls, i.e., 97.1% are boys and 2.9% girls (Ministry of Justice, 2018c).

In her 2017/18 Business Plan, the Children's Commissioner for England, Anne Longfield, reported that she, together with Dame Louise Casey, had visited 10 of the children in the secure estate 'to learn about their lives before entering custody and understand the factors that led to them being imprisoned and what, if anything, could have been done to change their trajectory', (Longfield, 2017), page 12. One can have little objection to this, it seems to be exactly what a Children's Commissioner should do. But she picked only girls, despite 97.1% of the children in question being boys, (Longfield, 2018b). An empathy gap, perhaps?

The report 'Fractured Families', (Centre for Social Justice, 2013), stated that 'their extensive research…..showed that 76% of children and young people in custody had an absent father and 33% an absent mother' (page 60). The Prison Reform Trust (2013) quotes the same figures. An earlier report 'Punishing Disadvantage: a profile of children in custody', (Prison Reform Trust, 2010), used a sample of 200 children receiving custodial sentences in 2008 to conclude the following description of the multifaceted disadvantages of this demographic – recalling throughout that children in custody are 97% boys,

- Around half were living in a deprived household or unsuitable accommodation prior to imprisonment (page viii);
- Just under half had run away or absconded at some point in their lives (page viii);
- Two-fifths are known to have been on the child protection register or had experienced abuse or neglect (page viii);
- 31% of boys had the literacy level, and 38% of boys the numeracy level, expected of a seven year old (page 4);
- Around one-quarter of boys and one-half of girls had been in care (page 3).
- 11% had attempted suicide (page 61).

8.3.2 Prisoners' IQ

There is a further disadvantage which receives less attention but should not be hidden: IQ. A decade ago, research by Liverpool University based on a cross section of male and female prisoners in the UK concluded that the average IQ of prisoners was 87, an intelligence which nearly three-quarters of the general public would exceed, (BBC News, 2007). Some 6,000 UK prisoners (about 7%) were estimated to have IQs below 70, some three times the prevalence of such extremely low IQs in the general public. Poor conduct in prison is also found to be worse for lower IQ prisoners. Diamond et al (2012) concluded that, 'individual's IQ, as well as the average IQ of the prison unit, was significantly and negatively related to violent prison misconduct'. In the USA, studies have found that, for chronic adult offenders, the average IQ is 85, one standard deviation below the population mean. A study of Texas inmates who entered the prison system in 2002 indicated that approximately 23% of the inmates scored below 80, an intelligence with a prevalence of only 9.1% in the general public, (Ellis and Walsh, 2003)

Many people will have little patience with what may seem like making excuses for people who have committed heinous crimes. How much intelligence does it take, they might argue, to know that savagely beating someone is wrong? Nevertheless, statistically speaking at least, most people are being incarcerated, in part, for the crime of lacking intelligence.

Harrington and Bailey (2005), page 38, report the IQ level of 301 children and young people in trouble with the law (in custody and in the community) aged between 13 and 18 years old. 36% were found to have a low IQ (70-79) and 23% to have an extremely low IQ (under 70). Note that in the general public, IQs in these ranges would apply for only 6.8% and 2.3% of the population respectively, so 59% of young offenders have an IQ that would have a prevalence in the general public of only 9.1%. Only 15% of the sample had an IQ in the average range (90 – 109), within which half the general population would lie, whilst fewer than 3% had above average intelligence (compared to 25% of the general public). Whilst a fractured family background, and the other disadvantages itemised above, will contribute to the educational failure of imprisoned children (and adults), it would be unwise to ignore the even more intractable issue of intelligence. This will be uncomfortable for some, but the challenge for a decent society is to find a beneficial and fulfilling occupation for everyone, regardless of intrinsic capacities – physical or mental.

8.4 Male Prisoners and Their Families

A Ministry of Justice report, (Williams, Papadopoulou and Booth, 2012), provided the following information on page iii (recalling that 95% of adult prisoners are men),

- 54% of all prisoners reported having children under the age of 18;
- 61% of prisoners reported being single when they entered custody;
- 24% were living with a partner;
- 8% said they were married;
- 74% of prisoners reported being close to their families;
- 63% reported providing, and 73% receiving, emotional support from their families;
- 88% reported wanting their families involved in their lives;
- 40% saw the support of their families as important to preventing them reoffending in future;
- 36% thought that being able to see their children was important to preventing them reoffending in future;

The small proportion of married prisoners compared with the many who have dependent children is noteworthy. The vast majority of prisoners felt they had let their family down by being sent to prison (82%). The Prison Reform Trust (2013), page 5, quoted research indicating that the likelihood of reoffending was 39% higher for prisoners who had not received visits whilst in prison compared to those who had. Unfortunately, despite the evident importance of contact with their families, the report 'Reducing re-offending by ex-prisoners', (Social Exclusion Unit, 2002), notes that over 40% of prisoners lose contact with their families after entering prison.

8.5 Self-Harming in Prison

Women prisoners have a higher incidence of self-harm, short of suicide, than male prisoners. In the year ending March 2016, 31% of female prisoners in England self-harmed, on average 6.7 times each, compared to 11% of male prisoners, an average of 3 times each (Ministry of Justice, 2018d). However, this disguises the scale of the problem with male prisoners. The numerical preponderance of male prisoners means that nearly eight times more male prisoners than female prisoners self-harmed in the year to March 2016 (8,842 men cf 1,170 women). Moreover, whilst the number of female prisoners self-harming has decreased somewhat over the last ten years, the number of men self-harming is rising steeply (Figure 8.14), nearly doubling in ten years.

Similarly, whilst the number of *incidents* of women prisoners self-harming has been decreasing, the number of incidents of male prisoners self-harming is rising steeply (Figure 8.15), doubling in the last seven years. This is a rather different reality to that depicted by Baroness Corston (section 8.1.2.6). The number of incidents of self-harm is roughly double the number of assaults on other prisoners, which in turn is about three times higher than the number of assaults on prison staff (in 2015/16).

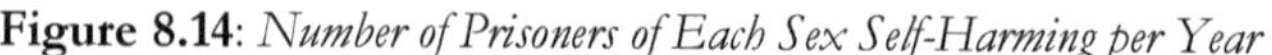

Figure 8.14: *Number of Prisoners of Each Sex Self-Harming per Year*

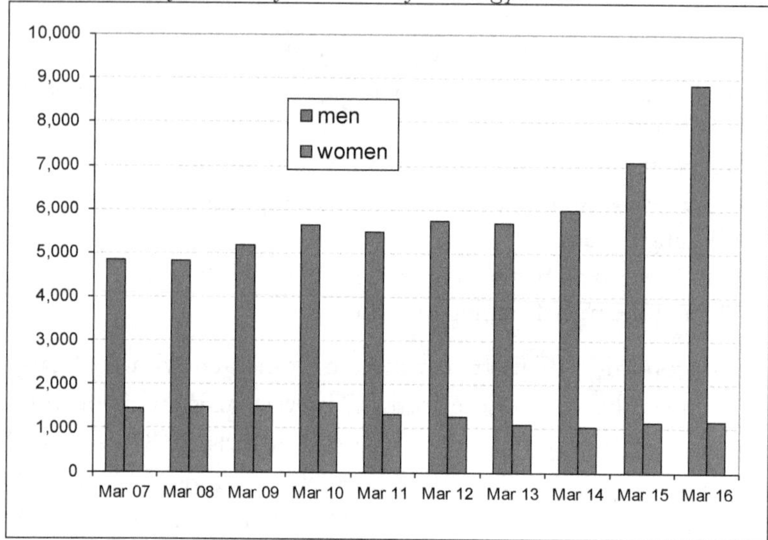

Figure 8.15: *Number of Incidents of Self-Harming in Prisons per Year by Sex*

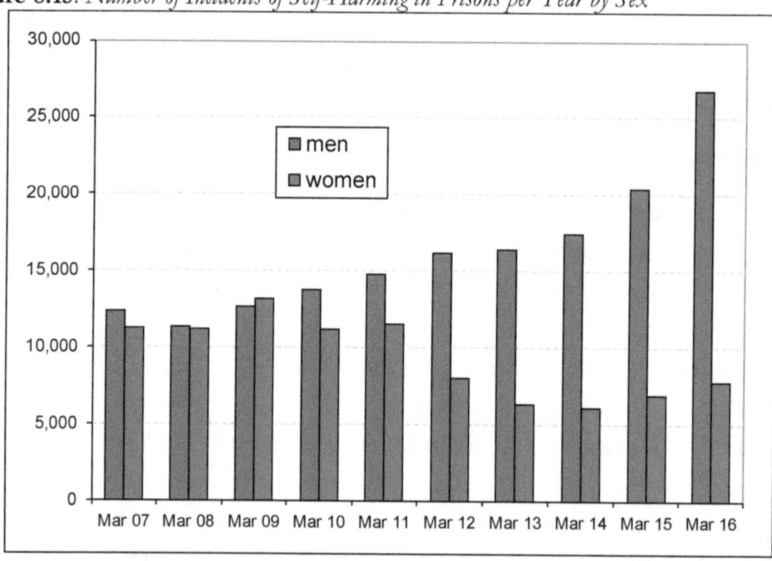

8.6 Deaths in Prison

Data on deaths in prisons in England and Wales have been taken from the charity Inquest (2018). Figure 8.16 shows how the number of deaths of men in prison has varied since 1990, distinguishing between self-inflicted deaths (suicide) and other causes. Figure 8.17 compares the total numbers of deaths of men and women in prison. Self-inflicted and non-self-inflicted deaths are discussed separated below.

8.6.1 Suicide in Prison

The number of suicides in prison fluctuates from year to year. In England and Wales, 2016 was the worst year for men with 108 suicides. 2003 was the worst year for women with 14 suicides. Over the last ten complete years (2008 – 2017) the average number of prisoner suicides in England and Wales was 71 men per year and 3.2 women per year. Over this ten year period the average suicide rate per 1000 prisoners was thus about 0.93 per year for men and about 0.8 per year for women. Hence, the suicide rates for men and women have been similar, but slightly worse for men, but 22 times more men than women have killed themselves in prison.

For both male and female prisoners, the rate of suicide far exceeds that of free individuals. In 2015 the UK-wide average (age adjusted) suicide rates were 0.16 per thousand and 0.05 per thousand for males and females respectively (Samaritans, 2017). Thus, a man in prison is about 19 times more likely to kill himself than a free women (0.93/0.05), and a woman in prison about 16 times more likely. Figure 8.16 indicates an upward trend in male prisoners' suicides. However, the really marked trend is the steep increase in deaths of male prisoners by natural causes (though one hesitates to use the word "natural" in a prison environment).

8.6.2 Deaths in Prison from 'Natural' Causes

Figure 8.17 compares the total deaths of men and women in prison. The contrast is stark. Not only are there far more deaths of men than women, but the former is increasing steeply, mostly due to "natural" causes. In 2017 some 284 men died in prisons in England and Wales, 181 of them from "natural" causes. For women the numbers were 8 and 3 respectively. Since the start of the millennium, the number of deaths of male prisoners from "natural" causes has nearly quadrupled (Figure 8.16).

Figure 8.16: *Deaths of Men in Prison in England and Wales by Cause*

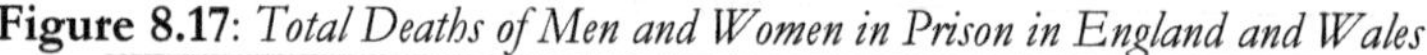

Figure 8.17: *Total Deaths of Men and Women in Prison in England and Wales*

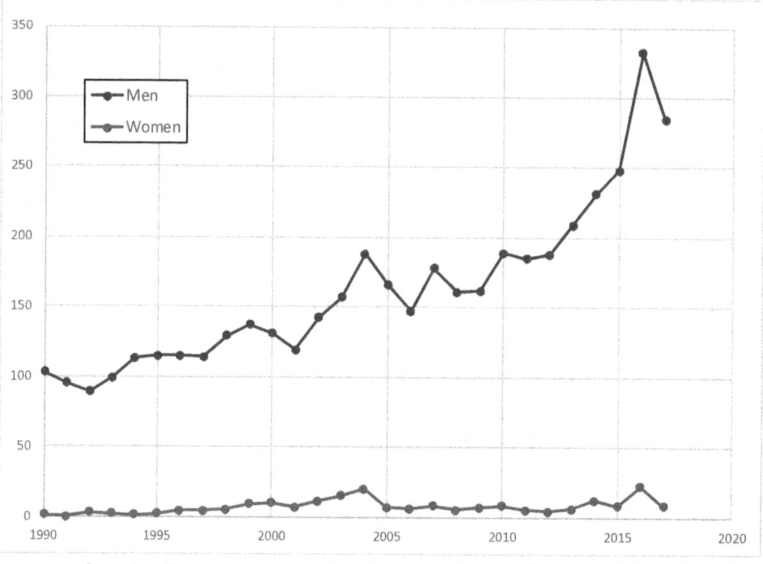

The reason for the huge increase in the number of non-self-inflicted deaths of male prisoners is due to the increased proportion of older male prisoners in gaol. The number of men over 60 in prisons in England and Wales has doubled in the last decade. It has been suggested that convictions for historic sex offences are the major contributor to this ageing male prison population. Increasing numbers of prisoners have mobility problems, using wheelchairs or Zimmer frames. These prisoners can find it impossible to access the exercise yard, or attend classes required for parole purposes. Some stop taking showers for fear of slipping. Some have dementia and no longer know where they are, or why, (Hill, 2017).

8.7 The Empathy Gap in Imprisonment

Imprisonment provides a perfect example of male disposability, gynocentrism and lack of male in-group preference. That men are far more readily incarcerated than women is emphatically clear from the data (male disposability), and a preferred treatment of women is now enshrined in policy at several different levels (gynocentrism). The public would probably agree that everyone should be equal before the law. Yet there is no public outcry, even from men, that this principle is violated in respect of sex (lack of male in-group preference). The hypothesis of male utility is consistent with the prevalence of low IQ prisoners. Men with low IQ will have greater difficulty in fulfilling a societal obligation regarding utility, but this obligation is inapplicable to women.

The traditional gendered psychology regards men as agentic, powerful and responsible, whilst women are regarded in this outmoded view as non-agentic, vulnerable, and in need of protection. If the agentic, powerful and responsible become criminal, clearly they deserve punishment. If the non-agentic, powerless and vulnerable become criminal, then society is more likely to regard a compassionate response, rather than punishment, to be appropriate. Hence, the traditional gendered psychology drives a disparate perspective to male and female offending. This becomes a pernicious, and unjust, phenomenon when the traditional gender norms no longer reflect social or political reality (if they ever did).

Feminists may appeal to "historical power imbalances" to rationalise different treatment of men and women. One may dispute that view of the past. But irrespective of that, the present reality is that women are far from powerless, even in the traditional male domains. In the context of criminal justice this is particularly marked. The Head of State in the UK has been a woman since 1952; our Prime Minister is (at the time of writing) a woman and a self-declared feminist; the Home Secretary has been a woman for 10 of the last 12 years; the head of the largest police force in the UK, the Metropolitan Police, is a woman; and the most senior judge in the land, the President of the Supreme Court, is a woman and an ardent feminist. Until November 2018, the Director of Public Prosecutions had also been a feminist woman for the previous five years. These women are leading a criminal justice system which is sex biased by policy. If any other group with such power were favouring their own, it would be called corruption.

Policy on imprisonment is driven by two themes. On the one hand there is the successful lobbying for a more lenient, compassionate, approach for women – driven by gynocentrism. On the other hand, there is the unwavering political necessity to be seen to be "tough on crime". If leniency is the policy for women, on whom is the policy of toughness to be enacted? In June 2018 the Government announced the new policy to avoid sending women to prison wherever possible (UK Government, 2018h), whilst simultaneously planning to expand the country's capacity to imprison men (Ford, 2018). Here we see the two strands of policy made explicit: compassion for women, punishment for men.

The entitlement of women to different treatment, in order to be "equal", is argued, at different times, on the following grounds. Firstly, that of historical power imbalance. A debate about past realities can be avoided. It is morally illiterate to claim present benefit based on injustice to someone else in history. Secondly, it is argued on the basis that women remain endemically disadvantaged in society generally. But this is a perspective which the entirety of this book challenges. In any case, injustice is not neutralised by more injustice. The third argument which is deployed is that women are currently treated more harshly by the criminal justice system, e.g., (Corston, 2016). This chapter has, I think, demolished this untruth. A fourth argument which is used is that women offenders have a background of being abused, by men, and that their offending is, in truth, at the behest of, or caused by, men. MP David Lammy tells us that 'Most Women in Prison Are There Because of a Man', (Wearmouth, 2019). This is a denial of female agency, stemming with painful obviousness from traditional gender norms. There is nothing progressive about it. This argument also raises the issue of the disadvantaged background of female offenders. But the demographic and personal characteristics of offenders are the same for men and women. Finally, it may simply be claimed that equal treatment is harsher for women and therefore unequal, (Corston, 2007). In truth, all these arguments are attempts to rationalise a deep seated bias, a prejudice, whose origin is gynocentrism and male disposability and their result: the empathy gap.

9

Violence and Abuse

Social scientists are often motivated by an ideologically based view of their subject that makes it hard for them to think beyond a narrow range of acceptable theoretical stances. This is particularly apparent in research on violence between intimate partners.
Louise Dixon, John Archer, Nicola Graham-Kevan (2012)

There are as many violent women as men, but there's a lot of money in hating men, particularly in the United States - millions of dollars. It isn't a politically good idea to threaten the huge budgets for women's refuges by saying that some of the women who go into them aren't total victims.
Erin Pizzey

During all the years that I specialised in working with violent women and their children, I could never come to terms with the fear men had of violent women.
Erin Pizzey, *Women or Men, Who Are the Victims?* (2000)

In this chapter the statistics on violent offences are reviewed, firstly looking at the overall data and then focusing on domestic violence and domestic abuse offences. The emphasis is on the breakdown by sex of the victims of violent crime. However, it would be misleading not to address also the sex of the perpetrators of violence. The chapter delves quite deeply into domestic abuse because this is such a major concern of women's advocates, and also because it features so prominently in the Family Courts. In the case of domestic abuse it is not only the statistics of offending which are of interest, but also the issue of service provision to victims and how this differs for the two sexes. A similar skew will be seen, in reverse, as regards provision of programmes assisting perpetrators to amend their ways. We will see that violence and abuse is perceived very differently according to the sex of the perpetrator and the sex of the victim. Sexual offences are not considered in this chapter (see chapters 19 and 20). Data in this chapter will be for England and Wales unless otherwise stated.

9.1 All Violence

9.1.1 Victims

In the last chapter we saw that the crime surveys for England and Wales indicate that the totality of crime has been falling since 1995 (Figure 8.3). The same is true when attention is restricted to violent crimes, see Figure 9.1, data taken from (Office for National Statistics, 2018x). In addition to these data from the Crime Survey for England and Wales (CSEW), the same source also provides data for police recorded crimes. These are also plotted on Figure 9.1.

Figure 9.1: *Violence Against the Person Offences, Comparing Police Recorded Incidents with CSEW Data, 1981-2018 (year ending March of that year)*

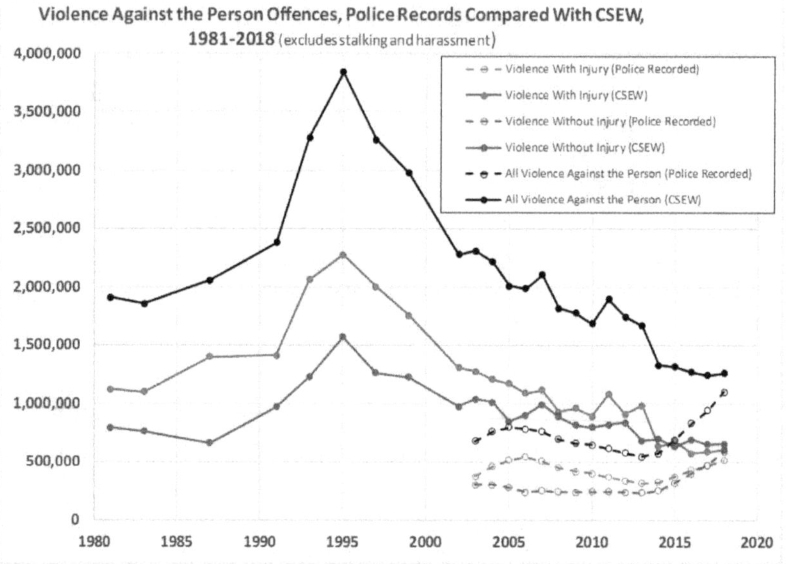

It is generally believed that the CSEW provides a better picture of crime prevalence than police records, due to variability and incompleteness in police recording – at least until very recently. The ONS Notes which accompany this dataset caution,

> 'The National Crime Recording Standard (NCRS) was introduced in April 2002, although some forces adopted NCRS practices before the standard was formally introduced. Figures before and after that date are not directly comparable. The introduction of NCRS led to a rise in recording in year ending March 2003 and, particularly for violent crime, in the following years as forces continued to improve compliance with the new standard.'

This may explain why the police records of violent crime shown in Figure 9.1 lie substantially below the CSEW estimates, until 2018. The ONS also note, (Office for National Statistics, 2018y),

> 'CSEW is the best measure of trends in the most common types of violence. For the offences that it covers, the CSEW provides the best measure of trends for the population. It has used a consistent methodology since the survey began in 1981.'

However, it now appears that the police data and the CSEW have converged to close agreement. It is worth emphasizing that the police recorded data prior to 2018 were probably underestimates. Thus, whilst Figure 9.1 shows that police records of violent crime have increased over the last 4 or 5 years, this may not be a genuine increase in the underlying rate of such crimes as the CSEW shows no such increase.

Figure 9.2: *Percentage of Adults Aged 16 or Over who were Victims of Violent Crime in the Indicated Year (CSEW data)*

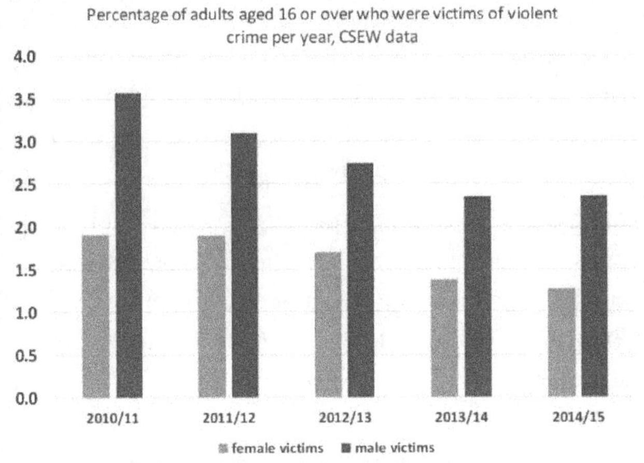

Figure 9.3: *Percentage of Adult Victims of Violence by Perpetrator Type*

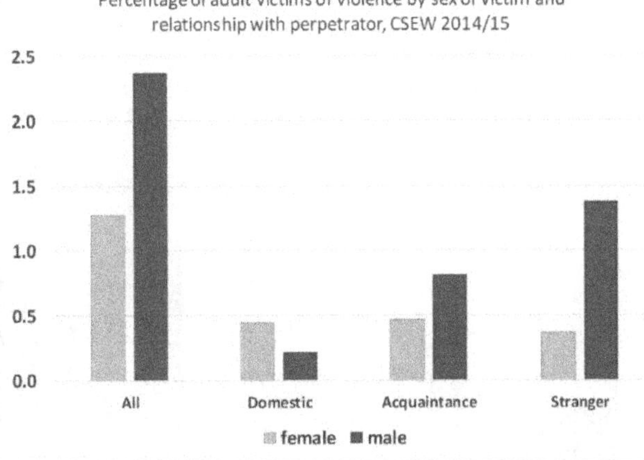

Based on the CSEW, violent crimes in 2018 have fallen to about one-third of their peak prevalence in 1995. (In contrast, the reader may wish to glance back at the increase in the prison population over that period, Figures 8.1 and 8.2). Figure 9.2 indicates the percentage of adults aged 16 or over who were victims of violent crime in each of the years 2010 to 2015, (Ministry of Justice, 2016b). Men are the victims of violent crime just under twice as frequently as women. Figure 9.3 breaks down adult victims of violence by three classifications of perpetrator: domestic, acquaintance or stranger. Women are about twice as often the victims of domestic violence (considered in more detail in the next section) but men are more often the victims of acquaintance or stranger violence, especially the latter, and these categories of perpetrator are more common.

The most serious crime is homicide. Figure 9.4 shows the number of victims of homicide by sex for years 1997 to 2017, (Office for National Statistics, 2018z). More than twice as many men are the victims of homicide as women (71% cf 29% in 2017). Homicides of men (but not of women) have increased over the period 2015 to 2018, though they are still below the rate prior to 2009. Figure 9.5, based on police recorded crime data, shows that this recent upward trend is shared by the other serious crime categories "attempted murder" and "causing death or serious injury by driving", (Office for National Statistics, 2018aa). Figure 9.5 gives homicide data both from the official Homicide Index and also from police records. The two can differ. Police recorded crime data on homicide represent the recording decision of the police based on the available information at the time the offence comes to their attention. Homicide Index data take account of the charging decision and the court outcome in cases that have gone to trial.

Figure 9.4: *Homicides in England and Wales, 1997 - 2017*

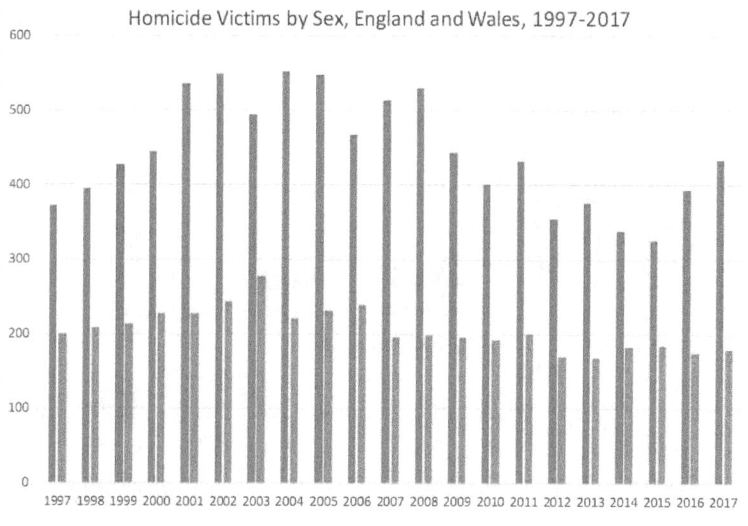

Figure 9.5: *Number of Police Recorded Serious Crimes, 2002-2018*

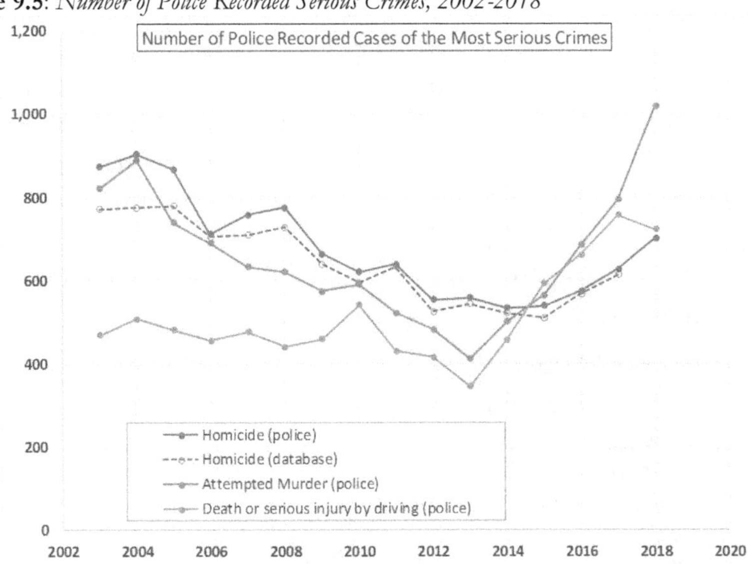

The data for homicides and attempted murders plotted in Figures 9.4 and 9.5 have been adjusted by subtracting certain exceptional homicides. These were, (i) in year 2002/3, 172 homicides attributed to Harold Shipman in previous years but coming to light in the official inquiry in 2002; (ii) in year 2005/6, 52 homicide victims of the 7th July 2005 London bombings, plus an estimated 230 attempted murders; (iii) in year 2016/17, 96 victims of the 15th April 1989 Hillsborough stadium fire, which were classified as unlawful killings at the inquest in 2016; (iv) in year 2017/18, 35 homicide victims of the Manchester Arena bombing together with the London Bridge/Borough Market and Westminster attacks. These attacks, combined with the terrorist-related incident at Parsons Green Underground station in September 2017, also accounted for about 337 attempted murders. All those figures have been subtracted from the raw data before plotting Figures 9.4 and 9.5.

The upturn in the number of the most serious crimes in the period 2013-2018, as shown in Figure 9.5, would appear to be genuine, rather than data collection inaccuracies – particularly in the case of homicides which is largely a matter of counting bodies. This is despite the continuing fall in violent crimes overall (Figure 9.1). Note, however, that the volume of the most serious crimes in Figure 9.5 is extremely small compared to the total violent crimes, Figure 9.1. And, despite recent rises, homicide rates remain below their peak rates in 2001 to 2009.

During 2018 and 2019 there has been much press attention to rising violent crime levels in London, particularly knife crimes, Figure 9.6. The volume of knife crime has indeed been rising in London, as it has in England and Wales as a whole. In the year ending September 2018, the rate of knife crime in London was 1.68 per 1000 population, compared with less that half that rate in England and Wales as a whole, 0.73 per 1000, (Office for National Statistics, 2018ab). The greatest incidence of knife crime outside London, at a rate of 1.1 to 1.2 per 1000, was in Greater Manchester, West Yorkshire and the West Midlands.

Figure 9.6: *Trend in Knife Crime, England and Wales, 2011 to 2018*

The same source indicates that, in the year ending September 2018, the homicide rate in London, at 16 per million, was higher than in England and Wales as a whole, but not dramatically so (13 per million), and was substantially lower than in the worst regions, namely Greater Manchester where the homicide rate was 29 per million. The second highest homicide rates in that year were in Sussex and Cleveland (21 per million), but low statistics will mean that this will vary from year to year. The increased number of homicides in England between 2016/17 and 2017/18 can be accounted for by the increases in London and Greater Manchester alone. The high level of homicides and knife crimes in these cities, and in West Yorkshire and the West Midlands, is likely to be demographic related, but exploration of that issue is beyond the scope of this book. (The nominal knife crime rate and homicide rate in the City of London are extremely high, but this is an artefact of the small number of people living there compared with the very large number of people working in, or visiting, the City. For example, the homicide rate was notionally 130 per million, but that corresponds to just one homicide!).

In summary, whilst there are some localised increases in some of the most serious violent crimes, the overall picture is of falling violent crime (Figure 9.1) and men account for roughly twice as many victims of violent crime as women (Figures 9.2, 9.3 and 9.4). This greater victimisation of men is particular to violent crime. When other crime is considered, there is little difference in the victimisation of men and women, Figure 9.7. In the umbrella category of "personal crime", men are again the majority of victims, but only by 26%, (Office for National Statistics, 2018ac).

Figure 9.7: *Adult Victims of All Crime and Personal Crime by Sex and Age (2018)*

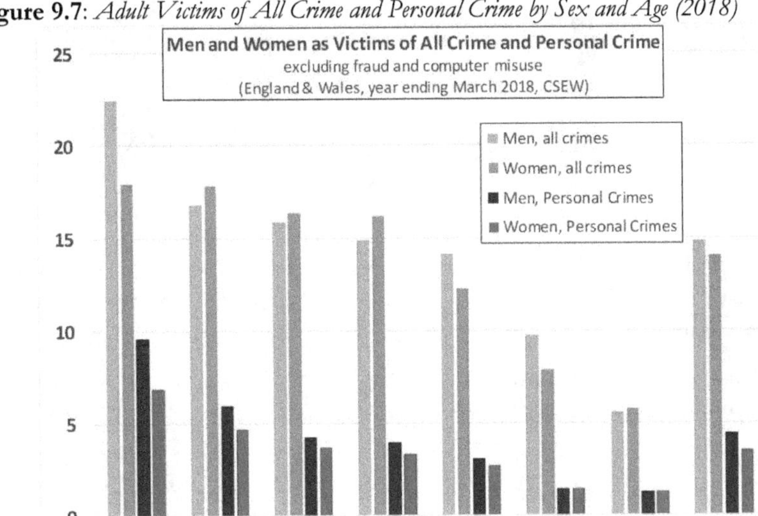

As children, the excess victimisation of males over females is especially marked, and now applies for all crime and non-violent crime and well as for violent crime, see Figure 9.8, (Office for National Statistics, 2018ad). The number of boys aged 10 to 15 who are victims exceeds the number of girls as follows: for violent offences by 93%; for robbery by 350%; for theft by 69%; and for all crime by 67%.

9.1.2 Perpetrators

In years 2007 to 2017, between 6.3 and 8.2 times more males than females were sentenced for violence against the person offences, (Office for National Statistics, 2018ae). For example, in 2017 there were 24,754 males and 3,088 females convicted and sentenced for violence against the person (VAP) offences in England and Wales. In 2014, and restricting to the adult age range, these figures were 18,145 men and 2,160 women sentenced for VAP offences.

Figure 9.8: *Percentage of Children Aged 10 to 15 as Victims of Crime, 2018*

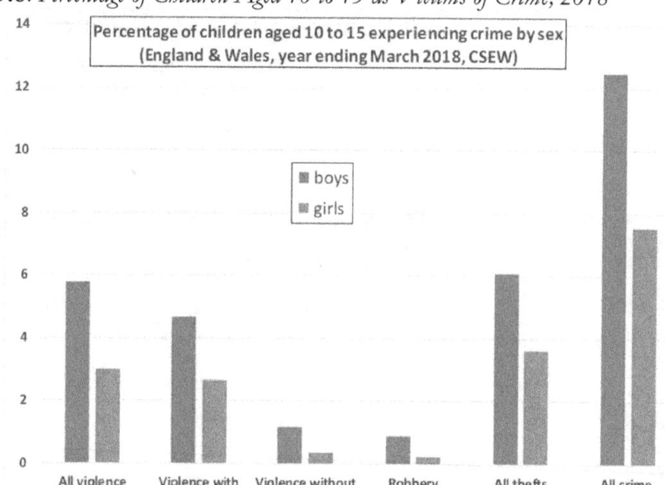

A slightly different picture emerges if MOJ reoffender statistics are used, (Ministry of Justice, 2016c). These data define "offender" as including, not just people who are convicted and sentenced in court, but also people accepting a caution, reprimand or warning. These data indicate the number of male VAP offenders in England and Wales in 2014 was 18,757, not much greater than the above sentencing figure. In contrast, the number of female VAP offenders in 2014 was 4,296, substantially larger than the number sentenced, implying that a much larger proportion of female VAP offenders receive a caution, warning or reprimand, rather than a court appearance. On this basis, the ratio of male to female VAP offenders was 4.4 in 2014.

A crude estimate of the percentage of men who commit a VAP offence at some time in their lives can be made using the 2014 reoffender data, (Ministry of Justice, 2016c). Of the 18,757 male offenders, 4,319 were reoffenders (the average number of reoffences for these recidivists was 2.78). Accounting for this, the number of first-time male VAP offenders in 2014 was 14,438. Multiplying this by a nominal average adult lifetime (say 79 – 16 = 63), and dividing by 2 to account for half of the offenders having died, gives about 450,000 men still living who have committed a VAP offence at some time in their life. This estimate is very crude because it fails to account for the varying rate of offending, which was greatest in 1995. Dividing by the adult male population of England and Wales of about 23 million suggests that about 2.0% of men in England and Wales have, at some time in their lives, committed a VAP offence. Around 77% of these will have committed only one such offence in their life. Thus, about 0.5% of men are repeat VAP offenders.

Carrying out an estimate on the same basis for female offenders (4,038 first-time VAP convictions in 2014) suggests that about 130,000 women in England and Wales have committed a VAP offence (0.55%).

9.2 Violence and Abuse Within the Home: Men as Victims

Violence within the home presents a very different gender distribution from violence outside the home. Compared to outside the home, within the home women are a larger proportion of both victims and perpetrators. There is a great weight of empirical evidence that the incidence of domestic abuse suffered by men is comparable to that suffered by women. Researchers have been reporting for over 40 years that domestic abuse (DA) of men is not rare, for example (Steinmetz, 1977) and the many early studies by Murray Straus, the history of which has been accessibly summarised by Linda Kelly (2003). And yet the narrative to which the public is exposed paints a very different picture, one in which domestic violence, or other domestic abuse, overwhelmingly involves female victims and male perpetrators.

There has been dispute within the academic literature for decades regarding the relative significance of domestic abuse against men and women, for example the rather highly charged rebuttal of Steinmetz by Straton (1994). There are too many academic exchanges to be summarised here, but the reference trail can be picked up from (Bates, Graham-Kevan and Archer, 2014) or (Bates, 2016).

The general public do not read the academic literature. Their views tend to be shaped by the media, which in turn is influenced on this topic by the women's refuge charities. This lobby, together with all governmental and international agencies, present a perspective on domestic abuse as a gendered crime, perpetrated overwhelmingly by men against women. For example, Women's Aid (2018a) informs us that 'in the vast majority of cases it (domestic abuse) is experienced by women and is perpetrated by men'. Similarly, Sandra Horley (2014), CEO of Refuge, said, 'the vast majority of domestic violence is perpetrated by men against women'. The same view is echoed by UNICEF (2006), as follows: 'although men are sometimes victims, the vast majority are women'. These claims regarding the "vast majority" of victims will be examined against the best available data in this chapter.

It is important to recognise that this gendered perspective on domestic abuse – including the claim that male victims are relatively rare – is a cornerstone of the dominant prevailing theory of gender, feminism. For example, Sandra Horley (2018) writes, 'domestic abuse needs to be considered within a broader context of VAWG (violence against women and girls), recognising the root causes as male power and control, gender inequality and discrimination against women'. Similarly, Women's Aid (2018b) state their belief as,

> 'Women are the overwhelming majority of victims of domestic abuse. Domestic abuse is a violation of women and their children's human rights. It is the result of an abuse of power and control, and is rooted in the historical status and inequality of women in society.'

(Refuge, 2018) states,

> 'Inequality between the sexes means that men have more power than women – inevitably some men abuse or exploit that power.'

And Women's Aid (2018a) again,

> 'Domestic abuse is a gendered crime which is deeply rooted in the societal inequality between women and men. It takes place "because she is a woman and happens disproportionately to women."'

The last quote also explains the usage of the term "gendered" in this context. Clearly, there is no room within this perspective for widespread domestic abuse of men, since the perspective itself denies it explicitly: domestic abuse, it is claimed, 'takes place because she is a woman, and is rooted in the inequality of women'. This perception of domestic abuse rests upon both universal female victimhood and also universal male culpability. Vera Baird, former Solicitor General for England and Wales and currently Northumbria Police and Crime Commissioner, expressed it thus,

> 'it was essentially the Refuge Movement that first counted the figures and demonstrated that domestic violence was not something that was done by a few cruel and unusual men', (Baird, 2011).

In other words, Baird claims that domestic violence towards women is a generic trait of men. In this she aligns with the dominant narrative on gender. A theory of gender which requires this interpretation is therefore refuted if the empirical evidence shows widespread domestic abuse of men. There will therefore be resistance to accepting such empirical evidence by proponents of the feminist patriarchal 'power and control' theory. Kelly (2003) expresses this viewpoint thus,

> 'Domestic violence can more broadly be described as the male "way of doing power".....Domestic violence is not viewed as just another tool used by men in the subordination of women. Rather, it is considered "one of the most brutal and explicit expressions of patriarchical domination." Such strong roots in patriarchy have produced an equally strong force against accepting female violence..... Despite the wealth and diversity of the sociological research and the consistency of the findings, female violence is not recognized within the extensive legal literature on domestic violence. Instead, the literature consistently suggests that only men commit domestic violence. Either explicitly, or more often implicitly, through the failure to address the subject in any objective manner, female violence is denied, defended and minimized.'

Kelly opines that a successful challenge to the patriarchal understanding of domestic violence would therefore fatally undermine the prevailing dominant discourse on gender (feminism). Male victimisation is therefore vigorously refuted by adherents of the dominant narrative.

It is often presumed that domestic violence was 'discovered' in the early 1970s with the opening of the world's first refuge for battered women in Chiswick, London, (Pizzey, 2011). In truth there was an attitude at that time that what went on between man and wife behind closed doors was their own affair. But that does not mean that domestic violence was entirely ignored and unpunished, even much earlier. Actually, tough measures, including flogging, were enacted by Parliament in the early Victorian era against men who beat their wives, including the 'Prevention and Punishment of Aggravated Assaults on Women Act', (Hansard, Aggravated Assaults Bill, 1853). Centuries earlier still, in the Elizabethan period, domestic disputes and violence were a considerable proportion of indictments for violence brought before Courts, (George, 2002). Nevertheless, it is certainly the case that there has been an immeasurably greater focus on domestic abuse since Erin Pizzey's work in the 1970s.

9.2.1 Incidence of Male Victims: Survey Data

The best source of data on the incidence of domestic abuse in England and Wales is the CSEW (Crime Survey for England and Wales). As the name implies, these data are obtained from surveys, not recorded police data or logged crimes. Except where otherwise indicated, the data below relates to the CSEW for the year ending March 2017 and has been taken from the dataset 'Domestic abuse in England and Wales - Bulletin tables' as well as the companion dataset 'Domestic abuse in England and Wales - Appendix tables', (Office for National Statistics, 2017p).

When interpreting the domestic abuse data from these surveys it is important to appreciate the questions asked which elicit positive responses recorded in the surveys. There are different sets of questions for domestic abuse, partner abuse, sexual abuse and stalking. Domestic abuse may be carried out by any family member upon any other family member, whereas "partner abuse" refers to intimate partners. "Family abuse" refers to domestic abuse excluding partner abuse. Partner abuse includes abuse by former partners. They may be former partners at the time of the abuse. There is no requirement that the partner is cohabiting with the victim, nor even that they have ever cohabited. An example of the type of questions asked is illustrated for partner abuse in Table 9.1.

Table 9.1: *Example of a Survey Question in the CSEW: "Indicate whether, in the last year, your partner or ex-partner"...*

- Prevented you from having your fair share of the household money
- Stopped you from seeing friends and relatives
- Repeatedly belittled you to the extent that you felt worthless
- Frightened you, by threatening to hurt you or someone close to you
- Pushed you, held you down or slapped you
- Kicked, bit, or hit you with a fist or something else, or threw something at you
- Choked or tried to strangle you
- Threatened you with a weapon, for example a stick or a knife
- Threatened to kill you
- Used a weapon against you, for example a stick or a knife
- Used some other kind of force against you
- None of these
- Have never had a partner / been in a relationship
- Don't know/can't remember
- Don't wish to answer

Not all the categories relate to physical violence, and there is a wide range of severities. The survey relates to people from age 16 to 59. Respondents are asked about incidents both in the last year and over life. In the data below, the "last year" refers to April 2016 to March 2017.

- 7.5% of women and 4.3% of men reported domestic abuse in the last year;
- 5.9% of women and 3.0% of men reported partner abuse in the last year;
- 2.0% of women and 1.6% of men reported family abuse in the last year;

- From the above, rather more than 1 in 3 victims of domestic abuse or partner abuse are men;
- 20% of incidents of violence against the person against men were domestic violence;
- At least 13.4% of victims in prosecutions for domestic abuse were men (17% of those where sex was stated);
- 8.2% of defendants in prosecutions for domestic abuse were women;
- Police reported prevalence of domestic abuse is 0.8% (average over England and Wales);
- Domestic abuse prevalence estimates from the CSEW have reduced by 33% between 2004/5 and 2016/17, contrary to the impression one often gets from the media. Thus, the CSEW indicates that domestic abuse is now at about one-fifth its peak incident rate in 1994 (see Figure 9.9);
- Only 5% of clients using IDVA (independent domestic violence advisor) services were male.

Figure 9.9: *The Reducing Number of Incidents of Domestic Abuse (1981 – 2018, CSEW) (Office for National Statistics, 2019b)*

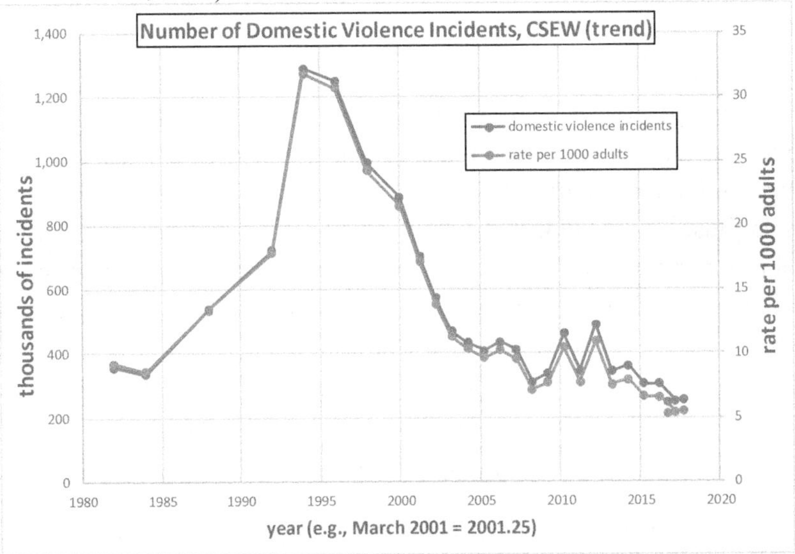

For the first time, the 2017 CSEW on domestic abuse includes extensive data provided by Women's Aid and Safelives, which are organisations with self-declared partisan positions on the nature of domestic abuse – see section 9.2. Although such data is not flagged as "National Statistics" most readers will interpret its presence in an ONS report as indicating some degree of official approval. Also for the first time, the 2017 CSEW uses the term "femicide", a term created by the feminist lobby to distinguish it from "homicide". The reason for distinguishing killing of females from killing of males by using a distinct term has not been explained. One might surmise that it is to facilitate a perspective, and perhaps ultimately a legal recognition, that femicide is more heinous than the mere killing of males.

9.2.2 Severe Force

The CSEW used to report the incidence of the most severe type of physical violence under a category "severe force". For male victims, between 2009/10 and 2012/13 the incidence of "severe force" increased from 0.8% to 1.0%, whilst for women it decreased from 1.5% to 1.1% (relating to incidence in the last year). Thus, incidence in the severe force category had become essentially equal for the two sexes by 2012/13. Incidence in this category has not been reported by the CSEW since. However, Mankind Initiative (2017) identify that,

> 'Of those that suffered from partner abuse in 14/15, 29% of men and 23% of women suffered a physical injury, a higher proportion of men suffering severe bruising or bleeding (6%) and internal injuries or broken bones/teeth (2%) than women (4% and 1% respectively). Only 27% of men sought medical advice whilst 73% of women did.'

In the year ending March 2018, a larger proportion of partner abuse against men was physical force (46%) than was the case for women victims (28%), (Office for National Statistics, 2018af). To put this in context, the majority of partner abuse victims (74.5%) did not sustain a physical injury as a result of the abuse, and for those that did sustain an injury, these were often relatively minor injuries. However, emotional/psychological effects of abuse may be severe. The same source reveals that 11.0% of men and 7.2% of women who reported partner abuse tried to kill themselves as a result of the abuse experienced in the last year (for adults aged 16 to 59 years).

9.2.3 Demographic Dependence of DA

The risk of domestic violence decreases with age. Teenage men are about three times more likely to suffer domestic abuse as men over 55. Teenage women are about twice as likely as women over 55 to suffer domestic abuse. Some DA support web sites will state that anyone can be a victim of domestic abuse, whether wealthy or poor. Whilst strictly true, this obscures a marked dependence of incidence upon socioeconomic class. In 2007, the published data suggested that where household income was greater than £40,000 a woman's risk of suffering domestic abuse was about one-third that for households with an income of less than £10,000. For men, the risk would be halved in the higher earning demographic, (Home Office Statistical Bulletin, 2009). The latest data indicates an even more marked effect of socioeconomic class. Where household income was greater than £50,000 a woman's risk of suffering domestic abuse was little more than one-fifth that for households with an income of less than £10,000. For men, the risk was about one-third in the higher earning demographic, (Office for National Statistics, 2018af).

9.2.4 Domestic Violence and Marital Status

An issue which is rarely brought out in discussions on DA statistics is that the overwhelming bulk of the survey respondents reporting DA are not married. Recall that partner abuse can relate to an ex-partner, and there is no requirement for cohabitation, either at the time of the incident or any other time. Of adult women reporting domestic abuse in the survey, only 5% were married. For men the corresponding figure is 7%. For both sexes, domestic abuse is most common for those who are divorced or separated, followed by single people. Married people have the lowest incidence of domestic violence for both sexes, see Figure 9.10, based on (Office for National Statistics, 2017u)

Figure 9.10: *Domestic Abuse by Marital Status (2016 CSEW)*

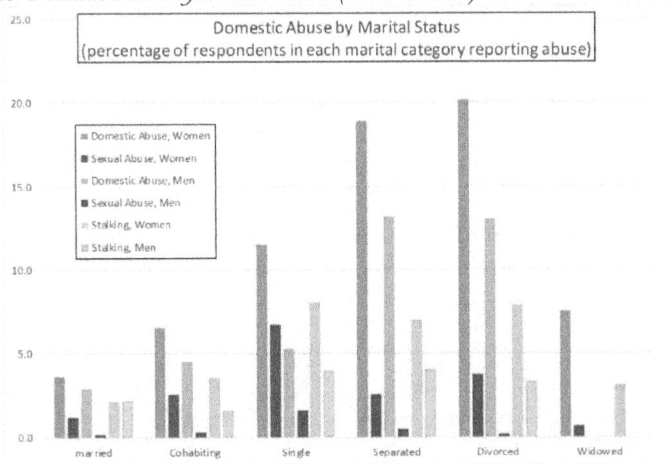

The peak in domestic abuse for those divorced or separated raises an obvious question: are they causally connected? If so, does the separation precipitate the abuse, or vice-versa? The CSEW does not enlighten us on this point. However it seems more likely that the separation precipitates the abuse rather than the reverse, because otherwise it is hard to understand why the incidence is not greater in the married/cohabiting categories. Another question which arises in this context is whether the abuse relates to the ex-partner or a new partner.

9.2.5. Repeated Domestic Abuse

Women's Aid (2018a) declare that, 'women are more likely than men to experience multiple incidents of abuse'. However, Figure 9.11 plots the data on repeat incidents of partner abuse from (Office for National Statistics, 2016b) and shows that there is very little difference between the sexes, except for a slight difference in the "more than 50 times" category, which is rare for both sexes. (Note that about two-thirds of survey respondents either declined to answer this question or replied "don't know". The data in Figure 9.10 has been renormalised to total 100%). Taking repeat incidents into account, men are the victims in about one-in-four incidents (as contrasted with being about one-in-three victims).

Figure 9.11: *Repeat incidents of partner abuse by sex of victim (2015 CSEW)*

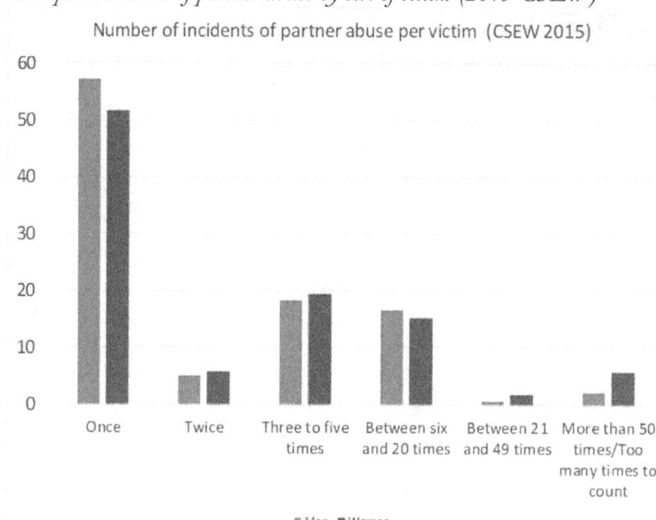

9.2.6 Reports to Police, Prosecutions and Convictions

Figure 6 of the 2017 CSEW Bulletin Tables indicates that 24% of all domestic abuse offences recorded by the police in England and Wales in 2016/17 were against male victims (hence 76% against female victims). The same percentages apply when confined to the "violence against the person" sub-category of domestic abuse. However, a very different gender split is found in prosecutions for domestic abuse. Table 24 of the 2017 CSEW Appendix

Tables indicates that 91.7% of defendants in such cases are men, and only 8.2% are women. The sex of the victims is not always recorded, but where it is recorded 17% of victims are men and 83% women. The 2018 Violence Against Women and Girls Report indicates very similar data: defendants 92.1% men, 7.9% women; victims 16.5% men, 83.5% women, (Crown Prosecution Service, 2018). The variation in these statistics since 2010 is shown in Figure 9.12.

The reason for the greater attrition of cases against male victims is unknown. It might reflect perceived severity of the offence (perceived, that is, by the police or prosecuting authorities), or it might reflect the judged likelihood of gaining a conviction. In either case it seems likely that such judgments are influenced by gender bias in the perception of the seriousness of violence perpetrated by men or by women, and also the gender bias in the perception of the harm of violence to male or female victims.

Figure 9.12: *Defendants and Victims in Prosecutions for Domestic Abuse*

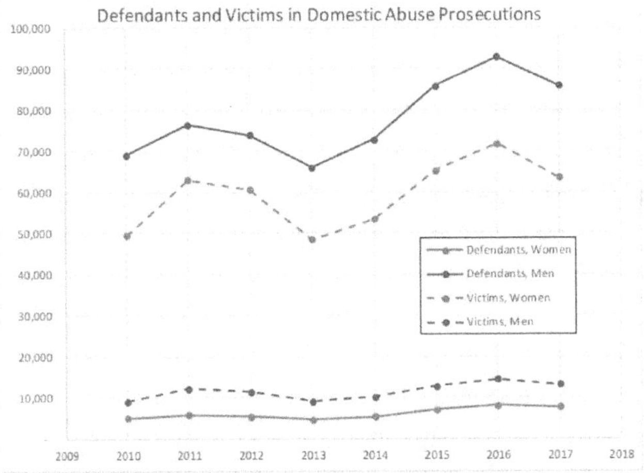

9.2.7 Domestic Homicides

Figure 9.13 plots the number of homicides in England and Wales by the sex of the victim, showing separately the data for different relationships with the perpetrator, using data taken from (Office for National Statistics, 2017v). In round terms, there are about twice as many female victims of domestic homicide as male victims of domestic homicide. In contrast, for homicide committed by acquaintances or by strangers, male victims are 5 or 6 times more numerous than female victims. Overall, in 2016, men accounted for 69% of all homicide victims, but 34% of domestic homicide victims. Note that the latter is consistent with the CSEW evidence on the relative prevalence of domestic abuse of male victims (i.e., one-in-three).

Figure 9.13: *Number of Homicides in England and Wales by Sex of Victim and Relationship with the Perpetrator (Office for National Statistics, 2017v)*

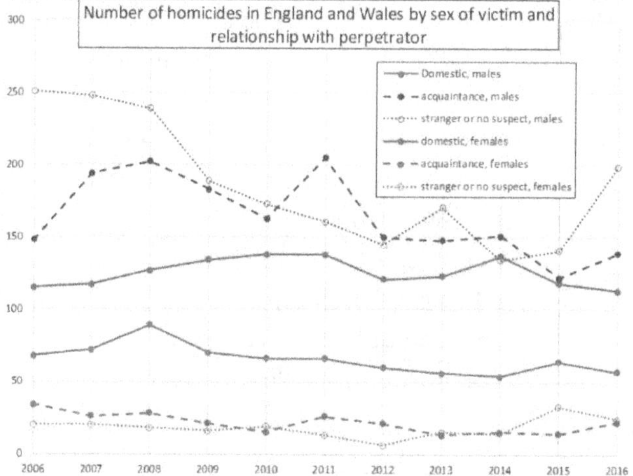

If attention is confined to homicides committed by partners or ex-partners, in 2015/16 there were 77 female victims and 28 male victims. It is sometimes stated that two women per week are killed by their partner or ex-partner in England and Wales (Women's Aid, 2018c). In recent years it would be more accurate to state that two *people* per week are killed by their partner or ex-partner, of which around one-quarter are men.

Perpetrators of partner homicides do not form a representative cross-section of the public. Bridger et al (2017) reviewed 188 cases of intimate partner homicide recorded in England and Wales between April 2011 and March 2013. The dataset contained 162 (86%) female and 26 (14%) male victims. These figures are reversed for perpetrators as all the relationships were heterosexual in nature. The perpetrators were 46% unemployed, 58% non-earning, and 29% employed in unskilled work. Hence, partner homicides are extremely skewed to the lowest socioeconomic groups.

Gender issues in relation to the homicide of children are less often discussed. In particular, data on the sex of perpetrators of child killing in the UK are difficult to obtain, not being specified in ONS datasets (though some information is available from Crown Prosecution Service reports, see section 9.3). This is odd in view of the prominence given to the sex of partner killers and the sex of perpetrators of homicide generally. Table 3 of the domestic abuse dataset, (Office for National Statistics, 2018c), gives a breakdown of the suspected perpetrators of domestic homicides. But this Table is grossly misleading as regards the cases where the perpetrator is a parent (i.e., the victim is their son or daughter), because the Table is restricted to adult victims,16 years or older, not children. Some data on the sex of perpetrators of child killing was obtained via a Freedom of Information enquiry to the Home Office (2018). The number of homicides of children under 16 per year by a parent, averaged over the 20 years 1998 to 2017, was 21 perpetrated by fathers and 11 perpetrated by mothers. However, there are some difficulties with this dataset. Firstly, as will be seen below, around 20% of child killings involve both parents, and it is not clear how this has been addressed. (If the homicide has been assigned to the father in such cases, then the killings by mothers and fathers would actually be much closer to parity). Also, cases where the suspect has committed suicide or died before trial have been assumed guilty. There are also issues related to the completeness of the homicide statistics in relation to infanticide and death through neglect, co-sleeping, etc., as discussed further below.

The following data is taken from (Office for National Statistics, 2016c) and (Office for National Statistics, 2018f). Table 9.2 gives the number of homicides of children and young adults by sex of the victim. These data have been averaged over a range of years to smooth the data because the statistics are small. There is a slightly greater number of boys than girls who are victims of homicide at all ages. This excess of male homicide victims becomes emphatic in the teenage years, and even more so in the early twenties.

Table 9.2 relates to all homicides. Between 2006 and 2017 an average of 62% of homicides of children under 16 in the UK were carried out by a parent or both parents (although there are signs in the last year of data that this proportion may be falling to less than half). A similar percentage (59.7%) is indicated across a range of countries, (Stockl et al, 2017).

Table 9.2: *Number of homicides per year of children and young adults by sex of victim, England and Wales*

Age range	Averaged over years	male	female
Under 1	2006-2017	10	8
1 - 4	2006-2017	9	8
5 - 15	2006-2017	12	7
15 - 19	2012-2015	29	7
16 - 24	2006-2017	90	24

The excess of fatalities of boys over girls is reflected in data from the USA, (NCANDS, 2016), which reports that, 'boys had a slightly higher child fatality rate than girls at 2.87 boys per 100,000 boys in the population compared with 2.11 girls per 100,000 girls in the population'. The same source informs us that, 'nearly three-quarters of child fatalities were attributed to neglect only or a combination of neglect and another maltreatment type'. In contrast, more than half of child fatalities involved no element of physical abuse. Neglect, in other words, is the principal child killer rather than violence (at least in the US).

Per year of age range, the homicide rate of children over one year old is substantially less than that for adults of pre-retirement age, see Figure 9.14. In sharp contrast, however, infants under one year old suffer by far the greatest homicide rate. US data confirm this same, very emphatic, pattern of high infant homicide rates (Figure 9.15). The greater prevalence of homicide of infants is of significance when considering the sex of perpetrators. In English law, infanticide is defined as the killing of a child under one year old by the child's mother. The purpose of introducing the law of infanticide was explicitly to facilitate mitigation for mothers killing their infant children, infanticide being regarded as a lesser offence than murder or manslaughter. Such mitigation, or the offence of infanticide itself, is not available for men.

Figure 9.14: *Number of homicides per year of victims' age range (England & Wales)*

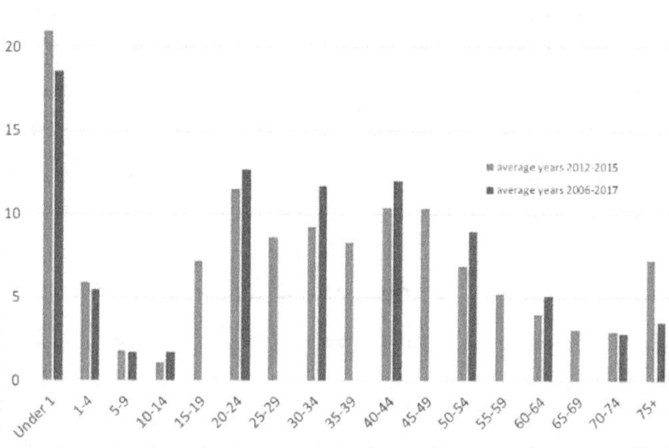

In the late 1960s / early 1970s, there were typically around 18 convictions for infanticide per year. In recent years there is perhaps one conviction for infanticide per year on average, (Office for National Statistics, 2018f). Moreover, the convictions for infanticide in recent years are almost always the outcome of an initial indictment for murder, (Crown Prosecution Service,

2014). Prosecution for an initial charge of infanticide almost never happens now. This begs the question: are infanticides being registered as homicides, as they should be? The sentence awarded for a conviction for infanticide is never imprisonment. Even a suspended sentence is unusual. Generally, a hospital sentence, probation or a supervision order is awarded.

Figure 9.15: *Number of homicides per year of victims' age range (USA). Copied from (Children's Bureau, 2018)*

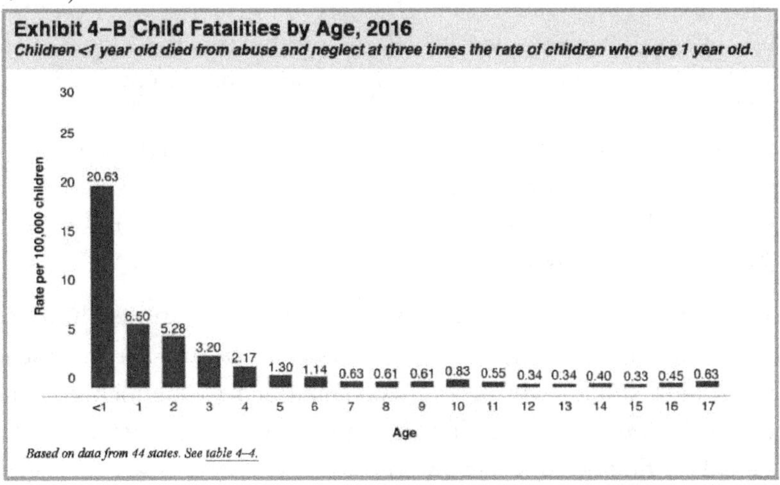

The sex of perpetrators of child homicide is less than clear in the general literature. For example, (Debowska et al, 2015) cite a number of sources which variously claim greater female perpetration, greater male perpetration, or about equal – although there appears to be a consensus regarding mothers being the predominant perpetrators of the homicide of younger children. The major USA study, (NCANDS, 2016b), is more helpful, concluding that,

> 'In 2016, parents - acting alone or with another parent or individual - were responsible for 78% of child abuse or neglect fatalities. More than one-quarter (27%) of fatalities were perpetrated by the mother acting alone, 16.8% were perpetrated by the father acting alone, and 20.1% were perpetrated by the mother and father acting together. Nonparents (including kin and child care providers, among others) were responsible for 16.7% of child fatalities, and child fatalities with unknown perpetrator relationship data accounted for 5.3% of the total.'

The corresponding report for the following year, (NCANDS, 2017), indicates that 80.1% of child fatalities due to abuse or neglect were the responsibility of one or more parent. Only 15.2% were attributed entirely to non-parents. The mother acting alone was responsible in 30.5% of cases, the father acting alone in 15.5% of cases, and the mother and father both responsible in 22.3%

of cases. The mother together with a non-parent were responsible for the child death in a further 10.8% of cases. All told, the mother was implicated in 63.6% of cases. The father was implicated in 38.8% of cases. This is a clear indication of greater perpetration by mothers than fathers based on a large USA dataset. For the UK, examination of all serious cases reviews over the 7 year period from 2009 to 2015, (Bradford R. , 332 Child Homicides, 2018a), provided the following conclusions,

- Where culpability was established, the mother was the lone perpetrator in 36% of cases and either a lone or a co-perpetrator in over half of cases (58%).
- Mothers were more likely to be responsible for a child death than fathers and male partners combined.
- Single mothers were the demographic most likely to be responsible for the deaths of children.

Another very large study, covering a wide range of countries, has recently been published in the BMJ, (Stockl et al, 2017). This involved a systematic review of 9431 studies which, after screening, led to the inclusion of 126 studies which all reported the number or proportion of perpetrators of child homicide. Key findings (medians) were,

- Over the 44 countries for which there was relevant data, parents committed 56.5% of child homicides, with parents killing rather more girls than boys;
- Data from 33 countries distinguishing the perpetrators of parental homicides of children under the age of 18 years showed that mothers committed just over half of all parental homicides (54.7%);
- Across all homicides of children (under 18), boys were the victims substantially more often than girls (70% cf 30%), the homicide of boys increasing dramatically in late adolescence;
- Over the 14 countries for which there was relevant data, parents committed 77.8% of homicides of children under one year old;
- Over the 12 countries for which there was relevant data, mothers committed 71.7% of parental homicides of children under one year old;
- Over the 13 countries for which there was relevant data, almost all neonaticides (killing within the first day of life) were committed by mothers (median 100%, inter-quartile range 92.9% to 100%). Fathers committed extremely few neonaticides (median 0%, inter-quartile range 0% to 6.7%).

The study found that acquaintances committed only 12.6% of child homicides, but this increased to 36.9% for adolescents. Step-parents committed only 7.2% of parental homicides (hence 4% overall).

A review of the serious case reviews to which the Children And Family Court Advisory and Support Services (CAFCASS) have contributed in recent years, (Green and Halliday, 2017), provided the following results, from 49 cases of child death. The father was involved in 33% to 41% of the child deaths, whereas the mother was involved in 47% to 55% of the child deaths (and the mother's partner in 12% of the deaths). All these sources concur that mothers are responsible for rather more child homicides than fathers, or men in general, especially as regards younger children.

Despite this, the advice of the London Safeguarding Children Board (2017b) in respect of protecting children from domestic abuse recognises only the dangers to children posed by men. In being so limited this procedure omits at least half the risk to children. And yet both the review of serious cases by Bradford (2018a) and that by Green and Halliday (2017) have highlighted many cases where exactly this refusal to acknowledge that mothers too can pose a risk to children has had fatal consequences. Some of these are celebrated cases which have been much in the news. The skewed perception of domestic abuse as "gendered", and hence the exclusive province of male perpetrators, is thus more than a male disadvantage: it permits children to be exposed to avoidable risk by a refusal to accept reality.

There are two further contributions to the overall homicide rate of infants which do not appear in the statistics. (I do not include abortion here, the statistics for which would render homicides statistically insignificant). These are neonaticides and covert homicides passed off as sudden infant death syndrome (SIDS), or "cot death". No one knows what proportion of SIDS is actually covert homicide. However, the variation of the rate of SIDS with marital status is rather alarming, see Table 9.3 based on (Office for National Statistics, 2018m). Here the term "joint registrant" refers to the father being named on the birth certificate, in contrast to "sole registrant" where that is not the case. The incidence of SIDS per 100,000 live births has a consistent trend with marital status. The rate is least for married couples, greater for cohabiting joint registrants, greater still for non-cohabiting joint registrants, but greatest for sole registrants (lone parents, generally single mothers). The rate of SIDS is 7 or 8 times greater for a single parent family than a married couple family.

Table 9.3: *Rate of SIDS ("Cot Death") by Marital Status (per 100,000 live births)*

<table>
<tr><th>Marital Status</th><th>2012</th><th>2013</th><th>2014</th><th>2015</th><th>2016</th></tr>
<tr><td>Married</td><td>8</td><td>7</td><td rowspan="2">17</td><td rowspan="2">15</td><td rowspan="2">17</td></tr>
<tr><td>Joint Registrants, Same Address</td><td>20</td><td>30</td></tr>
<tr><td>Joint Registrants, Different Address</td><td>40</td><td>44</td><td rowspan="2">66</td><td rowspan="2">67</td><td rowspan="2">82</td></tr>
<tr><td>Sole Registrant</td><td>55</td><td>58</td></tr>
</table>

Neonaticide is the killing of a new born baby within its first 24 hours of life. Debowska et al (2015) note,

> 'some women give birth unassisted, kill the neonate, and dispose of the body immediately after birth.'

Similarly, Craig (2004) observes,

> 'It is very difficult to get accurate figures on the incidence of neonaticide and infant homicide since many cases are never discovered; official figures are likely to be an underestimate'

Resnick (1970) opines,

> 'hundreds and possibly thousands of neonaticides still occur in Britain each year'

And Steven Pinker (1997), referring to the USA, rather graphically described it thus,

> 'Every year, hundreds of women commit neonaticide: they kill their newborns or let them die. Most neonaticides remain undiscovered, but every once in a while a janitor follows a trail of blood to a tiny body in a trash bin, or a woman faints and doctors find the remains of a placenta inside her.'

9.2.8 International Studies of Domestic Abuse

The academic literature on domestic violence is huge. It would not be appropriate to attempt a review here. However, there are a couple of references worth mentioning briefly. The first is the compendium of 'References examining assaults by women on their spouses or male partners: An annotated bibliography' by Martin Fiebert (2012). Quote,

> 'This bibliography examines 286 scholarly investigations: 221 empirical studies and 65 reviews and/or analyses, which demonstrate that women are as physically aggressive, or more aggressive, than men in their relationships with their spouses or male partners. The aggregate sample size in the reviewed studies exceeds 371,600'.

Earlier versions of this review have appeared as peer reviewed publications, each succeeding paper accumulating further evidence, e.g., (Fiebert, 1997), (Fiebert, 2004), (Fiebert, 2010).

The other international study which is particularly worth noting is the Partner Abuse State of Knowledge (PASK) Project. This was published in May 2013 in the journal 'Partner Abuse' and is the most comprehensive review of domestic violence research literature ever carried out, (PASK, 2013a). This unparalleled three-year research project was conducted by 42 scholars at 20 universities and research centres. John Hamel, PASK Director, said,

> 'The purpose of this project is to bring together, in a rigorously evidence-based, transparent and methodical manner, existing knowledge about partner abuse, with reliable, up-to-date research that can easily be accessed by anyone. PASK is grounded in the premises that everyone is entitled to their opinion, but not to their own facts; that these facts should be available to everyone, and that domestic violence intervention and policy ought to be based upon these facts rather than ideology and special interests.'

The headline finding of the PASK review was that,

> 'men and women perpetrate physical and non-physical forms of abuse at comparable rates, most domestic violence is mutual, women are as controlling as men, domestic violence by men and women is correlated with essentially the same risk factors, and male and female perpetrators are motivated for similar reasons.'

A key numerical result from the PASK Project was,

> 'Among large population samples, 57.9% of inter-partner violence (IPV) reported was bi-directional, 42% unidirectional; 13.8% of the unidirectional violence was male to female (MFPV), 28.3% was female to male (FMPV)'.

In contrast to the CSEW, which indicates that about 1 in 3 victims of partner abuse is male, the international PASK Project implies that men experience a rather greater amount of victimisation than women. Their conclusion is that, as regards unidirectional partner violence, men are victims twice as frequently as women.

It is claimed that women may be impacted more by domestic violence. Certainly, it is likely that a given degree of physical force may cause greater injury to a woman than to a man, though this will depend upon the individuals. But this should not, in my opinion, confuse the issue of equal culpability. In practice, however, it probably does. Moreover, the PASK project observes,

> 'There was a relative dearth of research examining the consequences of physical and psychological victimization in men, and the studies that have been conducted have focused almost exclusively on sex differences in injury rates….. Relatedly, there is limited research on the psychological consequences of abuse on male victims, and the research that does exist has yielded mixed findings (some studies find

comparable effects of psychological abuse across gender, while others do not).' (PASK, 2013b)

In this context, recall from section 9.2.2 that the 2017/18 CSEW reported that more men than women who reported partner abuse in the UK in that year tried to kill themselves as a result of the abuse. So the psychological impact of partner abuse on men is no less than that upon women.

9.2.9 Dads as Victims of Domestic Violence

Fathers who are subject to partner abuse whilst living with their children face a particular problem. In the context of partner abuse against women victims, it has long been unacceptable to ask, foolishly, "why does she not just leave?" Yet the same unthinking question is still acceptable in the context of abused men: why does he not just leave her? The complete answer is complex. But, where children are present, the answer may be very simple: he sticks around for fear that the children will become the target of abuse in his absence. Men face an acute difficulty in this respect because, not only are refuges for men a rarity, but there are almost none to which a father may flee with his children.

The Welsh Dads Survey carried out by the charity FNF Both Parents Matter Cymru (2017) provided many comments which alluded to domestic violence against the respondents themselves, or their children, by their partner. In 2018 the same charity conducted a survey specifically for male victims of domestic abuse, though not specific to Wales. Some results were,

- 681 men who responded identified as a victim / survivor of 'Domestic Violence & Abuse' as set out in the UK Government definition;
- 92.6% of the respondents were from the UK;
- 15% of respondents did not identify as white British (12.2% identified as black, Asian or mixed race). 13.7% declared a disability;
- 93.75% of victims were no longer living with their abuser;
- 95% of reported abusers were identified as female, 3% as male.

The survey obtained respondents' answers to questions relating to, (a) the nature and prevalence of any physical abuse, (b) the nature and prevalence of any non-physical abuse, (c) for those who did not seek help as a victim of domestic abuse, what prevented them from doing so?, and, (d) what sort of help would have made things better? A few salient findings were as follows,

- Just over half of male victims did not appreciate at the time that what they were experiencing was abuse, they didn't know where to turn for help, and they did not expect to be believed;

- 69.7% of respondents had faced prejudice or stereotyping as a victim of abuse because they were a man (e.g., police telling them to 'man up', social workers assuming that they must be the perpetrator, DV support services asking them questions to determine whether their partner was the 'real' victim, etc.);
- When asked how important it was that services for male victims should be grounded in the experience of men and separated from services primarily designed for women, 82.3% of respondents thought this Important or Essential.

9.2.10 Domestic Abuse Services: The Sexes Compared

Data from Women's Aid Federation of England, reported in (Office for National Statistics, 2017p), indicated there were 3,798 beds in women's refuges in England in 2017, up from 3,467 in 2010. Pro-rata this suggests nearly 4,500 bed places in women's refuges in the UK as a whole. In contrast, Mankind Initiative (2017) identifies only 105 refuge beds potentially available for male victims, of which only 31 are dedicated for male victims. There are no refuge or safe houses at all in London for male victims. Moreover, there is no provision for men to flee domestic violence with their children.

In Wales, in year 2015/16, a total of 1,518 women were referred to, and accommodated at, a refuge. The corresponding figure for male victims was 41. The extent of support provided to victims of domestic abuse in Gwent in 2015/16 has been provided in Table 7.3 of Appendix 3 to the Gwent Regional Violence Against Women, Domestic Abuse and Sexual Violence Strategy 2017-2022 (Gwent Partnership Board on VAWDASV, 2016). Support for victims of DA were provided to 2,478 women and 69 men. In North Wales the corresponding figures were 2,401 women and 32 men, as quoted by FNF Both Parents Matter Cymru (2018) and referenced by the National Assembly for Wales Petitions Committee (2018).

Clearly, there is a massive disproportion in service provision for male and female victims. The provision of refuge space for male victims is around 0.7% to 2.8% of that for female victims. This is glaringly inconsistent with the relative prevalence of abuse suffered by men (34% based on the CSEW; 24% of police reports in the UK; 17% of victims in prosecutions). Whilst there may not be a need for equal refuge space for men, there is an obvious and huge shortfall in service provision to men at present. The almost complete lack of facilities for fathers to flee with their children can be particularly problematic for abused men.

Figure 9.16: *The Duluth Model's 'Power & Control Wheel'*

9.2.11 Perpetrator Programmes

There are 'treatment' programmes to correct the behaviour of perpetrators of partner abuse. In the UK, as in most countries, these programmes – perhaps better called re-education programmes – are based on the Duluth model. The Duluth model originated from cases in Duluth, Minnesota, studied by Ellen Pence and Michael Paymar (1993). It is based on the patriarchal power and control theory of domestic violence which admits of no motive other than an assumed male desire for dominance over women. Consequently it does not, and cannot, recognise that men can be victims, or that women can be perpetrators. The mindset of the model is adequately portrayed by its (now infamous) power & control wheel, reproduced as Figure 9.15. It recognises only female victims and male perpetrators.

In the UK, perpetrator programmes are accredited through the charity Respect whose Accreditation Standard is explicitly applicable only to male perpetrators abusing female victims, (Respect, 2012). Moreover, the accreditation effectively ensures that only programmes conforming broadly, if not necessarily in name, to the Duluth "male power & control" theory can be accredited. For this reason, perpetrator programmes which are based on any other understanding or methodology will find it far harder to get funding, or to be accepted by authorities such as the courts or social services, due to lack of accreditation.

Unsurprisingly, given that male power and control is a false view of domestic violence in the great majority of cases, Duluth programmes have a woeful record of success, despite the man's further contact with his children often being dependent on completing such a programme. A thorough review of studies appraising the efficacy of Duluth-type programmes is beyond the scope of this book, but it is valuable to make some passing observations. Consider firstly the study by Dutton and Corvo (2006) from which the following are quotes,

> 'The Duluth model's negligible success in reducing or eliminating violence among perpetrators in tandem with the iron-grip of prohibition of other approaches is perhaps its most damaging feature.'
>
> 'Dutton (2003) argued that Duluth models had two major flaws that were contraindicative of effective treatment; they attempted to shame clients and, in taking a strong adversarial stance to clients (based on a view of male sex role conditioning as a major issue in domestic violence), failed to establish a therapeutic bond with their clientele.
>
> The single most predictive factor for successful therapeutic outcome (even those labelled "interventions") is the therapeutic bond. However, it becomes extremely difficult to form a positive relationship when the therapist is required to assume that strategic intentional domination is the sole motive for all clients and to presumptively disbelieve any claims of mutuality raised by clients.'

More recently the report, 'Transforming Rehabilitation: a summary of evidence on reducing reoffending', (Ministry of Justice, 2014), contains this statement,

> 'The most recent systematic review of US evidence indicates that the Duluth Model appears to have no effect on recidivism. However, this review also identified substantial reductions in domestic violence reoffending by offenders who had attended other interventions.'

The US reference in question was, 'What works to reduce recidivism by domestic violence offenders?', (Miller, Drake & Nafziger, 2013). A more recent review of the effectiveness of perpetrator programmes has reconfirmed the woeful record of Duluth, or feminist-patriarchy based, programmes, and also indicated that CBT (cognitive behaviour therapy) modalities are no better, (Voith et al, 2018).

In the UK in 2006/7, the programme DVIP (Domestic Violence Intervention Project) had 230 referrals but only 33 men completed the course, i.e., a completion rate of a woeful 14%, (DVIP Accounts, 2007). Moreover, taking into account its limited effectiveness even for men who completed the programme, as DVIP admitted before a Home Office Select Committee (2008), DVIP can be concluded to have been effective in 23 cases out of 230, i.e., 10%. In the absence of a control group this might even be consistent with zero effectiveness.

It is worth noting that one of the originators of the Duluth model, Ellen Pence, was ultimately to reject the model herself, based on hard practical experience. The following extracts are taken from 'Co-ordinating Community Responses to Domestic Violence: Lessons from Duluth and Beyond' by Melanie Shepherd and Ellen Pence (1999),

> 'He does it for the power, he does it for control, he does it because he can – these were the jingles that, in our opinion, said all there was to say.'

On the next page she clarifies how wrong they were,

> 'By determining that the need or desire for power was the motivating force behind battering, we created a conceptual framework that, in fact, did not fit the lived experience of many of the men and women we were working with. Like those we were criticising, we reduced our analysis to a psychological universal truism. The Domestic Abuse Intervention Programme staff - like the therapist insisting it was an anger control problem, or the judge wanting to see it as an alcohol problem, or the defence attorney arguing that it was a defective wife problem - remained undaunted by the differences in our theory and the actual experiences of those we were working with. We all engaged in ideological practices and claimed them to be neutral observations.
>
> I found that many of the men I interviewed did not seem to articulate a desire for power over a partner. Although I relentlessly took every opportunity to point out to the men in groups that they were so motivated and merely in denial, the fact that few men ever articulated such a desire went unnoticed by me and many of my co-workers. Eventually we realised that we were finding what we had predetermined to find.'

In the face of all these negative observations it is remarkable that the ideological stranglehold of Duluth on perpetrator programmes is still firmly in place in the UK (and elsewhere). This means that perpetrator programmes that could work, for either sex, have been pushed to the margins and all but eliminated.

9.3 The Empathy Gap for Men as Victims of Violence

"Men are violent" or "we need to talk about men's violence" are sentiments you can express publicly without fear of censure or disagreement. You would not be treated so kindly if you opined that Muslims are terrorists or black men are drug dealers. All these are examples of castigating the whole for the behaviour of a few. They are of the same type. The acceptability of one and the political incorrectness of the others is determined only by their respective identity group status: oppressor or oppressed. But this status is prejudice dressed up as politics. It relegates the individual to irrelevance, replacing them with an identity label. You are undeserving by virtue of an accident of your birth. I have worked all my life amongst men in an engineering environment and the number of incidents of violence I have witnessed is zero. Nor do I encounter any of great significance in my personal life, though I have occasionally seen young women slapping or kicking their boyfriends in shopping malls. Serious violence does occur, of course, as the statistics show. But the narrative which presents such violence as a norm is false. Having said that, it depends upon the sort of society within which you mix. Undoubtedly, the exposure to violence is strongly demographic related, and that also is clear from the statistics.

As an illustration of the double standards in operation in the context of partner violence, consider the cases of MPs David Ruffley, Sarah Champion and Layla Moran. In 2014, MP David Ruffley was obliged to stand down when it emerged he had been cautioned by the police for assaulting his former partner, (McGurran, 2014). Whether the assault was a one-off or part of a continuing behaviour pattern we do not know. Four years earlier Mr Ruffley 'fell in front of a train', (Geater and Jones, 2010) - see chapter 18 for the relationship between domestic violence and suicide. As soon as Mr Ruffley's abuse of his ex-partner became known, his career was over.

Contrast this with the case of Labour MP Sarah Champion. She was in the throes of divorcing her husband when an argument led to her assaulting him. Both were cautioned, though it was Mr Hoyland who called the police and Ms Champion spent time in a police cell. When the story emerged later, she was Shadow Secretary of State for Women and Equalities and also Shadow Minister for Preventing Abuse. Many accounts at the time presented Ms Champion's abuse as a one-off event following years of provocation.

However, friends claimed it was not the first time she had hit him, and that she had been harassing and abusive throughout their marriage. A picture emerged from some reports of an abusive bully who terrified her former husband, a classic partner abuse scenario. Mr Hoyland, they said, was terrified of her. His new partner stated that Mr Hoyland remained deeply disturbed by what happened in his marriage and still has nightmares about his former wife, (Powell and Jenkins, 2016). Nevertheless, Champion's Party Leader leapt to her defence. Mr Corbyn told the Labour Party's Women's Conference that Champion has 'our total, full and absolutely warm support'. As a result, Champion retained her job as Shadow Minister (though she lost it over another issue later). As of March 2019, she remains an MP and is Chair of the All Party Parliamentary Group on Sexual Violence and Adult Survivors of Childhood Sexual Abuse. She is also a member of the Women and Equalities Committee (what message does that send?). Whatever they may profess in public, there can be no one who doubts that a male MP in the same position would be sacked from his senior position immediately, be vilified by all, lose the whip and be deselected.

The tolerance of female violence towards men, even when the woman is in a position of authority, has been illustrated again recently by the case of Lib-Dem MP Layla Moran. In 2019 she admitted, via Twitter, that she had been arrested for assaulting her then-boyfriend six years earlier. (Both were initially detained, as also happened in the Sarah Champion case, illustrating how male complainants of partner abuse can expect to be arrested). Moran was charged, but charges were later dropped, (BBC News, 2019). Moran appears to have chosen public confession six years after the event only because rumours were beginning to circulate, and, it has been suggested, she might want to clear the decks in preparation for a Lib-Dem leadership bid. Colin Sutton, a retired Metropolitan Police detective chief inspector, branded the language Moran used in her "faux-confession" as a 'classic victim-blaming statement of a domestic abuser', (Ward, 2019). Lib-Dem commenters have praised Moran's courage and declared that she is brave and "an inspiration", (HEqual, 2019). A spokesperson for the Lib-Dems asked that her privacy be respected. Where a man would be sacked and disgraced, a woman is lauded and held up as a role model. What part of gynocentrism and male disposability do you not grasp?

All western countries have policy directives and specific legal provisions for a particular class of violent offences: violence against women and girls

(VAWG). So embedded have these sex-based provisions become that the acronym VAWG is a familiar one. Even if violence were overwhelmingly perpetrated against female victims this would be prejudicial. But even that is not so.

Ignoring location, violence is perpetrated against male victims roughly twice as frequently as against female victims. This is true as regards both men and boys. It is also true for the most extreme cases where homicide results. When attention is confined to homicides outside the home, men and boys are 5 or 6 times more often the victims of homicide than women and girls. Adherents of the dominant gender narrative will generally react to these observations with unconcern, citing (correctly) that men and boys are also the majority of the perpetrators of these offences. The implication appears to be that this observation somehow neutralises any need for concern or compassion for the victims. This is about as clear an example of victim blaming as one could have – the victim is to blame for his own injuries, or death, because he shares genital anatomy with his attacker. Such thinking is the product of the empathy gap, given wings by identity politics, which allows all males to be lumped together into an undifferentiated and undeserving mass, with no need to distinguish between villain and victim.

Within the home, women are more often both the victim and the perpetrator, compared to outside the home. Despite the strong media focus on domestic violence, the volume of domestic violence offending is significantly less than stranger or acquaintance violence outside the home (Figure 9.3). Nevertheless, one in three victims of domestic abuse or partner abuse are male. Where physical injury occurs, men may be rather more than one in three victims. One in three victims of domestic homicide are also male (and about one in four victims of partner homicide are male). But this prevalence of male victims of domestic abuse is subject to successive attritions, resulting ultimately in a tiny level of service provision to male victims. The percentages of men through the process diminish as follows: 34% from crime surveys; 24% from police reports; 17% of victims in prosecutions; but only about 1% - 3% of the service provision.

The aspect of domestic violence which is least well appreciated by the public or by social and political narratives, is the extent to which mothers are responsible for child deaths. Statistics on this issue are incomplete for the reasons discussed in section 9.2.7. The largest studies indicate that mothers are responsible for more child deaths than men. MOJ data does not confirm this but there may be shortcomings in these data. Many culpable child deaths may not feature in the official homicide records. Nevertheless, one-third of people prosecuted for child homicide in 2017/18 were female, (Crown Prosecution Service, 2018). Evidence from Serious Case Reviews supports the contention that mothers are responsible for more child deaths than are men.

How do these basic facts about violence align with the huge societal, legal and political focus upon VAWG – and indeed the very existence of the acronym itself? The facts betray that the VAWG perspective is not so much a product of compassion for women and girls as it is the product of deliberately withholding compassion from men and boys. VAWG is also a political propaganda weapon. This is amply demonstrated by the Crown Prosecution Service's series of VAWG reports, for example, (Crown Prosecution Service, 2018). The casual reader would be forgiven for thinking that Violence Against Women and Girls means violence against women and girls. But within the context of these CPS VAWG reports it does not. In this context, "Violence" does not mean violence, "Women" does not mean women, and "Girls" does not mean girls. Instead, VAWG is actually a formal term meaning a particular category of crime. The offence may not be violent, and the victim may be a man or a boy. Responding to pressure to clarify this obfuscation, the CPS have, since 2016, added a footnote stating 'includes data on men and boys' to this series of CPS VAWG reports.

But the designation of certain categories of crime as VAWG is, at best, misleading. If this false categorisation of a certain class of offences as Violence Against Women and Girls were acceptable, it would be equally acceptable to label it as Violence Against Men and Boys (VAMB), and to subsume all such offences against females under the label VAMB. But such a thing – which no one would wish to do - would rightly be seen as a concealment of offences against women and girls. Yet our society now condones this usage of the VAWG label as a concealment of offences against men and boys. It is a subterfuge, but is prevented from being perceived as such by the empathy gap – and lack of male in-group preference - which result in its toleration.

The mindset which legitimises VAWG results in the introduction of terms such as "femicide", surely a levering of the empathy gap to suggest that the killing of females is more serious an issue than the killing of mere males. The instantiation of the empathy gap as VAWG clearly demonstrates the operation of gynocentrism and male disposability. Violence suffered by females is perceived differently from violence suffered by males, and violence perpetrated by females is perceived differently from violence perpetrated by males.

Yet women can be both strong and violent, men can be weak and vulnerable, and immature boys have no physical advantage over girls – and still less over adult women. This minimisation of male victimisation is necessary to protect the dominant gender narrative; widespread male victimisation by females conflicts with its basic tenets. The empathy gap facilitates belief in an ideology which cannot countenance female perpetration and is indifferent to male victimisation.

Criticism of the presentation of domestic abuse as overwhelmingly men abusing women is invariably interpreted by those advocating this perspective as an attempt by reactionary forces to re-establish patriarchal power over women. My perspective is that the "gendered" interpretation of domestic abuse is another example of the empathy gap in operation. Here we see why the empathy gap must be kept in place. To allow that domestic violence is gender symmetric fatally undermines feminist patriarchy theory. To allow equal empathy for men would thus lead to the collapse of the whole feminist narrative.

10

Family Court Statistics

The feminisation of the state launches a new offensive in the gender war. It is now an orthodoxy that one of the primary duties of the state is to protect women's interests against men. Anna Coote and her colleagues write that fathers are no longer essential to the economic survival of family units. And Polly Toynbee can calmly incite women to forget about fatherhood and just look to the state for all the provisions needed to enable them to have careers and operate effectively without men. Quoting Toynbee: 'What it (the state) can do is shape a society that makes a place for women and children as family units, self-sufficient and independent.
Geoff Dench (1940-2018), *Transforming Men*

These fathers know that they need their families. But they are not making much impact, and at the level of general principles, in the public arena, the overwhelming mood, blending feminism and traditional sentiments, is that if women want to exclude men they should be allowed to.
Geoff Dench (1940-2018), *Transforming Men*

This short chapter provides some basic information about the operation of the family courts in the UK and acts as an introduction to the following chapter which will address whether the family courts are gender biased.

10.1 Family Court Statistics (England and Wales)

The family courts in England and Wales are within the civil jurisdiction, as contrasted with the criminal courts. Since 2014 the family courts have been in two branches: the Family Division of the High Court, and the Family Courts formed from the merger of the family court functions of the magistrates' courts and the county courts. Cases may be brought as "private law" or "public law". Public law cases are those brought by a local authority or the NSPCC (National Society for the Prevention of Cruelty to Children). These cases generally involve applications to intervene to protect a child in some way, such as being removed from their parents into independent care. Private law cases are brought by individuals, usually separating parents. These cases address divorce and associated financial matters, and "child arrangements" following parental separation. They also address certain aspects of domestic violence in as far as it relates to these matters. Here I shall be exclusively concerned with private law, and specifically child arrangements. The principal legislation under which the family courts operate in respect of child arrangements is the Children Act 1989, (UK Government,

1989), with various later additions. This gives rise to the jargon that the cases that interest us here are "Private Law Children Act" cases. Figure 10.1 shows the number of cases completing in the family courts of England & Wales, comparing divorce (including legal separation) cases and Private Law Children Act cases. In 2017 there were 103,382 and 42,307 such cases respectively. (Due to missing data, prior to 2011, Figure 10.1 estimates the number of Private Law Children Act cases completing as a fixed fraction (40%) of the number of matrimonial cases). Note that just under half of divorce cases involve children under the age of 16. But also note that roughly half of Private Law Children Act cases relate to parents who are not married.

Figure 10.1: *Divorce and Private Law Children Act Caseload in the Family Courts of England & Wales, 2006 – 2017 (cases completing)*

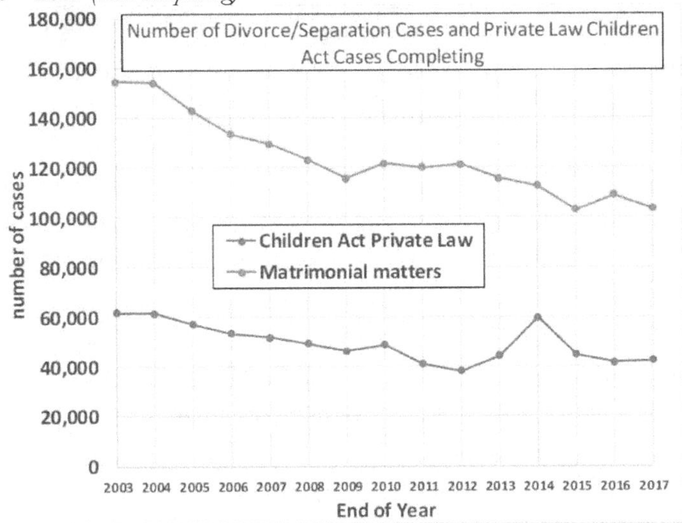

10.2 The Paramountcy Principle and the Perception of Risk

To quote Hunt & MacLeod, (2008),

> 'The legal position with respect to child contact after parental separation is that parents can agree arrangements informally, there is no requirement to seek a court order. The law does not explicitly seek to influence those arrangements and there is no statutory presumption that there should be contact. Parents who cannot agree can apply to the court for a contact order under Section 8 of the Children Act 1989, which is governed by the welfare principle, i.e., that when determining any question with respect to a child's upbringing, the child's welfare is the court's paramount consideration'.

This is the Paramountcy Principle: that it is the child's best interests and welfare that must be the court's first and paramount consideration. As far as

I am aware, no one disputes this principle. Where the contention lies is how this desirable objective is best fulfilled. We will see in chapter 11 that in over 90% of cases, the couple's children remain living with their mother, with a variable degree of lesser contact or visitation with the father being permitted or agreed, and often no contact at all. Fathers' groups will contend that this results from a conflation of "the best interests of the child" with the wishes of the mother, together with a societal bias towards assuming that children are best cared for by their mother.

Note the statement in the above quote that 'there is no statutory presumption that there should be contact'. Hence, if one parent leaves the other and takes the children, the remaining parent is not entitled to any contact with the children unless he, or she, obtains an order to that effect from the family courts. I note a peculiar tension between this legal position and the legal obligation on parents to care for their children, which includes providing them with a home, protection and essential maintenance. The abandoned parent has been rendered unable to fulfil these obligations in a manner which he, or she, cannot legally circumvent without a court ruling.

In the above, the term "parent" can be taken to mean a person with parental responsibility (PR). This is a legal status. The biological mother automatically has PR. However, biological fatherhood does not automatically confer PR. A man who was married to the mother at the time of the birth has PR. Note that this is independent of biological paternity. Also, a man named on the birth certificate has PR. A man who considers himself the father of a child, and who may indeed be the biological father, will not have PR if he is not married to the mother and his name does not appear on the birth certificate, unless he has obtained a court ruling granting him PR. A man without PR is in a disadvantaged position after parental separation in respect of obtaining contested child contact.

10.3 Legal Aid, LASPO and the Role of False Allegations

No understanding of the Family Courts is complete without appreciating the significance of allegations of domestic violence, and the associated issue of legal aid.

10.3.1 Legal Aid and LASPO

In April 2013 a new Act came into force, the 'Legal Aid, Sentencing and Punishment of Offenders Act 2012', generally referred to as LASPO, (UK Government, 2012a). A major purpose of the LASPO Act was to reduce the financial burden of legal aid on the public purse by withdrawing legal aid from civil court cases, and therefore from the family courts. However, it was recognised that some types of civil case should still be supported by legal aid provision, in particular, private family law cases involving allegations of domestic abuse. A "gateway" was introduced which set out precisely what would be accepted as sufficient justification to underwrite a claim for legal aid via a domestic abuse allegation. The stipulations within the gateway regarding what constitutes "evidence" do not meet the standards which one would normally associated with a court of law, after all, these provisions are intended only to guide the allocation of legal aid, not to decide upon criminal culpability.

10.3.2 The Domestic Violence Legal Aid Gateway

Legal aid is usually subject to means testing, (UK Government, 2018u). However, there is again an exception. The Legal Aid Agency (LAA) waives the means test in the case of applications for legal aid for an order for protection from domestic violence or forced marriage, (UK Government, 2018v). In 2015 the parliamentary Justice Select Committee held an inquiry into the impact of changes to civil legal aid under LASPO. In its submission to the inquiry, the Ministry of Justice summarised the types of evidence needed to activate the domestic violence gateway as follows, (UK Parliament, 2015),

- a conviction, police caution, or ongoing criminal proceedings for a domestic violence offence;
- a protective injunction;
- an undertaking given in court (where no equivalent undertaking was given by the applicant);
- a letter from the Chair of a Multi-Agency Risk Assessment Conference (MARAC);
- a finding of fact in court of domestic violence;
- a letter from a defined health professional (which includes a doctor, nurse, health visitor or midwife);
- evidence from social services of domestic violence; or,
- evidence from a domestic violence support organisation of a stay in a refuge.

The protective injunctions referred to above are court orders intended to prevent domestic violence, the so-called non-molestation orders (NMOs) and occupation orders. The system was later reviewed and new regulations were brought into force in April 2014 which extended the types of evidence accepted to include,

- police bail for a domestic violence offence;
- a bindover for a domestic violence offence;
- Domestic Violence Protection Notice/ Domestic Violence Protection Order;
- evidence of someone being turned away from a refuge because of a lack of available accommodation;
- medical evidence expanded to include evidence from practitioner psychologists; and,
- evidence of a referral to a domestic violence support service by a health professional.

Before April 2016 there was a 2 year time limit on evidence, except for convictions. A further review led to more changes which came into force in April 2016, the most significant of which was the extension of the evidence period from 2 years to 5 years. The latest issue has no time limit. This is significant because it means historical evidence of a great many years vintage, and perhaps relating to a different relationship, will also count. Also, the range of health professionals who may provide evidence has now been expanded to include social workers, dentists, paramedics and radiographers, (Legal Aid Agency, 2018).

Some of these sources of "evidence" are questionable. Evidence of having applied to, or been referred to, a refuge, irrespective of whether the applicant was admitted, clearly is not truly evidence of anything. Even a letter of support from a refuge cannot be taken as constituting evidence in the usual sense, since the declared policy of women's refuge charities is to "believe the victim" without question. Whilst this may be a perfectly valid and compassionate approach when providing support services, it invalidates any claim to constitute real evidence.

Following an allegation of domestic violence, it is common practice for a man's solicitor to advise that he sign an "undertaking" (listed above as one of the gateway evidence options). Such an "undertaking" will state that he will not threaten, harass, intimidate or pester his ex, or other such wording as appropriate, for example see (Stowe Family Law, 2017). This is advised on the grounds that the alternative is a more high risk strategy involving asking a judge to make a ruling on the matter, which may end up with the man being ruled as a domestic violence perpetrator. Solicitors may convince a man to go down the "undertaking" route on the grounds that it implies no admission that his ex's allegations are true. What the man is highly unlikely to be aware of is that, by doing so, he has just provided sufficient "evidence" to allow his wife to acquire legal aid to deploy against him. The *coup de grâce* is this additional ruling, see (UK Parliament, 2015),

> 'Legal aid is also available for proceedings which provide protection from domestic violence, such as protective injunctions, without the need to provide evidence of domestic violence.'

Putting all this together provides a charter for the false accuser. An application for a protective injunction following from an allegation of domestic violence will be funded by legal aid, without means testing, and without any need for evidence. Upon such an injunction being granted, the injunction itself then provides "evidence" to activate the DV gateway for the granting of further legal aid in the subsequent private family law proceedings, e.g., over child arrangements. To the lay person this seems like a well funded mechanism for creating "evidence" out of thin air.

10.3.3 Prevalence of Allegations of Domestic Abuse

The best data on the percentage of private family law cases involving allegations of domestic violence was provided by the Ministry of Justice research team as a private communication to the charity Families Need Fathers Both Parents Matter Cymru together with HMCTS (Her Majesty's Courts & Tribunals Service). This indicates that 49.2% of private family law cases in 2016 involved allegations of domestic abuse. We shall see in chapter 11 that academic studies based on data from 2004 and 2011 confirm that about 50% of private family law cases for child contact involved allegations of domestic abuse.

A report was published in July 2017 with joint research by Women's Aid and CAFASS, the Children and Family Court Advisory and Support Service, (CAFCASS and Womens Aid, 2017). It claimed that '62% of applications to the family court about where a child should live or spend time feature allegations of domestic abuse'. However, this study was based on a small sample of cases (216) in which CAFCASS had been involved and may not be representative. Moreover, it is possible that the definition of "allegation of domestic abuse" used in this study might have been rather broader than the Court's definition. The report notes that, 'this data includes all records of domestic abuse within the CAFCASS case file, including any allegations'.

Whether around 50% or 62%, a figure of this order appears anomalous when compared with the prevalence of domestic abuse estimated from surveys (see section 9.2.1), although it was noted in chapter 9 that domestic violence is far more prevalent amongst separated and divorced couples than other couples (see Figure 9.10). In view of the advantage that making such an allegation confers upon the accuser in the family courts, the implication is that many such allegations are fraudulent or wildly exaggerated. In this context, note that it is unusual for such allegations to ever be subject to a "finding of fact" within the family courts (see section 10.3.6 below).

10.3.4 Which Sex Gets Legal Aid in the Family Courts?

Prior to LASPO, women were awarded 60% of the legal aid in private family law cases and men 40% of such legal aid. Following LASPO, with the acquisition of legal aid now largely dependent upon allegations of domestic violence, one could anticipate that the proportion of legal aid granted to women would increase markedly. This indeed was the case. Immediately following the introduction of LASPO in April 2013, women were awarded 85% of the legal aid in private family law and men just 15% (see Figure 10.2, data provided by the Legal Aid Agency, private communication to the charity Families Need Fathers Both Parents Matter Cymru).

Figure 10.2: *Proportion of Legal Aid Awarded to Men and Women in Private Family Law*

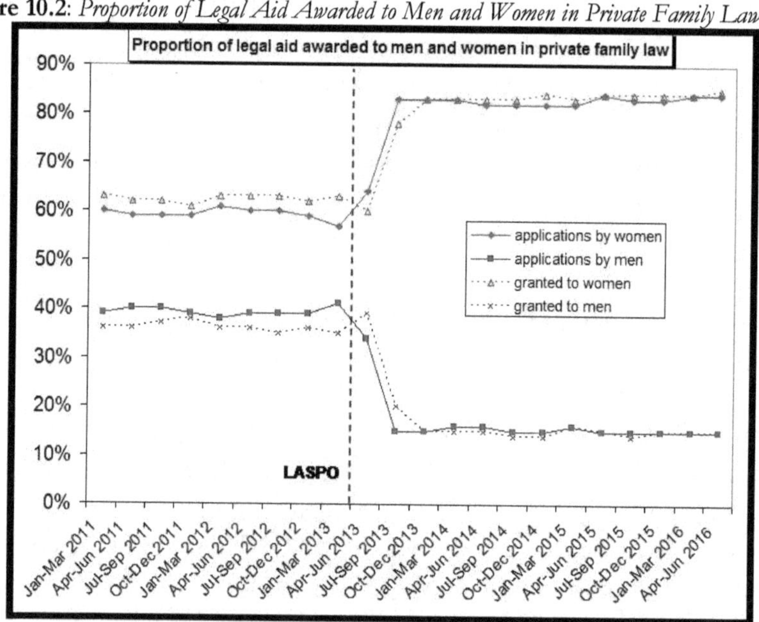

The result is an invidious but very common situation in which the accuser has legal representation but the accused does not, thus inverting the original purpose of legal aid – to allow the impecunious accused to mount a proper defence. The effect of legal aid being less commonly available in the Family Courts, especially to men, has led to the rise of Litigants In Person (LIPs). These are people, most often men, who have no professional legal representation to assist them in court. Instead, they have to manage the court process themselves, and this may include defending themselves against serious allegations. They may be aided by a so-called McKenzie Friend. This is a person without legal training who may advise the LIP, but cannot actually address the court on his behalf. In child contact cases, where LIPs are particularly common, the McKenzie Friend is often a man who has been through his own similar case in previous years and is often obtained via a fathers' group such as Families Need Fathers. The net result is that a subculture of amateurs has arisen in the Family Courts: unrepresented men trying their best to negotiate the system.

This situation has led to men accused of domestic violence being obliged to cross-examine their ex-partner – their accuser – in court. This is an undesirable outcome for both parties. Women's groups have presented this phenomenon from the woman's perspective. For example, under the lurid headline 'Revealed: how family courts allow abusers to torment their victims', Sandra Laville (2016) wrote in The Guardian,

> 'Violent and abusive men are being allowed to confront and cross-examine their former partners in secretive court hearings that fail to protect women who are victims of abuse, a Guardian investigation has found. Mothers involved in family court hearings have given graphic descriptions of the "torture" of being questioned by abusive men – a practice still allowed in civil cases but banned in criminal courts.'

The language here is highly partisan. It will be true in some cases that the man in question is indeed a violent abuser; he may even have been convicted of such an offence. But, commonly, this will not be the case. The man has been accused by the woman, but no court has yet ruled on the matter. His accuser should rightly be described as an "alleged victim" and he as the "alleged abuser" or simply as "the accused". This misuse of language is part of a process which is undermining the presumption of innocence in cases involving a woman accusing a man. We shall see below that only a very small proportion of these accusations will ever be critically examined.

The claim in the above quote that the accused man is "being allowed" to question his accuser is a loaded, and grossly misleading, presentation of the true position: the man has no choice but to do so because he has no legal representation to do it for him. It is not only a case of the practice being "allowed in civil cases but banned in criminal courts", it is also unnecessary in the criminal court because the man would have legal aid and be represented.

Following the media highlighting of "victims" being cross-examined by their "abuser", the matter was quickly taken up by the then-Justice Minister, Liz Truss who promised a rapid change in the law to ban the practice, (Truss, 2017). This was to be addressed via the Prisons and Courts Bill, (UK Parliament, 2017b), see para 31V of (UK Parliament, 2017c), but is now to feature in a new Domestic Abuse Bill, at the Committee stage as I write, (UK Government, 2019b).

Table 10.1: *The Number of Applications for Legal Aid via the Domestic Violence Gateway which use Various Types of 'Evidence', 2017/18*

Type of 'Evidence'	Number of Applications
Arrest for DV offence	67
Bind overs	68
DV injunction orders (NMOs or Occupation orders) plus protection notices (DVPN) or protection orders (DVPO)	3,934
Expert report for court/tribunal	26
Financial abuse	29
Finding of fact	72
Referral to DV support service	454
IDVA	134
Letter from health professional	2,240
Letter from local authority or housing association	75
Letter from DV support organisation	524
MARAC	979
Ongoing criminal proceedings	172
Police bail	126
Refuge admission or refusal	766
Relevant conviction or caution	516
Social services letter	354
Undertaking	331
TOTAL of above(1)	**10,869**
TOTAL applications(2)	**10,038**

(1)This will exceed the number of DV applications for legal aid because some will cite more than one type of evidence.

(2)Total applications including a DV component (see Sheet 6_8 of the Legal Aid Statistics Tables). 9,497 of these are for DV alone, plus a further 541 for both DV and child abuse.

10.3.5 Routes through the Gateway

In the year 2017/18, the number of applications for legal aid via the domestic violence gateway which deployed the various different types of evidence are listed in Table 10.1, (Legal Aid Agency, 2018). How the use of the various types of evidence has changed since 2013 is shown by Figure 10.3, for some of the larger contributors. Easily the most commonly cited "evidence" is a domestic violence injunction order or protection notice, used in 39% of applications for legal aid via the DV gateway in 2017/18. What emerged in 2017/18 as the clear second most deployed type of "evidence" is a letter from a health professional (used in 22% of applications).

Figure 10.3: *The Number of Applications for Legal Aid via the Domestic Violence Gateway which use Various Types of 'Evidence', 2013 to 2018*

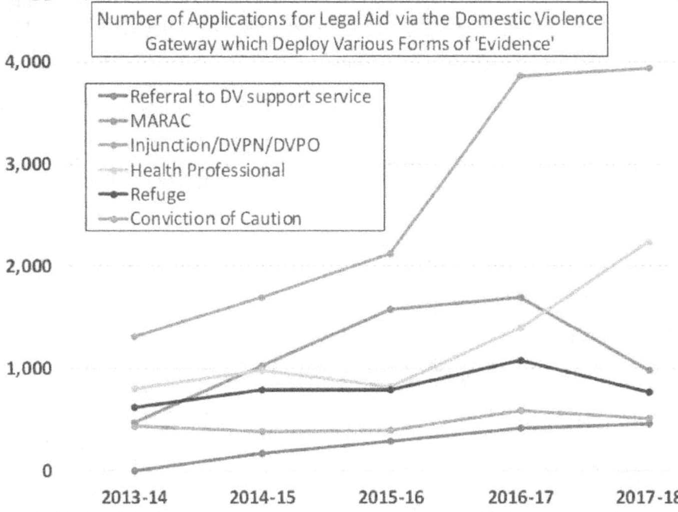

Findings of fact provide evidence in only 0.7% of applications. Despite the dominant influence that allegations of domestic violence exercise over the family court proceedings, it is relatively rare that the allegations themselves are critically examined (see next section). Relevant convictions or cautions are deployed as evidence in only 5% of applications. Even if arrests for a DV offence, finding of fact, and ongoing criminal proceedings are added to the relevant convictions or cautions, this still only accounts for 8.2% of applications (and many of those arrested, being proceeded against or cautioned will be innocent). This fact stands in stark contrast with the presumption which underlies Sandra Laville's article, above, namely that all the accused are guilty and that no allegations are false.

10.3.6 Statistics of Domestic Violence Remedy Orders

Fathers groups claim that there is evidence of an escalating rate of false allegations of domestic violence in the family courts, citing the increase in the number of domestic violence remedy orders made since LASPO was introduced in April 2013, (Bowcott, 2018). The data, taken from Family Court Statistics Quarterly to March 2018, do appear to bear out the claim, (Ministry of Justice, 2018f). Figure 10.4 plots separately both the so-called Non-Molestation Orders (NMOs) and the total orders for domestic violence remedies, which includes also the so-called Occupation Orders. Prior to LASPO the number of orders had been falling, probably due to a reducing rate of Children Act cases as a result of the falling divorce rate (see Figure 10.1). But after LASPO the number of orders does indeed increase. To gauge the effects of the simultaneous change in the number of Private Law Children Act cases going through the courts, Table 10.2 gives the ratio of the number of domestic violence orders to the number of Private Law Children Act cases. This suggests an increase in the proportion of domestic violence orders per case, even from a baseline of 2003 when the absolute number of such orders was larger.

Katie Ghose, CEO of Women's Aid, was quoted as stating that 'it is misleading to suggest that this increase in non-molestation orders granted by the courts is a result of false allegations of domestic abuse to secure legal aid', (Bowcott, 2018). She said "official reports" showed false domestic abuse allegations were rare. It is not stated to what "official reports" she was referring. Possibly Ghose meant the 2013 report from the Crown Prosecution Service Equality and Diversity Unit, 'Cases Involving Allegedly False Rape and Domestic Violence Allegations', (CPS Equality and Diversity Unit, 2013). This report is considered in more detail in section 19.6. It did give the impression of demonstrating that false allegations of domestic abuse are rare, but actually it merely showed that prosecutions for false allegations of domestic abuse are rare, which no one disputes.

Table 10.2: *Ratio of DV orders to Private Law Children Act cases*

Year	NMOs	All DV Orders
2003	42%	59%
2012 (just prior to LASPO)	51%	58%
2017	61%	66%

Figure 10.4: *Number of Court Orders made for Domestic Violence Remedies, Before and After LASPO*

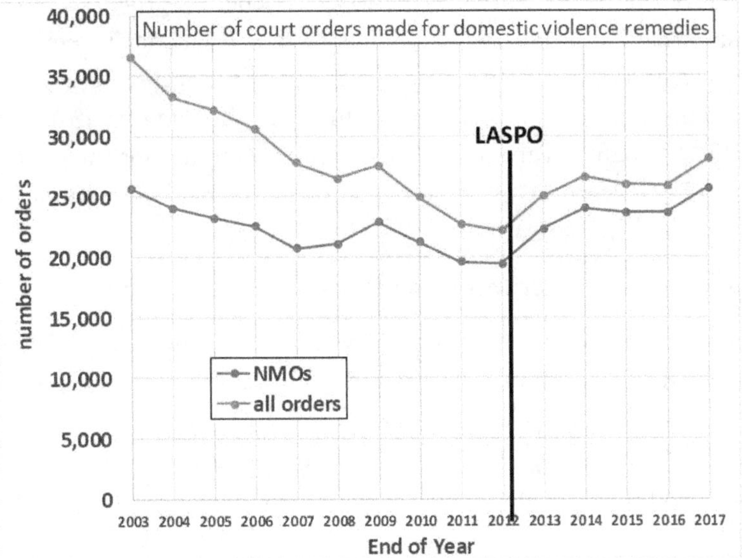

Figure 10.5: *Number of Non-Molestation Orders Issued in the Midlands Area, Showing a Marked Increase after LASPO*

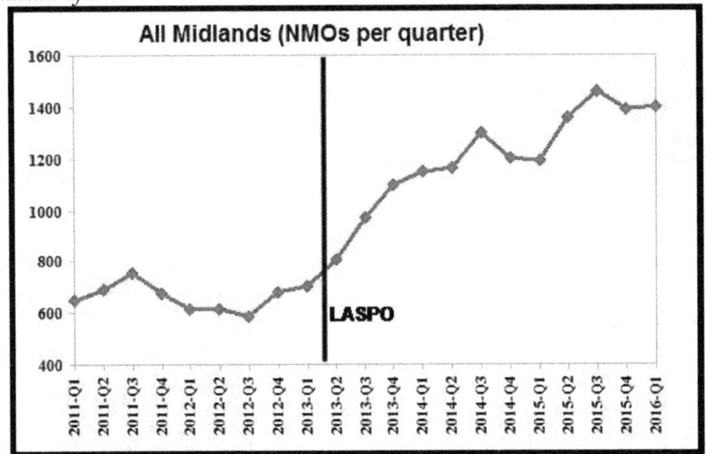

The increase in NMOs is more marked in some geographical regions than others. The increase is most marked in the Midlands (Figure 10.5) and this is driven predominantly by increases in Birmingham and Solihull.

Are the allegations which lie behind these NMOs valid or false? The review of Hunt and Macleod examined 308 private law child arrangement cases and found that exactly half (154) involved allegations of domestic violence. But in only 24 cases was a "finding of fact" hearing listed, of which

12 never took place. So, in this sample, only 8% of allegations were ever subject to a "finding of fact". Anecdotal evidence, (Barnett, 2014), is that "finding of fact" hearings may have increased in frequency recently, though opinions are mixed. In some quarters, the guilt of the accused is assumed, but this presumption has no legal basis in the overwhelming majority of cases. The tactical benefits of the allegation to the accuser are obtained without its truth ever being formally examined, even on a "balance of probability" basis, in the great majority of cases.

10.4 Lobbying and Serious Case Reviews

The family courts do not operate in a vacuum. They are subject to lobbying by interest groups, both directly and indirectly via the political process. This lobbying has been going on for decades and would form a study in its own right - see, for example, the book 'An Exercise in Absolute Futility: How falsehood and myth changed the landscape of family law', (Langford, 2015). I shall give just one recent example. In January 2016, the charity Women's Aid launched a campaign called 'Child First'. This campaign was underpinned by a report produced by Women's Aid entitled 'Nineteen Child Homicides', (Women's Aid, 2016). The organisation wrote,

> 'We have launched the Child First campaign to stop avoidable child deaths as a result of unsafe child contact with dangerous perpetrators of domestic violence.' (Women's Aid, 2015),

Women's Aid claim that their campaign report, 'Nineteen Child Homicides'…

> '…highlights the tragic stories of 19 children and 2 women in 12 families that were killed by perpetrators of domestic abuse in circumstances related to unsafe child contact within a ten year period. It's possible that these deaths could have been prevented if the domestic abuse had been considered as an ongoing risk factor.'

The cases in question are valid and terrible. However, what Women's Aid have done is to select 12 cases from 10 years of data to present a particular point of view. This is lobbying for a predetermined objective, based on extreme "cherry picking", not research. The campaign had no interest in presenting a balanced picture. The objective of the campaign was to put pressure on the courts to tighten their approach to ordering contact with fathers. Ostensibly this was in order to end, as the Foreword of 'Nineteen Child Homicides' put it, 'a deeply embedded culture that pushes for contact with fathers at all costs'. They succeeded. The relevant court procedure, so-called Practice Direction 12J, was revised, (Ministry of Justice, 2017b).

The source of information used to compile the report 'Nineteen Child Homicides' was the Serious Case Reviews (SCRs). These are reports produced by the child safeguarding authorities when children are killed or seriously harmed. The extreme degree of careful selection of cases reported in 'Nineteen Child Homicides' begs an obvious question: what would be the outcome of an unbiased review of all the Serious Case Reviews? This was reported by Bradford, (332 Child Homicides, 2018a). In the 7 years 2009 to 2015 there were 332 children culpably killed in the UK whose deaths have been subject to Serious Case Reviews by the child protection authorities (excluding suicides). The review attempted to establish the perpetrator or perpetrators, using a balance of probability judgment where there was no conviction. The conclusion was that mothers were responsible for at least as many child deaths as fathers and male partners combined, in fact, rather more (see also section 9.2.7).

Polly Neate, then the CEO of Women's Aid, wrote in the Foreword to 'Nineteen Child Homicides',

> 'While it is impossible to prevent every killing of a child, when the risks are known no other consideration should be more important – yet there is evidence here that other considerations were rated more highly.'

This admirable sentiment can take on a very different interpretation from that intended by Polly Neate, who assumes that only men can be a risk to children. The irony is that the Women's Aid mindset itself represents "other considerations" which are rated more highly than child safety, even when the "risks are known". By relentlessly pursuing the narrow interests of mothers, and wilfully ignoring the possibility that mothers can also pose a risk, the best interests of the child are made subsidiary, not paramount. The more complete examination of the same evidence base as used by Women's Aid shows that mothers can pose at least as much risk to their children as men. The Women's Aid campaign's conclusion is therefore in conflict with the paramountcy principle.

It is not only the review by Bradford (2018a) which has highlighted the potential risk that mothers may pose to their children. American data has long shown that mothers are responsible for more child fatalities by abuse or neglect than fathers or other men combined (see section 9.2.7). In addition, CAFCASS have published research which concurs with this conclusion. The report 'Learning from CAFCASS submissions to Serious Case Reviews' was made available publicly in November 2017, Green and Halliday (2017). The report derives lessons to be learnt from the 97 SCRs to which CAFCASS contributed from 2009 to 2016. These SCRs involve known or suspected abuse or neglect of a child where the child has died or the child has been seriously harmed. The key findings were,

- Mothers and fathers were suspected perpetrators of a similar number of incidents of child homicide;
- Allegations of domestic abuse had been made in 71% of cases, and almost all allegations of domestic abuse were against men, or included men, usually fathers;
- Of those cases where domestic abuse allegations had been made, only in about half of the cases was the person thought to have killed or harmed the child the alleged domestic abuse perpetrator;
- In some cases, the authorities' concentration on the alleged risk posed by the father or male partner may have masked a greater risk posed by the mother. Quote, 'In some cases where index incidents were perpetrated by the mother, SCRs found that the mother's history had not been sufficiently analysed, concerns about her being overshadowed by concerns about the father or other male. It is interesting to note that such SCRs do not show a simple relationship between male domestic abuse and the fatal/serious maltreatment of children.'

In summary, the dominant narrative, buoyed by powerful lobbying, that it is men in particular who pose a risk to children, is not borne out by the evidence. Allegations of domestic violence have a significant bearing on the outcomes of child contact applications (see chapter 11), but the relationship of such allegations to actual risk is in doubt, partly because of the prevalence of false allegations and partly because other people, including the mother, may pose a greater risk. The most disconcerting aspect of this is that the child safeguarding authorities display the same mindset, namely that domestic abuse is only ever a threat posed by a man to the mother and child. The result is that safeguarding guidance completely ignores the threat to the children which may be posed by the mother, see for example (London Safeguarding Children Board, 2017b). The evidence suggests that this ignores an equal or greater risk to the child in many cases.

10.5 The Empathy Gap Against Fathers in the Family Courts

Even today most people will refuse to believe that one of feminism's main aims is, and always was, to give women the power to rid their families of men.

There is a terrible arrogance here that sees only the female parent as significant. In the family courts we see this played out explicitly. Allegations of domestic abuse provide a convenient mechanism. Protestations that only abusive men are treated in this way are untrue, as the bald statistics illustrate. Unfortunately, the denigration of men over the last 50 years has been so successful that the public no longer balk at the preposterous notion that half of all fathers are abusers.

In the matter of child arrangements after parental separation we see most clearly how far culturally intensified gynocentrism has departed from evolved matricentrism. The child's best interests are elided with the mother's wishes, and the latter are truly made paramount. The invalidity of Family Courts' supposed protecting of the child's best interests has been expressed by Karen Woodall thus,

> 'In the UK there is a distinct lack of interest in family separation in social services, those with statutory responsibility for the wellbeing of children. This lack of interest in family separation stems largely from the feminist project to promote the rights of women and the manner in which the needs of children in society are seen as indivisible from the rights and wellbeing of their mother. Additionally, the promotion of single parenthood and the belief that families come in all shapes and sizes, means that the experiences of children through divorce and separation are seen as somewhat insignificant. Children are expected to 'get over it' and so long as their physical needs are met, there is not much concern about their emotional and psychological wellbeing.' (Woodall, 2019)

The powerful feminist lobby can mount campaigns such as 'Child First' and win debates in parliament which are not debates but monocultures of opinion, the feminist establishment being passed ammunition by the external lobbying to promulgate a gross distortion of reality, (Hansard, 2016). On another day, in another context, the same feminists will be arguing that men should do more childcare, so that women can pursue their fulfilling middle class careers. If this seems inconsistent – no, it is perfectly consistent with the feminist objective of increasing women's power in every circumstance. Only the arguments are inconsistent. Gynocentrism ensures that even a male dominated legislature and judiciary will acquiesce to the demands of the feminist lobby, because lack of in-group preference means the empathy gap operates between man and man as much as between woman and man. These combined psychosocial forces mean that the extent to which a man is permitted to be a father is defined by the mother, as we shall see next.

11

Are the Family Courts Biased Against Fathers?

The elimination of the father has always been an essential purpose of the sisterhood. The assaults they have mounted upon marriage and the 'bourgeois' family may be seen as strategic ploys, clothed in ideological humbug and mumbo-jumbo, which were intended to vitiate men's rights of paternity and to transfer all parental rights to women.
Neil Lyndon, 'No More Sex War' (1992)

Most societies have arranged matters so that a family surrounds and protects mother and child; our families having withered away so that only a male "partner" remains, we find ourselves in a situation where the mother and children need often to be protected from him rather than by him. Our consensual liaisons grow less durable every year and, if the evidence of wife-battery, rape-within-marriage and child sexual abuse is to be credited, it is to be hoped that they will soon wither away altogether. The State having taken over the duties of children towards their parents (and allowed the childless among us to face the future without dread) it had better finish the job and take over the duties of the father towards the child.
Germaine Greer, *Independent Magazine* (25 May 1991)

11.1. Introduction

It is not only fathers' groups, but also many in the general public who will readily agree that fathers get a rough deal from the family courts. And yet, in 2015, a report funded by the Nuffield Foundation was published, authored by academics from the Universities of Warwick and Reading, for which the associated press release was titled, 'study finds English family courts not discriminating against fathers', (Harding and Newnham, 2015). The press picked up the story and headlines followed such as 'Anti-father court bias is a myth', (Gibb, 2015), 'Men are treated fairly when trying to get access to their children in courts, study says', (Dutta, 2015), and, 'No anti-father bias in family courts, research finds', (Smith, 2015). These headlines were motivated by the report's findings, such as,

> '…the County courts showed no indication of gender bias in contested cases about where the child should live. Contact applications by fathers were overwhelmingly successful.'
>
> 'The County Courts actively promoted as much contact as possible even in cases of proven domestic violence, often combined with welfare concerns or strong opposition from older children.'

Dr Harding is quoted in the publicity release as saying,

> 'Whilst it's true that mothers were usually the primary care giver in contact applications, this was simply a reflection of the social reality that women are more likely to take on the role after a relationship breakdown. But there was actually no indication of any bias towards mothers over fathers by the courts; in fact we established there was a similar success rate for mothers and fathers applying for orders to have their children live with them.'

Are we to conclude that all those fathers who, over the last 40 years, have complained of being unfairly estranged from their children, are just making it up? I review the Harding-Newnham report below, after also reviewing an earlier study by Joan Hunt and Alison Macleod (2008). Before proceeding, there is a key factor to bear in mind. The issuing of a court order does not guarantee that it is obeyed. The studies reviewed here were able only to count the orders, of various types, produced by the courts. Whether the contact, or the extent of contact, ordered was actually forthcoming is another matter entirely. It may be that the chief criticism one could bring against the family courts is not so much their bias, but their inability to influence people's behaviour – and their toothlessness in enforcing their own orders. These issues are explored in this chapter. Before we blithely conclude there is no bias against fathers on the basis of counting court orders, there are a number of factors to which we should be alert and which may be obscured in some studies,

- Does a bias in outcome originate from societal norms, and the initial status quo, rather than from the courts?
- What is the extent of contact ordered? Is it what was requested, and, if so, was a modest request conditioned by societal norms and expectations?
- Is the court order obeyed, or does the resident parent frustrate contact? Does the court enforce its own orders?
- How long does it take for a court ruling to be made, from the time of separation? If this is several years, as is common, has the non-resident parent's relationship with his/her child been disrupted beyond repair?

In addition, note that the studies reviewed here did not interview the parents affected. Turning firstly to the earlier of the two studies I wish to review.

11.2 The 2008 Study of Hunt & MacLeod

In 2008, a report was published by the Ministry of Justice Family Law Division, 'Outcomes of applications to court for contact orders after parental separation or divorce', authored by Joan Hunt and Alison Macleod (2008) of the Oxford Centre for Family Law and Policy, University of Oxford. The study was based on a sample of 308 files covering cases heard in all three tiers of family court which then existed: the family proceedings courts, the county courts and the high court. The criteria for selection were a) that there was an application for a contact order, b) that the applicant was a parent and the child was living with the other parent, c) that the application was made in 2004 (the latter requirement giving sufficient time for most cases to have ended in time for publication in 2008). Where more than one child was involved in a case, one child was selected (randomly) as the index child on whom the data to be collected would focus. Interviews were conducted with magistrates, solicitors and other legal advisors, and officers of CAFCASS (Children and Family Court Advisory and Support Service). Interviews did not address the specific cases studied. No interviews with parents were carried out.

Of the 308 sample cases, 60% involved a single child, mean age 4.5 years (mean age of all children 5.5 years). The vast majority of children (279; 91%) lived for most or all of the time with their mothers; with 23 (7%) living with their fathers. Four children had recently temporarily changed residence (three from their mother and one from their father) and two appeared to be in a *de facto* shared living arrangement.

That 91% of children were living with their mother at the start of the proceedings is of central importance. It will be seen that the operation of the family courts is such that the initial status quo is the dominant factor in influencing the final outcome. To pre-empt our conclusion, the bias in the outcomes for fathers may not be so much a bias in the operation of the family courts as it is the intrinsic bias in society, and hence a bias in the status quo at the start of proceedings.

The average age of the fathers in the sample was 34, but the range was enormous, from 17 to 58. Nine were under 21 at the point they brought the application. The mothers were on average slightly younger (mean 31) but again there was a wide age range (18-50), with 14 being under 21.

In over half the sample cases (162 of 308; 53%) the parents were not married to each other, with 116 (38% of 308) having cohabited. In almost half of cases where information was available, the interval between parental separation and the court proceedings exceeded two years (46% 116 of 255); just over a fifth (56; 22%) had separated within the previous six months. Bear in mind the significance of a delay of the order of years in the life of a child under 5.

Applications were almost all (289; 94%) brought by the non-resident parent, typically the father (265 of 289; 92%) although there were also 24 cases brought by non-resident mothers (24 of 289, 8%). More than half the non-resident parent applicants (156 of 289; 54%) were also seeking other orders, typically a parental responsibility order (107 of 156; 69%), with 49 seeking sole or shared residence (31%). It is worth emphasizing at this point the bias that already exists before the courts begin to operate. The *de facto* position is that about 92% of non-resident parents before proceedings commence are fathers. Fathers are on their back foot from the start, a position of disadvantage from which they will (statistically speaking) never recover.

Another disadvantage, and a most egregious one, lies behind the large number of 'people' applying for parental responsibility orders. None of the 107 applicants for parental responsibility orders will have been mothers, because mothers automatically have parental responsibility: but unmarried fathers do not. Entering the court proceedings without the initial benefit of having legally recognised parental responsibility can only put the father at a significant disadvantage, and this is a disadvantage encoded in law. But perhaps this is less significant than one might imagine, the report noting that,

> 'Somewhat surprisingly, there was no association between whether the non-resident parent got face to face contact and whether the parents had previously been married, nor even between whether they had ever lived together. Those who had been previously married, however, were more likely than those who had not to get staying rather than visiting contact (57% compared to 47%)'

One could turn this around, though, and conclude that being married, or having parental responsibility, does mean much in practice. Where information was available (in 286 cases), 38% of resident parents (109 of 286) were known to have been opposed to any face to face contact, with a further 15% (44) wanting supervised contact only, i.e., a total of 53% of resident parents were opposed to anything beyond supervised contact. An additional 11% of resident parents were resistant to 'staying contact', i.e., overnight stays with the non-resident parent. These statistics are very important because, as we shall see, the initial position of the resident parent is the most significant factor in the contact outcome for the non-resident parent.

Consistent with other evidence (see chapter 10 and section 11.4), Hunt and MacLeod observed that, 'in exactly half the sample cases (154 cases of

308) allegations of domestic violence perpetrated by the non-resident parent had been made at some point'. Note the distinction between allegation and established fact, and recall that very few of these allegations will ever be subjected to meaningful investigation.

The outcomes in terms of court orders (as opposed to what may actually have transpired) were given by Hunt and MacLeod as follows. Where outcomes were known (286 cases), 49% resulted in "staying" orders, i.e., staying overnight at the non-resident parent's home; 20% resulted in orders for unsupervised visiting; and, 31% resulted in orders for supervised or conditional contact, indirect contact, or no contact at all. Indirect contact refers to contact by 'phone, letter, email, etc., but not face-to-face. No contact at all was ordered in 14% of cases. 95 resident parents initially opposed any form of contact at all (36% of those where this was known, 266). This was virtually equal to the number that did not oppose any form of contact (103, 36% of 286).

The number of cases in each outcome category are displayed in Figure 11.1, which distinguishes according to the resident parents' initial position on contact. Where the court order was for no contact at all, or for indirect contact only, this resulted overwhelmingly from the resident parent being opposed to any form of contact. Applicants for a staying order by both sexes were comparably successful: 100 being granted out of 124 fathers applying, and 10 being granted out of 12 mothers applying. Hence, 91% of staying order applications were granted to fathers.

Figure 11.1: *Court Ordered Contact Outcomes by Resident Parents' Initial Position*

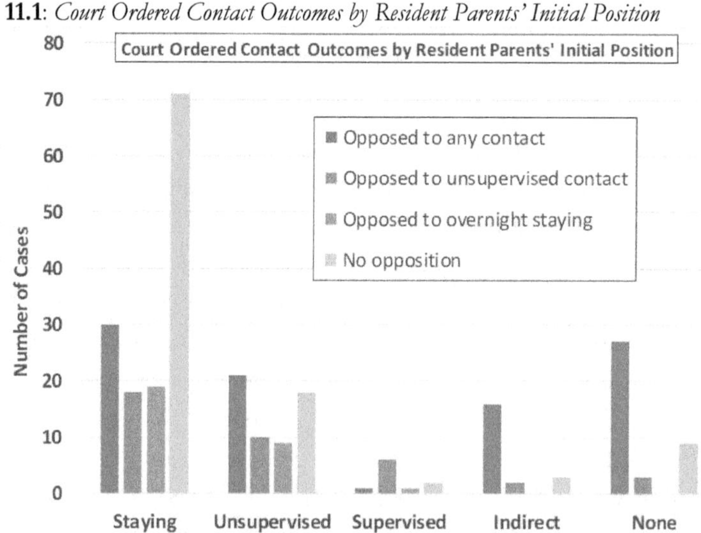

The ordered frequency of overnight staying was: at least weekly 30%; fortnightly 59%; monthly 11%. The number of overnight stays per instance was one (45% of cases) or two (43% of cases) or three (11% of cases). In these cases where staying contact was ordered, non-staying visits may also have been ordered, though in 79% of cases this was only one or two days per fortnight. In terms of total hours contact, staying plus non-staying, this amounts to between 25 hours and 72 hours (i.e., between 7% and 21% of the time) in 76% of cases. Recall that this is the time awarded by the courts, not necessarily what transpires.

Where the court order was for unsupervised visits, the number of hours contact per fortnight was far smaller than when staying contact was ordered, on average just 10.3 hours per fortnight. The range is broad, with any number of hours from just 3 hours per fortnight to 20 hours per fortnight being almost equally likely (see Figure 11.2). Again recall, this is the time awarded by the courts, not necessarily what transpires. These are the so-called McDads, whose contact with their children is barely sufficient for a visit to the park and a meal in McDonald's once per fortnight. In terms of having a fighting chance of maintaining a meaningful long-term involvement in your child's life a staying contact order must be the objective.

Figure 11.2: *Contact Hours Awarded Per Fortnight in Cases Where Unsupervised Visitation Has Been Ordered (not overnight staying)*

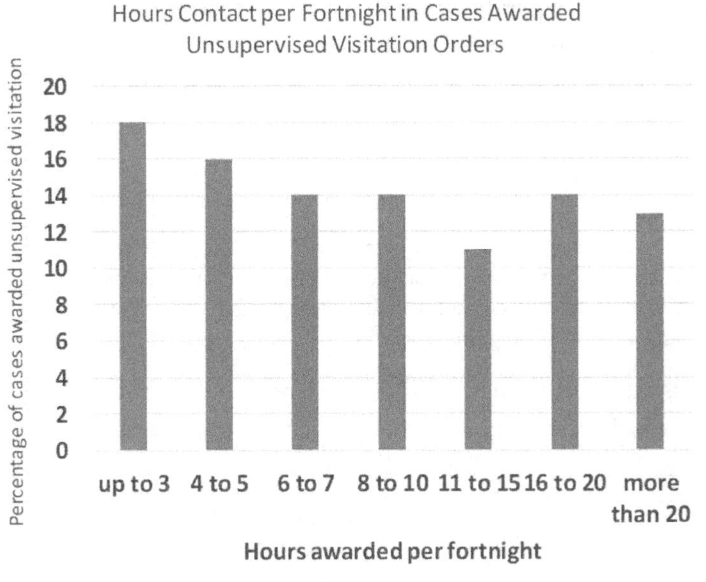

In almost half of cases in which the non-resident parent had come to court to achieve some form of face to face contact (128 of 269; 48%) the outcome fell short in some respect of what the applicant had originally sought. 85 (32%) did not achieve the type of contact they had initially sought (56 failed to achieve face to face contact; 25 got visiting contact rather than the staying contact they had sought; 4 got only supervised contact). 43 (16%) achieved the type of contact sought but not the quantum desired, i.e., less frequent overnights or less frequent or shorter duration visits.

Two factors most influence the outcome for the non-resident parent. The first is the initial attitude of the resident parent, the second is whether there is a claim of a "serious welfare issue" against the non-resident parent. These "serious welfare issues" include allegations of domestic violence, child abuse, neglect, drug or alcohol abuse or mental illness. More than four in five cases which ended with no face-to-face contact involved such issues.

In contrast, where serious welfare concerns were not raised, 90% of cases (112 of 125) ended with either staying (65%) or unsupervised visiting contact (25%). Hence, whilst allegations of domestic abuse do not necessarily prevent staying or unsupervised contact, these results do indicate a strong correlation between failing to gain such contact and a suspicion of 'welfare issues' against the non-resident parent, especially allegations of domestic abuse. What the data do not reveal is whether the refusal by the courts to order face-to-face contact aligns with a genuine risk, or only a concern created by allegation. It is worth noting in that context that "findings of fact" in regard to allegations of domestic violence are relatively rare, as noted in chapter 10. To quote Hunt & MacLeod,

> 'Asked why finding of fact hearings are not listed more often both CAFCASS officers and solicitors largely attributed this to the courts' reluctance.
>
> (Quote from Judge): We do our best to avoid them (findings of fact) if at all possible because they are totally unproductive and unhelpful, on the whole. It just raises the temperature. And how do you decide whether he hit her or not when it's her saying one thing and him saying the other?'

As regards the significance of the initial position adopted by the resident parent, this is illustrated by Figure 11.1. On the issue of the time it takes the courts to make an order, we read the following in Hunt & MacLeod,

> '...few of our sample cases were resolved quickly. The average duration was almost 11 months. Over a third of completed cases (35%) took more than a year and 6% more than two, the longest case having been continuously before the courts for four

years…..the average duration of cases which had not completed was 35 months, the shortest having started 29 months previously, the longest 43.'

'Some of the longest cases in the study were those where the resident parent had been initially opposed to any contact but the outcome of the proceedings was that this was expected to take place. Over half these cases (54%) took more than 12 months….Where the resident parent raises concerns about the safety of the child with the non-resident parent then those concerns have to be investigated. Fifty-eight per cent of such cases took more than 12 months.'

Perhaps there has been an improvement on these times in the last ten years. The Family Court Statistics Quarterly, January to March 2018, indicate in the first quarter of 2018 a mean time from start to completion in Private Family Law of 26 weeks (median 20 weeks), (Ministry of Justice, 2018f).

However, it must be borne in mind that these times are only the time taken from the point of application to a first order. It is common for parental separation to have occurred several years prior to the application being made, as illustrated by Figure 11.3 (from Hunt & MacLeod's Appendix Table 6). In addition, in some cases, there may be later enforcement applications (see section 11.3 and Figure 11.4).

Figure 11.3: *Interval between Parental Separation and Application to the Court*

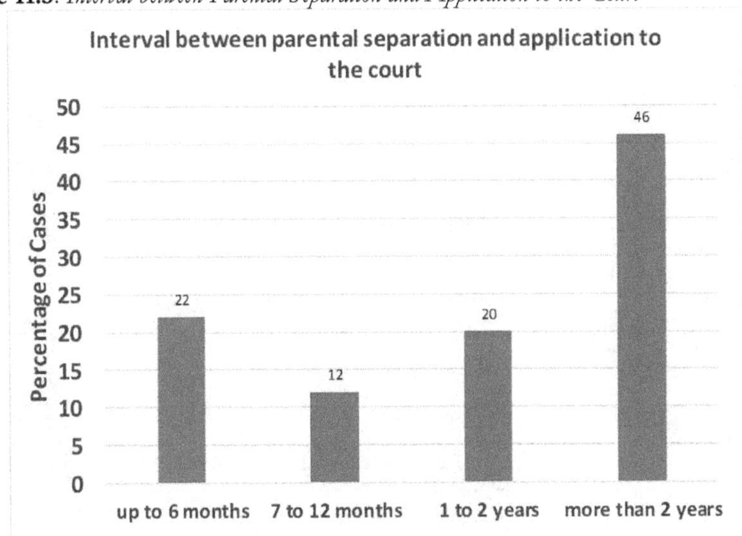

11.3 Lawyers', Judges' and Court Officers' Opinions

I cannot do justice to the full set of quotes reported by Hunt & MacLeod. However, here are a selection relating to the influence of the resident parent on the proceedings.

'Where we are highly ineffective are cases where the resident mothers take the view that they don't want contact to happen. And in those cases it is very, very difficult.' (Judge)

'There are certain resident parents and they're quite a big group I guess, who have the attitude that they're looking after the child and their relationship with the child is considerably more important than the relationship with the other parent. And therefore contact has a small part to play in the child's life, it's of relatively little importance and more of a nuisance than a benefit. That's a fairly common attitude.' (CAFCASS officer)

'I do think that most parents want what is best for their child but they just don't recognise that it is helpful to a child to grow up knowing both parents.' (Judge)

'Quite often we find that in contact cases the parents are just using the child as a pawn, and especially the resident mother because it's just a way of getting back at a partner she no longer has a relationship with other than through the child and it's the only way they can do that.' (Magistrate)

'They've got a new man and they want their happy family and father interferes with that. That's relatively common.' (Magistrate)

Figure 11.4: *Interval between Order being Flouted and Application for Enforcement*

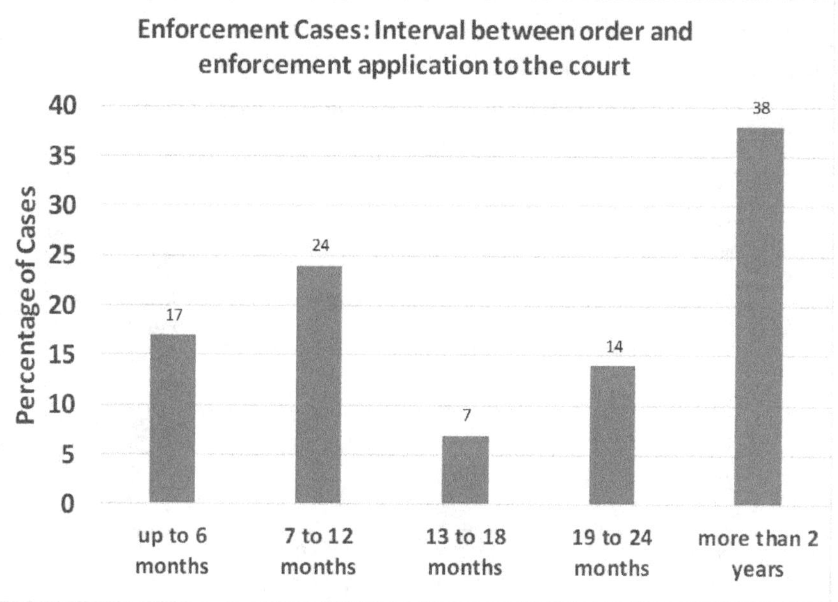

11.4 The 2015 Study of Harding and Newnham

I turn now to the study by Maebh Harding and Annika Newnham (2015) funded by the Nuffield Foundation. This is the study which provoked the press headlines quoted at the start of this chapter. The study was based on a sample of cases which they describe as follows,

> 'The research is based on document analysis of a retrospective sample of 197 case files from the County Courts. We examined case files from five different County Courts in England and Wales.....The sample was limited to Section 8 application cases which were disposed of by final order in a six month period between February and August in 2011.'

Here "Section 8" refers to the Children Act, (UK Government, 1989), and is the section which relates to child arrangement orders, parental responsibility orders, and associated orders. The authors selected just under half the relevant "Section 8" cases from the chosen courts over the six month period. They do not state how that selection was done, or claim that the sample is either representative or random. Instead they write, rather disconcertingly,

> 'At the time of selection there were 210 County Courts in the UK. It should be noted that our findings about the use of different Section 8 orders and the typical time patterns orders are not statistically representative of the general practice in 2011 but instead give us an idea of the different types of solutions being used in these five courts in 2011 in a range of circumstances.'

It is difficult to be certain what this ungrammatical sentence means, but it appears to admit that their sample is not representative. More disconcertingly, the authors appear to have selected cases on some undeclared basis. There are other reasons to suspect that this is the case, as we shall see.

Of the 197 cases selected by Harding & Newnham only 174 related to parents, and the rest of the report focuses on those. In common with other sources, Harding & Newnham note that 50% of cases involved allegations of domestic violence (40% against father, 2% against mother, 8% against both). They further note that, of the 86 cases in which allegations of domestic violence were made, the new LASPO evidential requirements (see Table 10.1) were satisfied in 45 cases (52%). Noting that the LASPO requirements are minimal, this may have a bearing on the likely validity of the remaining allegations.

The sample of cases addressed by Harding & Newnham include at least 30 applications by mothers for sole residency, and at least 32 cases by fathers for sole residency (Harding & Newnham section 2.2). It is striking, and unexpected, that these two figures should be almost equal. Father's applications for sole residency were 18% of the total cases considered (32 out of 174), and mother's applications for sole residency were 17% of the total. One would expect a substantially greater number of sole residency applications from mothers, an expectation confirmed by Hunt & MacLeod's sample which included just 9 cases of fathers seeking sole residency (3% of

308), compared to 44 mothers seeking sole residency (15%). This suggests that Harding & Newnham's sample has an uncharacteristically large proportion of cases in which fathers were seeking sole residency.

Another indication that Harding & Newnham's sample may be unrepresentative relates to where the child was living at the time of the court application. Their table in section 2.6.1 indicates the child was with the mother in 126 cases (76%) and with the father in 39 cases (24%), ignoring the few indeterminate cases. This contrasts with only 9% of cases involving residency with the father at the start of proceedings in Hunt & MacLeod's sample.

This concern that the child's residence at the time of application may indicate the unrepresentative nature of Harding & Newnham's sample relates particularly to fathers' applications for sole residency. Of the 32 such applications, to quote section 2.8.5 of Harding & Newnham, 'Dad was the pre-application status quo primary caregiver in only 7 of the 32 applications by fathers for residence….However, in 20 applications the child was in the care of the father at the time of the application'. This is an extraordinarily high proportion of residence with the father at the time of application (63%), compared with all cases (typically 8% or 9%). Clearly, these 32 are mostly self-selected cases in which the father has deemed he has an unusually great chance, or need, of winning sole residency.

It is worth clarifying how Harding & Newnham can claim that fathers were the "status quo primary caregiver in only 7 of the 32 applications by fathers for residence" when in 20 of those 32 applications the child was living with the father at the time of the application. This is explained simply by Harding & Newnham defining the "status quo primary caregiver" as 'the main carer of the child for over one year'. The peculiar circumstance that only 7 of the 32 fathers are labelled as "status quo primary carers", and yet 20 of the 32 cases involved children living with their fathers at the time of application, results from many children having very recently moved residence. Specifically we read,

> 'In 16 cases the child had been living with the mother and was now with the father. In 2 cases the child had previously lived with the father and was now with the mother. In 10 of these transfer cases the transfer had occurred because the child had been placed with the other parent following social services or police involvement. In 8 cases the change was because one of the parents had retained the child following contact. Most of these cases also cited child safety concerns as the reason for retaining the child.'

Consequently, the claim made by Harding & Newnham that, "fathers' applications for residence were mainly to change, rather than protect, the status quo or to reflect a recent change in care" could easily be misunderstood – largely as a result of the particular usage of the term "status quo". In fact, 20 of these 32 applications by fathers for sole residency were in order to consolidate the arrangements which prevailed at the time of application, and so were not 'mainly to change' existing arrangements at all.

A further concern that Harding & Newnham's sample may not be representative relates to the proportion of their sample which involved 'serious welfare issues' *excluding* domestic violence. More of these issues were raised against mothers than against fathers. Such issues were raised in 79 out of the 174 cases (45%), of which 30 were against fathers (17%), 34 against mothers (19%), and 12 against both (9%). Harding & Newnham themselves note that, as regards the 32 applications by fathers for sole residency,

> 'What stood out from these cases was how many of the fathers' residence applications featured quite serious fears about the children's safety (*i.e., from the mother*), which were usually shared by social workers or healthcare professionals. If we look at the reasons given by the fathers in the 32 applications for sole residence, 8 mentioned local authority involvement, 7 claimed that Mum was incapable and 3 were made to protect the child from the mother.'

This appears to be an abnormally large proportion of mothers deemed to be a risk to their children in this particular set of 32 cases. Recall the press headlines following publication of Harding & Newnham's study in 2015, quoted above. The publicity release by the (Nuffield Foundation, 2015) gives a key conclusion as,

> 'There was actually no indication of any bias towards mothers over fathers by the courts; in fact we established there was a similar success rate for mothers and fathers applying for orders to have their children live with them.'

This claim is based on the number of orders made for sole residency, namely 40 for mothers and 24 for fathers (Harding & Newnham section 4.2). One could reasonably argue that these figures do not support the claim (40 is significantly larger than 24), especially in view of the number of *applications* for residency by fathers in their sample exceeding the number by mothers.

But the more serious objection is the apparently unrepresentative nature of their sample cases. The preceding observations have indicated that Harding & Newnham's sample, (i) included an abnormally large proportion of applications for sole residency by fathers, (ii) that these applications involved an abnormally large proportion of children who were already resident with their fathers at the time of the application, and, (iii) that there were an abnormally large number of mothers in these 32 cases against whom there were serious child welfare concerns.

Consequently, Harding & Newnham's highly publicized claim that, 'we established there was a similar success rate for mothers and fathers applying for orders to have their children live with them' must be ruled as lacking valid substantiation. The cases chosen appear to be highly uncharacteristic.

11.5 Enforcement

The principal failing of the family courts is an almost total lack of enforcement of their own orders. I emphasised earlier the important distinction between what the court orders, and what happens in reality. It is common for the resident parent to frustrate, or deliberately obstruct, fulfilment of orders for contact by the non-resident parent. If the non-resident parent has spent years getting to the point of having an order for contact, having this flouted by the resident parent will understandably cause great irritation. But loss of temper will avail the non-resident parent nothing. Unfortunately, little else will either. At the start of the process the resident parent holds all the cards. At the end of the process the resident parent still holds all the cards – largely due to lack of enforcement of court orders.

The Family Court Statistics Quarterly, January to March 2018, (Ministry of Justice, 2018f), provides data for the number of children involved in applications for private law enforcement orders, and the number of children for whom such orders are made. The ratio of the latter to the former is plotted against year in Figure 11.5. In 2011 only 2% of enforcement applications actually resulted in an enforcement order; by 2018 this had decreased further to just 0.2%. In the first quarter of 2018, 1813 applications for enforcement were made, just 3 were ordered. Between 2011 and 2017 the number of applications for enforcement more than tripled, from 2078 to 6832 annually. But an enforcement order almost never emerges from the application, and this is now almost literally 'never'.

In 2011, the number of enforcement applications was 5% (2%) of the number of contact applications (orders); by the first quarter of 2018 this had increased to 17% (10%). This provides an indication of the *minimum* extent to which court orders for contact are being flouted. (I have made the assumption that enforcement orders relate overwhelmingly to contact orders).

Figure 11.5: *Enforcement Orders Granted as a Percentage of Enforcement Applications*

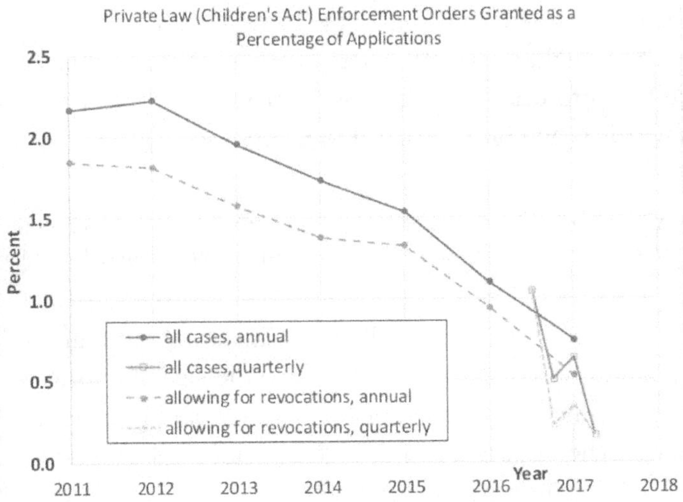

Of the sample cases studied by (Hunt and MacLeod, 2008) we read,

> 'Thirty applications by non-resident parents (10%), were brought, at least in part, because of the resident parent's alleged non-compliance with an order.....Most of the applicants in these cases (and all those seeking penal notices) were non-resident fathers.'

It is not clear what we can conclude from this regarding the percentage of cases for which court orders *are* obeyed, because it is likely that many disappointed non-resident parents simply do not raise an enforcement application. Similarly, it is not clear if the frequency of disobeying court orders is increasing, or whether non-resident parents are becoming more inclined to make enforcement applications. If the latter, one wonders why because, as we shall see, there appears to be no benefit – quite the opposite.

If an enforcement order does not result, what *does* happen after an enforcement application is made? In other words, what happens when a non-resident parent complains to the court that their own order is being disrespected? The answer is quite shocking if (Hunt and MacLeod, 2008) is any guide. The best you can realistically hope for is that your original order is reinstated. In only 2 of the 30 cases of enforcement applications in Hunt & MacLeod's sample was a penal notice issued. But in 4 cases the request for a penal notice was declined. But worse: in 14 of the 30 cases, even the original order was not reinstated. Instead a new order was issued for *reduced contact.* So, in about half of cases where a resident parent has refused to abide by the terms of a court order, and the non-resident parent has brought the matter formally to the attention of the court, the court responds by "rewarding" the resident parent with reduced contact by the non-resident parent. In Hunt & MacLeod's sample there were 19 initial orders for staying contact which were later subject to enforcement applications. The result was eight of these fathers had their initial staying order reduced to a non-staying order. To quote Hunt & MacLeod,

> 'In all, we calculate that 18 parents (62%) might consider themselves disappointed with the outcome of their application for 'enforcement', including 14 who failed entirely.'

These disappointed "parents" are all non-resident fathers. Hunt & MacLeod conclude, 'The court is ultimately impotent in the face of implacable hostility on the part of either resident parents or children and non-compliance with court orders'. The *de facto* position is that resident parents are a law unto themselves. The greatest problem with the family courts is their impotence in dealing with belligerent resident parents.

Hunt & MacLeod include many quotes from involved professionals. I include a few relating to the issue of enforcement below (there are other comments which may express differing opinions, see the report itself for the full set of quotations). One of the interesting things about these quotes is that, rather than use the cautious terminology "resident parent", as I have done, they generally simply refer to the mother.

- 'I suspect that your data will suggest that there is a reasonable amount of contact for fathers; that's what I would suspect. But what we get back in court is the reality that mothers don't cooperate and that's the biggest area where you get the argument that you don't get enough contact.' (Magistrate)
- 'The main problem is not getting a contact order but enforcing it if it is breached.' (Solicitor)
- 'I think the system is quite good at effecting an order and pushing people together and trying to get them to agree to try to compromise, the system is quite good at that. But the number of occasions when you come out of court with an order and six months later the client is back saying well I've got the order but it doesn't happen. In common with all other aspects of British law I think the enforcement side of all civil justice is very poor. In the bad cases you go round the loop again and again.' (Solicitor)
- 'It was really sad. An old client came a couple of weeks ago for another reason. We'd fought tooth and nail for four years, everything was thrown at us, sexual abuse allegations, neglect, you're not committed. And we got contact. Mother then moved away, never turned up and by then he'd lost the will and never came back

to enforce the order. I said to him it doesn't have to be that way, come back and I'll take it forward. But he hasn't come back.' (Solicitor)

- 'There was one particular case where we did take enforcement proceedings and mother started playing ball. But the client has got back in touch with me about another matter and I know contact isn't happening, so although mother started to comply when we took the proceedings she's not now. But I think he's just given up and thought 'it's such a battle'.' (Solicitor)
- 'The enforcement side is dreadful. There is a general perception among nonresident parents that 'this isn't worth the paper it's written on'.' (Solicitor)
- 'We are supposed to have a system where ultimately a parent who has physical possession of the child can be sent to prison but of course it very rarely happens and my experience is that a lot of non-resident parents go to court, get themselves an order, mum doesn't comply with the order, they come back to court to try and enforce it, and eventually they give up.' (Solicitor)
- 'You do feel that in certain circumstances the courts are timorous. I don't think the courts feel that they have the power to do anything about a mother (who fails to comply). There are a lot of fathers being advised just to give up if the mother has remained completely and implacably hostile.' (Solicitor)
- 'I have one case at the moment where the court needs to bite the bullet and put a penal notice on – 'thou shalt do this Mrs X'. But the court doesn't like doing it. The trouble is the court doesn't like saying you're out of order and you need to face up to reality and have a more reasonable approach. In the years we were before the court it didn't matter what they said to this mother it never happened. I think they could probably have taken a stronger stance with mother. There was no prison mentioned, no fine mentioned, they said it wouldn't be realistic to change residence. There was nothing really said to mother that was strong enough for her to do anything.' (Solicitor)
- 'Penal notices. I think sometimes they are not robust enough on that. They could be imposed more, they are a threat. And it may be sufficient for a parent to realise that they've got to take it in hand and they've got to encourage their child to have contact and they've got to also comply with the court orders. I had this case where I asked for a penal notice; it's been going on for 10 years- and still the court wouldn't do it.' (Solicitor)
- 'I've never seen any court fine anybody. There was a phase a few years ago where (X) court sent the odd mother to prison but I think the general accepted position at the moment is that they won't do it.' (Solicitor)
- 'The best way I've ever seen a contact order enforced was where the magistrates fined the mum by mistake, because they thought that they could. And I was acting for the mum and we appealed it, and we were successful on appeal, but that's the only time I saw that mum, I know it's my client, discuss contact sensibly, because she'd lost money.' (Solicitor)

- 'I'm not the sort of person who would be saying mum should be sent to prison, but on the one occasion that a mum did she purged her contempt and within a couple of days she was out of prison and contact worked from then on.' (Solicitor)
- 'She hasn't got two beans to rub together so a fine's impractical. Of course, he doesn't want to send her to prison, it's the last thing he wants.' (Solicitor)
- 'A financial penalty affects the child. Committal affects the child. I do wonder whether the suggestion that they might transfer residence might help, but having said that I'm not sure that would help either, because if that destabilises the child, their home life, what they're used to, their schooling, their friends...?' (Solicitor)
- 'A lot of fathers don't actually want the day to day care of the children so if your only sanction is you lose the children, how many fathers actually want it? There are some out there, my client today would gladly take the children. A lot of them I don't think would cope, so you have a toothless regime out there.' (Solicitor)

11.6 What Proportion of Separating Couples Apply to Court?

What proportion of divorcing or separating couples go to court for child arrangement orders? There is a mythology that the figure is 10%, i.e., that 90% of couples make private arrangements without involving the courts, for example see (Harding and Newnham, 2015). But it appears from MOJ data that the proportion of couples having recourse to the courts is far higher. The Family Court Statistics Quarterly, January to March 2018, (Ministry of Justice, 2018f), gives the following data for 2017. These relate to England and Wales,

- Private Law Children Act cases 50,651
- Children involved 76,780 (hence 1.52 children per case)
- Divorce, annulment, judicial separation cases 110,010
- Number of children involved in contact applications 44,267
- Dividing the above number by the average number of children per case gives 29,123 cases involving at least one contact application.

The number of divorces, annulments and separations indicated above is reasonably close to the number of divorces in 2017 given by (Office for National Statistics, 2017q), namely, 101,669. However, not all these involve dependent children. In 2013 only 48% of divorces involved children under 16, namely 55,323 cases out of 114,720, (Office for National Statistics, 2015c).

However, court orders for contact do not only relate to divorcing couples but also to previously cohabiting couples, or perhaps to a couple who were not even cohabiting. Despite cohabiting couples accounting for only around 20% of the total number of children, the Marriage Foundation (2018) estimates that cohabiting couples account for half of all family breakdown.

(This is broadly consistent with Hunt and MacLeod's sample of Children Act cases, of which 53% were unmarried). This suggests that there were around 203,000 family breakdowns in 2017, but that only about 100,000 involved dependent children (under 16).

Hence, the proportion of all family breakdowns involving dependent children where recourse to the courts is made for child contact arrangements appears to be roughly 29,123/100,000 or about 29%.

This may be an under-estimate as regards all child arrangement applications. The number of children involved in residence applications in 2017 was 29,149. One cannot simply add this to the number of children involved in contact applications because this will involve considerable double accounting. However, in England alone, in year 2017/18 CAFCASS received 41,844 new cases, (CAFCASS, 2017/18). Not all of these will relate to contact or residence applications, though around three-quarters probably will. Allowing also for Wales, the number of cases in England and Wales in which contact or residence applications were made in 2017 is perhaps closer to 33,000, or 33% of all family breakdowns involving dependent children. The "mythology" that the proportion is 10% therefore appears grossly inaccurate.

After I had made the above estimate (33%), and as stop press information in the final revision of this book, I became aware of information from CAFCASS. Teresa Williams, the Director of Strategy at CAFCASS, has drawn together data 'which indicate that around 38% of couples need to go to court to resolve disagreements over how they should care for their child post-separation'. This was reported by Sir Andrew MacFarlane, President of the Family Division, as part of his keynote address to the Resolution Conference in April 2019, (MacFarlane, 2019). It seems that even my 33% might be a slight under-estimate, though it is clear now that the figure is in this ball-park.

It is worth noting in passing that the number of child arrangements cases being received by CAFCASS is increasing. Over the five years 2014/15 to 2018/19 the numbers were 34,119; 37,415; 40,536; 41,844; and 44,141 respectively, (CAFCASS, 2017/18).

11.7 Actual Contact Outcomes

In reviewing the operation of the courts, I have emphasised the crucial distinction between what contact is ordered and what contact actually transpires. Moreover, we have seen in section 11.6 that around two-thirds of child contact arrangements occur without court involvement. For these reasons the statistics relating to court orders tell us very little about the reality of ongoing involvement of non-resident parents in their children's lives.

Quality data on the extent of contact by non-resident parents in the UK does not currently exist. This woeful lack of *quality* data is the main message in the review 'Shared Care After Separation in the United Kingdom: Limited Data, Limited Practice?', (Haux, McKay, and Cain, 2017), published in the Family Court Review. Despite lamenting this lack, the report does pull together what information is available, namely that derived from the UK Household Longitudinal Surveys (UKHLS, also widely known as the "Understanding Society" surveys) and its predecessor, the British Household Panel Survey (BHPS). Haux et al emphasise the manifold limitations of these sources, but they appear to be the best available guide at present. I reproduce their findings in Figures 11.6, 11.7 and 11.8. A few salient points from Figures 11.6-8 are,

- Almost equal shared care applies in at most 3% of cases, and less than this according to the nominally resident parents. Equal shared care has not increased since 2002;
- There are two sources of serious sample bias. The first is that resident parents are substantially more numerous in the surveys than non-resident parents, simply because the location of non-resident parents is harder to track;
- The other sample bias is that non-resident parents who have no contact at all with their children will be less likely to respond to surveys. This is probably why the estimate by the resident parent of the proportion of non-resident parents with no contact at all (27% to 33%) is substantially larger than the estimate based on the non-resident parents' responses (12% to 19%). This suggests the larger estimate is likely to be more accurate.
- Only 46% of non-resident parents have staying contact on a regular basis, but this may be an overestimate for the reasons discussed above. Note that this is similar to the proportion of court orders for regular staying contact identified by Hunt & MacLeod, i.e., 49%. It is not clear, therefore, that recourse to the courts significantly improves a non-resident parent's likelihood of achieving regular staying contact.
- 40% of non-resident parents have no staying contact, even on an irregular basis, and this is likely to be an underestimate for the reasons discussed above.

- The non-resident parent has contact once per week or more frequently in 57% to 61% of cases (non-resident parents' data), or 38% to 47% of cases (resident parents' data).
- The non-resident parent has contact more than once per month, but less often than once per week, in about 13% of cases.

Figure 11.6: *UKHLS 2013/14 (reproduced from Haux et al Table 3)*

Arrangements for Children—Parents' Reports

Question: Can you tell me how often you visit, see or contact your child(ren) under 16 living outside the household? *Column percentages*

Arrangement (NRP question)	*NRP %*	*Arrangement (PWC question)*	*PWC (term time) %*
Shared care 50–50	3		
Almost everyday	17	At least once per day	9
Several times a week	25	At least once per week	29
About once a week	16		
		At least once per fortnight	12
Several times a month	14	At least once per month	8
Once a month or less	5		
A few times a year	8	At least once per year	6
		Less often	3
Never	12	Never	33
Total	100	Total	100
N (parents)	781	N (children)	3,935

Source: UK Household Longitudinal Survey wave 5 (mostly 2013–14). Note that NRPs answer only for themselves, even if there are multiple children; PWCs answer separately about each child. This is another source of difficulties in making direct comparisons between accounts.
Notes: PWC = parent with care; NRP = nonresident parent.

Figure 11.7: *UKHLS 2009/10 (reproduced from Haux et al Table 4)*

Arrangements for Children—Parents' Reports for 2009–2010

Percentages are based on all with nonresident children (total percentages)

	Do they stay with you for weekends or school holidays on a regular basis, an irregular basis, or not at all?			
Can you tell me how often you visit, see or contact your child(ren) under 16 living outside the household?	*Regular basis*	*Irregular basis*	*Not at all*	*Total*
… never	-	-	**13.5%**	13.5%
a few times a year	1.5%	2.8%	7.5%	11.8%
once a month or less	1.4%	0.9%	2.3%	4.6%
several times a month	6.4%	2.3%	3.9%	12.5%
about once a week	**10.2%**	3.1%	5.9%	19.2%
several times a week	**15.4%**	2.9%	3.5%	21.8%
almost everyday	8.8%	2.0%	3.3%	14.1%
shared care 50–50	2.3%	0.1%	0.1%	2.6%
Total	46%	14%	40%	100%
N (Unweighted base)	598	196	554	1,348

Source: Own analysis of Understanding Society wave 1 (2009/10).
Note: Table omits nine cases with missing data (refused, not known) on either variable.

Figure 11.8: *BHPS and UKHLS (reproduced from Haux et al Table 5). I suspect the column headed UKHLS 2009-10 contains typographical errors. It's heading should read NRP not RP, and the first row should be 3 not 37 (the percentages then add to 100%).*

Arrangements for Children—Parents' Reports over Time Column percentages

Data Source	*BHPS 2002*		*BHPS 2007*		*UKHLS 2009–10*	*UKHLS 2013–14*
Respondent:	*PWC*	*NRP*	*PWC*	*NRP*	*RP*	*NRP*
Arrangement						
Shared care 50–50	1	3	1	2	37	3
Almost everyday	7	10	7	10	15	17
Several times a week	15	22	19	24	22	25
About once a week	16	22	20	22	19	16
Several times a month	14	13	13	14	13	14
Once a month or less	8	4	6	6	5	5
A few times a year	9	7	7	8	10	8
Never	32	19	27	14	13	12
N	870	423	647	308	1348	781

Source: Based on analysis of data from BHPS waves 12 and 17 (approximately 2002 and 2007) and UKHLS waves 1 and 5.
Note: PWC = parent with care; NRP = non-resident parent.

Does a father who was particularly involved with his child prior to separation, perhaps even the primary carer, benefit by obtaining a greater level of contact after separation? Some people express that opinion, if only indirectly, with such disparaging remarks as "perhaps he could have taken more interest in childcare prior to the divorce". But that view is ignorant. For one thing, direct childcare is not the only possible contribution to family welfare. In any case, there is no shortage of anecdotal evidence that fathers who shared care equally with their partner, or perhaps were the primary carer, can find ongoing contact after divorce just as difficult to obtain.

On the matter of highly involved fathers, (Haux, McKay, and Cain, 2017) write,

> 'In sum, fathers who were more involved in their children's care (in terms of active fathering or sole fathering) and who felt closer to them tended to engage in more frequent contact with their child post-separation and to have them for more overnight stays. Despite this, frequency of contact declines with time for both more- and less-involved fathers. We found somewhat less evidence that perceived parenting competence was linked to subsequent contact patterns, though this might be in part a consequence of the smaller sample size. Finally and importantly, none of the measures of pre-separation fathering were associated with lower chances of breakdown in contact.'

I interpret this to mean that a more involved father prior to separation tends to remain more involved after separation ***if*** contact takes place, but a father's prior involvement in caring does not lead to a greater likelihood of contact after separation, nor does it mitigate against loss of contact. However, there is evidence from an older study of Canadian and Scottish cases that the most involved fathers prior to separation have a greater tendency to end with no ongoing contact. The reasons would appear to be their greater difficulty in adapting to the reduced, and highly controlled, degree of contact after separation, since this cuts across their already-established, highly involved, mode of fathering, (Kruk, 1992), (Kruk, 1993).

11.8 Financial Issues

Financial matters are beyond the scope of this brief review, but a few of the more obvious inequalities need be mentioned. There is a glaring inequality in child maintenance payments. It is surely beyond dispute that if childcare were divided equally, 50/50, in all respects, then no party should be required to pay child maintenance to the other. But this is not the requirement of the UK's Child Maintenance Service, as their on-line child maintenance calculator confirms, (UK Government, 2018j). Instead the required payment from the non-resident to the resident parent reduces pro-rata with contact time to 50% at a 50/50 time division, rather than zero. The notionally "non-resident" parent must still pay 43% of the maximum pay to the notionally "resident" parent even if (s)he is actually caring for the child *most* of the time.

Whilst a reducing child maintenance payment in line with increasing contact time is only reasonable, it has the pernicious effect of acting as a disincentive to the resident parent in agreeing to greater amounts of contact.

On the other hand, any child maintenance received by the resident parent does not affect the resident parent's entitlements to benefits (welfare) in any way. There is therefore no direct public financial interest in ensuring child maintenance is paid.

A particular difficulty faces the non-resident parent after separation: the need to find, and pay for, additional accommodation now that (s)he no longer lives with the resident parent. For most people this will necessarily be very modest accommodation due simply to financial constraints (and might mean moving in with friends or the grandparents temporarily). But in order for overnight staying contact to be ordered, the court must be satisfied that the non-resident parent can offer the child appropriate accommodation. This may mean a separate bedroom. But a spare bedroom may be beyond the displaced parent's means under these circumstances. This is a particularly unfair constraint on separated fathers (as 92% of non-resident parents) and may prove an insurmountable problem. Moreover, if he can afford a place with a spare bedroom, and is receiving housing benefit (or the equivalent under universal credit) he may then face reduced benefit payments as a result (the so-called "bedroom tax"). Non-resident parents on social assistance under the age of 35 are only eligible for a "bedsit" (living with other adults) rather than a flat with a separate bedroom, which may prohibit stayovers entirely. All these constraints hit low-earners especially, and, of course, men especially as the mother usually retains the former joint accommodation.

11.9 The Empathy Gap Against Non-Resident Fathers

About 62% of child contact arrangements are made informally without involving the courts. About 92% of non-resident patents are fathers in the UK. Almost equal caring occurs in at most 3% of cases, probably rather fewer, and has not increased since 2002.

The courts order staying contact in less than half of cases on which they rule. The totality of cases, and by implication therefore also arrangements agreed privately without court involvement, have the same outcome: less than half involve staying contact. Typical staying orders are for one or two overnights per fortnight with one additional visiting day per fortnight. This is the extent of contact which the luckier 40%-50% of non-resident parents may hope to achieve.

The courts order no contact of any sort in 14% of cases. The courts order either no contact or only indirect or supervised contact in 31% of cases. These figures compare with surveyed outcomes which suggest that no contact at all results in about one in three cases. One could add to this a further 9% where contact occurs only a few times per year.

In Hunt & Macleod's analysis, more than four in five cases which ended with the court ordering no face-to-face contact involved "serious welfare issues", of which an allegation of domestic abuse is the most common. Hence, whilst such allegations do not prevent contact, they do make face-to-face contact significantly less likely. And this is despite very few such allegations being subject to any meaningful investigation.

Courts order unsupervised visits, but without overnight stays, in about 20% of cases. The average ordered contact time under these conditions is 10 hours per fortnight. Surveys of outcomes suggest that contact less than weekly but at least monthly occurs in about 20% of cases.

The uncertainties in all these figures are huge. The outcomes from the courts in terms of the content of orders is not dramatically different from the actual (surveyed) outcomes. Assuming cases going to court are the more problematic cases, this suggests that the courts' ordered outcomes encourage alignment with societal norms (no better, no worse). The numerical extent to which court orders are flouted is unknown. By early 2018 applications for enforcement were running at 17% of applications for contact orders. But since virtually no orders are ever enforced, regardless of applications to do so, it is likely that flouting of orders is far more common than 17%. Consequently, it is not known whether the actual outcomes for cases which go through the courts fall short even of the general societal norms arising from informal arrangements. Informally, court orders are routinely flouted so that the outcomes for non-resident parents having recourse to the courts may be significantly worse than for those who agree privately.

It appears that the actual outcome is "no contact" in a greater percentage of cases than the courts order, but this may be because orders for indirect or supervised contact ultimately lead to no contact longer term. The actual prevalence of no contact, or contact only a few times per year, may be as high as about 40%. A similar conclusion applies in the USA. Data reported in the 'Fragile Families and Child Wellbeing Study' indicates that, one year after separation, 37% of non-resident fathers had not seen their child in the last month, and after five years this had risen to 49%, and 28% had not seen their child in the last year, (Princeton, 2018).

The outcomes for non-resident parents – which term I will now replace with "fathers" - are clearly hugely inequitable. Fewer than half will achieve the arrangements which are (arguably) required for a meaningful ongoing relationship between father and child, namely staying contact. The *de facto* standard has become just three days per fortnight, which will include one or two overnight stays. So even the sought-for standard is inequitable; cases which are close to equitable (near 50/50) are rare (less than 3%). The majority of the other half of cases ultimately result in no contact, or very infrequent contact, as striving Dads morph into McDads and then into so-called deadbeat Dads under the action of societal forces largely beyond their control. The longer term outcomes for the intermediate 20% of cases with their 10 hours of non-staying contact per fortnight is in need of a study in its own right.

Economic strangulation is a major exacerbating factor in constraining separated fathers' options, particularly as regards preventing staying contact in practice, but the financial details of separation are beyond the scope of this book.

So, are the family courts biased against fathers? It may be that this is a misattribution of where the problem lies, though the reality is worse. The courts' chief failing is their impotence. At the start of the process the resident parent holds all the cards. At the end of the process the resident parent still holds all the cards. The anecdotes from legal professionals demonstrate that the courts are powerless to control the behaviour of a belligerent mother. It is not clear that the involvement of the courts makes a substantial difference, one way or the other, although the data are so uncertain that confidence in any conclusion is lacking. What is clear is that non-resident parents – about 92% of whom are fathers – are treated inequitably in almost all (97%) of cases.

Claims are sometimes made that fathers seeking contact via the family courts are overwhelmingly successful. However such claims are disingenuous: any contact at all, even if indirect or supervised, is counted as a "success" in such claims. The reality is that, despite the often modest applications by fathers who accept that equal shared care is unlikely, about half of fathers fail to achieve what they request. Either they fail to achieve the type of contact sought or they fail to achieve the quantum of time sought.

The data is consistent with a contention that the courts merely reflect societal bias, rather than introducing bias of their own. However, one might also argue that society operates "in the shadow of the law", with informal arrangements merely anticipating what would result from recourse to the courts. Which of these perspectives is more true is less important than the fact of fathers' evident disadvantage. It is not only the agreed or ordered extent of contact, in terms of time, but the financial and practical difficulties which non-resident fathers face which degrades the outcome and puts enormous strain on the father-child relationship, and sometimes destroys it.

That "male disposability" is an apposite term can hardly be disputed when around 40% of fathers are indeed disposed of virtually completely, and many of the rest partially. We see the operation of the empathy gap yet again in the equanimity of society with these conditions, a situation brought about by deliberate feminist policy.

In many cases the fathers may, in fact, be content with the extent of their contact. But in a large percentage of cases, not only are fathers far from content, the outcomes have the long term effect of severing the father-child relationship. This can no longer be presented as merely a fathers' rights issue (and hence unimportant due to the empathy gap). The influence of the breakdown of the paternal relationship upon the next generation is no longer contentious. The impact of the loss of a parent is emerging as a dominant issue of social disadvantage to the child. In this we see how culturally intensified gynocentric feminism has left family-positive evolutionary matricentrism a long way behind: child arrangements are too often the result of making the mothers' wishes paramount, not the best interests of the child. The issue of the impact of fatherlessness on outcomes for the children is addressed in the following chapters, 12, 13 and 14.

12

Parental Alienation, ACEs and the Woozling of Shared Parenting

If you want to wind up a feminist, talk about children's rights.
Geoff Dench (1940-2018), *Transforming Men*

The phenomenon of parental alienation is explained in this chapter. It is a form of child abuse and a form of partner abuse. The alienated parent is the target, but the child features as the more significant, though collateral, damage. Whilst alienation generally occurs within the context of parental conflict during separation, alienation should be viewed primarily in terms of its adverse impact on the child rather than only a feature of a child contact dispute. In chapter 13 I shall review the evidence supporting the contention that fatherlessness is detrimental to child development. In this chapter I shall claim that continued involvement of both parents in the life of their child after separation is generally beneficial even when there is ongoing parental conflict. What the general public does not appreciate is that there is a powerful lobby seeking to empower mothers to be able to marginalise, or eliminate entirely, a father's ongoing involvement in his children's lives. A case history study is provided as an illustration of the power politics involved. The concept of an Adverse Childhood Experience, or ACE, is also explained here. Both parental alienation and ACEs are damaging to children, and both are related to parental separation, a sociological epidemic whose adverse impacts on children society is tolerating.

12.1 What is Parental Alienation?

Parental Alienation (PA) is a phenomenon in which one parent turns a child against the other parent by negative portrayal. PA is primarily a form of child abuse. It is an induced mental health issue. The phenomenon was virtually unknown before the dramatic increase in the prevalence of parental separation. Dr Sue Whitcombe is a chartered psychologist and an expert in alienation. In a presentation to the Male Psychology Conference at UCL, (Whitcombe, 2017), she gave a simple definition of alienation for the lay person as follows,

- Unjustified or unwarranted rejection of a parent where there was previously a normal range, loving, "good enough" relationship;

- Intentional or unintentional actions by a parent (usually the parent with custody) to turn their child against the other parent (usually the non-resident parent).

Extensive research literature is now available, e.g., (Parental Alienation Research Institute, 2019). PA is sometimes described as a form of "programming" of the child: an unjustified campaign of denigration against the target parent aimed at causing the child to reject that parent utterly. Alienation is effectively a campaign of black propaganda, or psychological aggression, perpetrated by the alienating parent against the target parent in which the chid is used as a weapon without regard for the child's mental wellbeing. Not all attempts to alienate a child will succeed, but when it does the result is that the child becomes hostile, vitriolic and abusive towards the alienated parent without valid justification. The alienated child refuses contact with the alienated parent, but this attitude originates from an abnormal state of mind imposed upon the child by the alienating parent and this has a range of psychological harms to the child. The alienated child will then automatically side with the alienating parent in any conflict or dispute. The alienated child's view of the targeted parent is exclusively negative, without nuance, to the point that the parent is demonized and seen as entirely evil.

When an alienated child rejects a parent they do so with complete lack of ambivalence, showing no sign of guilt or remorse for their rejection. It is important to appreciate how unnatural this is. Children are wired to attach to their parents and caregivers, even if they are neglectful or abusive. There is a large body of research into child abuse which demonstrates that even the most physically abused children rarely reject an abusive parent with the vehemence that alienated children display. The alienated child's mind is an induced pathology. It involves a form of psychological splitting, which is traumatic and causes long term harm.

Because alienation arises in the context of parental separation, and because of the role of feminist lobbies in that context, the acceptance of alienation as a valid phenomenon has had a difficult history. However, that is rapidly changing as the psychological community begin to recognise that the evidence cannot be ignored. Quoting (Kruk, 2018),

> 'Research evidence of the many facets of parental alienation is much more robust than is often assumed. The most recent quantitative research raises some serious alarms. Harman (2017) found a staggering 13.4% of US parents reporting they had been victimized by parental alienation at some point in their lives. The large body of research by Baker and colleagues which focused on perspectives of now-young adult

> child victims of alienation and of targeted parents, details strategies of alienating parents and short- and long-term consequences of alienation. There is also concordance in the clinical and research literature in regard to core components of alienation. Slowly but surely, the misunderstanding and denial surrounding parental alienation is being washed away. A survey conducted at the Association of Family and Conciliation Courts 2014 Conference reported 98% agreement in support of the basic tenet of parental alienation: children can be manipulated by one parent to reject the other parent, who does not deserve to be rejected.'

The alienating parent may be of either sex, the alienated parent may be of either sex, and the child in question may be of either sex. Mothers are not intrinsically more likely to alienate than fathers. However, the resident parent has the greater opportunity to alienate after separation, and mothers are overwhelmingly more often the resident parent (92% in the UK). In principle, non-resident parents may also alienate. However, once they have become non-resident, they simply have far less opportunity to do the alienating than the resident parent. But parents will often have a long period of discontent or dispute before finally separating. The process of alienation may therefore start well before separation, in which case either parent may be the alienator. For these reasons it should not be assumed that the sex ratio of alienators is necessarily the same as that of resident parents, i.e., 92% alienating mothers and alienated fathers.

One of the mechanisms of enacting alienation is to frustrate contact with the child by the non-resident parent, for example by cancelling contact arrangements at the last moment, by blocking messages and gifts, by preventing communication, and by making the child feel bad about spending time with the other parent or his family. Because of this, alienation is sometimes presented as a child contact issue – because that is how it manifests to the non-resident parent. But it is primarily a child abuse issue. The child is being used as a weapon by the alienating parent against the target parent. The behaviours of the alienating parent cause the targeted child to become distant, and ultimately extremely hostile, towards the alienated parent, and this distortion of the child's perception is carried out careless of the impact on the child's psychological wellbeing.

The actions of the alienating parent may be described as situational aggression, and this will be facilitated by a lack of empathy for the former partner, exacerbated by anger. The more serious empathy gap is, disturbingly, that displayed towards the child by the alienating parent. The alienating parent's actions are likely to be accompanied by a conviction that the other parent is unnecessary to the child's wellbeing. The extent to which their alienating behaviours are excused by ignorance is debatable, but the motivation most often appears reprehensible: more arising from self-interest than concern for the child. The psychological types most susceptible to becoming alienators, and whether there are familial connections, are beyond the scope of this brief account.

It has become the practice in the family courts to take into account the wishes of the child ("the voice of the child"). The wisdom of this is questionable in any case – children are not the best judge of their own interests. But where a child has been alienated, the "voice of the child" is really the voice of the alienating parent, and the process is a subterfuge.

PA is not only child abuse; it is also abuse of the targeted parent. To quote (Harman, Kruk and Hines, 2018), 'Parental alienating behaviors do not just contribute to child abuse; they are direct and indirect attacks that an alienating parent makes on the target parent'. These authors itemise the reasons for regarding alienating behaviours as a form of intimate partner violence (IPV), perpetrated mostly through psychological aggression. This form of IPV includes attempts to control the partner or the relationship, damage the victim's sense of self, intimidate, emotionally wound, express anger, restrict or coerce a partner, and otherwise abuse their position of power. Sub-components of this type of aggression are described at length by the authors. A few examples are,

- "Expressive aggression" entails the use of name-calling, misrepresenting, degrading and humiliating the target parent;
- "Coercive control" refers to a wide range of tactics designed to disempower the target by controlling their behaviours. Having the loyalty of the children, and typically residency and legal control over the children, affords the alienating parent a considerable amount of power to wield over the target parent;
- "Invoking a threat of violence" by "exploiting perceived vulnerability" is also a form of psychological aggression. This can take the form of false allegations of domestic abuse, as we have seen already in chapters 10 and 11. More subtle stratagems are manifold. For example, an alienating mother may arrange to have an intimidating adult present at parenting time exchanges, as a "bodyguard", deliberately to create the impression that there is a threat of violence necessitating such protection;
- "Gaslighting" is a strategy aimed at destabilising the target's belief in themselves and their own memory by falsely portraying past events.

Harman, Kruk and Hines (2018) note that,

> 'Alienating parents often use the time period between the temporary and final orders (which can be months or years) as "proof" that they should be the primary custodial parent. This strategy is even encouraged by lawyers to obtain full custody for their clients, because many American and Canadian judges base final parenting orders on what the "normal" distribution of parenting time was prior to the final hearing. Creating an extended temporary order period with imbalanced parenting responsibility provides the alienating parent with power to exploit the targeted parent's limited parenting time in their favour.'

12.1.1 Prevalence of Alienation

By 2016, parental alienation and alienating behaviours in separated or divorced families had been well documented in over 500 references drawn from the professional literature across 30 countries, (Harman, Leder-Elder and Biringen, 2016). By 2018, more than 1,000 books, book chapters, and articles had been published in mental health or legal professional journals on the subject of parental alienation, (Kruk, 2018). Despite this rapid increase in research attention, the prevalence of PA remains uncertain. The reason for this is principally because there is no unique, universally accepted diagnostic criterion for the presence of PA. Its chief qualitative characteristics are widely accepted, but that does not constitute a definitive diagnostic criterion. However, there is consensus that the prevalence is alarmingly high.

A telephone survey of randomly sampled adults in North Carolina (USA) has been reported, (Harman, Leder-Elder and Biringen, 2016). Of those who were parents, 13.4% stated that they had been alienated from one or more of their children. Nearly three-quarters of respondents stated that they knew someone who had been alienated. The survey indicated that 30 fathers had been alienated out of 178 who answered the question (17%), compared with 25 mothers who had been alienated out of 226 who answered the question (11%). Thus, whilst more fathers than mothers reported alienation, the gender difference is nowhere near as marked as the gender difference that might have been expected based on resident versus non-resident parent status. However, there are known gender differences in the perception and reporting of abuses which are some years in the past, as can be seen in domestic abuse statistics, and half the sample were over 45 years old. Consequently, the gender ratio from this study may be misleading. Further studies are needed.

The incidence of PA will be greater where divorce has occurred. Harman, Kruk and Hines (2018) note, 'The prevalence of children who have been alienated from a parent has been challenging to calculate due to the need to accurately diagnose this outcome, but some estimates point to around 29% of children from divorced homes as being alienated from a parent to some extent'. According to Whitcombe (2017) the prevalence of alienation within the general community of separating parents has been estimated from random sampling to be up to about 15%, but in samples of the most intractable cases the prevalence can be up to 40%.

In July 2016, Sarah Parsons, Principal Social Worker and Assistant Director of CAFCASS, stated that 'parental alienation is responsible for around 80% of the most intransigent cases that come before the family courts', (Whitcombe, 2017). Whitcombe has estimated that this implies that parental alienation is likely to be a feature in a minimum of 9,000 family proceedings applications per annum involving more than 18,000 children (England & Wales).

In respect of the issue of who is alienated most, mothers or fathers, (Kruk, 2018) observes,

> 'There are no gender differences in regard to who is the perpetrator and who is the target of parental alienation. Custodial status, however, is a strong predictor of who is likely to alienate a child from a parent.'

This perspective is emphasised in (Harman, Kruk and Hines, 2018), for example,

> 'Experts have found that custodial status, rather than gender, is a more important predictor of who is likely to alienate....'
>
> 'Although some non-residential parents can alienate a child, the custodial parent is most often the alienating parent because they have a monopoly on the child's physical, mental, and emotional attention, regardless of gender. Non-residential targeted parents often have limited or no contact with their children (sometimes for years at a time), making it almost impossible to reciprocate many of the behaviors outlined above (*i.e., alienating behaviours*). The targeted parents we have studied have observed the negative outcomes of alienation in their children and report not wanting to make the situation worse. Despite being the target of severe IPV, none of the targeted parents in studies by the first authors reported wanting to take their children away from the alienating parent or reverse roles entirely; indeed nearly all of the targeted parents that we have interviewed and studied want the children to have a healthy relationship with both parents. These parents make the conscious decision not to reciprocate the aggressive behaviors of the alienating parent. These parents also know that if the targeted parent reciprocates the behavior of the alienating parent, it only serves to justify the child's negative feelings toward the targeted parent due to their enmeshment or alignment with the alienating parent.'

False allegations play a major role in the operation of the family courts (see section 10.3), and false allegations also play a major role in the operation of alienation, the two things being inextricably linked. Whitcombe (2017) reported the following data from her clinical practice, based on a sample of 47 men and 7 women, in which 70% of former partners had repeatedly broken court orders, 78% currently had no direct contact, and 56% had not seen their child in the last year. In answer to the question 'have you been subject to false allegations of domestic violence against your partner?', 67% of clients said yes, 33% said no. In answer to the question 'have you been subject to false allegations of child abuse?', 81% of clients said yes, 19% said no.

One must be cautious about assuming such very high incidence of claimed false accusations apply across all family court cases. Dr Whitcombe's clients are self-selected as having been subject to parental alienation, for whom false allegation rates will be higher. However, it appears that the "most intransigent" cases overwhelmingly involve alienation, so these levels of (claimed) false accusation are pertinent in those cases.

In October 2018, CAFCASS issued their 'CAFCASS Child Impact Assessment Framework', also known in the development stage as the 'High Conflict Practice Pathway', (CAFCASS, 2018). Amongst other things it presents their recommended approach to addressing alienation. It has not met with universal approbation. The guidance has been accused of attempting to entrench the status quo and avoid the issue by leaving the child with the alienating parent. For example, this extract,

> 'Despite these risks to the emotional wellbeing of the child, the risk of forcing them into time with the other parent may be higher……It can, very understandably, feel wholly unjust to a rejected parent. However, regardless of how they were formed, a child's wishes and feelings may be so entrenched against time spent with the other parent (and a change of where they live is also not viable), that time with that parent is not possible.'

Alienation expert Karen Woodall has responded to that with unambiguous condemnation, 'Is there any evidence in the world in 2018 that moving an abused child from the abuser to the healthy parent is more harmful to them than leaving them with the abuser? No there is not.' (Woodall, 2018). It is not helpful to a child being abused by alienation to confuse the issue of alienation with high conflict between the parents. They are separate issues. And where high parental conflict exists in the absence of alienation, shared parenting is still generally beneficial to the child, as we shall see in section 12.4.

12.2 Adverse Childhood Experiences

The 11 recognised Adverse Childhood Experiences (ACEs), and their prevalence in Wales in 2017, has been reported by (Public Health Wales, 2017). The survey results are summarised below, in order of the most common ACEs first,

- Parental separation (25%);
- Verbal abuse (20%);
- Mental illness - living with a sufferer (18%);
- Domestic violence (17%);
- Physical abuse (16%);
- Alcohol abuse - living with a substance abuser (13%);
- Emotional neglect (7%);
- Sexual abuse (7%);
- Drug abuse - living with a substance abuser (6%);
- Physical neglect (4%);
- Imprisonment of a parent (4%).

Figures in brackets are the prevalence in Wales of these ACEs in the childhood experiences of 2,500 surveyed adults in 2017. The most common ACE is parental separation. Parental separation is correlated with domestic abuse (see section 9.2.4) and this will further raise the ACE-count for those affected by parental separation.

The Welsh survey showed that 19% of the population surveyed had experienced one ACE; 17% two or three ACEs; and 14% four or more ACEs, (Public Health Wales, 2017).

Consistent with this, other UK data also suggests that around 50% of the population experience one or more ACEs, while about 12% experience four or more ACEs, (Bellis et al, 2014). In a small cohort of high risk young people involved in a project with Gloucestershire police, 69% had experienced 4 or more ACEs, and 29% had experienced 8 or more ACEs, (Gloucestershire Health and Wellbeing Board, 2018).

Interestingly, a study based on a British cohort born in 1958, and hence 60 years old in 2018, showed a substantially smaller prevalence of ACEs, (Kelly et al, 2013). No ACEs at all in 70% of cases, one ACE in 22% of cases, and two or more ACEs in only 8% of cases. The latter contrasts with 31% of people experiencing two or more ACEs from the 2017 Welsh survey. It may be relevant to note that while this 1958 cohort were children, the divorce rate and the prevalence of cohabitation had not yet undergone the rapid increases that later occurred.

12.2.1 Behaviour and Health Outcomes of ACEs

ACEs are claimed to influence subsequent behaviour and health outcomes which persist into adulthood. Compared with people who experienced no ACEs, those with four or more ACEs were found from the survey 'Adverse Childhood Experiences and their impact on health-harming behaviours in the Welsh adult population', (Public Health Wales, 2016), to be,

- 4 times more likely to be a high-risk drinker;
- 6 times more likely to have had, or to have caused, a teenage pregnancy;
- 6 times more likely to smoke;
- 6 times more likely to have had sex before age 16;
- 14 times more likely to have been a victim of violence in the last 12 months;
- 15 times more likely to have perpetrated violence in the last 12 months;
- 11 to 16 times more likely to have used illegal drugs, including Class A;
- 20 times more likely to have been incarcerated.

The mental health outcomes for people experiencing four or more ACEs, compared to those experiencing none, taken from (Public Health Wales, 2017) were,

- 3.7 times more likely to currently be receiving treatment for mental illness;
- 6.1 times more likely to have ever received treatment for mental illness;
- 9.5 times more likely to have ever felt suicidal or self-harmed

An ACE score above six is associated with a 30-fold increase in attempted suicide (Whitcombe, 2017). Michelle Kelly et al have investigated the effect of ACEs on premature death, before age 50, using the 1958 British birth cohort mentioned above, (Kelly et al, 2013). In men the risk of premature death was 57% higher among those who had experienced 2 or more ACEs compared to those with none. Women's premature death rate (before 50) displayed an even greater sensitivity to ACEs. Figure 12.1 illustrates the impact of increasing numbers of ACEs on physical health outcomes for a number of key diseases.

As always with correlations in the social sciences, the question of causality arises. Do ACEs cause subsequent disadvantages, or are both related to a third factor? Three mechanisms for how ACEs might cause harm have been suggested: health-harming behaviours, social determinants of health; and neurobiological and genetic pathways. These have been discussed, for example in (Scottish Public Health Network, 2016). ACEs are certainly related to deprivation, and deprivation is related to poorer health outcomes and associated behaviours (see chapter 3). However, it has been claimed that there is a relationship between ACEs and health harming behaviours independent of deprivation, (Bellis et al, 2014).

While individuals that suffer ACEs have an increased risk of poor outcomes as adults, many individuals who experience ACEs do not encounter these effects. An individual's ability to avoid harmful behavioural and psychological changes in response to chronic stress is known as resilience. Having a strong relationship with a trusted adult throughout childhood has been found to increase resilience and to reduce the long-term negative impacts of childhood adversity, (Ford et al., 2016).

Figure 12.1: *Increased Risk of Disease with History of ACEs, 2013. Reproduced from (UCL Institute of Health Equity, 2015), Crown copyright 2015.*

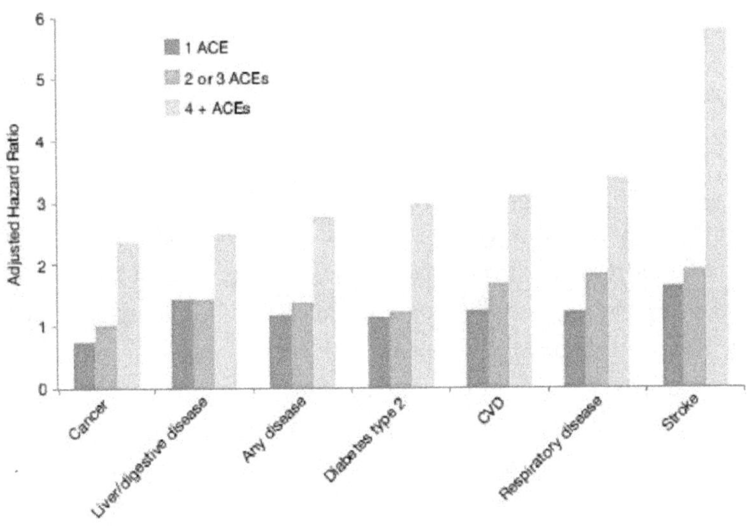

12.2.2 ACEs and Parental Involvement

Perhaps the most dramatic of the recent Welsh survey findings is the very clear, negative, correlation between a child receiving constant support from both parents and the number of ACEs to which the child is likely to be subject. This is shown by Figure 17 of the report 'Mental Illness - Welsh Adverse Childhood Experience (ACE) and Resilience Study', (Hughes et al, 2018), reproduced in Figure 12.2 below.

Figure 12.2: *Constant Adult Sources of Personal Support during Childhood, by ACE Count*

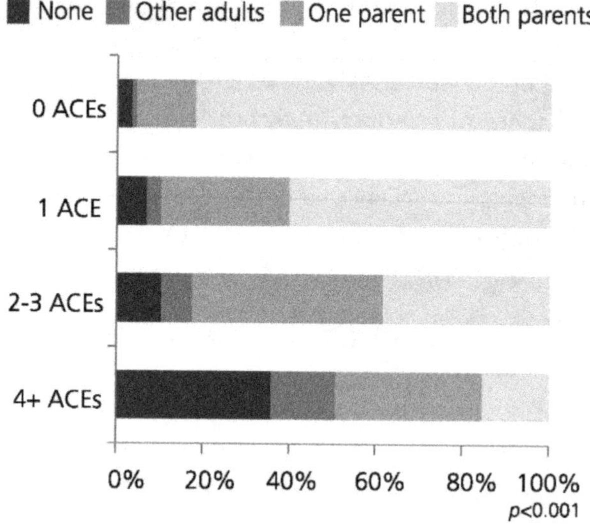

Finally, I note the inevitable relationship between parental alienation and ACEs. Alienation virtually always occurs within the context of parental separation, and hence there is immediately one ACE inflicted on the associated children. However, other ACEs will generally also occur. In high conflict separations, especially if parental alienation is occurring, verbal abuse is likely, as are allegations of domestic violence or sexual abuse, and the issue of mental health arises. Consequently, high conflict parental separation, and especially cases involving alienation, may impose a constellation of ACEs upon the affected children, raising them in one 'fell swoop' from zero ACEs to the dangerous 4+ ACEs category. But parental alienation is worse still as it also induces direct psychological harms which are not measured by ACEs.

12.3 Woozling Shared Parenting

Fathers groups have long advocated for shared parenting after parental separation. There is no strict definition of what this means, but it is usually taken to mean that the children would spend at least 30% of their time, including overnight stays, with each parent. Fathers groups have campaigned in the UK and elsewhere for legislation to oblige the family courts to adopt a rebuttable presumption of shared parenting, i.e., that shared care would be the default position unless reasons to oppose it were demonstrated. Despite assistance from members of the UK Parliament, such initiatives have always been thwarted. In this section I give a brief account of one such defeated attempt to legislate in favour of shared parenting. It is a case study in power politics and illustrates where the power lies. It is not with fathers. It illustrates how the feminist establishment, as it is manifest in academia, Government and the third sector, acts in concert to ends which have nothing to do with equality.

The continuing failure to adopt a presumption of shared care is a disadvantage to fathers because the status quo is that fathers are the non-resident parent in 92% of cases of separation (UK). They are likely to achieve no overnight stays, and even those who do almost always have contact at well below the 30% shared-care standard (see chapter 11). More importantly, however, the continued rarity of shared care disadvantages the children, for the reasons discussed in this chapter and the next on fatherlessness.

In section 8.2 I defined the useful term "woozle" - a widely quoted claim which has gained acceptance through repetition but which is untrue or not properly substantiated. Results from social science research are especially prone to being woozled. This is because social science research suffers particularly severely from reproducibility problems. This is not entirely the fault of the researchers but arises from the fact that social science is largely observational rather than experimental. As a result there is invariably a very large number of uncontrollable variables which confuse interpretation. Quoting results from a single study in social science may therefore be misleading. Review articles, or meta-analyses, which pull together many independent studies are to be preferred. Sometimes one is obliged to rely on single authoritative studies for lack of comparisons. However, there is less excuse to promulgate a skewed perspective on an issue when there is a balance of contrary evidence. In this case the woozle consists of ignoring the balance of evidence and instead promoting an outlier study which suits one's purpose. Such woozling played a significant role in the example case of thwarting a shared parenting initiative which I now present.

An Australian study by Jennifer McIntosh et al (2010) considered the outcomes for infants and other children of various post-separation parenting arrangements. This study considered separately school age children and pre-school children. For pre-school children the study reported finding deleterious effects of shared care on the children's psychology and behaviour. The negative findings for pre-school children were summarised on page 9 thus,

> 'Young infants under two years of age living with a non-resident parent for only one or more nights a week were more irritable, and were more watchful and wary of separation from their primary caregiver than young children primarily in the care of one parent. Children aged 2–3 years in shared care.....showed significantly lower levels of persistence with routine tasks, learning and play than children in the other two groups. Of concern, but as predicted by attachment theory, they also showed severely distressed behaviours in their relationship with the primary parent (often very upset, crying or hanging on to the parent, and hitting, biting, or kicking), feeding related problems (gagging on food or refusing to eat) and not reacting when hurt. Such behaviours are consistent with high levels of attachment distress.... Thus, regardless of socio-economic background, parenting or inter-parental cooperation, shared overnight care of children under four years of age had an independent and deleterious impact on several emotional and behavioral regulation outcomes.'

But they then added, 'by kindergarten or school entry at around age 4-5 years of age, these effects were no longer evident'.

The McIntosh et al study subsequently became the basis of a woozle, as will be described below. I emphasise that the McIntosh paper itself is not the woozle. It is the use of the paper by others which constitutes the woozle.

The key issue is whether the McIntosh pre-schooler results are consistent with other published studies. They are not.

A review of all relevant studies on shared care of young children, available at the time in question, has been presented by Linda Nielsen (2014). Up to 2014 there had been 31 studies which compared the outcomes for children who lived in shared parenting families (30% or more of the time) to children who lived with their mother and spent varying amounts of overnight time with their father. However, only eight of these 31 studies included infants and children under the age of 6 years. One of those was the 2010 McIntosh study. The remaining seven studies are those of interest here, since they are independent studies comparable to the McIntosh study. In the brief summary of these seven studies, below, I borrow liberally from Linda Nielsen's review paper. Three of the seven studies only included parents who had formerly been married. These data are the most applicable to divorced parents more generally.

The first study compared 58 children who lived with their mother and 35 who lived at least 35% of their time with their father, with half of them being 4-years-old or younger. One to two years after their parents' separation, there were no differences in social or behaviour adjustment between the two groups. The frequent overnighters, however, had better relationships with their fathers and were better adjusted emotionally.

The second study followed children from 1,100 divorced families over a period of 4 years. What made this study unique for its time was that the children in 150 of these families were overnighting 30% to 50% time with their fathers. In these families, 125 of the children were infants or preschoolers younger than 5 years. At the end of 4 years, the frequently overnighting children were better off than the others on all of the standardized measures of their academic, emotional, physical, and behavioural well-being. Three years after the parents' divorce, only 1.6% of the frequent overnighters' fathers were seeing less of their children compared to 56% of the other fathers.

The third study assessed children from nearly 600 shared parenting and 600 primary care families. Roughly 40% of the children were under the age of five years. Three years after their parents' divorce, children who were frequently overnighting (35%–50% of the time) had better relationships with their fathers, were happier and less depressed, and had fewer health problems than the less frequently overnighting children. There were no differences on measures of emotional health.

In the next group of three studies (which I shall call studies 4 to 6) the majority, but not all, of the parents had been married before separating. A sizable minority had separated before the child was born; and others had never lived together at all.

Study 4: The researchers compared infants 12- to 20-months-old in three types of families: 52 in intact families, 49 who never overnighted, and 44 who occasionally overnighted. Compared to non-overnighters, the overnighters were no less securely attached to their mothers. In the second part of the study one year later, the overnighters did as well as the non-overnighters on a challenging task to gauge attachment with their mothers.

Study 5: The researchers assessed 132 children between the ages of two and six years on several standardized measures of well-being. For the two and three year olds, the overnighters were no different from non-overnighters in regard to: sleep problems, depression, anxiety, aggression, or social withdrawal. For the four to six year olds, especially for the girls, the overnighters were better off in regard to attention problems and social withdrawal and were no different from the non-overnighters on the other measures.

Study 6: This study involved 7,118 separated parents, of which only 50% had formerly been married and 12% had never lived together, suggesting caution should be exercised in assuming these findings are applicable to divorced parents. The children were divided into those with frequent overnighting (35% to 50%) and those with less, or no, overnighting. The mothers reported no differences between the two groups of children on measures of physical health or socioemotional well-being. In contrast, the fathers of the frequent overnighters rated their children higher on health, learning skills, and overall progress than the other fathers. Overall the frequent overnighters had marginally better outcomes, even after accounting for parents' levels of violence, conflict, and education.

The seventh, and final, study can be discounted as inapplicable to the general run of divorced or separated parents. The cases were derived from severely disadvantaged families, 85% were African or Hispanic American, and 50% of the fathers and 10% of the mothers had served time in jail.

In summary, the conclusions of the 2010 McIntosh pre-schoolers' study conflict with all six of the comparable and relevant independent studies, none of which indicate a deleterious impact of shared parenting on pre-schoolers. In fact, they indicate the opposite: shared care has some beneficial outcomes for the child.

Moreover, Nielsen (2014) discusses several substantial limitations of the McIntosh study, including the fact that most of the parents in the McIntosh study had never been married to one another (90% of them in the case of infants, and 60% for toddlers). Moreover, 30% of the infants' parents had never even lived together. Such studies often vary in their findings, all studies have limitations, and there is no imputation regarding the competence or honesty of those involved in the McIntosh study. So none of this would matter much if it were not for the use to which the McIntosh study would be put.

In November 2011, the Ministry of Justice published a long awaited review of family justice, known as the Norgrove report, (Ministry of Justice,

2011). There had been hope amongst fathers' groups that this might pave the way for the adoption of a rebuttable presumption of shared parenting in some meaningful way. But hopes were dashed when the final report was issued. Key extracts are,

> 'We remain firm in our view that any legislation that might risk creating an impression of a parental "right" to any particular amount of time with a child would undermine the central principle of the Children Act 1989 that the welfare of the child is paramount.'
>
> 'Drawing on international and other evidence we opposed legislation to encourage "shared parenting"…..The thorough and detailed evidence from Australia showed the damaging consequences for many children. So we recommended that: no legislation should be introduced that creates or risks creating the perception that there is a parental right to substantially shared or equal time for both parents.'

The 'thorough and detailed evidence from Australia' refers, of course, to the McIntosh study. The reported deleterious effects of shared care, based on McIntosh, are used here to claim conflict with the principle which guides the family courts, namely that the best interests of the children are paramount. But the Norgrove report cited only three of the available studies, and placed particular emphasis on McIntosh (2010). Despite the balance of evidence to the contrary, the Norgrove report is predicated on shared parenting being harmful to the child. This perspective was reinforced by those who responded to consultation. On page 138 the Norgrove report notes that,

> 'Our opposition to legislation that might give rise to a shared parenting presumption attracted a large response in consultation. Charities, legal and judicial organisations and academics (including Professors Helen Rhoades, Liz Trinder, Rosemary Hunter and Judith Masson and the Network on Family Regulation) supported the panel's stance.'

Professor Helen Rhoades contributed Annex G to the Norgrove report, in which she writes, 'this submission argues that there should not be any formal legislative recognition of the importance of children having a meaningful relationship with both parents post-separation', basing her argument mostly on the potential of fathers to be abusive.

Professor Liz Trinder provided the following consultation response, quoted in the Norgrove report (page 138), 'I am encouraged that the Review has opted against a shared care presumption. That is entirely consistent with the research evidence on what works for children'. Except that it isn't, and wasn't at the time either, as I have outlined above. But at this point the research has been successfully woozled: McIntosh is now taken to be "the research", and the Norgrove report has laundered the woozle.

However, Norgrove was only a report; what matters is legislation. The legislation which followed was the Children and Families Act (UK Government, 2014). There were (and are) some Members of Parliament who are supportive of shared parenting, and this showed in the initial drafting of the Children and Families Bill. There was initial optimism that progress on shared parenting would at last be made. Specifically, this was to be addressed by Clause 11 of the Bill which originally read as follows,

> 'A court... is... to presume, unless the contrary is shown, that involvement of that parent in the life of the child concerned will further the child's welfare.'

The children's charities, Coram Children's Legal Centre and the NSPCC, formed the Shared Parenting Consortium. Despite the name, the Shared Parenting Consortium was firmly opposed to any presumption of shared care. They argued that a presumption of shared parenting would endanger children, (Family Law Week, 2014). Their lobbying particularly targeted Baroness Butler-Sloss. As a former President of the Family Division within the House of Lords, she was the perfect person to table a devastating amendment to the Bill. She duly did so. And who was going to gainsay her, given her authority in the area, and given the compelling direction from the children's charities, from the academics, and from the Ministry of Justice's own Norgrove report? By successfully woozling the research, a biased lobby is able to build up a seeming consensus of authoritative opinion supporting their desired outcome. The result was emasculation of Clause 11's attempt to open the door to shared parenting. The final Clause 11 of the Children and Families Act 2014 includes the clarification,

> '"involvement" means involvement of some kind, either direct or indirect, but not any particular division of a child's time.' (UK Government, 2014)

The final wording was a victory for the anti-shared parenting lobby – in this case misleadingly called the Shared Parenting Consortium. The above amendment makes clear that "involvement" may mean indirect contact – perhaps permission to write letters or to email the child. And even direct contact may mean only supervised contact once a fortnight in a contact centre for a couple of hours. The amendment killed completely the initiative for a presumption of shared parenting. It ensured continuance of the status quo.

It is worth considering briefly the words used by Lady Butler-Sloss in proposing the key amendment, referring to (Hansard, House of Lords, 2013a). She starts as follows,

> 'My Lords, it is with some regret that I have not sought to remove the presumption from the wording of Clause 11, although I still think it is unfortunate.'

She refers here to the initial part of clause 11, which was retained, namely the presumption that involvement of a parent in the life of the child will further the child's welfare, unless the contrary is shown. It is difficult to read into the Baroness's position on this anything other than a preference for the burden of proof to lie with the father to prove his benefit to the child. This is horribly reminiscent of the reversal of the principle of "innocent until proven guilty". She continued,

> 'I am, however, concerned about the message that separating parents may receive from the current wording of Clause 11. Originally the heading for this clause was "Shared parenting". That heading, thank goodness, was removed, but it had been picked up by the press, and this clause may be seen by some as containing the right to equal access to children. There is concern, not just on my part but on that of many of the agencies, including the NSPCC, Barnardo's and Coram.'

The Baroness's position is clear. She is implacably opposed to equality in parenting, whatever term is used to describe it. And yet still the public fail to grasp that feminism has always had, as one of its principal aims, granting mothers the right to get rid of the fathers of their children if that should be their wish. Do remember that when feminists call for fathers to "lean out" and do more childcare. And do remember that "equality does not mean treating everyone the same". Finally, there is this revealing paragraph from Butler-Sloss,

> 'The groups of parents whom I worry about in relation to Clause 11 are those who try to settle the arrangements for the children without going to court. In the absence of lawyers to advise either side, the stronger, more dominant parent may insist on an arrangement based on equality, or at least on disproportion which is not appropriate for the welfare of the children. We know from the Norgrove report of the fine line between children at risk in the private law sector and those seriously at risk in public law. The parents of some of those children at risk may well make their decisions outside court. I want the weaker parent to have something in statute to hold on to if browbeaten.'

Please do decode this judicial verbiage. The father is "stronger and dominant", the mother is "weaker and browbeaten". Is this the reality? Really? The Baroness appears to see the court process as a mechanism for mothers to attain ascendency over fathers. Recall that the noble Baroness was once the Head of the Family Division. She explicitly declares "an arrangement based on equality" as an adverse outcome: so much for the insistence that feminism is all about equality. And she uses Norgrove, that woozled misrepresentation of the research, as a means of raising a spectre of male violence ("seriously at risk in public law"). Is there any mystery as to why the outcomes for fathers are as they are? This is how the power politics of prejudice are played out.

Note this: at the start of the Bill's Report Stage, Butler-Sloss declared an interest - that she was, at the time, a Governor of Coram, (Hansard, House of Lords, 2013b).

To bring the story up to date, by 2018 there were 60 relevant studies on the impact on children of shared care. The Journal of Divorce & Remarriage published a special issue, under the editorship of Linda Nielsen, 'Shared Physical Custody: Recent Research, Advances, and Applications', (Nielsen, 2018). Key extracts from the Preface are,

> 'This Special Issue opens with my article summarizing the results of the 60 existing studies that compared the outcomes of children in joint physical custody (JPC) and sole physical custody (SPC) families. As these studies document, JPC children fare better than SPC children on a wide range of measures of well-being—above all, the quality of their relationships with both parents. More notably, independent of family income, the level of conflict between the parents, the quality of their relationships with each parent, and quality of the parenting skills, JPC children are still generally more advantaged. Still, as this article explains, there are situations where JPC is not more beneficial than SPC.'

> 'The 20 authors of the articles in this two-part special issue and the 12 experts at the international conference in 2017 reached the same conclusion—and reached it independently of one another without being commissioned by any organization to try to achieve a consensus. This body of scholars concludes that JPC is generally in the best interests of children, with some exceptions, including, but not limited to, children who need protection from a parent whose care is abusive, neglectful, or grossly inadequate. These conclusions are in accord with those reached by the 110 international experts who endorsed Warshak's 2014 consensus paper, (Richard Warshak, 2014), on shared parenting for children under the age of 4.' (Nielsen, 2018).

In the context of the USA, Nielsen also notes, encouragingly, that,

> 'Changes in custody laws are sweeping the country, too slowly and insufficient for some people and too quickly and ill-considered for others….. 20 states are in the process of revising custody statutes to be more favorable toward joint physical custody (JPC).'

Unfortunately, the recent history in the UK, as outlined above, has set us back rather badly.

12.4 Parental Conflict and the Benefit of Contact

There has been an unspoken presumption in the family courts that where there is a high level of conflict between the parents, the children's best interests are served by restricting, or eliminating entirely, contact with one parent. The empirical evidence, however, is not in favour of this presumption, except in the most extreme and persistent cases of conflict. In 2017 the ubiquitous Linda Nielsen published a review article, 'Re-examining the Research on Parental Conflict, Coparenting, and Custody Arrangements'. An extract from the Abstract reads,

> 'Recent research does not support the idea that conflict - including high legal conflict - should rule out joint physical custody as the arrangement that best serves children's interests. Parents with joint physical custody do not generally have significantly less conflict or more cooperative relationships than parents with sole physical custody. Conflict and poor coparenting are not linked to worse outcomes for children in joint physical custody than in sole physical custody. The quality of the parent–child relationship is a better predictor than conflict of children's outcomes, with the exception of the most extreme forms of conflict to which some children are exposed.' (Nielsen, 2017)

Nielsen rightly cautions against making exaggerated claims about all conflict being irrelevant to outcomes for children. Quote, 'these studies did not conclude that frequently being exposed to, or dragged into the middle of, intense, ongoing, frightening, or physically aggressive conflict will have little to no impact on children'. Nevertheless, she concludes that,

> 'Joint physical custody is associated with better outcomes for children than sole physical custody even when their parents do not initially both agree to the parenting plan and even when the conflict at the time of separation or in subsequent years is not low.'

> 'Limiting the time that children spend with one of their parents through sole physical custody is not correlated with better outcomes for children, even when there is considerable conflict and a poor coparenting relationship.'

These conclusions are broadly supported by Nicole Mahrer et al in 'Does Shared Parenting Help or Hurt Children in High-Conflict Divorced Families?', although these authors also stress the limitations where conflict is both high and persistent over many years. Extracts from the Abstract are,

> 'We review 11 studies of relations between parenting time and parenting quality with children's adjustment in high-conflict divorced families. Despite heterogeneity of methods used across the studies, some tentative conclusions can be made based on findings of multiple studies. Higher levels of shared parenting were related to poorer child adjustment in samples with high conflict many years following the divorce, but

typically not in samples that assessed conflict during the divorcing process or in the 2 or 3 years following the divorce.' (Mahrer et al, 2018)

12.5 Empathy Gap in Alienation and Shared Care

The phenomena underlying the imposition of ACEs take us beyond the empathy gap and into a broader range of sociological childcare issues. Similarly, alienation takes us beyond an empathy gap for the alienated parent because, whilst the alienated parent is the target and is harmed thereby, the greater damage is to the child. For the same reason, the issue of shared parenting is not only a fathers' rights issue because the absence of one parent has adverse effects on the child, including reduced resilience. All these things are primarily childcare and child welfare issues. Nevertheless, the empathy gap for the alienated or non-resident parent facilitates this abuse. The alienated or non-resident parent may be the father or the mother. But the alienated parent is more often the father, and the non-resident parent is far more often the father.

13

The Drivers of Fatherlessness

Women's Liberation, if it abolishes the patriarchal family, will abolish a necessary substructure of the authoritarian state; ... so let's get on with it.
Germaine Greer, *The Female Eunuch* (1970)

To understand what has happened to marriage and the family and the political implications of this we need to recognise that we have been in hock to an ideology which has actively sought to undermine the male breadwinner role within the family and the family within it for nigh on 70 years. And it is this male breadwinner role which middle class women, often feminists themselves, benefit from, both through marriage and then when they get divorced. Working class women, on the other hand do not get married as the forces ranged against their men mean they are unable to provide support. Feminists have always made it clear that they regard men providing financial support for women as the root of all evil.
Belinda Brown, *Feminism set out to destroy the family* (2019a)

Fathers experience a state funded system that sees mothers as important while men are often an irrelevance or a problem
Welsh Dad's Survey, 2017

Chapters 10, 11 and 12 have presented some of the mechanisms which lead to fathers becoming estranged from their children after parental separation. In this chapter I summarise the key statistics on marriage, divorce, cohabitation, partnership dissolution and living arrangements, with and without children. These provide an insight into the numbers of children growing up without their father. In particular they show that, whilst divorce is a significant contributor to fatherlessness, it is the decline of marriage which is the dominant cause of fatherlessness. This is not only because of the increased prevalence of lone mothers but even more due to the increased prevalence of cohabiting couples and the fact that cohabiting couples are far more likely to split than married couples.

I review the correlation between the decline of marriage and socioeconomic class. It is amongst the poorest people that marriage has become least common, whilst the well-off still marry almost as often as ever. This is the marriage gap. And the marriage gap in turn becomes a fatherhood gap. It is therefore amongst the less well-off that fatherlessness is most prevalent. All data in this chapter on marriage, divorce, cohabitation, households, etc., relates to England and Wales.

13.1 Marriage, Divorce, Cohabitation and Single Living: the Data

Since the late 1960s there has been a long-term trend of decreasing marriage rates and initially steeply rising divorce rates, Figure 13.1, (Office for National Statistics, 2015d). However, the divorce rate has been falling over the last 15 years as an inevitable response to the declining marriage rates. Part of the reduction in marriage rates so apparent in Figure 13.1 could be a transient effect of the trend towards later marriage (Figures 13.2a,b). But if this were the case, the marriage rate would eventually show an upturn and a return to earlier rates. This is not apparent, though the downward trend has (arguably) ceased since about 2005. In 2015 there were 239,000 marriages and 101,000 divorces, (Office for National Statistics, 2018p).

Figure 13.1: *Long Term Trend of Marriage and Divorce, England and Wales*

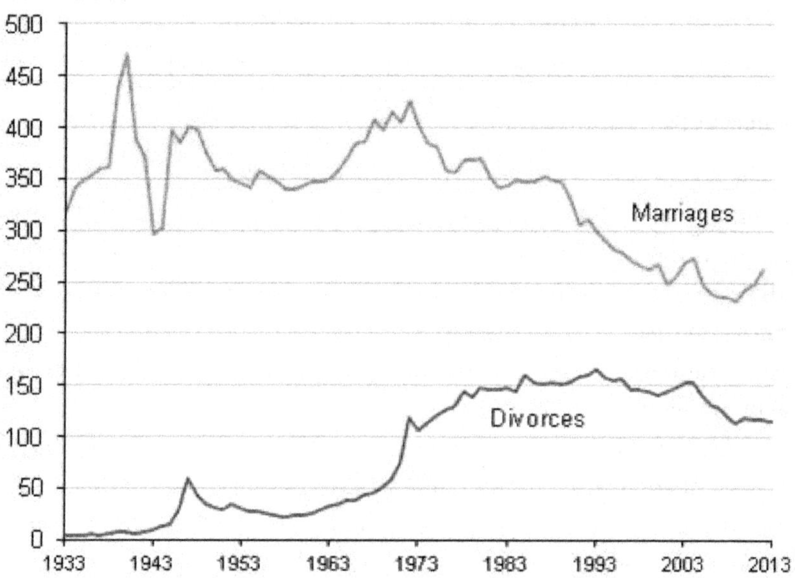

Figures 13.2a,b illustrate the trend towards marrying later, (Office for National Statistics, 2014). In 1981 the median age at first marriage was 22.0 for women and 24.1 for men. By 2015 these had increased to 29.7 and 31.5 respectively. Including re-marriages, the mean age at marriage in 2015 was 35.1 (women) and 37.5 (men), (Office for National Statistics, 2018r). In 2017, of all people aged 16 and over,

- There were about one million more women than men in the population;
- 11.6 million couples were married and living together;

- 11.1 million men and 12.1 million women were not currently married (noting that this includes young adults who are less likely to be married, and also widows/widowers);
- 3.0 million couples were cohabiting;
- 8.6 million men and 9.7 million women were not living as a couple;
- 8.8 million men and 7.6 million women had never been married;
- 1.5 million men and 2.2 million women were divorced and not then re-married;
- 0.8 million men and 2.3 million women were widowed.

(Office for National Statistics, 2018q)

Figure 13.2a: *Age of Men at First Marriage, 1981 to 2012*

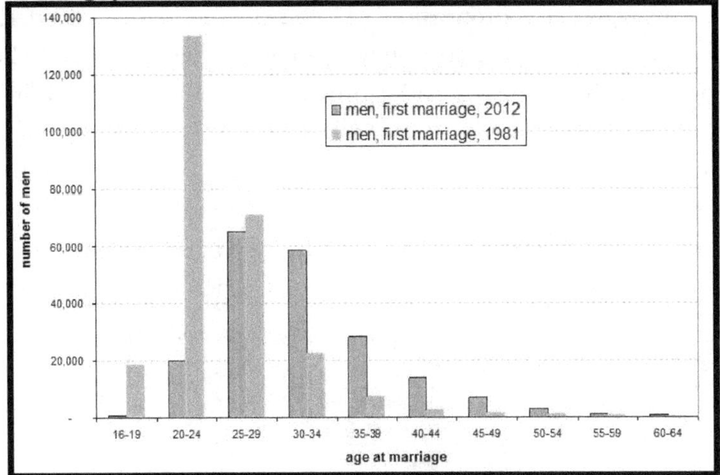

Figure 13.2b: *Age of Women at First Marriage, 1981 to 2012*

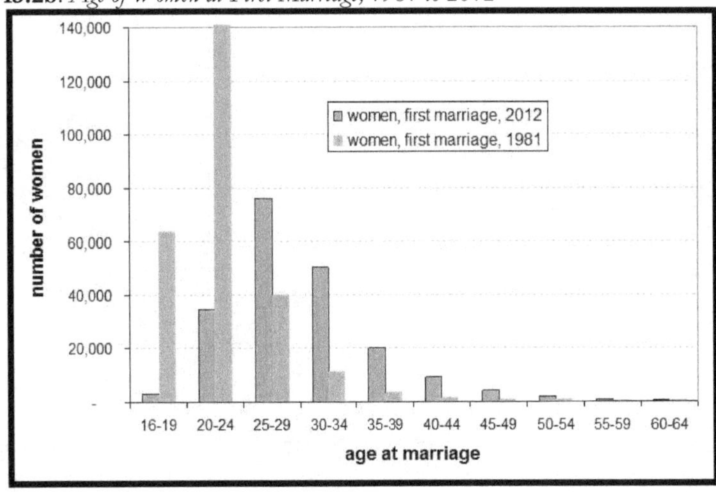

Note that whilst there are a million fewer men than women who are not currently married (because there are a million fewer men in the population), there are over a million more men than women who have never married. This implies that more men than women marry more than once, i.e., that a divorced man is more likely to remarry than a divorced woman. Hence, there are more unmarried women divorcees than unmarried men divorcees. This is consistent with the historic (and pre-historic) tendency for fewer men than women to leave progeny, (Wilder, Mobasher and Hammer, 2004), (Karmin et al, 2015). The greatest sex imbalance, however, is in the widowed category, due to men's shorter lifespan.

Figure 13.3 indicates the proportion of people of the same sex by marital status, versus age. The proportion of women who are married declines sharply in later life as the proportion who are widowed increases. In 2017, of people between their late 30s and retirement age, roughly two-thirds were married. This Figure, being a snapshot in time, underrepresents the proportion of people who have ever been divorced or widowed, since many of these have remarried and are thus counted as married. In 2017 more than 90% of people of retirement age had been married at some time in their lives. But this will change dramatically in future, as we shall see.

Figure 13.3: *Marital Status as a Percentage of Total Adult Population of the Same Sex, Versus Age, (Office for National Statistics, 2018q)*

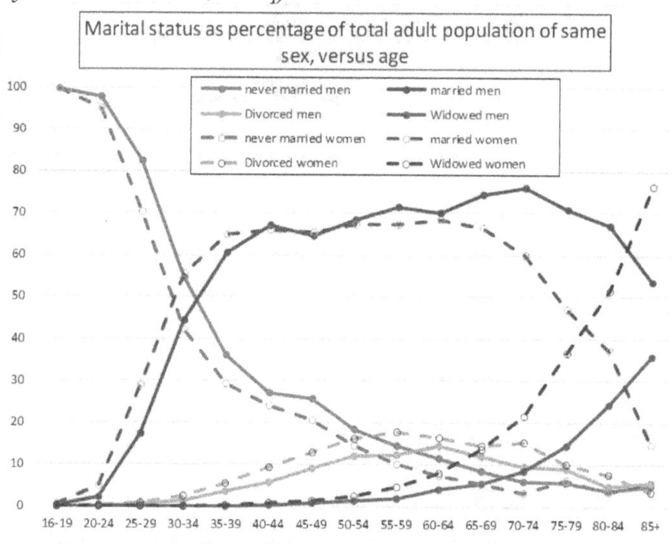

Figure 13.4 indicates the proportion of people who are living together, married or not, versus age. Young people, unsurprisingly, are most often not

living as couples. 20% to 30% of people over 30 do not live as a couple, and this rises after retirement age as widowhood intervenes. The median duration of marriages which end in divorce was 12 years in 2017, an increase from 10 years in 1997, (Office for National Statistics, 2018p).

Figure 13.4: *Living Arrangements as a Percentage of Total Adult Population of the Same Sex Versus Age, (Office for National Statistics, 2018q)*

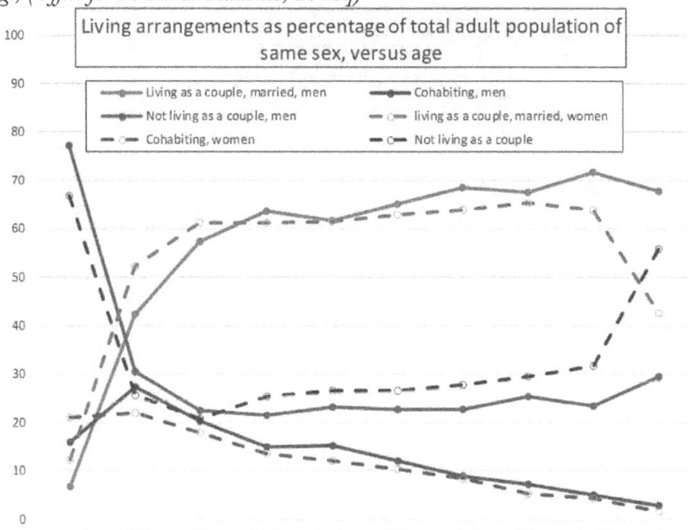

Figure 13.3 may mislead. It is easy to make the false assumption that as the current population ages, this age dependence of marital status will remain unchanged. For example, the Figure may be interpreted as implying that as people get older the percentage ever married will approach that of people currently over 70, and hence that more than 90% of young adults today will eventually marry. This, however, is false. It fails to account for a genuine decline in the popularity of marriage.

Figures 13.5 and 13.6 are the best indication of the long-term decline of marriage. Figure 13.5 plots the percentage of men who have ever married against age but does so separately for different birth cohorts. Thus, for men born in 1940, over 90% eventually married. Even for the 1950 birth cohort this was noticeably falling. For the 1960 birth cohort, about 80% eventually married, even though some may later have divorced. For the 1970 birth cohort this dropped to only around 70%. It is too early to say what the outcome will be for the 1980 birth cohort, but Figure 13.5 unambiguously indicates the proportion of men who ever marry is continuing to decline, and perhaps will be about 60% for this cohort. The downward trend continues for the 1990 birth cohort. These data are from (Office for National Statistics, 2018r).

Figure 13.5: *Percentage of Men Ever Married Versus Age: Different Birth Cohorts Compared, (Office for National Statistics, 2018r)*

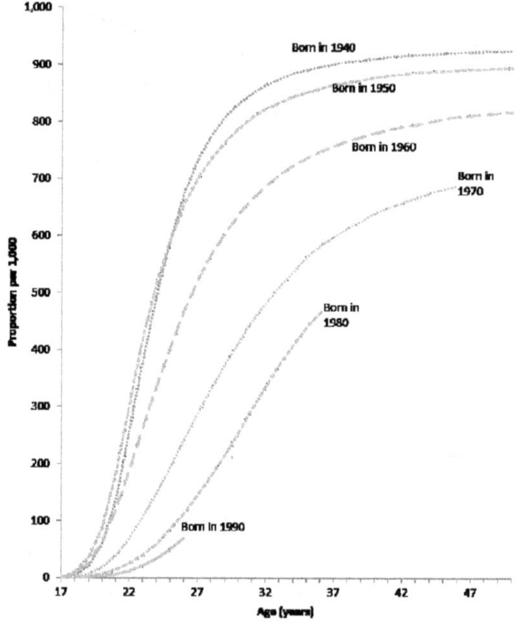

Figure 13.6: *Percentage of Women Ever Married Versus Age: Different Birth Cohorts Compared, (Office for National Statistics, 2018r)*

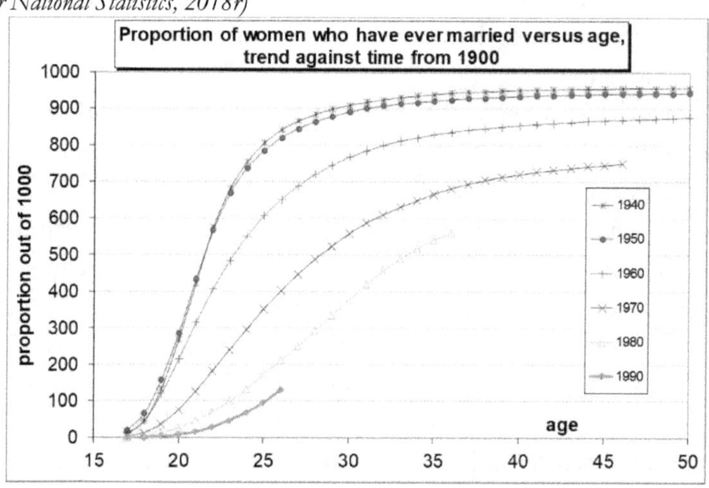

Figure 13.6 shows the same reducing popularity of marriage amongst women. 95% of the 1950 birth cohort were married at some time, whereas the 1980

birth cohort appears to be trending towards about 65%.

According to The Marriage Foundation (2014), when the current trends are extrapolated, it is predicted that only 52% of today's 20 year old men and 53% of today's 20 year old women are expected to ever marry. This is the truest measure of the decline of marriage.

13.2 Statistics on Children's Living Arrangements

Data in this section are taken from (Office for National Statistics, 2017r) and (Office for National Statistics, 2015e) except where otherwise noted. A family is defined as two married or cohabiting adults, with or without children, or a lone parent with at least one child who lives at the same address. Figure 13.7 shows the numbers of married, cohabiting and lone parent families. In this Figure "with or without children" refers to dependent age children. People who do not currently have dependent children, whether married, cohabiting or single-living, may have children in the future – or may have grown-up children. This should be borne in mind when interpreting Figure 13.7. Thus, the categories "married, cohabiting or lone parents without children" includes those living with adult children past the age of dependency. Hence the category "lone parent without children" is not really an oxymoron but denotes a parent living without a partner but with adult offspring. Figure 13.7 excludes adults living without a partner or children of any age (so non-resident parents not living with a new partner do not feature at all in these data). Such lone-living people are not classed as a "family".

Whilst the number of married couples without dependent children exceeds the number with dependent children at any one time, this does not imply that most married people do not have children. In fact, a very clear majority of married couples have at least one child at some time (in excess of 80% at the present time, though this is falling).

Of women born in 1971, 18% were childless in 2016, when they turned 45 and hence likely to remain childless. Almost half of women (48%) who turned 30 in 2016 did not have any children, (Office for National Statistics, 2017s). In contrast, for women born in 1945 only 10% of women remained permanently childless, and only 18% had no children by the age of 30.

Young males are more likely to be living with their parents than young females; around 32% of males aged 20 to 34 years were living with their parents compared with 20% of females aged 20 to 34 years in 2017.

There were 14.0 million dependent children living in 7.98 million families in the UK in 2017, an average of 1.75 children per family with dependent children. This figure is not the same as women's average fertility because, (a) some of these mothers will go on to have more children, (b) it does not count adult progeny, and, (c) it does not account for childless women. The average fertility of women in England and Wales is currently 1.90, based on the 1971 birth cohort, (Office for National Statistics, 2017s). Average fertility is currently falling at a rate of 0.1 per 13 years, though we have yet to see what the average fertility will be for today's young women. Fertility is strongly demographic-cultural dependent. In 2014 the average total fertility rate for women born in the UK was only 1.76, compared with a total fertility rate of UK resident women not born in the UK of 2.09, the proportion of live births to the latter mothers being 27% (Office for National Statistics, 2015f). Note that the UK-born fertility rate of 1.76 does not refer to indigenous whites only, but includes people of all ethnicities and parental country of origin.

Figure 13.7: *Number of Families by Family Type, 1996 – 2017 ("children" denotes those of dependent age only; "without children" may mean with children of adult age)*

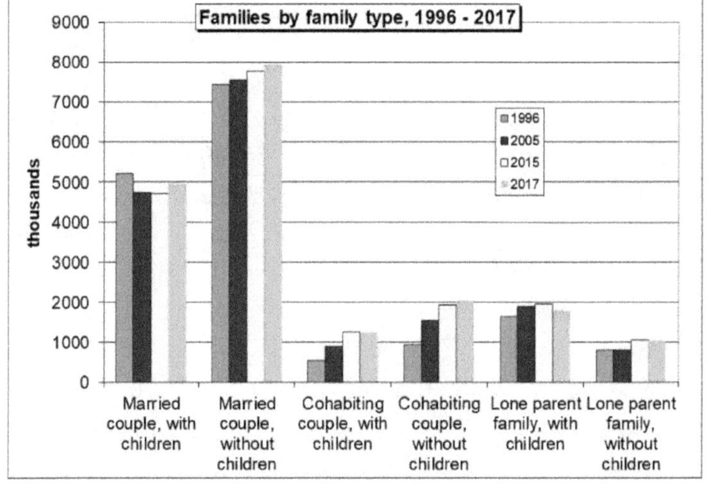

In order to reveal the statistics on adults living alone it is better to consider "households" rather than "families", from which latter category lone adults are excluded. Thus, in 2017, there were,

- 7.7 million single-person households;
- 15.7 million households with one family including two parents;
- 2.7 million households with a lone parent family;
- 1.1 million households with two or more families or two or more unrelated adults.

Figure 13.8 brings out most starkly the prevalence of lone living; 28% of all households consist of a single person living alone. The commonest arrangement is a household of just two people, which might be either a couple with no children living with them, or a lone parent with one child, or two unrelated adults. Households of just one or two people comprise nearly two-thirds (63%) of all households. The origin of the pressure on housing is clear.

Figure 13.8: *Proportion of Households by Household Size*

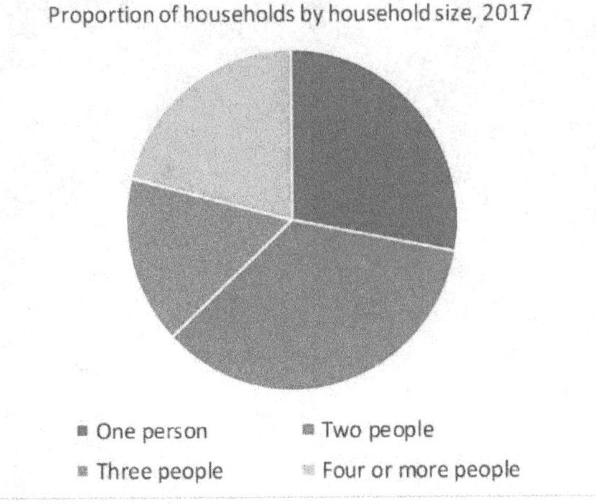

Of the 7.7 million one-person households in the UK, 53.8% of them in 2017 contained one woman and 46.2% of them contained one man. However, this is slightly misleading as half of these lone-living people are over 65, and the excess of women over men in this age range is primarily due to men's shorter longevity. Confining attention to those of working age, i.e., 16 to 64 years old, a larger proportion of people living alone are men, the number of lone-living men exceeding the number of lone-living women by 41%. This is because a larger proportion of men than women never marry, because men tend to marry when older, and because partnership dissolution most often involves a mother continuing to live with the children whilst the father starts a new living arrangement on his own (at least initially).

13.3 The Decline of Marriage Drives Fatherlessness

Historically, the overwhelming majority of children were born to married women. But now only about half of children are, at birth, born to a married woman, having reached 53% by 2012, see Figure 13.9, (Benson, 2015). Moreover, the prevalence of parental separation is strongly correlated with marital status at the birth of the child. For parents who were married when the child was born, 24% will split by the time the child reaches 15. In contrast, 69% of couples who never married will split by the time the child is 15. Perhaps most strikingly, even where the parents were unmarried at the birth of the child but subsequently married, 56% split by the time the child is 15.

Figure 13.9: *Marital Status of Couple at the Birth of the Child, and Birth Certification. Dual certification means the father is named; in sole registration no father is named. Reproduced from (Benson, 2015).*

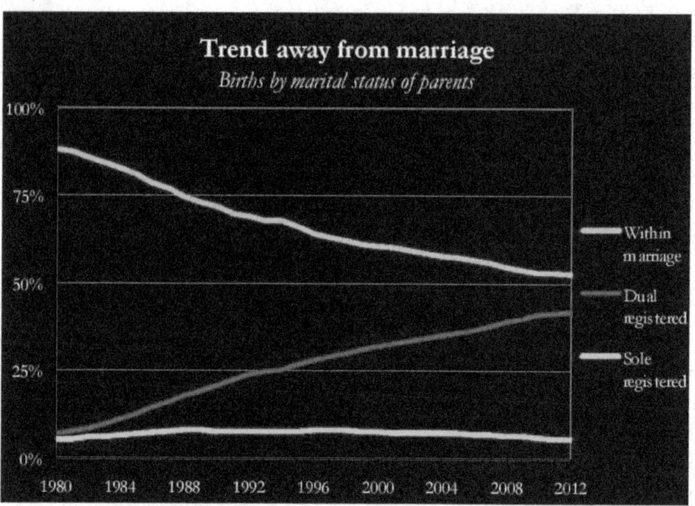

Significant though divorce is as a cause of family breakdown, the divorce statistics omit a crucial issue which is approaching dominance: the break-up of cohabiting couples with children. Whilst cohabiting couples account for only about 15% of dependent children, cohabiting couples are far more likely to split than married couples. In fact about half of family breakdowns relate to cohabiting couples. In addition, there are the lone parent families, overwhelmingly single mothers (noting that these may relate to sole or dual registration). Far more children fail to live with both parents as a result of the combined effects of lone parenting and cohabitation break-up than the result of divorce.

Only 55% of children live with both parents to age 15. If current trends continue, any child born today in the UK has only a 50/50 chance of being with both their birth parents by the age of 15. Nearly all parents (93%) who stay together until their children reach 15 are married. Hence, only 7% of children living with both parents at 15 will have unmarried parents. This statistic should be compared with the 20% of children initially living with both parents in a cohabiting family, (The Marriage Foundation, 2017), (The Marriage Foundation, 2016).

Of teenagers not living with both parents, just 32% of cases involved divorce – the rest were never married. Hence, twice as much fatherlessness is caused by the decline of marriage than is caused by divorce.

Recalling that barely half of today's teenagers will marry, (The Marriage Foundation, 2014), the ongoing decline in marriage is therefore of considerable concern as it implies increasing fatherlessness. As we shall see, this also implies increasing disadvantage to children and a downward spiral of social decohesion.

Marriage *per se* is not a magic bullet. We have seen, above, that couples who marry only after the birth of a child are twice as likely to split as couples who marry first. What protects against parental separation is the care, deliberation, planning and commitment to family stability which couples who marry before having children display.

13.4 The Socioeconomics of Marriage: The Marriage Gap

In this section I lean heavily on the report by Harry Benson and Stephen McKay (2015) from which the Figures are taken. Figures 13.10 and 13.11 show the huge dependency of the marital status of new mothers, and mothers of children under five, on household income. Figure 13.10 shows that only 24% of new mothers in the lowest family income range are married. In contrast, 87% of new mothers in the highest family income range are married. This is the marriage gap: the wealthy get married, the poor do not. Figure 13.11 shows that it is families in the middle income range whose likelihood of being married has reduced most markedly over the last twenty years. Marriage has become the wealthy persons' privilege. The reason for this relates to hypergamy, the Welfare State and feminist ideology, as explained by Belinda Brown, (2019a). Well educated professional women will generally only marry men who match, or over-match, them in earning power. Women in the lower socioeconomic strata also want a man who earns more than they can acquire on their own, with State assistance. The former define those who marry, the wealthy, whilst the latter define those who do not: the poor and increasingly the average earners. Feminist ideology and associated social changes have made it increasingly difficult for men to out-earn women, especially if women are State assisted. The irony here is that the men that women want to marry are those men who approximate best to what the feminists disparage as "patriarchs". I say "irony", but actually this is precisely the mechanism by which "patriarchy" came about in the first place: through women's own wishes.

But the outcome for children is that children of poor families may thus be doubly disadvantaged: by poverty and by potential father deprivation.

Figure 13.10: *Likelihood of New Mothers being Married by Household Income. Reproduced from (Benson and McKay, 2015)*

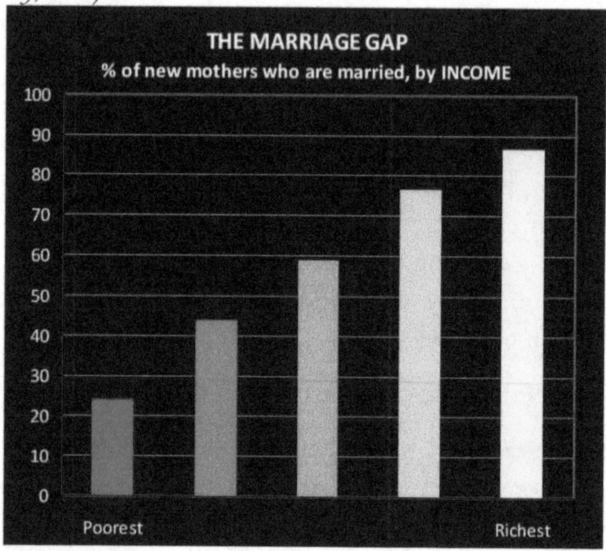

Figure 13.11: *Likelihood of Mothers of Young Children being Married by Household Income. Reproduced from (Benson and McKay, 2015)*

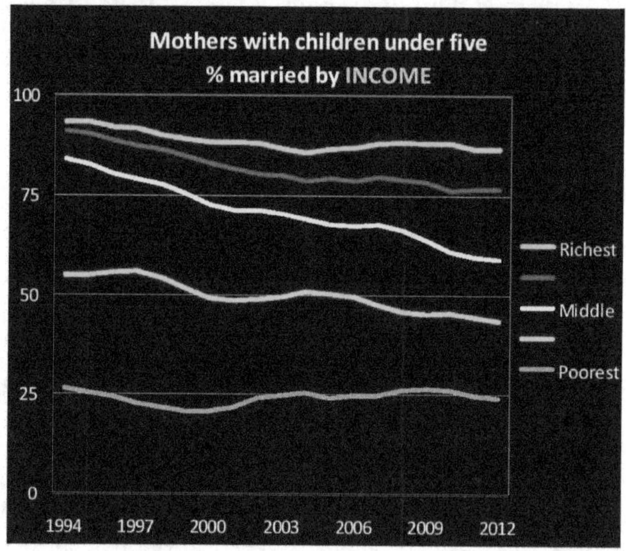

Figure 13.12: *Percentage of Mothers with Children under Five by Housing Status. Reproduced from (Benson and McKay, 2015)*

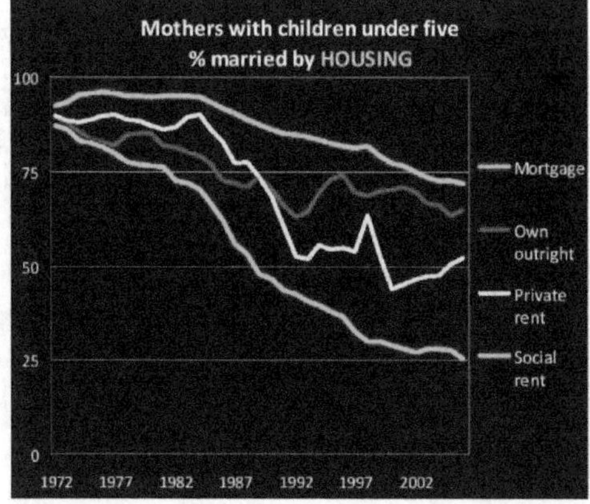

Figure 13.13: *Percentage of New Mothers who are Married by a Range of Socioeconomic Markers. Reproduced from (Benson and McKay, 2015)*

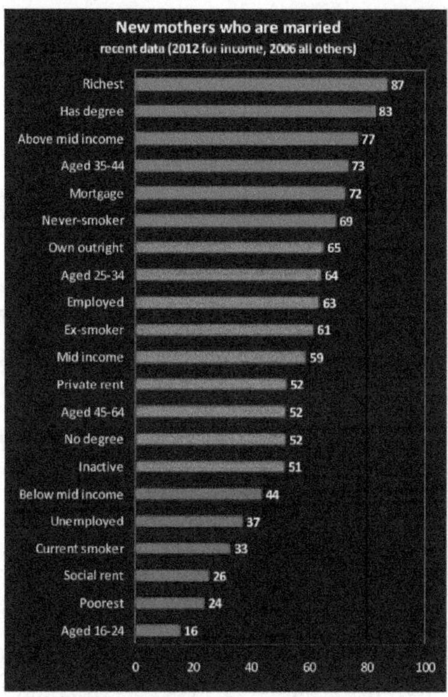

Housing status acts as a socioeconomic marker. Hence Figure 13.12 shows that whilst 70% of couples with a mortgage are married, only 25% of those in social housing are married. The Figure shows how marriage has collapsed in the latter group since the 1970s. Some 60% of lone parent families receive housing benefit (or the equivalent under universal credit) compared to 10% of couple families.

Figure 13.13 shows the relationship between marriage and a range of socioeconomic markers. It is clear that marriage itself is effectively a socioeconomic marker. The pattern of low income being associated with single parent families is universal. Figure 13.14 shows data from the US Department of Health & Human Services (2012) indicating a child poverty rate in single mother families which is more than four times that in married parent families.

Figure 13.14: *Percentage of Children in Poverty by Family Structure, USA (US Department of Health & Human Services, 2012)*

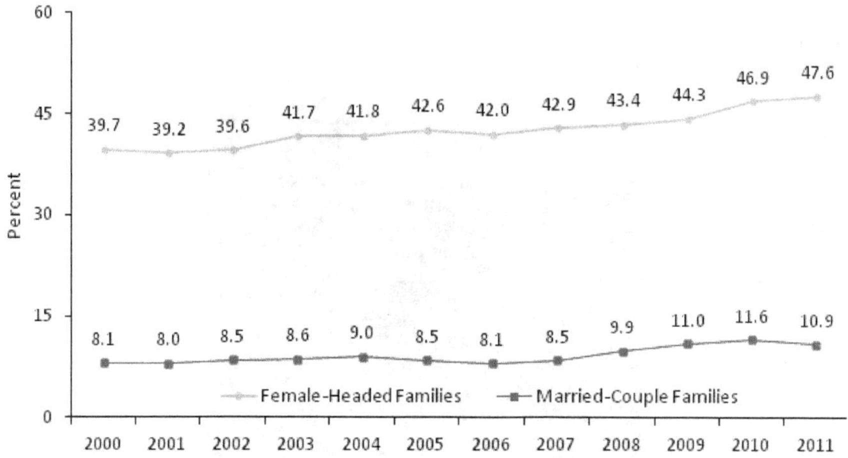

13.5 Summary of the Drivers of Fatherlessness

Fatherlessness results from two things: divorce and the decline of marriage. For teenagers not living with both their parents, divorce is responsible in only one-third of cases. In two-thirds of cases the parents were never married (to each other). About half of children born now are born outside marriage. At any time, about 15% of dependent children live in cohabiting families and about 23% in single parent families. However, cohabitees are far more likely to split than married couples. The result is that barely more than half (55%) of children aged 15 are still living with both their parents. The decline of marriage is the greater cause, rather than divorce, though both are substantial.

The genuine decline of marriage is best illustrated by Figures 13.5 and 13.6. Today's retirees were 90% to 95% likely to have been married at some time. These elderly people may not fully appreciate that, on current trends, only about 50% of today's 20 year olds will ever marry. Today's parents of 30 year olds may be wondering when their offspring will ever marry. The answer for nearly half of them will be "never".

Many children will retain meaningful contact with their fathers post-separation. But, as we saw in chapter 11, nearly 40% of fathers have no, or negligible, involvement with their children after separation. Many paternal grandparents discover only too late the disadvantage of being the parents of a son when they are estranged from their grandchildren's lives for the error of having a child of the incorrect sex.

The decline of marriage, and hence fatherlessness, is strongly related to demographic. Only 24% of new mothers in the lowest family income range are married. In contrast, 87% of new mothers in the highest family income range are married. This is the marriage gap: the wealthy get married, the poor do not. The children of unmarried parents are thus at greater risk of disadvantage by a double-whammy of poverty and fatherlessness.

Does being poor reduce the likelihood of marriage, or does being an unmarried parent make you poorer? Both, to a degree. Being a poor man can be expected to make your matrimonial chances slim. There are, of course, a host of covariates, including educational attainment, IQ and personality traits. The welfare state is certainly implicated. For example, it may be disadvantageous to cohabit or marry due to loss of housing benefit (or the equivalent under universal benefit). And whilst no one could pretend that getting married will automatically make you wealthy, there may be some truth to the old adage that "two can live as cheaply as one", a domestic economy of scale which appears to be less appealing today than it was. The result is a lose-lose scenario consisting of an epidemic of poor lone-mothers and socially isolated fathers. *Cui bono*? Well educated, middle class feminists with professional jobs, and probably with husbands, whose policies of family-destruction have brought about this disadvantage to the less well off.

14

The Effect of Fatherlessness on Outcomes for Children

Unless we reverse the trend of fatherlessness, no other set of accomplishments - not economic growth or prison construction or welfare reform or better schools - will succeed in arresting the decline of child wellbeing and the spread of male violence. To tolerate the trend of fatherlessness is to accept the inevitability of continued social recession.
David Blankenhorn, Fatherless America (1995)

A community that allows a large number of men to grow up in broken families, dominated by women, never acquiring any stable relationship to male authority, never acquiring any set of rational expectations about the future - that community asks for and gets chaos. Crime, violence, unrest, disorder - most particularly the furious, unrestrained lashing out at the whole social structure - that is not only to be expected; it is very near to inevitable. And it is richly deserved.
Daniel Patrick Moynihan, (1927 – 2003)

Chapters 10 to 13 have reviewed the prevalence of fatherlessness and its causes. This might be of little importance if fatherlessness had no great impact on children. The distress of the fathers themselves, of course, is of little consequence, thanks to the empathy gap. But if fatherlessness has a significant disbeneficial effect on children, the enormous scale of fatherlessness revealed in the preceding sections implies a similarly enormous scale of disadvantage to children. This chapter reviews the evidence for the impact of fatherlessness on children and their adult outcomes. As was the case for ACEs and alienation in chapter 12, it is too narrow to focus only on the implied empathy gap for men, as fathers. The more concerning impact is upon the children. But I shall argue that the empathy gap for fathers results in collateral damage to children which, as a society, we are tolerating.

What is not explored here, for lack of information, is the extent to which fathers' fecklessness contributes to the overall prevalence of fatherlessness. Undoubtedly, a society which minimises the importance of fathers can only encourage some dads to become genuinely deadbeat. Equally certain, though, is that this denigration is inapplicable to the many tens of thousands of fathers who exhaust themselves, emotionally and financially, every year in the UK in fighting for greater involvement with their children, or any involvement at all. After the introductory section, I start with a renowned, but now historical study from 1992, which sets the scene. The long section which follows provides a selection of references to studies indicating the disbenefits of father absence, though it is emphasised that this is a tiny fraction of the literature. The final two sections review specific studies notable for being very extensive and claiming a causal connection between fatherlessness and adverse outcomes for the children.

14.1 The Differing Perspectives on Fatherhood

There is no shortage of empirical studies which show the relationship between fatherlessness and adverse outcomes for children. Fathers' advocates will eagerly quote such sources and attribute the blame for fatherlessness to the exclusion of fathers from their children's lives after parental separation. The scale at which society has been disenfranchising fathers from their children's lives over the last half century, as outlined in chapters 10 to 13, lends credibility to that perspective.

Those wishing to promote more childcare by fathers, perhaps as part of a strategy to enhance women's standing in the workplace, will also eagerly quote such sources, though they will attribute blame differently. It is men who must change, they will opine, to take some of the childcare burden from mothers. That being more involved in childcare, perhaps even the primary carer, may avail fathers little when it comes to continuing involvement with their children after separation is a fact which such advocates find convenient to ignore.

And where fathers are no longer involved in their children's lives, the "deadbeat dad" mantra is deployed to place the blame squarely upon the fathers. For example, in the USA the Marriage & Religion Research Institute (2014) concludes, 'society will continue to remain in a crisis until fathers accept the responsibility of caring for and protecting their children'. Certainly, there will be feckless fathers who deserve such admonition. But perfectly good fathers who have been forcibly removed from their children's lives by injunctions and court orders may justly react to such statements with less than complete placidity. And those who are genuinely feckless, what if they are the second or third generation of fatherlessness? Where then does the blame lie?

Some people reject completely the claims that fathers bring any benefit to children at all, for example (The Liz Library, 2018). The attempt on this site to refute the relationship between fatherlessness and adverse childhood outcomes starts with a list of famous men who did well in life but, it is claimed, were fatherless. Any such selection of individual cases is fraudulent, of course. No one is claiming that the effects are deterministic and inescapable. Such spurious arguments are essentially straw men. It did amuse me, though, that the first mentioned man was George Washington. This is odd in view of the famous, if apocryphal, story concerning Washington being unable to lie to his father about the cherry tree incident. His father died when Washington was 10. Second on the list was Thomas Jefferson. In fact, he lived with his father too, until the latter died when Jefferson was 14. We shall see below that much, perhaps most, of the benefit of father involvement relates to younger children. I confess that surprised me, but it's what the empirical evidence suggests. So Washington and Jefferson are no refutations at all.

The weight of evidence is that fatherlessness is correlated with adverse outcomes for children, and that father involvement is correlated with improved outcomes. That is not to say that all studies report such an association: they do not. Some studies report no statistically significant effect. What does seem significant, though, is the absence of studies indicating that father absence is beneficial, which discounts any suggestion that the studies indicating the benefits of father involvement are mere statistical noise.

One must always be careful in social science research not to confuse correlation with causality. The correlation of fatherlessness with a whole range of serious adverse outcomes for children is clear, as we will see. But is this a causal relationship? The most obvious concern is that fatherlessness is correlated also with lower socioeconomic status, and poverty is correlated with poorer child outcomes. This is just one pathway by which a relationship between fatherlessness and adverse child outcomes might arise without direct causality. Of importance, therefore, are studies which control for relevant socioeconomic variables, or other significant variables such as parental educational attainment, before drawing conclusions about the father effect. There is no shortage of these either. Of greatest interest is the thorough review by Sara McLanahan et al, who are so bold as to claim causal connection explicitly. This paper is reviewed in detail in section 14.5.

Whilst this chapter concentrates upon harm to children, it is important to recall throughout that this arises as a collateral consequence of the empathy gap against men which facilitates the societal equanimity at endemic fatherlessness.

14.2 Families Without Fatherhood, Dennis & Erdos, 1992

I start with the classic work 'Families Without Fatherhood' by Norman Dennis and George Erdos (1992, 3rd ed 2000) for two reasons. It shows how long the deleterious effects of father absence have been known and also because it overturns expectations based on the authors' affiliations. Norman Dennis was a sociologist, lifelong Labour supporter and Labour councillor in Sunderland (he died in 2010). George Erdos, a psychologist at the University of Newcastle and elsewhere, styles himself an 'ethical socialist'. Raised in Hungary, he experienced both communism and fascism at first hand before moving to the UK. Dennis and Erdos's polemic is a long work. I will restrict myself to a few extracts because, as far as data analysis is concerned, there is an embarrassment of riches in more recent studies. They set the scene with this observation,

> 'One of the authors was invited to prepare a paper for a seminar based upon a very extensive study of the literature on the lone-parent family. Contrary to the near-consensus among his social policy colleagues that, in its strongest version, it was reactionary nonsense to allege that the lone-parent family was inferior to the two-parent family, he could find no study which did not show clearly that, over a whole range of outcomes, children in lone-parent families suffered disabilities as compared with the average child in the stable two-parent family. In a weaker version of the consensus it was assumed that, in so far as there were differences, these were not due to lone-parenthood as such, but merely to low income. Alternatively or additionally, they were due to the fact that the non-academic public erroneously believed that lone-parenthood was to the disadvantage of children, and this erroneous belief itself, this stigma, had the effect of creating disadvantage. There was nothing a dollar and a dose of enlightenment would not fix.
>
> Colleagues holding this view were asked for bibliographical details of the studies that supported either the stronger version or the weaker version - at that stage fully expecting that such studies were available. On one occasion this bona fide request was met, surprisingly, with a hostile, 'You know quite well that there are no such studies!'
>
> The success of the attack on the family was even more astonishing when the experience of children is considered; but it was even more vulnerable when the anti-family consensus began to be challenged. For the case that the family was not deteriorating only changing, so far as children were concerned not only flew full in the face of common experience. It also flew in the face of every empirical study that had ever been published on the subject that had yielded definite results on the benefits and drawbacks for children of families with fathers as compared with those households without them.'

Dismissing the above as the rantings of an antediluvian conservative is hardly possible in view of the authors' actual political leanings and academic subjects. Dennis & Erdos proceed to summarise a mass of data analyses (by other authors). I will confine myself to one example,

> 'All the 17,000 children born in England, Scotland and Wales in the week 3-9 March 1958 were (and are) the subject of periodic follow-up investigations by the National

> Child Development Study. Of these children, 600 were born outside of marriage. A principal author of the Crellin study of these (as they were called) 'illegitimate' children was Dr M.L. Kellmer Pringle, well-known for her publications on child development. What were the statistical associations between, on the one hand, birth taking place without the mother being married to the father (a central prohibition of the pre-1960s system) and, on the other, various aspects of the circumstances and personal characteristics of the mother and child?
>
> In Crellin's population, the proportions of the children of married and uncommitted fathers were spread evenly through the social classes. Whereas uncommitted fatherhood had in the past been associated with low social class, by the later-1960s this was no longer the case. Her findings confirmed that the rapid acceleration in the rise in the frequency of uncommitted fatherhood was not the result of the emergence of an 'underclass' which was repudiating the values of respectable society. Attitudes, law and conduct had been transformed within a decade. No underclass has at its disposal the means of moulding public opinion to achieve such a thing. It was a change throughout society of the evaluation of what respectable behaviour was. Those changes were being effected by members of society who had access to the means for communicating what is going to be accepted as true and virtuous - the effective intelligentsia.
>
> In remoulding attitudes and assumptions about what was factually true and ethically valid, at least as important was a part of the intelligentsia which was largely based in higher education and which made its influence felt most widely through serious newspapers and discussion programmes. Its prime commitment was to draw attention to, and remedy, the evils associated with the system of life-long monogamy. These evils included the subordinated and narrowly domestic life of the woman, the stereotyping of the roles of the son and the daughter at the cost of the latter, and of course in some cases sheer brutality and sexual abuse. Only people who were heartless, who were uncaring, would say anything that could be interpreted in any way as weakening the case for the removal of these evils.
>
> Factual surveys like Crellin's had shown (and continued to show for as long as they were considered worthy to be financed) that on average the life-long socially-certified monogamous family on the pre-1960s pattern was better for children than any one of a variety of alternatives practically applicable to large urban populations. These surveys undermined aspects of the arguments put by the defenders of the interests of the various problem groups. Certain of the righteousness of their respective causes, there must have been at least a few who consciously attacked what they suspected might well be true, but inconveniently and irrelevantly true.'

Allow me to paraphrase: the determination to undermine the nuclear family, based on a particular socio-political opinion, and which no one dared contradict, was effectively propagandised by the media and the empirically clear evidence of its detrimental effects ignored. There were left-leaning academics who were well aware of this 27 years ago.

14.3 The Big Picture - A Selection of Studies

The validity of the claim that there are a great many studies which show a significant deleterious effect on children of father absence or disengagement, or a beneficial effect of father involvement, is easily demonstrated with a few hours of Googling or reference chasing. In fact there are thousands of professional articles on the effect of fathers on child development. Not all studies identify a statistically significant disbeneficial effect of father absence. The review paper by McLanahan et al, summarised in section 14.5, selected a number of studies of particular quality. About half of the studies found a significant disbeneficial effect of father absence on education, whilst three-quarters of studies found a significant disbeneficial effect on mental health, externalizing behaviours, delinquency, substance abuse and early childbearing. The studies which did not do so merely found no statistically significant effect either way. This is significant in itself.

As far as I am aware, no studies appeared to find a beneficial effect of father absence. This is worth noting. There are many reasons why a father-effect might be hard to discern in data. For example, if the father absence occurred after a substantial period of co-residence and father involvement, does this count as fatherlessness or not? Similarly, if a study merely records divorce as the indicator, there may be no measure of the continuing involvement of a father via contact arrangements thereafter. Some studies may consider only biological father absence, without allowance for the involvement of other father figures. And even where a father is co-resident, his mere presence may not confer benefit if he is disengaged from the child. Consequently, the fact that many studies report a null result is not surprising. There will also be considerable 'noise' in the data. However, if those studies which report a significant disbenefit of fatherlessness were merely the result of random statistical noise, one might expect a similar number of studies spuriously reporting a beneficial effect of fatherlessness. The absence of such reverse results supports the reality of the disbeneficial effects reported.

In this section I give a rather random selection of a few published works as an indication of what the literature demonstrates. I emphasise that I have merely scratched the surface of the available literature. If you can afford academic book prices, probably the best summary of the overall scene in this area is "The Role of the Father in Child Development", 5th edition, (Lamb (editor), 2010). In sections 14.4 and 14.5 I shall review two studies in greater detail.

The UK Fatherhood Institute (2013) summarised the position in respect of the effect of fathers on children's educational outcomes thus,

> 'Major studies across the world which follow families over time have found fathers' involvement with their children linked with their higher educational achievement and higher educational /occupational mobility relative to their parents. For example, in the UK, fathers' involvement with their 7 and 11 year old children is linked with their better national examination performance at age 16 and their educational attainment at age 20. This is as true for daughters as for sons, across all social classes – and whether the mother is highly involved too, or not.'

In a Finnish study, Lyytinen et al (1998) found that the frequency of fathers' reading to children aged 14 to 24 months was linked with children's greater interest in books later. It is remarkable that an effect occurs at such a young age. In a low income American sample, and controlling for parent demographics and income, Ryan et al (2006) found that the cognitive development of two and three year olds was significantly improved when either parent was supportive, and to the same extent by mothers and fathers, and that cognitive development was highest when both parents were supportive.

Flouri and Buchanan (2004) used longitudinal data from the National Child Development Study which tracks people born in Britain in 1958. 7,259 cohort members with valid data on both mother and father involvement at age 7 were used in the analysis. Father involvement and mother involvement at age 7 independently predicted educational attainment by age 20. The benefit was the same for sons and daughters. The benefit of father involvement was additive to the benefit of mother involvement. The authors concluded that early father involvement is another protective factor in counteracting risk conditions that might lead to later low educational attainment levels.

Studies have found that a father's interest in his child's education has more influence on educational success than family background, the child's personality or poverty. The next two studies summarised found low fatherly interest similarly predictive, in the other direction: a father's low interest in his son's education, for instance, reduces his boy's chances of escaping poverty by up to 34%. In 2007, Darcy Hango (2007) published 'Parental investment in childhood and educational qualifications: Can greater parental involvement mediate the effects of socioeconomic disadvantage?'. An extract from the Abstract is,

> 'Data are from the National Child Development Study; a longitudinal study of children born in Britain in 1958. Results suggest that parental involvement does matter, but it depends on when involvement and economic hardship are measured, as well as type of involvement and parent gender. Father interest in education reduces the impact of economic hardship on education the most, especially at age 11. Both father and mother interest in school at age 16 have the largest direct impact on education. The frequency of outings with mother at age 11 also has a larger direct impact on education than outings with father, however, neither compare with the reduction in the effect of economic hardship as a result of father interest in school.' (Hango, 2007)

Under the auspices of the Department for Work and Pensions, during the Blair Labour Government, Jo Blanden (2006) published a report 'Bucking the trend: What enables those who are disadvantaged in childhood to succeed later in life?' The analysis was carried out by using data from the British Cohort Study (BCS) of children born in 1970 and included all babies born in Great Britain between 4th and 11th April 1970. This was an initial sample of 18,000 individuals. One of the benefits of using the BCS is the richness of the dataset, meaning that not only is the dataset large, but that it was possible to control for many other variables so that different influences were not confounded. The results showed that the level of parental interest is extremely important; with father's interest having a large influence on their sons, and mother's interest most important for their daughters.

Blanden's analysis was based on multivariate regressions. Her Table 5.1 gives the regression results where the predicted variable is the outcome for the child in terms of subsequent adult poverty status. Easily the largest negative beta coefficient (i.e., the largest cause of an adverse effect) is 'father's little or no interest in the child's education', indicating up to 34% greater chance of adult poverty for boys. Surprisingly, this analysis shows little effect of father's lack of interest in education on the outcomes for girls. Conversely, a mother's lack of interest in education adversely affects girls more than boys.

Blanden's Table 5.2 gives the regression results where the predicted variable is children's test scores at age 10. The results are qualitatively similar. In the case of boys, easily the largest negative beta coefficient is for 'father's little or no interest in the child's education'. Again this affects girls test scores very little, whilst the gender effect is reversed for mother's lack of interest in education. The key result is that it is the father's interest, or lack thereof, which is the largest determinant of both the educational attainment of the son, and the son's later financial success.

There are a number of further studies which consolidate the conclusion that high levels of interest by a father in his child's schooling and education, his high expectations for their achievement and his greater direct involvement in their learning, education and schools, are associated with the child's better exam results, greater progress at school, more constructive attitudes towards school, and higher educational expectations. This is not confined to middle-class families: whatever the father's educational level his interest and participation pay off for his children.

Fathers' higher levels of commitment to their child's education, and their involvement with the school, are also associated with children's better behaviour at school, including reduced risk of suspension or expulsion. Children's school behaviour is strongly linked with their educational attainment and fathers' influence on that behaviour is not only significant but may at times be more significant than mothers' influence, (Lloyd et al, 2003).

Not surprisingly, if fathers' positive involvement can be beneficial, fathers' negative parenting can be destructive also. For instance, fathers' harsh parenting is more strongly linked to children's (especially boys') aggression than is mothers' harsh parenting (Chang et al, 2003).

As regards language acquisition, to quote the UK Fatherhood Institute (2013) again,

> 'While within-gender variation is enormous, and parents' vocabulary use is far more powerfully affected by their education level than their sex, some studies suggest that fathers' verbal interactions with their children may differ from mothers'; and that this may sometimes be to their children's advantage. Fathers have been found to use different and longer words with their children and also more abstract words. Topics may also vary by gender, with mothers referring more frequently to emotions (this has been found to predict children's emotional understanding) and fathers more often using causal explanatory language, which predict their children's theory of mind.'

References supporting those contentions include 'Mother and father language input to young children: contributions to later language development', (Panscofar and Vernon-Feagans, 2006), and, 'Mothers' and fathers' use of internal state talk with their young children', (LaBounty et al, 2008).

High father involvement in reading, appropriate disciplining, social activities, trips out, etc., is associated with fewer child behavioural problems, lower criminality and lower substance misuse. All these behavioural benefits impact on subsequent school achievement. Children also tend to do better and behave better when they have high levels of self-respect and self-regulation. The quality and quantity of fathers' parenting impact strongly on these and other significant measures of adjustment. Further sources of these conclusions include the Swedish study, 'Fathers' involvement and children's developmental outcomes: a systematic review of longitudinal studies', (Sarkadi et al, 2008); the book 'Fathering & Child Outcomes', (Flouri, 2005); and, of course, 'The Role of the Father in Child Development', 5th edition, (Lamb (editor), 2010).

The report 'Prisoners' childhood and family backgrounds', based primarily on a survey of 1,435 prisoners serving sentences between 1 month and 4 years, indicated that 53% of prisoners had not lived with both natural parents as a child, (Williams, Papadopoulou and Booth, 2012). Many had changed living arrangements during their childhood. So, whilst 47% of prisoners reported living with both natural parents, this may not have been the case for their whole childhood. 24% of prisoners stated that they lived with foster parents or in an institution, or had been taken into care, at some point when they were a child, and hence did not enjoy the benefit of the involvement of either parent full-time. To put this in context, about 2% of the general population have spent time in care as children, (Full Fact, 2012).

The 2013 report 'Fractured Families', (Centre for Social Justice, 2013), stated that their extensive research 'showed that 76% of children and young people in custody had an absent father and 33% an absent mother'. The Prison Reform Trust (2013) quotes the same figures.

The Abstract of the 2003 study by Ellis et al (2003) into the impact of fatherlessness on early sexual activity is as follows,

> 'The impact of father absence on early sexual activity and teenage pregnancy was investigated in longitudinal studies in the United States (N = 242) and New Zealand (N = 520), in which community samples of girls were followed prospectively from early in life (5 years) to approximately age 18. Greater exposure to father absence was strongly associated with elevated risk for early sexual activity and adolescent pregnancy. This elevated risk was either not explained (in the US. study) or only partly explained (in the New Zealand study) by familial, ecological, and personal disadvantages associated with father absence. After controlling for covariates, there was stronger and more consistent evidence of effects of father absence on early sexual activity and teenage pregnancy than on other behavioral or mental health problems or academic achievement.'

The 2001 study by Kaye Wellings et al 'Sexual behaviour in Britain: early heterosexual experience' was based on a survey of 4762 men and 6399 women. They found that the odds of having first intercourse before age 16 was roughly doubled for children raised with only one, or neither, parent compared with children raised with both parents (x2.29 for boys, x1.65 for girls). A similar increase in odds applied to the likelihood of pregnancy before age 18, (Wellings et al, 2001).

A Swedish study reported in The Lancet in 2003, (Weitoft et al, 2003), used medical and mortality data from 65,085 children with single parents and 921,257 children with two parents. Analysis of risk was conducted using Poisson regression, adjusted for factors that might be presumed to select people into single parenthood, and for other factors, mainly resulting from single parenthood, that might have affected the relation between type of parenting and risk. Children with single parents showed increased risks of psychiatric disease, suicide or suicide attempt, injury, and addiction. After adjustment for confounding factors, such as socioeconomic status and parents' own addiction or mental illness, children in single-parent households had increased risks compared with those in two-parent households as follows,

- For psychiatric disease in childhood, relative risk for girls 2.1, and for boys 2.5;
- For suicide attempt, relative risk for girls 2.0, and for boys 2.3;
- For alcohol-related disease, relative risk for girls 2.4, and for boys 2.2;
- For narcotics-related disease, relative risk for girls 3.2, and for boys 4·0;

Boys in single-parent families also had a raised risk of all-cause mortality.

14.4 The Study of Radl, Salazar and Cebolla-Boado, 2017

I have selected the study 'Does Living in a Fatherless Household Compromise Educational Success? A Comparative Study of Cognitive and Non-cognitive Skills' by Jonas Radl, Leire Salazar and Hector Cebolla-Boado (2017) for special attention because of its size, involving over a quarter of a million subjects across 33 different OECD countries. The study addresses the relationship between various family forms and the level of cognitive and non-cognitive skills among school students aged 15 to 16. The cognitive skills were measured using standardised numeracy test scores. These data were obtained from the Programme for International Student Assessment (PISA) release for 2012 which provides data consistently across nations. Non-cognitive abilities were captured by a measure of "internal locus of control".

"Internal locus of control" is a term describing the belief that life events are causally attributable to one's own actions. A high degree of internal locus of control is thus the belief that the driving force of success is one's own ability and effort. In contrast, a high degree of external locus of control is the belief that fate or luck or some external "other" is the responsible factor for one's good or bad fortune. Whether locus of control is predominantly perceived as internal or external has been used extensively to explain differences in peoples' effort, especially among children. Lack of internal locus of control is believed to be related to several psychological problems including depression.

The authors of the study note that there is ample evidence that the absence of one of the parents, usually the father, is negatively correlated with educational success of students. Scholars have analysed the detrimental impact on a variety of outcomes such as test scores, grades, and attitudes about school and educational aspirations. When focusing on the final level of educational achievement and/or years of schooling attained, the negative influence exerted by father absence seems to be especially pronounced.

Radl et al's study considered only the presence or absence of the father in the household, but not the reason for his absence. Moreover, they were not able to distinguish between biological- and stepfathers. Their analysis controlled for basic socio-demographics (students' sex, age, and social background as measured by the mother's level of education and migrant status). The presence or otherwise of siblings and grandparents in the same household were also controlled via independent variables.

The study found that the absence of fathers from the household is associated with adverse outcomes for children in virtually all developed countries. This was generally true for both cognitive and non-cognitive skills, although the disadvantage was notably stronger in cognitive skills.

Figure 14.1 shows the numerical results for the regression beta coefficient associated with father absence, the two graphs showing the effect on cognitive and non-cognitive skills. The dependent variables were normalised to unit standard deviation, so the plotted beta coefficients can be regarded as fractions of a standard deviation. The central estimate for all 33 countries is negative, for both outcomes, i.e., that father absence is detrimental. However, the effect on cognitive skills is substantially larger in magnitude. For almost all countries the error band is fully within the negative range for cognitive skills. In contrast, for about two-thirds of countries, the error band for non-cognitive skills is consistent with zero effect.

To put the magnitudes in Figure 14.1 in context, note that the beta coefficient for the dependence of numeracy on age was 0.166, on average over the 33 countries. The average beta coefficient for the dependence of numeracy on the mother's years of education (a surrogate for socioeconomics) was 0.07. For most countries the effect of fatherlessness was greater than these effects, sometimes far greater.

Figure 14.1: *Effect of Father Absence on Cognitive and Non-Cognitive Outcomes from Radl et al, 2017*

Does Living in a Fatherless Household Compromise... **229**

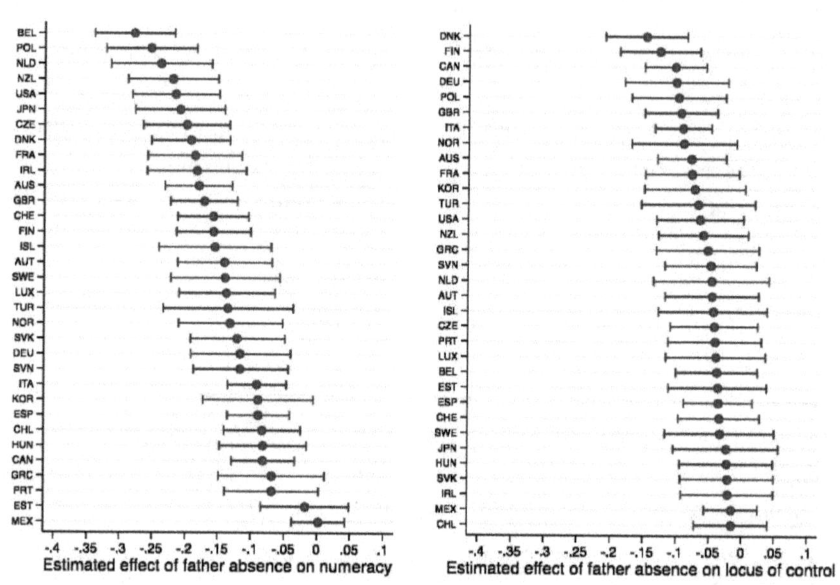

Fig. 1 Between-country variation in the estimated effect of father absence on cognitive and non-cognitive outcomes. *Note* Models control for gender, age, foreign born, mother's education as well as presence of grandparents and siblings in the household

I note in passing that the finding by Radl et al that father absence appears to affect cognitive skill outcomes more than non-cognitive skills is opposite to that found by other studies. Unfortunately many such results in the social sciences suffer from reproducibility problems.

It is also worth noting that Radl et al find the presence of other family members, especially grandparents and to a lesser extent siblings, to be deleterious to the subject child, especially in cognitive skills. However this is likely to be masking a socioeconomic effect.

As a by-product, the analysis also isolates the effect of being female on these outcomes. For the cognitive skill the beta coefficient was negative (an average of -0.136), but this will be because numeracy was chosen as the measure. A verbal cognitive measure could be anticipated to result in a positive beta coefficient. Of greater interest is that the beta coefficient for the dependence on being female of the non-cognitive skill (i.e., internal locus of control) was also significant and negative (-0.152). This suggests that girls have a greater tendency than boys to believe their fortunes are under the control of an external "other", making them more vulnerable to mental illness. It also suggests, speculatively, that feminists' insistence on men's controlling behaviour towards women might arise more from female psychology than from objective reality.

14.5 The Study of McLanahan, Tach and Schneider, 2013

I have selected the study 'The Causal Effects of Father Absence', (McLanahan, Tach and Schneider, 2013), for particular attention because it is a rare example in social science of explicitly claiming a causal connection. High quality regression analyses, which control for other implicated variables, are often suggestive of causality, though not conclusive, and hence authors rarely make an explicit claim for causality. McLanahan et al are a rare exception, and it is surely a measure of their confidence that they claim causality in the title.

McLanahan et al recognise that the literature on father absence is frequently criticised for its use of cross-sectional data and the application of methods that fail to take account of possible omitted variable bias. They give a careful account of the strengths and weaknesses of a range of techniques which attempt to address causal connections. The techniques they identified were,

- Various forms of regression analysis, which means fitting the dependence of outcome variables to a set of independent variables in an attempt to isolate the dependence on different factors;
- "Lagged Dependent Variable" models, which also deploy regression, but which use longitudinal data at two time points, before and after father absence, in an attempt to cancel-out unmeasured factors;
- "Growth Curve" models which use longitudinal data at more than two points in time in order to fit both before and after effects and also the rate-of-change of outcome data;
- "Individual Fixed Effects" models which concentrate on changes apparent over time in individual children;
- Three other models of increasing sophistication, making 7 model types in all.

McLanahan et al identified 47 articles of suitable quality that make use of one or more of these methods of causal inference to examine the effects of father absence on a range of outcomes for children, including educational attainment, mental health, and relationship formation and stability.

Studies of father absence effects on education were broken down into three categories. As regards effects on test scores, of 31 analyses 14 found statistically significant disbeneficial effects of father absence on test scores, whilst 17 found no significant effect. The father absence effect on general educational attainment was more emphatic. Of nine studies examining high school graduation using multiple methodologies, only one found null effects, and this study compared siblings in blended families. The rest provided strong evidence of a negative effect of father absence. In the broader category of attitudes, aspirations, engagement, coursework and courses failed the evidence was more mixed. Of 18 analyses, about half showed a significant disbenefit of father absence, and half did not.

Studies of father absence effects on children's mental health and behaviours were also broken down into three categories. As regards the effect on the mental health of children when adult, five studies out of six showed a significant negative effect of parental divorce. For the impact of father absence on children's social-emotional problems in childhood, McLanahan et al identified 27 separate analyses that examined the association between parental divorce and some type of externalizing behaviour or delinquency. Of these, 19 analyses found a significant disbeneficial effect of divorce or father absence on problem behaviour for at least one comparison group, whereas 8 found no significant association. McLanahan et al also identified six analyses that examined children's smoking, drug and alcohol use. The evidence for this set of outcomes was very robust, with only one analysis reporting a null effect of father absence, the rest indicating clear negative effects.

The effect of father absence on their offsprings' subsequent likelihood to marry, divorce or separate was mixed and limited to a very few studies. In respect of early childbearing, McLanahan et al identified only two analyses that examined the effect of father absence. Both analyses found an association between parental absence and a tendency for early childbearing, with divorce in early childhood having a stronger effect than divorce in middle childhood.

McLanahan et al's key conclusions were,

- Father absence negatively affects children's social-emotional development, particularly by increasing externalising behaviour. These effects may be more pronounced if father absence occurs during early childhood, and they may be more pronounced for boys than for girls.

- Effects on social-emotional development persist into adolescence, for which they found strong evidence that father absence increases adolescents' risky behaviours.
- They found strong and consistent negative effects of father absence on high school graduation, the effects on educational attainment appearing to operate by increasing problem behaviours rather than by impairing cognitive ability.

The longer-term effects of father absence included the strongest evidence for a causal effect on adult mental health, suggesting that the psychological harms of father absence experienced during childhood persist throughout the life course.

14.6 The Indirect Empathy Gap for Fatherless Children

There are thousands of professional articles on the effect of fathers on child development. Studies of the effect of father absence do not all identify a statistically significant disbeneficial effect. However, the majority of studies (perhaps between half and three-quarters) find statistically significant disbeneficial effects of father absence on education, mental health, externalizing behaviours, delinquency, substance abuse and early childbearing. Many studies, using a variety of methodologies and longitudinal data, contribute to an increasingly clear picture of a causal connection between father absences and these adverse effects. Nor is this a new finding. It has been known for over a quarter of a century, though further evidence has continued to accumulate.

In chapters 10 to 13 I outlined the mechanisms which drive father absence. Simply blaming men for being deadbeats will not do. A particular concern is the danger that a positive feedback mechanism will propagate the adverse effects of fatherlessness to the following generation, thus driving an increasing gradient in social capital which may operate differentially on males. Measures of this are the strong demographic dependence of the collapse of marriage (section 13.4), the strong demographic dependence of Adverse Childhood Experiences (chapter 12), and the prevailing post-separation arrangements which result in fatherlessness in far too large a percentage of cases (chapters 10 and 11).

Tens of thousands of fathers annually in the UK attempt, but often fail, to remain involved with their children. Blaming men is an inappropriate reaction because it must be acknowledged that external social factors largely determine the outcome. The individual working class man did not create the socio-political conditions which have led to the collapse of marriage. The individual working class man did not create the misandric culture which brands men as violent and predisposes judicial forces to separate him from his children. The individual working class man did not create the empathy gap which underlies the different perception of parents according to sex, and which drives much of fatherlessness after parental separation.

Whilst this chapter, like chapter 12, has concentrated upon harm to children, it is important to recall that this harm arises, at least in part, as a collateral consequence of the empathy gap towards men which facilitates the societal equanimity at endemic fatherlessness. In all these issues where there is collateral harm to children we see the crucial distinction between evolved matricentrism, whose function was to protect children, and feminist gynocentrism in which the woman, not the child, has been made the primary recipient of concern.

15

Paternity and Its Enemies

It is a piece of idle sentimentality that truth, merely as truth, has any inherent power denied to error, of prevailing against the dungeon and the stake. Men are not more zealous for truth than they often are for error, and a sufficient application of legal or even of social penalties will generally succeed in stopping the propagation of either. The real advantage which truth has, consists in this, that when an opinion is true, it may be extinguished once, twice, or many times, but in the course of ages there will generally be found persons to rediscover it, until some one of its reappearances falls on a time when from favourable circumstances it escapes persecution until it has made such head as to withstand all subsequent attempts to suppress it.
John Stuart Mill (1806 – 1873), *On Liberty*

In this chapter I consider men's fertility, what challenges it and what control men themselves exercise over it. I start with the absence of a convenient, reversible and "persistent" male contraceptive, comparable to the female pill. This leads to a discussion about the degree of influence men exercise over conception: just how accidental are those "accidental" pregnancies, and how common are they? Once conception has taken place, it is the woman's right to choose. But if men, in practice, have little influence over whether conception takes place, what control do men have over their own fertility at all? Only to be celibate, it seems – or, to express it as some do, "he should have kept his dick in his pants". The same people would hardly condone telling women to refrain from sex as their only available contraceptive. Equality? It would be a great thing.

Next the issue of declining male fertility, as measured by sperm counts, is discussed, both as regards the effects of ageing and also the controversial, but alarming, reports of steep declines in average sperm counts. I contrast the apocalyptic nature of some predictions (albeit uncertain) with the complete lack of interest at the level of the political medical establishment.

The largest part of this chapter addresses misattributed paternity, or paternity fraud, which refers to the situation in which a man who has assumed social fatherhood, or who has been asserted to be the biological father, is not in fact the biological father. The rate of mispaternity is one of the more controversial subjects in gender politics. Here I make an attempt to clarify the matter. There is a dominant narrative which seeks to minimise biological paternity in favour of social paternity alone. I examine critically the ethics of this position.

It is indisputable that men have historically been disadvantaged compared to women in respect of their lack of certainty that a given child is indeed theirs. The advent of cheap, convenient and highly reliable DNA testing has provided a technological means to eradicate this disadvantage. But legal, medical and societal norms are maintaining the previous status quo. It will be shown that a man in the UK has no legal right to know whether or not a given child is biologically his. The inequality between the sexes in the context of fertility is stark.

15.1 Men's Control Over Their Own Fertility

15.1.1 Male Contraception

The advent of the oral contraceptive pill for women was of such overwhelming significance that a large part of the social changes of the last half century can be attributed to its consequential effects. For men, there is no equivalent. Men have only the condom, which is not widely liked, though its use does confer significant benefit in terms of protection against infection. As well as being inconvenient, unpopularity arises from the fact that the condom decreases sensitivity. In circumcised men this can involve a double loss of sensitivity, and hence a further disincentive. Moreover, in long term relationships, the condom is generally forgone in favour of 'the pill', thus throwing all the burden for contraception upon the woman.

It is therefore a moot point whether the absence of a convenient "persistent" male contraceptive is more of a disadvantage for men or for women. What *is* clear is that the absence of a convenient, reversible, "persistent" male contraceptive is a gender inequality. For women the inequality lies in the unfair placing of the burden of responsibility. The pill is by no means free of side effects or medical disadvantages. It is becoming increasingly clear that many women would welcome the burden of contraception being shared by men.

For men the inequality lies in having little or no control over their own fertility. Should their partner become pregnant, the woman has the option of the morning-after pill or an abortion. The man has no recourse to such after-the-event preventatives: it is a woman's right to choose. That being the case, it is even more important that a man should be able to prevent an unwanted pregnancy in the first place.

The empathy gap is evident. Many people will have scant sympathy for a man who has contributed to a pregnancy he does not want. They will express the view that, in that case, he should not have had sex in the first place. But they will not apply the same harsh logic to women.

It is important to recognise that an effective "persistent" male contraceptive need not mean an hormonally based male pill, or, indeed, any sort of pill. For men, unlike women, the gonads are conveniently placed outside the body. Access is easy. This means that "mechanical" interventions which prevent sperm being ejaculated are relatively easy to engineer. There are many contraceptive options which show promise, including hormone based pills, non-hormonal or "herbal" pills, and a variety of vas occlusion methods, (The Male Contraception Initiative, 2018). The vas occlusive medical devices have the major advantage over a "male pill" that they avoid interference with the endocrine system, and thus avoid the associated adverse side-effects.

Arguably the major obstacle to bringing a male contraceptive to market is not technological but commercial. Getting candidate substances or methodologies across the so-called "valley of death" – the pre-clinical development stage – is expensive, (The Male Contraceptive Initiative, 2017). Following that, the legally obligatory clinical trials are even more expensive, something which only Big Pharma can finance. Hence Big Pharma needs to be convinced that there is a large market for the ultimate product.

The key question is therefore how many men would use a male contraceptive if it were brought to market? An Ipsos survey indicated that two-thirds of men would use a male contraceptive if in a long-term relationship, and more than half of men would do so outside such a relationship, (Ipsos, 2014). The same survey indicated that 80% of women in a long term relationship would trust a man to take the contraception. That far fewer women would trust a man with contraception in the case of short-term or casual relationships is not so relevant, because, in such cases, the man's motivation would be more to protect himself.

Another major driver for effective and persistent male contraception is that its widespread uptake would markedly reduce the need for abortions. It is one of the paradoxes of fertility that the abortion rate in the UK increased steadily from the 1960s when the use of the female contraceptive pill became common, (Abortion Statistics, England and Wales: 2017). In 2017 there were 197,533 abortions notified as taking place in England and Wales. In the USA there are over a million abortions annually. Some abortions will be for reasons of protecting the physical health of the woman, or due to concerns over the physical health of the foetus. But research published by Finet et al (2005) indicate that these physical health concerns are the primary motivation for abortion in the USA in only 7% of cases.

The paradoxical increase in the abortion rate since the availability of the pill is probably related to the delay in marriage and to the decline in marriage, with 81% of abortions in England and Wales relating to unmarried women. Consequently, there is no reason to expect another paradoxical outcome if a male contraceptive were to become widely used. On the contrary, a steep decline in the need for abortions is inevitable. Consequently, there would be multiple benefits to both sexes from the availability of an effective, persistent, reversible male contraceptive. At present society is insensitive to men's lack of control over their own fertility, an instance of the empathy gap.

15.1.2 Option Denied?

The effective lack of control which men exercise over their partners' pregnancies leads some people to be suspicious that many "accidental" pregnancies may not be quite so accidental. This is sometimes called "type two paternity fraud". In the popular press, and in women's magazines, stories abound which give succour to such suspicion. An infamous confession by journalist Liz Jones (2011) stoked the fires of concern,

> 'Because he wouldn't give me what I wanted, I decided to steal it from him. I resolved to steal his sperm from him in the middle of the night. I thought it was my right, given that he was living with me and I had bought him many, many M&S ready meals. The 'theft' itself was alarmingly easy to carry out. One night, after sex, I took the used condom and, in the privacy of the bathroom, I did what I had to do. Bingo. I don't understand why more men aren't wise to this risk - maybe sex addles their brain. So let me offer a warning to men wishing to avoid any chance of unwanted fatherhood: if a woman disappears to the loo immediately after sex, I suggest you find out exactly what she is up to.'

And in a later relationship,

> 'My husband was 14 years younger than me, and he had told me he was not ready for children. But I didn't listen......I do believe that any man who moves in with a woman in her late 30s or early 40s should take it as read that she will want to use them to procreate, by fair means or foul, no matter how much she protests otherwise.'

> 'Many girlfriends have told me how they have tricked their boyfriend or fiancé or husband. One found herself childless in her 40s, so she lied to a very new boyfriend that she was on the Pill. He is now in a new relationship having to pay support for a child he never sees.'

No one knows how common these hole-in-the-condom or turkey baster induced pregnancies might be, though the rising incidence of the 30-something woman who wants a child – quickly – but cannot find a man who is willing to commit, can only put the thought into more heads. However, these extreme measures will be far less common than the "accidental" pregnancies which follow ceasing to take contraception. In fact, the majority of "accidental" pregnancies occur, not due to contraception failure, but because birth control has been stopped, (Abrams, 2012), (Taft et al, 2018).

The degree of premeditation will be variable. I suspect that in many cases the woman is almost acting instinctively, though the extent to which that might mitigate against her culpability in ignoring her partner's wishes is something I will leave to the reader to decide. It seems in some cases that the woman delegates responsibility to fate,

> 'Dr Terri Foran, sexual health physician and lecturer in women's health at the University of New South Wales, says this version of "accidental pregnancy" is not uncommon. "Many women I see these days, I ask if they're using contraception and they'll say no. Then I'll ask if they're intending to fall pregnant and they'll say no but if it happens it happens."' (Hakim, 2018).

In a Psychology Today article titled 'Not-So-Accidental Pregnancies: Some accidental pregnancies aren't so accidental, especially if the guy could be a good provider', Michelle Bryner (2016) wrote,

> 'Melinda Spohn, a social worker and researcher at Spokane Falls Community College in Washington, decided to study why so many of her clients told her that their pregnancies were unplanned, despite the variety of easily available birth control. Some of the women admitted that they had not used birth control with guys who had appealing characteristics. To determine whether such behavior is widespread, Spohn surveyed nearly 400 women at two community colleges. More than a third of women said they had risked pregnancy in the past with men who had attractive qualities - such as commitment to the relationship, good financial prospects or the desire for a family - but hadn't discussed the possibility of pregnancy with their partner. It was unclear how many women actually became pregnant.'

Up to 2010 in the USA the proportion of births that were intended at conception was 63%, (U.S. Department of Health and Human Services, 2012). Unsurprisingly this varied with marital status. For married women 77% of all births were intended at conception, for cohabiting women this was 49% and for single women, 33%. A survey in Australia indicated that 38% of women who had become pregnant in the survey period had done so unintentionally, but of these unintended pregnancies 68% were reported as wanted, (Taft et al, 2018). There is clearly plenty of scope between "unintentional" and yet "wanted" to facilitate ignoring the man's wishes with a clear conscience.

A survey of 5686 women of childbearing age in Britain in the period 2010 – 2012, reported in The Lancet, indicated that only 55% of pregnancies were planned. A further 29% were classed as "ambivalent", (Wellings et al, 2013). Quite what "ambivalent" means is a moot point. A study 'Do Perceptions of Their Partners Affect Young Women's Pregnancy Risk? Further Study of Ambivalent Desires' involved collecting data from women, asking them to report on their perceptions of their partners' childbearing desires, (Miller et al, 2017). The women's perception of their partner's wishes were found to be statistically related to the outcome, i.e., pregnancy, which is reassuring – but this is only a statistical correlation. Again there is plenty of scope here for "ambivalence" to become "pregnancy", despite the lack of a partner's "affirmative consent". Yes, I use that phrase deliberately.

15.1.3 Men's Fertility

Male fertility is challenged by two factors: a general decline in average sperm counts in Western countries, and age. The former is less well established than the public have been led to believe, whilst the effect of age is more serious than the public appreciate.

Unlike women, whose fertility comes to a final full-stop at menopause, the saying goes that "men can have children at any age". Whilst technically true, this perception disguises the substantial decrease in sperm count which occurs continuously from age 20 throughout a man's life. Women are acutely aware of their biological clock. Men and women tend to be unaware that a man also has a biological fertility clock. The fact that the clock does not actually stop should not obscure the fact that it slows down a very great deal. It has been estimated that the average time to pregnancy for a woman under 25 if her partner is also under 25 is just 5 months but increases to two years if a man is over 40, and even longer if he is over 45, (Your Fertility, 2018). There is general appreciation that a woman who leaves her attempts at pregnancy too late will face increasing fertility difficulties. There is less general appreciation that the same is true for the man in the partnership. Thus, for a couple who marry when both are in their late 30s or early 40s, there is a double hit on their likelihood of conceiving.

But the fertility even of young men in Western countries may be reducing. There have been reports of falling sperm counts for decades. The most recent to cause a stir amongst the public was the 2017 meta-analysis 'Temporal trends in sperm count: a systematic review and meta-regression analysis' by Hagai Levine et al (2017). This examined thousands of independent studies and conducted a meta-analysis of 185 of them. The international team of researchers ultimately looked at semen samples from 42,935 men from 50 countries between 1973 and 2011. They concluded,

> 'This comprehensive meta-regression analysis reports a significant decline in sperm counts (as measured by sperm concentration and total sperm count) between 1973 and 2011, driven by a 50–60% decline among men unselected by fertility from North America, Europe, Australia and New Zealand. Because of the significant public health implications of these results, research on the causes of this continuing decline is urgently needed.'

This decline in sperm count in Western men was not matched by a significant decline in non-Western men. The cause is not currently known. The decline in sperm concentration appears to be worryingly large, a reduction by approximately 50 million/ml since 1973. The likelihood of conception begins to fall steeply below a sperm concentration of 40 million/ml, and sperm concentrations below 15 million/ml are regarded as nominally infertile.

The Levine et all meta-analysis also reported that unselected Western men had an overall drop in sperm concentration from 99 million/ml in 1973 to 47 million/ml in 2011. Taken at face value, these results are extraordinarily concerning. The study did not report any levelling off of the declining trend. Consequently, if this study is correct, low male fertility might soon be the norm in Western countries, with nominal infertility becoming the norm within 25 years at the current rate of decline. The best of studies can, of course, be wrong.

This is not an area in which a non-expert should be expounding opinions. Even the experts are ambivalent. An editorial addressing the findings of Levine et al in the Canadian Journal of Urology focused more on cautious concern than on disbelief, (Gomella, 2017). However, the briefest of searches reveals controversy in the informed academic literature. For example, Bonde and te Velde (2017) write,

> 'A recent systematic review on worldwide declining trends in sperm counts has fuelled alarming reports in national and international news media. However, methodological issues exist with data gathering and analysis precluding any conclusion and no solid data exist to indicate increasing frequency of couple infertility during past decades.'

Also expressing considerable scepticism were the Greek authors of 'Declining Sperm Counts… or Rather Not? A Mini Review' (Ravanos et al, 2018) whose view was,

> 'Temporal global trends of sperm quality remain a matter of debate. The aim of this study was to present a comprehensive review of studies reporting on sperm quality counts, summarize the main end points, and assess the main reasons for potential discrepancies. An evidence-based review of PubMed and Scopus databases was performed regarding studies reporting on modification of sperm quality counts, independently of study character, study language, or date. Since the meta-analysis of Carlsen et al in 1992 that suggested an annual decline in sperm count of 1%, several reports confirmed the decline in sperm quality, whereas others disproved them, suggesting a slight increase or absence of change in sperm count. Such controversies may be attributed to geographical and time-related variability in sperm values and also to several confounding factors that influence the semen parameters. Intrinsic weaknesses of the studies include heterogeneity of subjects recruited, lack of adjustment for confounding factors, and samples that do not always represent the general population. No consensus exists on whether sperm counts actually decrease because studies' results are often controversial or inconclusive with methodological deficiencies. More prospective, large-scale, population-based studies are needed in order to provide sound evidence of possible global trends in sperm count.'

On the other hand, Levine at al are far from being the only authors reporting dramatic falls in sperm counts and sperm concentrations. They could not be, since their report was a meta-analysis of other studies. Published the year before Levine et al, the meta-analysis of Sengupta et al (2016) also reports a similar steep decline in sperm concentrations, although they identify a different range of affected countries,

> 'The current study, following a previous report of massive fall in semen volume over the past 33 years, attempts to delineate the trend of altering sperm concentrations and factors responsible for this by reviewing articles published from 1980 to July 2015 with geographic differences. The current study identified an overall 57% diminution in mean sperm concentration over the past 35 years, which, when analyzed for each geographical region, identified a significant decline in North America, Europe, Asia, and Africa……It points to the threat of male infertility in times ahead.'

And as regards European men in particular, Sengupta, Borges and Dutta (2018) wrote,

> 'We analysed the data published in English language articles in the past 50 years in altering sperm concentration in European men. A time-dependent decline of sperm concentration in the last 50 years and an overall 32.5% decrease in mean sperm concentration was noted.'

A study on Danish men over a 21 year period (1996 – 2016) was intended to investigate the effect of *in utero* exposure to maternal smoking on sperm counts, (Priskorn et al, 2018). As expected the study confirmed that, 'exposure to maternal smoking was associated with lower sperm counts'. Surprisingly, then, given that exposure *in utero* to maternal smoking declined significantly over the period, no overall increase in sperm counts was observed despite the decrease in this exposure. Overall, there were no persistent temporal trends in semen quality, testicular volume or levels of follicle-stimulating hormone over the 21 years studied. Of more immediate concern, perhaps, is that they also observed that, 'throughout the study period, 35% of the men had low semen quality'. The authors conclude that their results suggest that 'other unknown adverse factors may maintain the low semen quality among Danish men'.

Despite the uncertainty, the credible threat that nominal male infertility could become the norm within 25 years is, one would expect, sufficient motivation for urgent attention – including at the political level of the medical establishment, not merely within the research literature. But in comparison with the similarly apocalyptic forecasts of climate change, which have spawned global academic, political, technological and commercial action, for male fertility we find nothing at all. Searching the annual reports of the Chief Medical Officer for England for years 2015, 2016, 2017 and 2018 reveals that neither "sperm" nor male fertility generally are mentioned in three of them, (Sally Davies, 2018). Only in 2017 does the word "sperm" appear, firstly in the context of endocrine-disrupting chemicals, where we read, 'a body of literature now documents an increasing incidence of breast cancer in women, decreased sperm counts and increasing incidence of testicular cancer in men', and secondly in the context of smoking, 'epigenetic changes in human sperm have been shown to be affected by environmental influences such as smoking behaviour'. The claims of dramatic and ongoing reductions in sperm counts are not mentioned at all in the Chief Medical Officer's reports, nor is the possibility of catastrophic effects on male fertility. Perhaps this is the result of a considered appraisal of the evidence and a decision to avoid an alarmist position. But one might also suspect that it results from a particular skew in the established focus of concern.

15.2 Mispaternity and Paternity Fraud

15.2.1 Terminology and Perception

I shall generally use the term "mispaternity", which is a contraction of "misattributed paternity", as an attempt to avoid the pejorative term "paternity fraud". However, even the term "mispaternity" may be criticised on the grounds that, in some cases, there may have been no particular claim of paternity asserted. However, one may reasonably take the view that either the mother is certain regarding the paternity of her child, or she is not certain. So if she pretends to be certain when, in fact, she is not, then this is less than honest – and hence an assertion of paternity in these circumstances does take on the characteristic of fraud.

Some opine that the term "paternity fraud" should be used only when the attempt is being made to gain financially from the false, or uncertain, claim – such as to obtain child support payments. However, in my view, this puts undue emphasis on financial issues whereas other harms, emotional, psychological and social, are of greater importance – both to the faux-father and the child.

Academic publications will refer to "extra-pair paternity", but this is not quite the same thing. Extra-pair paternity refers to a heterosexual couple in an established relationship in which the woman has a child by another man. Frequently this will involve mispaternity if the woman passes off the child as that of her partner, as will most often be the case. But mispaternity can also arise outwith an established relationship, and extra-pair paternity need not necessarily lead to mispaternity.

Terms such as "covert paternity" or "uncertain paternity" accurately describe the situation when the true biological father is not known, except possibly by the mother. But the mother does not necessarily make any assertion of paternity in such circumstances, so the term "mispaternity" is not strictly applicable.

In tests for paternity the term used in the scientific community is "paternity exclusion". This refers to a specific man being shown, generally with high confidence, *not* to be the father. The appropriateness of the term "mispaternity" then depends upon whether he was ever asserted to be the father. However there is a degree of disingenuousness about those who emphasise this distinction because, had there been no such suggestion, the man's paternity would not have been tested at all.

The term "paternity exclusion" has the benefit of clear meaning, though it should be noted that a failure to exclude paternity does not always mean the man in question is the father. Older tests, such as those based on blood groups, were capable of definite exclusion but were not capable of definite proof positive of paternity. Such tests would provide only a lower bound to the rate of mispaternity. (This effect has been allowed for and corrected in the database below). However, recent tests, especially those based on DNA, provide far more accurate data.

Hence, I shall use the term "mispaternity" but numerical estimates of its prevalence will be based primarily upon (appropriately corrected) paternity exclusions.

15.2.2 The Prevalence of Mispaternity

The prevalence of mispaternity has been subject to heated controversy. Part of the reason for this is that, prior to modern biochemical testing techniques becoming available and widely used in the 1990s and early 2000s, we could all live in the bliss of ignorance. It came as a shock, then, when large testing programmes began to report extremely high rates of mispaternity, approaching 30%. It would be foolish, however, to interpret these high rates as applicable to the whole population (say of the UK or the USA).

I should stress immediately that mispaternity rates depend extremely sensitively on two things: firstly on demographic, and secondly on whether there is disputed paternity or suspicions about paternity before testing. Mispaternity rates differ by more than an order of magnitude between the highest and lowest socioeconomic groups. And recall that the highest socioeconomic groups correlate with high rates of marriage, whereas the lowest socioeconomic groups correlate with high rates of single parenthood. Combine this with the distinction between the general population, and that sub-population of disputed paternity, and it becomes less surprising that reports of mispaternity rates range from fractions of 1% to 30%, or even 50%, rates. Without specifying the population to which the tests in question relate, the reported mispaternity rate is meaningless.

On the one hand, then, it is intemperate to suggest that rates like 30% apply generally to the population at large (in European or Anglophone countries). It is understandable that some people became irritated by such inflated claims, exemplified by the article 'Rampant misattributed paternity: the creation of an urban myth', (Gilding, 2005). On the other hand, commenters along these lines are perhaps insensitive to the fact that those people who promulgate concern about these high rates of mispaternity tend to be themselves of precisely that sub-population to which the high rates might be applicable: namely men after partnership dissolution and involved in paternity disputes.

Before turning to the evidence on mispaternity rates from paternity tests, it is worth briefly considering the proportion of women in a heterosexual relationship who have "extra pair copulations" with one or more other men. Such data are obtained from surveys. Table 15.1 presents these data for the UK, the USA and Australia, taken from (Gilding, 2007) and (Simmons et al, 2004), see those references for sources. Obviously, not all such "cheating" results in pregnancy, and even if it does a false claim of paternity does not necessarily follow (though that might be common in the case of married or cohabiting couples). The percentages in Table 15.1 do, however, put mispaternity rates in context. They are the necessary but not sufficient conditions for mispaternity, and thus provide upper bounds to possible mispaternity rates in the general public.

The UK data in Table 15.1 indicate the very strong demographic dependence of the likelihood of a woman having sex with a man not her usual partner. It is to be expected that this will be reflected in mispaternity rates. However, the very low percentage of reported cheating amongst married UK women may be regarded with some caution as married people might be less likely to admit it, even in confidential surveys.

Table 15.1: *Percentage of women in a heterosexual partnership reporting one or more extra-pair copulations. (Data relates to "in the last year" except for Australia which is "lifetime").*

Country	Demographic	Age Range		
		16 - 24	**25 - 34**	**35 - 44**
UK	Married	1.5%	2.2%	2.4%
UK	Cohabiting	10.3%	6.5%	7.5%
UK	Single	29.7%	23.7%	18.8%
USA	All	27.2% (1)	13.4% (2)	
Australia	All	13.0% (3)	46.0% (4)	

(1) ages 18-29; (2) ages 30-44; (3) ages 18-24; (4) ages 25-50

Mispaternity rates derived from paternity testing have been reported many times. Two review articles of note which compile a number of sources are (Bellis et al, 2005) and (Anderson, 2006). (Bradford, R, 2018b) has compiled a total of 134 sources of reported mispaternity rates. This latter reference partitions the 134 data according to the presence or absence of prior suspicion or disputed paternity, as follows,

[1] 43 data where testing was not done due to paternity dispute and where there was no reason prior to testing to expect a particularly high or particularly low mispaternity rate (35 cases from European or Anglophone countries and 8 cases from other countries);

[2] 72 data where there was disputed paternity or suspicion about paternity prior to testing (60 cases from European or Anglophone countries and 12 cases from other countries);

[3] 19 data which might have been anticipated to result in particularly low mispaternity rates, due to their subjects or because especially high paternity confidence was expressed prior to testing.

The complete set of sources for these 134 data can be found in (Bradford, R, 2018b). Figure 15.1 plots the mispaternity rate against year from the data without prior bias, i.e., data from [1], above, distinguishing the European and Anglophone data from other countries. Three data points with particularly high reported mispaternity rates are also distinguished in Figure 15.1, the refences being given in (Bradford, R, 2018b). The first of these is a reported mispaternity of 30% due to Philipp (1972), the provenance of which has been rightly criticised because its basis was never properly reported. The second is a reported mispaternity of 25% due to McLaren (1977) and refers to a study undertaken in certain flats in Liverpool. Again the provenance is lacking, having never been fully reported. The third is that due to Edwards (1950), a reported mispaternity of 50% which refers to premarital pregnancies only. It can be seen that these three data lie above the other European and Anglophone data in Figure 15.1 and are probably best ignored.

Figure 15.1 incudes horizontal dashed lines at the median levels of the European and Anglophone data alone. Including all 35 data gives a median of 8.0%. However, excluding the above three questionable data, leaving 32 data points, produces a median mispaternity of 5.4%. This is my best estimate of the median mispaternity rate in the general population, without biases due to particularly high or low expected results. However even this is questionable. The large scatter in the data may be due to differing demographic compositions of the samples. The appropriateness of the 5.4% median depends upon an assumption that the 32 sources taken together provide a representative cross-demographic sample of a population (say, of the UK). But this is unproved.

Figure 15.1: *Percentage of identified mispaterniy from data with no prior anticipation of bias*

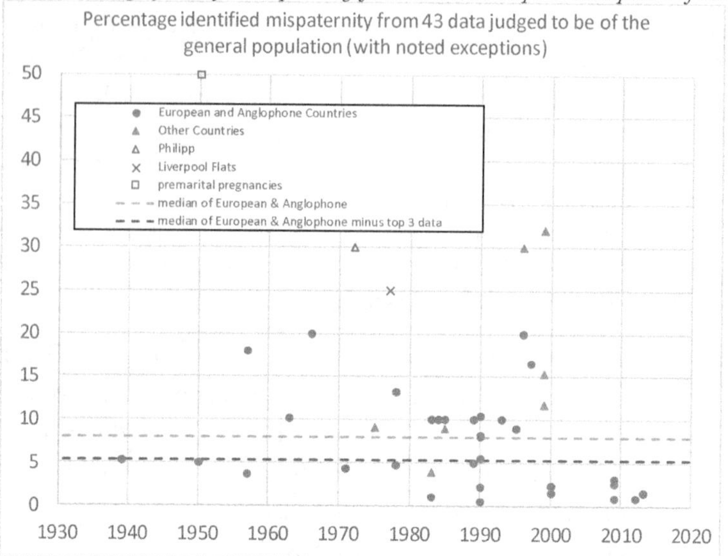

All 134 mispaternity data are plotted against year in Figure 15.2. This compares data from tests for disputed paternity with general population data and also with data where there was high prior confidence in paternity. It is obvious from Figure 15.2 that the three sets of data, denoted by [1], [2] and [3], above, are distinct statistical populations, consistent with expectations. The data from disputed paternity tests, set [2], lie at substantially higher mispaternity levels than the set [1] data, which are more representative of the general population. But the data with high prior paternity confidence, set [3], lie at substantially lower mispaternity levels. The medians for the three sets of data are given in Table 15.2, based on the European and Anglophone data only. That disputed paternity cases and the general public form distinct statistical populations is shown more clearly in histogram form in Figure 15.3, for European and Anglophone countries only.

Table 15.2: *Medians of the European and Anglophone Mispaternity Data Sets*

Dataset	Median Mispaternity
[1]	5.4%
[2]	25%
[3]	1.6%

The spread of mispaternity rates indicated by Table 15.2 serves to emphasise its sensitive dependence on the sub-population in question. It's worth noting that tests are carried out with respect to a given child, so Table 15.2 (and Figures 15.1,2) relate to the rate per child, not per putative father.

Figure 15.2: *All 134 mispaternity data, comparing data from tests with disputed paternity with general population data and with data where there was high prior confidence*

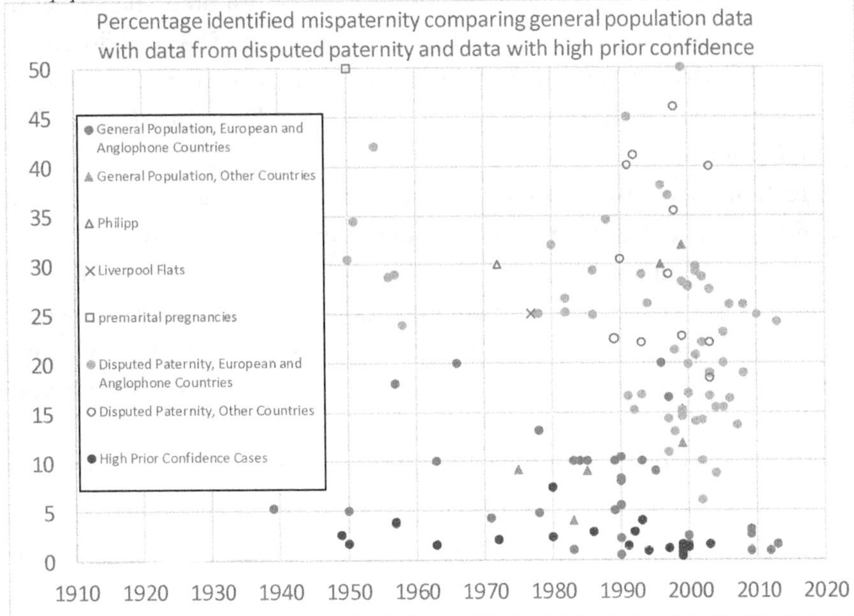

Figure 15.3: *Mispaternity data in histogram form*

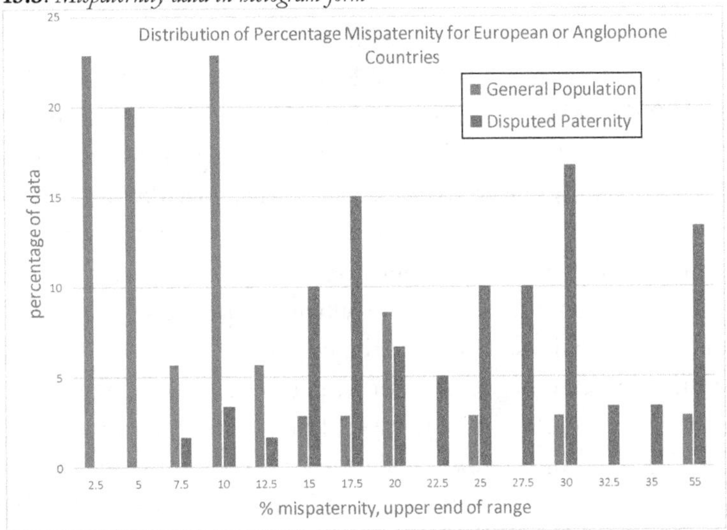

If the data are indicative, Table 15.2 suggests that, for a child picked at random from the whole population, paternity would be misattributed in 5.4% of cases. If the selection is made from a sample where there is reason to have a high prior confidence in paternity (and this may be on the basis of, say, an affluent married couple) then only 1.6% of children may have misattributed paternity. But for that sub-population selected on the basis of having a declared prior suspicion, or where paternity is being disputed, then we could expect the suspicion to turn out to be well founded in 25% of children. For a randomly selected man with four children, there is a 5.4% chance of mispaternity per child, and hence a 20% chance that at least one of the children is not his.

Much of the controversy over the rate of mispaternity is caused by failing to define the population to which the question relates. It may be perfectly appropriate for fathers' groups to place the emphasis on the 25% figure in as far as they represent fathers who entertain doubts about paternity, since this is precisely the population which gives rise to this elevated figure. And this is despite the fact that such a very high level of mispaternity is wildly inapplicable to the whole population.

In passing it is worth noting how extensive are some of the databases relating to disputed paternity. The largest by far are the annual reports from the American Association of Blood Banks. Between years 1998 and 2013 this source reported an average annual mispaternity ("paternal exclusion rate") of 27% and tested an average of around 360,000 cases annually, see Figure 15.4, (American Association of Blood Banks, 2010). This is a very large sample and may be compared with the number of divorces per year in the USA, e.g., 944,000 in year 2000 and 827,261 in 2016, (Centres for Disease Control & Prevention, 2017). Not all disputed paternity cases will relate to divorce, but the bulk of them will be associated with partnership dissolution. Bearing in mind also that roughly one-third of marriages will end in divorce, these figures serve to illustrate that the sub-population of disputed paternity cases is not a negligible fraction of the wider population, but on the contrary is a significant proportion of it. Consequently, the very high mispaternity rate of 27% does apply for a substantial proportion of the population.

The huge increase in the number of paternity tests being carried out in the USA over the last 30 years (Figure 15.4) indicates that increasing agitation over paternity fraud has a substantial motivation. With the order of 100,000 men annually in the USA discovering conclusively that their putative child is not, in fact, theirs, the determination of public discourse to minimise the issue is yet another example of the empathy gap – which, once again, also disadvantages the children.

Figure 15.4: *The increasing volume of paternity cases analysed annually by the American Association of Blood Banks, 1988 to 2010*

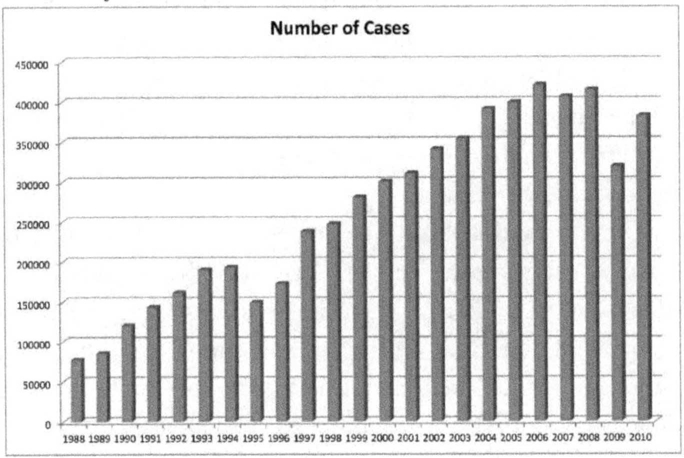

Figure 15.5: *Whose consent is required to carry out a DNA test?*

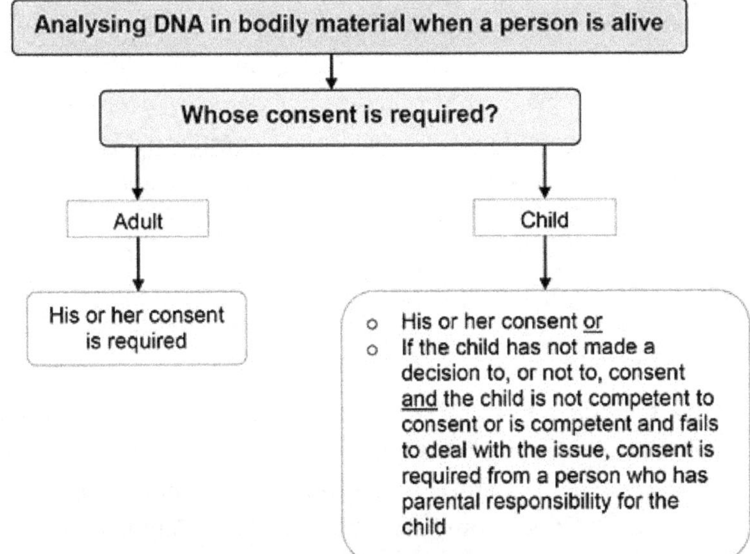

15.2.3 Men are Not Legally Entitled to Know if a Child is Theirs (UK)

In the UK, the legal aspects of DNA paternity testing are addressed by the Human Tissue Act (2004). The issue of consent in DNA paternity testing is addressed in Section 45 and Schedule 4 of the Act. Some sources give the impression that it is illegal for a man to carry out a DNA paternity test without the mother's permission. This is not true.

The Act makes it an offence to have human tissue, with the intention of carrying out a DNA test, without "qualifying consent". The maximum penalty for this offence is 3 years in prison. The legality of a DNA paternity test hinges upon consent. Qualifying consent is defined in a flowchart reproduced in Figure 15.5 and taken from the Human Tissue Authority (2018) web site. Essentially the man and the child must both consent. There is no legal requirement for the mother's consent.

However, a very young child will not be deemed capable of consent. In this case the man may consent on the child's behalf if he has legal parental responsibility (defined below). There is no hard and fast rule regarding whether a child is capable of consent. The Explanatory Notes to Section 2 of the Act state, 'Competence (of children) is not defined in the Act but will be established according to common law principles (the 'Gillick test')'.

The Gillick test requires a judgment on the minor's maturity, intelligence, understanding, experience, and ability to form a meaningful view of the implications of the decision in question, bearing in mind the potential for peer pressure, family pressure, fear and other misgivings. Whether a given child is Gillick competent is necessarily a subjective judgment. Moreover, the child's competence will depend upon the gravity and complexity of the decision. It is reasonable to argue that the issues involved in revealing paternity require a particularly advanced degree of maturity. Having said this, I have seen advice suggesting that children as young as 12 might be deemed Gillick competent, but there is no guarantee that third parties would agree, it will vary from case to case.

If the child is capable of consent but refuses consent, then holding material for the purposes of carrying out a DNA test would be illegal. If the child is not capable of consent and the putative father does not have Parental Responsibility then a paternity test cannot legally be carried out unless consent is obtained from someone who does have Parental Responsibility, usually the mother. Hence, a man in the UK does not in general have the right to know if a child is biologically his. He must wait until the child is old enough to give qualifying consent (and does consent). Otherwise, a man who does not have Parental Responsibility can legally discover if a child is his only with the mother's permission.

However, the salient feature of the 2004 Act is that the man does not require the mother's permission to carry out a legal DNA paternity test, provided that either the child is capable of consenting and consents, or, the child is not capable of consenting and the putative father has Parental Responsibility and consents on the child's behalf. A man qualifies as having Parental Responsibility if, (i) he is married to the child's mother, or, (ii) his name appears on the baby's birth certificate.

But, even a man with Parental Responsibility is at risk of being accused of a criminal offence if he carries out a DNA test without the child's consent, by consenting on behalf of the child, and the child is old enough to raise a question that the child might be deemed Gillick competent and has not explicitly consented.

Note that a mother equally cannot determine whether a given man is the father of her child without his consent. To obtain his DNA by subterfuge for the purposes of carrying out such a test would be against the consent requirements of the Act.

Prior to the 2004 Human Tissue Act, the custom and practice in paternity testing was generally in accord with the Department of Health's 'Code of Practice and Guidance on Genetic Paternity Testing in the UK (2001)'. One might have expected that the revision of this Department of Health Guidance following the 2004 Act would bring it into line with the Act, and hence deal with questions regarding the mother's consent consistent with the above discussion. The Guidance was indeed revised in 2008, but the relevant extract from the Department of Health's (Good Practice Guide on Paternity Testing Services, 2008) is,

> '3.33 The best interests of the child should be a primary concern when commissioning genetic paternity tests. This Guide reflects the view of the Human Genetic Commission that, in the majority of circumstances, motherless testing could prove harmful to the child, as well as to the family unit as a whole.
>
> 3.34 The British Medical Association advises doctors who are consulted by putative fathers about paternity testing without the mother's knowledge and consent to encourage those seeking testing to discuss their plans with the child's mother. Should the putative father reject this advice, the British Medical Association tells doctors not to become involved in the testing process.
>
> 3.35 We are aware too that, in cases where parentage is disputed, the Child Support Agency may offer genetic testing of all three parties – the child, the mother and the alleged father. It is unlikely that the Child Support Agency will accept motherless testing as a method of resolving a paternity dispute for the foreseeable future.
>
> 3.36 We are therefore of the view that motherless testing should not be undertaken by paternity testing companies, unless such a test has been directed by a court.'

Hence, despite the legality of a motherless test if qualifying consent prevails, the Department of Health advises that this is not done. Not only do they recommend that doctors do not facilitate motherless testing, but they express the view that independent testing companies should not undertake such tests either – which, frankly, is none of the DoH's business. The DoH's position is effectively that the mother should always be given power of veto over a man discovering if he is the father or not, despite this not being the lawful requirement.

The above extract from the DoH's guidance correctly indicates that the CSA (Child Support Agency), or the Child Maintenance Service (CMS) as it now is, will also not sanction testing without the mother, (Child Maintenance Service, 2018). Thus, even a man with Parental Responsibility cannot, in practice, obtain a test which will be recognised by legal or Governmental bodies. Proof via a DNA test that a man is not the biological father can obviate child support payments after parental separation, (Child Maintenance Service, 2018). But if the mother refuses permission, no test that the CMS will recognise will be undertaken. If such a man has PR, he might legally undertake an informal test and discover that he is not, in fact, the father. But this will not be recognised by the CMS and will not affect demands for child support payments. If the man does not have PR, but clandestinely carries out a test anyway and discovers he is not the father, he will risk a criminal charge by revealing his knowledge. In any case, the CMS will ignore an informal test not authorised by themselves. And such a man's demands for a formal test may simply be blocked by the mother. Equality? It would be a fine thing.

In the seven years from 1998 to 2005, the CSA sanctioned an average of only 2,692 DNA tests per year, (Child Support Agency, 2005), and in 2007/8 some 3,474 tests, (Wintour, 2008). These numbers compare with around 50,000 to 60,000 Children Act cases going through the UK family courts annually over this period (Figure 10.1), or around 100,000 family breakdowns involving dependent children annually (section 11.6). Hence CMS-sanctioned DNA testing occurs in only about 3% of family breakdowns in the UK. These tests reveal on average around a 16% mispaternity rate. Data are not currently available on how many men request DNA tests but are turned down by the CMS, either because the mother refuses consent or for other reasons. It is therefore unknown how many men are obliged to pay child maintenance for a child who is not biologically theirs, due to the mother withholding consent for testing. Whilst it is likely that most men with established social fatherhood will be willing to pay child maintenance irrespective of biological paternity, this does not negate concern over the lack of a right in principle to establish biological paternity. The following section addresses the ethics of this position, and how it exposes the empathy gap in operation once again.

15.2.4 A "Thin View" of Fatherhood?

In this section I consider the ethical issues around DNA paternity testing. An enormous amount has been written on the subject, but, oddly, given that ethicists have done much of the writing, a valid ethical analysis is notable by its absence. Instead we have seen expositions which list the problems and provide opinions, often skewed by ideology or by a desire to assert, or refute, "fathers' rights". I take the view here that these apparent difficulties arise from a prejudice and a preconception. The former refers to the mother's traditional power to choose social paternity between credible alternatives. But the traditional circumstance in which only the mother could know the father has no bearing upon the ethical question regarding the deployment of DNA testing now that it has become available. To confuse the two is to cling to a past which no longer applies. Elementary ethical analysis delivers a devastating critique of this refusal to yield traditional power.

The preconception which confuses the issue is the common assumption that DNA testing applies only upon partnership dissolution. That this is the situation in which the ethical question has most often arisen does not mean that it is valid to restrict attention to this situation in an ethical analysis. In fact, I shall argue that there is a simple means of slicing the Gordian knot apparently posed by the conundrums which arise in this situation. But first let us review a few of the opinions which have been voiced on the matter.

In 2010 Melanie McDonagh wrote in the Spectator, bemoaning the advent of the DNA test,

> 'At a stroke, the one thing that women had going for them has been taken away, the one respect in which they had the last laugh over their husbands and lovers......DNA tests are...a change in the balance of power between the sexes.... Many men have, of course, ended up raising children who were not genetically their own, but really, does it matter? You can feel quite as much tenderness for a child you mistakenly think to be yours as for one who is.' (McDonagh, 2010)

An hypothesis from evolutionary theory is that women have exploited sexual crypsis (that oestrus is not apparent) to defeat mate-guarding in favour of superior genetic material for their offspring, whilst retaining the usual mate as the better resource provider. Perfectly in tune with that idea, McDonagh wrote,

> 'Uncertainty allows mothers to select for their children the father who would be best for them.'

She refers, of course, to selection of a social father independent of the man involved in conception. In 2011 Marylin Stowe, at the time one of Britain's best known family lawyers, wrote,

> 'For all those tens of thousands of fathers who we are led to believe may be fretting about the paternity of their children, consider this: does it really matter whether a child is the biological offspring of his or her father? Does it really matter if a loving father and his child never find out? What harm is being done to the man, child or woman concerned – that is until they find out and the predictable fallout occurs?' (Stowe, 2011)

The following is the opinion of Dr Anna Smajdor, a medical ethicist specialising in ethical issues related to reproduction,

> 'I think it (DNA testing) is representative of a kind of overvaluing that we tend to do as a society in placing all this emphasis on the genetic relationships above others and I think that the reason we are able to think of this as fraud is only because we place so much value on that.....The issue should not be whose genes are in this child.' (Smajdor, 2016)

In 2007, medical ethicist Heather Draper published a paper in the Journal of Medical Ethics where she opined,

> 'Although children may result from infidelity, and paternity testing may be proof of infidelity, these issues (and the feelings they engage) need to be disentangled both from the interests of the children, and from our understanding of what fatherhood means. Paternity testing might be an effective test of genetic relatedness and infidelity, but it is an ineffective test of fatherhood.'
>
> 'Claims for reimbursement and compensation in cases of misattributed paternity produce the same distorted and thin view of what it means to be a father that paternity testing assumes, and underscores a trend that is not in the interests of children.' (Draper, 2007).

Leslie Cannold is an American-Australian philosopher and ethicist. In 2007, in an article on The Ethics Centre web site, she wrote,

> 'At the heart of cuckold paternity fraud discourse is the claim that real fatherhood is biological fatherhood.....The claim that only biological paternity is real paternity is asserted rather than argued in father's (sic) rights discourse.' (Cannold, 2008)

Actually, no claims about what constitutes "real fatherhood" are required to discuss the ethical issues arising from DNA testing. Even whether there is such a thing as "real fatherhood" is irrelevant to the ethical analysis. The common theme in the above quotes is clear: these ethicists, and other writers (all women), propose the view that biological paternity does not matter, only social paternity matters – including resource provision and the entirety of parental involvement with child rearing. To think otherwise is, apparently, to have a 'distorted and thin view of what it means to be a father'. But in so saying, are these women putting themselves in the position of the man in question or simply expounding what suits their own interests? I suggest they are failing to put themselves in the man's shoes, and are failing to feel what he might feel. And what is this but a failure of empathy?

At this point I introduce the first of two ethical analyses. I wish to address the ethical nature of the following proposition,

> Genetic paternity is relatively unimportant; the paternity on which attention should be focussed is social paternity, and hence whether a given social father is, or is not, the biological father is not of great importance.

I believe that is the position put forward in the above quotes.

Before proceeding with the ethical analysis I note that there is a tendency to pay too little respect to the influence of evolution. The stable pair bond would not exist if it did not provide evolutionary benefit to the male. Consequently, in an evolutionary steady state, cuckoldry can exist only to a limited degree. If cuckoldry became too common, the stable pair bond would cease to provide evolutionary benefit to the male's gene line, and the pair bond would cease to be an evolutionary steady state. In game theory terms, infidelity is reneging for individual advantage, and reneging must be managed to a sufficiently low level if the societal benefit of cooperation (in this case stable pair bonding) is to be accrued. It is therefore counter-evolutionary to expect fathers *en masse* to be unconcerned about whether the children they contribute to raising are genetically theirs. Unfortunately, evolution works on rather long timescales (though not necessarily as long as you might think).

For the ethical analysis I shall deploy Kant's Categorical Imperative. Kant argued that in order for a dictum to be a valid moral principle it must be adopted as universally applicable. If the proposition to be tested were a morally valid position, therefore, it must be universal. Amongst other things, this must mean valid for both sexes: what's good for the goose is good for the gander. The ethical nature of the proposition therefore requires that the following statement is also accepted,

> Genetic maternity is relatively unimportant; the maternity on which attention should be focussed is social maternity, and hence whether a

given social mother is, or is not, the biological mother is not of great importance.

In practice, due to the undeniable evidence of giving birth, there is no doubt who is the biological mother (only since the advent of surrogacy has dispute become possible). However, it is easy to create a Gedankenexperiment to test the acceptability of this second proposition. Suppose it was discovered that maternity wards throughout the country had been sending mothers home with the wrong baby, say in 5% of cases, and that this had been going on essentially forever. Would society react to this with an unconcerned shrug? I suggest the reaction would be more like the detonation of a sociological thermonuclear device. Even if just two women found they had been given the wrong baby it would make the news and cause a stir. And if we really believed the above proposition in the context of mothers, we could dispense with the wrist tags which babies wear in maternity wards and send the mothers home with any child – they're all the same.

But no one – and especially not those women commentators and ethicists quoted above – would endorse the proposition in the context of mothers. No one would accuse a mother who prefers to raise her own child, not someone else's, of having a "distorted and thin view of motherhood". Consequently, to contend that the proposition applies for fathers fails the Categorical Imperative. The proposition is unethical.

By way of an introduction to my second ethical analysis, I note that in the report 'The Health of the 51%: Women', the Chief Medical Officer for England, Sally Davies, included a chapter 'A human rights approach to women's health', (Davies, 2015). This included a list of 12 reproductive rights which were claimed as human rights. The context was women, but as men are humans too, the wording suggests an acknowledgement that these reproductive rights should apply also to men. One of those 12 rights was 'the right to enjoy the benefits of scientific progress'. The DNA test, which provides a virtually certain test of paternity, is an example of scientific progress in the area of reproduction. According the Chief Medical Officer, men have a right to enjoy the benefits of DNA testing. Currently this is being denied.

A further overture to my second ethical analysis relates to accidental discovery of mispaternity as a result of medical procedures, such as transplant operations. There is quite a sizeable literature in the transplant community about the ethical dilemma practitioners face when paternity mismatch is accidentally brought to their attention. One example is, 'The dilemma of unintentional discovery of misattributed paternity in living kidney donors and recipients', (Schroder, 2009). The Abstract reads,

> 'Previous study of professional attitudes in genetic counseling indicated a wide acceptance of nondisclosure of misattributed paternity. In 1994, the Committee on Assessing Genetic Risks of the Institute of Medicine recommended that only the mother be informed of the misattributed paternity information. Results from past surveys of geneticists and genetic counselors support this position. In an international survey of over 1000 medical genetic professionals (MDs and PhDs) conducted in 1985–1986, 96% of respondents indicated the belief that 'the protection of the mother's confidentiality overrides disclosure of true paternity.' Eighty-one percent of the 682 survey participants said that they would only disclose the information to the mother, 13% would lie about the findings, and 2% would tell the couple that a gene mutation was responsible for the disorder. Results from a 1989 survey of nondoctoral genetic counselors reflected a perspective similar to that of the medical geneticists.
>
> Although these previous surveys demonstrated overwhelming support for nondisclosure, a more recent survey suggests a shift in attitudes. A 2006 survey of 273 genetic counselors from the United States and Canada indicated little consensus about how the misattributed paternity information should be treated. Furthermore, 97.2% indicated that their institution did not have a policy to govern the disclosure of the misattributed paternity.'

Like professionals associated with family law and medical ethics, the more general medical fraternity has also, in the past, had a consensus around maintaining the status quo and "managing" information – which most often meant the mother may be informed, but not the father. Not everyone has been happy with this consensus, however. The Abstract from an article by Lainie Friedman Ross (1996) writing in "Bioethics" was,

> 'In 1994, the Committee on Assessing Genetic Risks of the Institute of Medicine published their recommendations regarding the ethical issues raised by advances in genetics. One of the Committee's recommendation was to inform women when test results revealed misattributed paternity, but not to disclose this information to the women's partners. The Committee's reason for withholding such information was that "genetic testing should not be used in ways that disrupt families". In this paper, I argue that the Committee's conclusion in favour of nondisclosure to the male partner is unethical. I argue that both parties ought to be informed.'

For my second ethical analysis I shall deploy utilitarian moral philosophy. This takes a practical stance in which the most preferred moral action is that which produces the greatest benefit (or avoids the greatest suffering) when integrated over all affected people: the maximising of utility. The proposition whose ethical status, as judged by this utilitarian approach, I wish to address is this,

> Legal paternity shall require the carrying out of a DNA test on the baby, or child, in question and the result made known to the putative father (and mother) prior to legal paternity (Parental Responsibility) being permissible, and hence prior to inclusion of the man's name on the birth certificate.

This is the sword-stroke which, I claim, severs the Gordian knot posed by the conflicts of interest which arise without it. There are many issues which would need to be set out clearly in legislation regarding the rights and obligations of married men versus biological fathers in order to forge a complete workable arrangement. However, the details of these arrangements will not undermine the key advantage of the above proposal, which is that a later revelation of biological paternity can no longer arise to cause conflict with the status of the man in terms of social or legal fatherhood. It can no longer arise because full disclosure applies from the start. By making the DNA test a legal obligation prior to the awarding of legal paternity, the issue is seen to involve the putative father and the child only.

Some of the problems associated with the existing arrangements are,

- Under the current arrangements, whether the percentage is 1% or 5% or 25%, the child and the father are both misled regarding the truth about paternity in a proportion of cases. This applies to the whole population, so even 1% is over half a million people in the UK, and in reality probably several million people have been thus misled;
- The status quo effectively maintains a sex-based power imbalance which is intrinsically inequitable. Narratives around minimising the significance of genetic paternity have been shown to be unethical;
- Under current arrangements, men have no right to know if a child is biologically theirs, and obtaining this information, even where legal, is being frustrated by State actors to bolster the status quo;
- Men are prevented from benefiting from DNA technology because a request for a DNA test on an individual basis is such a vote of no confidence in the partner that it is unlikely the relationship would survive. A legislative obligation applicable to all would avoid this problem and is probably the only way of doing so;
- Late revelations of mispaternity risk family dissolution, a situation which could be avoided if the truth were revealed from the start;
- Some of the disputes following partnership dissolution would be obviated if biological paternity had been established before paternity

obligations were accepted (e.g., around 360,000 cases annually in the USA);

- The concern that biological paternity may be raised by men on partnership dissolution in order to gain advantage is obviated;
- There is a peculiar double standard: children born of sperm donor sperm have a legal right to know the identity of their biological father once they turn 18, but children born from conventional sexual intercourse have no such right;
- Sometimes mispaternity is revealed as a by-product of medical treatments, which currently presents practitioners with a dilemma: to disclose or not to disclose? Maintenance of patient confidentiality and trust comes into conflict with the duty to tell the truth and the rights of the child to know their own genetic heritage;
- Children may be severely medically disadvantaged their whole lives by being unaware of their true father's medical history. Whilst the proposed process will not always reveal the true father, it will reveal if the social father is not the true father.

In short, the entirety of the controversies around paternity testing could be avoided if the proposition to require testing prior to assigning Parental Responsibility were adopted. This could be achieved by adopting radically new legislative arrangements around paternity rights and obligations, bringing them into line with the reality of available technology. Once embedded, it is hard to see where any counterbalancing disbenefit might lie. There would be resistance to change. Women would no doubt object that "compulsory" testing was presenting them as liars. But, in reality, the testing is little to do with the mothers: it is about the putative father and the child. Such attitudes are a hang-over from the days when the mother established paternity, but this is precisely what would change. The legislative requirement that testing must apply to all, and not be waived, prevents a mother being singled out as under suspicion. To be clear, even if a man turns out not to be the biological father, he may still claim legal paternity if the mother agrees and no other paternity candidate is forthcoming within some agreed period.

The utilitarian criterion for moral action requires that utility is increased, and the best moral action maximises utility. In obviating the whole tranche of current controversies, the adoption of a legislative requirement for paternity testing prior to the awarding of paternal rights and responsibilities is strongly motivated by utilitarian moral considerations.

15.3 The Empathy Gap Against Paternity and Male Fertility

Men have little control over their own fertility, a situation which is accepted by men with bovine forbearance. A woman's right to choose after conception means that men have an opportunity to choose only prior to conception. But in the absence of a convenient, persistent and reversible male contraceptive, men have little control over conception in practice. The frequency with which women might secretly plan to conceive expressly against their partners' wishes is unknown. But those ambivalent cases of not-quite-so-accidental accidental pregnancies are common, as evidenced by the fact that most unplanned pregnancies occur, not due to contraception failure, but following deliberately ceasing contraception. There would be major advantages to both sexes in having a persistent, reversible male contraceptive available. The barriers to this happening are not primarily technological.

A dominant narrative attempts to minimise the significance of biological paternity, a position that would be acceptable to no one if applied to mothers. The empathy gap facilitates a glaring inequality which I have shown to be unethical, despite claims to the contrary. Historically men have been disadvantaged compared to women in respect of their lack of certainty that a given child is indeed theirs. This situation persists despite cheap, convenient and highly reliable DNA testing technology having been readily available for over twenty years. Widespread application of the technology is frustrated partly by legislation and partly by medical, legal and government agencies protecting existing custom and practice, and rationalising these policies with terms like "protecting family stability" and "the interests of the child". But the right to benefit from advances in reproductive technology has been argued, by the Chief Medical Officer of England, to be a human right. And I have argued that retaining the ancient *status quo* in respect of the traditional uncertainty in paternity is unethical.

Whether reports of steeply declining sperm counts in Western countries are correct is unclear, though scientifically credible. If they are correct, however, nominal male infertility could be the norm in a few decades. Whilst alarmism is to be avoided, and the situation is less certain than the popular press may sometimes suggest, nevertheless there is a remarkable mismatch between the apocalyptic nature of this projected possibility and the complete lack of concern at the level of the political-medical establishment. The empathy gap for men may be facilitating ignoring a threat to society as a whole.

16

Homelessness and Loneliness

On being persuaded to give up sleeping with his mother at age 3, his sisters claimed firstly, "You're a big grown man. You'll be sleeping with Harold and Jack". When that did not work they said instead, "It'll only be for a bit. You can come back to Mum later on." I was never recalled to my Mother's bed again. It was my first betrayal, my first dose of ageing hardness, my first lesson in the gentle, merciless rejection of women".
Laurie Lee (1914 - 1997), *Cider With Rosie*

Men released from jails in the southwest and Wales have admitted that they would reoffend to get a roof over their head and regular meals. The Catch 22 charity said that prisoners being released without accommodation was a significant problem, with their data showing that 35 per cent of inmates leave with no fixed address.
Richard Ford, in *The Times* 13/2/19

The term "homeless" is ambiguous. In particular, the term is used in different ways by local authorities and by the general public. The latter often conflate the "homeless" with those sleeping rough. But local authorities recognise a much broader class of homeless people who have not (as yet) ended up on the streets: the statutory homeless. In reality, rough sleepers are the tip of this homeless iceberg. The statistics within the UK of both the statutory homeless and rough sleepers are reviewed here, identifying the differences by gender as appropriate. This culminates with the most distressing category: the deaths of rough sleepers. A brief review is then presented of the data on loneliness, an issue closely related to living arrangements. The chapter closes, as usual, by summarising aspects of these issues which illuminate the empathy gap.

16.1 Statutory Homelessness and "Single" Homelessness

The term "household" is used in discussions about statutory homelessness. A household may comprise a single adult. Not everyone who is without a home is classified as statutorily homeless. If classed as statutorily homeless, the local authority has a duty to house the household. But this is subject to an assessment of priority.

A necessary (but not sufficient) criterion for a household to be considered statutorily homeless is that they do not have a legal right to occupy accommodation that is accessible, physically available and which would be reasonable for the household to continue to live in, (Ministry of Housing, Communities and Local Government, 2018a). Local authorities have a duty to secure accommodation for unintentionally homeless households who fall into a 'priority need' category, and it is this additional priority assessment which determines the statutory homeless. Scotland has recently dropped the prioritisation process.

There is no duty to secure accommodation for all homeless people. For example, there is no statutory duty to secure housing for homeless single people or for couples without children who are not deemed to be vulnerable for some reason. The latter are often loosely termed the "single homeless", though this may be a misnomer in that the term really refers to any homeless people who are not deemed statutorily homeless, (UK Parliament, 2018d).

In most cases, households deemed statutorily homeless will currently be in some form of temporary accommodation or shelter, or be lodging informally with friends or relations. One of the key determinants of their statutory homelessness is that their current arrangements are "on sufferance": they have no legal right to remain, and in most cases will be under some pressure to leave. However, they are generally not currently living on the streets.

A brief definition of the 'priority need groups' is given by (UK Government, 2018k), namely,

- households with dependent children;
- pregnant women;
- those aged 16 or 17;
- those aged 18 to 20 who were previously in care;
- people who are vulnerable in some way, e.g., because of mental illness or physical disability;
- those who are vulnerable as a result of time spent in care, in custody, or in HM Forces;
- those who are vulnerable as a result of having to flee their home because of violence or the threat of violence.

These are the criteria which will lead local authorities to assess the "household" (or individual) as being in priority need, and hence being classed as the statutory homeless for which the local authority has an obligation to provide housing. The remainder are the "single homeless" for which there is no obligation on local authorities to provide housing. The "single homeless" are the feedstock for the community of rough sleepers.

There are huge quantities of data available on statutory homelessness in the UK, but accurately understanding what the data mean can be challenging.

One source of confusion is that the four nations of the UK use different definitions and processes. The (UK Statistics Authority, 2017) observes,

> 'Definitions of statutory homelessness across the UK countries differ, as a result of different policies aimed at reducing homelessness and defining those eligible for support. The main source for statutory homelessness statistics is administrative data, and because of differences in the legislative processes and systems, these statistics aren't directly comparable across the UK. There is limited explanation within these statistics publications about how these statistics differ across the UK, and they vary in their usefulness. Furthermore, while each of the statistics present contextual information about the specific policies within each of the UK countries, there is limited advice about the comparability of statutory homelessness across the UK, and existing advice is perceived as confusing and incoherent.'

The second potential source of confusion for the neophyte is the terminology associated with what might be dubbed a "triage system", as described by the (Ministry of Housing, Communities and Local Government, 2018a). The Housing Act 1996, the Homelessness Act 2002, the Localism Act 2011 and the Homelessness Reduction Act 2017 determine the legal duties on local authorities towards homeless households and households threatened with homelessness. Households which are statutorily homeless are owed legal duties that fall into three main categories,

- Prevention duty;
- Relief duty;
- Main Homelessness duty.

Prevention duties become relevant for qualifying households if they are within 56 days of being made homeless. If prevention measures fail, the household may fall into the "Relief duty" category. Relief duties are owed to households that are already homeless and require help to secure settled accommodation. The duty lasts 56 days. Main Homelessness duty describes the duty a local authority has towards an applicant who is unintentionally homeless, eligible for assistance and has priority need.

Hence, those owed a relief duty who are not successfully assisted within 56 days will only be promoted to the Main Homelessness category if they meet the above priority criteria. The rest may be on their own after expiry of the 56 days. Where households are found to be intentionally homeless, or not in priority need, the authority may provide advice and assistance, but the household must find accommodation for themselves.

A third potential confusion is that the Homelessness Reduction Act 2017 made a wider class of people eligible for housing, so that data thereafter is not comparable with that before.

I now turn to the data. Only people who notify their local authority through the appropriate channels will appear in the homeless data. The rest are the "invisible homeless" who are not represented in the data. The picture is highly complex. In reading the following account with a focus on gender, the principal feature is that, whilst there are comparable numbers, or greater numbers, of male than female applicants, men become the minority of those to whom a duty is recognised when prioritisation is deployed and the minority of those successfully assisted. If the reader finds the following nation-specific sections rather opaque, the big picture is reprised in section 16.1.5.

16.1.1 Statutory Homelessness in England

In year 2017/18 in England, 215,530 households were successfully assisted under prevention or relief duties: 93% prevented, and 7% relieved. The prevention cases consisted of securing continued residence in their existing home in 55% of cases, and arranging alternative accommodation in 45% of cases, (Ministry of Housing, Communities and Local Government, 2018e). Nearly half of applicants assessed under the "triage" system for prevention/relief have at least one support need. Data for 2018 quarter 2 (Ministry of Housing, Communities and Local Government, 2018f) indicates that, of all applicants for prevention/relief, 52% had no support needs identified whilst the support needs of the rest were as follows (the percentages being of those who had any support needs),

- Mental health issues, 22%;
- Physical ill-health or disability, 14%;
- Experience of, or risk of, domestic or sexual abuse, 12%;
- Support needs by virtue of youth, 7%;
- Offending history, 7%;
- History of repeat homelessness, 6%;
- Drug dependency needs, 5%;
- History of rough sleeping, 5%;
- Alcohol dependency needs, 4%;
- Learning disability, 4%;
- Access to education, employment or training, 4%
- Experience of, or risk of, abuse (non-domestic), 3%;

- Care-leaver, 2%;
- Old age, 1.1%;
- Former asylum seeker, 0.9%;
- Served in HM forces, 0.7%;

Unfortunately, no gender break-down of the English data at the prevent/relief stage is currently published.

As explained above, the Main Homeless Duty category, applicable only to those with priority, comes into play only after the "triage" represented by the initial prevent/relief process. In 2017/18 in England there were 109,470 decisions made regarding applications under the Main Homelessness category, of which 56,600 (52%) were accepted. These are the cases designated as unintentionally homeless and in priority need. Local authorities assessed that they did not have a duty to house the remaining 48%, which consisted of 8,700 (8%) intentionally homeless but in priority need, 18,450 (17%) homeless but not in priority need, and 25,720 (23%) not homeless, (Ministry of Housing, Communities and Local Government, 2018d).

The 56,600 households who successfully achieved the Main Homelessness Duty are broken down by sex in Table 16.1. Easily the most common demographic achieving this priority status are single mothers with dependent children. Of lone parents, mothers account for 92% of those achieving Main Homelessness Duty, which is consistent with the proportion of lone parents who are mothers in the general population (see chapters 11 and 12). Lone mother families account for nearly half of households achieving Main Homelessness Duty.

Table 16.1: *The Breakdown of Households Achieving Main Homelessness Duty in 2017/18 by Demographic (percentages of 56,600), England*

Couple with dependent children	Lone parent household with dependent children		One person household		All other household groups
	Male applicant	Female applicant	Male applicant	Female applicant	
20%	4%	47%	14%	10%	5%

Table 16.2 confirms that dependent children, or the expectancy of children, are overwhelmingly the reason for being assessed with a Main Homelessness Duty, almost all the remainder being due to mental illness or physical disability. Only 2% results from domestic violence, though a larger percentage (7.7%) at the prevent/relief stage were attributed to allegations of partner violence, (Prevention and Relief Tables, 2018e). Recall that Tables 16.1 and

16.2 do not include those people filtered out by the prevent/relief stages, nor do they include nearly half of applicants for Main Homelessness Duty who are filtered out by the prioritisation process.

In 2017, 38% of successful applicants for Main Homelessness Duty did not identify as white, (Ministry of Housing, Communities and Local Government, 2018d).

Table 16.2: *The Breakdown of Households Achieving Main Homelessness Duty in 2017/18 by Reason (percentages of 56,600), England*

Household with dependent children	Household member pregnant	Household member vulnerable through:						Homeless in emergency
		Old age	Physical disability	Mental illness	Young person	Domestic violence	Other	
66%	7%	1%	8%	10%	2%	2%	3%	1%

16.1.2 Statutory Homelessness in Scotland

Homelessness data for Scotland in 2017/18 has been taken from the charts and data tables obtainable from the (Scottish Government, 2018). The total number of applicants under Scotland's homelessness provisions in 2017/18 was 34,972, with 82% (28,792) being assessed as homeless or at risk of being homeless. The number of male applicants exceeded the number of female applicants by 21% (19,112 male versus 15,860 female).

The living arrangements of applicants at the time of application in 2017/18 were,

- Living with relatives, friends or partners, 42%
- Owning or renting, 37%
- Rough sleeping, 4% (but 8% of applicants had slept rough at some time in the previous 3 months)
- Institutional accommodation, 9%
- Temporary accommodation, 3%
- Not specified, 5%

The proportion of applicants who identified "fleeing domestic violence" as the reason for their homelessness was just under 3%.

Table 16.3 breaks down the applicants by demographic. By far the largest demographic were single males without children. Table 16.3 contrasts sharply with Table 16.1 for England. This is because Table 16.3 is the totality of applicants (not all successful) in Scotland, whereas Table 16.1 for England addresses only those people achieving the Main Homeless Duty. Recall that the bulk of English applicants are removed by the prevent/relief scheme and nearly half of those that are not removed in these stages are removed by the prioritisation process and hence do not feature in the Main Homeless register.

Table 16.3: *The Breakdown of Applicants under Scotland's Homelessness Provisions in 2017/18 by Demographic (percentages of 34,972)*

Couple with dependent children	Lone parent household with dependent children		One person household		Couple without dependent children
	Male applicant	Female applicant	Male applicant	Female applicant	
5%	4%	17%	46%	21%	3%

16.1.3 Statutory Homelessness in Wales

Local Authorities in Wales have duties under Part 6 (Allocations) of the Housing Act 1996 and Part 2 (Homelessness) of the Housing (Wales) Act 2014. For year 2017/18, Stats Wales (2018) provides data on Welsh households for which housing assistance has been considered, broken down by gender. The data are summarized in Table 16.4.

Table 16.4: *Welsh Households for which Housing Assistance has been Considered or Accepted, by Gender, 2017/18*

Category of need and/or outcome	male	female
Total (Wales)	13,950	14,847
...of which the total successfully housed	5,232	7,188
Ineligible households	234	153
Eligible, but not homeless or threatened with homelessness	2,022	2,085
Eligible, threatened with homelessness, prevention assistance provided	3,282	5,790
...of which those which were successful	2,127	3,894
Eligible, homeless, subject to duty to help to secure	6,315	4,959
...of which those which were successful	2,541	2,112
Eligible, homeless but not in priority need	1,206	360
Eligible, unintentionally homeless and in priority need	819	1,407
...of which those positively discharged	567	1,179

Salient features of Table 16.4 are,

- Similar total numbers of men (13,950) and women (14,847) were assessed, but substantially fewer men (5,232; 37.5%) than women (7,188; 48.4%) were housed, despite substantially more men (6,315) than women (4,959) being deemed "eligible, homeless, and subject to a duty to help to secure housing";

- Substantially more men (1,206) than women (360) were deemed "not in priority need" despite being eligible and homeless;
- Even for people deemed "eligible, unintentionally homeless and in priority need", men were less likely to be housed (69%) than women (84%).

16.1.4 Statutory Homelessness in Northern Ireland

Homeless data can be obtained from the links provided by the Northern Ireland (Department for Communities, 2018). In 2017/18 some 18,180 households applied for provision, of which 65% (11,877) were accepted as "full duty applicants", but only 1,837 (10% of the initial applicants) had this duty successfully discharged.

Table 16.5 indicates the demographic breakdown of the initial 18,180 applicants. Single males are the dominant category, exceeding "families" of all types (i.e., one or more adults with children). In absolute numbers, 5,971 single males and 5,805 families applied. Since only 1,837 duties were discharged it seems likely that very few of these would relate to single males.

Table 16.5: *The Breakdown of Applicants under Northern Ireland's Homelessness Provisions in 2017/18 by Demographic (percentages of 18,180)*

Families	Couples	One person household		Pensioners
		Male applicant	Female applicant	
32%	5%	33%	17%	13%

16.1.5 Statutory Homelessness: The Big Picture on Gender

It is difficult to extract a clear picture on gender from the preceding data on statutory homelessness, largely because the "longitudinal" picture is not generally provided, i.e., three of the UK nations do not publish the gender breakdown at application and also the gender breakdown either after prioritisation or at discharge of duty. (The exception is Wales).

The Scottish and Northern Irish data show that single male applicants are strongly dominant. In Wales, the total numbers of male and female applicants are comparable. A gender breakdown of applicants is not published for England, but the implication of the data from the other three nations is that single males are likely to be dominant, and the total number of male applicants likely to be comparable with, or exceed, the number of female applicants.

In contrast, after the "triage" stage of prevention/relief, and after prioritisation, the number of women entering the Main Homeless Duty in England considerably exceeds the number of men. The overwhelmingly dominant demographic in the Main Homeless Duty in England are families headed by a single mother (47%). 71% of households accepted for Main Homeless Duty include children.

Only Welsh data provide the gender breakdown both at application and discharge. These data confirm for Wales what has been implied above for England. Similar total numbers of men and women were assessed, but substantially fewer men than women were housed, despite substantially more men than women being deemed 'eligible, homeless, and subject to a duty to help to secure housing'. Even for people deemed 'eligible, unintentionally homeless and in priority need', men were less likely to be housed than women.

16.2 Rough Sleepers

16.2.1 Rough Sleeper Counts in England

Estimates of the number of people sleeping rough in England have been taken from (Ministry of Housing, Communities and Local Government, 2018b). For this purpose "sleeping rough" is defined as sleeping in the open air (such as on the streets, in the open fields, in tents, doorways, parks, bus shelters, subways, etc.). Also counted are people sleeping in places not designed for habitation (such as stairwells, barns, sheds, car parks, cars, derelict boats, bus or train stations, or makeshift shelters, often composed of cardboard boxes).

It should be noted that this definition does *not* include people in hostels or shelters, people in campsites or other sites used for recreational purposes or organised protest, nor are squatters or travellers counted. Not counting people in hostels or shelters for the homeless is a significant omission, since these people would be sleeping rough if this provision were not available. Consequently, I shall make an estimate of these additional people below.

I draw the readers' attention immediately to an ambiguity in what is meant by "the number of rough sleepers". This might mean the number of people sleeping rough on a given night, or it might mean the number of different people who have slept rough on one or more nights within a given period (say, within a given year). Popular news accounts rarely distinguish between these two things. It is easy to conflate the two though there is a huge numerical difference between them. National estimates of rough sleepers generally relate to single-night snapshots. This is a wild under-estimate of the problem.

Only in London has any attempt been made to estimate how many different people have slept rough at least once in the last year. I will present these data in the following section and use them to make a crude estimate for the nation as a whole. This is not usually done but is crucial in order to obtain a faithful picture of the true extent of rough sleeping.

The English data is based on a single night count, or an estimate for the number on a single night, in October or November. These 'single night' counts involve teams walking through areas and visibly spotting rough sleepers. It is important to appreciate the limitations of the counts. One limitation is that many rough sleepers deliberately hide themselves from sight, for fear of being attacked or robbed. Another limitation is that the entire local authority area clearly cannot be searched, so some sort of estimation is inevitable. Counts in rural areas will be particularly challenging. (Do you fancy trying to check every barn in Gloucestershire?). The counts will inevitably be lower bounds.

In 2017, of the 326 local authorities in England, only 54 (17%) conducted a count. The majority (272 authorities, or 83%) provided an estimate without a count. Moreover, 176 local authorities (54%) have not conducted a count in any of the last 8 years (2010 to 2017). This can only reflect badly on the accuracy of the data (not to mention reflecting badly on the local authorities themselves). Key results were,

- Local authorities' counts and estimates show that 4,751 people slept rough in England on a snapshot night in autumn 2017. This has increased rapidly from 1,768 in 2010 (see Figure 16.1);
- The rate of rough sleeping per 1,000 households is 0.31 for London and 0.18 for the rest of England;
- Nearly one-quarter (24%) of rough sleepers in England are in London;
- 14% of rough sleepers in England are women, 84% men (2% sex not recorded).
- 68% of rough sleepers identified in London had a support needs assessment recorded. Of these, 44% had alcohol support needs, 47% mental health support needs, and 35% drug support needs, with 14% having all three needs. Only 32% of rough sleepers had none of these three needs.

In terms of gender ratio and age, there is little difference between London and the rest of England. However, there is a large difference in nationality. In

London just under half of rough sleepers are not UK nationals. In the rest of England between 13% and 19% of rough sleepers are not UK nationals.

Figure 16.1: *Rough Sleepers in England Versus Year*

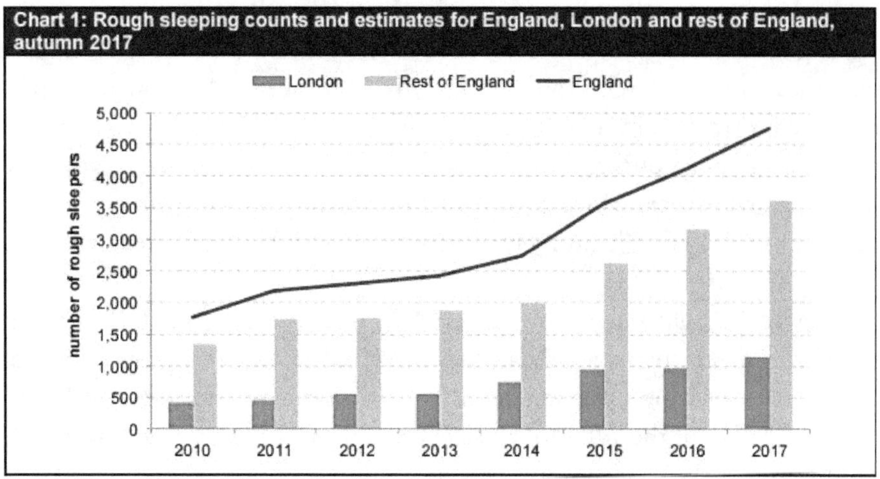

As explained above, the estimate of 4,751 refers to people sleeping rough on one specific night. A meaningful estimate of the number of different people commonly sleeping rough in the days or weeks before, or after, the night in question should be increased by the number who were in night shelters at the time. The number of night shelter places available increases in the winter months due to the Severe Weather Emergency Protocol (SWEP) which provides extra bed places triggered by forecasts of freezing, near freezing or otherwise severe weather conditions. The number of people reported as using SWEP and extended winter provision in the winter of 2017/18 was 6,502 across 145 service providers who responded to the survey, (Homeless Link, 2018). What is unclear is the extent of double-accounting between the local authority single night snap-shot figure of 4,751, and the number recorded in night shelters, 6,502 on the severest night, when fewer might remain on the streets. It is clear that many do remain on the streets, even in the severest of weather, so the number of rough sleepers on a single night including those in night shelters could be up to around 11,000.

16.2.2 CHAIN Data for London

There is an enormous difference between the number of people sleeping rough on any one night and the number who have slept rough at some time over a given year. People may spend some nights on the street, but other nights they may get a space indoors – for example sleeping on someone's floor or sofa. Their period of sleeping rough may be short. The Mayor of London's Combined Homelessness And Information Network (CHAIN, 2018) is the only source in the UK which attempts to identify everyone who sleeps rough at any time, but it is confined to Greater London.

Figure 16.2 shows the variation in the number of rough sleepers identified in the last ten years. In 2017/18 there were 7484 rough sleepers identified, down from a peak of 8108 in 2016/17. These figures serve to illustrate the huge difference between rough sleepers identified at any time during a given year, which is 7484 in London alone, compared with the number sleeping rough on a given night, which is far smaller even for the whole of England (4751).

Figure 16.3 illustrates why the CHAIN figures are so much larger than the single night snap-shot data. The pie chart shows the proportions of individuals seen rough sleeping on just one occasion, or twice, or three to five times, etc. 59% of the 7484 rough sleepers seen over the year were seen only once, and 87% were seen not more than 5 times. Collecting data on a given night would be unlikely to capture these people. However, caution is required: being seen only once does not mean the person in question slept rough only once. 4456 of the 7484 rough sleepers seen at some time during 2017/18 had not been seen in previous years, whereas the remainder (3,028) had been seen in previous years. Rough sleepers are not just a single homogeneous demographic: some are short-termers, some long term.

The CHAIN figures of 7484 (2017/18) and 8108 (2016/17) compare with the local authority single night snapshot estimates for London of 1137 and 964 respectively. Thus, the number of people experiencing rough sleeping at some time in a given year is roughly 7 or 8 times greater than single night snapshot numbers (at least in London). If this ratio is applicable to England as a whole, the local authority single night snap-shot of 4751 suggests that perhaps around 36,000 people in England have experienced rough sleeping at least once in 2017/18.

For comparison, Homeless Link (2018) estimate the number of people who are "single homeless" is on average, 77,000 on any one night. The low estimate is 52,000 and the high estimate is 111,000. This will include rough sleepers, but not all "single homeless" are rough sleepers (see section 16.1).

The CHAIN report indicates that, of all identified rough sleepers in London who provided information, 36% had been in prison, 11% had been in care, and 7% had been in the armed services. However, 'new' rough sleepers, i.e., those seen for the first time in 2017/18, are a distinct demographic. Of those who provided information, only 4% reported that prison had been their last long-term accommodation. 38% had been in private rented accommodation, and a total of 54% in some form of long term, non-institutional accommodation. 12% had been in short-term accommodation (including hostels and asylum-seekers accommodation), and 8% were newly arrived in the UK.

Figure 16.2: *Number of Rough Sleepers Seen in London at Least Once During 2017/18 (CHAIN data)*

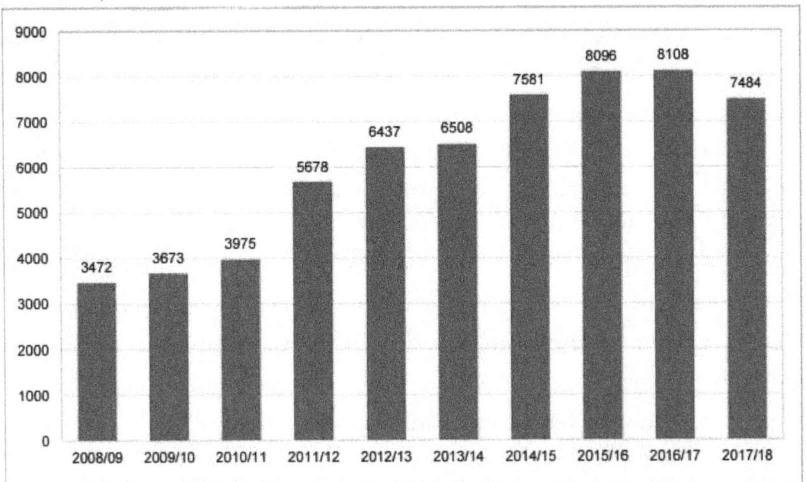

Figure 16.3: *Number of Rough Sleepers Seen in London by the Number of Times Seen During 2017/18 (CHAIN data)*

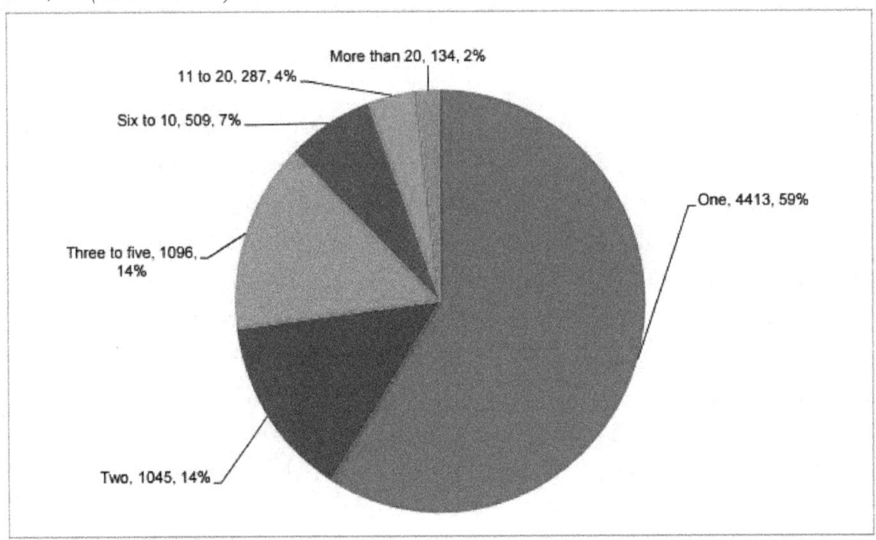

16.2.3 Rough Sleeper Counts in Wales

The Welsh Government reported a count of rough sleepers in Wales in 2017, (Welsh Government, 2018a). The count was conducted in two periods: a two-week period from the 16th to the 29th of October 2017, and a single night on 9th/10th November 2017. Each of the 22 unitary authorities submitted an estimate, (StatsWales, 2017). Six of these local authorities submitted zero rough sleepers. Eight reported having no emergency bed places for rough sleepers.

The 'single night' count involved teams walking through areas and visibly spotting rough sleepers. The counts are subject to the same limitations as the English counts. The two-week count included such visual identifications but also involved engaging with local agencies and services, including the voluntary sector, faith groups, the police, local residents, outreach workers, health agencies and drug and alcohol misuse and treatment teams. The counts will inevitably be lower bounds.

The number of rough sleepers identified in the single night counts was 188. Just over half of these are accounted for by Cardiff and Wrexham. The number of rough sleepers identified in the two-week survey, 345, was substantially greater. The difference between the two figures suggests that the number of people who have slept rough at some time over the last year will be far larger, but this figure is unknown.

On the survey night in November, there were 191 people sleeping in emergency accommodation. These people are not included in the above counts, although the people in question would most likely have been sleeping rough had they not found space in a shelter. Including these people, the two-week survey figure increases to 536.

Assuming 1.35 million households in Wales, (Welsh Government, 2018b), the counts of 188, 345 or 536 correspond to a rough sleeper rate of 0.14, 0.26 or 0.40 per 1000 households. The first, and lowest, of these figures, i.e., that for the single night count, may be compared with 0.31 for London and 0.18 for the rest of England obtained on the same basis.

The rough sleeper count in Wales has not been conducted to current standards for sufficiently many years to permit the long-term trend to be discerned. However, the same methodology was used in 2016. The 2017 count was 10% greater over the two-week period and 33% greater on the single November night. This is consistent with the trend in England for increasing numbers of rough sleepers (Figure 16.1).

The published Welsh data does not disaggregate by sex, although the proforma which is used to capture the data does request that sex is recorded.

16.3 Deaths of Rough Sleepers

There is no legislative requirement on the national government, nor on local authorities, to count or record numbers of rough sleeper deaths. Nevertheless, in recent years data has started to become available.

16.3.1 Bethany Thomas 2012 Data

In 2012, Bethany Thomas of the University of Sheffield produced a report on deaths amongst rough sleepers 'Homelessness kills: An analysis of the mortality of homeless people in early twenty-first century England', (Thomas, 2012). The analysis was based on death records, searching the records for cases where the address of the deceased was a homeless shelter, advice or day centre. The search would not identify homeless people for which the registered address had been recorded as a relative's address or hospital, or, in some cases, no address. The figures will therefore be under-estimates. The headline conclusions were,

- From the records of deaths in England between 2001-2009, 1,731 were identified as having been homeless people. Of these, 90% were male and 10% female;
- Nearly one-third of the identified homeless deaths were in London;
- The average age at death of the above was 47 for men and 43 for women.

Thomas's figure is equivalent to 192 rough sleeper deaths per year in England. ONS data (below) indicates that the true number is more than twice this estimate.

16.3.2 ONS Data

The ONS have been estimating rough sleeper deaths only since 2013. The methodology deployed by ONS is similar to that of Thomas, but more inclusive. It starts with death registration records and searches on terms like "no fixed abode", "homeless" and "night shelter" or the name or address of a known homeless hostel or project. Coroners' inquest reports are also used as a source. The ONS searches include homeless people who had been found in need of medical attention in the street and subsequently died in hospital, or other places of medical assistance. The ONS also deploy sophisticated statistical tools to include allowance for more deaths not captured by the direct searches. They state that, 'this is a robust but conservative (lower bound) model, so that the figures produced should be taken as the lowest probable estimates'.

Key findings from the December 2018 ONS report 'Deaths of Homeless People in England and Wales: 2013-2017' (Office for National Statistics, 2018ah) were,

- There were an estimated 597 deaths of homeless people in England & Wales in 2017 (an increase of 24% since 2013 when 482 rough sleeper deaths were identified);
- Men accounted for 84% of these deaths. Hence the gender ratio of rough sleeper deaths is essentially the same as the gender ratio of rough sleepers, to within one or two percentage points;
- The top three causes of deaths of the homeless in 2017 were drug poisoning (32%), suicide (13%) and alcohol-specific (10%);
- Although there is a concentration of homeless in London, and hence a concentration of homeless deaths in London, the rough sleeper death rate per million people (15.4) is not the largest, being exceeded by the West of England (21.0), Liverpool (20.5) and Greater Manchester (17.8);
- The mean age of the deaths of rough sleeping men was 44, whilst for women it was 42. The most common age range for deaths of male rough sleepers was 45 to 49, compared with 35 to 39 for women.

Rather remarkably, there is no seasonal trend in the rate of rough sleeper deaths, despite the freezing weather in winter months. Figure 16.4 shows the number of deaths per month, averaged over the five years 2013 to 2017.

Figure 16.4: *Deaths per Month: ONS data (England & Wales)*

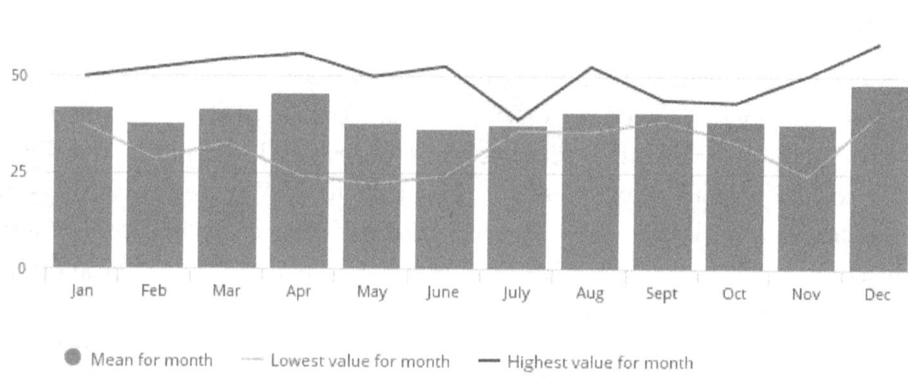

16.3.3 Data from the Bureau of Investigative Journalism

The Bureau of Investigative Journalism maintain a log of rough sleeper deaths in the UK, obtaining their information essentially from "crowd sourcing". Recall that despite many vulnerable people being known to the authorities, the authorities are under no obligation to report or record their deaths, so local journalists and charities are often the only ones to do so. To compile their list, the Bureau makes use of their extensive network of local journalists to report to the Bureau's central register cases which appear in local papers. In addition, the Bureau speaks to councils, hospitals, coroners' offices, police forces, charities, GPs and NGOs. This is a "bottom up" approach and will inevitably miss many of the deaths. What the Bureau's list includes, which ONS data lack, are the names of the deceased (where available), and, in some cases, a brief biography, (Bureau of Investigative Journalism, 2018).

The Bureau's data is updated continually. The data given here was obtained on 27/12/18. The Bureau started collecting data in October 2017, so the data for England, Scotland and Wales relate to 14 month period. However, the data for September to December 2018 appears incomplete. The Northern Irish data relate to October 2017 to August 2018 (11 months). Table 16.6 shows how the 546 deaths identified by the Bureau breakdown by nation. Also shown are the death rates per million of the population. I believe the data from Northern Ireland uses an inconsistent definition of "homeless", the Bureau's database recording that the definition used in this case was, 'officially recognised as homeless and died while waiting to be housed by the Northern Irish Housing Executive', i.e., this probably includes statutory homeless, not only rough sleepers. For this reason the Northern Ireland data has been omitted from Table 16.6.

Table 16.6: *Summary of Bureau of Investigative Journalism's Data by Nation*

Nation	Deaths	Deaths per million population
England & Wales	294	5.1
Scotland	103	19.1
UK	546	8.4

Of the 546 deaths identified by the Bureau's list, two-thirds were either "unnamed" or "anonymous" or had only a first name or nickname given. No doubt many of these people did have known names which were simply not reported. But it seems that a very large proportion died without their full identities being known.

The high incidence of ex-offenders, drug addicts and alcoholics amongst rough sleepers creates a perception that all of them can be so described. Not only is that not true, but it is easy to lose sight of the fact that even those who end up in such straits were not necessarily always ne'er-do-wells or drop-outs. Whilst this book generally eschews personal anecdotes, a few brief biographies of deceased rough sleepers is appropriate to illustrate that the background of many of these unfortunates was productive, even laudable, a fact that is rightly disconcerting. These accounts are taken from the (Bureau of Investigative Journalism, 2018).

- Istvan Kakas died in Bath, on October 16, 2018, aged 52. He had been a chef working under both Gordon Ramsay and Michael Caines. Kakas had completed more than 250 parachute jumps while on military service. He received a heroism award from the mayor of Bath after he helped save a man and his daughter from drowning. He began selling the Big Issue in 2010.
- Craig Cunningham died sleeping rough in Chester, on October 25, 2018. He used to manage a Kwiksave store before falling on hard times.
- Rob O'Connor died in Chelmsford, on February 23, 2018. He died in a shop doorway on a night when temperatures dropped to -2C. Rob had recently undergone treatment for cancer and had his voice box removed.
- Colin Ellis was found dead behind the steering wheel of his car, in which he lived, in late autumn 2017. By the time he was discovered, he had been there for several days. Charity workers recalled Mr Ellis regularly bought food and gave his own cash to other people on the streets.
- Darren Greenfield died in Edinburgh, in December, 2017, aged 48, after years of sleeping rough. He had served with the 2nd Royal Tank Regiment, the Royal Army Pay Corps and the Adjutant General's Corps. He became homeless after leaving the army.
- Anthony Barnard died in Lowestoft, on December 28, 2017, aged 57. Mr Barnard was found dead in the garden of his former home.
- Allan "Scotch" Alexander died while sleeping rough in a car park in Taunton, on Boxing Day 2017. The day before his death Allan was seen giving away a Christmas meal to a homeless woman by a member of the public.

- Henryk Smolarz died in Plymouth city centre, on March 12, 2018, aged 62. He was believed to have been Polish and friends say he was a physicist and mathematician.
- Hamid Farahi died in Church Langley, in March, 2018, aged 55. Hamid, a physicist who fought in Iraq, was living in the back of his car in a Tesco car park.
- Stephen Kinghorn was born in South Shields, Country Durham. He attended a sailing school in Hull for five years where he took part in the 93/94 tall ships race, and was a qualified skipper of small vessels. His team helped to build a school in a remote village in Zimbabwe. Things started going downhill when his first child was stillborn and continued to slip further downwards. Stephen went to London and was involved with Love Activists and a homeless kitchen trying to get food for fellow homeless. Then his second child died, which was the catalyst to sending him rock bottom. Stephen died in London on 19th March 2018. He was 39 years old.
- Remigiusz Boczarski had been living in a bus shelter in Malvern when he died, apparently from suicide, on October 30, 2018, aged 40. A local woman who befriended him told press: "He would turn up at my door and I would wash his clothes and give him a meal. He was always a really nice guy. He never overstayed his welcome."

None of these men, living or dead, would get any sympathy from Professor Erin Dej of Wilfrid Laurier University in Canada who would dismiss them all as perpetuating hegemonic masculinity, performing hypermasculinity to fortify the dominance of men and the subordination of women, and adopting a "compensatory masculinity" to cope with their failed status, (Dej, 2018), (Airaksinen, 2018). No empathy gap there, then.

16.4 Loneliness

Loneliness impacts directly on wellbeing, but also impacts via its relationship to physical health (as we will see). There is no objective measure of loneliness. Measures of loneliness are inevitably subjective, being based on the subjects' self-reports of their own inner state, for example the DeJong Gierveld Loneliness Scale. Moreover, two people subject to identical conditions may have radically different perceptions of loneliness. Being alone, even for long periods, does not induce loneliness in everyone. The resilience to being alone without suffering the negative emotion of loneliness is highly individual.

Government-sponsored surveys of loneliness have been carried out in both England and Wales. These studies used very different survey questions and so are not directly comparable. Nevertheless, it is of interest to compare their outcomes to identify aspects of similarity and difference, which are more likely to be due to the differing methodologies than any major underlying national differences. This is done in the follow sub-sections.

16.4.1 Loneliness Survey in England

The English survey was published by ONS as 'Loneliness: What characteristics and circumstances are associated with feeling lonely?', (Office for National Statistics, 2018ag). Respondents were asked the question 'how often do you feel lonely?', with possible answers being often/always, some of the time, occasionally, hardly ever or never. (We will see below that the contrast with the Welsh survey is that respondents themselves were left to judge what psychological states or feelings corresponded to "feeling lonely").

In 2016/17, 5% of adults (aged 16 years and over) in England reported feeling lonely often/always, 16% of adults reported feeling lonely some of the time, and 24% occasionally. 55% of adults reported feeling lonely hardly ever or never. The English survey indicates a slightly greater incidence of loneliness amongst women than amongst men (Figure 16.5), though a more nuanced picture will emerge from the Welsh data when different types of loneliness are distinguished. In passing I note that Figure 16.5 does not fit well with a stereotypical view of women as more gregarious and men as more likely to be 'loners'. However, the data may be skewed by the excess of widows over widowers.

Far more marked, however, is the age dependence of loneliness (Figure 16.6). One might reasonably have guessed that old people would suffer most from loneliness, after being pre-deceased by their partners. But it is young people who are the most likely to be lonely, especially those under 25, but also those under 35 to a lesser extent. What is not clear is whether this is an effect of age, or is a change in societal behaviour which has, as yet, only manifested in the young. There is some evidence that it is the latter. Society may be becoming lonelier.

Figure 16.7 shows how loneliness depends upon marital status, divorce/separation or being widowed. It would appear that being married protects against loneliness, not surprisingly. One might reasonably postulate that the prevalence of loneliness amongst the young is a result of the delay of, and decline of, marriage. If so, it is not really due to age, but due to a change in society, and so is likely to persist as today's young people grow older. Loneliness appears set to become more common.

Figure 16.5: *Sex Dependence of Loneliness According the ONS-English Survey Definition*

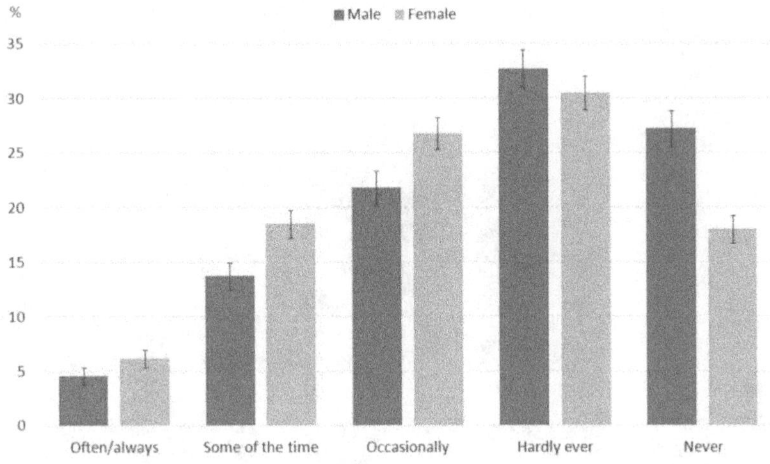

Figure 16.6: *Age Dependence of Loneliness (ONS-English survey)*

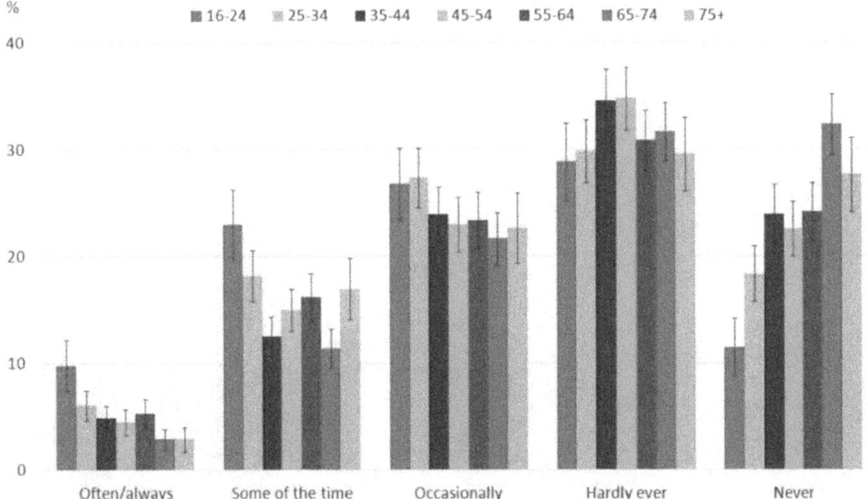

However, the starkest correlation with loneliness was general health, see Figure 16.8. People who reported their general health to be bad or very bad were far more likely to report feeling lonely, often or always, and substantially less likely to say they hardly ever, or never, felt lonely. Conversely, people who said their general health was good or very good were significantly less likely to report feeling lonely often/always, or even some of the time, and significantly more likely to report hardly ever, or never, feeling lonely. This confirms the correlation claimed above between loneliness and general health.

Figure 16.7: *Loneliness Dependence on Marital Status and Living Arrangements (England)*

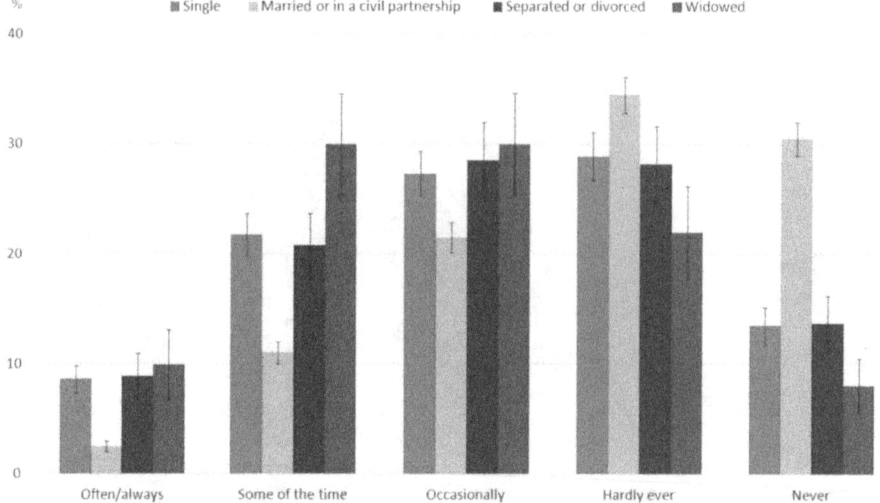

Figure 16.8: *Loneliness Relationship with General Health (England)*

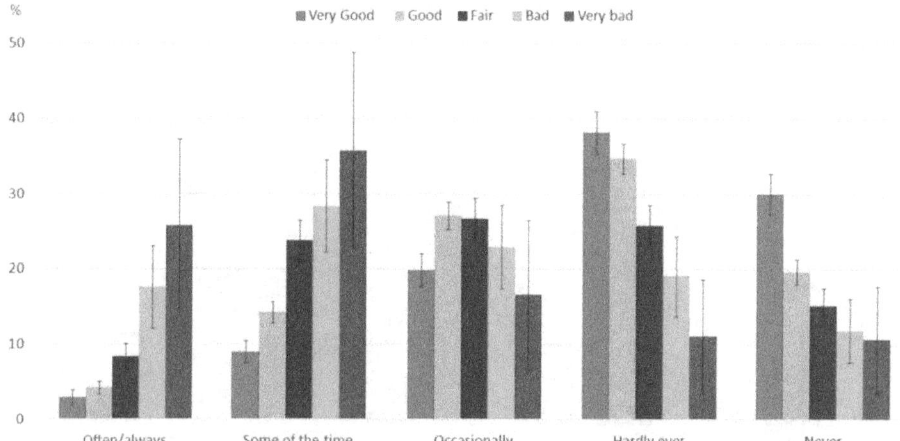

16.4.2 Loneliness Survey in Wales

Loneliness in Wales was measured for the first time in the 2016/17 National Survey, using the De Jong Gierveld 6-point loneliness scale, (Welsh Government, 2018c). This was very different in methodology from the English survey. Respondents were asked to state which, if any, of the following six statements applied to them,

- 'I experience a general sense of emptiness'
- 'I miss having people around'
- 'I often feel rejected'
- 'There are few people I can rely on when I have problems'
- 'There are few people I can trust completely'
- 'There are not enough people I feel close to'

For each respondent this results in a score from 0 to 6 depending upon how many statements apply. A score of 4 or more was defined as "lonely". 17% of respondents were found to be lonely based on this definition.

The De Jong Gierveld questions permit two distinct types of loneliness to be captured separately: emotional loneliness, defined by questions [1-3], and social loneliness defined by questions [4-6]. This distinction turns out to be crucial in extracting gender dependence of loneliness.

As with the English survey, loneliness was found to be significantly more common amongst the young than the old. Double the proportion of people under 45 were identified as lonely (20%) compared to people over 65 (11% or fewer).

Again as found in the English survey, there is a very clear relationship between loneliness and general health (Figure 16.9). Physical ill health is strongly correlated with being lonely, but this effect disappears in the oldest age group. For the youngest age group (16-24), having a limiting long-term illness increases the probability of loneliness from 15% to 46%. For the over 75s, the probability of loneliness is 10% irrespective of health issues.

Figure 16.9: *Loneliness in Wales (2016/17) Against General Health*

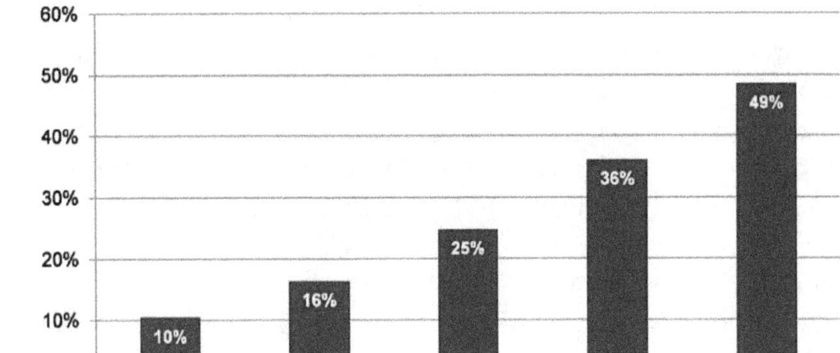

A strong association was found between loneliness and mental well-being as measured using the Warwick-Edinburgh Mental Wellbeing Scale (WEMWBS), Figure 16.10. Mental well-being is measured based on four issues: being less satisfied with life, thinking that things you do in life are less worthwhile, having lower levels of happiness, and raised levels of anxiety. After controlling for other factors identified as related to loneliness, the first three of these wellbeing measures were all found to be related to loneliness.

Figure 16.10: *Loneliness in Wales Versus Subjective Wellbeing*

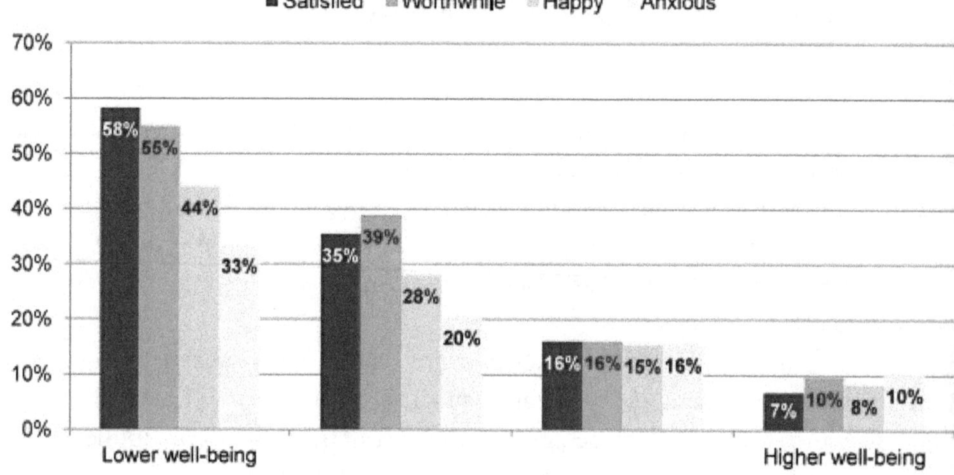

As regards the overall loneliness scale, in contrast to the English survey there was no significant effect of household type. Nor was there a significant effect of gender when the overall loneliness scale was used. However, a more interesting picture emerges when considering emotional and social loneliness separately. For this purpose, emotional loneliness was defined as scoring 2 or more out of questions [1-3], above, whilst social loneliness was defined as scoring 2 or more from questions [4-6].

What now emerges is that emotional loneliness is very strongly related to household type and age (Figure 16.11), whilst social loneliness is related to gender, being worse for men. Social loneliness is more prevalent (34%) than emotional loneliness (20%).

43% of single parents reported emotional loneliness compared with 16% of adults in a two-adult household with children (reducing to 10% for married pensioners without children), see Figure 16.11. However, some of the factors found not to be associated with emotional loneliness, after controlling for other factors, were gender, educational attainment, economic status or rural versus urban living.

However, a gender effect was found in respect of social loneliness. Recall that the social loneliness subscale is based on the relevance of the statements: "there are few people I can rely on when I have problems", "there are few people I can trust completely", and, "there are not enough people I feel close to". When controlling for other factors, social loneliness was found to be increased by being a man, by being middle aged, by being single, separated, divorced or widowed, by being an internet user, and (perhaps most unexpectedly) by having higher level qualifications.

Figure 16.11: *People who are Emotionally Lonely, by Household Type*

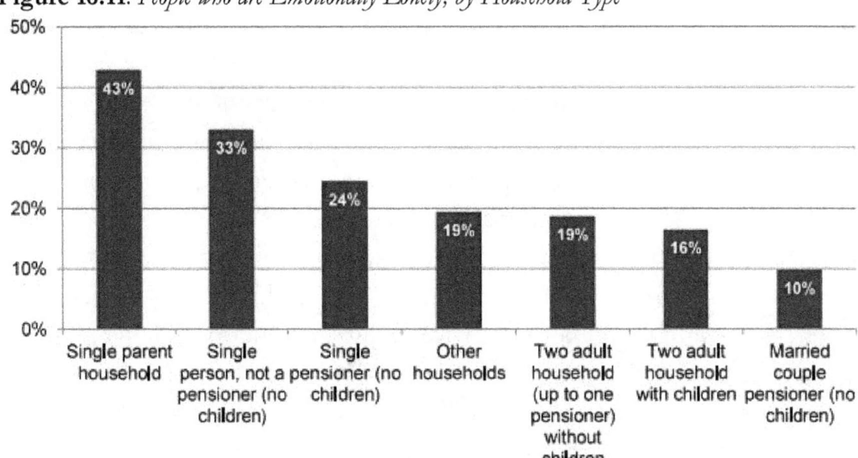

16.5 The Empathy Gap in Homelessness and Loneliness

There are three levels of homelessness: the statutory homeless, the "single homeless" who have failed to attain a designation as statutorily homeless, and a sub-set of the latter, the rough sleepers. The number of the statutory homeless considerably exceeds the number of rough sleepers. Details are incomplete for all UK nations but the number of men applying for housing assistance is at least comparable with the number of women. The Scottish and Northern Irish data show that single male applicants are strongly dominant at the point of application. Despite the reverse gender ratio at application, those actually housed, or placed on the priority register, tend to be skewed towards women. This is predominantly due to prioritisation where children are involved, and the fact that 92% of single parents are mothers.

The overwhelmingly dominant demographic in the Main Homeless Duty in England are families headed by a single mother (47%).

However, there may be a gender bias in addition to this effect. In Wales, similar total numbers of men and women were assessed, but substantially fewer men than women were housed, despite substantially more men than women being deemed 'eligible, homeless, and subject to a duty to help to secure housing'. Even for people deemed 'eligible, unintentionally homeless and in priority need', men were less likely to be housed than women.

The numerical dominance of men among rough sleepers may be one of the outcomes of the above process. The result is that 84% to 86% of rough sleepers are men. The same sex ratio applies to those who die as rough sleepers. This is the ultimate "bottom line" of homelessness, and it is overwhelmingly male.

Perhaps against expectation, loneliness is more prevalent in young people rather than older people. Emotional loneliness is strongly related to living arrangements, being far more prevalent amongst single parents or adults living singly. The decline of marriage (see chapter 13) therefore suggests that loneliness will increase. Social loneliness, resulting from having an insufficient social network, is more prevalent in men and in middle age. Social isolation is severely exacerbated in men after partnership dissolution, and being ejected from an ex-partner's home is one of the possible causes of homelessness.

Consequently, gender skews in homelessness and loneliness are related to gender skews in parental roles and presumptions, and to parental separation. These imbalances work through the system and are ultimately visible to us all on the streets, including deaths, primarily of men.

17

Mental Ill-Health and Substance Abuse

Compare yourself to who you were yesterday, not to who someone else is today.
If you think tough men are dangerous, wait until you see what weak men are capable of.
When you have something to say, silence is a lie.
Jordan Peterson, *12 Rules For Life* (2018)

In this chapter I present a brief review of the prevalence of mental ill health, concentrating on data from surveys in England. The review breaks down into five parts, the first four being general mental disorders in adults, general mental disorders in children, substance abuse, and then the most acute mental illnesses which lead to being detained under the Mental Health Act (colloquially termed being "sectioned"). There are particular difficulties with mental health data, especially if differences due to age or sex are of interest, as they are here. Unlike physical illness, mental illnesses are not generally diagnosed by objective measurements. Whilst it is readily apparent to an observer that acute mental illness is a serious morbidity, diagnosis may be uncertain even in these cases. In less acute cases, diagnosis often relies on the sufferer's self-reported symptoms. Consequently, differences in apparent prevalence of a given disorder between the sexes, or between age groups, may reflect differences in subjective perception due to sex or age, rather than a genuine difference (whatever "genuine" might mean in this context). The reader should bear this in mind throughout this chapter.

A further source of uncertainty relates to the mental disorders themselves. There is a degree of arbitrariness in partitioning symptoms into constellations which are then taken to define a specific named disorder. The symptoms could be divided in alternative ways, and the boundaries between disorders may be ill-defined. This arbitrariness is considerably exacerbated by the use of differing diagnostic criteria for the same (or similar sounding) conditions by different investigators or different psychiatric bodies. This can lead to wide variations in reported prevalence, resulting in different sources being incomparable. In addition, comparison of mental disorders in children and adults may be frustrated by the use of different defined disorders. For example, "personality disorders" are not normally considered an appropriate category for children, whilst "behavioural disorders" are not usually considered appropriate for adults.

The final section considers the male-specific diagnostic guidelines published by the American Psychological Association (APA), and a document published by the British Psychological Society (BPS) which also includes male-specific diagnostic advice. I explain how these new initiatives are based on the currently dominant narrative on gender and why they conflict with the most elementary aspects of the empirical evidence. I examine how their perspective is an example of the empathy gap.

17.1 Mental Ill Health in Adults

Unless otherwise stated all the data given in this section will be taken from the report 'Mental Health and Wellbeing in England: Adult Psychiatric Morbidity Survey 2014', (McManus et al, 2016), based on a survey carried out for NHS Digital by NatCen Social Research and the Department of Health Sciences, University of Leicester, by 49 authors. Previous surveys had been carried out in 1993, 2000 and 2007, and results from these are included where appropriate to indicate trends. This reference should be consulted for the various screening procedures and diagnostic criteria used for the different disorders.

The severity of disorders was recorded using the revised Clinical Interview Schedule (CIS-R). A score of 12 indicates "symptoms warranting clinical recognition", whereas a score of 18 or more is considered severe and requiring intervention.

Before looking at individual disorders, the overall picture is one of generally increasing prevalence of mental disorders in both sexes (with some exceptions), with the prevalence in women generally exceeding that in men and also increasing faster in women (again with notable and important exceptions). For many conditions, there is a spike in prevalence for young women in the age range 16 to 24.

Virtually all mental disorders are strongly demographic dependent, being far more common in people living alone, in people with poor physical health, and in people who are unemployed or economically inactive. There is also a strong dependence on IQ, with mental ill health being substantially more prevalent amongst those with low IQ.

17.1.1 Common Mental Disorders

The following common disorders are collected together under the designation CMD (Common Mental Disorders),

- Generalised anxiety disorder (GAD)

- Depression
- Phobias
- Obsessive compulsive disorder (OCD)
- Panic disorder
- CMD-NOS (not otherwise specified)

Figure 17.1 shows that the prevalence of CMDs has increased in both men and women since 1993, but less so in men since 2000. Based on all disorders upwards in severity from "warranting clinical recognition" (CIS-R 12+), the prevalence in 2014 was 20.7% in women and 13.2% in men. So, as an average over all ages, adult women are more than 50% more likely than men to experience CMD symptoms.

Figure 17.1: *CMD Symptoms Reported in the Previous Week by Sex, 1993 – 2014, Adults (16 – 64). Severities measured by CIS-R of 12+ and 18+ shown separately.*

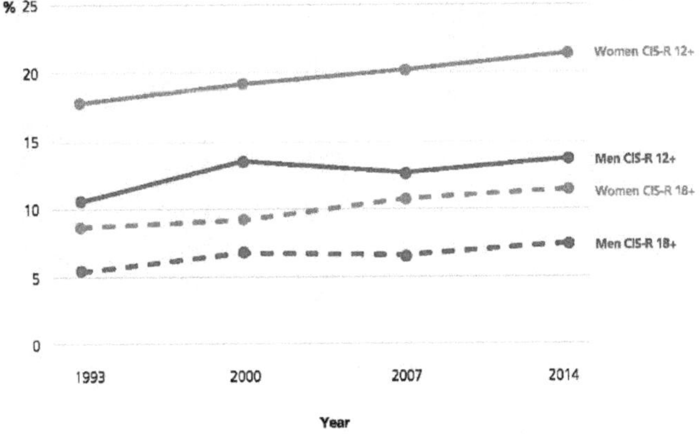

Figure 17.2: *CMD Symptoms Reported in the Previous Week by Age and Sex in 2014, Adults (16 – 64), for CIS-R of 12+*

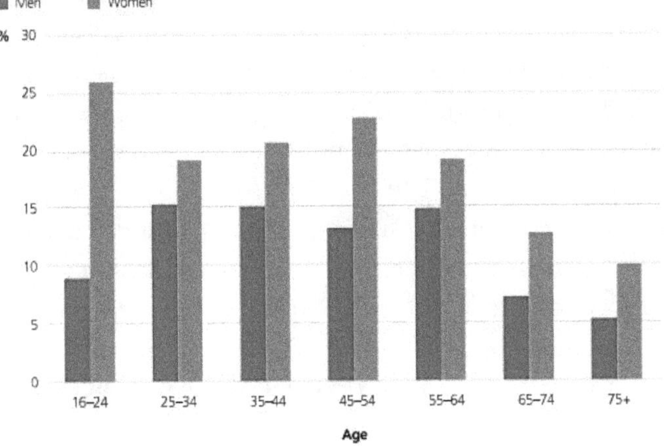

Figure 17.2 breaks down the prevalence of CMDs by age. Women experience more CMDs than men at every age. But there is a particularly pronounced 'spike' in the prevalence of CMDs in women aged 16 to 24. This pattern will be seen in other mental disorders, below.

The most common of the CMDs are those in the non-specific category, followed by generalised anxiety disorder and then depression. The prevalence of OCD is less than 2% at all ages, and panic disorders less than 1%.

Figure 17.3 shows the prevalence of CMDs against an estimate of verbal IQ (estimated based on performance in the National Adult Reading Test). People with a verbal IQ less than 80 are nearly twice as likely to suffer CMDs as those in the above-average intelligence range (110+).

Figure 17.3: *Presence of Any CMD Versus Predicted Verbal IQ*

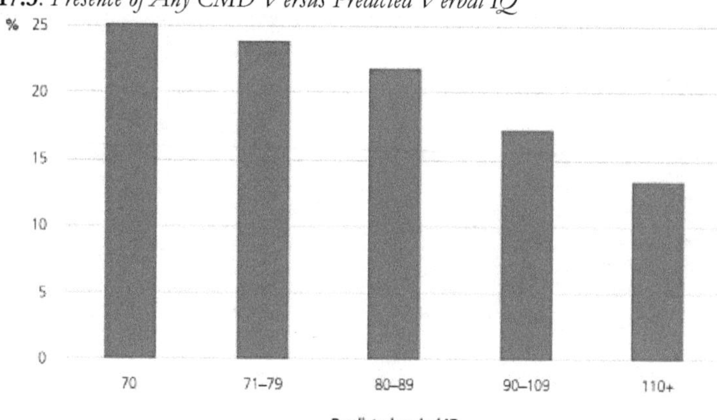

17.1.2 Personality Disorders

Personality disorders are of particular interest in the context of gender because they can play a major role in relationship conflicts, and hence in issues relating to the family courts, child contact, domestic abuse allegations and parental alienation. The two most serious forms of personality disorder are Antisocial Personality Disorder (ASPD) and Borderline Personality Disorder (BPD). There is a broader class of personality disorders but I shall confine attention here to ASPD and BPD.

ASPD is defined as a pervasive pattern of disregard for, and violation of, the rights of others that has persisted in the individual since the age of 15 or earlier. Diagnostic criteria generally require at least three of the following symptoms: failure to conform to social norms, irresponsibility, deceitfulness, indifference to the welfare of others, recklessness, failure to plan ahead, irritability and aggressiveness.

The ASPD rate was found to be higher in men (4.9%) than women (1.8%). Age dependence was significant. In 18 to 24 year old men the prevalence was 6.4%-6.6% and in 18 to 24 year old women the prevalence was 3.3%. In the oldest age range (55-64) the prevalence reduces to 4.1% and 0.4% for men and women respectively. The variation with age is shown in Figure 17.4.

Figure 17.4: *Screening Positive for ASPD and BPD in the Last Year (both sexes combined)*

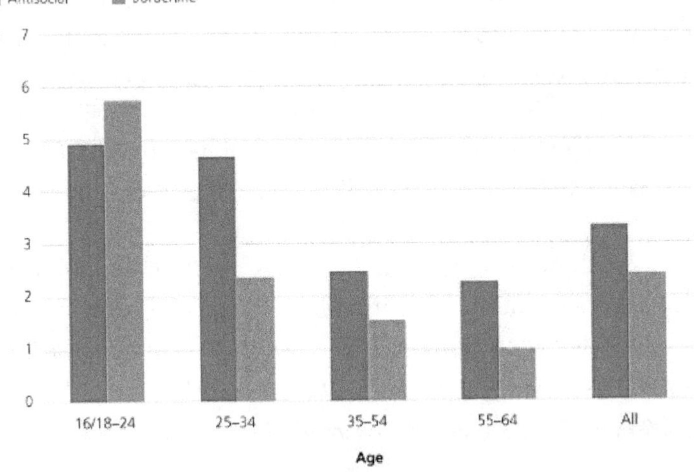

BPD is characterised by unstable relationships with other people, unstable sense of self and unstable emotions combined with marked impulsivity, and these indicators start in early adulthood. Diagnostic criteria usually require five or more of the following symptoms,

- Frantic efforts to avoid real or imagined abandonment;
- Pattern of unstable and intense personal relationships;
- Unstable self-image;
- Impulsivity in more than one way that is self-damaging (e.g., spending, sex, substance abuse, binge eating, reckless driving);
- Suicidal or self-harming behaviour;
- Affective instability;
- Chronic feelings of emptiness;
- Anger;
- Paranoid thoughts or severe dissociative symptoms (quasi-psychotic).

More women (2.9%) than men (1.9%) screened positive for BPD, but the 95% confidence intervals overlapped (i.e., the difference was not deemed statistically significant). Younger people were more likely to screen positive for BPD than older people, and this age dependence was more marked in women than in men. Positive BPD screening was nearly six times more common in the 16-24 age range than the 55-64 age range (Figure 17.4).

This marked age dependence of the prevalence of BPD contrasts with stability being a defining feature of the condition. But Figure 17.4 is cross-sectional, not longitudinal, data. It may be tempting to interpret Figure 17.4 as implying that as the current 16-24 cohort ages into middle age the prevalence of BPD will reduce substantially. If so, then the condition is not stable (i.e., not always persistent) as is usually claimed. However, this assumption is not justified. If, alternatively, the condition genuinely is stable, then the ~6% prevalence of BPD in the 16-24 cohort will persist as this cohort ages into middle age and beyond, and BPD will increase in the population as a whole. Only time will tell which of these interpretations is correct.

Figure 17.5 shows that age dependence is also marked in the totality of personality disorders and that the incidence in the two sexes is very similar. The exception is for women in the 16-24 age range which shows the spike in prevalence which is common in many mental disorders.

Figure 17.5: *Screening Positive for Any Personality Disorder by Age and Sex*

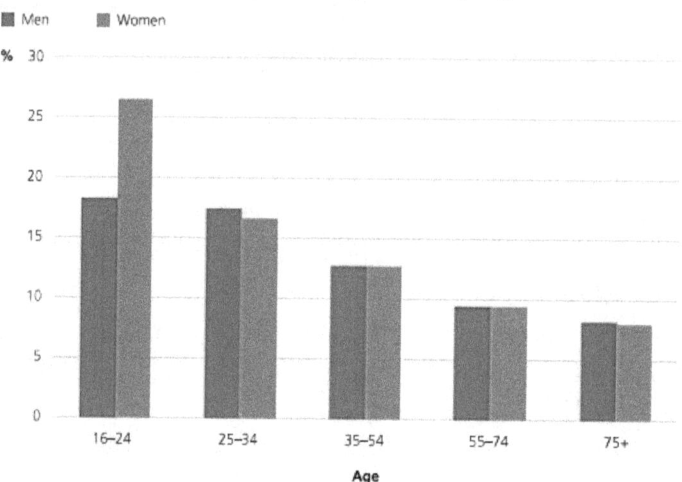

17.1.3 Autism Spectrum Disorders

Autism spectrum disorders (ASDs) are developmental disorders characterised by widespread abnormalities of social interaction and communication, as well as severely restricted interests and highly repetitive behaviours. Practices have varied, but currently (and in this section) such subtypes as Asperger's syndrome are included within the ASD category. There has been some public concern over the apparently rising incidence of ASDs. To quote the 'Mental Health and Wellbeing in England: Adult Psychiatric Morbidity Survey 2014' (McManus et al, 2016),

> 'The number of diagnosed cases of autism increased steeply throughout the 1990s. It is quite possible that this was due to changes in public and professional awareness of the condition, different diagnostic definitions and practices, availability of services and referrals, and earlier age at diagnosis. Nevertheless, the current evidence available does not rule out the possibility that the prevalence of ASD has increased.'

Figure 17.6 shows the prevalence of ASDs in adult men and women in 2007 and 2014. The apparent decrease in prevalence is not statistically significant due to relatively low statistics.

Figure 17.6: *Prevalence of Autism Spectrum Disorders in Adults, 2007 and 2014*

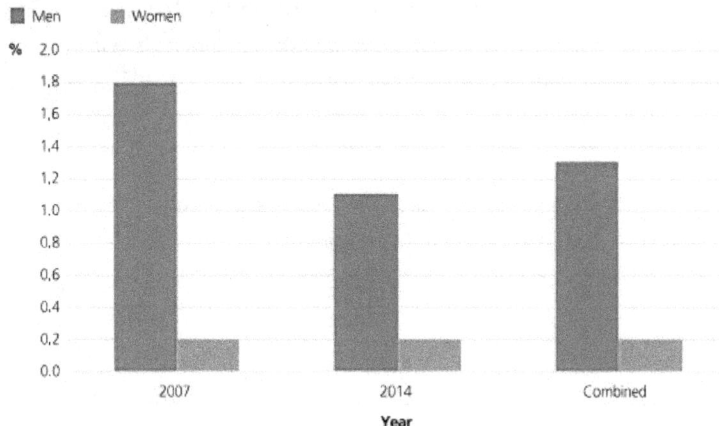

The incidence of ASDs in men is at least six times greater than in women. The association of ASDs with males, and the nature of some of the symptoms, has even led some researchers to regard autism as being the result of an "extreme male brain", (Baron-Cohen, 2012).

There is a caricature of the autistic as a savant: a person with extraordinary ability in some very narrow area. Another caricature, of the Asperger's personality, is a young man with non-existent social skills and dubious personal habits who rarely leaves his IT-rich man-cave but has an IQ of 160 and can hack into the Kremlin and the Pentagon at will. The reality for the overwhelming majority of people with ASDs is rather different from either caricature. ASD is known to be strongly associated with learning disabilities. Amongst all people with a degree the prevalence of autism was found to be only 0.2%. In contrast, amongst men with no educational qualifications the prevalence was 3.2%. The caricature of the autistic as a nerdy genius is not generally true, though these types also exist.

17.1.4 Psychotic Disorders

Psychotic disorders produce disturbances in thinking and perception that are severe enough to distort the subject's perception of reality. The main types are schizophrenia and affective psychosis. Organically induced psychoses, such as dementia and Alzheimer's disease, are not included in this section.

Figure 17.7 indicates the prevalence of psychotic disorders by sex and age. For both men and women, psychosis is most common in the age range 35 to 44. This is unusual, as it is most often the 16 – 24 age range in which mental disorders are most common, especially for women. Across all ages, 0.5% of men and 0.6% of women were identified with psychosis in the last year. Figure 17.7 indicates that there is little difference in the prevalence in men and women over 35, but that women under 35 are more than twice as likely as men to suffer psychotic complaints. However, the text of the Mental Health and Wellbeing in England: Adult Psychiatric Morbidity Survey 2014, (McManus et al, 2016), states that, over all ages, there was no statistically significant difference in incidence between the sexes.

In general I do not focus on ethnic differences. However, in the case of psychotic disorders there is such a marked ethnic dependence that it would be remiss to omit any mention of it. The prevalence of psychotic disorders in black men was ten times higher than that in white men (3.2% cf 0.3%). Amongst Asian men it was four times higher (1.3%). But there was no significant variation by ethnic group among women. These facts suggest a strong genetic component to psychotic disorders.

Figure 17.8 plots the prevalence of psychotic disorders against an estimate of verbal IQ (based on performance in the National Adult Reading Test). People with a verbal IQ less than 80 are between 4 and 9 times more likely to suffer psychosis than people with above average intelligence (110 and above).

Unsurprisingly, suffering from a psychotic illness is negatively correlated with employment. Economically inactive people were far more likely to have a psychotic disorder (2.3%) than those in employment (0.1%). 80% of people suffering from psychotic disorders were receiving treatment, almost all of whom were on medication, though about half of such people were also in active psychological therapy. Very few were in counselling without medication. This high treatment rate contrasts with other forms of mental disorder for which treatment rates are far lower, and this reflects the more serious nature of the condition.

Figure 17.7: *Psychotic Disorders in the Last Year by Age and Sex (2007 and 2014 data combined)*

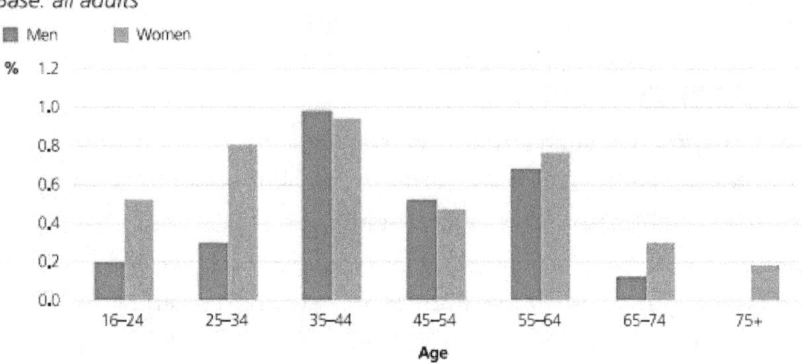

Figure 17.8: *Prevalence of Psychotic Disorders Against Estimated Verbal IQ*

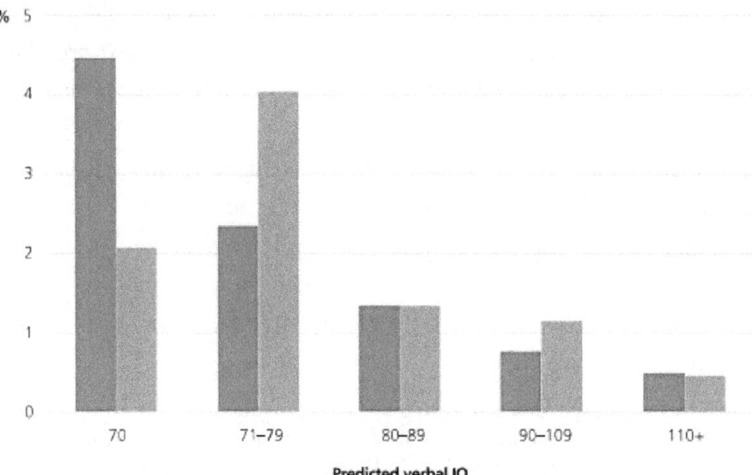

17.1.5 Attention Deficit Hyperactivity Disorder (ADHD)

The Mental Health and Wellbeing in England: Adult Psychiatric Morbidity Survey 2014, (McManus et al, 2016), states that, '9.7% of adults screened positive for ADHD, with similar rates for men and women'. Such high prevalence is surprising, as is the equality between the sexes. This is probably due to the particular diagnostic criteria deployed. Discussion of hyperactivity disorders is deferred to section 17.2.4 where data for children and young adults is presented, including a discussion of the differing diagnostic criteria.

17.1.6 Post-Traumatic Stress Disorder (PTSD)

The Mental Health and Wellbeing in England: Adult Psychiatric Morbidity Survey 2014, (McManus et al, 2016), defines traumatic events as,

> 'an event or experience like a major natural disaster, a serious automobile accident, being raped, seeing someone killed or seriously injured, having a loved one die by murder or suicide, or any other experience that either put you or someone close to you at risk of serious harm or death.'

Individuals exposed to such trauma may subsequently develop post-traumatic stress disorder (PTSD). This is a severe and disabling condition, characterised by flashbacks, nightmares, avoidance, numbing and hypervigilance.

Figure 17.9 shows the percentage of people in each age range who have experienced trauma at least once in their life. Positive screening for PTSD is far less common than the experience of trauma itself (4.4% cf 31.4% across all ages and sexes), see Figure 17.10.

The study states that 'screening positive for PTSD did not vary by sex'. However, Figure 17.10 suggests this is only true for people older than 24. In contrast, women in the age range 16 to 24 were three times more likely than men to screen positive for PTSD, and also about three times more likely than older women. This is despite the incidence of trauma being essentially the same for women of all ages (Figure 17.9). This suggests that young women in the age range 16 – 24 are more susceptible to an adverse psychological effect arising from a given traumatic event than are older women (or men of any age). This would be consistent with the spike in the prevalence of many other mental disorders in young women of this age. In this respect it is worth noting that the study observes that,

> 'research has shown that subjective appraisal of threat is more important for the development and maintenance of PTSD than objective trauma severity….. Epidemiological studies of PTSD typically rely on a subjective assessment by the participant as to whether a particular event was sufficiently severe to justify being a trauma and self-reported assessment of their symptoms – raising the possibility of reporting bias.'

The converse effect is apparent in older people. Both men and women are subject to substantially reduced rates of PTSD when over 65, despite experiencing comparable levels of trauma. PTSD therefore appears to be partly a measure of susceptibility or perception or resilience.

What remains to be seen is whether the current 16-24 cohort of young women will retain their vulnerability as they age, and so continued to be identified with PTSD at elevated rates compared to older women currently, or whether they will become more resilient with age as Figure 17.10 suggests.

Figure 17.9: *Percentage of People Who Have Experienced at Least One Trauma in Their Lifetime (by age and sex)*

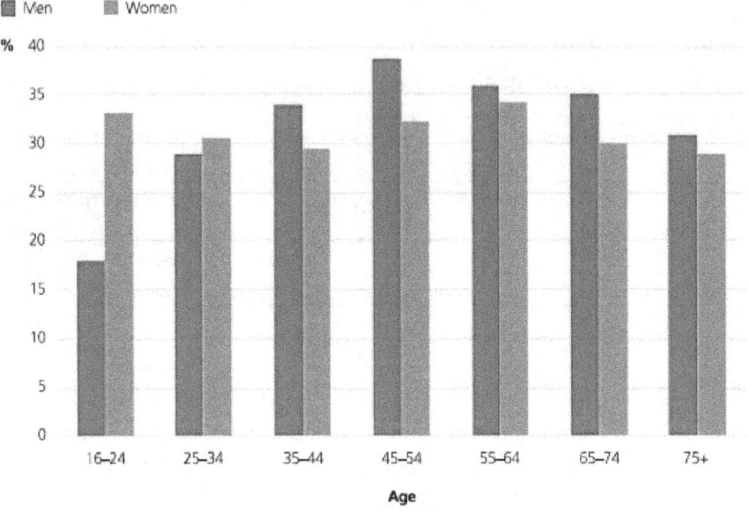

Figure 17.10: *Screened Positive for PTSD by Age and Sex*

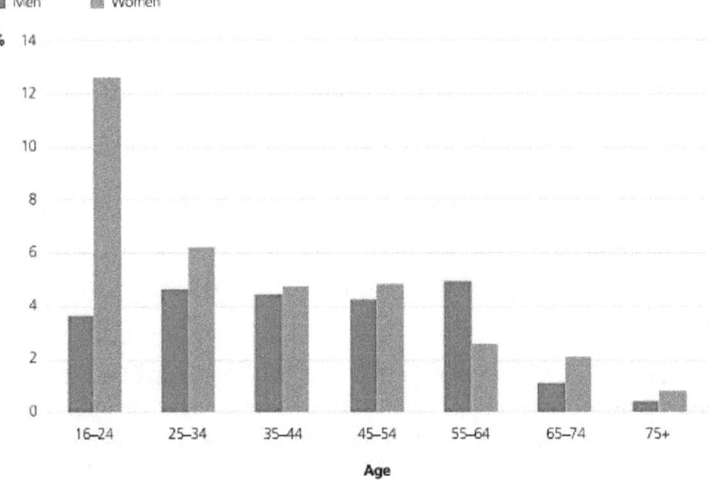

17.1.7 Bipolar Disorder

Bipolar disorder, previously known as manic depression, is a common, lifelong, mental health condition. It is characterised by recurring episodes of depression and of mania (feelings of elation and overactivity). Prevalence is around 2% with no significant difference between the sexes. It is more common when young (3.4% at 16-24) but decreases linearly to very low rates in the over-65s (<0.4%)

17.1.8 Mental Disorders and Employment

There is a very strong relationship between mental illness and unemployment or economic inactivity, see Table 17.1. This may be because the mental disorder frustrates gaining, or retaining, employment, or it may be because unemployment promotes mental ill health.

Table 17.1: *The Relation Between Employment Status and Prevalence of Mental Illness*

Mental Illness	Employed		Unemployed or Economically Inactive	
	Men	**Women**	**Men**	**Women**
CMD	11%	20%	24%	34%
PTSD	2.5%		10%	
Psychotic disorders	0.1%		2.3%	
Autism spectrum	0.7%		1.2%	
Personality disorders	12%		31%	
ADHD	7.5%	7%	24%	15%
Bipolar disorder	2%	1.8%	5.6%	3.3%
Drug dependency	4.5%	2%	9.5%	3%
Suicide attempts	4%	8%	20%	13%
Accessing treatment for those with CIS-R = 12+	27%		53%	

17.1.9 Access to Treatment by Demographic

Women are generally more likely to be receiving treatment for mental health conditions than men. In part this is due to a slightly greater overall incidence of mental disorder in women. But women receive significantly more treatment even after controlling for this factor. The Mental Health and Wellbeing in England: Adult Psychiatric Morbidity Survey 2014 (McManus et al, 2016) notes,

> 'In unadjusted analysis, women in the population were more likely to report mental health treatment than men. This was true both for medication and for psychological therapy. Overall, 16.5% of women and 9.6% of men received treatment of some sort. The mean CIS-R score in women was 1.8 points higher than that in men. The treatment gap was, however, more evident among those with fewer CMD symptoms (CIS-R 11 or less). After controlling for differences in CIS-R, women remained significantly more likely to get treatment than men (OR 1.58 compared to unadjusted OR 1.80).' (NB: OR = odds ratio)

Despite the incidence of mental disorders being greater in the lower socioeconomic classes nevertheless poorer people are less likely to be receiving treatment. For people with a CIS-R score of 12+, it is more than twice as likely they will be receiving treatment where the household income is above £36,228 than where it is below £17,868.

In respect of the relevance of race in receiving treatment for mental disorders, the Mental Health and Wellbeing in England: Adult Psychiatric Morbidity Survey 2014, (McManus et al, 2016), notes, 'After further controlling for other factors in the final model, people in the Black/Black British group had the lowest odds of being in receipt of treatment (OR 0.27, compared with the White British group).' Most people will interpret this as arising from discrimination or another form of race-based disadvantage. Fewer people will interpret the reduced frequency of treatment for men in a similar way.

17.2 Mental Ill Health in Children and Young Adults

The data in this section on mental disorders in children and young adults is taken from official statistics published by NHS Digital and the UK Government Statistical Service. The survey from which these data were collected involved 9,117 children aged 2 to 19 in England between January and October 2017. The summary report is (NHS Digital, 2018a). Behind the summary there are a sequence of topic reports, available from (NHS Digital, 2018b), which have also been used as sources here.

17.2.1 All Disorders

Childhood disorders are classified differently from those in adults. In the reports found in (NHS Digital, 2018b) the categories used were,

- Emotional disorders
- Behavioural disorders
- Hyperactivity disorders
- Autism spectrum disorders, eating disorders and other less common disorders

These will be discussed in turn in the following subsections. Nearly two-thirds of those aged 5 to 19 who exhibited one disorder also displayed at least one other disorder (possibly within the same category).

Perhaps the most important of all the findings in respect of gender is illustrated by Figure 17.11, which shows the prevalence of all mental disorders by sex and by age. Recall that section 17.1 has shown that the prevalence of mental disorders in adults is greater in women than in men. Contrast this with

Figure 17.11 which shows that boys under 11 suffer a greater incidence of mental disorders than girls the same age. In the early teenage years (11 to 16) the incidence becomes the same. But, consistent with section 17.1 for adults, by young adulthood, ages 17 to 19, the prevalence of disorders has become more than twice as great in females as in males.

Figure 17.11: *Percentage of Any Mental Disorder by Age and Sex, 2017*

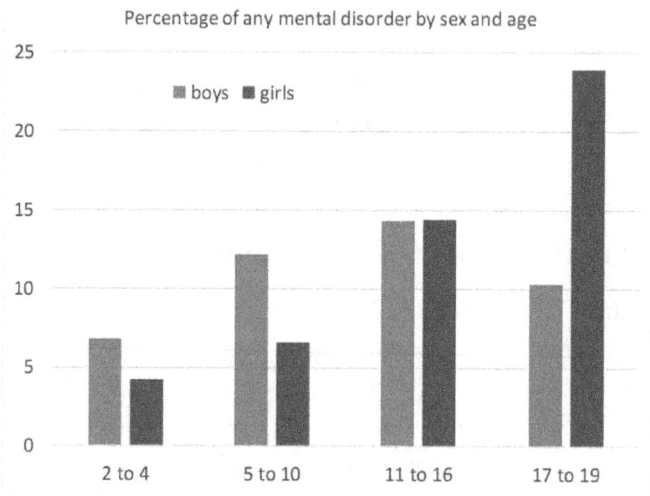

Figure 17.12 shows that the incidence of disorders is higher in boys in age range 5 to 15 and that the prevalence in both boys and girls has increased since 1999.

Figure 17.12: *Trend in All Mental Disorders, 1999 – 2017, by Sex, Ages 5 to 15*

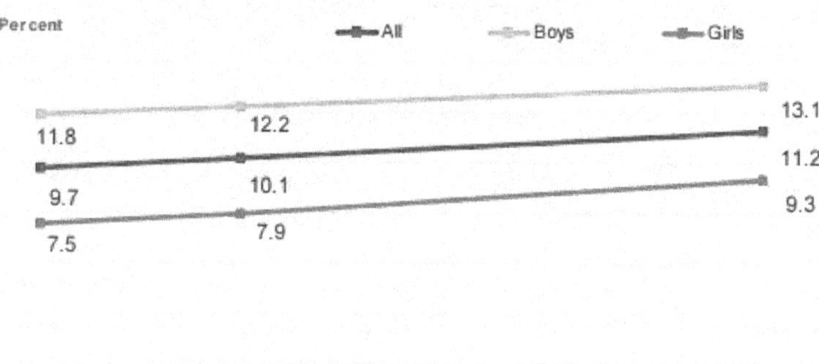

Figure 17.13 shows that emotional disorders are dominant in terms of prevalence in teenagers. We shall see that this is what leads to women having

the greater overall prevalence of disorders in the 17 to 19 age range, as it is women who experience emotional disorders most. In contrast, up to age 10 it is behavioural disorders which dominate, and the majority of these are boys.

Figure 17.13: *Rates of the Different Mental Disorders, Ages 2 to 19*

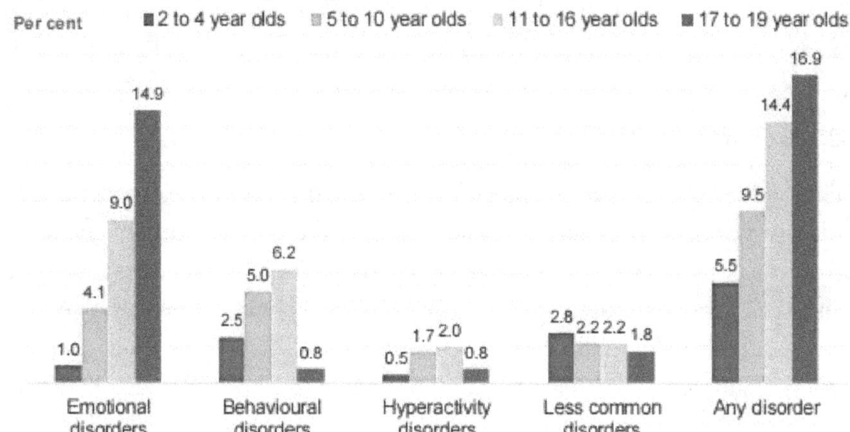

17.2.2 Emotional Disorders

Emotional disorders comprise anxiety disorders, depression and bipolar disorder. The anxiety disorders include OCD, phobias, panic disorder, PTSD and body dysmorphia. Consistent with the preceding discussion, Figure 17.14 shows that, whilst the prevalence of emotional disorders are comparable between the sexes prior to age 10, thereafter there is an increasing difference. In the age range 17 to 19, women are nearly three times more likely to experience emotional disorders.

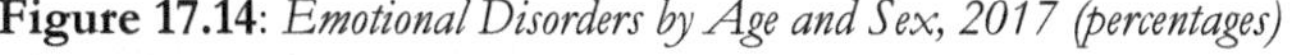

Figure 17.14: *Emotional Disorders by Age and Sex, 2017 (percentages)*

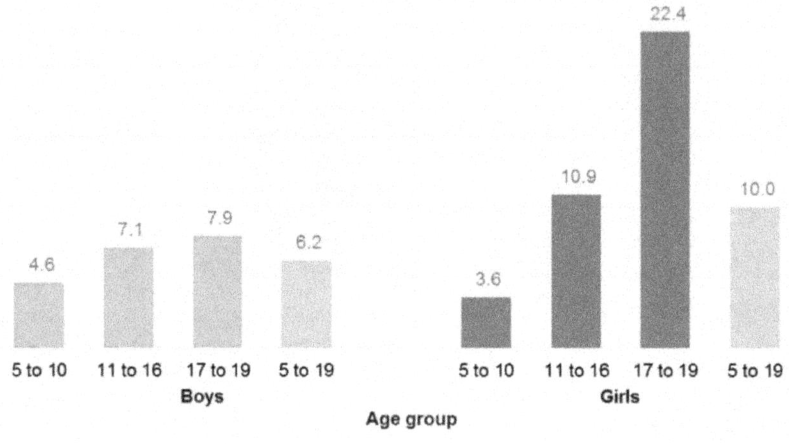

The prevalence of emotional disorders is strongly related to family circumstances. Family functioning was measured using the General Functioning Scale of the McMaster Family Activity Device. It comprises 12 statements that parents rate on a four point scale. A score was derived, with scores above 2 considered to indicate 'unhealthy' family functioning. Emotional disorders were found to be five times more prevalent for family functioning scores above 2.5 than for scores below 1.5.

17.2.3 Behavioural Disorders

Behavioural disorders are characterised by repetitive and persistent patterns of disruptive and antisocial behaviour in which the rights of others and social norms or rules are violated. Their presence in childhood is required for certain adult psychiatric diagnoses, such as antisocial personality disorder. The main subtypes are oppositional defiant disorder (ODD) and conduct disorder. ODD is characterised by temper outbursts, arguing with adults, disobedience, deliberately annoying others, passing on blame, being easily annoyed, resentful, spiteful and vindictive. Conduct disorder consists of engaging in antisocial behaviours such as shoplifting or stealing cars.

Behavioural disorders are more common in boys than girls (see Figure 17.15) but reduce markedly in those aged 17 to 19 for both sexes. ODD is nearly six times more prevalent if special educational needs are present, and nearly four times more prevalent in the lowest quintiles of family income compared with the top quintile.

Figure 17.15: *Behavioural Disorders by Age and Sex, 2017*

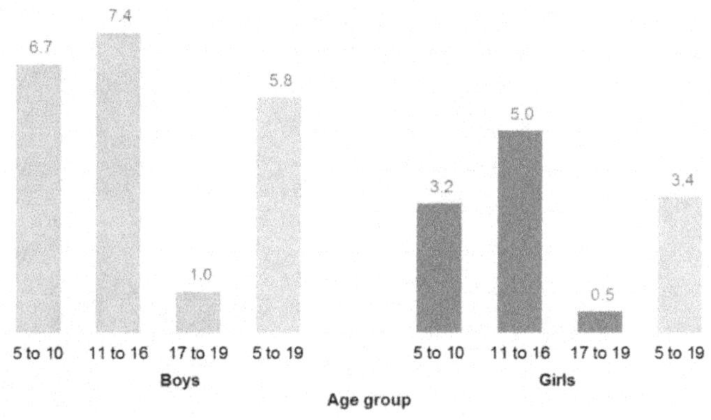

17.2.4 Hyperactivity Disorders

In section 17.1.5 I deferred discussion of ADHD (attention deficit hyperactive disorder) because of a need to clarify the different diagnostic criteria which lead to wildly differing reported prevalence rates. The status of differing diagnostic standards has been explained in (NHS Digital, 2018b) thus,

> 'Hyperactivity disorders can be identified by two official sets of diagnostic criteria: the International Classification of Diseases 10th Revision (ICD-10) and the Diagnostic and Statistical Manual of Mental Disorders fifth edition (DSM-5). The results in this survey are based on the ICD-10 classification of hyperactivity disorders. ICD-10 is the official classification system in the UK, and has been used in the 1999 and 2004 surveys of the mental health of children and young people in England.
>
> The ICD-10 classification of hyperkinetic disorder is similar to the DSM-5 classification of ADHD. Both classification systems require symptoms to present themselves in several settings such as school or work, home life and leisure activities. However, the ICD-10 criteria for hyperkinetic disorder tends to be more restrictive than the DSM-5 criteria for ADHD in identification of hyperactivity disorders. For example, an ADHD diagnosis requires symptoms to be present by twelve years of age while symptoms of hyperkinetic disorder must be present by the age of seven. As a result, the rates of hyperactivity disorders presented in this report (based on ICD-10 criteria for hyperkinetic disorder) are likely to be lower compared to other surveys which utilise DSM-5 criteria (ADHD).'

For this reason the prevalence rates of hyperactive disorders in children to be discussed here, and based on ICD-10, will be substantially lower than the adult rate of 9.7% stated in section 17.1.5 and based on DSM-5/ADHD. Moreover, the more restrictive ICD-10 criteria will reveal a marked sex dependence for children which was absent from the adult data based on the DSM-5/ADHD measure.

Hyperactivity disorder is over four times more prevalent amongst boys than girls, Figure 17.16. About 3% of boys under 17 have a hyperactivity disorder to ICD-10. Hyperactivity disorder was also found to be substantially more prevalent amongst white British children than other ethnicities.

The prevalence of hyperactivity disorders is strongly related to family circumstances, being nearly six times more prevalent for family functioning scores above 2.5 than for scores below 1.5 (recalling that scores above 2 are taken to imply unhealthy family functioning). As always, causality must not be assumed. To quote the survey report, 'while problems with family functioning may contribute to the onset of hyperactivity disorders, the presence of hyperactivity disorders could also lead to problems with family functioning.'

Figure 17.16: *Hyperactivity Disorders by Age and Sex, 2017*

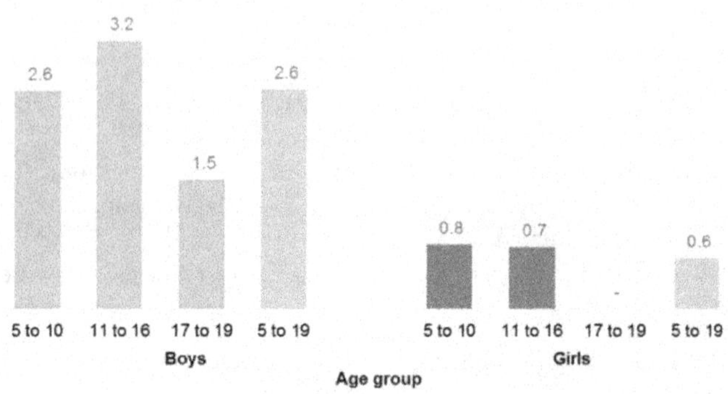

Children who were living with a parent in receipt of disability benefit were nearly five times more likely to have a hyperactivity disorder (5.8%) than children whose parents were not receiving disability benefits (1.2%).

17.2.5 Autism, Eating Disorders and Less Common Disorders

The other less common disorders assessed by the survey, (NHS Digital, 2018b), include autism spectrum disorders (ASD), eating disorders, and other types of disorder, including tics. The latter includes Tourette's syndrome.

ASD was five times more prevalent in boys (1.9%) than girls (0.4%). The survey data apparently indicated a decreasing prevalence of ASD with age, see Figure 17.17, but this is believed to be an artefact of the lack of third-party reports in the older age range. ASD is a persistent condition, so a longitudinal age dependence is not expected. The prevalence of ASD in boys in the age range 5 to 10 was 2.5% and this may be a better indicator of the true prevalence at all ages.

Tics and related disorders were twice as common in boys (1.1%) as in girls (0.6%). Eating disorders were seven times more common in girls (0.7%) than boys (0.1%). In young women, ages 17 to 19, the prevalence of eating disorders was 1.6%.

Across this whole class of disorders, and in the age range 5 to 19, boys showed higher prevalence (2.6%) than girls (1.6%). There is some indication that this class of disorders has had increasing incidence, but this was reported as not statistically significant. White British children were nine times more likely to have this class of disorder than black children, and more than three times more likely than Asian children.

The prevalence of this class of disorder was five times greater in the poorest functioning families (score > 2.5) compared with the best functioning families (score < 1.5). All three subtypes (ASD, eating disorders and tics) displayed substantial family functioning dependence.

Figure 17.17: *Autism Spectrum Disorders by Age and Sex, 2017*

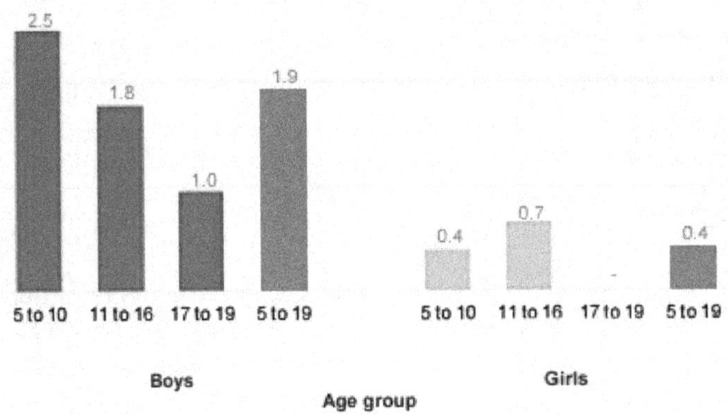

17.2.6 Mental Health Medication of Children

Psychotropic medication was being taken by about 2.5% of 5 to 19 year olds at the time the interviews were conducted, (NHS Digital, 2018b),

> 'The most commonly reported drugs were those used for treating hyperactivity disorders (stimulants 0.8%, atomoxetine 0.1%) and emotional disorders (antidepressants 0.9%). Melatonin, which is a hormone found naturally in the body and used to treat sleep disturbance, was reported for 0.7% of children.'

One in six children with a disorder was taking psychotropic medication. Prescribing rates were 14.8% for children with a behavioural disorder, 15.2% for emotional disorders, and approaching half (45.9%) of those with a hyperactivity disorder.

In 5 to 16 year olds with a disorder, stimulants and melatonin were the most likely types of medication to be prescribed, reflecting the higher rate of hyperactivity disorder in this age group (of which more than 80% are boys). The (NHS Digital, 2018b) survey reports that hyperactivity disorder has 'remained stable' between 1999 and 2017. But this does not sit easily with the fact that NHS prescriptions of stimulants and other drugs for use against ADHD has doubled between 2007 and 2017, (Sylvester and Bennett, 2018).

17 to 19 year olds with a disorder were most likely to be prescribed antidepressants. This is consistent with emotional disorders being the most common type of disorder identified at this age (of which 74% are girls).

17.2.7 Demographic, Lifestyle and Sexuality Factors

Taking into account the entire range of mental disorders, the following relationships between prevalence and demographic and other factors were found in 5 to 19 year olds.

17.2.7.1 Income

The prevalence of any disorder was 6.8% in the highest quintile of family income, but over twice as great in the lowest, and second lowest, quintile of income.

17.2.7.2 Ethnicity

White British children had the highest incidence of mental disorders (14.9%), larger than white non-British (8.3%), and nearly three times that of black or Asian children (5.2%-5.6%).

17.2.7.3 Sexual Identity

One in ten 14 to 19 year olds (10.2%) described themselves as lesbian or gay (1.7%), bisexual (6.3%), or "other" (2.2%). Girls were more likely to identify with a non-heterosexual identity (13.2%) than boys (7.1%). Young people who identified as lesbian, gay, bisexual or "other" were substantially more likely to have a mental disorder than those who identified as heterosexual. A disorder was present in 34.9% of young people who identified as non-heterosexual, compared to 13.2% of those who identified as heterosexual.

17.2.7.4 School Exclusion

Children with a disorder were ten times more likely to play truant (8.5%) than children without a disorder (0.8%). School exclusion was nearly 14 times more common in children with a disorder (6.8%) than in those without (0.5%). Boys with a disorder were four times more likely to be excluded from school (9.9%) than girls with a disorder (2.4%).

17.2.7.5 Family Functioning

Family functioning was associated with the presence of mental disorder. Over a third (38.2%) of children living in families with the least healthy functioning (score >2.5) had a mental disorder, compared to 8.3% in the most healthily functioning families (score <1.5).

17.2.7.6 Caring Responsibilities

Many children have caring responsibilities, despite their own tender age. This can consist of looking after family members, friends or neighbours because of either long-term physical or mental ill-health, disability, or old age. 18.4% of 11 to 19 year olds were identified with caring responsibilities, with similar rates in boys and girls. Overall there was not a significant impact of caring responsibilities on incidence of disorders.

Figure 17.18: *Percentage of Adolescents Aged 12 – 17 Who Had at Least One Major Depressive Episode in the Last Year (USA), after (Lukianoff and Haidt, 2018)*

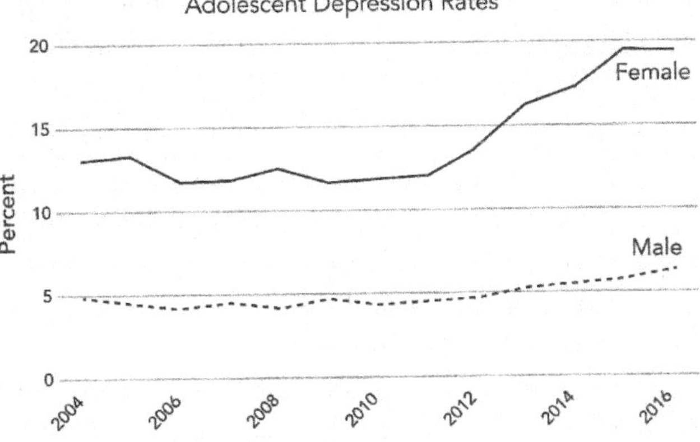

Figure 17.19: *Percentage of College Students Responding in the Affirmative to the Question "do you have psychological disorder?", after (Lukianoff and Haidt, 2018)*

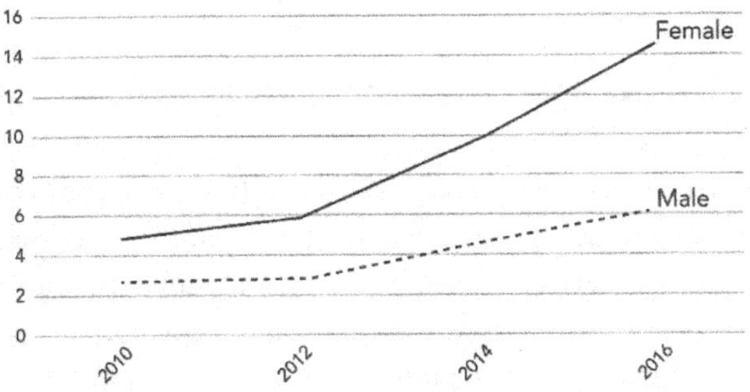

17.2.8 Teenagers and Students in the USA

In the book 'The Coddling of the American Mind', Lukianoff and Haidt (2018) present graphs reproduced above as Figures 17.18 and 17.19 which show recent steep increases in depressive episodes amongst adolescents and even steeper increases in psychological disorders amongst students in the USA. These increases have been concentrated on the years since 2011/12.

17.3 Substance Abuse

The issue of drug and alcohol abuse is extremely complex and it is not appropriate to attempt to tackle it here. Just a few bald statistics are given. It is possible to slip into addiction through recreational use of drugs or alcohol – they are, after all, pleasurable – at least initially. However, well-adjusted people without exacerbating factors will generally be alert to the dangers of slipping into addictive behaviours – though not always, and excessive alcohol usage in older and more affluent people without exacerbating factors has become increasingly prevalent, i.e., simply as a bad habit.

Alcohol abuse may result from a combination of genetic, psychological, environmental and social factors. Top risk factors are (i) stress, which may be work related, (ii) starting drinking at an early age, (iii) self-medication for a mental health condition, such as depression, (iv) family history of alcoholism, which may act genetically or through learnt behaviour, (v) normalisation of excessive consumption through peer group pressure. Illicit drug abuse shares most of these same characteristics. In the USA, a route to opiate addiction is via prescription drugs. Many illicit drugs are characterised by very rapid toleration, increasing required dosage and very high levels of addictiveness.

In chapter 14 the evidence was presented for parental separation, and specifically fatherlessness, increasing substance abuse amongst children. Not surprisingly, there are also many studies which show a link between alcohol abuse and a greater likelihood to divorce/separation. However, there remains a key question: does parental separation cause increased alcohol abuse? Anecdotally this seems likely, as in "drowning one's sorrows". But academic studies are now beginning to emerge which confirm the effect, for example (Kendler et al, 2017). This study was based on 950,000 Swedes born between 1960 and 1990 who married in or after 1990. The authors reported that, after divorce, the rates of alcohol use disorder (AUD) increased six-fold in men and seven-fold in women. These rates remained greatly elevated even after controlling for potential confounding factors, including prior problem behaviour, low parental education, and familial risk of AUD. It is much more common for research to concentrate on alcohol abuse as a causal factor in divorce. However one can discern indications in earlier work that people who are divorced consume the greatest amounts of alcohol while the lowest levels of alcohol consumption are found in those who are married, e.g., (Clarke-

Stewart, 2007). However, the extent to which parental separation or divorce precipitates alcohol abuse appears to require greater research attention.

17.3.1 Alcohol Abuse

Given the association of alcohol with increasing the prevalence of diseases, especially cancers, it is a moot point whether severe (alcoholic) levels of abuse cause more deaths than more common but lower levels of alcohol consumption. In fact, it would require premature death (before age 75) by cancers and cardiovascular diseases to be increased due to alcohol consumption by only 7% among people with "non-alcoholic" levels of drinking for this to dominate over premature deaths due to acute conditions among alcoholics. But only epidemiology can identify the increased risk to people from cancers and cardiovascular diseases: one cannot attribute the death of any individual from these common conditions specifically to alcohol. In contrast, the severe abuse of the alcoholic leads to specific, acute conditions which can be diagnosed and attributed unambiguously to alcohol abuse. Consequently, these acute alcoholic mortalities can be recorded and counted, and these form the basis of the statistics given here.

The ONS provides data for these alcohol related deaths disaggregated by sex, (Office for National Statistics, 2017k). In 2016 in England and Wales, there were 4,416 premature deaths of men (before age 75) attributed directly to alcohol abuse. The corresponding figure for women was 2,232. Hence, twice as many men than women die prematurely due to severe conditions unambiguously attributable to alcohol abuse. There are several different specific causes of death in this category. The conditions which account for virtually all premature deaths due to alcohol are,

- Alcoholic liver disease, 68%
- Fibrosis and cirrhosis of liver, 17%
- Mental & behavioural disorders due to alcohol use, 7%
- Accidental poisoning by alcohol, 6%
- Alcoholic cardiomyopathy, 2%

In addition, a large proportion of deaths in car accidents can be attributed to alcohol and these do not appear in the statistics for the overall destructiveness of alcohol abuse.

17.3.2 Drug Abuse

The ONS publish data on drug related deaths disaggregated by sex, (Office for National Statistics, 2017m). They distinguish between all drug poisoning, in which the underlying substance may be illicit or a prescription drug, and deaths due specifically to illegal drugs. In 2016 there were 2,572 deaths of men from drug poisoning, of which 1,899 involved illegal drugs. The corresponding figures for women were 1,172 and 697 respectively. Consequently there are more than double the number of drug poisoning deaths of men than women, and 2.7 times as many from illegal drugs.

17.4 People Detained under the Mental Health Act

People who are judged by qualified professionals to be a danger to themselves or to others may be detained in secure accommodation. The legislation covering such involuntary detainment is the Mental Health Act 1983, (Legislation UK Government, 1983), as amended by the Mental Health Act 2007, (Legislation UK Government, 2007). Involuntary detainment is colloquially referred to as "being sectioned", in reference to Sections 2 and 3 of the 1983 Act which address this legal procedure. The Act has separate provision in Sections 4 and 5 for Short Term Orders, which include an element of consent, and also Community Treatment Orders which are subject to recall to hospital for assessment. The statistics of people treated under the Mental Health Act gives an indication of the prevalence of the most serious disorders. The following data were taken from the 'Mental Health Act Statistics, Annual Figures 2016/17: Data Tables', (NHS Digital, 2017). The data relate to England only.

The number of people involuntarily detained ("sectioned") has increased each year from 2012/13 to 2016/17. In 2012/13 there were 50,408 detentions, increasing to 63,622 in 2015/16 (the last year for which complete data is available at the time of writing). Known detention rates were higher for males (83.2 per 100,000 population) than females (76.1 per 100,000 population). Note that this contrasts with the greater prevalence of most common mental disorders in adult women rather than adult men, including psychotic disorders, and the greater access to treatment services by women.

The number of people subject to Short Term Orders under Sections 4 and 5 of the Act has also increased each year from 2012/13. In 2012/13 there were 25,112 such orders, increasing to 35,955 in 2015/16 (the last year for which complete data is available at the time of writing). Known rates were higher for males (29.3 per 100,000 population) than females (22.3 per 100,000 population). Again this contrasts with the greater prevalence of most mental disorders in adult women and their greater access to treatment services.

Community Treatment Orders are less used, some 4,966 in 2016/17, but these again involve more men than women (corresponding to rates of 11.4 per 100,000 for men and 6.6 per 100,000 for women). The greater use of "sectioning", Short Term Orders and Community Treatment Orders for men than women, despite the apparently greater demand from women, may reflect a perception by the responsible authorities that men tend to pose a greater risk (though this is supposition on my part).

17.5 APA and BPS Guidelines for the Psychological Practice with Boys and Men

The American Psychological Association (APA) published their 'Guidelines for Psychological Practice with Girls and Women' some 12 years ago as I write, (American Psychological Association, 2007). The APA's equivalent 'Guidelines for the Psychological Practice with Boys and Men' was published only 11 years later, (American Psychological Association, 2018). The two documents read rather differently, though both are consistent with the dominant narrative on gender. The APA's guidelines for boys and men focus strongly on masculinity as a social construct and traditional masculinity as a source of harm. This met with widespread criticism when the guidelines were published. The criticism did not escape the APA's notice and they felt it necessary to issue a statement 'Addressing Media Misrepresentation of the Men's Guidelines', (MacDermott, 2019). The criticisms were not just from the media but also from some psychologists, for example John Barry (2019), one of the leading lights of the new Male Psychology Section of the British Psychological Society (BPS).

The BPS has not published formal guidelines on psychiatric treatment for boys and men, but it has published a large and radical document called the 'Power Threat Meaning Framework', with lead authors Dr Lucy Johnstone and Professor Mary Boyle, (British Psychological Society, 2018). This initiative seeks to overturn the whole basis of psychiatric diagnosis. The proposed radical alternative to conventional mental disorder diagnosis starts with questions such as, 'how is power operating in your life?' and 'what kind of threats does this pose?'. Therapy starts by asking, 'what did you have to do to survive?' and 'what access to Power resources do you have?' I do not intend to be drawn into a digression on the philosophical origins of this slant on mental ill health other than to note that, as these examples demonstrate, it puts victimhood and power at the centre of the proposed new conception of mental disorder.

The relevance of the 'Power Threat Meaning Framework' is that it includes a section on men. In this respect it is broadly similar to the APA guidelines for boys and men, being firmly based on the prevailing dominant gender narrative. The 'Power Threat Meaning Framework' has also attracted criticism, again including some psychologists, for example Martin Seager (2018).

The different approaches to the two sexes proposed by these professional institutions could not be more stark. Stripped down to its essentials, both claim that mental disorders suffered by men and boys are, in large part, due to "traditional masculinity", or patriarchy. Moreover, the mental disorders suffered by women and girls are also perceived as commonly the product of patriarchal society, i.e., "traditional masculinity". The 'Power Threat Meaning Framework' expresses how women's oppression under patriarchy is reinterpreted as mental disorder, noting the existing criticisms of…

> 'the psychiatric diagnostic system for systematically pathologising what are seen as women's rightful and reasonable responses to unreasonable events occurring in repressive, dangerous and damaging social contexts…..(some) psychologists have challenged abnormality as a construct and gender bias within psychiatric diagnosis, arguing that it is the "pathologies" of patriarchy, of racism, classism, heterosexism and ableism that are the "disorders" women suffer from, not "disorders of mental illness"'.'

It is startlingly bold to suggest that women do not, in fact, have mental illnesses, but that their appearance of mental illness is actually an artefact of their oppression – but this hypothesis appears to be seriously entertained. The APA's guidelines on women and girls also allude to men as culpable for women's mental disorders,

> 'Salient mental health statistics reveal that women are two times more likely than men to be depressed, and girls are seven times more likely than boys to be depressed. Women who are subject to group and individual discrimination are even more likely to experience depression. Girls and women are also roughly nine times more likely to have eating disorders than boys and men. Compared with men, women are two to three times more likely to experience many types of anxiety disorders. The abuse and violence in U.S. society (e.g., abuse, battering, rape) may contribute to the development of dysfunctional behaviors, such as eating disorders, depression, anxiety, and suicidal behavior, whereas discrimination against women and girls of color can result in lowered self-expectations, anxiety, depression, and negative attitudes toward self. In general, the physical and mental health concerns of women and girls are related to complex and diverse economic, biological, developmental, psychological, and sociocultural environments.'

No evidence is offered to support "abuse and violence" being responsible for women's elevated rates of "dysfunctional behaviours, eating disorders, depression, anxiety, or suicidal behaviour".

If I may indulge in personal opinion for a moment, I find it quite extraordinary that anyone can seriously entertain the idea that women in general lack agency. Perhaps it comes of being raised in a family with three older sisters. But neither the young women nor the grandmothers of my acquaintance align well with being helpless before an onslaught of ubiquitous abuse, as depicted in the APA's Guidelines.

Nevertheless, the APA claim that the origin of the mental health problems experienced by women and girls lie in society – and specifically patriarchal society - but not in the individuals themselves and certainly not in any generic problem inherent in "femininity". This contrasts sharply with the perceived origin of much of the mental ill health in men and boys, which is explicitly put down to men themselves, as individuals or as male society. Men are victims of their own pathology (traditional masculinity) and women too are victims of men's pathology. I will let the APA guidelines speak for both documents in some extracts which follow (omitting references, for which see the original).

> 'boys and men, as a group, tend to hold privilege and power based on gender' (see the Introduction)

It is not my intention to critique gender theoretical ideas such as this. However this perspective is relevant because of the claimed causal connection between "power", or lack thereof, and mental disorder (made explicit in the 'Power Threat Meaning Framework'). Attempts to refute that all men are powerful are futile: even homeless men, at the very bottom of our society, exhibit hegemonic masculinity, so we are told (Dej, 2018). The APA are clear in attributing blame for much of men's and boy's mental disorders on "traditional masculinity", e.g.,

> '...socialization for conforming to traditional masculinity ideology has been shown to limit males' psychological development, constrain their behavior, result in gender role strain and gender role conflict and negatively influence mental health and physical health.' (see section 'Need for Professional Practice Guidelines for Boys and Men')

What the APA mean by "traditional masculinity" is as follows,

> 'Masculinity ideology is a set of descriptive, prescriptive, and proscriptive of cognitions about boys and men (sic)......including: anti-femininity, achievement,

> eschewal of the appearance of weakness, and adventure, risk, and violence. These have been collectively referred to as traditional masculinity ideology.' (Definitions)
>
> 'traditional masculinity ideology can be viewed as the dominant (referred to as "hegemonic") form of masculinity that strongly influences what members of a culture take to be normative.' (Guideline 1)

One assumes that "anti-femininity" refers to homophobia, or to a reluctance to engage in touching or affectionate behaviour with other men.

These extracts are important because they make clear that what is being called "traditional masculinity" is assumed by APA to be the norm for men. Hence, in asserting that "traditional masculinity" is harmful, this carries the implication that essentially all men are culpable. The APA does not think at all highly of "traditional masculinity". Under Guideline 3 ('the impact of power, privilege, and sexism on the development of boys and men and on their relationships with others') we read,

> 'Researchers in the psychology of men and masculinity have identified that insecurities stemming from early childhood experiences (such as attachment insecurities) are linked to adherence to traditional masculinity ideology. Research also suggests that insecurely attached men not only rigidly adhere to sexist gender role ideology, that they may act on those schemas in ways that promote or justify intimate partner violence.' (sic)
>
> 'Traditional masculinity ideologies have also been linked to parenting concerns, including work-family conflicts.'

Based on the errors noted above, it seems that the Guidelines have not even been well edited to ensure grammatical English. Under Guideline 4 we read,

> '...several studies have identified connections between adult attachment insecurity and men's adherence to traditional masculinity ideologies.'
>
> 'Additionally, traditional masculinity ideology encourages men to adopt an approach to sexuality that emphasizes promiscuity and other aspects of risky sexual behavior….. Indeed, heterosexual men's adherence to traditional, sexist aspects of masculinity has been connected to sexual assault perpetration.'

Of the many harmful features which (we are told) are inherent within "traditional masculinity", emotional control – or stoicism – comes in for particular criticism, as does the (alleged) reluctance to express affection, or even to touch, other men, as follows,

> '...traditional masculinity ideology discourages men from being intimate with others…… Because of the pressure to conform to traditional masculinity ideology, some men shy away from directly expressing their vulnerable feelings and prefer building connection through physical activities, talking about external matters….. and seeking and offering practical advice with their male friends.' (Guideline 4)

> '...men experience conflict related to four domains of the male gender role.....(including) restrictive emotionality (discomfort expressing and experiencing vulnerable emotions); restrictive affectionate behavior between men (discomfort expressing care and affectionate touching of other men)' (Introduction)

> 'Psychologists can discuss with boys and men the messages they have received about withholding affection from other males to help them understand how components of traditional masculinity such as emotional stoicism, homophobia, not showing vulnerability, self-reliance, and competitiveness might deter them from forming close relationships with male peers.' (Guideline 4)

There is something disingenuous about the ostensible favour bestowed upon intra-male bonding in the above extracts, given that the same ideological lobby has vetoed the formation of men's groups on countless university campuses in the USA, Canada and the UK in recent years. The claims of homophobia, and men's inhibitions against affectionate friendships with other men, seem painfully out of date. For example, in their book 'Men and Maculinities', Eric Anderson and Rory Mcgrath (2019) write,

> 'Dozens of other ethnographic and qualitative studies show that young men today associate much more freely with symbols that were once coded as gay. As they do, those symbols lose their stigma.'

> 'In 2016 Anderson and McCormack.....utilized several large-scale surveys from several nations to show that decreasing cultural homophobia from the 1980s was sustained and profound. They next highlighted that.....qualitative research on gay and bisexual men show(s) that their lives are dramatically better now than they were in the 1980s.'

> '... the decline of cultural homophobia in the West means the stigma attached to homosexuality - and any behaviors related to homosexuality - has been largely removed. In such a context, men are no longer culturally compelled to perform a rigid form of masculinity or avoid behaviors which would traditionally feminize them. Accordingly, the narrow range of gendered presentation has been extended, meaning that men are able to embrace a same-sex friendship to the point of a bromance.'

The difference between the APA guidelines for males and for females could hardly be more startling. Mental ill health in females is due to their mistreatment by society, especially its male component, whilst men are to blame for their own ills. Nor can this be evaded by appeal to it being applicable to only a few pathological men. The text makes clear that "traditional masculinity", complete with its array of claimed pathologies, is the dominant form of masculinity which society takes to be normative. The different treatment of men and women recommended by the APA has formed the basis of a Title IX complaint against Harvard University, who partner with the APA and whose program in clinical psychology is accredited by the APA, (Airaksinen, 2019). (Title IX is a US federal law prohibiting discrimination on the basis of sex in an educational institution's programs or activities).

Bringing all the above extracts together, we see that the APA are claiming that "traditional masculinity" causes men to be prone to partner violence, family problems, sexual assault perpetration, and being emotionally stunted, homophobic loners - not forgetting being the cause of women's mental ill health as well. Absolutely no sexism or empathy gap there, then.

Did the authors ask themselves what effect these views were likely to have on prospective male patients? I can only speak for myself: should I ever suffer from a mental disorder, I am now firmly deterred from seeking help from these professionals. This is ironic in view of the APA writing,

> 'Research suggests that socialization practices that teach boys from an early age to be self-reliant, strong, and to minimize and manage their problems on their own yield adult men who are less willing to seek mental health treatment.' (Section 'Need for Professional Practice Guidelines for Boys and Men')

The APA guidelines attribute to stoicism, not just reluctance in help seeking, but also many of the ill effects themselves. Harvard psychologist and famous author, Steven Pinker, has referred to the APA's guidelines for boys and men as being 'blinkered by dogmas'. One of the dogmas is that gender is entirely a social construct, without regard to biological and genetic factors. The other dogma, Pinker argued,

> 'is that repressing emotions is bad and expressing them is good - a folk theory with roots in romanticism, Freudian psychoanalysis, and Hollywood, but which is contradicted by a large literature showing that people with greater self-control, particularly those who repress anger rather than "venting," lead healthier lives: they get better grades, have fewer eating disorders, drink less, have fewer psychosomatic aches and pains, are less depressed, anxious, phobic, and paranoid, have higher self-esteem, are more conscientious, have better relationships with their families, have more stable friendships, are less likely to have sex they regretted, and are less likely to imagine themselves cheating in a monogamous relationship.' (Edsall, 2019)

A paper published in February 2019, by the APA's PsychNET, comes to a very different view of traditional masculinity to the APA's guidelines for boys and men. Based on a survey of 1,233 people including a large percentage of transgender men and women (34%), Levant et al (2019) conclude, 'traditional masculine ideology may be a general and mental health protective factor for self-identified men, and a mental health protective factor for women, regardless of assigned sex at birth'.

I do not wish to be drawn into debates about gender theory, but some aspects are impossible to avoid in this context as the APA guidelines, for both sexes, are overtly gender political. For example, in the Guidelines for Psychological Practice with Girls and Women (2007) we read,

> 'Good practice requires that psychologists remain abreast of new developments in contemporary social forces and their interaction with gender and other social identities. Many contemporary issues could be cited here; however, four particularly salient and recent examples include (a) the increasing prevalence of global terrorism, violence, and war in which women are particularly victimized by vulnerability to rape, assault, and poverty; (b) the effects of the media in popular culture, which portrays an image of woman as thin, White, sexualized, and victimized; (c) biopsychosocial realities and changes relevant to women's reproductive experiences; and (d) the phenomenon of increasing lifespan with an aging population that consists mostly of women.'

Three of these four "social forces" impact adversely on men and boys even more than upon women, and yet there is no mention of them in the APA's Guidelines for the Psychological Practice with Boys and Men (2018). Why would that be? It is worth a digression to consider how these examples betray the depth and extent of the empathy gap.

To claim that women are victimised in violence and war is true; to claim they are *particularly* victimised is false. In simple statistical terms, men are the primary victims of war. As regards the direct deaths of combatants, this needs no defending (see section 7.3.2). Men are also the majority of the victims of violence generally, as we have seen for the UK in chapter 9. As for worldwide, the World Health Organisation confirms that the number of deaths of men associated with war and conflict in 2004 exceeded that of women by over five times (155,000 versus 29,000), and for violence outside of war, men's deaths exceed that of women by more than four times (485,000 versus 115,000), (Global Burden of Disease: 2004 Update).

Death is not the only measure of the impact of violence. "Disability-adjusted life year", or DALY, is calculated as the sum of the years of life lost due to premature mortality and the healthy years lost due to disability resulting from the violence. The impact of war on men in 2004, as measured by DALY, was nearly six times that upon women, whilst violence outside of war impacted men nearly five times as much. Similarly the DALY data for 2016 indicates that men are 2.4 times more victimised by "collective violence and legal intervention" and 3.5 times more impacted by "interpersonal violence", (World Health Organisation, 2018a).

Even war rape, which is usually assumed to be the particular province of female victims, is not confined to women and girls. One of the primary purposes of war rape is to humiliate the vanquished. In some conflicts, particularly those in Africa, the war rape of men is widespread. Anyone citing war rape is obligated to be familiar with the work of the Refugee Law Project, 'Gender Against Men' (Refugee Law Project, 2008), 'Investigating Conflict-Related Sexual Violence against Men in Africa' (Dolan, 2014), 'They Slept With Me' (Refugee Law Project, 2015) and 'The Rape of Men: the Darkest Secret of War' (Storr, 2011) and the associated TV documentary, 'An Unspeakable Act (Part2)' (BBC World Service, 2012).

I labour these off-topic points not only to emphasise that the APA's claim that women are particularly victimised by war and violence is false but also to illustrated that the absence of any mention of their impact upon men in their 2018 Guidance can only be interpreted as a disturbing asymmetry of empathy.

Some might opine that empathy is inappropriate because men start wars in the first place. But this is an example of the apex fallacy: blaming all men for the actions of a few. Exceedingly few men engaged in war ever want to be there. Down through the ages, the majority of fighting men would have preferred not to be the target of other men's violence. But men at war are either professional servicemen doing their duty, without option, or they have been conscripted to fight, without option. And the implied claim that female leaders would be less inclined to start wars and send men (yes, predominantly men) into battle is not born out by history, (Dube and Harish, 2017). In more recent UK history, the majority of female MPs in 2003 voted in favour of the UK joining the Iraq war (83 out of the 104 women who voted, a larger proportion of women MPs in favour of the war than male MPs). A majority of female MPs also voted in favour of bombing Syria (98 women in favour, 83 against).

As for the second of the APA's "social forces", some women may be unhappy about being portrayed in the media, in adverts and in dramas, etc., as unfailingly thin and sexualised, but for men this would be a considerable improvement on being almost always either a despicable villain or a bumbling oaf. Heroes these days are almost always heroines, (Nathanson and Young, 2001). And as for the APA's complaint that the media portrays women as victimised, this is remarkably hypocritical given that the entirety of their Guidelines for Psychological Practice with Girls and Women (2007) presents women as victimised.

The final "social force" which the APA mention as disadvantageous to women is their ageing population. There are, of course, many valid health concerns relating to the elderly, both mental and physical. And this ageing population, especially the over-80s, mostly comprises women. But it is rather peculiar to single out this phenomenon as a disadvantage to women, since the alternative – which applies to men – is being dead. It is not a particular disadvantage to women that they remain alive longer than men.

17.5.1 APA Versus Data

Rather than critique the hypotheses presented by APA and the 'Power Threat Meaning Framework' we can take a different approach: the scientific method. We can confront the implications of these hypotheses with the broad aspects of the data on mental disorders, in particular their gender dependence. What follows is not rigorous, it is heuristic: a "reasonableness check". I fully realise that different disorders have widely differing prevalence between the sexes.

Observation 1

If social constructionism were correct, as APA assume, there would be no difference between the prevalence of mental ill-health in very young boys and girls. In fact, there is a difference as indicated by Figure 17.11. Boys exhibit a significantly greater prevalence of mental disorders even at pre-school age (2-4) and up to age 10. This suggests an innate difference in the sexes. The far greater prevalence of behavioural disorders, hyperactivity and autism spectrum disorders in boys also points to innate sex differences.

Observation 2

If masculinity were entirely socially constructed and also largely to blame for men's and boys' mental ill-health, as APA propose, then the ratio of men's to women's prevalence of such mental ill-health should increase with age through childhood because the masculine cultural conditioning will not have occurred in very young children but will become far more marked towards puberty and throughout adolescence. In fact we see the opposite (Figure 17.11). Whilst boys show greater prevalence of mental disorders before the age of 10, in the age range 11 to 16 there is equality of prevalence, but after age 16 it is women who have the greater prevalence (Figures 17.2 and 17.11), and this is especially marked in the age range 17 to 24. Greater prevalence in young women is further illustrated by Figure 17.5 (personality disorders), Figure 17.7 (psychotic disorders) and Figure 17.10 (PTSD). Though there are disorders where males predominate, notably autism spectrum, hyperactivity and behavioural disorders, the latter two are largely childhood disorders whereas autism is probably largely genetic. There is nothing in these broad-brush observations to support the idea that socially constructed masculinity is a substantial cause of mental ill-health.

Observation 3

If traditional masculinity were a major cause of mental disorders in boys and men, as APA suggest, then over recent decades the prevalence of disorders in men and boys would be expected to have declined because boys and young men have become less 'macho' acculturated and more accepting of a softer, more emotive, nature, including markedly reduced homophobia, see (Anderson and Magrath, 2019). But actually the prevalence of disorders in men and boys has increased (Figures 17.1 and 17.12 for England, Figures 17.18 and 17.19 for the USA).

Observation 4

Over the last several decades, young women have become markedly more assertive, confident and often dominant in many social, educational and workplace settings. Violence in society generally has reduced, and domestic abuse in particular has reduced. If abuse were a central cause of mental disorders in girls and young women, as APA have proposed, then their prevalence would be expected to have reduced. In fact, the incidence of mental disorders in young women has increased markedly, substantially more than for young men (Figures 17.1 and 17.12 for England, Figures 17.18 and 17.19 for the USA).

Conclusion: The feminist theories of the APA and BPS's 'Power Threat Meaning Framework', based on the hypothesis that traditional masculinity is damaging, fail elementary reasonableness checks.

Here is an alternative hypothesis, offered by Barbara Kay, (The American Psychological Association goes to war against boys and men, 2019),

> 'All this depression and anxiety "may" come from female ideologues, who as educators and role models: routinely tell girls they can "be anything" and "have it all," which causes anxiety when "all" fails to emerge, as it almost invariably does; who encourage girls to explore their sexuality without letting emotion get in the way of healthy pleasure, but fail to warn them that promiscuity can leave them feeling sad and empty and humiliated; who valorize abortion, but fail to warn of abortion's frequent psychological impact; who deplore early commitment, even when a young woman and man happen to be right for each other; who encourage misandry by belittling or ignoring men's legitimate concerns, or fail to acknowledge men's legitimate contributions to society; who value career ambitions over motherhood; who confuse girls regarding the difference between being wooed and sexual misconduct; and of course who persuade girls and women that if they are unhappy, the reason never lies within, or from poorly-considered choices, but is always the

> fault of a "traditional" male asserting his privilege, or "social construction" that thwarts their self-realization.'

This perspective of Barbara Kay's does a better job than the hypothesis that "masculinity is harmful" in explaining the greater prevalence of mental disorders amongst women than amongst men. Note that Kay's last point, that young women are being taught to believe that all their woes are caused by men, is an encouragement to believe in a pervasive external locus of control. But this is known to be associated with mental ill-health. Teaching young women to adopt this exaggeratedly negative attitude towards men is therefore not only misandric, it is also imposing mental fragility upon women. If you are brought up to believe that the other half of the human race is dedicated to finding ways to abuse and assault you, it probably would not do your peace of mind much good. You might just suffer from an anxiety disorder.

On the other hand, if you are brought up to believe that you are the heir to an unbroken line of violent abusers, and that you are under universal suspicion of having acquired similar behavioural habits, then you are also unlikely to be in good psychological shape. This perspective is consistent with the most striking feature of recent data, namely the increasing prevalence of mental disorders in both sexes. In short, the APA's hypothesis originates from an ideology which may be driving increasing mental ill-health rather than the opposite, and the APA have adopted a position of complicity.

17.6 The Empathy Gap in Mental Health Perceptions

In adults, women are diagnosed with more mental disorders than men. However, even after controlling for this greater prevalence, women remain significantly more likely than men to be receiving treatment (by 58%). After controlling for other factors, including disorder prevalence and severity, lower rates of treatment were indicated by being poor, being black and being male.

In contrast, the prevalence of mental disorders is greater in boys under 11 than in girls the same age. The prevalence becomes the same in the early teenage range, 11 to 16. By late teenage, 17 to 19, the prevalence of mental disorders increases markedly in young women but falls in young men (Figure 17.11). This is confirmed by the adult surveys which show a very marked spike in the prevalence of many disorders in young women aged 16 to 24. The reason for this turn-around is that, up to age 10, it is behavioural disorders, hyperactive disorders and autism spectrum disorders which dominate, and in these boys are the majority. But in the teenage years, emotional disorders dominate, and in these girls are the majority.

Psychotropic medication was being taken by about 2.5% of 5 to 19 year olds when the survey was conducted in 2017. Below the age of 16 most of the medication was for hyperactivity, generally stimulants, around 80% of which are boys. In the 16 to 19 age range, prescriptions were mostly antidepressants for young women.

The incidence of disorders was strongly related to lower income and to disfunctional families. The incidence was also nearly three times greater in teenagers who identified as non-heterosexual.

School exclusion was nearly 14 times more common in children with a disorder than in those without. Boys with a disorder were four times more likely to be excluded from school than girls with a disorder.

The rate at which people are detained under the Mental Health Act is greater for men than women, despite the greater prevalence of mental disorders amongst women, and women's greater use of treatment services.

I have critiqued the APA's guidelines on psychological practice for boys and men, in contrast with those for girls and women. Mental disorders in the latter are claimed to arise largely from the assaults which society imposes on the psyches of women and girls. They need and deserve our assistance, which will include protecting them from these externally imposed harms. Mental disorders in men and boys, in contrast, are said to arise largely out of the pathologies of their own "traditional masculine" psychologies; men and boys are the architects of their own suffering – as well as the suffering of others. They are broken and need to concentrate on fixing themselves. In the different perceptions of male and female sufferers from mental disorders we see a particularly emphatic example of the empathy gap. It is disturbing that this is manifest in an area in which the subjects are so vulnerable. Yet the APA themselves note that,

> '...many men report experiencing gender bias in therapy...'

> '...investigations have identified systemic gender bias toward adult men in psychotherapy...'

> 'A disparity exists between the occurrence and severity of men's mental health problems and the disproportionately low number of men served by psychological services. It has been suggested that many men do not seek psychological help because services are not in alignment with masculine cultural norms that equate asking for assistance for psychological and emotional concerns with shame and weakness.'

Have the APA asked themselves whether blaming traditional masculinity might reinforce these perceptions of shame? Remarkably, the APA do not interpret these observations as a salutary lesson for their own practice. Instead of aiming to provide a therapeutic service aligned to the needs of the patient, the APA consider it more appropriate to demand that the patient change to align with their diagnostic preconceptions.

It is a pity the APA takes such a pejorative attitude towards men. A pernicious aspect of this stems from the refusal to contemplate an innate component to male psychology. As a result, they replace a man's shame at failing to achieve success in a perceived gender role with a profounder shame of his own nature. This is where the dearth of empathy takes you. The ultimate irony is that the APA's attitude, indeed the feminist position, is profoundly traditional itself, being based upon assumptions of men's agentic nature, and hence their culpability, as contrasted with women's lack of agency, and hence that their ills are imposed upon them by the agentic within society, namely men.

18

Suicide, Suicidality and Self-Harm

There is but one truly serious philosophical problem, and that is suicide.
Albert Camus, *The Myth of Sisyphus* (1942)

This chapter presents the statistics on suicide in the UK. It has become fashionable to lament the high rates of male suicide. This gives the impression, which one suspects the general public believe, that male suicide rates have increased in recent years. Is this correct? The data are presented here and provide a less simple picture than this suggests.

Whenever male suicide is mentioned in public utterances one can guarantee that reference will immediately be made to men's reluctance to talk about their feelings or to seek help. Is this valid? Or is it another example of the oblique victim blaming which so often follows any acknowledgement of male disadvantage? In this chapter I concentrate on the alternative, exogenous, factors which increase suicide rates: intimate partner separation and domestic abuse. The effect of separation or divorce on suicide rates will be seen to be more marked for men than for women. I then critique the dominant narratives which seek to rationalise high male suicide rates, confronting theoretical explanations based on hegemonic masculinity with elementary empirical observations.

Before turning to these aspects of completed suicides, I review the data on self-harm, suicidal ideation and suicide attempts. Together with data on mental disorders, the contrast between the female dominance in relation to these problems, and the emphatic male dominance as regards completed suicides, constitutes the suicide paradox. It is pointed out that this ceases to be paradoxical if, instead of assuming that suicide is always a result of mental illness, that instead exogenous factors might be dominant, especially for men.

Suicide in prison is not covered here as it has been addressed already in section 8.6.1.

18.1 Self-Harm, Suicidality and Suicide Attempts (England)

Data on self-harming, suicidal ideation and suicide attempts have been taken from McManus et al (2014), which is Chapter 12 of the Adult Psychiatric Morbidity Survey 2014, based on the English survey carried out for NHS Digital by NatCen Social Research and the Department of Health Sciences.

The data is based on answers obtained from both face to face interviews and self-completion questionnaires. For reasons of comparability, trends over time draw on the face to face reports, which tend to be lower. See the source for further details of the methodology.

Figure 18.1 shows the percentage of people who have ever self-harmed by age and against year. Self-harming has increased markedly between 2000 and 2014 for all age ranges. However, self-harm is far more prevalent amongst the youngest adults (ages 16 to 24) and reduces with age. People of retirement age are nearly 14 times less likely to self-harm than those aged 16 to 24. It is worth noting how remarkable this is. Whilst Figure 18.1 presents cross-sectional data, it has a longitudinal implication because the question asked by the survey related to having *ever* self-harmed. For those who were of retirement age in 2007, the answer was virtually zero – implying that even 40 or 50 years earlier, when they were at the most susceptible age, self-harming was extremely rare. This suggests that self-harm is almost entirely a recent phenomenon.

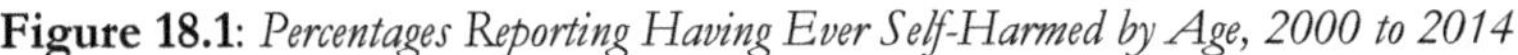

Figure 18.1: *Percentages Reporting Having Ever Self-Harmed by Age, 2000 to 2014*

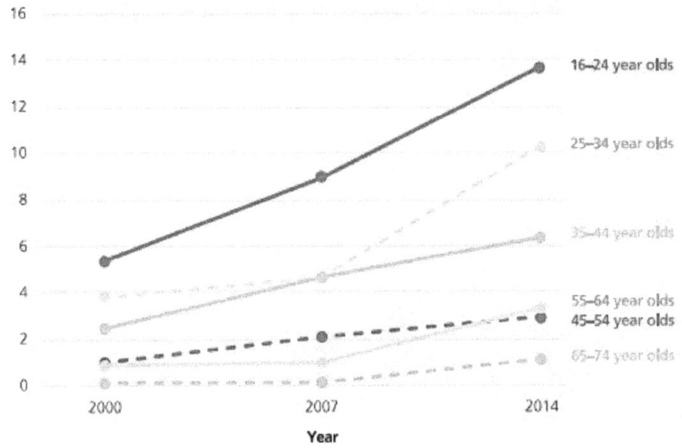

Figure 18.2 shows the prevalence of self-harming by sex in the most susceptible age range, 16 to 24. Self-harming has increased steeply for both sexes, doubling for men between 2000 and 2014, but tripling for women. Women were 65% more likely than men to self-harm in 2000. By 2014 they were 150% more likely.

Figure 18.3 shows the percentages of people who have ever had suicidal thoughts, broken down by sex and by age range. Figure 18.4 displays, in the same format, the percentages who have attempted suicide. These histograms illustrate a feature which was seen in chapter 17 to be typical also of mental disorders: there is a very clear 'spike' in prevalence amongst women in the age range 16 to 24. Apart from that, suicidal ideation is very similar between the two sexes, and quite flat until retirement age when it reduces substantially.

Figure 18.2: *Percentages of 16 to 24 Year Olds Reporting Having Ever Self-Harmed, by Sex, 2000 to 2014*

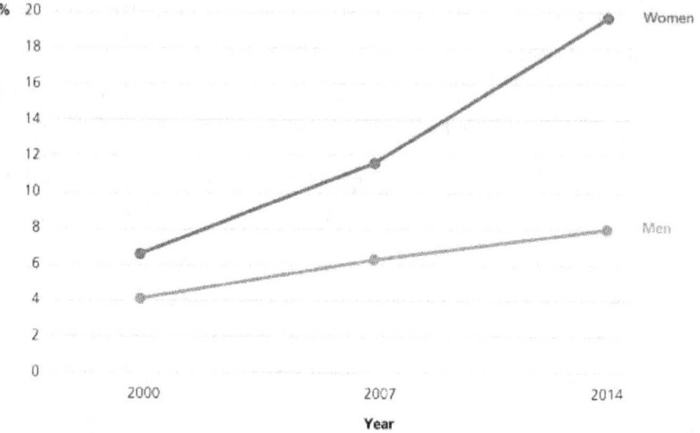

Figure 18.3: *Percentages Reporting Ever Had Suicidal Thoughts by Age and Sex, 2014*

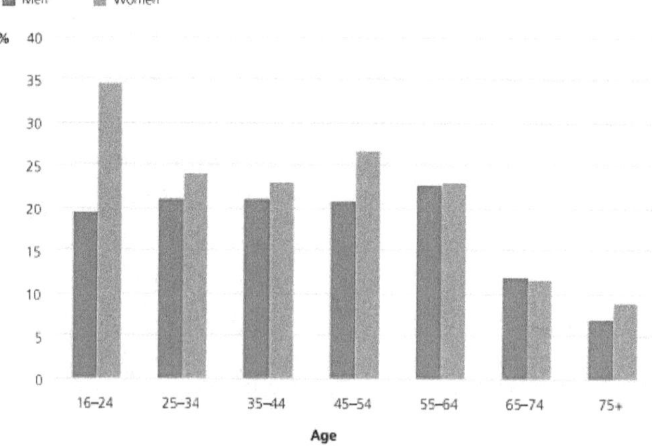

Suicide attempts by men peak in young men aged 25 to 34. This will be seen to contrast with completed suicides which are substantially less common below 30 than in the age range 30 to 60, peaking in the mid-40s.

Figure 18.5 shows the trends, between 2000 and 2014, in suicidal ideation and suicide attempts within the last year, comparing with self-harm at any time. Both self-harm and suicidal ideation have increased significantly. In contrast, suicide attempts have remained relatively stable. To quote the source, 'between 2007 and 2014, reporting of a suicide attempt in the past year remained stable at 0.7% of 16 to 74 year olds. Since 2000 there has been a slight increase, but only among women (0.5% in 2000, 1.0% in 2007)'.

Figure 18.4: *Percentages Reporting Ever Attempted Suicide by Age and Sex, 2014*

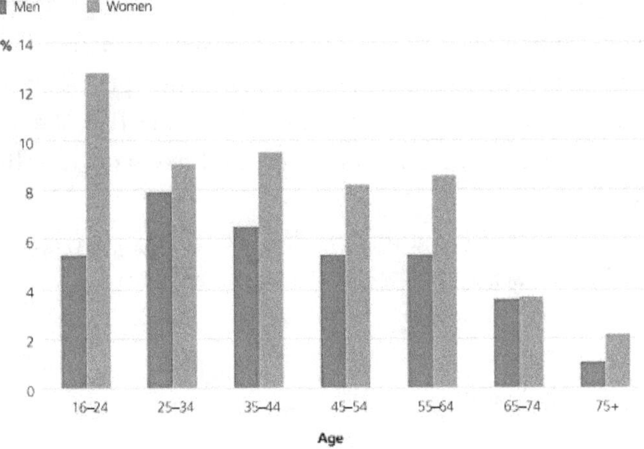

Figure 18.5: *Trends in Self-Harm (ever), and Suicidality and Suicide Attempts within the Last Year, 2000-2014 (all adults, 16 – 74)*

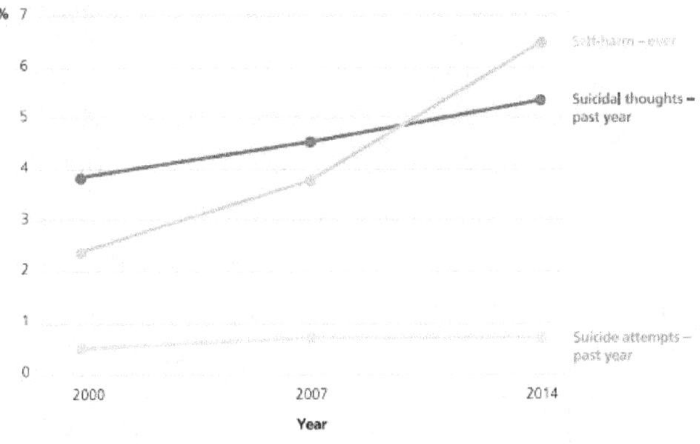

It is worth emphasising the huge difference in annual rates of suicidal ideation, suicide attempts and completed suicide. Over all adult age ranges and both sexes, these rates are 5.4% (suicidal ideation, 2014), 0.7% (suicide attempts, 2014) and, as we shall see in the next section, 0.01% (completed suicide, 2012-2016). Hence, only 13% of people with suicidal thoughts go on to attempt suicide, and only 1.4% who attempt suicide actually succeed. In the next section, when I address completed suicide, the reader might wish to bear in mind that suicide data is actually the extreme tail of a distribution of unhappiness.

Finally in this section I consider the relationship between self-harm, suicidal ideation, suicide attempts and indicators of mental disorder. In chapter 17 the CIS-R score was introduced as a measure of the severity of common mental disorders. Figure 18.6 plots the prevalence of self-harm, suicidal ideation and suicide attempts against CIS-R (larger scores indicate greater severity of disorder). There is a very clear relationship between mental disorder severity and self-harm, suicidal ideation and suicide attempts. The relationship appears to be roughly linear. For ages 11 – 19, Table 18.1 shows a similarly clear relationship between mental disorders and having ever self-harmed or attempted suicide.

Figure 18.6: *Suicidal Ideation, Suicide Attempts and Self-Harm (Ever) by Severity of Symptoms of Common Mental Disorders in the Last Week, 2014 (as measured by CIS-R score)*

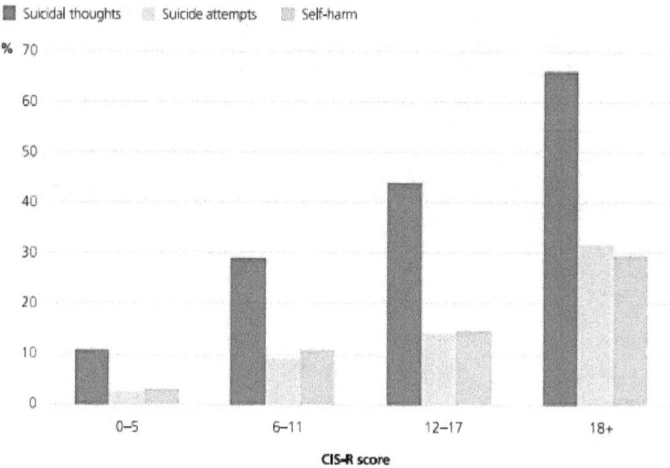

Table 18.1: *Percentages Ever Self-Harming or Attempting Suicide by Sex and by Reporting Any Mental Disorder*

Any Mental Disorder?	Ages 11 to 16		Ages 17 to 19	
	Boys	Girls	Boys	Girls
No	2.0%	4.0%	6.9%	11.7%
Yes	18.6%	31.2%	34.1%	52.7%

18.2 Suicide

18.2.1 UK Suicide Statistics and Trends

Suicide data for England and Wales has been taken from (Office for National Statistics, 2018s) for the years 1981 to 2016. These data refer to suicides of people aged 10 and over. Some suicide rate data from 1950 is also quoted and this was taken from Gunnell (2003). Suicide rates are defined per 100,000 of the population of the same sex and age range. Figures 18.7 and 18.8 give the number of suicides in England and Wales respectively, separately for males and females, between the years 1981 and 2016. The most striking feature of the data is that suicides of women have reduced markedly over this period, to about half their 1981 level, in both nations. In contrast, the number of male suicides in England has remained fairly flat. In Wales, however, the number of male suicides has increased, by perhaps 25% over the period (based on a running average).

Figure 18.7: *Number of Suicides in England, by Sex, 1981-2016*

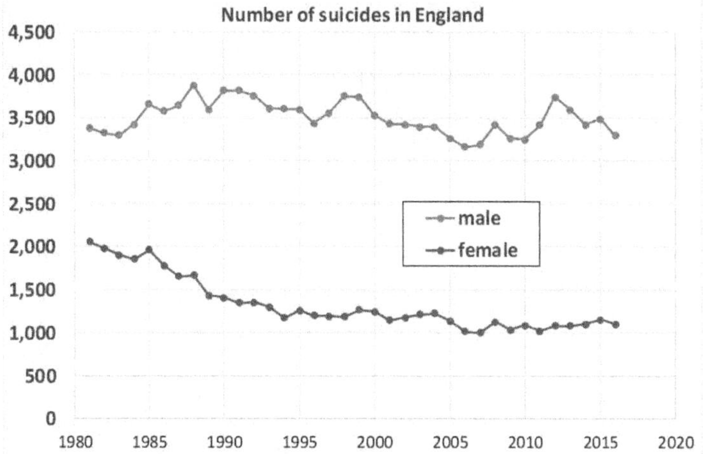

Figure 18.8: *Number of Suicides in Wales, by Sex, 1981-2016*

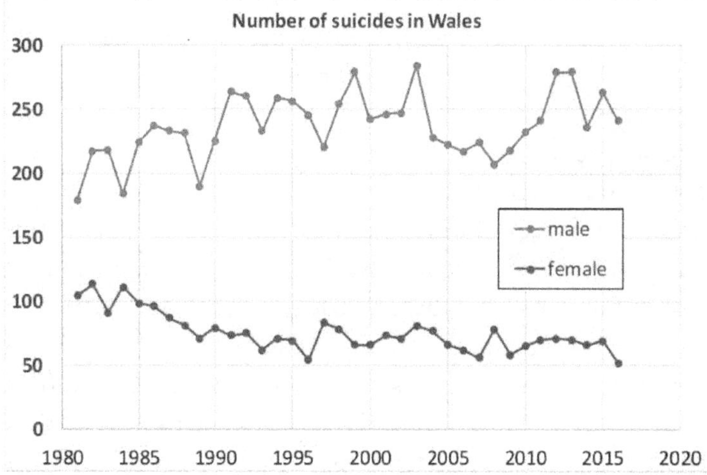

However, in contrast to Figures 18.7 and 18.8, the male suicide *rate* in England and Wales combined has *reduced* between the early 1980s and recent years, from around 19 to around 15. Figure 18.9 shows the ratio of male to female suicide rates over the same period, for England and Wales separately. This ratio has increased markedly over the period. In England the suicide rates, averaged over a five year period to 2016, were 15.2 for men and 4.6 for women, hence an average of 3.3 male suicides to every female suicide. The suicide rate for men in Wales averaged over the same five year period was substantially worse than in England, namely 20.0, whilst that for women was 4.7, hence 4.3 male suicides in Wales for each female suicide.

Figure 18.9: *Ratio of Male to Female Suicide Rates in England and Wales, 1981-2016*

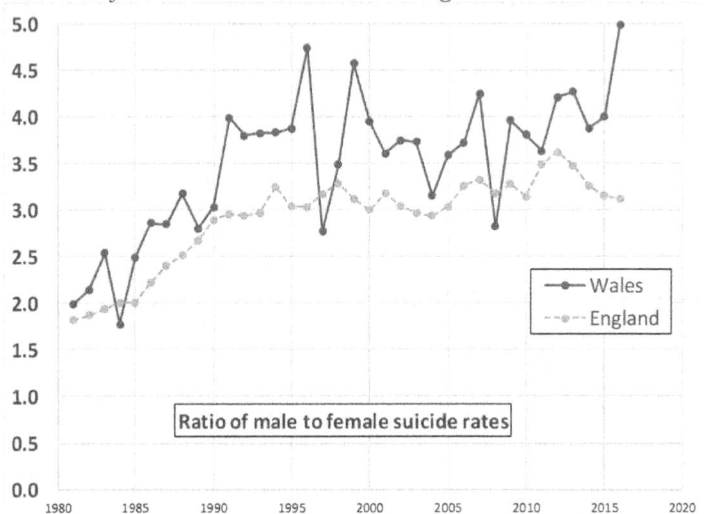

For both nations, the increase in the male:female suicide rate ratio since 1981 was primarily due to the reduction in the number of female suicides, rather than the increase in male suicides. This fact tends to be elided in popular accounts of suicide. But it has a significant implication. A rational approach to suicide prevention would start by asking what has caused the reduction in female suicides? If this can be identified, perhaps it can be rolled out to men. But there appears to be a reluctance to acknowledge that something beneficial has been done for women, so this approach is never considered.

Figures 18.7-9 are not disaggregated by age. Carrying out that disaggregation reveals some surprising long-term trends. Figure 18.10 shows the male suicide rate in England and Wales combined from 1951 to 1998, and Figure 18.11 shows the rate from 1981 to 2016. These show the trends separately for various age ranges (though the age ranges differ between the two graphs). In the second half of the 20th century, Figure 18.10 shows that the suicide rate for men over 54 in England and Wales *reduced* quite dramatically. That for men aged 45 to 54 also reduced significantly. In stark contrast, the suicide rate for younger men, from age 15 to 44, *increased* significantly over the same period. Over the later period, 1981 to 2016, Figure 18.11 shows that there has been little discernible trend in male suicide rate for men below the age of 60 (consistent with Figure 18.7). However, men aged 60 and older showed markedly reduced suicide rates over the period, roughly halving between 1981 and 2016.

The popular perception that men's suicide rate has substantially increased in recent years is false (though there may be local increases, such as that in Wales). Moreover, the reduction in older men's suicide rates goes largely unremarked.

Figures 18.12 and 18.13 present the same data for women. Here the story is simpler, at least if we consider changes from the mid-1960s. For women, the suicide rate has decreased for all age ranges above 30, whilst for women younger than 30, for whom the suicide rate is much smaller, there has been little change.

It should be recalled from the previous section that there have been large increases in rates of self-harm and suicidal ideation, for both men and women since 2000. Yet in contrast we see relatively steady, or falling, rates of suicide, especially for women. This indicates that there is no simple relationship between completed suicide and what might have been assumed to be precursor indicators: self-harm and suicidal ideation.

To reiterate: the marked increase in the male:female suicide rate ratio (Figure 18.9) is primarily due to the reduction in the female suicide rate. Moreover, any increase in male suicide rate is concentrated in young and middle-aged men, with older men having seen reductions in suicide rates. Attempting to explain these observations based on statistical modelling, Gunnell (2003) concluded,

> 'The factors most consistently associated with the rises in young male suicide are increases in divorce, declines in marriage and increases in income inequality. These changes have had little effect on suicide in young females. This may be because the drugs commonly used in overdose - their favoured method of suicide - have become less toxic or because they are less affected by the factors underlying the rise in male suicide.'

The impact of intimate partner separation or divorce on suicide rates will be examined in greater depth in section 18.2.3.1, and the role of domestic abuse in section 18.2.3.2.

Figure 18.10: *Male Suicide Rates in England and Wales by Age Range, 1951-1998*

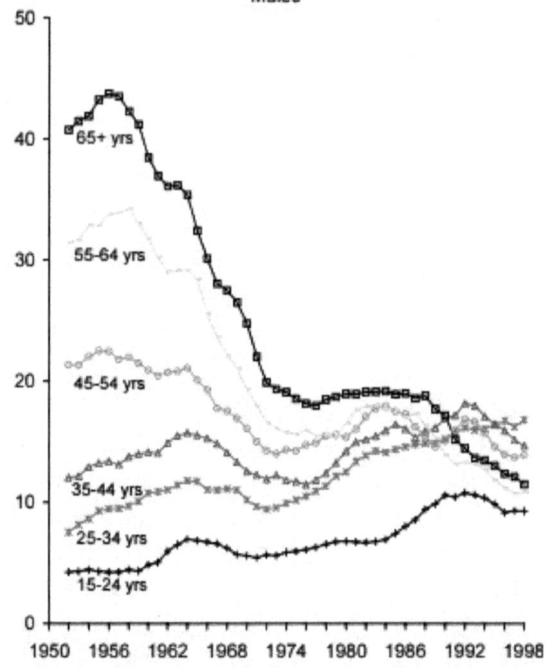

Figure 18.11: *Male Suicide Rates in England and Wales by Age Range, 1981-2016*

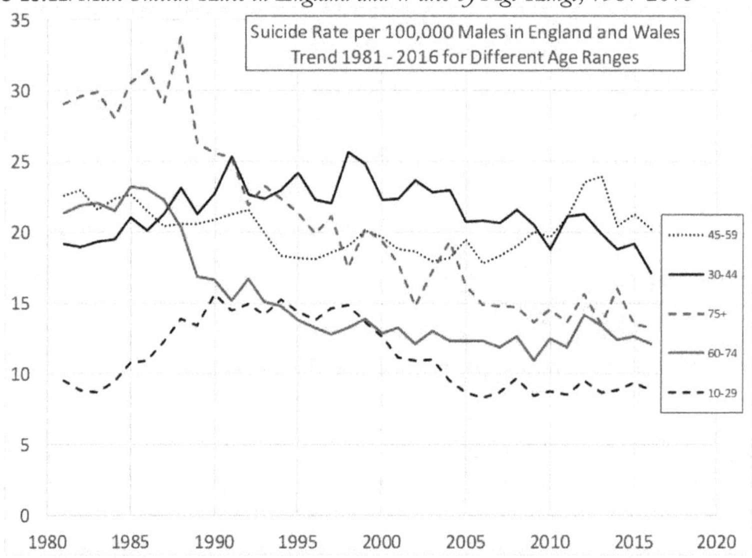

Figure 18.12: *Female Suicide Rates in England and Wales by Age Range, 1951-1998*

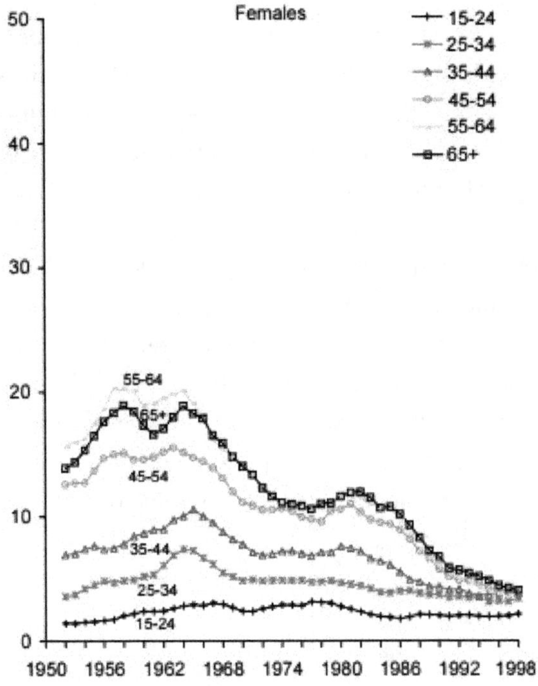

Figure 18.13: *Female Suicide Rates in England and Wales by Age Range, 1981-2016*

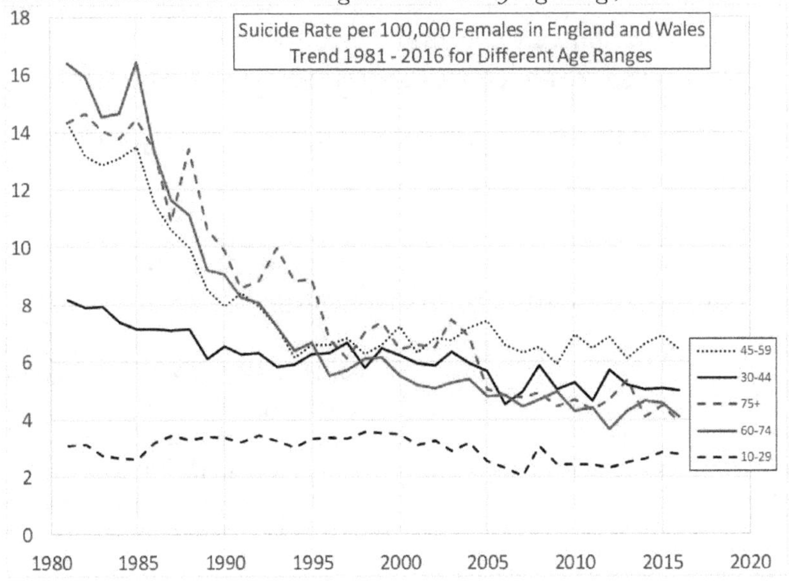

18.2.2 The Suicide Paradox

The term "gender suicide paradox" is often used to describe the fact that women have a higher prevalence of reported mental disorders than men, but a far lower suicide rate. The "paradox" can be widened to include self-harm, suicidal ideation and suicide attempts – all of which are more prevalent among women than men, despite women's substantially lower rate of completed suicide.

But this supposed paradox is not only a gender issue. The prevalence of self-harming and suicidal ideation by both sexes has increased substantially, as has the prevalence of mental disorders (chapter 17). Yet the suicide rate in the UK has not increased overall, in fact it has decreased, even for men alone, and has reduced markedly for women. Consequently, the suicide paradox relates to a disconnect between increasing mental disorders, self-harming and suicidal ideation and reducing rates of completed suicides. The paradox applies also to men, though it is even more marked for women.

In this respect it is worth recalling the relative rarity of completed suicide compared with self-harming, suicidal ideation or even suicide attempts. To recap: over all adult age ranges and both sexes, the relevant yearly rates are 5.4% (suicidal ideation, 2014), 0.7% (suicide attempts, 2014) and 0.01% (completed suicide, 2012-2016). Completed suicide is at the extreme tail end of the distribution of misery underlying these phenomena.

18.2.3 Reasons for the High Male Suicide Rate

A number of factors which elevate suicide rates can be identified. The role of intimate partner separation/divorce is considered in some detail in section 18.2.3.1, and the effect of domestic abuse in section 18.2.3.2. A major correlate of suicide, however, is socioeconomic class. The report 'Men, Suicide and Society', (Samaritans, 2012), summarises it thus,

> 'There are systematic socio-economic inequalities in suicide risk. Socio-economic position can be defined in many ways – by job, class, education, income, or housing. Whichever indicator is used, people in the lower positions are at higher risk of suicide. As you go down each rung of the social ladder, the risk of suicide increases, even after taking into account underlying mental health problems. There is debate over precisely how low social position increases suicide risk. Suggestions include having many more adverse experiences, powerlessness, stigma and disrespect, social exclusion, poor mental health and unhealthy lifestyles.'

Male suicide is particularly strongly associated with socioeconomics. This is hardly surprising. For those in poorly paid, or irregular, employment, it can be difficult to pay for the basics of life in the modern world. And if the only means you have to do so involves long hours of laborious work in unpleasant conditions, with no hope of your lot improving, succumbing to despair may be hard to avoid. Financial pressures on men are likely to be greater than on women, there still being an expectation that the man is the family's main breadwinner. It does no good to disparage this as "hegemonic masculinity" if it is simply a man's daily lived experience. And the sheer unpleasantness of much of the work that men in the lower socioeconomic classes are obliged to do is a factor which seems to receive little attention.

Section 18.2.3.3 will critique the various narratives which surround the issue of high male suicide rates. But first I shall look at the relationship between suicide and partner separation, followed by the impact of domestic abuse.

18.2.3.1 Partner Separation and Suicide Rates

There is a wealth of research evidence regarding the relationship between partner separation or divorce and subsequent suicide rates. To pre-empt the conclusion of this section, it is clear that separation results in increased suicide rates in men, and most studies show increased suicide rates in women also, though the increase for men is substantially greater. As usual we must be cautious and refer to "correlation". However, a causal connection is almost certain in this case. The usual proviso is that suicidality might be related to the precipitation of separation/divorce. Whilst this cannot be completely dismissed, it is made less credible by the fact that the separation might be initiated by one partner but the suicide by the other. This is, in fact, the most common permutation, since women initiate most separations/divorces, but men kill themselves far more often.

Evans, Scourfield and Moore (2016) have performed a thorough literature search for reputable publications addressing associations between relationship breakdown and suicide or suicide risk, and how this is differentiated by sex. Confining attention to Western and Anglophone countries, from a coarse sort of 1,066 articles, they examined the full texts of 52. Of these, 19 were considered of the appropriate quality and level of detail and presented data at the "individual level". A further 10 papers were "ecological studies" which the same authors had considered in an earlier publication. This earlier publication appears as an Appendix to the report 'Men, Suicide and Society', (Samaritans, 2012). The authors are cautious about over-stating their conclusions, the 2016 article concluding that,

> 'Nineteen published articles that included individual-level data were identified. Twelve reported a greater risk of suicide in men following relationship breakdown, two indicated a greater risk in women, and a further five showed no clear gender differential. Although there are possible indications of increased risk for men, no definitive conclusion about gender differential can be drawn.'

The 2012 report, which included more studies, concludes,

> 'This paper presents a systematic review of the evidence on gender differentials in suicide risk after breakdown in intimate relationships (including divorce and separation). Twenty-nine published papers were identified, which included analysis of individual-level data and ecological studies. Of these, 17 found suicide risk to be higher in men, six found risk to be higher in women and six had no consistent findings on gender difference.'

A simple counting of how many reports indicate a greater, or equal, effect of separation on suicide rates in the two sexes may not, however, be the best indicator. Differences may be small or large in magnitude and will vary in statistical significance. Consequently, I have used the sources quoted in these two studies by Evans, Scourfield and Moore (plus one more, namely Wyder 2009) to compile two sets of results, given in Tables 18.2 and 18.3.

Table 18.2 lists those studies which provide an explicit numerical factor by which separation, divorce or widowhood increased the rate of suicide or suicidality, separately for the two sexes. These factors measure the enhancement after separation with respect to the base rate for non-separated persons of the same sex. (The non-separated reference might be married people or single people, usually the former). Most of the data relate to completed suicide, though some refer to suicidality or suicide attempts. Data in italics in Table 18.2 had a 95% confidence interval consistent with no effect. The rest indicated a statistically significant effect at the 95% confidence level, or better. None of the data of Table 18.2 relate to Great Britain and only one study to Northern Ireland.

Figure 18.14 uses the data of Table 18.2 to plot the factor of suicide rate increase due to separation for men against that for women. The black line is the line of equality. Only two points lie below the line (and only one significantly so). Several points lie on, or very close to, the line of equality. But a substantial number of data points lie well above the line, indicating a larger effect of separation/divorce on men's suicide rates than upon women's. Of the 27 data points on Figure 18.14, 2 lie below the line, 7 lie very close to the line, while 18 points (67%) lie clearly above the line. Despite the professional reticence of Evans, Scourfield and Moore, I suggest that

Table 18.2: *Increase in Suicide or Suicidality after Separation, Divorce or Widowhood for Men and Women Separately. Note that the reference base rate for non-separated people is markedly greater for men than for women. Data in blue italics indicates that the effect is not significant at the 95% confidence level. Sources Fekete and Kolves gave only the relative rates for separated men and women, hence the X in the female column is unknown.*

Reference	Country	Category	Male	Female
(Trovato, 1991), 1981	Canada	Suicide	1.67	1.61
(Rodríguez-Pulido, 1992)	Canary	Suicide	8.06	8.6
(Cantor, 1995)	Australia	Suicide	6.2	1.6
(Burgoa, 1998)	Spain	Suicide	2.99	*1.5*
(Kposowa, 2000)	USA	Suicide	2.38	*1.27*
(Agerbo, 2005) divorced	Denmark	Suicide	1.75	1.68
(Agerbo, 2005) separated	Denmark	Suicide	1.93	1.97
(Masocco, 2008)	Italy	Suicide	1.79	1.96
(Denney, 2009) separated/divorced	USA	Suicide	1.39	*1.42*
(Denney, 2009) widowed	USA	Suicide	1.6	*1.18*
(Petrovic, 2009)	Serbia	Suicide	3.79	*1.47*
(Masocco, 2010) 24-44	Italy	Suicide	1.47	2.67
(Masocco, 2010) 45-64	Italy	Suicide	1.77	1.62
(Corcoran, 2010)	N.Ireland	Suicide	2.61	*2.57*
(Wyder, 2009) separated,15-24	Australia	Suicide	12.1	3.07
(Wyder, 2009) separated,25-44	Australia	Suicide	8.45	3.15
(Wyder, 2009) separated,45-64	Australia	Suicide	5.25	4.08
(Wyder, 2009) separated, 65+	Australia	Suicide	2.82	1.58
(Wyder, 2009) widowed,25-44	Australia	Suicide	2.7	2.08
(Wyder, 2009) widowed,45-64	Australia	Suicide	1.87	1.63
(Wyder, 2009) widowed, 65+	Australia	Suicide	1.98	0.85
(Kovess-Masfety, 2011)	Spain	Suicidality	*1.68*	*1.14*
(Kovess-Masfety, 2011)	France	Suicidality	*1.43*	*0.96*
(Kovess-Masfety, 2011)	Spain	Attempts	*8.04*	*0.9*
(Kovess-Masfety, 2011)	France	Attempts	*4.46*	*0.78*
(Fekete, 2005)	Hungary	Suicidality	*1.64X*	X
(Kõlves, 2010)	Australia	Suicidality	2.06X	X

Figure 18.14 indicates convincingly that the increase in suicide rate due to separation tends to be significantly greater for men than for women. However, more obviously still, Figure 18.14 shows that the suicide rate for

both sexes is increased by separation. Of the 27 data points, all show an increase for men, and 22 (81%) are significant at the 95% confidence level or better. For women, of the 27 data points, 14 to 16 (52%-59%) show an increase which is significant at the 95% confidence level or better. The median factor by which separation/divorce increases the suicide, or suicidality, rate for men is 2.1 (mean 3.5). For women the median is 1.6 (mean 2.0).

The reader should bear in mind when interpreting the data in Table 18.2 and Figure 18.14 that the factors given are with respect to the base suicide rate for the same sex, and that the base suicide rate for men is substantially higher than that for women. For example, in England in recent years we have seen in section 18.2.1 that the suicide rate for men was 3.3 times that for women. For such a base rate ratio, Figure 18.14 implies a relative suicide rate for men and women after separation as given in Figure 18.15 (which is obtained from the suicide data of Figure 18.14 by multiplying the y-axis by 3.3). Hence, Figure 18.15 gives the suicide rate for men and women after separation normalised by the base rate for non-separated women. Separated men are 8 times more likely to commit suicide than non-separated women (based on the median, or 12 times more likely based on the mean).

Figure 18.14: *Increase in Suicide or Suicidality due to Separation, Divorce or Widowhood Comparing the Increase for Men and Women. Note that the reference base rate for non-separated people is markedly greater for men than for women.*

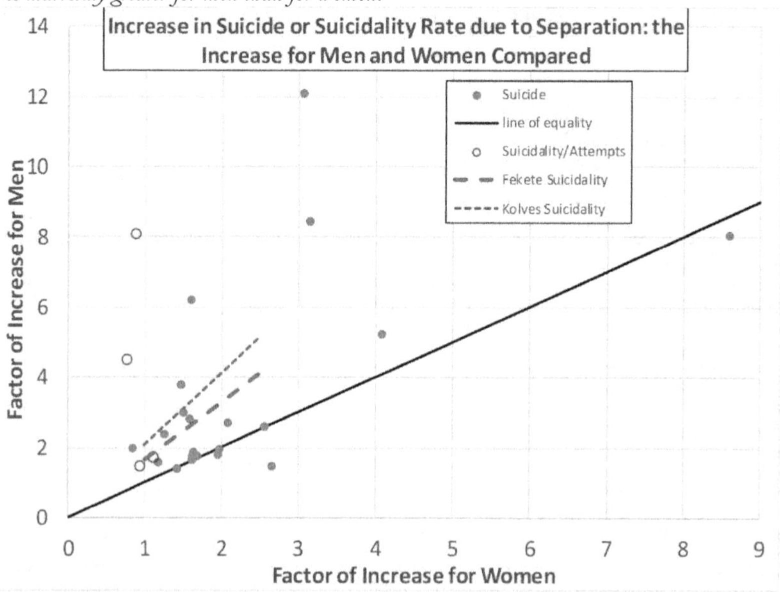

Figure 18.15: *Suicide Rates for Separated Men and Separated Women Compared. The rates plotted for both sexes are normalised by a base rate for non-separated women. This Figure assumes a male:female suicide rate ratio of 3.3, representative of England in recent years.*

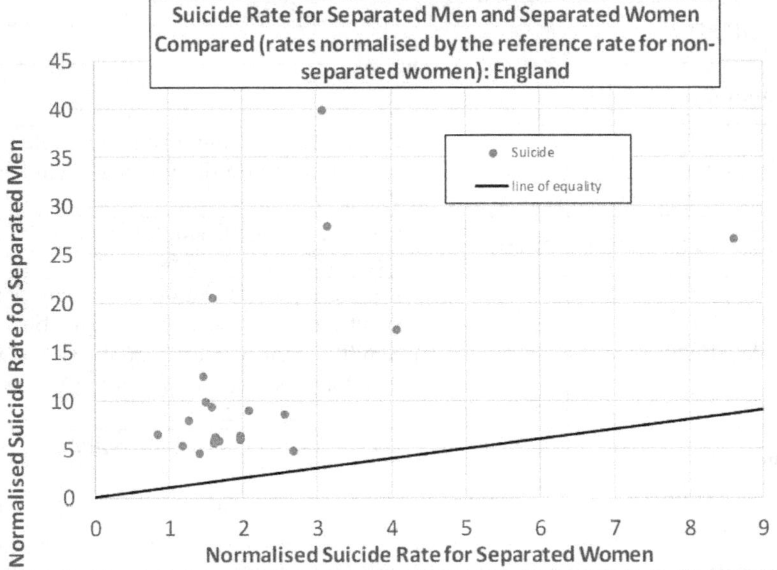

Those studies identified in (Evans, Scourfield and Moore, 2016) or (Samaritans, 2012) which did not provide a quantification of the increase in suicide or suicidality rates, but which did provide a qualitative indication of the relative enhancement for the two sexes, are listed in Table 18.3 together with their principal results. (One further source has been added, namely the Centers for Disease Control and Prevention, 2012). Of these additional 16 studies, 12 indicated a significant association of separation/divorce with suicide rate for one or both sexes. Of the 16 studies, 10 indicated a greater effect on men than on women, whilst only 2 indicated a greater effect on women. Hence these qualitative results are broadly consistent with the quantitative results of Table 18.2. Across the 43 studies listed in the two Tables, 28 (65%) indicate a greater adverse effect of separation/divorce on men than on women, and only 4 (9%) a greater effect on women.

A striking thing about these studies is how very few use contact with children, or even the existence of children, as a covariate in their statistical analyses. One cannot help but think that the authors might have profited from spending some time attending meetings of the charity Families Need Fathers Both Parents Matter Cymru. Here they would see first-hand that men's distress after separation is very evident, freely expressed, and almost exclusively concerned with child contact.

Table 18.3: *Sources Indicating Relative Suicide or Suicidality Incidence for the Two Sexes after Separation or Divorce where Rates are Not Quantified.*

Reference	Country	Result
(Zeiss, 1981)	USA	Significantly fewer suicidal feelings amongst women
(Kposowa, 2003)	USA	Divorced men 9.7 times more likely to kill themselves than divorced women
(Walsh, 2009)	USA	Departure of an intimate partner cited as a factor in significantly more male than female suicides
(Rossow, 1993)	Norway	Correlation significant for men (0.35) but not significant for women (0.25)
(Burnley, 1995)	Australia	For ages 15-24 and 65-74, correlation significant for men (0.52-0.56) but not significant for women (0.26-0.28). For ages 25-39, correlation significant for both: men 0.53, women 0.52.
(Lester, 1995)	USA	Correlation significant for both: men 0.42, women 0.50
(Gunnell, 2003)	UK	Significant association for both sexes at ages 25-34, but for neither sex for ages 60+
(Andres, 2005)	Europe	Significant association for men but not for women
(Barstad, 2008)	Norway	Significant association with separation for both sexes but larger for men (0.42 cf 0.25)
(Andres, 2010)	Denmark	Association not significant for either sex (but best estimate greater for men, 0.33 cf 0.16)
(Fernquist, 2003)	Many	In highly religious countries, significant association for both sexes but greater for men (0.53 cf 0.45)
(Agerbo, 2011)	Denmark	Significant association and twice as great an effect on women
(Heikkinen, 1995)	Finland	Sex difference not significant
(Cutright, 2005)	USA	Sex difference not significant
(Lester, 1992)	Australia	No significance association for either sex
(Centers for Disease Control, 2012)	USA	Men's suicide rate is enhanced more than women's by partner separation

Data from the USA (Centers for Disease Control, 2012) is also given in Table 18.4. The majority of men who committed suicide in the USA (~60%) had no known mental health problem, whereas the majority of women who committed suicide (~61%) did have a known mental health problem. This is consistent with a greater role of exogenous factors in male suicide. Overall there were 3.6 male suicides for each female suicide (broadly like the UK and most other Western countries). A larger percentage of men who committed suicide had a known problem with their intimate partner (33%) than did women who committed suicide (25.5%). Bearing in mind that an intimate partner problem is likely to be mutual, these data imply that men with such a problem are 4.6 times more likely to commit suicide than women in the same position (2,289/493).

Table 18.4: *Suicide Data from the USA (Centers for Disease Control, 2012)*

Reason for Suicide	Men		Women	
	number	% of total	number	% of total
All reasons	6,931	100	1,931	100
Current mental health problem	2,724	39.3	1,184	61.3
Physical health problem	1,419	20.5	442	22.9
Intimate partner problem	2,289	33.0	493	25.5
Other relationship problem (non-intimate)	659	9.5	267	13.8
Suicide of family member or friend within past 5 years	127	1.8	34	1.8
Other death of family member or friend within past 5 years	443	6.4	110	5.7

The large number of sources prohibits a detailed discussion of their findings beyond the broad outcomes recorded in the above Tables and Figures. However, a few quotes are appropriate. (Rossow, 1993), Norway, concludes,

> 'Times series analyses on differenced data from 1911 to 1990 showed that both alcohol consumption and divorce were independently and statistically significantly associated with the male suicide rate, but not with the female suicide rate.'

(Gunnell, 2003), UK, concludes,

> 'The factors most consistently associated with the rises in young male suicide are increases in divorce, declines in marriage and increases in income inequality. These changes have had little effect on suicide in young females.'

(Andres, 2005), Europe, concludes,

> '…the effect of divorce rate is specific to gender.'

(Andres, 2005) finds the influence of divorce on men's suicide rate is significant at the 99% confidence level (i.e., $p < 0.01$). In contrast, the influence for women is not statistically significant ($p > 0.1$). (Walsh, 2009), USA (Kentucky), concludes,

> 'In 2005, intimate partner problems were documented as a contributing factor in 128 (29%) of all suicide cases where the circumstances were known. In 54 (42%) of the 128 cases, the coroner noted that the decedent's intimate was in the process of leaving, breaking up, had recently left, had recently separated, had recently filed for divorce, was awaiting divorce, or had a divorce recently finalized. Of those 54 cases involving intimate partner problems most (87%) of the suicide victims were men and were significantly different from the women.'

This suggests that separated, or separating, men are 6.7 times more likely to suicide than women in the same position. (Wyder, 2009), Australia, concludes,

> 'During the examined period, 6062 persons died by suicide in Queensland (an average of 551 cases per year), with males outnumbering females by four to one. For both males and females separation created a risk of suicide at least 4 times higher than any other marital status. The risk was particularly high for males aged 15 to 24 (relative risk 91.62). This study highlights a great variation in the incidence of suicide by marital status, age and gender, which suggests that these variables should not be studied in isolation. Furthermore, particularly in younger males, separation appears to be strongly associated with the risk of suicide.'

(Kposowa, 2000), USA, concludes,

> 'Divorced and separated persons were over twice as likely to commit suicide as married persons. Being single or widowed had no significant effect on suicide risk. When data were stratified by sex, it was observed that the risk of suicide among divorced men was over twice that of married men. Among women, however, there were no statistically significant differentials in the risk of suicide by marital status categories. Conclusions: Marital status, especially divorce, has strong net effect on mortality from suicide, but only among men.'

While (Kposowa, 2003) concludes,

> 'Divorced men were over eight times more likely to commit suicide than divorced women. After taking into account other factors that have been reported to contribute to suicide, divorced men still experienced much increased risks of suicide than divorced women. They were nearly 9.7 times more likely to kill themselves than comparable divorced women. Put another way, for every divorced woman that committed suicide, over nine divorced men killed themselves.'

18.2.3.2 Domestic Abuse and Suicide Rates

There is evidence that domestic violence is related to suicide, and that domestic violence has at least as great, or greater, impact on male suicide than on female suicide. Published data are still sparse, but emerging indicators are that male victims of domestic violence are more likely to kill themselves than female victims. In the book 'You Can Stop Male Suicide', (Poole, 2017) observes that,

> 'UK government data suggests that male victims of domestic violence are 50% more likely to attempt suicide than female victims, while US researchers have found that men who were sexually abused in childhood are up to 11 times more likely to suicide…..Another form of abuse that men are more prone to is false allegations of physical and sexual assault. A recent survey of 30 victims of false allegations (24 men and 6 women) by the University of Oxford's Centre of Criminology, found that over a quarter reported being suicidal.'

The Oxford survey which Poole refers to here is that by Carolyn Hoyle, Naomi-Ellen Speechley and Ros Burnett, (2017). Based on the observation that 'men in mid-life are dependent primarily on female partners for emotional support', (Samaritans, 2012), it is reasonable to expect that men would be particularly susceptible to psychological harm as a result of abuse by their female partner. This can only be exacerbated by the dearth of provision for male victims of domestic abuse (see chapter 9) and further exacerbated by the disbelief and lack of sympathy which male victims face from the public generally. All these societal factors amplify the natural tendency of men not to disclose their abuse to others, which in turn can only increase their silent distress.

Moreover, it is not just the victims but also the perpetrators of domestic violence who have elevated rates of suicidal ideation. For example, 22% of a sample of 294 men attending a batterer's intervention programme in the USA had experienced suicidal ideation in the two weeks prior to entering the programme, (Wolford-Clevenger et al, 2015). This is less surprising than it initially appears given that roughly half of domestic violence is reciprocal. However, as usual, one needs to be cautious about assuming causal connection. Mutual correlates are likely and causality may be more complex.

Causality has been investigated in the context of the suicidality of domestic violence offenders by (Cero et al, 2015) and (Wolford-Clevenger et al, 2017). Both support the association of suicidal ideation in domestic abuse perpetrators with "perceived burdensomeness". Perceived burdensomeness is the belief that one is a burden on others or society, generally accompanied by feelings of self-hatred and of being a liability. The sufferer believes that he (or she) will assist others best by dying, in other words that their suicide is a socially beneficial act.

The study of (Wolford-Clevenger et al, 2017) was based on 312 men and 84 women with an average age of 35 who were arrested for domestic violence and mandated to attend batterer intervention programmes in Rhode Island. No gender differences emerged for suicide ideation, drug use, alcohol use, depression or borderline personality disorder symptoms. Men reported greater capability for suicide than women, whereas more women reported a suicide attempt history than men. ("Suicidal capability" refers to being fearless about death and tolerant of physical pain, factors which are believed to be associated with suicide attempts and completions). Men and women did not differ in levels of perceived burdensomeness (though it should be recalled that the subjects were far from being a typical cross-section of the public). The authors conclude, 'the present study adds to the suggestion that perceived burdensomeness may be a more salient risk factor for suicide ideation than thwarted belongingness and showed that association held in both men and women'. ("Thwarted belongingness" refers to involuntary social isolation).

Another emerging observation, as yet with limited published support, is that male perpetrators are significantly more likely to kill themselves than they are to kill their partner. It must be recalled that men labelled as perpetrators are often also victims, though this may not be recorded. Indeed, the true perpetrator and victim might be entirely the reverse. It has been suggested that the number of male deaths resulting from partner abuse would exceed the number of female deaths, if suicides due to such abuse were included. Direct support for this corollary comes from the study by Davis (2010) which concludes,

> 'When domestic violence-related suicides are combined with domestic violence homicides, the total numbers of domestic violence-related deaths are higher for males than females. This paper recommends that to understand the broad scope and tragic impact of domestic violence, further research is needed concerning domestic violence-related suicide.'

This is an extremely significant finding given the powerful influence that accusations of domestic violence have in determining the outcomes of Family Court cases, and the manner in which related deaths have been used for lobbying purposes (see chapters 10 and 12).

What has been well established in the UK is perhaps the most surprising finding of all, namely that suicidal ideation by potential perpetrators is the best predictor of partner homicide. This has been revealed by the analysis of Bridger et al (2017) which reviewed 188 cases of intimate partner homicide recorded in England and Wales between April 2011 and March 2013. Offenders in these cases were 86% male and 14% female, and vice-versa for the victims. Whilst perpetrators had high rates of substance abuse (mostly alcohol) and prior offending, the most disproportionately prevalent characteristic was suicidal ideation, self-harm or suicide attempts by the perpetrator. Prior to the homicide, 40% of the male offenders were known by someone, but often not to police, as suffering suicidal ideation, self-harm or attempted suicides. For female offenders the figure was 28%. Post-offence suicide attempts occurred in 33.4% of cases with a 'success' rate for the perpetrator of 24.2% of those attempts. It is striking how dramatically higher this success rate is than amongst the general public (see sections 18.2.1-2). The authors conclude, rather remarkably, that,

> 'Of all of the characteristics (considered) suicide ideation appears to be the most over-represented in relation to the general population. Chronic substance abuse, cohabitation and even prior crime against the victim are so widespread and prevalent in the population generally that they would massively over-predict domestic homicide. Suicidal ideation or attempts, however, appear to be much rarer in the population. Thus, a 40% rate of suicidal indication among the male offenders may be the most useful of any of these characteristics in distinguishing people who are much more likely to kill their partners than other offenders.'

And also,

> 'It is plausible that many more intimate partner homicides might be accurately predicted, and perhaps prevented, with more public investment in obtaining data on suicidal indicators and more proactive treatment of domestic abuse offenders known to suffer suicidal tendencies.'

This is particularly noteworthy as research by the police in Thames Valley and in Dorset have shown that tools such as the Domestic Abuse Stalking and Harassment instrument (DASH) have failed to predict most cases of domestic homicide, see Bridger et al (2017) for details.

18.2.3.3 Lack of UK Research

It is striking that none of the studies in Table 18.2 relate to Great Britain, and only one to Northern Ireland. As for the sources given in Table 18.3, there is just one UK study, Gunnell et al (2003), and this provided no quantification of the effect of separation on suicide, only showing it to be significant. The UK's leading male-specific suicide charity (CALM) appears not to carry out research into causes.

Wales has a national suicide prevention strategy, 'Talk to me 2', (Welsh Government, 2015a), but the Objectives, (Welsh Government, 2015b), and the Key Activities, (Welsh Government, 2015c), make no mention of the male sex despite this being the demographic of concern. The Key Activities recognise domestic abuse as a suicide risk for women but not for men, which is odd.

It may well be that this absence of UK research is because research funding gets deflected onto anything but the elephant in the room: men. For example, the UK Government made £1.5M available for suicide research starting in November 2012 and running for 3 years. Despite initial strategy documents paying appropriate lip-service to male suicide, (UK Government, 2012b), the invitation to tender which emerged, (Department of Health, 2012), called for proposals against the following five categories only,

- How to reduce the risk of suicide in a key high-risk group: people with a history of self-harm;
- How approaches and interventions can be tailored to improve mental health in specific groups;
- How self-harm can be better managed and suicide reduced in children and young people, including looked-after children and care leavers;
- How the media can be better supported in delivering sensible and sensitive approaches to suicide and suicidal behaviour;
- How the health and social care system can provide better information and support to those bereaved or affected by a suicide.

There is no mention of the demographic which accounts for 77% of the suicides in the UK in these proposals, the male sex. Observations on these tender categories are,

- The focus on self-harm and mental disorder seems inappropriate since these phenomena appear to be very poor predictors of suicide. By focussing on self-harm and mental disorder, focus will shift primarily onto women, who suffer more from these issues, and away from men, who are the main victims of suicide.
- Whilst the focus on children and young people stirs one's sentiments, suicide peaks in adult men of middle age: men in their mid-forties. So the research areas again deflect attention away from the demographic upon which suicide is concentrated.
- The proposed research areas fail to address the most obvious and pressing question: why do the majority of people committing suicide do it? And this means adult men.
- Two of the five work areas relate to the media and "providing better information". But better information needs to be acquired before it can be disseminated, and the information which is still sadly lacking is quality

UK data on the motivations for adult men's suicide, how it relates to life events and the implied causalities.

There appears to be a reluctance to approach the question of what lies behind the high male suicide rate. Is it because this is a loose thread that the Department of Health has no desire to pull? Is it because there is a political wish to avoid drawing attention to the known exogenous factors: unemployment, deprivation, homelessness, imprisonment, domestic abuse, divorce, separation and child contact? Or is it simply the empathy gap which relegates adult male suicide to a lesser status, regardless of the suicide arithmetic?

18.2.4 Methods of Suicide and Suicide Attempts

Data on the method adopted for completed suicides in the UK in 2017 has been published, (Office for National Statistics, 2018t), and are reproduced in Table 18.5 below. Hanging is the most common method leading to a successful suicide, for both sexes. However this is misleading as regards the relative frequency of the methods used for suicide attempts. Recall that the overwhelming majority of suicide attempts do not succeed. Those which succeed tend to be those which opt for the most lethal methods, e.g., hanging. For the same reason, Table 18.5 is misleading as regards the choice of method by sex. Actually, a far smaller proportion of women than men who attempt suicide opt for hanging, but those who do are more likely to be successful.

Table 18.5: *Proportion of Suicide Deaths by Method and Sex, UK 2017.*

Method	Men	Women
Drowning	4.0%	5.2%
Fall and Fracture	3.7%	3.1%
Poisoning	18.2%	38.3%
Hanging	59.7%	42.1%
Other	14.4%	11.3%

As an indication of the methods used in suicide attempts I shall quote the results of a Swedish study because it has particularly large statistics and a very long follow-up period. The study identified 48,649 individuals admitted to hospital in 1973-82 after attempting suicide, but surviving. Over a period of up to 31 years after the index event, the study also identified whether these individuals subsequently succeeded in killing themselves, (Runeson et al, 2010). The number of women attempting suicide exceeded the number of men by 6.7% (noting that the data relates to failed attempts only). Within the follow up period, 13.8% of these men and 9.9% of the women subsequently succeeded in killing themselves. (Because these data relate to people with a history of suicide attempts they are not indicative of the general public).

Table 18.6 reveals a very different relative prevalence of methods used in unsuccessful suicide attempts, as compared with Table 18.5 for completed suicides. Poisoning was overwhelmingly the most common method for attempted, but failed, suicide (77% of men and 90% of women). In contrast, hanging, strangulation or suffocation accounted for only 2.0% of men's suicide attempts and only 0.9% of women's attempts. This stands in stark contrast with Table 18.5.

Table 18.6 also gives an indication of the degree of determination shown by those using the various methods as indicated by the percentage of each which subsequently resulted in a successful suicide. Hanging, strangulation or suffocation appears as easily the most successful, with a second attempt success rate of 53.9% for men and 56.6% for women (although more than twice as many men chose this method).

The data on subsequently completed suicides in Table 18.6 should not be conflated with data applicable generally, because this is a skewed sample of people who have attempted, but survived, earlier suicide attempts. Thus, for example, people who previously opted for hanging will be under-represented in Table 18.6 because most will have succeeded first time around.

It may be that the relative prevalence of the various methods is culture dependent. A much smaller scale study in Poland, involving 234 failed suicide attempts, (Tsirigotis et al, 2011), indicated the following method statistics,

- Drugs/poisoning: 48% of women and 25% of men;
- Exsanguination (wrist-cutting): 29% of women and 13% of men;
- Hanging/asphyxia: 11% of women and 56% of men;
- Jumping from height: 10% of women and 6% of men.

In Poland over the relevant period the suicide rate for men was more than six times that for women. This aligns with men opting far more often for the most lethal method – hanging.

I note in passing that USA data on methods of suicide, or suicide attempts, might be misleading if assumed to be indicative of European countries due to the prevalence of suicide/attempts in the USA using firearms, something which is rarer in countries with less readily available firearms.

Table 18.6: *Methods of Attempted Suicide, and Ultimate Successful Suicide, from Swedish Study (Runeson et al, 2010). The number of attempts is given as a percentage of the total attempts. The number of subsequently completed suicides is given as a percentage of the number of attempts using the same method, giving an indication of lethality.*

Suicide attempt method	**Men**		**Women**	
	No (%) of attempts	**No (%) of suicides during follow-up**	**No (%) of attempts**	**No (%) of suicides during follow-up**
Poisoning	18 225 (77.4)	2247 (12.3)	22 521 (89.7)	2023 (9.0)
Cutting or piercing	1686 (7.2)	219 (13.0)	737 (2.9)	79 (10.7)
Gassing	318 (1.4)	69 (21.7)	101 (0.4)	15 (14.9)
Hanging, strangulation, or suffocation	479 (2.0)	258 (53.9)	221 (0.9)	125 (56.6)
Drowning	165 (0.7)	50 (30.3)	161 (0.6)	70 (43.5)
Firearm or explosive	287 (1.2)	99 (34.5)	40 (0.2)	3 (7.5)
Jumping from a height	467 (2.0)	155 (33.2)	335 (1.3)	74 (22.1)
Other method	1403 (7.7)	125 (8.9)	579 (2.3)	58 (10.0)
Late effect of suicide attempt/other self inflicted harm	508 (2.8)	38 (7.5)	416 (1.7)	33 (7.9)
All methods	23 538	3260 (13.8)	25 111	2480 (9.9)

18.3 Male Suicide: Narratives, Rationalisations and Blaming

Rather than attempt an impossibly open-ended literature review, in this section I shall take the report 'Men, Suicide and Society', (Samaritans, 2012), to be indicative. This report contained a series of chapters written by leading social scientists in psychology, sociology, economics and gender studies. One of these has already been employed in the foregoing section on the effect of partner separation. Here I extract the salient features from the remaining four chapters which address, in turn, psychological factors, economic issues, private troubles and their relationship to larger society, and finally "masculinities".

Firstly, the chapter written by Olivia Kirtley and Rory O'Connor which addresses psychological factors. They ask why men of low socio-economic position in mid-life may be at higher risk of death by suicide. They note that the data shows that males who are suicidal are more likely to be unemployed or in low paid manual work. Despite a brief to focus on psychological issues, these authors note the major influence of unemployment, financial and housing difficulties, and relationship issues on suicidality in men. The key psychological issues they identify are a lack of skill in problem solving, and, in particular, "socially prescribed perfectionism".

Social perfectionism is defined as the perception that one must always meet the expectations of others, with these perceived prescribed standards often being unrealistic. Personally, I find the use of the word "perfectionism" in this context to be inappropriate. I suggest a better term for this psychological orientation would be "socially prescribed or perceived obligation" or "socially prescribed or perceived burden". Indeed, it is revealing to meditate upon a key distinction between "perfectionism" and "burden". The former implies an origin within the mind of the man in question: a character flaw or psychological weakness. In contrast, the word "burden" clearly indicates an imposition upon the man from society. The distinction is therefore between victim blaming and being victimised. Narratives surrounding male disadvantages almost always favour the former. This is male disposability and male agency, the flip side of gynocentrism, in action. Why? Because this judicious choice of wording, in suggesting a man's own failing is responsible for his suicidality, relieves society of any obligation beyond instructing men to improve.

Kirtley and O'Connor find a significant association between this so-called "perfectionism", or perceived social burdening, and suicidality. However, given that their brief was to investigate psychological factors, it is telling that they actually emphasise external factors, concluding,

> 'At the point of contact with psychiatric or other support services, more careful attention should be paid to individuals' life circumstances, particularly financial, employment or housing difficulties – and how these impact one's well-being.'

They also lament the lack of research thus,

> '…from the perspective of psychological research, the potential routes to suicide for males in their middle years remain "roads less travelled" and there is a distinct dearth of literature relating to this population. Those in middle age are a neglected population within psychological research and with little or no research within suicidology giving substantial focus to age or gender (as opposed to simply controlling for it); there are significant gaps in our knowledge, which must be addressed as an urgent priority.'

Brendan Kennelly and Sheelah Connolly address the relevance of economic issues on suicide. As is generally the case with social science research, different studies adduce contradictory findings. Kennelly and Connolly review a wide range of studies and highlight these conflicts. Nevertheless, they conclude,

> 'The balance of evidence suggests that, controlling for other risk factors, including the presence of psychiatric illness, being unemployed, having a low income, or living in a socio-economically deprived area, increase one's risk of dying by suicide. In addition, most researchers have found that deaths by suicide tend to increase during recessions.'

However, perhaps surprisingly, the effect of gender was less clear. A study on suicide in the UK found…

> '…a clear social gradient, with a four-fold difference in mortality between social classes I and V….this was mostly associated with excess mortality in social class V…..There was also evidence of a step-change in risk between non-manual and manual social classes.'

I suggest it might not only be pay that is the issue here, but also the sheer unpleasantness of hard manual labour. Kennelly and Connolly also make the following observations,

> '…some researchers have pointed out that regular fluctuation between suicide and economic conditions could be regarded as evidence that suicide is not solely due to irrational behaviour.'

Indeed, and exogenous factors generally have been underplayed in the narratives around male suicide. In respect of the impact of economic issues on suicide, the authors observer that,

> 'This point has not been adequately recognised in suicide prevention strategies which tend to be dominated by psychiatric and mental health research.'

In this context they ask a reasonable question,

> 'Is it feasible or sensible for the Samaritans to alter their longstanding approach to callers by becoming more adept at helping people think through financial problems as well as emotional problems?'

Julie Brownie takes a sociologist's view of male suicide, concentrating on emotional issues. She asks what it is about men from lower socioeconomic groups in their middle years which produces emotional vulnerabilities. There is a degree of presumption by Brownie that suicide must be related to emotional problems, though it is clear from the discussions above that exogenous factors play a significant role. There can be a confusion between the two, with external issues being reinterpreted through an emotional or psychological lens. For example, we read 'where children are involved…..relationship breakdowns are likely to have an impact on men's identity as fathers'. But the problem is not 'men's identity as fathers', an internal issue, but rather the external issue of men's access to children. It is being *permitted* to be a father that is actually the issue. This is another example of how a form of words is used to make an exogenous factor seem like a psychological factor, and thus to facilitate its transmogrification into a failing of the man himself, rather than a socially imposed disadvantage.

Brownie quotes other researchers regarding the significance of shame and self-respect, noting that the latter is, 'derived from being able to work hard and to provide for and protect their families'. Indeed, this is a major source of a man's self-respect, and it is an aspect of matricentrism in its family-centric form, as explained in chapter 1. Consistent with the evidence for the significance of partner separation/divorce presented in section 18.2.3.1, she writes,

> 'Increasing levels of partnership dissolution and re-partnering contribute to the complexity of relationships experienced in mid-life, including an increase in the number of men living apart from their children. These shifts potentially place men from lower socio-economic backgrounds at risk from a lack of emotional support at a time when they may also be facing considerable economic pressures.'

Exactly so. Brownie also observes the potential significance of men ending up living alone, and that 'there is some evidence that this is more likely for men than women to result from choice than from circumstances'. This choice may, however, be the aftermath of painful separation. And this observation about living arrangements may be significant if it is also true, as Brownie claims, that 'men of all ages and classes continue to remain dependent on women – mothers and then partners – as their main emotional conduits'.

The significance of "emotions talk" in male suicide is, however, more problematic and I do not think that Brownie makes a particularly compelling case. She states,

> 'The inability to express distressing emotion has been viewed as a risk factor for suicide and the argument that some forms of masculinity position men as stoical and unwilling to seek help has meant that emotions talk by men has come under scrutiny.'

But the evidential support she offers for the thesis that stoicism and reluctance to express emotions is a risk factor in men's suicide is weak. I refer the reader back to the quote from Steven Pinker in section 17.6 . He states that the idea that repressing emotions is bad and expressing them is good is merely a folk theory which is contra-indicated by abundant evidence. The main source which Brownie quotes in support of the contention is (Cleary, 2012), an extract from the Abstract being,

> 'This inquiry, based on in-depth interviews with 52 young Irish men who made a suicide attempt, examines suicidal behaviour at the individual level. The findings demonstrate that these men experienced high levels of emotional pain but had problems identifying symptoms and disclosing distress and this, along with the coping mechanisms used, was linked to a form of masculinity prevalent in their social environment. Dominant or hegemonic masculinity norms discouraged disclosure of emotional vulnerability, and participants used alcohol and drugs to cope – which exacerbated and prolonged their distress. Over time this led to a situation where they felt their options had narrowed, and suicidal action represented a way out of their difficulties. These men experienced significant, long-lasting, emotional pain but, in the context of lives lived in environments where prevailing constructions of masculinity constrained its expression, they opted for suicide rather than disclose distress and seek help.'

The problem with this is that it docs not establish any causal connection. One does not doubt the emotional stoicism or the drinking. But one suspects that hegemonic masculinity was in the dock in a show trial. As Pinker has emphasised, there is plenty of evidence against the thesis that stoicism is harmful. Recall from chapter 17 that Levant et al (2019) concluded that traditional masculine ideology provides protection against mental illness, not the reverse.

There are some obvious problems with the theory that "emotions talk" is beneficial to men in respect of suicide. For example, the concentration of suicide on the lower socioeconomic groups does not sit well with Brownie's observation that,

> 'men from lower socio-economic backgrounds are not especially resistant to the idea of discussing their feelings – at least, no more so than their middle-class counterparts.'

The dependence of suicide prevalence on age is also in conflict with the theory that "emotions talk" is beneficial to men. Brownie writes,

> 'Those currently in mid-life have grown up in an era in which emotions culture has been changing. Unlike those born in the first half of the twentieth century – referred to above as the 'silent generation' – they are less likely to maintain a stoical 'mustn't grumble' attitude in the face of emotional difficulties. Certainly, their own children will have broken decisively with such a culture.'

If talking of feelings was a significant preventative, suicide would have become less prevalent among younger men and would not have reduced amongst old men, those unreconstructed patriarchs. If fact, as Figures 18.10 and 18.11 show, the reverse is the case. There is no indication from suicide data that the softer, less macho, orientation of younger men has proved beneficial, just as there was not either from the data on mental illness (chapter 17): quite the opposite. But Brownie's closing shot seems eminently sensible,

> 'Given the continuing stigma attached to seeking help for mental distress, however, and given the centrality of relationships to wellbeing, helpline organisations might want to think how they can use their contact time with men to encourage them to develop sustainable sources of support in their own lives and communities. In other words, although talk might be the medium for accessing support, working with men on developing their own support networks (not all of which will be talk based) or helping them identify other non-talk-based ways of managing distress might be more effective, and might be perceived by men as being so.'

Amy Chandler explored the role of masculinities in men's suicidal behaviour. She examined 'the claim that suicide might be related to the failure of hegemonic masculinity'. Specifically, she proposes that the reason why men in lower socioeconomic groups suffer greater suicide rates is that they find it harder to achieve the hegemonic masculine ideal. From this perspective, unemployment or a man's estrangement from his children can lead to increased risk of suicide because these issues prevent successful alignment with the hegemonic masculine ideal.

One notes immediately a conflict between this view and the APA's perspective on mental ill-health (chapter 17). It seems men have a choice: achieve hegemonic masculinity and risk a mental disorder, or fail to achieve it and risk suicide instead. There is something unconvincingly elastic about this position.

Chandler's position on hegemonic masculinity is yet another example of converting exogenous causes into internal causes by verbal legerdemain. Unemployment or separation from partner or children is recast as failure to achieve hegemonic masculinity. The failure to achieve hegemonic masculinity is then held to be the cause of increased suicide risk. You see how that works? Why not simply say that unemployment or separation causes increased suicide risk? Why bring the concept of hegemonic masculinity into the picture at all? I suggest the answer is because it reallocates blame from society back onto the man himself.

18.4 The Empathy Gap in Suicide

In the book 'How You Can Stop Male Suicide', (Poole, 2017) advises that, 'we need to look beyond male suicide as a mental health issue to the role of exogenous factors'. We have seen that these exogenous factors include separation, the associated child contact issues, domestic abuse, low socioeconomic social class, and unskilled manual labour.

I have reviewed the plentiful and convincing evidence that separation/divorce significantly increases suicide rates for both sexes, but more so for men than for women. Since men have a base suicide rate 3.3 times that of women in England, after separation/divorce men's suicide rate is 8 times that of a non-separated women (based on the median, or 12 times based on the mean). In Wales these figures would be higher still. Remarkably, despite a large number of studies which analyse such suicide data, almost none have considered the significance of children or child contact. Anyone with experience of supporting fathers undergoing separation where there is a child contact dispute will confirm that this is the pre-eminent issue, to the exclusion of all else. In surveys of the experiences of such fathers, disclosure of suicidality does occur, (Both Parents Matter, 2017). The Welsh Assembly member Neil McEvoy has personally testified that suicidality is a very common feature of people coming into his constituency surgeries on matters relating to child contact, (McEvoy, 2019).

(Kposowa, 2003) speculates, following other authors, on the reasons for the high male suicide rate after separation/divorce,

> '…while social, psychological, and even personal problems facing women are readily denounced, societal institutions tend to ignore or minimise male problems as evident in suicide statistics. For instance, in many jurisdictions in the US there seems to be an implicit assumption that the bond between a woman and her children is stronger than that between a man and his children. As a consequence, in a divorce settlement, custody of children is more likely to be given to the wife. In the end, the father loses not only his marriage, but his children. The result may be anger at the court system especially in situations wherein the husband feels betrayed because it was the wife that initiated the divorce, or because the courts virtually gave away everything that was previously owned by the ex-husband or the now defunct household to the former wife. Events could spiral into resentment (toward the spouse and "the system"), bitterness, anxiety, and depression, reduced self-esteem, and a sense of "life not worth living"….. it may well be that one of the fundamental reasons for the observed association between divorce and suicide in men is the impact of post-divorce (court sanctioned) "arrangements".'

We have also seen that there is clear evidence of an association between suicide and domestic abuse, for the suicides of both victims and perpetrators. In many cases a man designated as a perpetrator may also be the victim of abuse, because rather more than half of partner abuse is mutual but the man is more likely to be identified as the abuser.

Suicide is also strongly associated with the lower socioeconomic classes. This relationship is probably not linear but disproportionately affects the lowest socioeconomic group (social class V). Men in this class are frequently unskilled labourers. Remarkably, none of the studies I reviewed considered the nature of men's employment as implicated in suicidality. There were many studies which addressed income, unemployment and socioeconomic class – and a few did explicitly identify the lowest class of manual worker to be especially vulnerable. But none made the obvious connection with the sheer unpleasantness of a man's daily work.

One hardly needs an academic study to spot the gendered nature of manual work in the outdoors: we all see it every time we go out. Whether it is an urban environment, where it is exclusively men digging holes in the road, removing garbage, working on scaffolding, etc., or in the countryside. More women than men study agriculture at college. But I walk around the countryside frequently and those I see working in the fields are all men.

How much imagination does it take to understand that doing dirty, laborious, and potentially hazardous work outside in all weathers, and earning little from it and even less respect, might impact adversely on one's equanimity when one reaches middle age with no expectation from life beyond being decreasingly able to sustain the physical effort? And then your wife throws you out, makes an allegation of violence against you, refuses to let you see the kids, and you are now homeless and not the local authority's priority to assist. This is not a rare scenario.

How is it that the hordes of academics carrying out suicide studies were unable to make the cognitive leap to the obvious: that men in the lowest socioeconomic classes tend to kill themselves more frequently because their lives are crap. After all, you can see them. They are not hidden. Could it be an empathy gap which blinds us to the staringly obvious?

And even the minimal encouragement of slightly better pay than more congenial jobs, typically favoured by women, is being eroded, by design. For example, consider the legal actions against supermarkets which claim equivalence of out-of-town warehouse work with in-town jobs in stores. The former employ almost entirely men, whereas the latter employ more women. These claims tend to be successful, but – from my own personal experience working in both environments as a student – I'd say the claimed equivalence is spurious.

It is clear, then, that there are multiple exogenous factors which contribute substantially to male suicide. Nevertheless, the persistent popular narrative, reinforced by parts of academia, attempts to deflect the blame back onto men themselves. This can be achieved by verbal legerdemain which recharacterizes external factors as psychological states (for example, a child contact problem becomes a man's "problem with identifying as a father", or a man's obligation to support his family becomes "perfectionism"). But the shortcomings of masculinity itself provide the most common scapegoat.

By relating suicide to hegemonic masculinity, culpability is laid squarely at the door of the man himself. If only the silly thing had not been so wedded to an outdated notion of what it means to be a man, he need not have died! If hegemonic masculinity were not smuggled into the picture we might be obliged to acknowledge that it was societal disadvantage which precipitated the suicide. But this is the conclusion which our society ties itself into cognitive knots to avoid. We must, at all costs, preserve the notion of men as autonomous and invulnerable to societal harm, because men's neediness would detract from those whose neediness is actually sanctioned. The worldview sanctioned by gynocentrism, male agency and feminism must be protected, if necessary by reconfiguring the world through whatever lens of verbiage is required to distort it to fit our preconceptions.

In section 18.3 we have seen that the deception is exposed by the fact that hegemonic masculinity may be held to blame (as championed by Brownie), or the failure to achieve hegemonic masculinity may be blamed (as proposed by Chandler). It works either way, just so long as exogenous causes can be redirected so that only the man himself is culpable.

By positing that hegemonic masculinity, or its lack, is to blame, society as a whole – and dominant gender narratives in particular – ensure that men continue to be perceived as autonomous, self-sufficient, agentic and in control of their own lives. Feminism pretends to speak against this supposed hegemonic masculinity, but actually it depends upon this mythology to delegitimise men from social concern. It cannot be admitted that men could be harmed by societal processes in which women might play a significant part. That men could be harmed by women cannot be admitted: it would reverse gynocentrism and male agency and challenge male disposability.

Only by his own failings can a man be harmed, not by others' doings: that is the fiction which must be maintained. By redirecting the blame back onto the man, society is absolved from any need to assist such men. Instead, the message to men is to improve themselves because their problem is that they are broken. By such a device, any need to acknowledge or address exogenous factors which disadvantage men is avoided. And any such acknowledgement must be avoided because men are required to function within society, not to impose a burden upon it. Men are not authorised to be needy. This is the operation of gynocentrism and male agency and disposability. This is the empathy gap.

19

Rape and False Allegations

Male sexuality is apparently activated by violence against women and expresses itself in violence against women to a significant extent.
Catharine MacKinnon, *Pleasure under Patriarchy*, in *Ethics* (1989)

Referring to men who are unjustly accused of rape: 'They have a lot of pain, but it is not a pain that I would necessarily have spared them. I think it ideally initiates a process of self-exploration. "How do I see women?", "If I didn't violate her, could I have?", "Do I have the potential to do to her what they say I did?"
Catherine Comins, former Assistant Dean at Vassar College. *Time Magazine*, 24/06/01

I feel that man-hating is an honourable and viable political act, that the oppressed have a right to class-hatred against the class that is oppressing them.
Robin Morgan, *Going Too Far: The Personal Chronicle of a Feminist*, (1977)

I believe that women have a capacity for understanding and compassion which man structurally does not have, does not have it because he cannot have it. He's just incapable of it.
Barbara Jordan (1936 – 1996) former US Senator.

Sexual assault is often considered to be the particular province of female victims. Indeed, sexual assault and rape are the pre-eminent feminist evidence for the toxicity of masculinity. And yet it is in sexual assault that we also find the most extreme discrimination against men. This discrimination lies in incredulity of the general public that a woman offending sexually against a man is a possibility. Some people even have difficulty in accepting that an adult woman can commit a sexual offence against a male minor. And almost everyone will baulk at the idea of a woman sexually assaulting an adult man. And yet, sexual offences are defined by lack of consent, not by force. The psychological disposition of the majority of the public is that the issue of a man's consent simply does not arise. But this is not the position of the *de jure* law. Unfortunately, it *is* the position of the *de facto* law.

The offence of rape is a rare example of an English law which is explicitly sexist. In English law, rape is defined as penetration using a penis. Hence a biological female cannot rape. But the definition of rape requires no use of force; the offence of rape hinges entirely upon lack of consent. And it is only the consent of the penetrated party which is required.

In this chapter I review the statistics of rape in England and Wales, covering CSEW estimates, police reports, prosecutions and convictions.

Males and females can both be raped and statistics for both sexes of victim are presented. Prison rape is excluded but will be considered in the next chapter. Attention is drawn to the obfuscation of which the CPS is culpable in their annual VAWG reports. The number of convictions for rape is a small fraction of the number of reports to the police of rape, known as attrition. The attrition rates for male and female complainants are compared. It is often implied that the attrition for rape cases is particularly large, i.e., compared with other offences. The veracity of this claim is examined here. Concern by women's groups that too many rapists are allowed to "get away with it" have led to calls for changes in the trial process for rape. These are reviewed and critiqued.

False allegations of rape occur. A perennial question is what percentage of rape complaints are false? This contentious issue is discussed. Finally, and closely linked to false allegations, is a long section on failures of the disclosure process in sexual offence trials.

This is the first of two chapters on sexual assault. The following chapter will concentrate upon the less told story of sexual offences against males, including perpetration by women. As for the present chapter, I start with the legal definition of the main sexual offences.

19.1 Definition of Sexual Offences

Within the UK, sexual offences are defined by the Sexual Offences Act 2003, (UK Government, 2003). There are a great many of them. Some are specific to minors, some relate to people in positions of trust, or offences within the family, or offences against people with a mental disorder, and many more, including offences related to prostitution, trafficking and indecent photographs of children. I cannot address all of them here, and it is not necessary to do so. The main offences are rape, assault by penetration, sexual assault and 'causing a person to engage in sexual activity without consent'. The key elements of the definition of the offence of rape are that person A commits rape against person B if,

- A intentionally penetrates the vagina, anus or mouth of person B with his penis,
- B does not consent to the penetration, and,
- A does not reasonably believe that B consents.

- Whether a belief is reasonable is to be determined having regard to all the circumstances, including any steps A has taken to ascertain whether B consents.

Only a biological male, i.e., someone possessing a penis, can commit rape in this jurisdiction. The victim, however, may be of either sex. Rape carries a maximum sentence of imprisonment for life. The Act includes some stipulations about what constitutes "consent". One of these is that a person consents if he (or she) agrees by choice, and has the freedom and capacity to make that choice. The issue of what constitutes "capacity" or "incapacity" then arises, and is problematical.

The offence of 'assault by penetration' is essentially the same as rape except that, (i) penetration is not carried out with a penis but any other body part (such as a finger) or with an object, and, (ii) the orifice penetrated must be a vagina or anus. Assault by penetration also carries a maximum penalty of imprisonment for life. Adolescent fumbling in which a young man's finger touches a girl's vagina, and inevitably "penetrates" a millimetre or two, constitutes the offence of assault by penetration, a crime almost on a par with rape. It also carries a maximum penalty of imprisonment for life.

The offence of sexual assault is defined as follows: Person A commits sexual assault if,

- He intentionally touches person B,
- The touching is sexual,
- B does not consent to the touching, and,
- A does not reasonably believe that B consents.
- Whether a belief is reasonable is to be determined having regard to all the circumstances, including any steps A has taken to ascertain whether B consents.

Conviction carries a maximum sentence of 10 years. Clearly this offence hinges upon what sort of touching is regarded as "sexual". Article 78 of the Act is intended to clarify this, but to my non-legal mind it is incomprehensible. This means that any touching of another person without their consent carries a risk of being regarded as sexual assault.

The offence of 'causing a person to engage in sexual activity without consent' is defined as: Person A commits the offence if,

- He intentionally causes person B to engage in an activity,
- The activity is sexual,

- B does not consent to engaging in the activity, and,
- A does not reasonably believe that B consents.
- Whether a belief is reasonable is to be determined having regard to all the circumstances, including any steps A has taken to ascertain whether B consents.

Where the activity involves penetration, the offence reiterates the terms under rape and assault by penetration. The offence is distinct when these conditions do not apply (e.g., there is no penetration), in which case the maximum sentence becomes 10 years, though it is unclear what then constitutes an activity which is sexual.

The characteristic of all four of the above sex offences is similar: person A is agentic, whilst person B is passive. Person A does the penetrating, or does the touching, or induces the other person to take part in an activity. Person B is passive and is acted upon. In the old gendered mindset, males are presumed agentic and females are presumed passive. There is therefore a strong psychological bias towards male culpability. But what if the ancient gender norms were never quite fully aligned with reality, and what if the old gender norms are now less indicative than ever?

In rape or assault by penetration, the person being penetrated cannot be culpable in English law. But what if a biological female coerces, or even physically forces, a biological male into a penetrative act against his wishes? Being "made to penetrate" or "non-consensually enveloped" is not covered by these laws. In the case of adult women carrying out sexual acts upon male minors, there are specific laws related to the victim's minor status, although we shall see that there is evidence that extremely few of these offences come to light.

For adult men, being "made to penetrate" is addressed, in principle, by the offences of sexual assault and 'causing a person to engage in sexual activity without consent'. But in the case of an adult woman coercing an adult man into sexual activity against his wishes, few men would know that they had any legal grounds for raising a complaint. Few would complain even if they knew in principle that they could. Men are not socialised to recognise their sexual victimisation by women, even when they feel violated by it. In this context, people who criticise men for their alexithymic tendencies may like to imagine what would happen if men were as sensitive to their emotional assaults as women. They may like to meditate upon the relationship of men's alexithymia to their toleration of disposability.

In cases involving women who have been drinking, or taking drugs, the issue of their capability to consent arises. The Crown Prosecution Service has offered the following advice, (CPS, 2017a),

> '...if, through drink, or for any other reason, a complainant had temporarily lost her capacity to choose whether to have sexual intercourse, she was not consenting, and subject to the defendant's state of mind, if intercourse took place, that would be rape. However, where a complainant had voluntarily consumed substantial quantities of alcohol, but nevertheless remained capable of choosing whether to have intercourse, and agreed to do so, that would not be rape. Further, they identified that capacity to consent may evaporate well before a complainant becomes unconscious.'

> 'Prosecutors and investigators should consider whether supporting evidence is available to demonstrate that the complainant was so intoxicated that he/she had lost their capacity to consent. For example, evidence from friends, taxi drivers and forensic physicians describing the complainant's intoxicated state may support the prosecution case.'

Hence, the loss of capacity to consent has been tied, legally, to some level of intoxication which is entirely ill-defined and will inevitably vary wildly from one case to another. A man is therefore at risk if he has sex with a woman who has drunk any alcohol at all. However, the most disturbing guidance is this,

> 'The Act imposes an evidential burden on the defendant to adduce sufficient evidence to raise an issue that the complainant consented' (CPS, 2017a)

Taken literally, one needs *evidence* of consent for every sexual encounter – and this need not mean full intercourse but applies for any sexual touching or sexual activity (whatever those terms might mean).

As regards the *de jure* law, a woman could, in principle, be guilty of assault by penetration, or sexual assault, or 'causing a person to engage in sexual activity without consent'. But at this point we run hard up against the distinction between the *de jure* law and the *de facto* law. In principle, a woman commits an offence if she touches a man sexually without his consent, or if she initiates a sexual act without his consent. In principle she too must 'adduce sufficient evidence of consent'. In principle, a man too should be deemed incapable of consent if he has consumed alcohol (to some unspecified degree), and hence a woman having sex with such a man commits an offence even if she believed him to be consenting.

But the *de facto* law could hardly be more different when the sex roles are reversed. Our profound, ancient prejudice overrules the *de jure* law. Men will rarely even perceive that they have been importuned by a woman; they are prevented by their upbringing, by society and by evolved psychological disposition. With sex and relationship education about to become obligatory in schools in the UK, it would be a good thing if boys were told about the legal fragility of their position if they have sex with, or even make intimate overtures to, a female. To quote from the book 'Legalising Misandry: From Public Shame to Systemic Discrimination against Men', (Nathanson and Young, 2006),

> 'Ewanchuk exposed a problem of profound importance – one that goes far beyond rape cases that come up in court. If implied consent is so difficult to argue in court, why would any man have sexual relations with any woman in any circumstances without written proof of her consent? Even that would be legally irrelevant. A woman could change her mind in the few minutes or seconds between signing a consent form and engaging in sexual activity. And "no", of course, means "no". Perhaps unintentionally, this doctrine severely erodes the kind of trust that is necessary for healthy sexual relations. We would have said "destroys" except for the fact that most men and women, ignorant of the law, continue to copulate on the basis of trust that has no legal standing whatsoever.'

19.2 Prevalence of Rape and Police Reports

It is frequently stated that rape is under-reported: that the rate of reporting of rape to the police is substantially smaller than its actual incidence. The surveys certainly bear this out, though recent data suggest that this under-reporting has an unacknowledged implication, which I will elucidate in due course. The true prevalence of rape is taken to be that estimated from the Crime Surveys for England and Wales (CSEW). It should be noted, however, that this estimate necessarily involves extrapolation from a small sample. There have been two major changes in recent years. The first is that the CSEW estimate of the incidence of rape of adult women has reduced markedly. (It is odd that we have not heard that reported in the press). The second is that the rate at which rapes are recorded by the police has increased steeply (for both sexes of victim).

Figure 19.1 shows how the CSEW estimate of the incidence of rape of adult women has varied from 2005 to 2016, (Office for National Statistics, 2017t). Note that the CSEW is confined to adults in the age range 16 to 59. In years 2005 to 2012, inclusive, the average incidence of rape of adult women was 0.93%. In the three reported years 2014 to 2016 the estimated incidence has fallen to about one-third the previous rate, 0.3%. This contrasts sharply with the steep increase in the rate of reporting of rape to the police, as shown by Figure 19.2, (Office for National Statistics, 2019b). Figure 19.2 refers to victims of all ages. Note the different scales for males and females in Figure 19.2. The Figure illustrates that the steep increase in reporting of rapes applies to victims of both sexes, the percentage increase for males being even larger than for females. However, the overall incidence remains far lower for males (6,218 in 2018) than for females (50,480). Hence males currently account for 11% of rape victims reported to the police.

Figure 19.1: *CSEW Estimate of Incidence of Rape of Adult Women, 2005 to 2016*

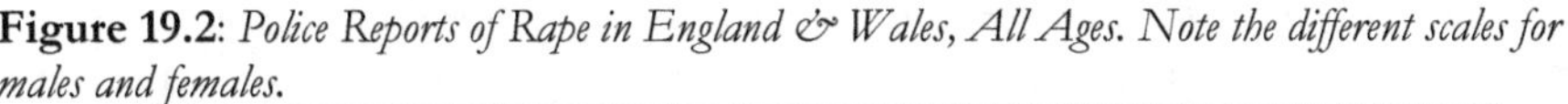

Figure 19.2: *Police Reports of Rape in England & Wales, All Ages. Note the different scales for males and females.*

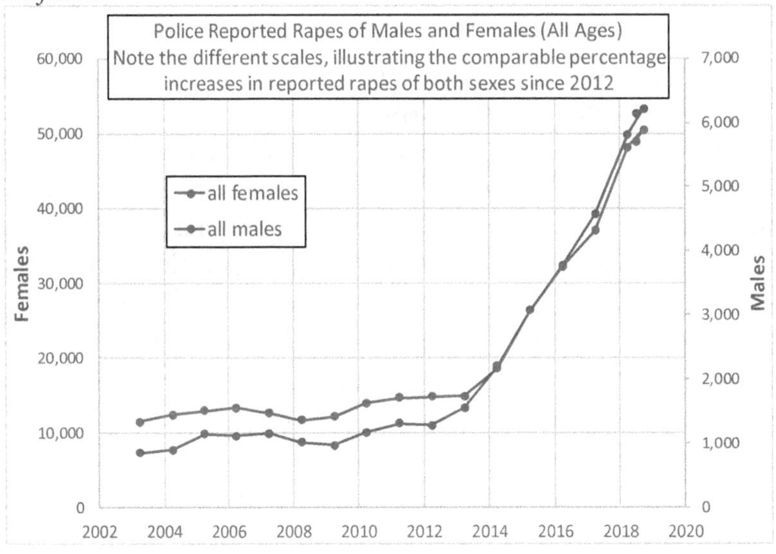

Figure 19.3: *CSEW-based Estimates of the Incidence of Rape of Adult Women Compared with the Rate of Police Reports of Rape of Adult Women*

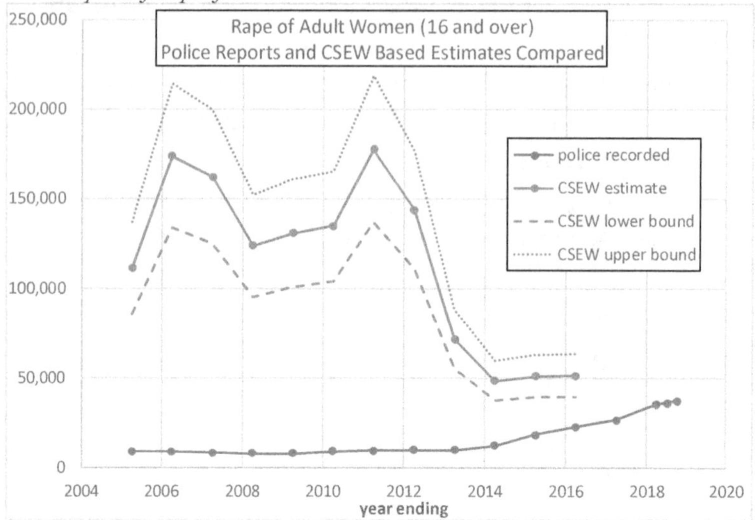

It is of interest to compare the CSEW estimate of the incidence of rape of adult women to the reported incidence. For this purpose the CSEW incidence, expressed as a percentage of women aged 16 to 59, can be converted to total incidents by multiplying by 160,000. The error in the CSEW estimate is perhaps about +/-23%, based on Figure 1.1 from (Ministry of Justice, 2013a). Figure 19.3 shows the CSEW-based estimate of the number of rapes of adult women compared with the number of police reports of the same. The upper and lower bound CSEW estimates, based on the above error, are also shown. The CSEW estimates do suggest a very large under-reporting of rape in year 2012 and earlier. But the position now appears to be rather different. The CSEW based estimate of the number of rapes of adult women in the year ending March 2016 is in the range 40,000 to 63,000. This compares with the number of police reports of rapes of adult women in the latest year (ending September 2018) of 37,369. The rate of police reports of rape of adult women is now closely approaching the lower bound of the rate estimated from the CSEW. This might suggest that the rape of women is no longer substantially under-reported. Alternatively, if rape of adult women ***is*** still substantially under-reported, then the near-convergence of the data in Figure 19.3 would imply a large prevalence of false allegations. I shall argue later that the latter appears to be the case.

The error in the CSEW estimate is inevitably large. To see why consider year 2015 when the female 'unweighted base' (i.e., the number of women contributing to the 0.3% estimate) was 10,363. But 0.3% of 10,363 is just 31 women who stated in their survey response that they had been raped in the previous year – a rather small statistic. Estimating the order of 50,000 victims from just 31 is quite an extrapolation.

How does the CSEW estimate of the incidence of rape of adult males compare with the reporting of rape of males to the police? The comparison is shown in Figure 19.4. The CSEW estimates vary wildly from year to year because the statistics are too small for stability. Over the years plotted, the average incidence was 0.032%, an order of magnitude smaller than the female incidence. Consequently, the number of men surveyed who report having been raped, from a typical 'unweighted base' of around 10,000 is only 3 per year. This could easily be 0 or 6 in any given year, hence the wild swings. (NB: The projected number of adult male rapes in Figure 19.4 has again been estimated by multiplying the percentage incidence by 160,000). The estimated average number of rapes of adult men per year is thus about 5,100. This is still about double the most recent annual rate of police reports of adult male rape, namely 2,609 in the year ending September 2018.

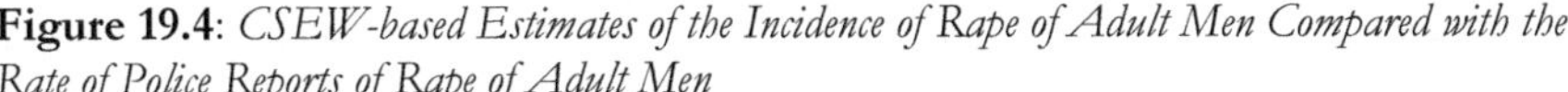

Figure 19.4: *CSEW-based Estimates of the Incidence of Rape of Adult Men Compared with the Rate of Police Reports of Rape of Adult Men*

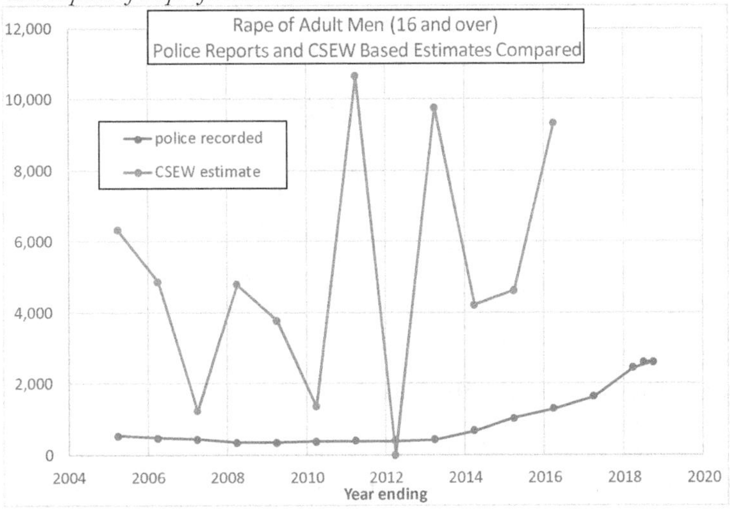

One of the differences between male and female rape victims, apart from the absolute volume of offences, is the differing age profile. Rape of females is concentrated in the adult age range, 16 and over (Figure 19.5). Rape of males is concentrated in the age range under 13 (Figure 19.6), although adult male rape is catching up, (Office for National Statistics, 2019b).

Figure 19.5: *Police Reports of Rapes of Females by Age Range*

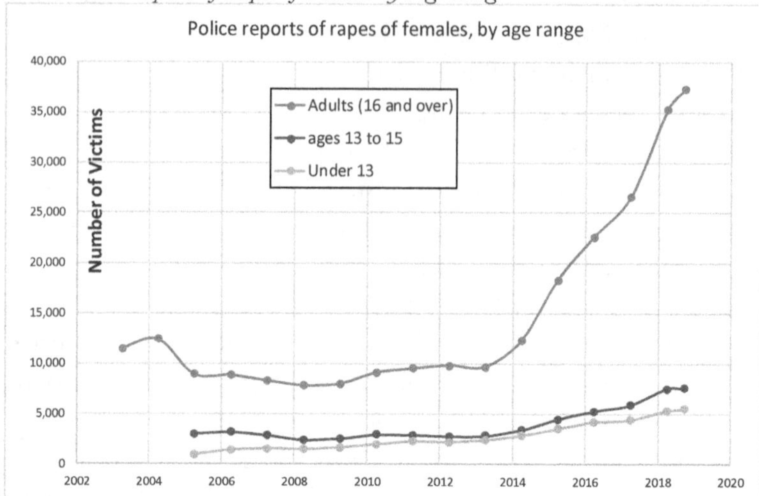

Figure 19.6: *Police Reports of Rapes of Males by Age Range*

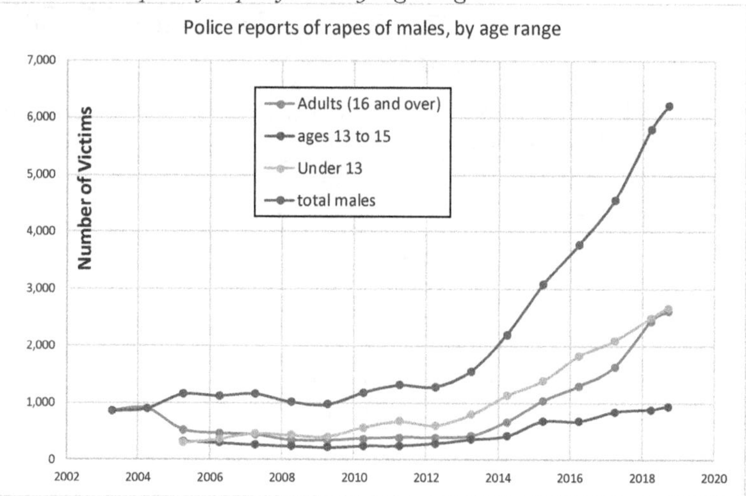

19.3 Conviction Statistics for Rape

Each year the Crown Prosecution Service (CPS) produces a report titled the 'Violence against Women and Girls Report', or the annual VAWG report. At the time of writing the latest is the 11th in the sequence, (CPS, Violence against Women and Girls Report, 2018a). Links to previous editions are (CPS, 2017b), (CPS, 2016). In this section I use all these reports back to year 2008/9. The purpose of these reports is to give special focus to females as victims.

The reader can be forgiven for assuming that VAWG, or "Violence Against Women and Girls", refers to violence against women and girls. Not so. In the CPS VAWG reports, "Violence" does not mean violence, "Women" does not mean women, and "Girls" does not mean girls. Rather, VAWG is defined as a certain category of crimes, namely: domestic abuse, child abuse, sexual offences and rape, stalking, harassment, human trafficking and modern slavery, pornography and obscenity offences, so-called 'honour-based' violence, forced marriage, female genital mutilation, and offences related to enforced prostitution. The victims of crimes classed as VAWG may be of either sex. So "Women" subsumes men, and "Girls" subsumes boys. But genital mutilation of males is not a VAWG crime, though that of females is.

Until the 2015/16 VAWG report, the reader would have needed to be very astute to realise that "Violence Against Women and Girls" also included crimes against men and boys. Since the 2015/16 report, the VAWG reports have carried a note on the title page reading "inclusive of data on men and boys" (a concession won after a number of people expressed their disquiet to the CPS). However, within the document the data still generally relate to both sexes under the banner "VAWG". It is hard to attribute this peculiar convention to any noble motive. As well as inflating the statistics which ostensibly apply to females, by including the male victimisation within them, it also rather neatly hides away male victimisation. The VAWG subterfuge is a ruse to make victimisation a female monopoly. And the insistence that females retain a monopoly of public concern is precisely male disposability and the empathy gap made manifest.

The data on prosecutions and convictions for rape in this section, being based on the VAWG reports, therefore relate to victims of both sexes combined unless otherwise stated. There is a further potential source of confusion due to the definitions employed within the CPS VAWG reports. The CPS place the emphasis on convictions arising from so-called "rape flagged" cases. Cases which enter the process as potential rape cases are "flagged" as rape cases and retain this designation even if the eventual prosecution is not for rape, or an initial charge for rape is later amended. Convictions obtained in rape flagged cases are not, therefore, necessarily convictions for rape. The conviction is frequently for a lesser offence (which therefore implies either an outcome of "not guilty" against the charge of rape, or that rape was never tried). The distinction is numerically large. For example, in the VAWG report for year 2017/18 there were 2,635 convictions which followed from rape flagged cases, but only 1,127 convictions for rape (and this includes attempted rape). This has led many people to conflate the larger number with the number of rape convictions, which is incorrect. Many people will also make the mistake of assuming that these numbers refer exclusively to female victims, which is also false.

It is difficult not to ascribe to the VAWG reports a desire willfully to mislead the reader. For example, the caption to Graph 11 of the 2014/15 VAWG Report is 'Rape volumes 2008-09 to 2014-15'. It contains the title 'Total Rape Crime', and the Key describes the conviction data as being 'Rape Convictions'. However, the conviction data plotted (up to 2,581 in 2014/15) are not all convictions for rape at all: most of these 2,581 convictions are for lesser offences. The 2015/16 VAWG Report is hardly much better. The caption of its Table 3 is 'Completed rape prosecutions by outcome', which hardly encourages the reader to interpret correctly the data which follows under 'Convictions'. In the latest 2017/18 VAWG Report, the corresponding Table caption is 'Completed rape-flagged prosecutions by outcome', which is strictly accurate though the reader must be aware that a conviction for a rape-flagged offence does not mean a conviction for rape, and hence continues to invite misunderstanding by the general reader.

However, for the last few years the VAWG reports have also included Ministry of Justice (MOJ) data for the number of prosecutions where the principle charge was rape, and the number of convictions for rape. The VAWG reports state that these data include attempted rapes as well as completed rapes. Figure 19.7 plots these data against year. The number of convictions for rape, including attempts, has not varied markedly since 2010, being an average of 1,180 per year over the years 2010 to 2017 with an average of 37% of those prosecuted on a principal rape charge being convicted of rape or attempted rape. This covers victims of both sexes. The conviction rate, assuming prosecution, for defendants accused of rape of males is shown in Table 19.1 for sample years. The conviction rate for adult male rape is especially low.

Table 19.1: *Conviction Rate for Male Rape Assuming Prosecution*

Offence	2014	2015	2017
Rape of male under 13	50%	54%	46%
Rape of male aged 13 to 15	29%	21%	47%
Rape of male aged 16 or over	15%	35%	21%

In contrast, Figure 19.8 plots the prosecution and conviction data given most prominence within the CPS VAWG reports, i.e., prosecutions of rape flagged cases and the resulting convictions, which may relate to any offence, generally a lesser offence than rape. Unlike the data which strictly relates to rape (or attempts), the number of "rape flagged" prosecutions has been trending upwards since 2006/7, as have the number of convictions resulting from such prosecutions, though an increasing proportion of these convictions is not for rape. Note the far larger conviction rate for these prosecutions (average 59%) compared to that for rape or attempted rape (37%).

Figure 19.7: *The Number of Convictions for Rape or Attempted Rape (of Both Sexes), and the Number of Prosecutions for a Principal Charge of Rape, and the Percentage Convicted (MOJ data)*

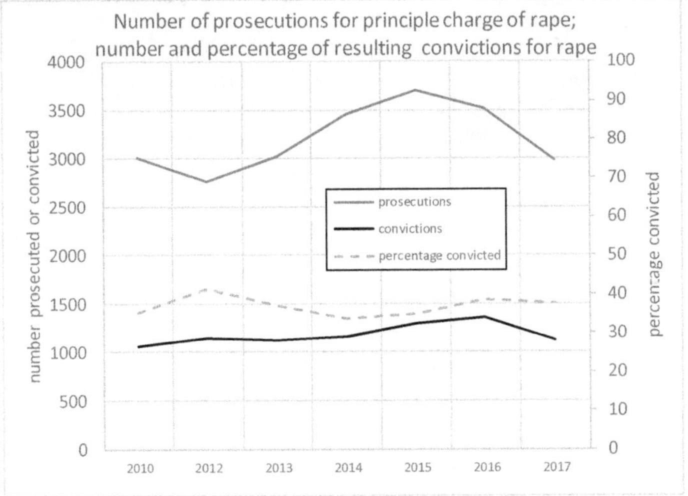

Figure 19.8: *The Number of Convictions for Any Offence Resulting from Prosecutions of Rape Flagged Cases, and the Number of Such Prosecutions, and the Percentage Convicted of Any Offence (CPS data)*

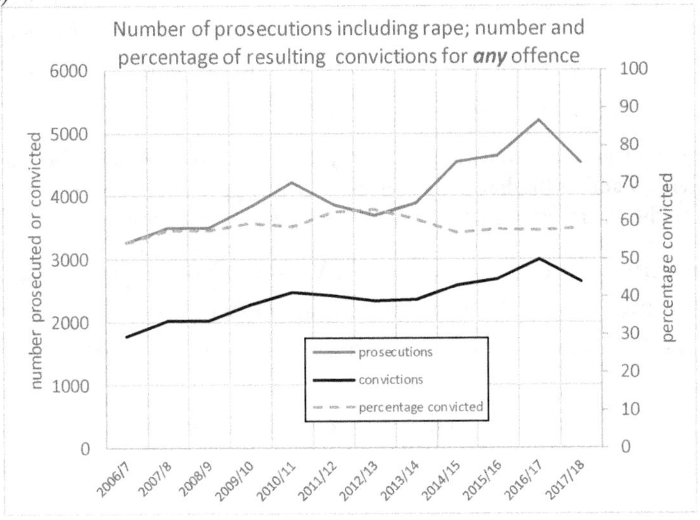

An interesting feature of the data is the marked increase in the proportion of all acquittals which arise from being acquitted by a jury at trial, when all rape flagged prosecutions are considered. (Note that there are many reasons for acquittal which do not involve exoneration by a jury, the main one being the prosecution dropping the case). The percentage of such acquittals-by-jury is plotted against year in Figure 19.9. It has increased from 36% in 2007/8 to 63% in 2014/2017.

Figure 19.9: *Jury Acquittals as a Percentage of All Acquittals for All Prosecutions of Rape Flagged Cases Versus Year*

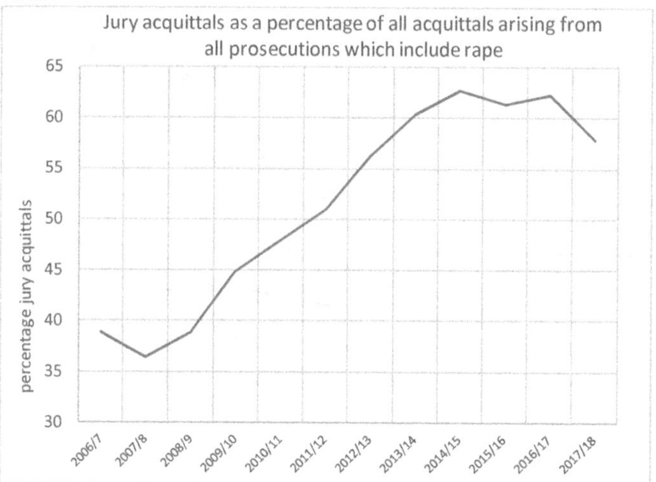

This increase in exonerations by juries has not escaped the attention of the CPS, or rape activists. The remarks made in the VAWG Reports on the matter make clear that the CPS regard it as axiomatic that increasing jury acquittals simply means that juries are failing to convict the guilty. For example, the 2010/11 VAWG Report states,

> 'The rise in jury acquittals tends to suggest that more work may be needed with partners to address public awareness and challenge myths and stereotypes, which have traditionally led to high jury acquittal rates in sexual cases.'

The same remarks are repeated in other VAWG Reports (e.g., 2012/13). It is worth recalling that in CPS terminology any verdict other than "guilty" is an "unsuccessful outcome" (and hence the conviction of an innocent man is a "success").

The CPS view that the high jury acquittal rate is due to juries "getting it wrong" fails to explain why this acquittal rate has increased substantially. There is, however, a consistent and simpler explanation of the data. Suppose that the actual incidence of rape is reasonably constant, as indeed is implied by Figure 19.7. But we know that the CPS have been prosecuting a growing number of rape-flagged cases (Figure 19.8). It would follow that a correct outcome (i.e., one aligned with truth) would be an increasing acquittal rate, as seen in Figure 19.9. If this view is correct, i.e., that the increasing jury acquittal rate is due to the CPS pursuing a greater number of weak cases, we would expect the jury acquittal rate, as a percentage of all acquittals, to be correlated with the volume of prosecutions. This is indeed the case, as displayed graphically by Figure 19.10. The Pearson correlation coefficient between the percentage of acquittals due to juries and the volume of prosecutions, for years 2006/7 to 2017/18, is 0.80: a strong correlation. There appears to be no reason to suppose that rape juries are any more lenient now than in earlier years, only that a greater percentage of cases are too weak to convict because of the CPS's over-zealous pursuance of cases which *should* fail.

Figure 19.10: *Jury Acquittals as a Percentage of All Acquittals for All Prosecutions of Rape Flagged Cases Versus the Volume of Prosecutions*

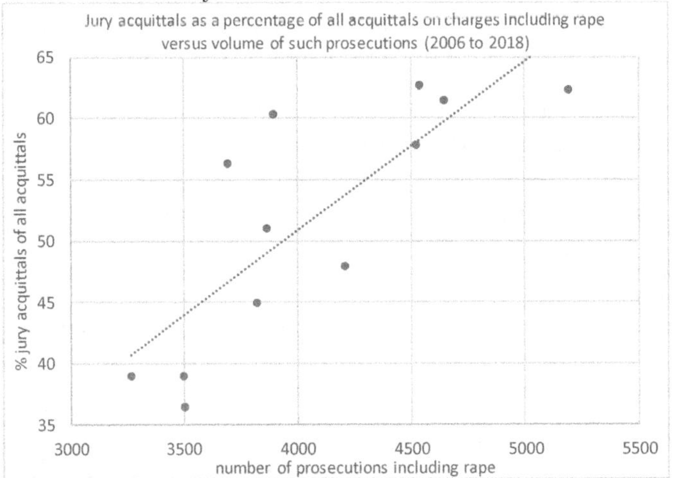

Table 19.2: *Outcome of Rape-Flagged Prosecutions*

Outcome	2006/7	2007/8	2008/9
Jury acquittal	578	539	575
All other acquittals*	908	943	902
Jury conviction	701	786	788
Guilty plea	1,077	1,235	1,230

**Almost all due to prosecution dropping the case, most often because they had no evidence to offer*

As an illustration of outcomes not determined by juries, Table 19.2 is derived from the 2008/9 VAWG report and relates to rape-flagged prosecutions (which, you will recall, may not involve a charge of rape, and, even if they do, a conviction may be for a lesser offence). In these years, juries most often returned a guilty verdict (for some offence or other).

At the time of writing we await a new review by Professor Cheryl Thomas of UCL into the effectiveness of juries in rape trials. In her 2010 review of this subject, (Thomas, 2010), she concluded that, contrary to popular belief and previous official reports, but consistent with Table 19.2, juries in rape trials convict more often than they acquit, with a 55% conviction rate in crown court rape trials. In 2010 Professor Thomas also concluded that,

> 'Jury conviction rates for rape vary according to the gender and age of the complainant, with high conviction rates for some female complainants and low conviction rates for some male complainants. This challenges the view that juries' failure to convict in rape cases is due to juror bias against female complainants.
>
> Juries are not primarily responsible for the low conviction rate on rape allegations.'

However, it remains to be seen what Professor Thomas will make of the latest data. I expect she will spot the much-reduced conviction rate. It remains to be seen whether the Professor will identify, as I have above, that this appears to be a simple consequence of the CPS pursuing an increasing number of weak cases, rather than a failure of juries to reach the correct verdict as dictated by the evidence and the principle of "innocent until proven guilty". I draw readers' attention to the especially low rates of conviction when the complainant is male. We shall see this again below when we look at attrition.

19.3.1 Sex of Rape Victims and Defendants

It may seem odd to address the sex of rape defendants, since rape is defined as an offence committed using a penis and hence can only be committed by a biological male. However, women appear in the rape defendant statistics for aiding and abetting rapes or conspiring to rape. Each year there are a certain number of such prosecutions of women. In years 2015/16, 2016/17 and 2017/18 there were respectively 65, 64 and 83 women prosecuted for aiding, abetting or conspiring to rape.

The Witness Management System records the sex of (alleged) rape victims for the majority of complaints. The data are given in Table 19.3. Note that 12.1% to 13.9% of alleged victims are male. This is broadly similar to the proportion from police reports (11% male, see Figure 19.2). Recall that none of the data in this section include prison rapes.

Table 19.3: *Sex of Rape Victims as Recorded by the Witness Management System*

year	female	male	unknown	% male where known
2015/16	4,312	608	1,734	12.4%
2016/17	4,657	754	1,790	13.9%
2017/18	4,067	560	1,607	12.1%

19.4 Attrition

The issues which most exercise rape activists are, (i) that rape is massively under-reported, and, (ii) that only a very small proportion of rapes reported to the police result in a conviction. As regards under-reporting, I have noted above that the CSEW estimated incidence of rape of adult women is beginning to align with the number of police reports of such rapes in England & Wales (Figure 19.3). However, severe under-reporting is still indicated by the CSEW and this suggests that a large proportion of police reports are false (as will be discussed in more detail below).

The second issue, that only a small proportion of reported rapes result in a conviction, is known as "attrition". An example of this attrition is provided by Figure 1.1 of (Ministry of Justice, 2013a) which gives the average of the data for years 2009/10, 2010/11 and 2011/12. Of 15,670 cases of alleged rape recorded by the police, 3,850 were flagged as "detected" in that the police were content that the crime had taken place and a perpetrator had been identified. Of these, 2,910 were prosecuted for rape and 1,070 were convicted of rape. Hence, only 6.8% of the police recorded rape allegations resulted in a conviction for rape. Some women's advocates insist that all the police reports of rape are genuine, as women never lie about rape. That is certainly untrue as one can readily identify many specific cases where women have lied about being raped (see section 19.6). However, the percentage of rape allegations which are false is a more contentious issue. This is reviewed in section 19.6. For now, two questions arise. Firstly, what is the reason for the large attrition between police reporting of rape and conviction? Secondly, how does the attrition for rape cases compare with the attrition for other serious crimes, say violence against the person (VAP) crimes? I take these two issues in order.

A Bristol criminologist specialising in the study of sexual offending has emphasised that attrition in rape cases is 'not all about criminal justice system failure', (Phil Rumney, 2018). He has listed 22 reasons for the high levels of attrition in sexual assault cases, as follows,

1. The complainant reports with no wish for a police investigation;
2. The complainant reports but decides not to do a victim interview;
3. The complainant reports and s/he decides specialist help/practical support is preferable to a criminal investigation, at least for now;
4. The complainant is uncertain or confused. Even after investigation it's not clear what has happened and there is no basis for criminal prosecution;
5. The report does not legally constitute rape;
6. The report is contradicted by other evidence;
7. Equally credible accounts are given by complainant & suspect and there is no other evidence;
8. Suspect cannot be found;
9. Suspect is dead;
10. Reported by a 3rd party, but the complainant who disclosed does not wish for the case to be formally investigated;
11. The complainant wants to move on;
12. The complainant decides s/he cannot cope with the criminal justice process at this time;
13. The complainant is worried that family members or friends might find out about the rape and has general anonymity concerns;
14. Withdrawal from the investigative process (many, many reasons for this, some listed above);
15. A recorded offence of rape is cancelled or transferred in line with the Home Office Counting Rules;
16. Retraction of the allegation because it is untrue;
17. Retraction of the allegation resulting from intimidation/manipulation by the suspect or 3rd party;
18. The report includes a false account that is so significant it undermines the complainant's credibility as a witness;
19. The case does not meet the CPS test for charging;
20. CPS discontinues the prosecution;
21. Jurors acquit on the basis that the standard of proof is not met;
22. Jurors acquit because they conclude that the defendant has a reasonable belief in consent.

To these one should add "perpetrator is unknown and investigation fails to identify him". The attention given to the high attrition rate in rape cases gives the impression that this attrition is greater than for other crimes – but is it? A study by the Ministry of Justice compared the attrition for rape offences, and for other sex offences, with GBH offences, both with and without intent, (Burton et al, 2012). Within each of these four serious offence types, a random sample of files of cases reported in eight police force areas were chosen to include a mix of urban and rural locations (though not claimed to be statistically representative of the whole of England and Wales). The sample comprised the following number of police reports: rape 292, sexual assault 287, GBH with intent 270, and GBH without intent 266. Figure 19.11 shows the attrition through the criminal justice process of this sample of serious cases. The striking thing is that the overall attrition is very similar for all four offence types. At the end of the process, the percentage of initial reports which led to convictions for the original reported offence were: rape 9%, sexual assault 11%, GBH with intent 10.5%, and GBH without intent 8.9%.

Based on this study it would appear that the presumption that rape cases, or other sexual assault cases, are subject to especially high attrition is not true. The attrition is comparable to that for serious VAP offences, with comparable final conviction rates as a proportion of initial reports. This is quite remarkable when one considers the particular difficulties in prosecuting sex offences which, by their nature, rarely have independent witnesses and often have no physical evidence, or even independent evidence that the offence has occurred at all.

Figure 19.11: *Comparison of the Attrition at Various Stages Through the Criminal Justice Process for Sex Offences and GBH*

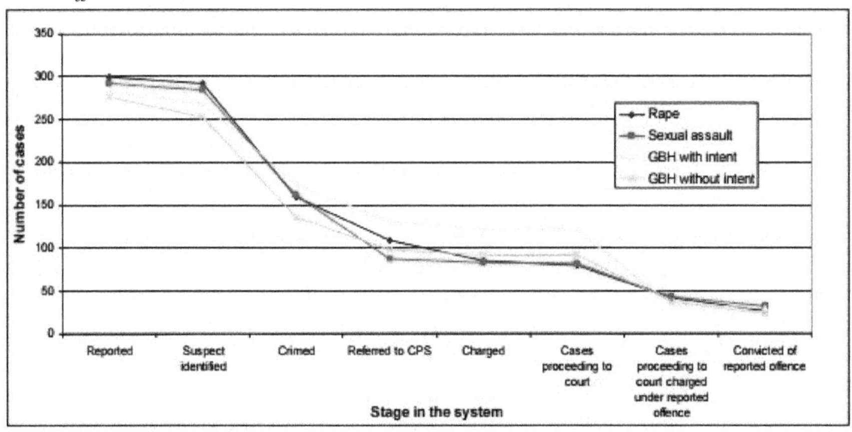

An aspect of attrition that is not usually brought out is that the attrition rate for sexual offences against males is greater than that for sexual offences against females. The overall attrition is measured by the percentage of reports to the police which fail to result in convictions for the reported offence. Attrition data for rape in England and Wales are given in Tables 19.4a-c. Table 19.4a gives the number of police reports of rape in 2013/14 and the number of convictions for rape in 2014. The latter as a percentage of the former is a measure of attrition. It is acknowledged that not all of the cases initially reported in 2013/14 will reach a verdict in 2014, so these attrition percentages are a rough indication only. Table 19.4b has the corresponding data for 2014/15 and 2015, whilst Table 19.4c has that for 2016/17 and 2017. These Tables have been compiled using the police recorded data given in (Office for National Statistics, 2019b) and the conviction data given in (Ministry of Justice, 2018e).

These Tables give the data separately for rape offences against the two sexes, as well as in different age ranges. It can be seen that the attrition for rape of males is greater than the attrition for rape of females in every age range and in every year (i.e., a smaller percentage of defendants are convicted for cases involving male victims). Recall that prison rape is not included in any of the data of this chapter.

Table 19.4a: *Attrition for Rape Offences, the Sexes Compared; Police Recorded Rape Allegations in 2013/14 cf Convictions in 2014*

Offence	Police Recorded 2013/14	Convictions in 2014	Convictions as Percentage of Recorded
Rape of female aged 16 and over	12,307	525	4.3%
Rape of male aged 16 and over	661	7	1.1%
Rape of female aged 13 to 15	3,407	321	9.4%
Rape of male aged 13 to 15	416	22	5.3%
Rape of female under 13	2,835	234	8.3%
Rape of male under 13	1,125	55	4.9%
Total (female victims)	18,549	1,080	5.8%
Total (male victims)	2,202	84	3.8%

In conclusion, we have found that attrition in rape cases involving female complaints is comparable with that for VAP offences, not especially high as suggested by rape activists. In contrast, the attrition in rape cases involving male complainants ***is*** especially great, but that receives no attention, concern or acknowledgement.

Table 19.4b: *Attrition for Rape Offences, the Sexes Compared; Police Recorded Rape Allegations in 2014/15 cf Convictions in 2015*

Offence	Police Recorded 2014/15	Convictions in 2015	Convictions as Percentage of Recorded
Rape of female aged 16 and over	18,328	616	3.4%
Rape of male aged 16 and over	1,023	19	1.9%
Rape of female aged 13 to 15	4,462	343	7.7%
Rape of male aged 13 to 15	667	24	3.6%
Rape of female under 13	3,527	226	6.4%
Rape of male under 13	1,382	69	5.0%
Total (female victims)	26,317	1,185	4.5%
Total (male victims)	3,072	112	3.6%

Table 19.4c: *Attrition for Rape Offences, the Sexes Compared; Police Recorded Rape Allegations 2016/17 cf Convictions in 2017*

Offence	Police Recorded 2016/17	Convictions in 2017	Convictions as Percentage of Recorded
Rape of female aged 16 and over	26,602	573	2.2%
Rape of male aged 16 and over	1,630	11	0.7%
Rape of female aged 13 to 15	5,897	266	4.5%
Rape of male aged 13 to 15	837	34	4.1%
Rape of female under 13	4,426	187	4.2%
Rape of male under 13	2,098	57	2.7%
Total (female victims)	36,925	1,026	2.8%
Total (male victims)	4,565	102	2.2%

19.5 Rape Trials and Juries

Numerous suggestions have been made by women's advocates to increase the number of rape convictions. It is axiomatic to this lobby that every man found not guilty of rape is a wicked villain who has got away with it. Three suggestions to modify the trial process have been made. The first is to permit the complainant to testify by video, rather than face cross-examination in court. This has already been adopted. The second is a suggestion to "train" juries in rape trials prior to the commencement of the trial. The third suggestion is to do away with juries in rape trials altogether. These latter two suggestions would be serious corrosions of the principles of justice.

19.5.1 Video Evidence by Complainants

By custom and practice it is usually considered the accused's right to face his accuser. This is no longer the case. Complainants are now permitted to give evidence via pre-recorded video in rape cases, and also in domestic abuse cases. The overturning of the precept that the accused has a right to face his accuser would appear to conflict with the Human Rights Act 1998, Article 6, which states 'everyone charged with a criminal offence has the following minimum rights....to examine or have examined witnesses against him and to obtain the attendance and examination of witnesses on his behalf under the same conditions as witnesses against him'. Is permitting the accuser to give evidence by pre-recorded video consistent with this precept? As a minimum it would appear to imply that if the accuser is allowed to pre-record her evidence, then the accused should be afforded the same privilege (i.e., 'under the same conditions'). In the USA the situation is clearer, I think, as the 6th amendment states 'In all criminal prosecutions, the accused shall enjoy the right ...... to be confronted with the witnesses against him'. The phrase 'be confronted with' effectively prohibits pre-recorded witness evidence. There is something to be said for a written constitution: it is not so easily overridden as constitution by precedent and Parliamentary fashion.

19.5.2 "Training" Rape Trial Juries

"Training" juries prior to trial is a terribly disturbing suggestion. Who will provide the material with which to do the "training"? It will clearly fall to those who claim to be expert in the area: the feminist/rape activist lobby. This "educating" will merely provide an opportunity for the trainers to impose their desired bias on perceptions. The purpose of the jury system is to allow the accused to be judged by his peers: ordinary untainted citizens. Any "education" prior to the trial is prejudicial to this ideal, even if it were of benign motivation. It would not be of benign motivation – it would be motivated by the objective of gaining more convictions, not a more accurate verdict. As just one example, what if the jury were told, as they almost certainly would be, that "false allegations of rape are extremely rare"? If the jurors believe it, the verdict would be assured.

19.5.3 Rape Trials Without Juries?

Those who interpret any not-guilty verdict in a rape trial as the jury's error have long called for juries to be scrapped in rape trials, for example (Bindel, 2016). But now that Members of Parliament have started calling for the abolition of juries in rape trials, as MP Ann Coffey has done, (Topping, 2018), the situation is becoming very worrying. A recent debate in Parliament on the matter increases one's concern, (Hansard, 2018). "Debate" in this case means feminist MPs agreeing with each other. Coffey also suggested "specialist rape courts" and referred to juries being "reluctant to convict young men". She stated that, "the most common cause of unsuccessful prosecutions in rape cases is jury acquittal". But she is here using the prosecutors' definition of success, i.e., conviction. She has absolutely no way of knowing how "successful" juries are if success is judged by the correlation between their verdict and the truth. Like all feminists, Coffey simply assumes male guilt and she has not taken the trouble to look critically at the reduced conviction rates for rape and its relationship with increased volumes of weak cases being prosecuted, as I have discussed above.

The system of trial by jury is a central principle of justice which I had thought to be inviolate. This is even more especially the case given that a guilty verdict can carry a sentence of life imprisonment. But I failed to account for the growth of anti-male prejudice within the corridors of power and influence, which is what lies at the heart of this latest attempt to erode the fundamentals of our system of justice.

QC and tax barrister, Jolyon Maugham, has expressed sympathy for the idea of scrapping juries in rape trials. 'We might start by asking, as Julie Bindel has urged, whether trial by jury serves the public interest in rape cases', he suggested, in an article titled, 'No, the legal system isn't biased against men - it allows them to rape with near impunity', (Maugham, 2018). He also offered this perspective on justice, 'it is not good enough for us to repeat the saying that it is better for ten guilty men to escape than one innocent man to suffer'. I beg to differ. I think it was far wiser men than Jolyon Maugham who created that principle in the first place. I find it extremely concerning that such a view is held by a QC. Mr Maugham is perhaps overly confident that he will not be accused himself.

At least one barrister blogger failed to be impressed by Mr Maugham's opinions, namely Matthew Scott (2018a). Amongst other criticisms, Mr Scott observed, wisely I think, that if juries were abolished for rape trials, their abolition in other trials would surely follow thereafter. Here is the same author, a criminal barrister at Pump Court Chambers, writing in The Spectator in response to Ann Coffey's suggestion and reminding us that scrapping juries in rape trials would be a mistake. He left us with a stark warning,

> 'A future Labour government may be very receptive to the abolition of juries in rape cases. It would be taken up by many on the left as a progressive measure to help rape victims. What's more, because jury trials are more expensive than judge-only trials, it would be enthusiastically implemented by a civil service long inclined to seeing juries (and even legal representation itself) as a dispensable luxury. Once rape juries have gone, juries in all other cases will not be far behind', (Scott, 2018b).

19.6 False Allegations of Rape

Few things are as contentious as claims regarding the percentage of rape allegations which are false. I had considered including here a Table of estimates of false allegation rates made in various studies, of which there are many. On reflection, however, I am of the view that this would give such estimates a credence which is undeserved. Instead I give a discussion which sets estimates in context. However, I will say at the outset that the rate of false allegations is certainly not trivial, as some try to claim. Towards the end of this long section I will give an estimate of the rate of false allegations which is both alarming and also hard to discredit.

For many years a figure of 2% was cited by many people. This derived from Susan Brownmiller's 1975 book 'Against Our Will: Men, Women and Rape'. This is the delightful work in which the author opines that rape is 'a conscious process of intimidation by which all men keep all women in a state of fear'. This is a statement which I can categorically refute immediately. It is a claim about *all* men and is stated to be a *conscious* process. Because I am a man and I am not conscious of any such thing, the statement therefore stands refuted (sorry to deploy patriarchal logic on you). Brownmiller's 2% figure turns out to have no credible basis, being a remark made in a speech by a judge in 1974 but of provenance there is none, (Greer, 2000).

The most egregious piece of misinformation about the frequency of false rape accusations is that put about by the CPS when Kier Starmer was the Director of Public Prosecutions (DPP, head of the CPS). In March 2013 the CPS published a report titled 'Charging Perverting the Course of Justice and

Wasting Police Time in Cases Involving Allegedly False Rape and Domestic Violence Allegations', (CPS Equality and Diversity Unit, 2013). It was co-authored by Alison Levitt QC. As a matter of personal history, it was this report, together with some VAWG documents, which caused me to become a blogger on men's issues in 2013. It opened my eyes to the degree to which the establishment were committed to misinformation and bias.

The Foreword, by Kier Starmer, notes that 'closer working with the police and specialist services has helped to address the types of ingrained practices which can ignore, or even add to, the victimisation of women and girls'. This is a rather odd message in a report about prosecuting false allegations of rape and DV, given that most false allegations are against men and made by women, i.e., it is a report ostensibly investigating male victimisation but expresses particular sympathy for women. This makes the mindset clear.

The Foreword continues, 'In recent years we have worked hard to dispel the damaging myths and stereotypes which are associated with these cases', and states that, 'One such misplaced belief is that false allegations of rape and domestic violence are rife. This report presents a more accurate picture'. It does not. It does exactly the opposite, and deliberately so.

The report takes data from a 17 month period between 2011 and 2013. The relevant data are contained in this quote, 'In the period of the review, there were 5,651 prosecutions for rape and 111,891 for domestic violence. During the same period there were 35 prosecutions for making false allegations of rape, 6 for making false allegations of domestic violence'. Hence, of all prosecutions for rape, only 0.6% (i.e., 35 out of 5,651) result in a prosecution for false allegation of rape, a very small percentage. The report deliberately misleads by concluding as follows,

> 'The review has allowed us to examine the suggestion that false allegations of rape and/or domestic violence are rife. It is plain that there were a large number of prosecutions for rape and domestic violence but that only a very small number of individuals were prosecuted for having made a false complaint.'

The juxtaposition of these two sentences gives the impression that the claim made in the first sentence is justified by the second sentence. It is not. The second sentence is not in the least surprising to anyone: no one has disputed that the rate of prosecution for false allegation of rape is very low. However the first sentence is false. The reader is being led by the presentation to conflate the number of prosecutions for false accusation with the actual number of false accusations. But it is the claimed huge disparity between these two things which is actually in dispute. The report has not addressed the issue at all. It is not true that the review 'has allowed us to examine the suggestion that false allegations of rape and/or domestic violence are rife'. Actually the rate of false rape or DV allegations has not been addressed by this report at all. The DPP's claim that 'this report presents a more accurate picture' is untrue. It presents a grossly misleading picture, and does so deliberately because the authors are not so foolish as to be ignorant of the distinction between false allegations and prosecutions for false allegations. The success of this misinformation is proved by the number of people since March 2013 who have been quoting a false allegation rate of 0.6% on the basis of this report. It was always the intention of the report to create a woozle. This is the degree of institutionalised dishonesty we are dealing with.

In a study primarily about anonymity for those accused of rape, the MOJ noted that 'various studies have estimated that 8% to 11% of rape allegations in England and Wales are false' and refers to a range of sources, (Ministry of Justice, 2010a). However it adds that 'the lack of a consistent definition of what constitutes a false rape allegation, as well as variations in recording practices by police and others in the CJS, make accurate assessment of the true extent of such allegations very difficult'.

One of the oft-repeated claims is that false allegations of rape are no more common than false reports of other crimes. Another MOJ report, (Burton et al, 2012), makes the following observation on a sample of cases examined in detail,

> '"False allegation" is not an officially recorded case outcome. However casefiles were reviewed to identify those cases that were seen as false. Files indicating a false allegation were then coded by the research team using the broad and narrow definitions highlighted by practitioners as part of the qualitative research. Taking the broader definition of false allegations would classify 12% of cases in the database reported as rape as false. However, the narrower definition focusing on 'malicious' complaints only would suggest a much lower figure of 3%. The prevalence of false allegations in GBH cases was lower than for rape and sexual assault. Some 2% of our sample of cases reported as GBH were considered false by police taking the broad definition covering both 'malicious' and 'non-malicious' allegations.'

The quest to determine the rate of false allegations of rape is like hunting the snark: one does not even know what it is one is looking for, let alone where to find it. Exactly what constitutes a false allegation? Certainly an allegation which is entirely fabricated, where no sexual encounter at all ever took place. But what if sexual intercourse did take place and is not disputed, but consent is disputed? What if the inebriation of the complainant is the issue? Because rape hinges upon consent, whether the crime of rape took place at all is not objectively verifiable. This little problem is brushed under the carpet. Consequently, those, like myself, who seek a factual position are ultimately frustrated by the nature of the crime itself: it has been rendered ineffable. The hard-line feminist position is that rape took place if the woman says it did – full stop. And that is why they want to see all accused men convicted – because they are all guilty as soon as accused. The conflict in perspectives is epistemological: the feminists have no truck with the idea that there is an objective truth. Truth is what they say it is.

Even if one could agree on a definition and quantification of false allegations, as a percentage of what should it be expressed? As a percentage of those prosecuted? Or as a percentage of all reports to the police? The latter is the only meaningful measure (since it is perfectly possible – in fact quite likely – that the number of false allegations considerably exceeds the number of prosecutions for rape).

The reader may wish to pursue the matter further, in which case I will reference a couple of studies as a place to start. Firstly, Lisak et al (2010) which, on the basis of their own study and also reviewing other referenced studies, concluded that 'the prevalence of false allegations is between 2% and 10%.'. Their paper may be consulted for a review of a number of other studies, many of which report far higher rates of false allegations (such as in the 30s or 40s of percent). However, Lisak et al remind us of the definition recommended by the International Association of Chiefs of Police (IACP), which emphasises the need to determine falsity through evidence of absence (as opposed to absence of evidence),

> 'The determination that a report of sexual assault is false can be made only if the evidence establishes that no crime was committed or attempted. This determination can be made only after a thorough investigation. This should not be confused with an investigation that fails to prove a sexual assault occurred. In that case the investigation would be labelled unsubstantiated. The determination that a report is false must be supported by evidence that the assault did not happen.'

Hence, studies reporting higher rates than about 10% tend to fall foul of this criterion. The other review the reader may wish to peruse is that of Rumney (2006). His Table 1 quotes the results of 20 studies which give false allegation rates ranging from 1.5% to 90%, which demonstrates rather well that the true rate is almost totally unknowable from such studies. 17 of the 25 quoted rates are in the range 10% to 47%. Rumney also critiques his sources and, rightly, indicates that the higher percentages result from studies in which either the reasons for designation of reports as "false" were unclear, or the reason fell well short of an actual demonstration of falsity.

My interpretation of this sea of confusion is that, if care is taken to include only cases where falsity is demonstrated, then the rate lies in the 2% to 10% range. However, all this establishes is a lower bound to the actual rate of false allegations. Even in the small percentage of cases which are tried in court one cannot be sure if a false allegation has been made. A conviction does not prove that the allegation was not false: there are plenty of case histories of such miscarriages of justice. Similarly, a not-guilty verdict does not prove that the allegation was false, or even that the man was innocent. And these are the cases which have received most investigative attention. We have seen above that the large majority of reports of rape do not result in prosecutions. It is not the focus of the police to compile evidence that the complaint is untruthful. Their focus is to attempt to compile evidence which makes a prosecution case for rape, and if they cannot do so, then the case does not go forward to the CPS. In many cases it will be difficult to find evidence that the allegation is false, and in most cases the attempt to do so is not made. It is sufficient for police purposes, as regards not proceeding with a case, that evidence supporting a rape prosecution is not sufficient. In short, for the bulk of cases, evidence of falsity is not sought and may not exist if it were. Consequently, the 2% to 10% estimate for the rate of false allegations is not only a lower bound, but may well be a wildly conservative lower bound, i.e., the actual rate may be far greater since the police make no attempt to find evidence which demonstrates falsity.

If the CPS takes the prize for the most reprehensible misinformation, Laura Bates, proprietor of the web site Everyday Sexism, takes the prize for the silliest. She is currently touring UK schools telling boys that 'a man is 230 times more likely to be a victim of rape than to be falsely accused of rape'. She adds, 'they're being fed all these misleading lies', (Aitkenhead, 2019). Indeed they are, and Ms Bates is responsible for some of them. To see how silly her claim is, suppose for sake of argument the CPS's figure of 0.6% were the correct rate of false rape allegations. In the year ending September 2018 there were 50,470 reports to police of rape of females (or 56,688 if rape of males is included). The number of false allegations would thus be 340. If a man were truly 230 times more likely to be a victim of rape than to be falsely accused of rape, there would have to be 340 x 230 = 78,000 rapes of males annually, 28 times the actual current rate of reporting adult male rapes to the police. But, I have argued above, the *lower bound* to the false allegation rate is in the range 2% to 10%. That gives us 1,134 to 5,669 false allegations per year, and hence – if Bates were right - an implied number of male rapes annually of 261,000 to 1,300,000, the latter being 470 times greater than the reporting rate to the police of adult male rapes. Err, no, I don't think so. Bates's claim is absurd. The false allegation rate only has to exceed 5%, as seems almost certain, for the probability of an adult man being falsely accused to exceed his probability of being raped. Ms Bates was attempting to minimise the significance of female offenders (false accusers) by eclipsing them with male offenders (rapists). This is what feminists always do.

The incidence of false rape allegations is certainly not a trivial percentage, as is sometimes claimed. Aileen McColgan claimed the rate of false allegations of rape to be 'infinitesimal', for example, (Rumney, 2006). That lower bound estimates lie in the range 2% to 10%, and that these estimates leave the bulk of allegations uninvestigated, is sufficient to prove the point that false allegation rates are not a trivial percentage. Personally, though, I was convinced of the matter by my own exercise to identify cases of false allegation.

I confined my search to the UK and to recent years. My only source was newspaper articles, which will severely limit what can be found. My expectation is that most cases of false allegation will not be reported in newspapers (or even identified as such). Hence, my trawl could only possibly pick up a small fraction of cases. Yet I easily found 146 cases, not including politicians or celebrities. My review, together with all 146 case histories, can be found in (Collins, W, 2018b). The 146 cases involved 16 deaths. 12 of these were the suicide of the wrongly accused, one was the suicide of the falsely accused's mother, one was the suicide of the alleged false accuser, one was a homicide due to vigilante action, and one was the death in prison of an innocent man. At least 28 of these cases involved disclosure failures, possibly more but news reports are not always explicit. Disclosure is discussed further in the next section. 25 cases involved serial accusers, 14 of them had accused more than two men.

I also reviewed allegations of rape or sexual assault against politicians, (Collins W. , 2018c), and celebrities, (Collins W. , 2018d), looking for all such allegations not just false allegations. I identified 25 cases of alleged sex offences against senior politicians (not including councillors), 24 men and one woman. Whilst I cannot be certain, my judgment was that 21 of these 25 were not guilty of any criminal offence, with 4 being guilty. You may judge differently. For celebrities I identified 45 cases, all men. My opinion was that 12 men were probably guilty, 29 men were innocent, and in 4 cases the matter was not clear. So, of the 70 cases against politicians or celebrities, the allegations appeared to be false, or below the criminal level, in at least 71% of cases. I had hoped that this would provide a handle on the rate of false allegations among the general public, but on reflection this can hardly be claimed. Politicians and celebrities have a target on their back and will potentially attract accusations to a far greater extent than an unknown member of the public. Nevertheless, the 71% figure is salutary. Of course, you may disagree with my reading of the cases.

To close this section I make a simple estimate of the rate of false allegations of rape of adult women. The estimate is alarming, but is difficult to fault as all the figures which are used are official figures from the MOJ or the ONS. We have seen in section 19.2 that the CSEW central estimate was 51,200 rapes of adult women in the latest survey year (year ending March 2016), derived from (Office for National Statistics, 2017t) as 0.32 times 160,000 (see also Figure 19.3). This rate appears steady over the last few years. But in (Office for National Statistics, 2018u) we read that the CSEW also identifies the following,

> 'Those who had experienced rape or assault by penetration (including attempts) since the age of 16 were asked who they had personally told.... Around one in six (17%) had told the police.'

Hence, these two CSEW-derived figures together imply that the number of genuine rapes of adult women reported to the police is expected to be 17% of 51,200, or 8,700 cases. But we have also seen in section 19.2 that the actual number of reports to the police of rape of adult women in the latest reported year (year ending September 2018) was 37,369, (Office for National Statistics, 2019b), see also Figure 19.5. These data imply that only 8,760 of the 37,369 cases of adult rape of women reported to the police were genuine, i.e., a false allegation rate of 77%. Since all three figures used in the estimate are MOJ or CSEW figures it is difficult to dismiss this result, despite its alarming nature.

To return to Laura Bates's preposterous claim, the above argument suggests there are 28,609 false rape allegations annually, some 11 times greater than the number of reports of adult male rape to the police, or nearly 6 times the estimated incidence of adult male rape based on the CSEW. It is fairly clear that false allegations represent a greater risk to men than rape. To express that differently: women are a greater sexual hazard to men than other men.

It is worth emphasising that the number of police reports of rape of adult women was far smaller, around 10,000, in 2013 and earlier (Figure 19.5), and the CSEW estimate of the rape incidence rate was substantially larger. Consequently, in these earlier years the same method would not provide evidence for a false allegation rate. This suggests that the alarmingly high false allegation rate of 77% or thereabouts is a recent phenomenon. The huge increase in reports of rape to the police since 2013, evident in Figure 19.5, would seem to have been the result of a massive escalation in false allegations. Patrick Graham has opined that the ready availability of victim compensation may be at least part of the reason, especially as compensation payment is not even dependent upon securing a conviction, (Graham, 2018).

It is also worth noting that Figure 19.6 shows a similar steep increase in the reporting of rape by adult males since 2013, suggesting that it is not only women making false allegations, but also men who may be seeking victim payouts. However, whatever the sex of the accuser, it is overwhelmingly men who are the accused. It is reasonable to hypothesise that this apparent dramatic increase in the incidence of false allegations since 2013 is a result of the post-Savile Operation Yewtree, which started in October 2012.

These observations put the increased frequency of jury exonerations of rape defendants (Figure 19.9) in a rather different light. The considerably increased exoneration rate since 2013 may be simply because juries are failing to be fooled by fraudsters, as indeed one would wish, rather than because an increasing number of rapists are "getting away with it", as the rape activists and our political establishment would have us believe, (Hansard, 2018). This further discredits calls for juries to be scrapped in rape trials. Not only would this be a profound erosion of a basic principle of justice, but it would remove the final barrier against injustice which has not yet fallen.

19.6.1 The Harm Done by False Allegations

Rape allegations are mud that sticks indelibly. Consider a totally innocent man, he need not even have met the accuser, (Graham, 2018). He will have his life ruined for perhaps two or three years whilst the case comes up, and probably for ever after as well. He is likely to be socially ostracised by his friends, relatives and neighbours, and perhaps even subject to attacks. During that time he may be suspended from work, or actually sacked. He may be prohibited from having any access to children, which may mean that he is obliged to leave his own home as he is deemed to be a risk to his own family. He may be subject to a curfew and made to wear an electronic tag. He may be forced to pay tens of thousands of pounds in legal defence for a case which is never heard because the prosecution announces the day before the trial is due that they have no evidence to offer. If the trial proceeds he might have to sell his house to pay legal bills in six figures, even for a case where the accusation is palpably ridiculous. He may end up bankrupt, homeless and unemployed as a result. If this description seems far fetched, take a look at the case histories linked from my review, (Collins, W, 2018b).

In terminating the case, the prosecution will generally use a form of words such as, 'we consider there is insufficient evidence to secure a conviction', thus leaving the impression that the man is guilty, they just cannot muster quite enough evidence to prove it conclusively. They will not reveal that they never had any independent evidence whatsoever and were just hoping something would turn up, a second accuser, perhaps. And even if the accused is tried and exonerated by a jury, there will be no shortage of voices – especially from feminist groups – that justice has miscarried, that he is actually guilty. Newspaper reports prior to trial will refer to him as a rapist. The same newspapers will most often report nothing when he is found not guilty or charges are dropped. Internet searches for the rest of his life will bring up the stories which accuse him of rape, but often without the ending of the story – the exoneration. And even if the exoneration is clear, in the minds of many the mud will stick. He may find that his former employers refuse to re-employ him even after he is exonerated, and when he attempts to get a new job, the Disclosure and Barring Service (DBS) may very well reveal his acquittal at a rape trial because the police 'think he might have been guilty', (Gibb, 2017).

However, these few words do not do justice to the devastating psychological impact of false accusation of sexual abuse. Oxford criminologists Carolyn Hoyle, Naomi-Ellen Speechley and Ros Burnett have produced a report on the severity of this impact, specifically covering people in positions of trust, especially teachers, against whom allegations are common, (Hoyle et al). Of broader scope is the anthology edited by Burnett (2016) 'Wrongful Allegations of Sexual and Child Abuse'. These studies confirm the account I have given above. They also identify an ongoing fear of being accused again. A few extracts are worth repeating,

> 'In the majority of accounts, an overwhelming sense of anger and betrayal emerged. More often this was not directed at their accusers, but at employers who were thought to have encouraged the allegations, at the police for what our participants

saw as treating them as guilty from the outset, and at a 'victim-centred' criminal justice system, with its provisions for complainants on one hand, and what they felt was a failure to recognize rights or due process of the accused on the other.'

'In our view, the cumulative impact of these interviews is both shocking and immense….until we conducted this study we had little grasp of the extent to which a false allegation is likely to affect every aspect of a person's life, psychological, material and physical. Most of the participants, it should be recalled, were able to refute the accusations made against them at a relatively early stage of the legal process. Despite this, their lives were, to put it simply, wrecked. It need hardly be stated that for factually innocent defendants who are wrongly convicted and imprisoned, but who cannot legally demonstrate this, the consequences will be still greater.'

'It is also of deep concern that the experiences described by the participants in this study are far from rare. A 2015 survey by the Association of Teachers and Lecturers of 685 of its members found that 22% of school and college staff had been the subject of a false allegation of abuse by a pupil…..The survey also found that, not surprisingly, the prevalence of false allegations and the publicity given to them is driving experienced staff out of teaching, and, presumably, deterring others from seeking to enter it.'

At this point the reader may wish to recall the decline in the male teacher and the associated discussions in chapter 2. Burnett et al conclude,

'The authors of this study hope that it will provide a valuable corrective to the somewhat uncritical discourse that has dominated media, political and policy-making discourse over the past 20 years – the discourse which states that victims will, almost invariably, be telling the truth. It is worth here repeating the Metropolitan Police statement on Operation Midland, 'our starting point with allegations of child sexual abuse is to believe the victim until we identify reasonable cause to believe otherwise.' No doubt the intentions behind that statement were honourable: a desire to right an historic wrong, and to give victims who had been previously ignored a voice. But this study suggests that in the process, a whole new and growing class of victims is being created, whose suffering is intense – all the more so for having been, until now, largely ignored. The road to hell, it is said, is paved with good intentions. Unfortunately, that is where the victims of false allegations of abuse are likely to find themselves – in a living hell.'

19.7 Disclosure

The exposure of allegations as false is not aided by the criminal justice process as it has been practiced in recent years. In late 2017 and early 2018 there were a rash of failed prosecutions of young men for rape, the common denominator being late, or improper, disclosure – see for example (Collins W. , 2017b). It would be hard to overstate the importance of disclosure. It is the process by which evidence is made available to the court, and hence is a central aspect of justice. Formally, the prosecution is in charge of disclosure, though they are obliged to pass on all relevant material to the defence. However, it is not lawyers who do the leg work to uncover evidence. That is the job of the police. Evidence includes witness statements, physical evidence and electronic communications. The latter are now extremely important in sex cases. The police are supposed to collect all evidence pertinent to the case, whether it might assist the prosecution or the defence, and "disclose" it, i.e., pass it on, via the prosecution team. Unfortunately, it has emerged that the disclosure process is seriously flawed in many cases.

Bluntly put, if you have been charged with rape, the only thing standing between you and a 10 year stretch might be whether a single policeman, or policewoman, can be bothered to unearth the key exculpatory evidence. Unfortunately, it is not only police laziness which may condemn you. There is also a culture which has taken root within the police that their job is to get a prosecution. The false allegation cases I reviewed, (Collins, W, 2018b), are full of examples of the police sitting on evidence which would have cleared the accused man, but they did not disclose it. Worse, the informal adoption of a mindset of "believe the victim" has meant that the accused is put in the position of having to prove his innocence: a reversal of the hallowed principle of "innocent until proven guilty". Having to prove your innocence is bad enough, but disclosure failures may then deny you access to the evidence to enable you to do so.

The celebrated case of Liam Allan, one of those which emerged at the end of 2017, is a typical example of a disclosure failure. Fortunately, in this case, the key evidence was revealed at the last moment, (Hartley-Parkinson, 2017). The case against Liam Allan collapsed when former conservative MP Jerry Hayes, the prosecution barrister – yes, the prosecution barrister – insisted that the police hand over the evidence from the complainants 'phone. Some 50,000 messages were finally revealed on the first day of the trial itself. The defence advocate, Julia Smart, to her great credit, spent the rest of that day, and undoubtedly all night, reviewing the contents of the new disclosure. Among them were messages to Mr Allan pestering him for sex and fantasising about 'rough sex and being raped'. One message read simply 'it wasn't against my will or anything'. The prosecution advised the case be withdrawn. It was. It should never have come to court. In an excellent résumé of the Liam Allan case, Matthew Scott, the Barrister Blogger, sums it up: 'Despite the magnificent performance of Mr Hayes, a case like this ought to shatter any remaining illusions that the English and Welsh criminal justice system is fit for purpose', (Scott, 2017).

But the Liam Allan case was just one in a string of failed rape cases which received publicity at that time due to similar shortcomings in process. Nor is this new. In 2006, solicitor Chris Saltese believed that there were 'certainly scores, and very possibly hundreds of men who have been convicted of sexual crimes who are rotting in prison with no prospect of release, but who are not guilty and should never have been sentenced. They were convicted on their accusers' word alone. The records that might prove their innocence have been lost or destroyed. There is literally nothing they can do to prove that they did not do what they have been accused of doing except reiterate that they did not do it. And that, of course, is not enough.' (Palmer, 2006).

It is surely damning when lawyers are so critical of the system in which they themselves are employed. Here is a coruscating piece by solicitor Matthew Graham, following the trial failures in late 2017,

> 'This isn't a story of a few rogue cops gone bad, or a crumbling, underfunded criminal justice system overwhelmed by national austerity (though both get blamed daily in courts and the press to cover a wider, more difficult truth). This is a story of a state funded system designed with political ends in mind to convict those accused of crime, because once a person is charged they must be guilty, if only the Crown can prove it.
>
> The job of the police is to investigate whether or by whom an offence has been committed. They have a legal duty to investigate all reasonable lines of enquiry, whether they point towards the guilt or innocence of a particular suspect. It sounds simple, but if you are a suspect in a criminal case you need to understand that this isn't how it works.....
>
> Inconvenient evidence that would undermine a prosecution or assist a suspect doesn't achieve either of those aims, so it doesn't have any real importance. As soon as the police think it is their job to catch the criminals, the system goes wrong, because it is they, not a court or a jury or anyone independent, who is deciding on who is a criminal and then setting about proving it....
>
> Pity those, and there are many, who didn't get the disclosure they deserved. Pity those suspects where the police hold or could hold evidence that helps their case that they don't know about. An extra witness here. A useful 999 call there. Social services records. School reports. Text messages. Emails and social media content. And ever on. And more fool those who expect a court to help their quest for fair disclosure. Expect to be met with apathy at best, more likely positive resistance. Expect to be told you are simply fishing for a loophole. Expect to have to justify the relevance of the material you have never seen. Expect the court to wholly accept a bland assurance of a prosecutor in court that never comes to fruition. Expect excuse after excuse after excuse and expect no one in authority to care one bit. And when you reach the day of trial without having received what the

> law says you should, expect the trial to carry on all the same. Because this is what happens in cases every day, all over the country, in magistrates and crown courts.' (Graham, M, 2018)

Lawyer Nick Freeman has called for people who make false rape and sexual assault allegations to be stripped of their statutory anonymity and named on a public register: 'The time has come for there to be a register where the names of those who make these disgraceful and disgusting allegations are added. Sadly, Mr Allan's case is not a one off. It is one of many – the tip of the iceberg. False allegations are made on a daily basis, and those who make them can hide behind a lifelong veil of anonymity', (Green, 2017).

On BBC Radio 4's 'Today' programme on 18/1/18, the then-DPP, Alison Saunders, was interviewed about the rash of failures of disclosure in recent rape cases. Sarah Montague opened with the simple direct question, 'Is it possible that there are people in prison today because of failures of disclosure by the police and CPS?'. Alison Saunders replied, 'I don't think so because of the safeguards which are in place'. One can immediately assert, with confidence approaching mathematical certainty, that the DPP's reply was false. Saunders failed to provide a politician's response to that tricky question and that was career terminal. Most surprisingly, on 27/1/18, John Humphrys on Radio 4's 'Today' programme effectively called for Alison Saunders' resignation by suggesting she should 'consider her position' and that it might be 'time to step aside'. On the same day it was announced that all rape and serious sexual assault cases in England and Wales would be reviewed to ensure evidence had been properly disclosed, (BBC News, 2018). Shortly after, Saunders announced she would be stepping down as DPP and did so on 31st October 2018. But the problem was never one person but an endemic mindset and institutionalized practices inimical to justice. Nor is the problem confined to the CPS but is principally an issue with the police, upon whom the burden of unearthing and disclosing evidence rests. In the matter of sexual offences, the police have been trained by feminist lobbyists.

In June 2018 the CPS issued their review of prosecutions of 'Rape And Serious Sexual Offence' (RASSO) cases, (CPS, 2018b). It includes the obligatory contrition,

> 'We deeply regret every case where mistakes have been made. Our priority, working closely with the police, is to put in place effective measures that bring about a sea-change in how disclosure is managed so that complainants and suspects alike can have confidence that every case is fair.'

However, the report is an unsatisfactory affair. It was confined to cases in progress, not cases already with a verdict. It refers to a review of 'all rape or serious sexual assault prosecutions being handled by the RASSO units and which were already set for trial, or in which a plea of not guilty was anticipated.....By February 13, a total of 3,637 cases had been assessed by RASSO lawyers. Some cases were at an early stage, while others were close to trial'. It also states that, 'the principal reason for undertaking this assessment of RASSO cases was to confirm that they were being progressed properly, and to address any concerns'. And yet, incredibly, the report omits to inform us of the outcome of this review of 3,637 cases. Instead it states that after this main review had concluded, 'the CPS conducted a further exercise to identify the extent to which disclosure issues were a factor in the decision to stop RASSO cases during that period'. The period in question was a mere six weeks, namely between 1 January and 13 February 2018. The report does not tell us how many cases were stopped in that period.

The only review outcomes which were reported were confined to this sub-review of cases which had been stopped. Even that is limited in extent. We are informed that 47 cases stopped during the period had issues with disclosure of unused material. But what this is as a percentage of the number of stopped cases we do not know. We are also informed of the following results of the review of stopped cases,

> 'This analysis has found examples of communications evidence that ought to have been reviewed by the investigator and prosecutor not being examined until after the case had been charged. In some of the cases that were stopped this evidence was so undermining that there was no longer a realistic prospect of conviction.'
>
> 'The failure to identify relevant third parties and to obtain material from them in a timely way was a feature in some of the cases that were stopped during the review period.'

But the report does not tell us to how many of the stopped cases these serious failings relate. Why not?

Even confining attention to cases which are stopped by the prosecution, since 47 disclosure failures were found in a period of six weeks, the implication might be that about 400 stopped cases per year would have disclosure problems. The actual number in 2017 was 916, (Graham, M, 2018). And what about cases which had not been stopped but were continuing to proceed? We are told nothing whatsoever about these, and yet these are the cases which matter most as regards potentially unsafe convictions. The report does nothing to reassure and a great deal to consolidate one's concern.

Accountability lies with the Attorney General, who is either asleep on the job or just hoping to get away with it.

However, the Commons Justice Select Committee, whose job it is to oversee such matters independently of the Ministry of Justice line management, took a rather more robust approach. Their inquiry report into disclosure was issued the month after the CPS's own report, on 20th July, (HOC Justice Committee, 2018). It is almost enough to restore one's faith in the democratic process (savour this moment, you will not hear me praising politicians again very soon). Some of the key findings of the Select Committee are worth reiterating at some length,

> 'We note that disclosure errors have been damaging for many people affected, including for complainants who might have waited years to have their case heard only for it to be delayed or for it to collapse. Fundamentally, however, disclosure errors have led to miscarriages of justice and - as the Director of Public Prosecutions told us - some people have gone to prison as a result.'

Note that Saunders appears to have changed her mind on this crucial fact since January. The Select Committee report continues,

> 'It is disappointing that we have heard the same issues raised throughout this inquiry as have been noted by inquiries as far back as 2011, and it is further disappointing that the Attorney General in place at the time of inquiry stated to us that he was aware of problems going back as far as 1996 but yet the problem had persisted and apparently worsened under his watch. We are also surprised and disappointed that the DPP, who should be closer to these problems on a day-to-day basis, does not appear to have pressed for more urgent action to address the worsening situation during her time in post.'

> 'We conclude that disclosure failures have been widely acknowledged for many years but have gone unresolved, in part, because of insufficient focus and leadership by Ministers and senior officials. This was not aided by data collected by the Crown Prosecution Service which might have underestimated the number of cases which were stopped with disclosure errors by around 90%.'

> 'The Code for Crown Prosecutors is clear "Prosecutors must be fair, independent and objective… Prosecutors must always act in the interests of justice and not solely for the purpose of obtaining a conviction". The fact that performance metrics do not fully reflect the purpose of the CPS is compounded by a significant underestimation of the number of cases that stopped due to disclosure errors in the CPS' internal data.'

> 'It is surprising and concerning that the Director of Public Prosecutions did not know that the case against Liam Allan had not been recorded as a disclosure error at the point that it was stopped. The Director has not acted as quickly and proactively as required and this, it appears to us, has permeated throughout the organisation.'

> 'It is fundamentally important that all police officers recognise both that they are searching for the truth; and that they have core disclosure duties which are central to the criminal justice process and are not merely an administrative add-on….. It is vital that disclosure is embedded at every stage in the process and not delegated to the most junior person as has all too often been the case in the past.'
>
> 'It is important that those who come forward to report serious offences, particularly those of a sexual or otherwise sensitive nature, are treated by investigators with respect and sensitivity. Their personal information should be handled in the same way and in accordance with their rights to privacy, where that is consistent with the interest of justice. The law is clear in that the right to a fair trial is an absolute right which cannot be violated to protect the right to privacy.'
>
> 'We do not agree with the DPP's assertion that disclosure in the Magistrates' Courts is not an issue and we are concerned that disclosure errors in the Magistrates' Courts will be left to continue if effort is not also focussed there.'
>
> 'We welcome the National Disclosure Improvement Plan, and note that it names the people responsible for ensuring that it follows into real and lasting change. We expect these people to be personally accountable for delivery of the plan.'
>
> 'We expect the next Director of Public Prosecutions to proactively address disclosure throughout their tenure.'

The last point refers to Max Hill who took over as the new DPP on 1st November 2018. Unfortunately, Mr. Hill does not seem to have got the message. I refer to the specific message in the Select Committee's guidance, above, that 'the law is clear in that the right to a fair trial is an absolute right which cannot be violated to protect the right to privacy'. Contrary to that guidance, in his first public speech as DPP, Mr Hill emphasised the complainants' right to privacy above the interests of justice and indicated clearly that searching social media records – a key issue in disclosure – will continue to be incomplete. An article in The Times reports his speech as follows,

> 'Rape complainants must have their personal privacy, including mobile phone records, protected, the new chief prosecutor said last night as he addressed his department's failings on disclosure of evidence.
>
> He said that there needed to be a lasting change in culture when it came to disclosure. However, he insisted that prosecutors were not obliged to trawl through the mobile phone records of all rape complainants as they struggled to cope with the rise in the volume of digital evidence.
>
> "We are very clear that seeking to examine the mobile telephones of complainants and witnesses is not something that should be pursued as a matter of course in every case," he said. "It is of vital importance that the personal information of those who report sexual offences is treated in a way that is consistent with both their right to privacy and with the interests of justice."' (Gibb, 2018)

So, it appears that the new DPP's view is that ensuring that any exculpatory evidence is found is rather too much trouble, and the complainants' privacy provides a suitable excuse for not being thorough. How much trouble would the accused man think was worthwhile to avoid ten years in prison and his reputation ruined forever? And do recall that Liam Allan's defence barrister found the relevant evidence overnight, in a haystack of 50,000 messages. If the police cannot be bothered to search thoroughly, the defence should be permitted to do so for themselves. Max Hill's attitude is appalling and inexcusable. It gives one no faith that there is any acknowledgement of the seriousness of the failings of the prevailing culture.

The 2017/18 CPS VAWG report contains a number of brief accounts of rape cases. On page 9 we read this one, (CPS, Violence against Women and Girls Report, 2018a),

> 'A young man was convicted of rape and controlling or coercive behaviour of his 16 year old girlfriend. The early disclosure of communications evidence, including thousands of pages of social media messages, led to the defendant pleading guilty to the controlling or coercive offence. A trial was held for the rape offence – the victim gave her evidence via video link after a pre-trial meeting with Counsel who provided support and reassurance. The defendant was sentenced to a total of four and a half years' imprisonment and made subject to a restraining order for 10 years.'

It seems, then, that 'early disclosure of communications evidence, including thousands of pages of social media messages' is not a problem when it is prosecution evidence being sought. Only when exculpatory evidence is in question does searching social media become too much trouble.

19.8 The Empathy Gap in Accusations of Sexual Assault

Sexual assault is generally regarded as victimisation of women and nothing more. Indeed, in feminist patriarchy theory, sexual abuse is said to be used as a tool by men for their oppression and domination of women. Radical feminists even assert that all penis-in-vagina sex is rape. But there are some issues in the context of sex offences in which men are disadvantaged. In this chapter I have concentrated upon the position of accused men and whether they receive fair treatment when accused.

We have seen that the CPS VAWG reports are an exercise in obscuring male victimisation whilst amplifying female victimisation, accomplished through a form of Newspeak in which "Violence" does not mean violence, "Women" does not mean women, and "Girls" does not mean girls. Claims that attrition of rape cases where the complainant is female is particularly large are challenged by a study which shows such attrition to be comparable to that for VAP offences. In contrast, attrition of rape cases where the complainant is male is indeed unusually large, but this goes unremarked by rape activists.

Feminists insist that women do not lie about rape, a claim that is palpably false. The percentage of rape allegations which are false continues to be highly controversial, but it is clearly not a trivial percentage. There is evidence which is difficult to refute that, at least in recent years, the false allegation rate has become an alarmingly large percentage, specifically that most police recorded rapes are false allegations. There is no shortage of case histories testifying to the egregious treatment of entirely innocent men. The psychological impact of false allegations is devastating, often leading to suicide. Feminists are unconcerned about this, even opining that falsely accused men might regard the experience in a positive light. For example, Deborah Orr writing in the Guardian,

> 'I'd like to hear just one person, exonerated after a sexual offences trial, declare that despite their personal suffering, they are proud to live in a society that takes people seriously when they say they have been sexually abused, and that if occasionally people have to undergo ordeals like theirs, in order to ensure that others who have committed such crimes are less likely to get away with them, then so be it.' (Orr, 2013)

I paraphrase: a man should be glad to have suffered at the hands of a woman in order to prevent suffering to women. Well, if the man were truly saintly, then yes. But this is an expectation of self-sacrificial behaviour by men, which is precisely what "male disposability" means. And the attitude of a woman who expects such self-sacrifice from men, for the benefit of women, is precisely what "gynocentrism" means.

One of the signs of a society which is slipping into authoritarianism is a creeping erosion of the processes of justice. This erosion will serve the interests of those in power to the detriment of those against whom they exercise their animus. In the context of men accused of sexual offences, there are five fundamental principles of our justice system which either have been eroded already or are under imminent threat of such erosion. They are,

- Everyone is equal before the law, irrespective of race or creed or sex;
- Everyone has the right to be regarded as innocent until proven guilty;
- Everyone accused of an indictable criminal offence, and pleading not guilty, has the right to be judged by his, or her, peers – the right to a trial by jury;

- Everyone has a right to expect all available evidence and testimony to be brought before the court;
- And, arguably, the right to face one's accuser.

Equality before the law has already been demolished in respect of sex, as discussed at length in chapter 8.

The *de facto* position in respect of males accused of sex offences against females is that the principle of innocence until proven guilty has also already been overturned. Whilst this is not a formally recognised position, in practice sex offences often reduce to "he-said, she-said". The trial then becomes a beauty contest between the complainant and the defendant. If the defendant is not guilty, he is put in the position of having to prove the fact. Proving a negative is intrinsically difficult, and all the more so when what he has to prove is some else's state of mind (i.e., their consent).

Having to prove your innocence is already a reversal of the basic principle of justice, but this is made even worse by disclosure failures denying the defendant access to the material that would furnish the crucial exculpatory evidence. The new DPP appears determined to continue to facilitate disclosure failures. In practice the right to have all evidence brought before the court has long since been violated by a woeful disclosure process tainted by a bias towards gaining a conviction, rather than promoting justice.

The right to a jury trial is perhaps the most sacrosanct principle. That removal of this right in the specific context of sex offence cases is being seriously promoted in Parliament is deeply disturbing. An alternative strategy to increase conviction rates which is being promoted by rape activists is to require the jury to be subject to prior manipulation ("training"), which would negate the purpose of an untainted random selection of jurors. But I have not exhausted the issue of sexual offences yet. There is another side to sexual offences which has not been addressed in this chapter: women offenders. This is addressed next.

20

Sexual Assault: The Story Less Told

We can't destroy the inequities between men and women until we destroy marriage.
Robin Morgan, *Sisterhood is Powerful* (1970)

I feel what they feel: man-hating, that volatile admixture of pity, contempt, disgust, envy, alienation, fear, and rage at men. It is hatred not only for the anonymous man who makes sucking noises on the street, not only for the rapist or the judge who acquits him, but for the men women share their lives with - husbands, lovers, friends, fathers, brothers, sons, coworkers.
Judith Levine, *My Enemy, My Love: Women, Men, and the Dilemmas of Gender* (1992)

Men's sexuality is mean and violent, and men so powerful that they can reach within women to fuck/construct us from the inside out. Satan-like, men possess women, making their wicked fantasies and desires women's own. A woman who has sex with a man, therefore, does so against her will, even if she does not feel forced.
Judith Levine, *My Enemy, My Love: Women, Men, and the Dilemmas of Gender* (1992)

As long as some men use physical force to subjugate females, all men need not. The knowledge that some men do suffices to threaten all women….He can beat or kill the woman he claims to love, he can rape women, whether mate, acquaintance, or stranger; he can rape or sexually molest his daughters, nieces, stepchildren, or the children of a woman he claims to love. The vast majority of men in the world do one or more of the above.
Marilyn French, *The War Against Women* (1992)

We are, as a sex, infinitely superior to men
Elizabeth Cady Stanton, (1815 – 1904)

The previous chapter considered rape, which, in English law, is necessarily committed by males whatever the sex of the victim. In this chapter I address categories of sexual offence which were not covered in the preceding chapter. Sexual offending by females is the main category I tackle here. In some cases this involves full intercourse without the consent of the man or boy in question, which only the definition adopted by English law prevents me from calling rape. It is here we meet the full force of sex-bias in the form of the general public's incapability to conceptualise a female coercing sex with a male. And if they can do so, they struggle to regard it as reprehensible let alone criminal. The incredulity reaches greater heights still if it is suggested that such a thing might deserve many years in prison. This is, in my opinion, where inequality of the sexes is greatest in our society. A simple sex reversal turns one of the most heinous of crimes – rape – into an event which most people do not recognise as being especially improper, let alone criminal, despite all other aspects being identical.

The other categories of offence considered here include rape in men's prisons, and sexual assaults of minors in juvenile correctional facilities, by either males or females. War rape is often assumed to be an issue for females only. It is not. Where war rape is endemic, the victims are invariably of both sexes, as we will see. But first I take a look at the statistics of people in prison for sex offences.

20.1 Sex Offender Prisoner Statistics (UK)

The statistics of people in prison for sex offences appears to confirm the societal prejudice regarding the sex of such offenders. About 99% of prisoners for sex offences are men. Hence, in the following paragraph, "people" can be interpreted as "men" to a very good approximation.

In June 2005 there were 6,951 people in prison for sexual offences in England and Wales, but this rose to 10,935 by June 2011, (Ministry of Justice, 2013a). By July 2014 this had risen further to 11,150 people, (Slack, 2014). By March 2015 this had increased again to just under 11,600, (Barrett, 2015). At this time 17% of the sentenced prison population was a sex offender, compared with just 10% in 2000. A total of 6,402 sex offenders were convicted in the year ending March 2015, (UK Government, 2015a). At 30 June 2017 the number of people in prison for sex offences had climbed further to 13,324, (Ministry of Justice, 2017a). By 31 December 2018 there were more still, some 13,512 prisoners, or 19% of the sentenced prison population, (Ministry of Justice, 2019). Hence the number of people in prison for sexual offences has nearly doubled in 13 years. The reasons for the increase are, (i) a larger number of men are being tried, most likely due to the police and the CPS pursuing a policy of increasing prosecutions, (ii) a larger proportion of those convicted are being sentenced to custody, (iii) the average sentence length for sex offences has increased (by policy), and, (iv) there is an influx of older men being imprisoned for historic sex offences following Operation Yewtree (the police purge on historic sex offences following the revelations about Jimmy Savile). Recall the discussion of false allegations in the previous chapter. How many of these imprisoned men are innocent? Certainly at least hundreds, but perhaps thousands.

By March 2015 the average sentence length for sex offences had become longer than it had ever been before, reaching 5 years 3 months. This average sentence length had increased from 3 years 4 months in 2003, an increase by

58% in 12 years. Note that the number of convictions for rape in 2015 was 1,295, compared to the total of 6,402 convicted for any sex offence, so 80% of the men contributing to that 5 year 3 month average sentence were convicted for a lesser offence than rape. By 2014 there were already at least eight men's prisons housing only sex offenders, (Slack, 2014).

There has been a slight rise in the number of women in prison for sexual offences, but the volume of female prisoners for sexual offences remains very small. In 2009 there were just 56 female child sex abusers in custody (49 sentenced and 7 on remand). Another 84 were under supervision in the community, (Townsend and Syal, 2009). Fewer than 2% of people on the sex offenders register were then women. In 2010 and 2011 there were respectively 121 and 103 female prisoners in custody for sexual offences, (Ministry of Justice, 2013a). In June 2015, about 2.5% of the female prison population were sex offenders, see Figure 7.08 of (Ministry of Justice, 2016a). The female prison population in 2015 was about 3,900, so the number of female sex offenders in prison was around 100. There will be slightly more now as the conviction rate has increased in recent years, though the absolute volume remains very small compared with convictions of male sex offenders.

Between the years 2007 and 2014, the number of women being convicted annually of sexual offences rose from 31 to 63, but in years 2015, 2016 and 2017 this rose further to 100, 120 and 108 respectively (the number of women prosecuted being 216, 211 and 186 respectively). Between years 2007 and 2014, the number of women being sentenced to immediate custody rose from 11 to 31, but in years 2015, 2016 and 2017 this rose further to 57, 63 and 58 respectively, (UK Government, 2018m). The average sentence length in years 2015-17 was 51 months. By the end of 2017 there would have been around 120 women in prison for sexual offences, or roughly 3.2% of the female prison population.

It is worth noting the far larger number of women who are arrested for sex offences than are prosecuted. In 2017, some 2,512 women required legal aid prior to being charged, e.g., whilst in a police station, in association with sexual offences (up from 1,632 in 2007), (UK Government, 2018n). Only a small proportion of these proceed to prosecution. The same is true for male offenders, of course, and the corresponding volume of identified male offenders is proportionally greater.

20.2 Examples of Women's Sexual Abuse of Minors

A question which arises is whether the above statistics on identified female sex offending are a true reflection of its underlying prevalence: are female sexual abusers really a hundred times rarer than male sexual abusers? Before turning to that issue, however, there is an even more fundamental problem: many people simply cannot believe that female sex offending is to be taken seriously, even when against minors. Barbara Ellen, responding to the case of Madeleine Martin, summarises this view well. She wrote in the Guardian,

> 'Do we seriously think that a female teacher sleeping with a male pupil is on a par with a male teacher sleeping with a girl pupil? I don't. And neither, I'd wager, would most 15-year-old boys….If anything, one would have thought they might be jealous. The internet is awash with sites dealing with "older woman teacher-pupil" fantasies. And there lies the rub – should the law be treating male and female pupil victims equally when male and female teenagers are so different?' (Ellen, 2009).

Barbara Ellen's position, simply put, is that 'he enjoyed it and he should be grateful for the attention'. She would readily agree that these same sentiments would be unthinkable in the context of a male teacher's sexual exploitation of an underage girl pupil. Equality only when it suits. As women become more powerful in all aspects of public life, in addition to their traditional social and domestic power, and as boys become less and less regarded, especially at school, Ellen's position sounds increasingly like an aristocrat declaring that the lower orders should be grateful for any acknowledgement of their existence, even if exploitative. It won't do. The powerful deserve especial punishment when they abuse their power, and this is now applicable to women.

Not all female sexual offending is of this teacher-on-pupil kind. Marie Black was convicted of being at the centre of a paedophile ring which raped and sexually abused two boys and three girls repeatedly and routinely over a ten year period. Two men and another woman were also convicted on a range of charges, but Black was declared the "common denominator" and ring leader, despite attempts by her defence to deflect all the blame onto the men, (Baker, 2015). Then there was the case of Vanessa George, a nursery worker, who took advantage of her position to photograph herself sexually abusing small children, passing the photos to a man, who passed them on to another woman, (BBC News, 2010).

If you missed the case of Nicola Fox it might be because it arose while the media were obsessing about male MPs putting their hands on women's knees or attempting to kiss them or otherwise importuning women. Fox forced a 13 year old boy with no previous sexual experience to have sex with her. She lured the boy into her house, saying she wanted a chat with him. She then slammed the door shut and barricaded it with a table so he could not escape. Fox pinned the boy down to the bed using her weight (she's a large woman). She removed her trousers and lower clothing then held the boy's hands over his head and forced sexual intercourse on him. He made it absolutely clear he did not want her to do what she did, telling her to stop and to get off. He struggled and was crying at one point, (Burns, 2017). Her response was to tell him, in an annoyed and aggressive tone, to stop crying. He felt upset and embarrassed but nevertheless the boy treated Fox with dignity because of her gender, and did not want to hurt her by using violence to free himself. This is a common reaction of males when subject to sexual assault by women (e.g., see section 20.9). This offence cannot be legally classed as rape because in English law rape is defined as penetration using a penis, so a biological woman cannot rape. But, legal niceties aside, this was forcible rape. Fox has been sentenced to 4 years in prison. At the Court of Appeal in London, prosecution counsel Louise Oakley claimed that Fox had been treated more leniently because of her sex. Lady Justice Hallett, presiding at the appeal, agreed that leniency had been shown but argued that mitigation was justified due to Nicola Fox's mental health problems. She declined to alter the sentence, (Bristow, 2017).

Not all women's sexual offending is as grievous as the above cases. I have compiled a list of 39 more typical case studies of women in the UK who have been convicted of sex offences against minors, (Collins, W, 2017c). All are reasonably recent (2010 to 2017). In 23 out of these 39 UK cases the female offender did not go to prison (59%). Suspended sentences were the most common outcome. Bear in mind that only the more serious cases are likely to feature in the press, my only source of material. Two of the 16 women who did go to prison were originally given suspended sentences – only to be sent to prison by the court of appeal. This leniency is worth bearing in mind because, even in this list of typical cases, there are some pretty serious ones. Three involve young lesbian women who fooled underaged girls into thinking they were male and raped them with rubber or wooden dildos. One such woman raped three different girls in this way (though technically this would not be rape but "assault by penetration"). Then there were the sisters who started abusing a boy sexually when he was six and continued throughout his boyhood. And the 24 year old woman who "assaulted by penetration" a three year old girl and circulated the pictures of her doing so. And the 39 year old mother who regularly had sex with six different 13 to 15 year old boys in her house after plying them with drink and drugs. And the 35 year old woman who groomed two boys, aged 12 and 13, to achieve her aim of having full sex with them. And the 44 year old female teaching assistant who had sex with "a string" of 15 and 16 year old boys, sometimes in the school premises, and continued even after she had been gaoled for it.

Then there was the delightful 44 year old mother of two who took advantage of being offered a bed in a friend's house after a party to sexually assault her son, aged 14, his mother later being outraged that the woman did not go to prison. And the 36 year old single mother who had sex with a 12 year old boy 191 times, keeping a diary of the events. And the 21 year old female babysitter whose idea of 'looking after' an 11 year old boy included full sexual intercourse. She simply stripped off, then stripped him, then straddled him. And the list includes two cases of middle-aged women taking sexual advantage of vulnerable 17 year old boys in special needs establishments. And a nationally acclaimed head teacher who was gaoled for historic offences involving grooming two boys and inducing them to have sex with her over a number of years (in one case with her husband in the adjacent tent whence she had evicted him). And on, and on.

It is of interest to compare these cases with that of Rolf Harris. If you are not familiar with his case I suggest you look back at some newspaper reports to see what he was accused of doing (and I shall assume for this purpose that he was guilty as found). The complainants in the Harris case were described in the newspapers as "brave victims" who had undergone "terrifying ordeals". The boy victims of the women in my 39 case studies were never described in such terms in the newspaper reports. And the words used to described their abuser's exploits were typically "affair" or "tryst" or "fling", not "abuse" or "assault" - or, indeed, "rape" - as would be the case if the sexes were reversed. Most of the above cases of female sexual offenders are a good deal worse than the Rolf Harris case, even if you believe he was guilty as found. And yet Harris was immediately declared a non-person, all his previous work negated. No punishment was harsh enough. He was cast into the furthermost pit of hell. Yet reverse the sexes and many members of the public will have difficulty regarding these women's exploits as deserving much more in the way of punishment than a bit of a ticking off. This is the gynocentric premium which makes "male privilege" a sick joke.

The 39 case studies, (Collins, W, 2017c), demonstrate that women's offending commonly displays the following characteristics: plying victims with drink or drugs, persistent grooming which continues for years, offences against multiple victims, offences against pre-pubescent victims (hence physically as well as legally children), and threats in the event of disclosure. Counter-accusations were sometimes deployed by the female abusers: that the boy victims raped them. The words used by judges in their summing-up at the trials have included statements such as, 'a disgraceful abuse of power', 'a case of gross child abuse', 'serious abuse of trust' and 'very serious offences indeed'. And yet a leniency which would cause public outrage in the case of male offenders is often displayed, despite these observations, in respect of sentencing female offenders. It could not be clearer. In sex cases you are not punished for what you have done, you are punished for what you are. This is prejudice.

In the USA there are several hundred cases annually of women teachers being convicted of sexual offences against underage boys in their schools, a collection of 275 examples can be found in (Collins, W, 2014).

A major study commissioned by the U.S. Department of Education, 'Educator Sexual Misconduct', reviews various other studies. One study, from the American Association of University Women in 2001, indicated that 57.2% of all students reporting sexual abuse specified a male offender and 42.4% a female offender. Another referenced study, by Cameron *et al,* reported nearly identical proportions: 57% male offenders vs. 43% female offenders, (US Department of Education, 2004).

Jenni Murray, the long-standing presenter of BBC radio's 'Woman's Hour', has difficulty understanding why women do it, (Murray, 2015). She questions whether they would be treated so leniently if they were male. I will not be straying into the psychology of offenders here, which will certainly be both complex and varied. In particular, it is likely that women in the role of carer, offending in the domestic environment against young children (paedophiles), have a distinct aetiology from that of (say) teachers offending against pubescent boys or girls in the 11 to 15 age range (hebephiles). In regard to the latter, this is the opinion of Anthony Beech, criminological psychology professor at the University of Birmingham,

> 'The teachers feel entitled. They think they can have sex with anyone they want. It's power imbalance and manipulation. There's a narcissism – I can do what I want because I'm the most important person going', (Sanghani, 2015).

In short, the motivation may be the same as it is for male offenders. Jenni Murray's difficulty in understanding is because she starts from a position of incredulity based on the old gendered mindset of female innocence, aided and abetted by the relative rarity with which female sexual offending comes to light.

20.3 The Prevalence of Female Sexual Abuse of Minors (UK)

It is ten years since Esther Rantzen, the TV presenter, caused public shock with this Guardian article, (Rantzen, 2009). It reported on calls to the UK's ChildLine. Extracts are as follows,

> 'The figures released by ChildLine demonstrate that sexual abuse by women is not nearly as rare as we would hope. There has been a dramatic rise in the number of women reported by child callers to ChildLine as abusers. This rise is partly due to the fact that many more boys are ringing us.
>
> Suicide is the biggest single cause of death for boys in their late teens and early 20s, even outnumbering deaths in road accidents. So ChildLine counsellors believed that far too many boys and young men were reluctant to disclose a problem until it became so overwhelming that they felt life was not worth living. That is why we have focused on boys – with so much success that the number counselled has reached an all-time high of more than 58,000.
>
> Last year, more than half the boys who rang disclosing sexual abuse reported that they had been abused by women. The most common female perpetrator – in almost 1,000 cases – was the boy's mother. Among the boys who reported being sexually abused by a man (almost the same number of callers), the most common perpetrator was the father – again, in about 1,000 incidents. Both shocking statistics.'

The accompanying article reports that '2,142 children had told ChildLine last year they had been sexually abused by a woman', (Press Association, 2009). Yet the phenomenon of sexual abuse by women was hardly unknown before 2009. You can find a massive bibliography of around 650 publications related to female sexual abusers or their victims, in alphabetical order here, (Collins W. , 2017d), or in chronological order here, (Collins, W, 2017e). The number of publications per year remained sparse until the mid-1980s when it started to take off considerably. It was then that Michele Elliott started the charity Kidscape.

Evidence is beginning to accumulate that around 20% – 25% of paedophiles are women. Michele Elliott has long been of this opinion. Elliott's book 'Female Sexual Abuse of Children, The Ultimate Taboo' was published in 1993, over a quarter of a century ago, (Elliott, 1993). The Man, Woman & Myth videos with Elliott are strongly recommended viewing, links here (MWM, circa 2013). The story of Elliott's own awakening to the reality of sexual abuse perpetrated by women is revealing. In the late 1980s she gave a talk at an RAF base, claiming, as she believed at the time, that abusers were all men. But an RAF officer came up to her privately afterwards and told her, with tears in his eyes, *'it isn't only men, you know, my mother did it to me'*. Shortly afterwards Elliott appeared on a radio phone-in show hosted by Philip Hodgson. She raised the issue of sexual abuse by women. She was unaware that she was opening a floodgate.

The radio station's switchboard was jammed with calls from people disburdening themselves of their own experience of sexual abuse at the hands of women – almost always the first time they had told anyone. Over the following week, Elliott's office at Kidscape was inundated with letters bearing similar tales (this was before email). This experience led to Elliott hosting the Kidscape First National Conference on Female Sexual Abuse. The event was invaded by 30 or so feminists intent on preventing witnesses speaking - and they largely succeeded. There is nothing new about feminists shutting down events. Not deterred, Michele Elliott appeared on the TV programme 'This Morning' to talk about the issue. Again the TV station was flooded with telephone calls, over a thousand. 90% of callers had never told anyone of their abuse at the hands of women before.

And yet nearly a quarter of a century later, the social narrative still resists acknowledging the reality of female perpetrated sexual abuse. The public is resistant to the notion because it transgresses against the matricentric belief that women are invariably caring, nurturing and benign. Men and women are both powerfully disinclined to believe that some women might deploy their social power in harmful ways. The pernicious effect of this mindset has been stressed in 1999 by Jacquie Hetherton in 'The idealization of women: its role in the minimization of child sexual abuse by females', (Hetherton, 1999). She wrote,

> 'these theories .... become problematic when they are used to endorse a "males do and females don't" gender dichotomy ...... The literature suggests that a gender dichotomy is exactly what some individuals, particularly those within the feminist movement, have attempted to cultivate. This has been evidenced by sustained efforts to suppress and derogate discussion of child sexual abuse perpetrated by women. The world's first conference on female sexual abusers in 1992 was scathingly described in The Guardian as misogynist in motivation.'

More recently a UK study by the Lucy Faithfull Foundation has come to the view that up to 20% of paedophiles are women, leading to an estimate that there might be 64,000 women in the UK who have committed sexual offences against children, (Townsend and Syal, 2009). Studies in the USA by the National Center on Child Abuse and Neglect have reached a similar conclusion: 'the sexual abuse of children by women, primarily mothers, once thought to be so rare it could be ignored, constituted 25% of the sexually abused victims (approximately 36,000 victims). This statistic is thought to be underestimated due to the tendency of non-disclosure by victims', (Boroughs, 2004). Like Michele Elliott's work, this knowledge goes back over a quarter of a century. It is not news, but it is only in recent years that it has begun to surface in public discussion. From (Boroughs, 2004),

> 'The crime of sexual child abuse by women seems so unnatural that it offends moral human instinct. Generally, it is a phenomenon that society finds difficult to accept socially and professionally. Women are viewed as sexually harmless to children, the common thought being, 'What harm could be done without a penis?' Simply put, it is difficult to understand how a woman is physically capable of sexually abusing a child in the traditional concept of rape without a genital organ for penetration. Women are more often viewed as victims rather than perpetrators of abuse. Men have long been viewed as both capable of sexually abusing children and as being the main perpetrators. That remains true, but there is increasing evidence that many more women sexually abuse children than previously thought. Women are perceived to be the gentler sex; however, half the women in a recent survey of 50 convicted female abusers stated they derived sadistic pleasure from inflicting pain on their victims.'

In a study of 17,337 subjects of childhood sexual abuse, 'Long-Term Consequences of Childhood Sexual Abuse by Gender of Victim', (Dube et al, 2005), 23% had a female-only perpetrator and 22% had both male and female perpetrators, i.e., 45% involved women. Males were 39% of those victimized, and men reported female perpetration nearly 40% of the time. The long-term impact of childhood sexual abuse on multiple health and social outcomes was found to be similar for males and females. A 2014 US study based on anonymous online self-reporting of sexual interest in children also indicated that about 25% of people admitting to such interest were women, (Wurtele et al, 2013)

20.4 Male Offenders' History of Childhood Sexual Abuse

Male sex offenders have an abnormally high prevalence of sexual abuse in their own childhood. Moreover, this sexual abuse is frequently perpetrated by women. Evidence supporting this contention follows.

The article 'Heterosexual molestation of children who later become rapists' studied a sample of 83 adult (male) rapists in the USA and found 59%

had been heterosexually molested as children. Most of these men (77%) reported sexual abuse on more than one occasion and that the abuse involved intercourse. Note that the 59% statistic relates specifically to sexual abuse as children by women perpetrators. The boys' mean age at the time of the sexual activity was 11.5 years, (Petrovich and Templer, 1984).

The paper 'Sexual trauma in the life histories of rapists and child molesters', (Groth, 1979), concluded the following,

> 'This study examined the life histories of 348 men convicted of sexual assault. The subjects were mostly recidivists, men who either had previous records of sexual assault or who admitted to similar prior offenses for which they had not been caught. Of these subjects, 170 had sexually assaulted adult victims, while 178 had victimized children. Evidence of some form of sexual trauma during their developmental years (ages 1 through 15) was found in the life histories of 31% of the offenders. In contrast, a control group (of law enforcement officers) reported similar experiences in only 3% of cases. The predominant type of trauma experienced by child molesters was a forcible sexual assault, whereas for rapists the abuse had taken the form of being pressured into sexual activity by an adult. In many cases the sexual assaults appear to replicate the offender's own victimization….. Incidences of sexual assault perpetrated by adult women against children appear far higher than that reflected by official crime statistics'

This point about "replicating the offender's own victimisation" was confirmed by O'Brien (1989) who reports that sex offenders against male victims who had themselves a history of having been abused were more likely to have been abused by a male. Similarly, and even more emphatically, of sex offenders against female victims who had themselves a history of having been abused in childhood, 93% had been abused by a female. The 1993 paper 'Childhood Sexual Abuse and Subsequent Sexual Aggression Against Adult Women', by Brière and Smiljanich, presented at the 101st annual convention of the American Psychological Association also suggests a very high (80%) prevalence rate of sexual abuse by females in the background of male sex offenders, (Matthews, 1996). The paper 'Parameters of sexual contact of boys with women', indicates a prevalence rate of female-perpetrated abuse against male sex prisoners as children of 46%, (Condi et al, 1987)

Table 2 of (Matthews, 1996) gives the prevalence rates of sexual abuse of males, both in general populations and in populations of sex offenders. Male US undergraduates were reported to have an anomalously high prevalence of sexual victimisation (the average of two samples being 28%). Ignoring this, the prevalence rate of sexual victimisation of males was 13% averaged over 8 samples of general population. In contrast, the prevalence rate of sexual abuse of males was 47% averaged over the 4 samples of sex offenders (and greater than 50% when confined to cases of abuse by women).

An extract from the Abstract of 'Sexual victimization in the history of sexual abusers: A review', by Hanson and Slater, (1988), reads, 'The present paper reviews the empirical literature on the proportion of child sexual abusers who were themselves sexually victimized as children. While findings in individual studies ranged between 0% and 67%, on average about 28% of the offenders reported being sexually victimized as children. This rate is higher than the base rate for community samples of non-offending males (about 10%)'. A more recent paper 'Characteristics of Perpetrators of Child Sexual Abuse Who Have Been Sexually Victimized as Children' reports on a study of all convicted child sexual abusers in S.E. London. They conclude that 'almost half the offenders reported experiences of sexual victimization in childhood', (Craissati et al, 2002). This paper, and the previous one, are not specific regarding the sex of the offender.

The paper 'Cycle of child sexual abuse: links between being a victim and becoming a perpetrator', (Glasser et al, 2001), studied 843 subjects attending a specialist forensic psychotherapy centre. They concluded,

> 'A high percentage of male subjects abused in childhood by a female relative became perpetrators. Having been a victim was a strong predictor of becoming a perpetrator, as was an index of parental loss in childhood'. However, abuse in childhood was not found to be a significant indicator of future perpetration by females, only by males. Detailed results were as follows. Of the 41 females attending the forensic psychotherapy service who were victims of sexual abuse, only one was also a perpetrator. However, of the 135 male victims, 79 were perpetrators (59%). Twenty-four male subjects reported having been sexually abused by females, 23 of whom were identified as female relatives. Seven of the 24 were also abused by male relatives. Of these 24 males, 19 went on to become perpetrators of sexual abuse (79%). Of the 111 male subjects abused by males, 60 became perpetrators (54%). This indicates that abuse of males by female relatives may be more likely to contribute to the male victim becoming an abuser than abuse by male relatives or persons outside the family.'

In summary, multiple studies show that the incidence of childhood sexual abuse in the history of adult sex offenders is significantly higher than that in the general population. Not surprisingly there is a spread of estimates, ranging from 28% to 80%. There is a particularly marked correspondence between male sex offenders against women and the offender's history of childhood sexual abuse specifically by a woman. The best estimate at present is that around half of male sex offenders against women have a childhood history of sexual abuse by a woman.

Naomi Murphy is a psychotherapist working at HM Prison Whitemoor, a top security prison housing serious violent and sexual offenders (men, obviously). She has 15 years experience working with some of the most disturbed and most serious sex offenders. She reports that 70% of these men were sexually abused as children, and 54% of these specifically by a woman. Moreover, this was generally women acting alone, not typically in conjunction with a man, as is sometimes claimed. Mothers feature large in this abuse, but other female relatives, neighbours, baby sitters, etc., also feature, (Murphy, 2017), (Murphy, 2019).

Let the implications of that sink in. As always, we must be careful about the distinction between correlation and causality. But it would be perverse not to suspect a causal connection in this case (though not deterministic, no one is condemned to become an abuser due to having an abusive history). Women in a caring capacity are naturally the arbiters of right and wrong to children in their care. So what effect will sexual behaviour with a mother, or other carer, have upon a child? It is hardly surprising that the victim may become confused as to what is acceptable. And if the victim comes to understand that he has been inappropriately treated, resentment at the breach of trust may set in. Either way, it is reasonable to expect that the resulting psychological state might predispose the former victim to become an offender. To emphasise: this is not deterministic. Victims are not doomed to become offenders. We are all responsible for our behaviour. But some, due to their history, may be prone to predispositions that others are not.

We constantly hear calls to "teach boys not to rape" as a means of reducing the rape of females. But society already does this very effectively, which is why rape is universally regarded as a particularly heinous crime. What society does not do so effectively is to acknowledge that women may sexually abuse children – girls or boys. It appears that boys abused by women have a significantly enhanced likelihood of later becoming sex offenders against women. Consequently, even if one's sole concern were the protection of women, a strategy which is more likely to be effective in reducing rape than "teach boys not to rape" might be to acknowledge more widely women's own sexual offending against boys and its harmful effects. The current refusal to accept female culpability for sex offences against boys may well be significant in increasing sex offences against women.

20.5 Perceptions of Female Perpetration and the Damage Done

The Guardian article by Barbara Ellen, referred to above, (Ellen, 2009), demonstrates the attitude of many members of the public to female perpetration of sexual abuse against male minors. Regrettably the same bias is common amongst professionals in the therapeutic community, the very people who should provide assistance to the abused. What harm is done by female sexual abuse of male minors? Its apparent link to later sexual offences against females is one answer. The abused are not doomed to be permanently damaged by their abuse, and that is equally true for female victims. But there are indications that male sexual abuse victims do suffer long-term psychological effects in some cases. The Abstract of the review article 'Female-perpetrated sexual abuse: a review of victim and professional perspectives', (Clements et al, 2013), reads,

> 'Professional attitudes towards female-perpetrated sexual abuse (FPSA) reportedly reflect the gender-role expectations found in broader society, which cast males almost exclusively as sexual aggressors or willing sexual recipients, females as sexually non-coercive or victims and male-perpetrated sexual abuse as particularly significant or injurious. Such views, however, appear to stand in contrast to the perspectives of individuals who have experienced FPSA. This paper details a systematic review of peer-reviewed quantitative and qualitative literature examining these different (professional and victim) perspectives. Although the methodological shortcomings of primary papers limit the conclusions that can be drawn, the findings suggest that victim and professional perspectives of FPSA remain discrepant; professionals generally considered FPSA as less serious, less harmful and less deserving of investigation than male-perpetrated abuse; while victims of FPSA felt their experiences influenced significantly their psychological wellbeing and abilities to form and maintain interpersonal relationships.'

Extracts from the conclusions of the review paper 'Female perpetrators of sexual abuse of minors: What are the consequences for the victims?', (Tsopelas et al, 2012), are,

> 'Although sexual abuse by female perpetrators, according to the data available, is less frequent than that of sexual abuse by males we really do not know if the smaller number of cases reflects the reality….The majority of such cases are not reported. Sometimes sexual abuse by female perpetrators is considered more acceptable than sexual abuse by males…. More disturbingly, literature suggests that victims of female abusers are very rarely taken seriously when they make their allegations. The vast majority (86%) of the victims that reported abuse were not believed…. Victims of sexual abuse by female perpetrators are usually friends or relatives of the abuser and find themselves sometimes under persuasion and psychological coercion to participate in sexual acts. The percentage of male victims is growing. There are severe and longstanding psychological consequences for the victims.'

> 'The research reviewed up to date suggests that in adult life there are similar psychiatric problems in the victims of sex abuse irrespective of the perpetrator's sex. These problems are commonly alcohol and substance abuse and addiction, self harm, anorexia, bulimia and agoraphobia. The development of borderline personality disorder has also been implicated….The similarity in the consequences of child sexual abuse perpetrated by both female and male offenders suggests that the former should not be taken lightly. There is no research suggesting that sexual abuse perpetrated by females causes less harm in any of the domains studied. This is the main message this review has for the general public.'

The study 'The Long-Term Effects of Child Sexual Abuse by Female Perpetrators: A Qualitative Study of Male and Female Victims', (Denov, 2004), was based on interviews with 14 victims of childhood sexual abuse by women, seven female and seven male. The 14 female abusers comprised: six mothers, two mothers together with grandmothers, one mother with sister, one sister with a female neighbour, three female babysitters, and one nun. 12 of the 14 victims reported that the frequency of the abuse was between once per month and more than once per week. The average age when the abuse started was five, and its average duration was six years. All 14 victims, i.e., all seven males and all seven females, reported the psychological effect of their abuse was rage, mistrust of women and discomfort with sex. 11 reported suicidal ideation and six had made suicide attempts. 12 reported they had a fear of abusing children whilst four (two of each sex) admitted to actual sexual victimisation of children. Other identified adverse outcomes were comparable between the two sexes. Denov noted that,

> 'Although many of the effects of female sexual abuse appear to be similar to those of victims of male sexual abuse, the current study highlights the long-term effects that are unique to being sexually victimized by a woman. For example, victims in the current study who experienced sexual abuse by men and women maintained that the sexual abuse by women was more damaging and led to a deeper sense of betrayal than similar abuse by men.'

Finally, a paper from Australia which highlights the media's role in reinforcing stereotypical views of the sex of offenders, and minimisation of the significance of female perpetration: 'Coming Clean on Duty of Care: Australian Print Media's Representation of Male Versus Female Sex Offenders in Institutional Contexts', (Landor and Eisenchlas, 2012). The Abstract tallies with the remarks I made previously regarding the UK media's reporting,

> 'Public opinion about sexual abuse of minors is greatly shaped by mass media and the way individual cases are reported. This paper examines Australian print media's representation of sex offenders, focussing particularly on the sex of the offenders

> and aiming to shed light on some of the misconceptions and deep-rooted prejudices within the population at large. Given the multi-faceted nature of sexual offences, this paper focuses on sexual offences committed by both males and females against minors in the context of a companion breach of duty of care. In order to explore the effect that linguistic tools can have in the Australian print media's way of reporting sexual abuse cases, twenty-nine newspaper articles published in Australian dailies were selected for analysis. The analysis of these articles reveals a marked bias in the manner in which sexual offences perpetrated by males, as opposed to females, are reported, suggesting a male monopoly on sexual abuse. We argue that this biased representation, which hinders adequate profiling of sexual offences against minors, may stem from an androcentric view of sexuality and from the systematic denial of female agency when it comes to sex.'

20.6 The Sex of the Victim

It is not only in respect of the sex of the perpetrator that perceptual bias arises, but also in respect of the sex of the victim. We saw in chapter 19 that the attrition rate for reports of male rape are consistently higher than for female victims, at all ages.

Another indication of this bias in relation to the sex of the victim is that the public are largely unaware that not all the victims of the Rotherham and Oxfordshire grooming and rape gangs were girls: at least 50 and 80 respectively were boys. The report by the independent inquiry into the Rotherham abuses noted that none of the boy victims had been flagged by social workers as "risky business" and stressed the importance of 'making sure that judgments about child sexual exploitation are consistent and gender neutral, for example by asking if the same level of risk would be acceptable if the child was the opposite gender', (Jay, 2014).

This bias in the perception of sexual abuse according to the sex of the victim reappears in the context of sexual trafficking and exploitation of minors. In the USA, a 2008 report from New York City revealed that about 50% of the victims of commercial sexual exploitation of children were boys, (Curtis et al, 2008). In 2013 a report by the organisation 'End Child Pornography and Trafficking' extended this conclusion to the USA as a whole in a report 'Boys: The Under-mentioned Victims of Child Sex Trafficking and Sexual Exploitation', (Keziah, 2013). A corresponding exposé in the UK came in 2014 from the charity Barnardo's which criticised the stereotypical belief that boys are less vulnerable to child sexual exploitation, observing that this has led to boys receiving insufficient protection from front-line services. Barnardo's stated that new findings indicate up to a third of child victims in the UK are male, (Malik, 2017).

I give just one example from the academic literature which identifies this bias against boy victims of sexual abuse in the US legal arena, 'Differences in Legal Outcomes for Male and Female Children Who Have Been Sexually Abused', (Edelson and Joa, 2010). The Abstract reads,

> 'The goal of the present study was to determine whether or not there were sex differences in legal outcomes for children who were sexually abused. Using the methodology of Joa and Edelson (2004), the results indicated that males who were sexually abused had poorer legal outcomes than females. Specifically, it was found that cases involving male victims were less likely to be filed with the District Attorney (DA) than cases involving female victims and had fewer criminal counts charged. For those children seen at a Child Abuse Assessment Center, cases involving female victims were significantly more likely to be filed by the DA's office than were cases involving male victims.'

20.7 Female Offender Sentencing

Criminal sentencing should be based only upon what you did, not upon who or what you are. In practice in the UK, and all Western countries, men are treated far more harshly in the criminal justice system (see chapter 8). In the context of sex offences we have already seen the female mitigation-bonus applied to Nicola Fox. Many instances of the same phenomenon can be seen in my 39 UK examples of female sex offenders, (Collins, W, 2017c). Here I take a look at a couple of academic publications which confirm this bias. The Abstract of the paper 'Sex-Based Sentencing: Sentencing Discrepancies Between Male and Female Sex Offenders', published in 'Feminist Criminology', (Embry and Lyons, 2012), reads,

> 'The current research examines the utility of the evil woman hypothesis by examining sentencing discrepancies between male and female sex offenders. National Corrections Reporting Program data are used to identify sex offenders for the years 1994 to 2004 and the sentences they received for specific sex offenses. Statistical analyses reveal a significant difference in sentence length between men and women, but not in the expected direction. The evil woman hypothesis would assume women are sentenced more harshly, but data show men receive longer sentences for sex offenses than women. Support is provided for the chivalry hypothesis to explain immediate sentencing disparity.'

Leaving aside the fact that 'Feminist Criminology' sounds to my ears rather like 'Aryan Criminology' – not something to be encouraged - the authors' puzzlement regarding the "expected direction" is remarkable. Anyone with even a passing acquaintance with sentencing data knows that men are sentenced more harshly than women for the same offence category. There is no reason to expect sexual offences to differ in this respect, indeed every reason to expect the bias against men might be even greater. The authors' findings are entirely expected. For "chivalry hypothesis" we can, of course, read "gynocentrism". Yes, feminists seem to have discovered gynocentrism – but, of course, it appears in the guise of benign sexism against women. It must be exhausting constantly having to contort one's brain into such configurations. Who was it called it 'pretzel logic'? Deering and Mellor, (2009), came to the same conclusion in 'Sentencing of Male and Female Child Sex Offenders: Australian Study'. Their Abstract,

> 'Research suggests that, in line with the chivalry hypothesis of female offending, a range of mitigatory factors such as mental health problems, substance abuse, and personal experiences of abuse are brought into play when women who offend against children are brought to trial. This is reflected in sentencing comments made by judges and in the sanctions imposed on the offenders, and as a result female offenders are treated differently to male offenders. The current study investigated this in an Australian context. Seven cases of female-perpetrated child sexual abuse were identified over a 6-year period through the Austlii database. Seven cases of male-perpetrated child sex abuse matched as far as possible to these were identified. Court transcripts were then located, and sentencing comments and sanctions imposed were analysed. All offenders were sentenced to imprisonment, but in general the women were more likely than the men to receive less jail time and lower non-parole periods because their personal backgrounds or situation at the time of the offending (i.e., difficulties with intimate relationship, male dependence issues, depression, loneliness and anger) were perceived as worthy of sympathy, and they were considered as likely to be rehabilitated. Further investigations are needed to support these findings.'

These observations are very much in line with the qualitative indications from my 39 UK examples of female sexual offenders. It is striking how judges manage to find mitigations for female sexual abusers to justify suspended sentences. Here's another which involved assault by penetration and abuse of three girls aged between five and eight, (Higgins, 2019).

20.8 Female Sexual Offending in Correctional Facilities in the USA

Without doubt, male-on-male sexual assault occurs all too frequently in prisons (see section 20.10). What is less well known is that female-on-male sexual abuse also occurs with alarming frequency in juvenile detention facilities, at least so reports from the USA indicate. In recent years, abuse of detained male juveniles by female guards has been revealed as a major problem in the USA. Information from the UK is lacking. Women's advocates will often cite "power differential" as being an aspect of culpability. This applies, of course, in cases where women teachers commit sexual offences against underage boys in their schools. But as an example of taking advantage of a power differential it is difficult to imagine anything more extreme than a guard abusing her prisoner. The key findings from a USA-wide survey of juvenile inmates, (Bureau of Justice Statistics, 2013), were,

- An estimated 9.5% of youths in state juvenile correctional facilities reported experiencing one or more incidents of sexual victimization by another youth or by staff in the last 12 months, or since admission if less than 12 months;
- Sexual abuse by staff was three times more common than that by another inmate. About 2.5% of youth reported an incident involving another youth, and 7.7% reported an incident involving facility staff;
- Among the youths who reported victimization by staff, 89.1% were males reporting sexual activity with female staff and 3.0% were males reporting sexual activity with both male and female staff. In comparison, males comprised 91% of youths in the survey and female staff accounted for 44% of staff in the sampled facilities;
- 8.2% of males and 2.8% of females reported sexual activity with staff. 5.4% of females and 2.2% of males reported forced sexual activity with another youth at a facility;
- Overwhelmingly the most common form of sexual offending in juvenile facilities in the USA is male juveniles being sexually abused by female staff;
- Most victims of staff sexual misconduct reported more than one incident (85.9%). Among these youths, nearly 1 in 5 (20.4%) reported 11 or more incidents.
- About 20% of the victims of staff sexual misconduct reported experiencing physical force or threat of force, 12.3% were offered protection, and 21.5% were given drugs or alcohol to engage in sexual contact.

An account of a typical case is,

> 'One former inmate said in an interview that a nurse gave him perks, such as soda and candy, and flirted with him. That led to sex on several occasions in the medical clinic, he said. She gave him money, then threatened to turn him in for having contraband – the money – if he refused her advances, he said. He was 18 at the time and the nurse, who is accused of having sex with other juveniles at Nampa, was in her mid-30s. "You're an easy target," said the college student, now 24."', (Reynolds, 2015)

As one mother of an abused son put it, you hear about male offenders in the Boy Scouts or the Catholic Church, where the boys are at least free to walk away. We don't hear so much about female offenders where the youths in question cannot walk away.

A recent study of the factors which increase a juvenile's risk of being sexually victimised, (Ehlin, 2018), indicated that prior victimisation was the strongest indicator, but also highly, and roughly equally, significant were being a gang member, being non-heterosexual, and being male. As an example of the cognitive contortions in which some people are willing to engage, consider the following extracts from the Abstract of a paper by Professor of Law, Brenda Smith, 'Uncomfortable places, close spaces: Female correctional workers' sexual interactions with men and boys in custody', (Smith, 2012). The first part acknowledges the problem,

> 'It is well known that sexual abuse occurs within the correctional system. That female correctional staff commit a significant proportion of that sexual abuse is met with discomfort bordering on disbelief. This discomfort has limited the discourse about female correctional workers who abuse men or boys under their care. Scant scholarship exists that addresses the appropriate response to sexual abuse by women; even less addresses sexual abuse by female correctional workers. Likewise, feminist jurisprudence on sexuality and desire does little to illuminate the motivations of women who engage in sexual misconduct or abuse, much less women who abuse men or boys in custodial settings. What the literature does acknowledge is that female sex offenders receive less-harsh sanctions overall than male sex offenders; they are even less likely to be prosecuted or punished when the victim is male and in custody.'

Remarkably, though, Smith then neutralises any suggestion of female staff culpability with the following reversal,

> '...although female correctional workers have access to significant power by virtue of their roles, that power may be diminished by a confluence of gender, race, and class. The literature also acknowledges that female correctional staff's entry into the correctional system was a great success for reformist feminists and that women have become power players within the correctional system because of their ability to supervise both women and men. Despite this status, however, women still experience sexual discrimination and harassment, both from male staff members and from male inmates. For black female correctional workers, gender discrimination is compounded by race and class discrimination.'

One wonders in what sense women have the "ability to supervise both women and men"? Male staff would have every bit as much ability to supervise both sexes, if one were equally willing to ignore sexual abuse. This is a fine illustration of the inability of mere statistical facts to cut through the gynocentric imperative to rearrange reality in the shape of female innocence.

20.9 Sexual Assault of Adult Men by Women

If many people have trouble believing that female sexual offending against male minors is of any great significance, how much more incredulous they become when one introduces the idea that women can commit sexual offences against adult men. And yet sexual offences are defined by lack of consent, not physical force. A problem with English law, however, is that the emphasis is placed on the consent of the penetrated party. Thus, whether your consent is regarded as relevant depends upon the convex or concave geometry of your genitalia.

Leaving aside the legal nicety that defines away the possibility of female rapists, let us consider for the purposes of this section an egalitarian definition of rape which includes non-consensual "envelopment", or being made to penetrate, as well as non-consensual penetration. There are two myths that suggest men are not able to be raped by women: men always want sex, so consent can be assumed, and men must be aroused to have an erection, so he clearly wanted it and so it's not rape, is it? But men do *not* always want sex. That is just the image of men promulgated in our society. In any case, sexual desire is not the same as consent. And, much like female genital response, male erectile response is involuntary, meaning that a man need not be consenting for his penis to become erect and be placed in a woman's vagina; mechanical stimulation is all that is necessary. In fact, men can be scared or intimidated into an erection, especially if the person is older or an authority figure. Arousal and stimulation are not the same thing, and, in any case, neither imply consent. If a women were to become lubricated during a rape, would it be a valid defense for the rapist to claim she was aroused and therefore wanted sex? No, it would not. For precisely the same reason, a man's erection is not an indication of consent. What it is, though, is a convenient rationalisation of widespread prejudice.

If a man is forced or coerced into sex without his consent, this should be regarded as rape. Any other view is sexist since grossly different standards are being applied to men and women. Unfortunately, both our law and our society are sexist in exactly this respect. People who know perfectly well that sex offences hinge upon consent, not force, will attempt to rationalise their prejudice regarding females offending against adult men by scoffing at the notion of a big, strong man being raped by a petite woman. They will also refuse to believe that any such man – or boy – could come to any harm at the hands of a female. The rape of men by women, i.e., non-consensual intercourse, is simply not recognised as a possibility by either the public or the *de facto* law. Whilst there is a gender-neutral offence of 'causing someone to engage in a sexual act without their consent', I suggest that any adult man making such a complaint against a woman is unlikely to be believed unless there was evidence of physical injury. Of the hundred or so women in prison for sexual offences in the UK, how many of the victims were adult men? I do not know, but I suspect the fingers of one hand would suffice for the counting, perhaps after an accident in a saw mill. This asymmetry in the *de facto* law has become acute since the standards being adopted in respect of the rape of women have become increasingly stringent (e.g., affirmative consent). How many men would be rape victims if the same standards were applied? The answer appears to be comparable with the number of women, as we will see.

The steadfast refusal to acknowledge female perpetrated sexual abuse, especially upon adult men, in contrast to the readiness with which minor infringements of sexual etiquette are now interpreted as abuse by men, are prime examples of the tenacity of stereotypical gender norms. Men are agentic, women are passive. Men are sexually predatory, women are harmless. Women cannot be abusers because they are nurturing and submissive. To claim that some women can be sexually manipulative and even violent is to invite accusations of misogyny. Anyone making such a claim is clearly just trying to minimise male sexual abuse, some might opine. Not so. The last chapter presented the bald statistics on rape in the UK, and the studies in this chapter reveal perpetrators of both sexes. There is no hiding of male perpetration going on here, only exposure of female perpetration. We will see that evidence is accumulating that female perpetrated sexual abuse is not only comparably as widespread as male perpetrated abuse, but can be just as severe, including non-consensual penetrations of any of the bodily orifices with finger or object, as well as coerced or forced intercourse, including violence which leaves injury.

The interested reader could start with the book 'When Women Sexually Abuse Men', (Cook and Hodo, 2013), or with Martin Fiebert's compilation of references to 40 empirical studies and 2 reviews that demonstrate that men also experience sexual coercion, Martin Fiebert (2012), or with the massive bibliography of about 650 references relating to female perpetration, (Collins,

W, 2017e). However, I shall use the more recent analysis by Stemple, Flores and Meyer, (Sexual victimization perpetrated by women: Federal data reveal surprising prevalence, 2017). This review built on earlier work, (Stemple and Meyer, 2014), and is summarised for the general reader in a Scientific American article, (Stemple and Meyer, 2017). The main review analysed data from four major surveys in the USA carried out by the Centers for Disease Control and Prevention and the Bureau of Justice Statistics (BJS) in the period 2008 to 2013. Their findings are a remarkable debunking of the popular notion that female perpetrated sexual abuse is rare. The National Intimate and Sexual Violence Survey (NISVS) found that men and women had a similar incidence of non-consensual sex, the survey implying an estimated 1.6 million women and 1.7 million men in the USA were raped or made to penetrate in 2011. Being "made to penetrate", the form of non-consensual sex that is particularly applicable to men, was found to be perpetrated by women in 79% of cases.

Another source used by Stemple et al, the National Crime Victimization Survey (NCVS), is more limited in that it does not include forms of abuse involving coercion rather than force. Bearing this limitation in mind, this survey found that female perpetrators acting alone accounted for 28% of rape/sexual assault incidents involving male victims. Incidents of rape/assault involving at least one female perpetrator were reported in 34.7% incidents involving male victims and 4.2% of incidents involving female victims. For cases of rape/sexual assault by a female perpetrator, 57.6% of male victims and 41.4% of female victims reported that the incident involved an attack, meaning the offender hit, knocked down, or otherwise attacked the victim physically. Of those who were attacked, 95.7% of male victims of female offenders and 47.0% of female victims of female offenders were physically injured in the incident.

Stemple, Flores and Meyer (2017) also quote a large range of other studies. I include some extracts, below. Note how many of these female perpetrated abuses would, if the sexes were reversed, earn the perpetrator perhaps ten years or so in prison.

> '...a 2003 study of coercive and forced opposite-sex sexual experiences among 268 male and 355 female college students solicited written descriptions of tactics from male and female victims and perpetrators. Female perpetrators reportedly bit, slapped, and hit male victims. In some cases female college students got on top of aroused men and forced the men to penetrate them. One male victim wrote, "Alcohol was involved. She undressed me, tried to arouse me by touching my genitals, oral sex, and trying to force me inside of her". One female perpetrator

> described her actions as follows, "I locked the room door that we were in. I kissed and touched him. I removed his shirt and unzipped his pants. He asked me to stop. I didn't. Then, I sat on top of him".'
>
> 'Another recent study of college and high-school aged men and boys also detected a high prevalence of female perpetration. The 2011 survey of 302 male college students found that 51.2% reported experiencing at least one sexual victimization experience since age 16. Of those victimized, 48.4% reported female perpetrators.'
>
> 'A 2014 study of 284 men and boys in college and high school found that 43% reported being sexually coerced, with the majority of coercive incidents resulting in unwanted sexual intercourse. Of them, 95% reported only female perpetrators. The authors defined sexual coercion broadly, including verbal pressure such as nagging and begging, which, the authors acknowledge, increases prevalence dramatically. Male respondents described incidents that included statutory rape, e.g., "I was coerced into sleeping with an older woman because I was told it would make me a big boy. I was only 12 at the time and the girl was 18 I believe", and, "she told me she could drink a ton and was giving me double shots to 'see if I could keep up.' After a couple hours things got blurry and I woke up next to her".'

Stemple et al also quote various sources of perpetrator self-reports, which are also revealing, as some extracts show,

> 'A 2012 study using data from a sample of 43,000 adults showed little difference in the sex of self reported sexual perpetrators. Of those who affirmed that they had "ever forced someone to have sex against their will", 43.6% were female and 56.4% were male.'
>
> 'One 2008 literature review looked at five studies of female perpetrated sexual victimization within relationships. The review found that between 1.2% and 19.5% of adolescent girls and 2.1% to 46.2% of college women self-reported that they perpetrated some form of sexual victimization.'
>
> 'A 2013 survey of 1058 male and female youth ages 14 to 21 found that 9% self-reported perpetrating sexual victimization in their lifetime; 4% of youth reported perpetrating attempted or completed rape, which, again is defined to include any unwanted intercourse regardless of directionality (i.e., respondent reported that he/she "made someone have sex with me when I knew they did not want to").While 98% of perpetrators who committed their first offence at age 15 or younger were male, by age 18-19 self-reports of perpetration differed little by sex: females comprised 48% of self-reported perpetrators of attempted or completed rape.'

In the UK there is far less information about "made to penetrate" as the national surveys do not ask questions related to this issue. The first UK study of the phenomenon is that by Weare, Porter and Evans, (Forced to Penetrate Cases: Lived Experiences of Men, June 2017). This was based on an online survey which resulted in 153 usable completions from men across the UK. 87% of respondents were heterosexual, 11% bisexual and 2% gay. Respondents were of ages between 18 and 77. Some 90% of respondents indicated their abuse occurred when they were adult (age 16 or over), the most common age being 16 to 25 (44% of respondents). The percentages of respondents answering in the affirmative to a range of questions were as follows,

- Forcing you to penetrate her after you had been drinking alcohol and were conscious but too intoxicated (drunk) to give her your consent to or stop what was happening, or when you were asleep or unconscious from consensually drinking alcohol or taking drugs, and when you came to (regained consciousness) you could not give consent to, or stop, what was happening, (26.8%);
- Telling lies, threatening to end the relationship, threatening to spread rumours about you, making promises you knew were untrue, or continually verbally pressuring you after you said you didn't want to, (22.2%);
- Using force, for example holding you down with their body weight, pinning your arms, restraining you, or having a weapon, (14.4%);
- Showing displeasure, criticizing your sexuality or attractiveness. getting angry after you said you didn't want to, (11.1%);
- Acting together with two or more people to force you to penetrate her where you had made it clear that you did not give your consent to what was happening or were unable, or threatening to physically harm you or someone close to you, (7.8%).

It is well known in rapes of women that thc perpetrator is most often someone they know. The same is true in made-to-penetrate cases. Only four percent of men reported that the perpetrator was unknown to them. The majority (69%) were friends, acquaintances, girlfriends, fiancées, wives or ex-wives. 95% of respondents reported some degree of emotional/psychological harm resulting from the non-consensual penetration event. They were asked to respond on a scale of severity, from one (no harm) to ten (severe harm). Replies were spread across this whole spectrum of severities (average six), but the commonest was level 10, severe harm. 81% of men who responded had told no one about the event. Only two men out of the 115 men who answered the question said they had reported the incident to the police. Neither resulted in a prosecution.

The men were asked to pick a single word or phrase which best described the incident. The phrases "non-consensual sex" and "forced sex" were commonly chosen, but easily the most commonly chosen was "rape". The unqualified word "sex" was chosen by only two of the men. 48% of respondents reported that they had experienced more than one such incident of sexual assault perpetrated by women. You can read a first-hand account of a man's experience of made-to-penetrate here, (Kulze, 2013). An aspect of his account which rings very true to me is his concern for his abuser, even while she is abusing him,

> 'Charlie woke up to a blank-faced girl straddling him. He had been disrobed, was erect, and as her hips began to shift in short, quick movements, he realized he was inside of her. Frozen with disbelief, Charlie laid still. He faked climaxing, hoping it would prompt her to dismount and leave the room. Eventually she did, but only after he rolled to his side and pretended to sleep. The next morning Charlie wasn't sure what to think. Had an underclassman he knew only by name really entered his dorm room and had her way with him as he slept? It all seemed so absurd, like the makings of an awkward wet dream. Except Charlie had zero interest in this girl. He had never spoken to her, kissed her or even tried to catch her eye. He felt neither lucky nor flattered, just extremely perturbed. "The most traumatic part was the complete assumption of consent," he said. "I was physically revolted by the experience. It just felt so shockingly wrong. It was just a really invasive experience. All I could think was, How can I get this to end? How can I get this to end without hurting her?"'

This is what gynocentrism and male disposability looks like: the primacy of Charlie's concern for the girl, rather than himself, even during her act of sexual assault against him.

20.10 Adult Prison Sexual Assault

Data on sexual assaults in prison are sparse. Official statistics are almost certainly woefully underestimated. People who are sexually assaulted or raped in prison are very unlikely to say anything because they are too scared, have been traumatised and will be bullied and victimised further if they make a report. The report 'Coercive Sex in Prison', (Howard League, 2014), laments the lack of large-scale research on coercive sex in prison. It quotes a 2003 UK study which reported that 'less than two percent of the 590 men they interviewed reported that they had been sexually assaulted while in prison, while three percent had been threatened sexually and two percent had witnessed an assault'. On the other hand, the study observed that 'three quarters of their interviewees thought that, in the British penal system at least, sexual assaults either did not occur at all or were very rare'. A further study in 2004 'found that of 208 former male and female prisoners, one percent had been anally or vaginally raped and 5.3 percent were victims of coerced sex'. In the USA, a survey of inmates by the Bureau of Justice Statistics in 2013 found that 'four percent of prisoners had experienced one or more incidents of sexual victimisation by another prisoner or by staff in the past year, and two percent of prisoners had been a victim of a non-consensual sexual act with another prisoner or unwanted sexual contact with prison staff''. Stemple, Flores and Meyer, (2017), quote a range of US sources to conclude that,

> 'For women prisoners and girls in detention, the staff perpetrators are overwhelmingly male, and for men and boys the staff perpetrators are overwhelmingly female. Because men and boys are vastly disproportionately incarcerated they are overrepresented among victims; women are therefore disproportionately represented among all staff abusers. Among all adult prisoners reporting any type of staff sexual victimization, 80.0% reported only female perpetrators. An additional 5.1% reported both male and female perpetrators. Among all juveniles reporting staff sexual victimization, 89.3% reported only female perpetrators. An additional 3.1% reported both male and female perpetrators…..The disproportionate abuse by female staff members does not occur because women are more often staffing facilities. Men outnumber women by a ratio of three to one in positions requiring direct contact with inmates.'

Her Majesty's Inspectorate of Prisons conducts an annual survey of a sample of prisoners, including asking whether they have been sexually abused by another prisoner or by prison staff. Across most security categories of prisons, one percent of UK prisoners respond that they have been sexually abused in prison. This is larger than the prevalence of sexual assaults on free men and larger than the prevalence of rape of free women. The Howard League report estimates that in 2014 this corresponded to between 850 and 1,650 "people" being sexually abused in UK prisons (although the number of incidents could be much larger as some victims will be assaulted multiple times). "People" here means overwhelmingly men. In 2012 and 2013, of the official reported cases, only 6% and 2% respectively related to women's prisons.

Since the 2014 Howard League report, the incidence of reporting of sexual assaults in UK prisons has increased steeply. The number of sexual assaults officially registered by the prison service will remain a small fraction of the underlying incidence. But even the officially reported figures have been growing rapidly. Between 2011 and 2015 the annual number of reports in the UK increased from 137 to 300, (Fenton, 2016). Almost all these will be assaults on men.

Finally, in respect of female prisoners' experience of sexual victimisation, Stemple, Flores and Meyer, (2017), observe,

> 'Despite the common assumption that, for women prisoners, male staff members pose the greatest sexual threat, BJS studies have consistently shown instead that women are much more likely to be abused by other women inmates than by male staff. For instance, in contrast to the 4.4% of former women prisoners who reported custodial sexual misconduct, 13.7% reported sexual victimization by inmates. A large, statistically significant difference between the threat posed by female inmates versus male staff has been found across BJS surveys on this topic.'

20.11 War Rape

You may think there is nothing much to say about men as victims of war rape? Quite the contrary, though I can cut it short. War rape is sometimes called a "weapon of war". That is inaccurate. War rape occurs once a military victory has been achieved. The purpose of war rape is to humiliate the vanquished. This can be accomplished just as well by raping the defeated men as by raping their womenfolk. In areas where female war rape is endemic, especially in Africa, the rape of men is also endemic. To avoid undue length I refer you to (Collins, W, 2015a). The most important function of that article is to point the reader to sources which expose the truth about the war rape of men, in particular the work of the Refugee Law Project (RLP). I will reproduce these sources here though I can hardly hope to do justice to the issue without excessive length. Will Storr's article in the Observer, 'The rape of men: the darkest secret of war', (Storr, 2011), is essential reading, but you will need a strong stomach. Here's an extract as a taster,

> 'Later on I speak with Dr Angella Ntinda, who treats referrals from the RLP. She tells me: "Eight out of 10 patients from RLP will be talking about some sort of sexual abuse."
>
> "Eight out of 10 men?" I clarify.
>
> "No. Men and women," she says.
>
> "What about men?"
>
> "I think all the men."
>
> I am aghast.
>
> "All of them?" I say.
>
> "Yes," she says. "All the men."'

The accompanying BBC documentary, An Unspeakable Act, (BBC World Service, 2012) is also essential viewing. Conflicts in the eastern Democratic Republic of the Congo have been reported to involve very high rates of war rape,

> 'Of the 1005 households surveyed 998 households participated, yielding a response rate of 98.9%. Rates of reported sexual violence were 39.7% among women and 23.6% among men. Women reported to have perpetrated conflict-related sexual violence in 41.1% of female cases and 10.0% of male cases.', (Johnson and Scott, 2010)

One of the few academics to have looked into the issue in any detail is Lara Stemple, of the University of California's Health and Human Rights Law Project. Her study 'Male Rape and Human Rights' notes incidents of male sexual violence as a weapon of wartime or political aggression in countries such as Chile, Greece, Croatia, Iran, Kuwait, the former Soviet Union and the former Yugoslavia. Of Sri Lankan males who were seen at a London torture treatment centre, 21% reported sexual abuse while in detention. In El Salvador, 76% of male political prisoners surveyed in the 1980s described at least one incidence of sexual torture. A study of 6,000 concentration-camp inmates in Sarajevo found that 80% of men reported having been raped, (Stemple, 2008/9). During the conflict the Western media were full of reports of the war rapes of women. Still today Googling "Sarajevo rape victims" will bring up any number of reports of the rape of women, but you will have to work harder to find mention of male victims.

The research by Lara Stemple at the University of California not only shows that male sexual violence is a component of wars all over the world, it also suggests that international aid organisations are failing male victims. Her study cites a review of 4,076 NGOs that have addressed wartime sexual violence. Only 3% of them mentioned the experience of men in their literature. "Typically," Stemple says, "as a passing reference."

Stemple's findings on the failure of aid agencies is no surprise to Chris Dolan of RLP, who you can see delivering a lecture on the subject here, (Dolan, 2014). He was quoted in Will Storr's article as saying, 'The organisations working on sexual and gender-based violence don't talk about it (men's sexual victimisation), he says. "It's systematically silenced. If you're very, very lucky they'll give it a tangential mention at the end of a report. You might get five seconds of: Oh and men can also be the victims of sexual violence." But there's no data, no discussion.'

As part of an attempt to correct this, the RLP produced a documentary in 2010 called 'Gender Against Men', (Refugee Law Project, 2012). Dolan says that attempts were made to stop him screening it. Quoting the Observer article,

> "'Were these attempts by people in well-known, international aid agencies?" I ask. "Yes," he replies. "There's a fear among them that this is a zero-sum game; that there's a pre-defined cake and if you start talking about men, you're going to somehow eat a chunk of this cake that's taken them a long time to bake." Dolan points to a November 2006 UN report that followed an international conference on sexual violence in this area of East Africa. "I know for a fact that the people behind the report insisted the definition of rape be restricted to women," he says, adding that one of the RLP's donors, Dutch Oxfam, refused to provide any more funding unless he'd promise that 70% of his client base was female. He also recalls a man whose case was "particularly bad" and was referred to the UN's refugee agency, the UNHCR. "They told him: 'We have a programme for vulnerable women, but not men.'"

Just as with domestic violence, it is really all about money. The NGOs keep men's victimisation suppressed because they don't want their funding reduced. And who, if you dig deep, do you find at the back of it all? Hilary Clinton. This is the same Hilary Clinton who opined that women had always been the primary victims of war, (Clinton, 1998). In the Observer article, Lara Stemple was quoted as describing a 'constant drum beat that women are the rape victims and a milieu in which men are treated as a monolithic perpetrator class'. She continued,

> 'International human rights law leaves out men in nearly all instruments designed to address sexual violence. The UN Security Council Resolution 1325 in 2000 treats wartime sexual violence as something that only impacts on women and girls… Secretary of State Hillary Clinton recently announced $44M to implement this resolution. Because of its entirely exclusive focus on female victims, it seems unlikely that any of these new funds will reach the thousands of men and boys who suffer from this kind of abuse. Ignoring male rape not only neglects men, it also harms women by reinforcing a viewpoint that equates "female" with "victim", thus hampering our ability to see women as strong and empowered. In the same way, silence about male victims reinforces unhealthy expectations about men and their supposed invulnerability.' (Storr, 2011)

The latest video I know of from the Refugee Law Project is (They Slept With Me, 2015). The war rape of men continues, unremarked by the public.

20.12 The Empathy Gap in Sexual Assault

Sexual assault is the pre-eminent area which feminists claim as their own province, the centre of patriarchal oppression of women by men. This chapter has told a different story. Whilst sexual abuse of females by males is not denied or minimised, either by society in general or by the present author, the sexual abuse of males by females certainly *is* denied and minimised. The empirical evidence stands in stark contrast to the deeply resistant societal prejudice.

The evolutionary origins of this asymmetry are obvious: the severe consequences of pregnancy by rape for a woman, as contrasted with the relatively insignificant *physical* consequences for a male victim of a woman's sexual abuse. The historical origin is also clear: when sexual assault was defined by physical force, this naturally tends to focus upon male culpability (though this hardly works in respect of the abuse of male minors). But both of these are now largely anachronisms. As soon as sexual offences became defined by lack of consent the distinct treatment of the two sexes lost any coherence it ever had. And the increasing recognition of the significance of psychological harms, and their influence on future behaviours, reduces the emphasis on purely physical harms.

The empirical evidence of coercive sex, or unwanted sexual touching, being perpetrated upon adult men by adult women is clear and not much less in magnitude than the reverse. But this bald fact is unlikely to reduce the incredulity of the bulk of the public regarding such experiences being potentially harmful to a man. The story of Charlie, above, is more likely to provoke amusement than outrage. Yet reverse the sexes and the event would be a particularly serious rape scenario which would certainly see the perpetrator go to prison for a very long time. Empathy gap, anyone? And Charlie's reaction in being less concerned about himself and more concerned about not hurting his rapist is very telling in respect of men's internalisation of their own disposability.

Women's sexual offending against male minors is somewhat more likely to provoke public calls for punishment, though even here it may depend upon the exact age of the boy. Many people are still of the opinion that a 35 year old teacher grooming a 15 year old boy pupil for sex does not deserve a harsh punishment: more of a ticking off. The distinct perception of the sexes in respect of both perpetrator and victim is ancient in origin but feminism has done nothing to diminish it. On the contrary, feminism in the form of MeToo and similar sentiments have inflamed intolerance of male words and actions to an extreme degree. We are nearing the point at which simply looking at a woman in a way she does not like might become a criminal offence. A venerable male professor being so unwise as to tell a female colleague that she is beautiful can result in his being excommunicated by his university, declared a sex abuser and rendered a non-person, his name being expunged as an undesirable. I, on the other hand, must tolerate women I barely know hugging or kissing me in public. I cannot recoil and reject their advances (which are sometimes, if not always, unwelcome) without being regarded as unforgivably rude. Who is privileged under these conditions? And who was originally possessed of the power required to bring this abjection of men about?

There are more than a hundred times more men in prison for sexual offences than there are women in prison for sexual offences. But there is a gross mismatch between this ratio and the known high incidence of male sex offenders who have a background of being sexually abused by a woman themselves as children (perhaps about one-third to one-half of all such men in prison). So, given the 13,500 men in prison in the UK for sex offences, why are there only about 100 women? Where are the several thousand missing women who have sexually offended against male minors? (Not to mention the women offending against female minors). The answer is that they go undetected, because women are trusted with children, it happens behind closed doors, and children generally do not tell. Esther Rantzen's Childline experience, and Michele Elliott's experiences, started to reveal the extent of the problem of female sexual abusers. But society does not want to know. It appears that at least 20% of sexual offending against minors is perpetrated by women, and perhaps almost 50%.

The starkest warning about adult women's potential for sexual exploitation of male minors comes from juvenile detention facilities in the USA where female staff perpetrating sexual abuse on male inmates is the commonest form of sexual assault. The power differential in this case is at its most extreme. But there is also substantial power differential between a teacher and her pupils, and one wonders at the true extent of sexual abuses in this scenario. More teacher-on-pupil sexual abuses have come to light in recent years than the public might have thought possible. Even war rape is not a female victim monopoly, as is generally supposed – a presumption encouraged by governmental policies and NGOs wishing to retain control of funding.

The societal view of sexual victimisation being a female monopoly, rather than being true, is actually a pre-eminent example of male disposability and the empathy gap which are so extreme in the scenario of female perpetrators of sexual abuse against males that few in society can conceptualise it as abuse at all.

21

Reprise: The Case for the Empathy Gap

With us, heretical opinions do not perceptibly gain, or even lose, ground in each decade or generation; they never blaze out far and wide, but continue to smoulder in the narrow circles of thinking and studious persons among whom they originate, without ever lighting up the general affairs of mankind with either a true or a deceptive light. And thus is kept up a state of things very satisfactory to some minds, because, without the unpleasant process of fining or imprisoning anybody, it maintains all prevailing opinions outwardly undisturbed, while it does not absolutely interdict the exercise of reason by dissentients afflicted with the malady of thought. A convenient plan for having peace in the intellectual world, and keeping all things going on therein very much as they do already. But the price paid for this sort of intellectual pacification, is the sacrifice of the entire moral courage of the human mind.
John Stuart Mill (1806 – 1873), On Liberty

In this final chapter I summarise the case for the empathy gap and its correlates, male disposability and gynocentrism. But first let's reprise the two schools of thought. Stripped down to their barest outline, the two oppositional positions are crudely as follows.

The feminist position is that men are powerful and privileged, and that women are oppressed by men because men are taught to do so by a cultural norm called "patriarchy" and because it is to men's (perceived) advantage to conform to this patriarchal system. Women are disadvantaged in multiple ways by the system of patriarchy, including being the particular victims of violence and sexual assault, which serve to reinforced women's subservience to men - by force when necessary, and by fear otherwise. Women are also disadvantaged in the workplace, facing discrimination in hiring and progression due to entrenched discrimination and 'glass ceilings'. This is especially egregious to women in feminist thought because financial freedom from men is the key to women escaping from their patriarchal oppressors.

Under patriarchy, men are misogynistic and this stems from a deep seated hatred of women and a conviction of women's inferiority. Men are commonly unaware of their privilege, and this is said to be because privilege is invisible to the privileged. Whilst some feminists may accept that some men suffer some disadvantages, they only recognise this as possible as a product of patriarchy itself, i.e., "patriarch hurts men too". Men's power means that men can be disadvantaged only by men, either by other men or by themselves through self-destructive behaviours, both of which emanate from patriarchy and the nature of masculinity. Women cannot be sexist, and endemic harms to men arising from the organisation and operation of society as a whole can only occur via patriarchy, i.e., only the male hegemony can harm or disadvantage individual men – and only then when it benefits the patriarchy as a whole. In contrast, the idea that female influences on society can cause endemic disadvantages to men is an impossibility in feminist philosophy. Under feminist patriarchy theory, women are powerless and innocent and can be culpable for no harms suffered by males. Feminism denies women's agency whilst paradoxically also asserting that women are strong and capable of being fully independent.

The perspective presented in this book, in contrast, is that women are indeed strong and capable of being independent, and that they also enjoy very considerable agency. In this perspective the key to understanding gender issues in society is not oppression of women by men (now or historically), but a deep seated preferencing of women, by both sexes. In its original form, matricentrism, this preferencing of women is of evolutionary origin, the functioning of which is to enhance reproductive success by flows of resource from men to women, where the latter are proxies for children. The logical corollary of matricentrism is relative disadvantaging of men, and hence "male disposability", a term which refers to a preference, by both sexes, to have dangerous or harmful activities carried out by men. Unlike feminism, in which the mindsets of the two sexes are oppositional, in this matricentric view the mindsets of the two sexes are aligned and consistent. Women expect to receive, men have a predilection to provide, and men are happy to acquiesce to their own "disposability" in return for the societal reward of respect which accompanies conformance to this expectation.

Matricentrism imbues women with considerable power as a birthright. But in traditional societies, systems of respect are in place to reward men for conformance to a norm in which they behave altruistically, namely stable pair-bonding and provisioning to family. This social respect provides a form of male power which balances intrinsic female power and constitutes the truth of "patriarchy". The system of patriarchy, the conferring of respect and status upon males for socially beneficial, family-centric behaviour, arose to even out the burden on the sexes. This is a consistent and harmonious system, as opposed to the oppressive patriarchal system envisaged under feminism.

However, evolved matricentrism has given way to cultural gynocentrism, by various historical processes including the rise of feminism. Whilst matricentrism originated for the benefit of children (reproductive success), under gynocentric feminism the focus shifts to woman, *qua* woman, and the child disappears from the picture. The danger of an intensified gynocentrism is that it grants women the power to define the moral right unopposed, a true hegemony.

Feminism is profoundly disrespectful of men. The feminist attack on masculinity has taken root in many men as well as women, and not just those who identify as feminists. The success of this attack is due to gynocentrism gifting women the power to define the moral right, together with men's ancient acquiescence to their own disposability and acceptance of women's moral authority. The latter is manifest in men's intense discomfort with female disapproval.

The disenfranchising of men from societal respect has caused men also to lose the social power which stemmed from it, a power that was necessary to balance women's intrinsic matricentric power. And this has been brought about at just the time that matricentrism has morphed into its intensified form, gynocentrism. The result is a rampant and limitless disadvantaging of men which goes unrecognised because it has been brought about by a mindset which reconceptualises gynocentrism as female oppression and disadvantage. In reality, the purpose of the illusion of female disadvantage is to rationalise female preferencing without it being perceived as such. As a result, female preferencing can never be sated whilst suffering under this delusion. This phenomenon is amplified by the wider deployment of identity politics and political correctness.

In this anti-feminist perspective, men can be, and are being, endemically disadvantaged by female influences within society. In this perspective, women can be, and are being, sexist. Women are now possessed of both an intensified gynocentric power and also, increasingly, political and economic powers previously the province primarily of men. The powers are unbalanced as men have been depowered in both spheres, deliberately. Feminism is incapable of recognising this, and will forever remain convinced that women "still have a long way to go", because the phenomenon of gynocentrism will always present women as deserving. Gynocentrism therefore conceals itself: gynocentric invisibility. The result is that the ancient empathy gap is now maturing into an outright prejudice against men as a class.

The question is: which of these two perspectives – the feminist or the anti-feminist - performs best as explanations of the empirical evidence presented in chapters 2 to 20? The discriminating factors are, (i) which sex is disadvantaged in each sphere?, and, (ii) are females being presented as disadvantaged when the evidence suggests the opposite (consistent with gynocentric invisibility)? To address the question I reprise each of the major topic areas covered in the book.

21.1 Education

The All-Party Parliamentary Group, the 'Women and Equalities Committee', has a remit which explicitly focuses on one sex only. This focus on equality issues for women and girls but not men and boys could be consistent with the Equality Act if females were truly disadvantaged compared with males, and in every sphere. This book shows that this is not the case in most areas. In the specific case of education, the common practice that the Minister (or Shadow Minister) for Education is also, or has recently been, the Minister (or Shadow Minister) for Women and Equalities, betrays a flagrant disregard for the serious, and worsening, educational disadvantage of males. This is reinforced by government policy documents which continue to focus on female education, when gender is raised at all, rather than upon the sex which is indubitably that disadvantaged. In what way can "patriarchy hurts men too" account for Government policies, now driven mainly by women Ministers, which ignores the education of males?

The relentless striving to achieve more "women in STEMM" continues, whilst senior politicians appear to be unaware that women now dominate in STEMM as undergraduates, as indeed women dominate as university staff in STEMM at all but the highest levels. In contrast, there is no political will to address boys' educational disadvantage, beyond telling them to "pull their socks up" (the obligation of male utility). These are clear illustrations of female preferencing contrasted with the disposability of males who fail to assist themselves. The latter is, of course, the presumption of male agency and autonomy. This situation is emphatically reflected by the contrast between the concerns of the professional institutes and the teaching unions. The professional institutes for engineering and physics, for example, spare no efforts to promote women's and girls' interests. In contrast, the teaching unions are entirely unconcerned about the disappearing male teacher and actively promote only "women's equality" issues. If the failure of boys in education is due to their toxic "laddishness", how exactly does boys' laddishness explain the behaviour of representative, and female dominated, professional bodies?

21.2 Health and Longevity

Across all causes there is a 43% excess of premature deaths of men over that of women in England and Wales. The probability of a man dying before age 45 is 78% greater than for a woman. More men than women die prematurely from all the non-sex-specific cancers. When it comes to disadvantage, being dead takes some beating. Yet this glaringly obvious disadvantage to men excites little public concern. What does the "Women and Equalities Committee" say about it? What does the Equality and Human Rights Commission say about it? Globally, many NGOs focus exclusively on the health of women and girls; none focus on men and boys. When the matter of men's health disadvantage is raised, the response will generally be that men should look after themselves better. In other words, "it's their own fault", the essence of male agency and autonomy. Is this not a clear lack of empathy?

There is a willingness to attribute men's indisputable health disadvantages to men's lesser use of healthcare services, and to attribute this to men's destructive masculine characteristics. However, this hypothesis does not survive inspection. Not only is men's reduced access to healthcare not as marked as is often supposed, but the part of this reduced access which is not explained by valid sex differences in need may be explicable by working patterns. Whilst it might be argued that men's working patterns are an individual choice, it would be disingenuous not to concede a societal – and practical/financial - obligation which acts in this respect. This is an example of the obligation for male utility driving male disposability.

Moreover, healthcare spending on women exceeds that on men, even after allowance for issues related to contraception, pregnancy and childbirth. Female-specific medical research funding exceeds that on male-specific medical research substantially, well over twice as much in the USA for example. In the UK, breast cancer and prostate cancer kill similar numbers of people, but breast cancer receives three times as much research funding. Public funding events, e.g., fun-runs, attract far more support for breast cancer than for prostate cancer (I speak from experience). How is this skewed focus explained given that it does not align with the evidence on mortality? But it *is* consistent with gynocentrism. It is not consistent with "it's men's own fault". Funding reflects societal concern, not the behaviour of the afflicted themselves.

Of course there are psychosocial factors which significantly impact male longevity, not least substance abuse, but innate biological sex differences also play a part, such as the immunosuppressant characteristics of testosterone (an instance of biologically instantiated male disposability perhaps). Biological effects are evident in the death rate for male babies and young boys which exceeds that of females of the same age by about 10% to 30%.

Both sexes suffer reduced longevity as a result of socioeconomic deprivation, but the empirical evidence shows that the demographic effect is significantly more marked for men. The intersection of deprivation and being male leads to the greatest health disadvantage. This is again an instance of reduced male utility, as manifest by being poor, driving male disposability. Crudely put: for men, it's perform or die.

Perhaps the most glaringly obvious example of male disposability in healthcare is the saga of the HPV vaccination. HPV infections are responsible for similar numbers of premature cancer deaths in both sexes. This was well known and not in dispute. Yet the authorities saw fit to instigate a vaccination programme for girls only. The disturbing aspect of the HPV vaccination saga is the amount of pressure, from a range of authoritative bodies - and ultimately the spectre of legal action - which was necessary to overturn a transparently sexist policy. Empathy gap, at all? Let those who are convinced that males are privileged, and incredulous at the idea of male disposability and gynocentrism, explain why the vaccine was not rolled out to boys only – and the spurious rationalisation of "herd immunity" claimed to be sufficient for girls. Let them explain why no one would ever have dreamed of suggesting such a policy.

Let them also explain why the Chief Medical Officer for England saw fit to produce the report "The Health of the 51%: Women" but refused to produce an equivalent for men. Let them explain how this can be consistent with the empirical evidence of men's health disadvantages other than simply female preferencing.

Men in the UK account for 97% of fatal accidents in the workplace. Non-fatal accidents at work are also dominated by men, especially those resulting in serious injury. This is because the occupations in which the most serious accidents happen are virtually all-male. Women are not queuing up to work in these DAD jobs (Dirty And Dangerous jobs), which are often not well paid and yet they are the jobs that most need doing if society is to function. This is male utility and male disposability at its most explicit. This is contribution, not privilege or oppression of women, to anyone not blinded by ideology.

The feminist professor who might be very willing to detect hegemonic masculinity in the attitude of such working men has an existence which is sustained by them. It is long overdue to recognise that these well-heeled feminists are the new bourgeoisie, parasitic upon the labours of the working class, as ever they were. At least the traditional bourgeoisie created the means of production and hence contributed to the economy, exploitative though it may have been. The new bourgeoisie contribute nothing but bitterness and division, sitting in their tenured chairs.

21.3 Male Genital Mutilation

It is hateful to mutilate the genitals of girls for no valid medical purpose. In the West very few people would demur, and certainly not those who call themselves intactivists and campaign against male genital mutilation. But our culture – in fact almost all cultures worldwide – accept mutilation of boys' genitals as if there were something natural about it. Claims of medical benefit are rationalisations which do not bear scrutiny. But, for some men if not all, circumcision causes very clear, persistent, harms, particularly as regards sexual function. Indeed, the amelioration of male sexual function is the original purpose of circumcision. In what way can this be contorted into oppression of women?

In the UK, MGM is almost certainly illegal under assault laws, yet it is being tolerated. It is an object lesson in how the public can be brought to accept anything so long as everyone else they know regards it as OK – even cutting body parts off babies, providing they are boy babies. How much clearer an example of a sex-based empathy gap do you want?

Lord Justice Munby, former head of the Family Division, has ruled that MGM is a harm. The medical evidence concurs. It is remarkable, then, that a non-consensual violation of the bodily integrity of a child, which has been judicially ruled to constitute a harm, nevertheless is still to be treated as legal. This position is arrived at by rationalisations which do not bear scrutiny and which are actually for the purpose of protecting the status quo rather than the child. What facilitates this peculiar illogic is a society which will readily accept such harms to males, of however tender an age, which are (rightly) socially and legally intolerable if perpetrated upon females.

Whilst intactivists are equally opposed to FGM, those people who are most vociferously opposed to FGM are often angered by campaigning against MGM. This curious inconsistency is made more curious by the impassioned anger of their response to intactivist campaigners. It is difficult to understand this reaction other than as a deep seated prejudice that the spotlight of concern should never be shone upon males. Males are not the proper recipients of concern. Females must retain their monopoly on victimhood and its attendant benefits. This is feminist intensified gynocentrism and its correlate, male disposability: the empathy gap.

The situation in African countries is especially distressing, though I have no wish to instruct other cultures how they should behave. However, even if we must refrain from comment on coming-of-age rituals in traditional African cultures, there is still no excuse for Westerners treating these brutal spectacles as a tourist attraction. There is no chance that these same people would regard female genital mutilation as a suitable tourist attraction even if the locals did (which they certainly do not). These MGM rituals, and the circumcision mobs that forcibly cut men in the street in these countries, cannot be simply dismissed as phenomena of the patriarchy. Anyone making such a claim will have to explain why it is that, in these cultures, it is just as often the women who insist that men are cut – so as to render them "fit to be our husbands". Male disposability is not specific to the West.

21.4 Work, Pay, Tax and Pensions

It is remarkable that the pay gap is presented as a disadvantage to women when the actual position on work, pay, tax and pensions is a transfer of money from men to women, consistent with ancient male provisioning and the pair bond. But the feminist objective is to make women independent of men, and the pay gap is their propaganda strategy to this end.

Feminists may delight in presenting the gender pay gap as women "doing the same work for less pay" but even they do not believe it. The full time, all-age median pay rate gap is currently about 9% in favour of men, whilst the part time median pay rate gap is about 5% in favour of women. The full time gender pay rate gap for people under 40 years of age is essentially zero. The pay rate gap after age 40 is a product of women having children and/or opting to work part time. Everyone knows this, it is not contentious. But feminists want to increase women's power by increasing their presence in the workplace, especially at senior levels. The motivation for the pay gap propaganda is the drive to increase female power and make women financially independent of men.

Over the UK as a whole, men work 52% more paid hours than women and work for more continuous years. 77% more men than women work full time, whilst nearly three times more women than men work part time, and average pay rates are higher for full time workers (regardless of sex). As a result, men earn 91% more than women and men pay nearly three times more income tax than women, despite women being 47% of those employed.

But women now spend more money than men – or influence the spending of more money than men - so there is a net flow of money from men to women for the purposes of spending. Please explain to me why the person working to earn the money is an oppressor whilst the person spending more of the money is oppressed? It is not so, of course. But feminism presents it as such because the objective is to make women financially independent of men, and hence to have the freedom to eject men from the home. *That* is the true goal about which feminists are careful to avoid being forthright.

Feminists endlessly claim that men do not pull their weight as regards housework. But surveys indicate that in terms of total work, paid work and housework, men do rather more work in total. Men and women also do similar amounts of unpaid voluntary work. Nor is unpaid caring the sole province of women. In fact men do 42% of unpaid caring, despite also doing 52% more paid working hours. A larger proportion of men over 65 are unpaid carers than women over 65. More men than women are in full time employment whilst also providing 50 hours or more of unpaid care per week.

What would happen if men did what feminists appear to want: simply declined to work so many paid hours in order to decrease their earnings and stay at home more? Would women pick up the slack and work longer hours? Does anyone really think so? Or would women simply tell men to get back to work? Who would ever do the DAD jobs other than men?

The 2012 British Social Attitudes Survey revealed that 69% of people believe that fathers should be the primary earner for the family, and 73% believe that fathers should work full time. No respondents (to within rounding) thought the mother should be the primary earner, and only 9% thought that mum and dad should share the responsibility for earning equally.

The feminist "diversity" project, ostensibly to get equal numbers of men and women in all employment, and at all seniority levels, is disingenuous. They have no intention of agitating for such an outcome where women are in the majority. In any case the project is preposterous as, taken literally, it would require an enormous proportion of people, of both sexes, to be forced into employment contrary to their wishes or ability. This is evident from the existing gender asymmetries in employment. 78% of occupations have an excess of one sex over the other exceeding 30%, and 41% of these involve an excess of female employees over male employees exceeding 30%. There has been no demonstration of any benefit from the proposed draconian policy of equalisation, and it is clear that it cannot happen. But the feminists are really interested only in using this overt policy as leverage to get more women into positions of influence. It is about power, not equality.

In respect of pensions, how can one interpret the WASPIs who claim that the equalisation of the State pension age for the two sexes is inequality? Did they campaign against injustice for all those years when men's retirement age was 5 years later? In 1951 the mean life expectancy of males at birth was only one year greater than men's State retirement age, whilst for women it was 12 years greater. A man who lived to 65 to start drawing his State pension in 1970 could expect to live another 12 years. A woman who lived to 60 to start drawing her State pension in the same year could expect to live another 21 years, hence drawing her pension some 9 years longer than the man. Where were feminist complaints about inequality then? And now that the gold standard of pensions, the defined benefit pension, has all but disappeared from the private sector, but still prevails in the public sector, note that two-thirds of public sector staff who will benefit from this far superior pension are women – and that this will be funded from taxes, provided overwhelmingly by men.

So we see that the ultimate fraudulence of the feminist drive for ostensible independence from men is that they never can be - not so long as men continue to do virtually all the DAD jobs which are required to keep society functioning, and not so long as men continue to pump three times more tax revenue into the Exchequer to pay for the female-dominated public sector and its pensions. In truth, what feminists really want is not independence from men, but rather not having to give anything back to men in return, not even acknowledgement of reality.

21.5 Imprisonment

Imprisonment provides a perfect example of male disposability, gynocentrism and lack of male in-group preference. That men are far more readily incarcerated than women is emphatically clear from the data (hence - male disposability). A preferred treatment of women is now enshrined in policy at several different levels (hence - gynocentrism). The public would probably agree that everyone should be equal before the law. Yet there is no public outcry, even from men, when this principle is violated in respect of sex (observe the lack of male in-group preference).

The traditional gendered psychology regards men as agentic, powerful and responsible, whilst women are regarded in this outmoded view as non-agentic, vulnerable, and in need of protection. If the agentic, powerful and responsible become criminal, clearly they deserve punishment. If the non-agentic, powerless and vulnerable become criminal, then society is more likely to regard a compassionate response, rather than punishment, to be appropriate. Hence, the traditional gendered psychology drives a disparate perspective on male and female offending. This becomes a pernicious, and unjust, phenomenon when the traditional gender norms no longer reflect social or political reality (if they ever did).

The entitlement of women to different treatment, in order to be "equal", is argued, at different times, on the following grounds. Firstly, that of historical power imbalance. We need have no debate about the past. It is morally illiterate to claim present benefit based on injustice to someone else in history. Secondly, it is argued on the basis that women remain endemically disadvantaged in society generally. But this is a perspective which the entirety of this book challenges. In any case, injustice is not neutralised by more injustice. The third argument which is deployed is that women are currently treated more harshly by the criminal justice system. Chapter 8 has demolished this untruth. A fourth argument which is used is that women offenders have a background of being abused, by men, and that their offending is at the behest of, or caused by, men. This is a denial of female agency, stemming with painful obviousness from traditional gender norms. There is nothing progressive about it. Finally, it may simply be claimed that equal treatment is harsher for women and therefore unequal. All these arguments are attempts to rationalise a deep seated bias, a prejudice, whose origin is gynocentrism and male disposability and their result: the empathy gap.

21.6 Violence and Abuse

On the subject of violence and abuse, are we not obliged to admit that the feminists have a point? This, together with sexual assault, are feminism's trump cards. This is manifest in the huge focus on VAWG – Violence Against Women and Girls. But wait: violence is perpetrated against male victims roughly twice as frequently as against female victims. And this is true as regards both men and boys. It is also true for the most extreme cases where homicide results.

Adherents of the dominant gender narrative will generally react to this observation with unconcern, citing (correctly) that males are also the majority of the perpetrators of these offences. The implication appears to be that this observation somehow neutralises any need for concern or compassion for the victims. This is about as clear an example of victim blaming as one could have – the victim is to blame for his own injuries, or death, because he shares genital anatomy with his attacker. Such thinking is the product of the empathy gap, given wings by identity politics, which allows all males to be lumped together into an undifferentiated and undeserving mass. There is no need to distinguish between villain and victim because both are infected with the blight of masculinity.

"Men are violent" or "we need to talk about men's violence" are sentiments you can express publicly without fear of censure or disagreement. You would not be treated so kindly if you opined that Muslims are terrorists or that we need to talk about black men's drug dealing. All these are examples of castigating the whole for the behaviour of a few. They are of the same type. The acceptability of one and the political incorrectness of the others is determined only by their respective identity group status: oppressor or oppressed. But this status is prejudice dressed up as politics. It relegates the individual to irrelevance, replacing them with an identity label. You are undeserving by virtue of an accident of your birth. Consider a 65 year old man who has never exercised violence upon anyone in his life and who has been steadfast in supporting his family over that long life. Is it his own fault that society regards him as dangerous and toxic? Or is it a prejudice which has been imposed upon him without due reason?

How are we to react to VAWG when "Violence" does not mean violence, "Women" does not mean women, and "Girls" does not mean girls? What does it imply when crimes against men and boys are hidden by being referred to as VAWG? Is the VAWG perspective about compassion for women and girls, or is it about withholding compassion from men and boys?

Despite the strong media focus on domestic violence, the volume of domestic violence offending is significantly less than stranger or acquaintance violence outside the home. Nevertheless, one in three victims of domestic abuse or partner abuse are male. Where physical injury occurs, men may be rather more than one in three victims. One in three victims of domestic homicide are also male (and about one in four victims of partner homicide are male). But this prevalence of male victims of domestic abuse is subject to successive attritions, resulting ultimately in a tiny level of service provision to male victims. The percentages of men through the criminal justice system diminish as follows: 34% from crime surveys; 24% from police reports; 17% of victims in prosecutions; but only about 1% - 3% of the service provision.

As an illustration of the double standards in operation in the context of partner violence, consider the cases of MPs David Ruffley, Sarah Champion and Layla Moran. All were arrested for assaulting their partners. But where a man is sacked and disgraced, a woman is lauded and held up as a role model. What part of gynocentrism and male disposability do you not grasp?

The aspect of domestic violence which is least well appreciated by the public or by social and political narratives, is the extent to which mothers are responsible for child deaths. Statistics on this issue are incomplete (and one wonders why). The largest international studies indicate that mothers are responsible for more child deaths than men. Evidence from Serious Case Reviews in the UK support this contention. Yet the danger represented by men is the mantra which leads to fathers being sundered from their children in society-destroying numbers by the family courts.

The mindset which legitimises VAWG is also responsible for the introduction of terms such as "femicide": a levering of the empathy gap to suggest that the killing of females is a more serious issue than the killing of mere males. The instantiation of the empathy gap as VAWG clearly demonstrates the operation of gynocentrism and male disposability. Violence suffered by females is perceived differently from violence suffered by males, and violence perpetrated by females is perceived differently from violence perpetrated by males. Yet women can be both strong and violent, men can be weak and vulnerable, and immature boys have no physical advantage over girls – and still less over adult women. This minimisation of male victimisation is necessary to protect the dominant gender narrative; widespread male victimisation by women conflicts with its basic tenets. The empathy gap facilitates belief in an ideology which cannot countenance female perpetration and is indifferent to male victimisation.

Criticism of the presentation of domestic abuse as overwhelmingly men abusing women is invariably interpreted by those advocating this perspective as an attempt by reactionary forces to re-establish patriarchal power over women. My perspective is that the "gendered" interpretation of domestic abuse is another example of the empathy gap in operation. Here we see why the empathy gap must be kept in place. To allow that domestic violence is gender symmetric fatally undermines feminist patriarchy theory. To allow equal empathy for men would thus lead to the collapse of the whole feminist narrative. The empathy gap is the fulcrum of the feminist lever.

21.7 Family Courts

Even today most people will refuse to believe that one of feminism's main aims is, and always was, to give women the power to rid their families of men. There is a terrible arrogance here that sees only the female parent as significant. In the family courts we see this played out explicitly. Allegations of domestic abuse provide a convenient mechanism. Protestations that only genuinely abusive men are treated in this way are untrue, as the bald statistics illustrate. Unfortunately, the denigration of men over the last 50 years has been so successful that the public no longer balk at the preposterous notion that half of all fathers are abusers.

The dominant narrative, buoyed by powerful lobbying, that it is men alone who pose a risk to children, is not borne out by the evidence. Allegations of domestic violence have a significant bearing on the outcomes of child contact applications, but the relationship of such allegations to actual risk is in doubt, partly because of the prevalence of false allegations and partly because other people, including the mother, may pose a greater risk. The most disconcerting aspect of this is that the child safeguarding authorities display the same mindset, namely that domestic abuse is only ever a threat posed by a man to the mother and child. The result is that safeguarding guidance completely ignores the threat to the children which may be posed by the mother. The evidence suggests that this ignores an equal or greater risk to the child in many cases.

In the matter of child arrangements after parental separation we see most clearly how far culturally intensified gynocentrism has departed from evolved matricentrism. The child's best interests are elided with the mother's wishes, whilst the latter are truly made paramount.

Gynocentrism ensures that even a male dominated legislature and judiciary will acquiesce to the demands of the feminist lobby, because lack of in-group preference means the empathy gap operates between man and man as much as between woman and man. These combined psychosocial forces mean that the extent to which a man is permitted to be a father is defined by the mother.

In respect of childcare and contact arrangements post-separation, there is no legal obligation on parents to involve the courts. They can agree informally between them. But recourse to the family courts for child contact arrangements are made in about 38% of cases, a very high level of inability of parents to agree. About 92% of non-resident patents are fathers in the UK.

The courts order staying contact in less than half of cases on which they rule. The totality of cases, and by implication therefore also arrangements agreed privately without court involvement, have the same outcome: less than half involve staying contact. Typical staying orders are for one or two overnights per fortnight, perhaps with one additional visiting day per fortnight. This is the extent of contact which the luckier 40% or so of non-resident parents may hope to achieve.

Courts order unsupervised visits, but without overnight stays, in about 20% of cases. The average ordered contact time under these conditions is 10 hours per fortnight. Surveys of outcomes suggest that contact less than weekly but at least monthly occurs in about 20% of cases. These are the McDads.

The courts order no contact of any sort in 14% of cases. The courts order either no contact or only indirect or supervised contact in 31% of cases. These figures compare with surveyed outcomes which suggest that no contact at all results in about one in three cases. One could add to this a further 9% where contact occurs only a few times per year.

It appears that the actual outcome is "no contact" in a greater percentage of cases than the courts order, but this may be because orders for indirect or supervised contact ultimately lead to no contact longer term. A meaningful relationship is unlikely to be sustainable on such a basis. The actual prevalence of no contact, or contact only a few times per year, may be as high as about 40%, especially after the first year or two.

All these figures are extremely uncertain, but as far as can be judged on present information, the courts order contact roughly in line with what transpires in practice, i.e., including the 62% of cases which do not go through the courts. However, there is no guarantee that contact ordered by the courts is what actually happens. The extent to which the family courts enforce their own orders is virtually zero. The chief criticism one can, with justification, bring against the family courts is not so much their bias as their ineffectuality. At the start of the process the resident parent holds all the cards. At the end, the resident parent still holds all the cards. A belligerent resident parent, the mother in 92% of cases, can flout court orders with complete impunity.

Claims are sometimes made that fathers seeking contact via the family courts are overwhelmingly successful. However such claims are disingenuous: any contact at all, even if indirect or supervised, is counted as a "success" in such claims. The reality is that, despite the often modest applications by fathers who accept that equal shared care is unlikely, about half of fathers fail to achieve what they request. Either they fail to achieve the type of contact sought or they fail to achieve the quantum of time sought. And even this relates to what the courts order, not what actually happens.

The dominant factor in fathers' success in seeking meaningful child contact is whether the mother agrees. Whilst there will be individual cases which depart from the norm, in the typical case the mother calls the shots and the courts do not alter that reality. Fatherhood is a status which mothers have the power to nullify. This is not male privilege, male power, or toxic masculinity. It is gynocentric feminism undermining the basis for an ongoing civilisation.

In some cases fathers may, in fact, be content with the extent of their contact. But in a large percentage of cases, not only are fathers far from content, the outcomes have the long term effect of severing the father-child relationship. That "male disposability" is an apposite term can hardly be disputed when around 40% of fathers are indeed disposed of virtually completely after separation, and many of the rest partially. We see the operation of the empathy gap yet again in the equanimity of society with these conditions.

This can no longer be presented as merely a fathers' rights issue (and hence unimportant to a society operating under the empathy gap). The influence of the breakdown of the paternal relationship upon the next generation is no longer contentious. The impact of the loss of a parent is emerging as a dominant issue of social disadvantage to the child. In this we see how culturally intensified gynocentric feminism has left family-positive evolutionary matricentrism a long way behind: child arrangements are too often the result of making the mothers' wishes paramount, not the best interests of the child.

21.8 Alienation, ACES and Shared Care

The phenomena underlying the imposition of ACEs take us beyond the empathy gap and into a broader range of sociological childcare issues. It is becoming ever clearer that the loss of one parent decreases a child's resilience to withstand the challenges of life. In the phenomenon of alienation we see the interests of one parent triumphing over the interests of the child. Whilst either parent may be alienated, the child is robbed of one parent most conclusively when the alienated parent is also the non-resident parent, which is the father in 92% of cases. The rarity of truly shared care, and the prevalence of effective fatherlessness, is being permitted in our culture, reckless of the effects on the next generation. Alienation and the elimination of the father are primarily childcare and child welfare issues. But gynocentric feminism overlays this reality with "women's rights".

21.9 Drivers of Fatherlessness

Fatherlessness results from two things: divorce and the decline of marriage. For teenagers not living with both their parents, divorce is responsible in only one-third of cases. In two-thirds of cases the parents were never married (to each other). About half of children born now are born outside marriage. At any time, about 15% of dependent children live in cohabiting families and about 23% in single parent families. However, cohabitees are far more likely to split than married couples. The result is that barely more than half (55%) of children aged 15 are still living with both their parents. The decline of marriage is the greater cause, rather than divorce, though both are substantial.

On current trends, only about 50% of today's 20 year olds will ever marry, and these will be strongly skewed to the relatively well-off. The decline of marriage, and hence fatherlessness, is strongly related to demographic. Only 24% of new mothers in the lowest family income range are married. In contrast, 87% of new mothers in the highest family income range are married. This is the marriage gap: the wealthy get married, the poor do not. The children of unmarried parents are thus at greater risk of disadvantage by a double-whammy of poverty and fatherlessness.

The result is a lose-lose scenario consisting of an epidemic of poor lone-mothers and socially isolated fathers. It is the well educated, well heeled middle class feminists with professional jobs and high earning husbands, whose policies of family-destruction have brought about this disadvantage to the less well off. Feminists are, as noted above, the neo-bourgeoisie.

21.10 Effects of Fatherlessness on Children

There are thousands of professional articles on the effect of fathers on child development. The balance of evidence is clear: the majority of studies find statistically significant disbeneficial effects of father absence, variously on education, mental health, externalizing behaviours, delinquency, substance abuse and early childbearing. Many studies, using a variety of methodologies and longitudinal data, contribute to an increasingly clear picture of a causal connection between father absence and these adverse effects. Nor is this a new finding. It has been known for over a quarter of a century, though further evidence has continued to accumulate.

Tens of thousands of fathers annually in the UK attempt, but fail, to remain involved in their children's lives. Blaming men will not wash. The individual working class man did not create the socio-political conditions which have led to the collapse of marriage, the key driver of fatherlessness. It is not toxic masculinity which has been assiduously working towards the destruction of marriage for 50 years; it is feminism. Feminism had the destruction of fatherhood, subject to the wishes of the mother, as its goal from the start. Feminism must now be squarely blamed for the resulting disadvantage to children, of both sexes.

Nor will it wash to blame men's violence. The statistics are preposterous. The individual working man did not create the misandric culture which brands men as violent and predisposes judicial forces to separate him from his children. The bad-mouthing of men, and their resulting disenfranchisement from equal status as parents has been constructed deliberately by feminists, and they continue to do so, e.g., (Barnett, 2014). What truly underlies this wholesale disadvantaging of children is a form of arrogance, a toxic femininity which sees fathers as unnecessary.

21.11 Men's Fertility and Paternity Fraud

Men have little control over their own fertility, a situation which is accepted by men with bovine forbearance. A woman's right to choose after conception means that men have an opportunity to choose only prior to conception. But because of the absence of a convenient, persistent and reversible male contraceptive, men have little control over conception in practice.

The frequency with which women might secretly plan to conceive, expressly against their partners' wishes, is unknown. But those ambivalent cases of not-quite-so-accidental accidental pregnancies are common, as evidenced by the fact that most unplanned pregnancies occur, not due to contraception failure, but following deliberately ceasing contraception.

There are advantages to both sexes in having a convenient, persistent, reversible male contraceptive on the market. The barriers to this are not primarily technological. But it will happen only if driven by women or for women, because a benefit to men is no motivation at all.

A man in the UK has no legal entitlement to know if a child is biologically his. This fact alone is enough to motivate the smashing of windows, knocking off policemen's helmets, chaining ourselves to railings, and being imprisoned. But men have no in-group preference, so it does not happen.

The dominant narrative attempts to minimise the significance of biological paternity, a position that would be acceptable to no one if applied to mothers. The empathy gap facilitates a glaring inequality in biological parenthood which I have shown to be unethical, despite claims to the contrary by those calling themselves ethicists.

Historically men have been disadvantaged compared to women in respect of their lack of certainty that a given child is indeed theirs. This situation persists despite cheap, convenient and highly reliable DNA testing technology having been readily available for over twenty years. Widespread application of the technology is frustrated partly by legislation and partly by medical, legal and government agencies protecting existing custom and practice, and rationalising these policies with terms like "protecting family stability" and "the interests of the child". But this attitude is actually created by gynocentrism, in which the mothers' wishes are law. In truth, the child's interests are ignored every bit as much as the father's.

Whether reports of steeply declining sperm counts in Western countries are correct is unclear, though scientifically credible. If they are correct, however, nominal male infertility could be the norm in a few decade's time. Whilst alarmism is to be avoided, and the situation is less certain than the popular press may sometimes suggest, nevertheless there is a remarkable mismatch between the apocalyptic nature of this feasible prediction and the complete lack of concern at the level of the political-medical establishment. The empathy gap for men may be facilitating ignoring an existential threat to our whole culture.

21.12 Homelessness and Loneliness

There are three levels of homelessness: the statutory homeless, the "single homeless" who have failed to attain a designation as statutorily homeless, and a sub-set of the latter, the rough sleepers. The number of the statutory homeless considerably exceeds the number of rough sleepers. Details are incomplete for all UK nations but the number of men applying for housing assistance is at least comparable with the number of women. The Scottish and Northern Irish data show that single male applicants are strongly dominant at the point of application. Despite this reverse gender ratio at application, those actually housed, or placed on the priority register, tend to be skewed towards women. This is predominantly due to prioritisation where children are involved, and the fact that single parents are 92% mothers. The overwhelmingly dominant demographic in the Main Homeless Duty in England are families headed by a single mother (47%). Single men or women without children are far less likely to achieve Main Homeless Duty, and hence assistance, and there are far more men than women in this category.

However, there may be a gender bias in addition to this effect. In Wales, similar total numbers of men and women were assessed, but substantially fewer men than women were housed, despite substantially more men than women being deemed 'eligible, homeless, and subject to a duty to help to secure housing'. Even for people deemed 'eligible, unintentionally homeless and in priority need', men were less likely to be housed than women.

The numerical dominance of men among rough sleepers may be one of the outcomes of the above process. The result is that 84% to 86% of rough sleepers are men. The same sex ratio applies to those who die as rough sleepers. This is the ultimate "bottom line" of homelessness, and it is overwhelmingly male.

21.13 Mental Health

The APA's guidelines for mental health practice with boys and men, and the similarly inspired Power Threat Meaning Framework from the BPS, fail the most elementary tests against prevalence data. If social constructionism were correct, as APA and feminism assume, there would be no difference between the prevalence of mental ill-health in very young boys and girls. In fact, there is a difference. Boys exhibit a significantly greater prevalence of mental disorders at pre-school age (2-4) and up to age 10.

If masculinity were entirely socially constructed and also largely to blame for men's and boys' mental ill-health, as APA propose, then the ratio of men's to women's prevalence of such mental ill-health should increase with age through childhood because the masculine cultural conditioning will not have occurred in very young children but will become far more marked towards puberty and throughout adolescence. In fact we see the opposite. Whilst boys show greater prevalence of mental disorders before the age of 10, after age 16 it is women who have the greater prevalence, and this is especially marked in the age range 17 to 24. If traditional masculinity is so prejudicial to mental ill-health, why are mental disorders substantially more prevalent in young women?

If traditional masculinity were a major cause of mental disorders in boys and men, as APA suggest, then over recent decades the prevalence of disorders in men and boys would be expected to have declined because boys and young men have become less 'macho' acculturated and more accepting of a softer, more emotive, nature, including markedly reduced homophobia. But actually the prevalence of mental disorders in men and boys has increased.

Over the last several decades, young women have become markedly more assertive, confident and often dominant in many social, educational and workplace settings. Violence in society generally has reduced, and domestic abuse in particular has reduced. If lack of power and the prevalence of abuse were the central causes of mental disorders in girls and young women, as APA have proposed, then mental illness would be expected to have declined. In fact, the incidence of mental disorders in young women has increased markedly, substantially more than for young men.

Feminist theories, as embodied in the APA guidelines, resoundingly fail to be consistent with the most obvious features of the epidemiological data.

The APA themselves have noted that men report experiencing gender bias in therapy. Remarkably, the APA do not interpret this as a salutary lesson for their own practice. Instead of aiming to provide a therapeutic service aligned to the needs of the patient, the APA consider it more appropriate to demand that the patient change to align with their feminist-based diagnostic preconceptions.

The APA criticise men, in general, in respect of their tendency to feel shamed by a failure to achieve success in their perceived gender role. Like feminism more broadly, the APA fail to appreciate that this shame, and the associated obligations, may be imposed by society rather than a pathology of "traditional masculinity". The ultimate irony is that the APA's attitude, indeed the feminist position, is profoundly traditional itself, being based upon assumptions of men's agentic nature, and hence that no ills may befall them that are not of their own making. In truth, there will be no mental or social health for anyone until female agency and its attendant responsibilities is acknowledged.

21.14 Suicide

We have seen that exogenous factors play a significant role in suicide, especially male suicide. It is not just about mental health. These exogenous factors include separation, the associated child contact issues, domestic abuse, low socioeconomic social class, and unskilled manual labour.

There is plentiful evidence that separation/divorce significantly increases suicide rates for both sexes, but more so for men than for women. Since men have a base suicide rate 3.3 times that of women in England, after separation/divorce men's suicide rate is 8 times that of a non-separated women (based on the median, or 12 times based on the mean). In Wales these figures would be higher still. Remarkably, despite a large number of studies which analyse such suicide data, almost none have considered the significance of children or child contact. Anyone with experience of supporting fathers undergoing separation where there is a child contact dispute will confirm that this is the pre-eminent issue, to the exclusion of all else.

We have also seen that there is clear evidence of an association between suicide and domestic abuse, for the suicides of both victims and perpetrators. In many cases a man designated as a perpetrator may also be the victim of abuse, because rather more than half of partner abuse is mutual but the man is more likely to be identified as the abuser.

Suicide is also strongly associated with the lower socioeconomic classes. This relationship is probably not linear but disproportionately affects the lowest socioeconomic group (social class V). Men in this class are frequently unskilled labourers. Remarkably, none of the studies I reviewed considered the nature of men's employment as implicated in suicidality. There were many studies which addressed income, unemployment and socioeconomic class – and a few did explicitly identify the lowest class of manual worker to be especially vulnerable. But none made the obvious connection with the sheer unpleasantness of a man's daily work.

One hardly needs an academic study to spot the gendered nature of manual work in the outdoors: we all see it every time we go out. Whether it is an urban environment, where it is exclusively men digging holes in the road, removing garbage, working on scaffolding, etc., or in the countryside. More women than men study agriculture at college and Radio 4's Farming Today finds no shortage of women to interview. But I walk around the countryside frequently and those I see working in the fields are all men.

How much imagination does it take to understand that doing dirty, laborious, and potentially hazardous work outside in all weathers, and earning little from it and even less respect, might impact adversely on one's equanimity when one reaches middle age with no expectation from life beyond being decreasingly able to sustain the required physical effort? And then your wife throws you out, makes an allegation of violence against you, and refuses to let you see the kids. You are now homeless and not the local authority's priority to assist. This is not a rare scenario.

How is it that the hordes of academics carrying out suicide studies were unable to make the cognitive leap to the obvious: that men in the lowest socioeconomic classes tend to kill themselves more frequently because their lives are crap. After all, you can see them. They are not hidden. Could it be an empathy gap which blinds us to the staringly obvious?

It is clear, then, that there are multiple exogenous factors which contribute substantially to male suicide. Nevertheless, the persistent popular narrative, reinforced by parts of academia, attempts to deflect the blame back onto men themselves. This can be achieved by verbal legerdemain which recharacterizes external factors as psychological states (for example, a child contact problem becomes a man's "problem with identifying as a father", or a man's obligation to support his family becomes "perfectionism"). But the shortcomings of masculinity itself provide the most common scapegoat. Men are disconnected from their emotions; men do not talk or seek help; men stubbornly insist on managing alone without degrading their status by asking for support – so the popular message goes.

By relating suicide to hegemonic masculinity, culpability is laid squarely at the door of the man himself. If only the silly thing had not been so wedded to an outdated notion of what it means to be a man, he wouldn't have been so distressed at his failure to achieve it. But why are the progenitors of this opinion so sure that these expectations are not imposed on a man externally? They are. That is what "exogenous factors" means. You see, if hegemonic masculinity were not smuggled into the picture we might be obliged to acknowledge that it was societal disadvantage which precipitated the suicide. But this is the conclusion which our society ties itself into cognitive knots to avoid.

We must, at all costs, preserve the notion of men as autonomous and invulnerable to societal harm, quintessentially agentic, because men's neediness would detract from those whose neediness is actually sanctioned. The worldview imposed by gynocentrism, namely male agency and power, must be protected, if necessary by reconfiguring the world through whatever lens of verbiage is required to distort it to fit our preconceptions. We have seen that these deceptions are exposed by the fact that both hegemonic masculinity, and the failure to achieve hegemonic masculinity, may equally be held to blame.

By positing that hegemonic masculinity, or its misguided pursuit, is to blame, society as a whole – and dominant gender narratives in particular – ensure that men continue to be perceived as autonomous, self-sufficient, agentic and in sole control of their own lives. Feminism pretends to speak against this supposed hegemonic masculinity, but actually it depends upon this mythology to delegitimise men from social concern. It cannot be admitted that men could be harmed by societal processes in which women might play a significant part. That men could be harmed by women cannot be admitted: it would reverse gynocentrism and male agency.

Only by his own failings can a man be harmed, not by adverse social conditions: that is the fiction which must be maintained. By redirecting the blame back onto the man, society is absolved from any need to assist such men. Instead, the message to men is to improve themselves because their problem is that they are broken. By such a device, any need to acknowledge or address exogenous factors which disadvantage men is avoided. And any such acknowledgement must be avoided because men are required to function within society, not to impose a burden upon it. Men are not authorised to be needy. This is the operation of gynocentrism and male agency and disposability. This is the empathy gap.

21.15 Rape and False Allegations

Sexual assault is generally regarded as victimisation of females, by men, and nothing more. Indeed, in feminist patriarchy theory, sexual abuse is said to be used as a tool by men for the oppression and domination of women. But there are a number of ways in the context of sex offences in which males are disadvantaged.

We have seen that the CPS VAWG reports are an exercise in obscuring male victimisation whilst amplifying female victimisation, accomplished through a form of Newspeak in which "Violence" does not mean violence, "Women" does not mean women, and "Girls" does not mean girls. Claims that the attrition of rape cases where the complainant is female is particularly large are challenged by a study which shows such attrition to be comparable to that for violence-against-the-person offences. In contrast, attrition of rape cases where the complainant is male is indeed unusually large, but this goes unremarked by rape activists.

Feminists insist that women do not lie about rape, a claim that is palpably false. The percentage of rape allegations which are false continues to be highly controversial, but it is clearly not a trivial percentage, contrary to claims by the CPS which are shockingly dishonest. There is evidence which is difficult to refute that, in recent years, the false allegation rate has become an alarmingly large percentage, specifically that *most* police recorded rapes are false allegations. There is no shortage of case histories testifying to the egregious treatment of entirely innocent men. The psychological impact of false allegations is devastating, often leading to suicide.

A popular view amongst rape activists is that a man should be pleased to be falsely accused, as evidence that he lives in a society that takes women's complaints seriously. In other words, a man should be glad to have suffered at the hands of a woman in order to prevent suffering to women. Well, if the man were truly saintly, then yes. But this is an expectation of self-sacrifice by men which is precisely what "male disposability" means. And the attitude of a woman who expects such self-sacrifice from men, for the benefit of women, is precisely what "gynocentrism" means.

Feminist activists are driving an erosion of the most fundamental principles of justice, namely that everyone is equal before the law, innocence until proven guilty, the right to trial by jury, the right for all evidence to be heard, and the right to face one's accuser. Equality before the law has already been demolished in respect of sex. The *de facto* position in respect of males accused of sex offences against females is that the principle of innocence until proven guilty has also already been overturned. The unjust requirement for the accused to prove his innocence is made even worse by inadequate, or corrupt, disclosure practices denying the defendant access to crucial exculpatory evidence. The signature of encroaching totalism is the perverting of justice to meet the ends of those who would take total power.

21.16 Sexual Assault: The Story Less Told

Sexual assault is the pre-eminent area which feminists claim as their own province, the centre of patriarchal oppression of women by men. But there is another story, less told. Whilst sexual abuse of females by men is not denied or minimised, either by society in general or by the present author, the sexual abuse of males by women certainly *is* denied and minimised. The empirical evidence stands in stark contrast to society's incredulity at women's sexual offending. But as soon as sexual offences became defined by lack of consent the distinct treatment of the two sexes lost any coherence it ever had.

The empirical evidence of coercive sex, or unwanted sexual touching, being perpetrated upon adult men by adult women is clear and not much less in magnitude than the reverse. But this bald fact is unlikely to ameliorate the public resistance to regarding such events as assault when the victim is a man. Even situations where reversing the sexes would reveal a serious aggravated rape, which would see the perpetrator go to prison for a very long time, the public will still view it as more amusing than criminal. Men's internalisation of their own disposability is especially marked in such cases. The man's priority is quite likely to be avoiding hurt to his rapist rather than concern for himself.

Women's sexual offending against male minors is somewhat more likely to provoke public calls for punishment, though even here it may depend upon the exact age of the boy. Many people are still of the opinion that a 35 year old teacher grooming a 15 year old boy pupil for sex does not deserve a harsh punishment: more of a ticking off. The distinct perception of the sexes in respect of both perpetrator and victim is ancient in origin but feminism has done nothing to diminish it. On the contrary, feminism in the form of MeToo and similar sentiments has inflamed intolerance of male words and actions to an extreme degree.

A venerable male professor being so unwise as to tell a female colleague that she is beautiful can find himself excommunicated by his university, declared a sex abuser and rendered a non-person, his name being expunged from all records as an undesirable. I, on the other hand, must tolerate women I barely know hugging or kissing me in public. I cannot recoil and reject their advances (which are sometimes, if not always, unwelcome) without being regarded as unforgivably rude. Who is privileged under these conditions? And who was possessed of the power required to bring about this abjection of men?

There are more than a hundred times more men in prison for sexual offences than there are women in prison for sexual offences. But there is a gross mismatch between this ratio and the known high incidence of male sex offenders who have a background of being sexually abused themselves as a child by a woman (perhaps about one-third to one-half of all such men in prison). So, given the 13,500 men in prison in the UK for sex offences, why are there only about 100 women? Where are the 4,500 to 7,000 missing women who have sexually offended against male minors? (Not to mention the women offending against female minors). The answer is that they go undetected, because women are trusted with children. And society does not want to know that caring, nurturing women can also sometimes be abusers.

It appears that at least 20% of sexual offending against minors is perpetrated by women, and perhaps far more.

The starkest warning about adult women's potential for sexual exploitation of male minors comes from juvenile detention facilities in the USA where female staff perpetrating sexual abuse on male inmates is the commonest form of sexual assault. The power differential in this case is at its most extreme. But there is also a substantial power differential between a teacher and her pupils, and one wonders at the true extent of sexual abuses in this scenario. More teacher-on-pupil sexual abuses have come to light in recent years than the public might have thought possible

Even war rape is not a female victim monopoly, as is generally supposed – a presumption encouraged by governmental policies and NGOs wishing to retain control of funding. On the contrary, where war rape is endemic, it is always commonly deployed against male as well as female victims.

The societal view is that sexual predation is a male monopoly, and sexual victimisation of adults is a female monopoly. But rather than being true, these perceptions are actually pre-eminent examples of male disposability and the empathy gap. These psychological biases are so extreme in the case of female perpetrators of sexual abuse against males that few in society can conceptualise it as abuse at all.

21.17 In Conclusion

The empirical evidence for an empathy gap against males, associated with a widespread gynocentric orientation, is overwhelmingly strong. It is remarkable that this remains imperceptible to the general public, and to feminists in particular. The reason is gynocentrism itself, which promotes its own invisibility.

Key evolved traits are generally motivated in the individual by emotions. One does not consciously eat in order to fulfil the evolutionary function of remaining a viable organism until genetic transmittal has been accomplished. One eats because one is hungry. But, in truth, the latter is the trick that evolution plays upon one in order to accomplish the former objective. Hunger, and the pleasure of eating, are proximate causes of a behaviour whose distal origin is successful genetic promulgation.

In the same way, there is a complex of emotions which promotes the pair bond. It includes lust but also compassion and tenderness and many other elements, traditionally summarised as love. This complex of emotions is the proximate cause of the pair bonding behaviour whose distal origin, or function or "purpose", is successful genetic propagation.

The genetic basis of our impetus to eat or procreate does not impose itself upon our consciousness. It would be counterproductive to do so since the fate of strands of DNA would hardly motivate us. Instead, those same strands of DNA have found a means of conning us to serve their needs, enacting the con by appropriate emotional drives and rewards. We see only the façade of the building, not its structural elements.

Evolved matricentrism is enacted by those same emotions which drive the pair bond. This includes, for example, the key element of the ceding of moral authority to mothers, and by extension to women in general. One of the associated correlates of this moral authority is men's discomfort at female disapproval. The veil which has obscured this matricentrism is the traditional patriarchy which the feminists are so intent on smashing. The societal respect which patriarchy embodied hid, and hence made tolerable to men, the underlying matricentric subservience.

As matricentrism has intensified into feminist gynocentrism, and the veil of respect for men has been withdrawn, another mechanism of obscuration has become necessary. This is the doctrine of female oppression and poisonous masculinity. For most people now, this new perspective on the sexes serves very effectively to hide gynocentrism. But it is a step too far. One cannot sweeten the pill by making it more bitter still. Some people are now rejecting a pill so bitter that it requires service to those who will continue to despise you.

Matricentrism was never truly invisible to the enquiring mind, more of an invisibility of convenience. And gynocentrism can be, and is being, perceived and resisted by many people, of both sexes. For women, resisting gynocentric tendencies may be equated with the responsible use of their power, motivated by the recognition of feminism's corrosive effects.

Inevitably one wonders where our present social malaise will lead. It is not a prediction but an observation that the peoples in whom Western culture is instantiated are failing to reproduce themselves. The relationship of this with feminism is clear. Strangely this excites little comment or concern. The feminist-progressive axis does appear to regard the death of Western peoples and their culture with approval. It will end, it seems, with the usual Pyrrhic victory of getting what you wished for.

Acronyms

Acronyms will generally be decoded in each chapter where they apply. However, for convenience I collect them here. Where relevant the UK may be assumed unless otherwise stated.

AAP	American Academy of Pediatrics
ACE	Adverse Childhood Experience
ADHD	Attention Deficit Hyperactivity Disorder
ASD	Autism Spectrum Disorders
ASHE	Annual Survey of Hours and Earnings
ASPD	Anti-Social Personality Disorder
AUD	Alcohol Use Disorder
BAME	Black Asian and Minority Ethnic
BBC	British Broadcasting Corporation
BHPS	British Household Panel Survey
BJS	Bureau of Justice Statistics (USA)
BMA	British Medical Association
BPD	Borderline Personality Disorder
BSP	Basic State Pension
CAFCASS	Children and Family Court Advisor and Support Services
CALM	Campaign Against Living Miserably
CDC	(US) Centers for Disease Control (and Prevention)
CHD	Coronary Heart Disease
CIS-R	Clinical Interview Schedule - Revised
CJS	Criminal Justice System
CMD	Common Mental Disorder
CMS	Child Maintenance Service
CPS	Crown Prosecution Service, or, Canadian Paediatrics Society
CSA	Child Support Agency
CSEW	Crime Survey for England and Wales
CVD	Cardiovascular Disease
DA	Domestic Abuse
DASH	Domestic Abuse Stalking and Harassment (instrument)
DBS	Disclosure and Barring Service
DfE	Department for Education
DoH	Department of Health
DPP	Director of Public Prosecutions
DSM-5	Diagnostic & Statistical Manual of Mental Disorders 5th ed
DV	Domestic Violence
DVPN	Domestic Violence Protection Notice
DVPO	Domestic Violence Protection Order
DVIP	Domestic Violence Intervention Project
ECU	Equality Challenge Unit
EGGSI	Expert Group on Gender Equality and Social Inclusion
EHRC	Equality and Human Rights Commission

ERCD	Elastic Radial Compression Device
EU	European Union
FOI	Freedom Of Information (Act enquiry)
FSM	Free School Meals
GAD	Generalised Anxiety Disorder
GBH	Grievous Bodily Harm (one of the VAP offences)
GDP	Gross Domestic Product
GP	General Practitioner (doctor in primary healthcare)
HE	Higher Education
HEPI	Higher Education Policy Institute
HESA	Higher Education Statistics Authority
HIV	Human Immunodeficiency Viruses
HMCTS	Her Majesty's Courts & Tribunals Service
HMRC	Her Majesty's Revenue & Customs
HOC	House of Commons
HPV	Human Papilloma Viruses
ICD-10	International Classification of Diseases 10th Revision
IDVA	Independent Domestic Violence Advisor
IPV	Intimate Partner Violence
JCVI	Joint Committee on Vaccination and Immunisation
LAA	Legal Aid Authority
LASPO	Legal Aid, Sentencing and Punishment of Offenders (Act)
LGBT	Lesbian, Gay, Bisexual and Transgender
LIP	Litigant In Person
LSCB	London Safeguarding Children Board
MARAC	Multi-Agency Risk Assessment Conference
MC	Male Circumcision
MGM	Male Genital Mutilation
MHRM	Men's Human Rights Movement
MOJ	Ministry of Justice
MP	Member of Parliament
MRI	Magnetic Resonance Imaging
mpMRI	Multi-Parametric MRI
NCANDS	National Child Abuse and Neglect Data System (USA)
NCRS	National Crime Recording Standard (USA)
NCVS	National Crime Victimization Survey (USA)
NEET	Not in Employment, Education or Training
NGO	Non-Governmental Organisation
NHS	National Health Service
NI	National Insurance
NIH	National Institutes of Health (USA)
NMO	Non-Molestation Order
NSPCC	National Society for the Prevention of Cruelty to Children
NISVS	National Intimate and Sexual Violence Survey (USA)
OCD	Obsessive Compulsive Disorder
ODD	Oppositional Defiant Disorder
OECD	Organisation for Economic Cooperation and Development
ONS	Office for National Statistics

OR	Odds Ratio
PA	Partner Abuse or Parental Alienation
PASK	Partner Abuse State of Knowledge (project)
PAYE	Pay As You Earn
PISA	Programme for International Student Assessment
PIAAC	Programme for the International Assessment of Adult Competencies
PR	Parental Responsibility
PSA	Prostate-Specific Antigen
PTSD	Post-Traumatic Stress Disorder
PV	Partner Violence
RACP	Royal Australasian College of Physicians
RAF	Royal Air Force
RASSO	Rape And Serious Sexual Offences
RCT	Randomised Controlled Trial
RCUK	Research Councils UK
RLP	Refugee Law Project
SAT(s)	Standard Attainment Test(s)
SCR	Serious Case Review
SEN	Special Educational Needs
SIDS	Sudden Infant Death Syndrome ("cot death")
SPA	State Pension Age
STEM	Science, Technology, Engineering and Mathematics
STEMM	STEM plus Medicine and subjects allied to Medicine
STI(s)	Sexually Transmitted Infection(s)
SWEP	Severe Weather Emergency Protocol
TUC	Trades Union Congress
UCAS	Universities and Colleges Admissions Service
UCL	University College London
UKHLS	UK Household Longitudinal Surveys
UN	United Nations
UNAIDS	United Nations Programme on HIV/AIDS
UNHCR	United Nations High Commission for Refugees
UNICEF	United Nations International Children's Emergency Fund
UTI	Urinary Tract Infection
VAP	Violence Against the Person
VAWG	Violence Against Women and Girls
WASPI	Women Against State Pension Inequality
WEF	World Economic Forum
WHO	World Health Organisation

References

Abrams. (2012, July 26). *Why We Keep Accidentally Getting Pregnant.* Retrieved December 21, 2018, from The Atlantic: https://www.theatlantic.com/health/archive/2012/07/why-we-keep-accidentally-getting-pregnant/260370/

Adams. (2019, February 16). The Guardian. *Labour would end free market in higher education, says Rayner.* Retrieved March 11, 2019, from https://www.theguardian.com/education/2019/feb/16/labour-would-end-free-market-in-higher-education-says-rayner

Adams, Bengtsson and Weale. (2017, August 17). *A-level results show rise in top grades despite tougher exams.* Retrieved April 16, 2018, from The Guardian: https://www.theguardian.com/education/2017/aug/17/a-level-results-show-first-rise-in-top-grades-in-six-years

Adams, S. (2018, March 10). *New threat to vital HPV jab as advisers to Health Secretary Jeremy Hunt say extending the vaccine to boys would not be 'cost effective'.* Retrieved April 22, 2018, from Mail Online: http://www.dailymail.co.uk/health/article-5486421/Jeremy-Hunt-advisers-say-HPV-vaccine-boys-not-cost-effective.html

Agerbo. (2005). Midlife suicide risk, partner's psychiatric illness, spouse and child bereavement by suicide or other modes of death: a gender specific study. *Journal of Epidemiology and Community Health, 59*(5), 407-412. doi:http://dx.doi.org/10.1136/jech.2004.024950

Agerbo. (2011, December). Social integration and suicide: Denmark, 1906–2006. *The Social Science Journal, 48*(4), 630-640. doi:https://doi.org/10.1016/j.soscij.2011.06.004

Ahmed et al. (2017, February 25). Diagnostic accuracy of multi-parametric MRI and TRUS biopsy in prostate cancer (PROMIS): a paired validating confirmatory study. *The Lancet, 389*(10071), 815-822. doi:https://doi.org/10.1016/S0140-6736(16)32401-1

Airaksinen. (2018, August 6). *Professor Slams 'Hegemonic Masculinity' of Homeless Men.* Retrieved April 24, 2018, from pjmedia: https://pjmedia.com/trending/professor-slams-hegemonic-masculinity-of-homeless-men/

Airaksinen, T. (2019, January 17). APA's 'Masculinity' Guidelines Now Facing Title IX Challenge. *PJ Media.* Retrieved January 20, 2019, from https://pjmedia.com/trending/apas-masculinity-guidelines-now-facing-title-ix-challenge/

Aitkenhead. (2019, February 17). The Interview: Everyday Sexism founder Laura Bates on how teenage boys are being raised on a diet of misogyny. *Sunday Times.* Retrieved March 5, 2019, from https://www.thetimes.co.uk/article/the-interview-everyday-sexism-founder-laura-bates-on-how-teenage-boys-are-being-raised-on-a-diet-of-misogyny-k0mk05c0w

al-Akiti, M. A. (1996, March 24). *Circumcision.* Retrieved August 3, 2018, from http://www.iol.ie/~afifi/Articles/circumcision.htm

American Academy of Pediatrics. (2012, August 27). *Newborn Male Circumcision.* Retrieved August 3, 2018, from https://www.aap.org/en-us/about-the-aap/aap-press-room/pages/Newborn-Male-Circumcision.aspx

American Association of Blood Banks. (2010). Annual report for testing in 2010, prepared by the relationship testing program unit. Retrieved from https://tinyurl.com/yxe5tr33

American Psychological Association. (2007, December). *Guidelines for Psychological Practice with Girls and Women.* Retrieved January 17, 2019, from https://www.apa.org/practice/guidelines/girls-and-women.aspx

American Psychological Association. (2018, August). *Guidelines for the Psychological Practice with Boys and Men.* Retrieved January 17, 2019, from https://tinyurl.com/yysu2o9j

Anderson and Magrath. (2019). *Men and Maculinities.* Routledge. Retrieved from https://www.routledge.com/Men-and-Masculinities-1st-Edition/Anderson-Magrath/p/book/9781138081819

Anderson, K. (2006, June). How Well Does Paternity Confidence Match Actual Paternity? Evidence from Worldwide Nonpaternity Rates. *Current Anthropology, 47*(3), 513-520. doi:https://doi.org/10.1086/504167

Andres. (2005). Income inequality, unemployment, and suicide: a panel data analysis of 15 European countries. *Applied Economics, 37*(4), 439-451. doi:https://doi.org/10.1080/0003684042000295304

Andres. (2010, December). Determinants of suicides in Denmark: Evidence from time series data. *Health Policy, 98*(2-3), 263-269. doi:https://doi.org/10.1016/j.healthpol.2010.06.023

Andrews, K. (2017, November 10). *The Gender Pay Gap: A Briefing.* Retrieved June 19, 2018, from Institute of Economic Affairs: https://tinyurl.com/yax5fqjo

Athena SWAN. (2017, April). *ASSET 2016: experiences of gender equality in STEMM academia and their intersections with ethnicity, sexual orientation, disability and age .* Retrieved April 18, 2018, from Equality Challenge Unit: http://www.ecu.ac.uk/wp-content/uploads/2017/04/ECU_ASSET-report_April-2017.pdf

Athena SWAN Charter. (2018). *Athena SWAN Charter.* Retrieved April 18, 2018, from Equality Challenge Unit: https://www.ecu.ac.uk/equality-charters/athena-swan/

Auvert et al. (2005, October 25). Randomized, Controlled Intervention Trial of Male Circumcision for Reduction of HIV Infection Risk: The ANRS 1265 Trial. *PLOS Medicine, 2*(11), e298. doi:https://doi.org/10.1371/journal.pmed.0020298

Baby Centre. (2013, February). *Circumcision.* Retrieved August 2, 2018, from https://www.babycentre.co.uk/a25005373/circumcision

Bailey et al. (2007, March 2). Male circumcision for HIV prevention in young men in Kisumu, Kenya: a randomised controlled trial. *The Lancet, 369*(9562), 643-656. doi:https://doi.org/10.1016/S0140-6736(07)60312-2

Baird. (2011, September 5). *Feminism in London Conference.* Retrieved September 3, 2018, from http://verabaird.biz/2011/09/05/feminism-in-london-conference/

Bakalar, N. (2016, April 19). Circumcision May Not Reduce Sensitivity of Penis. *The New York Times.* Retrieved July 28, 2018, from https://well.blogs.nytimes.com/2016/04/19/circumcision-may-not-reduce-sensitivity-of-penis/?_r=0

Baker. (2015, July 27). Female rapist faces jail after being found guilty of running paedophile ring which subjected five young children to horrific abuse over more than a decade. *Daily Mail.* Retrieved from https://www.dailymail.co.uk/news/article-3176340/Woman-faces-jail-guilty-running-paedo-ring.html

Banks and Baker. (2013, September). Men and primary care: improving access and outcomes. *Trends in Urology and Men's Health*, 39-41. Retrieved April 29, 2018, from https://onlinelibrary.wiley.com/doi/pdf/10.1002/tre.357

Barnett. (2014, March). *Contact at all Costs? Domestic Violence, Child Contact and the Pracicess of the Family Courts and Professionals.* Retrieved April 14, 2019, from PhD Thesis, Brunel University Law School: https://bura.brunel.ac.uk/bitstream/2438/8753/1/FulltextThesis.pdf

Baron-Cohen, S. (2012). *The Essential Difference: Men, Women and the Extreme Male Brain.* Penguin. Retrieved from https://tinyurl.com/y5hmvkoq

Barrett. (2015, April 30). Number of convicted sex offenders in jail reaches record high. *Telegraph.* Retrieved April 7, 2019, from https://www.telegraph.co.uk/news/uknews/crime/11573580/Number-of-convicted-sex-offenders-in-jail-reaches-record-high.html

Barstad. (2008, May). Explaining Changing Suicide Rates in Norway 1948–2004: The Role of Social Integration. *Social Indicators Research, 87*(1), 47-64. doi:https://doi.org/10.1007/s11205-007-9155-x

Bates, E. (2016, September 5). Current Controversies within Intimate Partner Violence: Overlooking Bidirectional Violence. *Journal of Family Violence, 31*(8), 937-940. doi:10.1007/s10896-016-9862-7

Bates, Graham-Kevan and Archer. (2014). Testing Predictions from the Male Control Theory of Men's Partner Violence". *Aggressive Behaviour, 40*, 42-55.

Baumeister, R. (2010). *Is There Anything Good About Men? How cultures flourish by exploiting men.* Oxford University Press. Retrieved from https://tinyurl.com/yybnv924

BBC. (2016). Diversity and Inclusion Strategy 2016-20. Retrieved March 23, 2019, from http://downloads.bbc.co.uk/diversity/pdf/diversity-and-inclusion-strategy-2016.pdf

BBC News. (2007, February 15). Many inmates 'have very low IQs'. Retrieved April 2, 2019, from http://news.bbc.co.uk/1/hi/education/6364809.stm

BBC News. (2010, November 4). *Little Ted's was 'ideal' place for Vanessa George abuse.* Retrieved April 8, 2019, from https://www.bbc.com/news/uk-england-devon-11682161

BBC News. (2012, November 27). *Manchester baby boy 'bled to death after circumcision'.* Retrieved August 2, 2012, from https://www.bbc.co.uk/news/uk-england-manchester-20503660

BBC News. (2013, January 17). *Sheffield circumcision cuts spark backstreet op fear.* Retrieved August 2, 2018, from https://www.bbc.co.uk/news/uk-england-south-yorkshire-21057581

BBC News. (2015, August 11). Kenyan men in hiding fearing circumcision. Retrieved March 15, 2019, from https://www.bbc.co.uk/news/world-africa-28746101

BBC News. (2015, October 12). *UK military deaths in Afghanistan: Full list.* Retrieved March 22, 2019, from https://www.bbc.co.uk/news/uk-10629358

BBC News. (2016, July 7). *UK military deaths in Iraq.* Retrieved March 22, 2019, from https://www.bbc.co.uk/news/uk-10637526

BBC News. (2018, January 27). All current rape cases to be 'urgently' reviewed over disclosure fears. Retrieved March 5, 2019, from https://www.bbc.co.uk/news/uk-42841346

BBC News. (2019, March 25). Lib Dem MP Layla Moran slapped partner at conference. Retrieved from https://www.bbc.com/news/uk-england-oxfordshire-47686844

BBC World Service. (2012, July 31). An Unspeakable Act (Part 2). Retrieved January 20, 2019, from https://www.bbc.co.uk/programmes/p00vxx55

BBC World Service. (2012, August 4). An Unspeakable Act (Part 2). Retrieved April 11, 2019, from https://www.bbc.co.uk/programmes/p00vxx55

Beaugé, M. (2005, April 28). *Conservative Treatment of Primary Phimosis in Adolescents.* Retrieved July 28, 2018, from The Circumcision Reference Library: http://cirp.org/library/treatment/phimosis/beauge/

Becci Newton and Joy Williams. (2013, December). *Under-representation by gender and race in Apprenticeships: Research summary (Research paper 18).* Retrieved March 22, 2019, from TUC: https://www.tuc.org.uk/sites/default/files/UnderRepresentationInApprenticeships.pdf

Beer, J. (2016, April 23). *Liverpool v-c calls for funding link to improve gender balance.* Retrieved April 18, 2018, from Times Higher Education: https://www.timeshighereducation.com/news/university-of-liverpool-vice-chancellor-janet-beer-calls-for-funding-link-to-improve-gender-balance

Bellis et al. (2005). Measuring paternal discrepancy and its public health. *Journal of Epidemiology and Community Health, 59*(9), 749-754. doi:10.1136/jech.2005.036517

Bellis et al. (2014). National household survey of adverse childhood experiences and their relationship with resilience to health-harming behaviors in England. *BMC Medicine, 12*, 72. Retrieved from https://bmcmedicine.biomedcentral.com/articles/10.1186/1741-7015-12-72

Bensley and Boyle. (2001). Physical, Sexual, and Psychological Effects of Male Infant Circumcision. In D. e. al, & F. M. Eds. George C. Denniston (Ed.), *Understanding Circumcision: A Multi-Disciplinary Approach to a Multi-Dimensional Problem* (pp. 207-239). doi:https://doi.org/10.1007/978-1-4757-3351-8

Benson. (2015, April). *The cost to Britain's children of the trend away from marriage, Harry Benson, Marriage Foundation.* Retrieved November 20, 2018, from The Marriage Foundation: http://www.marriagefoundation.org.uk/wp-content/uploads/2016/06/pdf-08.pdf

Benson and McKay. (2015, August). *The Marriage Gap The rich get married (and stay together). The poor don't.* Retrieved November 20, 2018, from http://www.marriagefoundation.org.uk/wp-content/uploads/2016/06/pdf-07.pdf

Bianchi, Milkie, Sayer and Robinson. (2000, September 1). Is Anyone Doing the Housework? Trends in the Gender Division of Household Labor. *Social Forces, 79*(1), 191-228. Retrieved June 27, 2018, from https://academic.oup.com/sf/article/79/1/191/2233934

Bignell. (2013, March 24). Shopping? It's all in the gender. *The Independent.* Retrieved March 21, 2019, from https://www.independent.co.uk/news/uk/this-britain/shopping-its-all-in-the-gender-8547059.html

Bindel. (2016, August 12). Juries have no place at rape trials – victims deserve unprejudiced justice. *The Guardian.* Retrieved March 4, 2019, from https://www.theguardian.com/commentisfree/2016/aug/12/juries-no-place-rape-trials-victims-deserve-unprejudiced-justice-judge

Blanchard. (2019, April 25). 'We must build an NHS that works for women': Health Secretary Matt Hancock pledges to close gender pay gap in the health service. *MailOnline*. Retrieved from https://www.dailymail.co.uk/health/article-6955957/We-build-NHS-works-women-says-Health-Secretary-Matt-Hancock.html

Bleustein et al. (2005, April). Effect of neonatal circumcision on penile neurologic sensation. *65*(4), 773-777. Retrieved April 27, 2017, from https://www.sciencedirect.com/science/article/pii/S0090429504013433

Bodkin. (2018, December 9). Universities launch drive to recruit more white males as low numbers give them 'minority group' status. *The Telegraph*. Retrieved February 24, 2019, from https://www.telegraph.co.uk/news/2018/12/09/universities-launch-drive-recruit-white-males-low-numbers-give/

Bollinger and van Howe. (2011, May). Alexithymia and Circumcision Trauma: A Preliminary Investigation. *International Journal of Men s Health, 10*(2), 184-195. doi: 10.3149/jmh.1002.184

Bollinger, D. (2010). Lost Boys: An Estimate of U.S. Circumcision-Related Infant Deaths. *Thymos: Journal of Boyhood Studie, 4*(1), 78-90. Retrieved August 2, 2018, from https://www.academia.edu/6394940/Lost_Boys_An_Estimate_of_U.S._Circumcision-Related_Infant_Deaths

Bonde and te Velde. (2017, September 26). Declining sperm counts — the never-ending story. *Nature Reviews Urology, 14*, 645-646. Retrieved December 22, 2018, from https://www.nature.com/articles/nrurol.2017.153

Boroughs. (2004, May). Female sexual abusers of children. *Children and Youth Services Review, 26*(5), 481-487. Retrieved April 8, 2019, from https://www.sciencedirect.com/science/article/pii/S0190740904000349

Bossio et al. (2016, June). Examining Penile Sensitivity in Neonatally Circumcised and Intact Men Using Quantitative Sensory Testing. *The Journal of Urology, 195*(6), 1848-1853. Retrieved July 28, 2018, from https://www.sciencedirect.com/science/article/pii/S0022534715055354

Bossio, J. (2015). *Examining Sexula Correlates of Neonatal Circumcision in Adult Men.* PhD Thesis, Queen's University, Kingston, Ontario, Canada, Deptarment of Psychology. Retrieved July 29, 2018, from https://qspace.library.queensu.ca/bitstream/1974/13627/1/Bossio_Jennifer_A_201509_PhD.pdf

Both Parents Matter. (2017). *Welsh Dads' Survey.* Retrieved October 6, 2018, from https://www.fnf-bpm.org.uk/article/research-223/index.html#.XMfvpfZFyM8

Both Parents Matter. (2018, September 18). *Senedd Assembly Wales.* Retrieved from http://www.senedd.assembly.wales/documents/s78555/18.09.18 Correspondence - Petitioner to the Committee.pdf

Bowcott, O. (2018, October 15). *Parents 'weaponising' domestic violence orders, claims charity.* Retrieved October 17, 2018, from The Guardian: https://www.theguardian.com/law/2018/oct/15/parents-weaponising-domestic-violence-orders-claims-charity

Boyd and Richerson. (1992). Punishment Allows the Evolution of Cooperation (or Anything Else) in Sizable Groups. *Ethology and Sociobiology, 13*(3), 171-195. doi:Boyd, R., & Richerson, P. J. (1992). Punishment Allows the Evolution of Cooper10.1016/0162-3095(92)90032-Y

Boyd and Richerson. (2009). Culture and the evolution of human cooperation. *Phil. Trans. R. Soc. B, 364*(1533), 3281-3288. doi:10.1098/rstb.2009.0134

Boyle and Hill. (2011, December 1). Sub-Saharan African randomised clinical trials into male circumcision and HIV transmission: methodological, ethical and legal concerns. *Journal of Law and Medicine*, 316-334. Retrieved August 7, 2018, from https://europepmc.org/abstract/med/22320006

Boyle and Hill. (2012, February 7). Circumcision-generated emotions bias medical literature. *BJUI, letter to editor.* doi:https://doi.org/10.1111/j.1464-410X.2012.10917.x

Bradford, R. (2015, January 5). *STEM versus Teaching.* Retrieved April 17, 2018, from Academia: https://www.academia.edu/37560970/STEM_versus_Teaching

Bradford, R. (2018a, October 6). 332 Child Homicides. *Academia.* Retrieved from Academia: https://www.academia.edu/37539591/332_Child_Homicides

Bradford, R. (2018b, December 23). *Database of Sources for Mispaternity Rates.* Retrieved from Academia: https://www.academia.edu/38028322/Database_of_Sources_for_Mispaternity_Rates

Bradford, R. (2019). Group Extinction in Iterated Two Person Games with Evolved Group-Level Mixed Strategies. *J.Mathematical Sociology.* doi:10.1080/0022250X.2019.1602045

Bradshaw et al. (2007, December). *Achievementof 15-year-olds inEngland: PISA 2006 National Report.* Retrieved February 23, 2019, from https://www.nfer.ac.uk/publications/NPC02/NPC02.pdf

Breda and Hillion. (2016, July 29). Teaching accreditation exams reveal grading biases favor women in male-dominated disciplines in France. *Science, 353*(6298), 474-478. doi:10.1126/science.aaf4372

Brent & Kilburn Times. (2012, June 22). *Queen's Park baby bled to death two days after being circumcised.* Retrieved August 2, 2018, from Brent & Kilburn Times: http://www.kilburntimes.co.uk/news/queen-s-park-baby-bled-to-death-two-days-after-being-circumcised-1-1419367

Bridger et al. (2017, September). *Cambridge Journal of Evidence-Based Policing, 1*(2-3), 93-104. Retrieved February 11, 2019, from https://link.springer.com/article/10.1007/s41887-017-0013-z

Bristol University HR Equality and Diversity Team. (2014). *University of Bristol: Annual Equality Monitoring Report 2013/14.* Retrieved February 24, 2019, from Bristol University: http://www.bristol.ac.uk/media-library/sites/hr/documents/equality-and-diversity/1314.pdf

Bristow. (2017, November 2). Top lawyer says Nicola Fox who forced boy, 13, to have sex was 'treated leniently' because she's a woman. *Hull Love.* Retrieved April 8, 2019, from https://www.hulldailymail.co.uk/news/hull-east-yorkshire-news/top-lawyer-says-nicola-fox-715043

British Academy. (2014, July). *A Presumption Against Imprisonment, Social Order and Social Values.* Retrieved July 4, 2018, from https://www.britac.ac.uk/sites/default/files/A Presumption Against Imprisonment updated 2016.pdf

British Heart Foundation. (2018). *Cardiovascular Disease Statistics 2018.* Retrieved April 21, 2018, from https://www.bhf.org.uk/research/heart-statistics/heart-statistics-publications/cardiovascular-disease-statistics-2018

British Medical Association. (2006, June). *The law and ethics of male circumcision: Guidance of doctors*. Retrieved August 3, 2018, from https://www.bma.org.uk/advice/employment/ethics/children-and-young-people/male-circumcision

British Psychological Society. (2018, January). *Power Threat Meaning Framework*. Retrieved January 18, 2019, from https://www.bps.org.uk/news-and-policy/introducing-power-threat-meaning-framework

British Social Attitudes Survey. (2012). *30th British Social Attitudes Survey*. Retrieved June 25, 2018, from http://www.bsa.natcen.ac.uk/latest-report/british-social-attitudes-30/key-findings/introduction.aspx

Britton, P. (2013, October 5). *Salford nurse struck off after baby died in Oldham home circumcision*. Retrieved August 2, 2018, from Manchester Evening News: https://www.bbc.co.uk/news/uk-england-manchester-21374643

Brown. (2019a). *Feminism set out to destroy the family and has largely succeeded*. Retrieved April 19, 2019, from Academia: https://www.academia.edu/38380550/Feminism_set_out_to_destroy_the_family_and_has_largely_succeeded.docx

Brown. (2019b, April 11). From Hegemonic to Responsive Masculinity: the Transformative Power of the Provider Role. *Quillette*. Retrieved April 14, 2019, from https://quillette.com/2019/04/11/from-hegemonic-to-responsive-masculinity-the-transformative-power-of-the-provider-role/#_edn12

Bryner, M. (2016, June 9). Not-So-Accidental Pregnancies: Some accidental pregnancies aren't so accidental—especially if the guy could be a good provider. *Psychology Today*. Retrieved December 21, 2018, from https://www.psychologytoday.com/us/articles/200509/not-so-accidental-pregnancies

Buchanan, M. (2015, July 30). *Justice for Men and Boys*. Retrieved April 15, 2018, from https://j4mb.org.uk/wp-content/uploads/sites/46/2015/07/150730-dept-for-education-foi-response.pdf

Burda, Hamermesh and Weil. (2013, January). Total work and gender: facts and possible explanations. *Journal of Population Economics, 26*(1), 239-261. Retrieved June 27, 2018, from https://link.springer.com/article/10.1007/s00148-012-0408-x

Bureau of Investigative Journalism. (2018, December). *Dying Homeless: Counting the deaths of homeless people across the UK*. Retrieved from https://www.thebureauinvestigates.com/stories/2018-04-23/dying-homeless

Bureau of Justice Statistics. (2013, June). *Sexual Victimization in Juvenile Facilities Reported by Youth, 2012*. Retrieved April 11, 2019, from US Dept of Justice: https://www.bjs.gov/content/pub/pdf/svjfry12.pdf

Burgoa. (1998, March 1). Mortality by cause of death and marital status in Spain. *European Journal of Public Health, 8*(1), 37-42. doi:https://doi.org/10.1093/eurpub/8.1.37

Burnett. (2016). *Wrongful Allegations of Sexual and Child Abuse*. OUP Oxford. Retrieved March 9, 2019, from https://tinyurl.com/y2njg7yd

Burnley. (1995, September). Socioeconomic and spatial differentials in mortality and means of committing suicide in New South Wales, Australia, 1985–1991. *Social Science & Medicine, 41*(5), 687-698. doi:https://doi.org/10.1016/0277-9536(94)00378-7

Burns. (2017, September 9). Woman paedophile, 33, who lured 13-year-old boy to her home and forced him to have sex with her is jailed for four years. Retrieved April 8, 2019, from https://www.dailymail.co.uk/news/article-4868122/Woman-paedophile-33-jailed-forcing-boy-sex.html

Burns, L. (2017, May 8). *Local history - Woodhead's forgotten tragedy*. Retrieved June 20, 2018, from Glossop Chronicle: https://glossopchronicle.com/2017/05/local-history-woodheads-forgotten-tragedy/

Burton et al. (2012, July). *Understanding the progression of serious cases through the Criminal Justice System Evidence drawn from a selection of casefiles*. Retrieved March 4, 2019, from Ministry of Justice Research Series 11/12: https://assets.publishing.service.gov.uk/government/uploads/system/uploads/attachment_data/file/217471/understanding-progression-serious-cases.pdf

CAFCASS. (2017/18). *Private law data*. Retrieved April 15, 2019, from https://www.cafcass.gov.uk/about-cafcass/research-and-data/private-law-data/

CAFCASS. (2018, October). *The Child Impact Assessment Framework and its development*. Retrieved October 20, 2018, from https://www.cafcass.gov.uk/grown-ups/parents-and-carers/divorce-and-separation/the-child-impact-assessment-framework-and-its-development/

CAFCASS and Womens Aid. (2017, July 25). *Allegations of domestic abuse in child contact cases*. Retrieved October 18, 2018, from https://www.cafcass.gov.uk/2017/07/25/cafcass-womens-aid-collaborate-domestic-abuse-research/

CALM. (n.d.). *Campaign Against Living Miserably*. Retrieved from https://www.thecalmzone.net/

Canadian Jewish News. (2013, September 30). *Circumcision ban introduced in Sweden*. Retrieved March 14, 2019, from https://www.cjnews.com/news/international/circumcision-ban-introduced-sweden

Canadian Medical Association. (1996). Neonatal circumcision revisited. *Canadian Medical Association Journal, 154*(6), 769-780. Retrieved Augsut 3, 2018, from https://tinyurl.com/y5ykdqrl

Cancer Research UK. (2014a). *Anal cancer mortality*. Retrieved April 22, 2018, from Anal cancer statistics: http://www.cancerresearchuk.org/health-professional/cancer-statistics/statistics-by-cancer-type/anal-cancer#heading-One

Cancer Research UK. (2014b). *Lung cancer incidence over time*. Retrieved from http://www.cancerresearchuk.org/health-professional/cancer-statistics/statistics-by-cancer-type/lung-cancer/incidence#heading-Two

Cancer Research UK. (2014c). *Lung Cancer (C33-C34), European Age-Standardised Mortality Rates, UK, 1971-2014*. Retrieved April 22, 2018, from Lung cancer mortality trends over time: http://www.cancerresearchuk.org/health-professional/cancer-statistics/statistics-by-cancer-type/lung-cancer/mortality#heading-Two

Cancer Research UK. (2014d). *Lung Cancer (C33-C34), European Age-Standardised Incidence Rates, UK, 1993-2015*. Retrieved April 22, 2018, from Lung cancer incidence trends over tiem: http://www.cancerresearchuk.org/health-professional/cancer-statistics/statistics-by-cancer-type/lung-cancer/incidence#heading-Seven

Cancer Research UK. (2015). *Prostate cancer statistics*. Retrieved from http://www.cancerresearchuk.org/health-professional/cancer-statistics/statistics-by-cancer-type/prostate-cancer#heading-Zero

Cancer Research UK. (2016a, September 2). *HPV and Cancer.* Retrieved April 22, 2018, from http://www.cancerresearchuk.org/about-cancer/causes-of-cancer/infections-hpv-and-cancer/hpv-and-cancer

Cannold, L. (2008, December 1). *Who's the Father?* Retrieved December 18, 2018, from http://www.ethics.org.au/on-ethics/blog/february-2008/who's-the-father

Cantor. (1995). Marital Breakdown, Parenthood, and Suicide. *Journal of Family Studies, 1*(2), 91-102. doi:https://doi.org/10.5172/jfs.1.2.91

Carlin, E. (2016, June 13). *HPV vaccination for adolescent boys.* Retrieved April 22, 2018, from The HPV and Anal Cancer Foundation: https://www.analcancerfoundation.org/press/the-times-hpv-vaccination-for-adolescent-boys/

Carvel. (2005, April 22). Women 'will own 60% of UK's wealth within two decades'. *The Guardian.* Retrieved March 21, 2019, from https://www.theguardian.com/business/2005/apr/22/money.genderissues

Casalicchio, E. (2018, April 4). *Theresa May decries 'burning injustice' of gender pay gap as deadline to reveal figures looms.* Retrieved June 19, 2018, from https://www.politicshome.com/news/uk/social-affairs/discrimination/news/94109/theresa-may-decries-burning-injustice-gender-pay

Ceci et al. (2014). Women in Academic Science: A Changing Landscape. *Psychological Science in the Public Interest, 15*(3), 75-141. doi:10.1177/152910061454123

Centers for Disease Control. (2012, September 14). *Morbidity and Mortality Weekly Report (MMWR): Surveillance for Violent Deaths — National Violent Death Reporting System, 16 States, 2009.* Retrieved February 8, 2019, from https://www.cdc.gov/mmwr/preview/mmwrhtml/ss6106a1.htm

Centers for Disease Control and Prevention. (2014). *Recommendations for Providers Counseling Male Patients and Parents Regarding Male Circumcision and the Prevention of HIV Infection, STIs, and other Health Outcomes* . Retrieved from https://www.regulations.gov/document?D=CDC-2014-0012-0003

Centers for Disease Control and Prevention. (2018). *HIV Surveillance Report: Statistics Overview.* Retrieved August 6, 2018, from https://www.cdc.gov/hiv/statistics/overview/index.html

Centre for Social Justice. (2013, June). *Fractured Families: Why Stability Matters.* Retrieved July 4, 2018, from http://www.centreforsocialjustice.org.uk/core/wp-content/uploads/2016/08/CSJ_Fractured_Families_Report_WEB_13.06.13.pdf

Centres for Disease Control & Prevention. (2017, March 17). *Marriage & Divorce.* Retrieved December 17, 2018, from https://www.cdc.gov/nchs/fastats/marriage-divorce.htm

Cero et al. (2015, June 11). Perceived burdensomeness, thwarted belongingness, and suicide ideation: Re-examination of the Interpersonal-Psychological Theory in two samples. *Psychiatry Research, 228*(3), 544-550. doi:10.1016/j.psychres.2015.05.055

CHAIN. (2018, March). *CHAIN Annual Report Greater London April 2017 to March 2018.* Retrieved 1 1, 2019, from https://data.london.gov.uk/dataset/chain-reports

Chang et al. (2003). Harsh parenting in relation to child emotion regulation and aggression. *Journal of Family Psychology, 17*, 598-606. Retrieved October 29, 2018, from https://www.ncbi.nlm.nih.gov/pmc/articles/PMC2754179/

Chapman, B. (2018, April 5). *Gender pay gap: 78% of large UK companies and public sector bodies pay men more than women, figures reveal.* Retrieved June 19, 2018, from The

Independent: https://www.independent.co.uk/news/business/news/gender-pay-gap-deadline-latest-reporting-uk-companies-pay-men-more-than-women-a8289606.html

Chaturvedi et al. (2011, Nov 10). Human papillomavirus and rising oropharyngeal cancer incidence in the United States. *J Clin Oncol, 29*(32), 4294-301. Retrieved April 22, 2018, from https://www.ncbi.nlm.nih.gov/pubmed/21969503

Child Maintenance Service. (2018). *Disagreements about parentage.* Retrieved December 18, 2018, from https://www.gov.uk/child-maintenance/disagreements-about-parentage

Child Support Agency. (2005, August 16). *letter to Barry Pearson.* Retrieved December 18, 2018, from Child Support Analysis: http://www.childsupportanalysis.co.uk/guest_contributions/csa_paternity_1.htm

Children's Bureau. (2018, February 1). *https://www.childwelfare.gov/pubPDFs/fatality.pdf#page=3&view=What groups of children are most vulnerable?* Retrieved September 7, 2018, from https://www.acf.hhs.gov/cb/resource/child-maltreatment-2016

Chinegwundoh, F. (2018, April 10). *Prostate cancer: Four in 10 cases diagnosed late, charity says.* Retrieved April 22, 2018, from http://www.bbc.co.uk/news/health-43669439

Christina Hoff Sommers. (1994). *Who Stole Feminism?: How Women Have Betrayed Women.* Simon & Schuster. Retrieved from https://tinyurl.com/y49vbwec

Circinfo. (2013, January). *Incidence and prevalence of circumcision in Australia.* Retrieved August 3, 2018, from https://www.circinfo.org/statistics.html

Circinfo.org. (2014). *Phimosis and paraphimosis.* Retrieved August 5, 2018, from Curcinfo.org: https://www.circinfo.org/phimosis.html

Circumcision News. (2010, May 8). *Fatally flawed: Bollinger's circumcision death calculations.* Retrieved August 3, 2018, from http://circumcisionnews.blogspot.com/2010/05/fatally-flawed-bollingers-circumcision.html

Circumcision Reference Library. (2012, January 14). *United States Circumcision Incidence.* Retrieved August 3, 2018, from http://www.cirp.org/library/statistics/USA/

Circumcision Resource Centre. (2018). *Circumcision Resource Centre.* Retrieved from http://circumcision.org/studies-on-circumcision/

CIRP. (2006, August 8). *United Kingdom: Incidence of Male Circumcision.* Retrieved August 3, 2018, from http://www.cirp.org/library/statistics/UK/

CIRP. (2013, February 22). *Complications of circumcision.* Retrieved August 2, 2013, from CIRP: http://www.cirp.org/library/complications/

CIRP. (2016, March 21). *Circumcision: Medical Organization Official Policy Statements.* Retrieved August 3, 2018, from http://www.cirp.org/library/statements/

Clark. (2008, June 4). Top university is first in Britain to make students sit entrance exams - because A levels are 'worthless'. Retrieved February 24, 2019, from https://www.dailymail.co.uk/news/article-1023992/Top-university-Britain-make-students-sit-entrance-exams--A-levels-worthless.html

Clarke-Stewart. (2007). *Divorce: Causes and Consequences.* Yale University Press.

Cleary. (2012). Suicidal action, emotional expression, and the performance of masculinities. *Social Science & Medicine, 74*, 498-505.

Clements et al. (2013, May 17). Female-perpetrated sexual abuse: a review of victim and professional perspectives. *Journal of Sexual Aggression, 20*(2), 197-215. doi:https://doi.org/10.1080/13552600.2013.798690

Clinton. (1998, November 17). Hillary Clinton and the Victims of War. Retrieved from https://www.snopes.com/fact-check/hillary-clinton-victims-of-war/

Cobley. (2018). *The Tribe: The Liberal Left and the System of Diversity.* Societas.

Cold and Taylor. (1999). The prepuce. *British Journal of Urology, 83*(1), 34-44. Retrieved July 27, 2017, from https://onlinelibrary.wiley.com/doi/abs/10.1046/j.1464-410x.1999.0830s1034.x

Collins, N. (2013, Feb 12). *Boys do worse at school due to stereotypes.* Retrieved May 3, 2018, from The Telegraph: https://www.telegraph.co.uk/education/educationnews/9862473/Boys-worse-at-school-due-to-stereotypes.html

Collins, W. (2014). *275 women teachers sexually offending against boy pupils in the USA.* Retrieved April 8, 2019, from EmpathyGap.uk: http://empathygap.uk/Women Teachers Sexually Offending Minors USA.pdf

Collins, W. (2015a, September 18). *Global Summit to End Sexual Violence in Conflict.* Retrieved April 11, 2019, from The Illustrated Empathy Gap: http://empathygap.uk/?p=604

Collins, W. (2015b, February 10). *Feminisation and Decline of Physics A Level.* Retrieved February 24, 2019, from The Illustrated Empathy Gap: http://empathygap.uk/?p=379

Collins, W. (2016, May 17). *The EHRC.* Retrieved April 14, 2018, from The Illustrated Empathy Gap: http://empathygap.uk/?p=906

Collins, W. (2017a, November 17). *Gender Pay Gap.* Retrieved June 29, 2018, from http://empathygap.uk/?p=2010

Collins, W. (2017b, December 22). *Rape – Part 1 (Statistics).* Retrieved March 5, 2019, from The Illustrated Empathy Gap: http://empathygap.uk/?p=2073

Collins, W. (2017c, November). *Women sexual offending against minors in the UK: 39 case studies, 2010 to 2017.* Retrieved from EmpathyGap.uk: http://empathygap.uk/Women Sexual Offending Against Minors in the UK.docx

Collins, W. (2017d, November). Bibliography of female sex offenders and their victims Alphabetical Order. Retrieved from http://empathygap.uk/Bibliography Female Sex Offenders and Their Victims Alphabetical.docx

Collins, W. (2017e, November). Bibliograph Female Sex Offenders and Their Victims Chronological Order.docx. Retrieved from http://empathygap.uk/Bibliography Female Sex Offenders and Their Victims Chronological.docx

Collins, W. (2017f, March 25). *MGM: Claimed Medical Benefits – Part 1.* Retrieved Augsust 5, 2018, from The Illustrated Empathy Gap: http://empathygap.uk/?p=1604

Collins, W. (2017g, April 12). *MGM: Claimed Medical Benefits – Part 2.* Retrieved August 8, 2018, from The Illustrated Empathy Gap: http://empathygap.uk/?p=1655#_Toc479773952

Collins, W. (2018a, October 24). *Sex Bias in Criminal Justice.* Retrieved from The Illustrated Empathy Gap: http://empathygap.uk/?p=2561

Collins, W. (2018b, January 28). *Rape – Part 2 (Case Histories of False Allegations).* Retrieved March 5, 2019, from The Illustrated Empathy Gap: http://empathygap.uk/?p=2176

Collins, W. (2018c, February 12). *Rape – Part 3 (Politicians)*. Retrieved March 5, 2019, from The Illustrated Empathy Gap: http://empathygap.uk/?p=2232

Collins, W. (2018d, February 28). *Rape – Part 4 (Celebrities)*. Retrieved March 5, 2019, from The Illustrated Empathy Gap: http://empathygap.uk/?p=2274

Collins, W. (2018e, February 6). *Teachers' Bias in Key Stage 2 SATS*. Retrieved from http://empathygap.uk/?p=2206

Complete Man. (2018, July 27). *Circumstitions*. Retrieved from http://www.circumstitions.com/completeman/sidegif.gif

ComRes. (2015, August). *BBC Woman's Hour – Household Chores Survey*. Retrieved June 27, 2018, from http://www.comresglobal.com/wp-content/uploads/2015/04/BBC_Womans_Hour_Housework_Survey_October_2014.pdf

Condi et al. (1987, October). Parameters of sexual contact of boys with women. *Archives of Sexual Behaviour, 16*(5), 379-394. Retrieved April 8, 2019, from https://link.springer.com/article/10.1007/BF0154142

Connolly, K. (2012, June 27). *Circumcision ruling condemned by Germany's Muslim and Jewish leaders*. Retrieved August 8, 2018, from https://www.theguardian.com/world/2012/jun/27/circumcision-ruling-germany-muslim-jewish

Cook and Hodo. (2013). *When Woen Sexually Abuse Men*. Praeger, Santa Barbara, California.

Coppola, F. (2016, July 31). The WASPI campaign's unreasonable demand. Retrieved March 28, 2019, from http://www.coppolacomment.com/2016/07/the-waspi-campaigns-unreasonable-demand.html

Corcoran. (2010, August). Suicide and marital status in Northern Ireland. *Social Psychiatry and Psychiatric Epidemiology, 45*(8), 795-800. Retrieved February 8, 2019, from https://link.springer.com/article/10.1007/s00127-009-0120-7

Cornwell et al. (2013). Noncognitive Skills and the Gender Disparities in Test Scores and Teacher Assessments: Evidence from Primary School. *The Journal of Human Resources, 48*, 236-264. Retrieved May 3, 2018, from http://jhr.uwpress.org/content/48/1/236.abstract

Corston. (2016, August 14). *Philip Davies' claim that courts favour women 'not backed by evidence'*. Retrieved April 1, 2019, from https://www.theguardian.com/world/2016/aug/14/philip-davies-claim-courts-favour-women-no-evidence-jean-corston

Corston, B. J. (2007). *The Corston Report*. Retrieved April 15, 2018, from http://webarchive.nationalarchives.gov.uk/20130206102659/http://www.justice.gov.uk/publications/docs/corston-report-march-2007.pdf

Council of Europe. (2011). *The Istanbul Convention: Action against violence against women and domestic violence*. Retrieved March 31, 2019, from https://www.coe.int/en/web/istanbul-convention/

CPS. (2016). *Violence against Women and Girls Report*. Retrieved March 2, 2019, from https://www.cps.gov.uk/sites/default/files/documents/publications/cps_vawg_report_2016.pdf

CPS. (2017a). *Rape and Sexual Offences - Chapter 3: Consent*. Retrieved March 7, 2019, from https://www.cps.gov.uk/legal-guidance/rape-and-sexual-offences-chapter-3-consent

CPS. (2017b). *Violence againsy Women and Girls Report.* Retrieved March 2, 2019, from https://www.cps.gov.uk/sites/default/files/documents/publications/cps-vawg-report-2017_0.pdf

CPS. (2018a). *Violence against Women and Girls Report.* Retrieved March 2, 2019, from https://www.cps.gov.uk/sites/default/files/documents/publications/cps-vawg-report-2018.pdf

CPS. (2018b, June). *Rape and Serious Sexual Offence Prosecutions: Assessment of disclosure of unused material ahead of trial.* Retrieved March 6, 2019, from https://www.cps.gov.uk/sites/default/files/documents/publications/RASSO-prosecutions-Assessment-disclosure-unused-material-ahead-trial_0.pdf

CPS Equality and Diversity Unit. (2013, March). *Charging Perverting the Course of Justice and Wasting Police Time in Cases Involving Allegedly False Rape and Domestic Violence Allegations.* Retrieved March 5, 2019, from https://www.cps.gov.uk/sites/default/files/documents/publications/perverting_course_of_justice_march_2013.pdf

Craig, A. (2016, April 13). Circumcision does not reduce penile sensitivity, research finds. *Queen's gazette.* Retrieved July 28, 2018, from https://www.queensu.ca/gazette/stories/circumcision-does-not-reduce-penile-sensitivity-research-finds

Craig, M. (2004, February). Perinatal risk factors for neonaticide and infant homicide: can we identify those at risk? *JRSM Journal of the Royal Society of Medicine, 97*(2), 57-61. Retrieved from https://www.ncbi.nlm.nih.gov/pmc/articles/PMC1079289/

Craissati et al. (2002, July 1). Characteristics of Perpetrators of Child Sexual Abuse Who Have Been Sexually Victimized as Children. *Sexual Abuse, 14*(3), 225-239. doi:https://doi.org/10.1177/107906320201400303

Crown Prosecution Service. (2014). *Statistics Regarding Offences and Convictions of Infanticide; Freedom of Information Act 2000 Requests, Disclosure Ref: 13/2014.*

Crown Prosecution Service. (2018, September). *Violence Against Women and Girls 2017-18.* Retrieved October 8, 2018, from https://www.cps.gov.uk/publication/violence-against-women-and-girls

Culhane, A. (2018, February 2). *Prostate cancer deaths overtake those from breast cancer.* Retrieved April 22, 2018, from http://www.bbc.co.uk/news/health-42890405

Curnock Cook, M. (2015, December). *Universities and Colleges Admissions Service.* Retrieved April 17, 2018, from End of Cyce report 2015: https://www.ucas.com/sites/default/files/eoc-report-2015-v2.pdf

Curtis et al. (2008, December). *Commercial Sexual Exploitation of Children in New York City, Volume One: The CSEC Population in New York City: Size, Characteristics, and Needs.* Retrieved April 9, 2019, from https://www.ncjrs.gov/pdffiles1/nij/grants/225083.pdf

Cutright. (2005, September). Marital status integration, psychological well-being, and suicide acceptability as predictors of marital status differentials in suicide rates. *Social Science Research, 34*(3), 570-590. doi:https://doi.org/10.1016/j.ssresearch.2004.05.002

Cylus et al. (2011, January 1). Pronounced Gender And Age Differences Are Evident In Personal Health Care Spending Per Person. *Health Affairs, 30*(1). doi:https://doi.org/10.1377/hlthaff.2010.0216

Darby. (2005). *A Surgical Temptation: The Demonization Of The Foreskin And The Rise Of Circumcision In Britain.* University of Chicago Press.

Dave et al. (2003, December). Male circumcision in Britain: findings from a national probability sample survey. *Sex Transm Infect., 79*(6), 499-500. doi:10.1136/sti.79.6.499

Davies, S. (2015, December). *Annual Report of the Chief Medical Officer 2014*. Retrieved April 14, 2018, from Department of Health: https://assets.publishing.service.gov.uk/government/uploads/system/uploads/attachment_data/file/595439/CMO_annual_report_2014.pdf

Davis. (2010). Domestic violence-related deaths. *Journal of Aggression, Conflict and Peace Research, 2*(2), 44-52. doi:10.5042/jacpr.2010.0141

Davis and Weller. (1999, December). The Effectiveness of Condoms in Reducing Heterosexual Transmission of HIV. *Family Planning Perspectives, 31*(6), 272-279. Retrieved August 6, 2018, from https://www.jstor.org/stable/2991537?seq=1#page_scan_tab_contents

Debowska et al. (2015, April). Victim, perpetrator, and offense characteristics in filicide and filicide–suicide. *Aggression and Violent Behavior, 21*, 113-124. doi:https://doi.org/10.1016/j.avb.2015.01.011

Deering and Mellor. (2009, October 14). Sentencing of Male and Female Child Sex Offenders: Australian Study. *Psychiatry, Psychology and Law , 16*(3), 394-412. doi:https://doi.org/10.1080/13218710902930291

Dej, E. (2018). When a Man's Home Isn't a Castle: Hegemonic Masculinity Among Men Experiencing Homelessness and Mental Illness. In J. M. Dej, *Containing Madness* (pp. 215-239). Springer. Retrieved January 18, 2018, from https://link.springer.com/chapter/10.1007/978-3-319-89749-3_10

Demurtas. (2018, April 26). Ban On Circumcision In Iceland To Be Dismissed In Parliament. *The Reykjavik Grapevine*. Retrieved March 14, 2019, from https://grapevine.is/news/2018/04/26/ban-on-circumcision-to-be-dismissed-in-parliament/

Dench. (1996). *Transforming Men*. Transaction Publishers. Retrieved from https://tinyurl.com/y37tdwp4

Dench, G. (2010). *What Women Want: Evidence from British Social Attitudes*. London: Hera Trust.

Denney. (2009, October 14). Adult Suicide Mortality in the United States: Marital Status, Family Size, Socioeconomic Status, and Differences by Sex. *Social Science Quarterly, 90*(5), 1167-1185. doi: https://doi.org/10.1111/j.1540-6237.2009.00652.x

Dennis and Erdos. (1992, 3rd ed 2000). *Families Without Fatherhood*. Retrieved October 28, 2018, from Civitas: http://www.civitas.org.uk/pdf/cs03.pdf

Denniston. (2017, June 25). Doctors Opposing Circumcision. Retrieved March 15, 2019, from http://neonatalcutting.org/2017/06/25/doctors-opposing-circumcision/

Denov. (2004, October 1). The Long-Term Effects of Child Sexual Abuse by Female Perpetrators: A Qualitative Study of Male and Female Victims. *Journal of Interpersonal Violence, 19*(10), 1137-1156. doi:https://doi.org/10.1177/0886260504269093

Department for Communities. (2018, December 4). *Northern Ireland Housing Statistics 2017-18*. Retrieved 1 1, 2019, from https://www.communities-ni.gov.uk/publications/northern-ireland-housing-statistics-2017-18

Department for Education. (2013, April 30). *School Workforce in England: November 2012.* Retrieved April 17, 2018, from Department for Education: https://assets.publishing.service.gov.uk/government/uploads/system/uploads/attachment_data/file/223587/SFR15_2013_Text_withPTR.pdf

Department for Education. (2016, March). *Education Excellence Everywhere.* Retrieved April 17, 2018, from Department for Education: https://assets.publishing.service.gov.uk/government/uploads/system/uploads/attachment_data/file/508447/Educational_Excellence_Everywhere.pdf

Department for Education. (2019, January 24). *Apprenticeship demographic and sector subject area PivotTable tool: starts and achievements 2014 to 2015 to Q1 2018 to 2019.* Retrieved from https://www.gov.uk/government/statistical-data-sets/fe-data-library-apprenticeships

Department for Education and Skills. (2007). *Department for Education and Skills.* Retrieved April 17, 2018, from Gender and education: the evidence on pupils in England: http://webarchive.nationalarchives.gov.uk/20090108131527/http://www.dcsf.gov.uk/research/data/uploadfiles/RTP01-07.pdf

Department of Health. (2008, February 4). *Good Practice Guide on Paternity Testing Services.* Retrieved December 18, 2018, from https://www.wales.nhs.uk/documents/DH_082624.pdf

Department of Health. (2012). *Invitation to Tender, Research Initiative to Support the Implementation of the National Suicide Prevention Strategy.* Department of Health Policy Research Programme.

Department of Health and Social Care. (2018, December 11). *Abortion Statistics, England and Wales: 2017.* Retrieved December 21, 2018, from https://assets.publishing.service.gov.uk/government/uploads/system/uploads/attachment_data/file/763174/2017-abortion-statistics-for-england-and-wales-revised.pdf

Devlin, K. (2010, February 17). Medical school selection tests 'favour white, middle-class boys'. Retrieved February 24, 2019, from https://www.telegraph.co.uk/news/health/news/7251676/Medical-school-selection-tests-favour-white-middle-class-boys.html

Diamond, Morris and Barnes. (2012, March). Individual and group IQ predict inmate violence. *Intelligence, 40*(2), 115-122. Retrieved April 2, 2019, from https://doi.org/10.1016/j.intell.2012.01.010

Dickens, C. (1843). *A Christmas Carol.* Chapman & Hall.

Dictionary.com. (2018, July 27). *Dictionary.com.* Retrieved from https://www.dictionary.com/browse/mutilation

Dieleman et al. (2016, December 27). US Spending on Personal Health Care and Public Health, 1996 - 2013. *JAMA, 316*(24), 2627-2646. doi:10.1001/jama.2016.16885

Diver. (2018, February 1). Oxford University extends exam times for women's benefit. *The Telegraph.* Retrieved February 24, 2019, from https://www.telegraph.co.uk/education/2018/02/01/oxford-university-extends-exam-times-womens-benefit/

Dolan. (2014, May 23). Investigating Conflict-Related Sexual Violence against Men in Africa. Retrieved January 20, 2019, from https://www.youtube.com/watch?v=7ADpH7VkbbY

Dolan. (2014, May 23). Investigating Conflict-Related Sexual Violence against Men in Africa (video). Retrieved April 11, 2019, from https://www.youtube.com/watch?v=7ADpH7VkbbY

Donna Laframboise. (1996). *The Princess at the Window: A new gender morality.* Penguin Books. Retrieved from https://tinyurl.com/yxohz6zu

Donnelly, L. (2014, December 16). *Jeremy Hunt: Women make better leaders.* Retrieved May 9, 2018, from https://www.telegraph.co.uk/news/uknews/11297302/Jeremy-Hunt-Women-make-better-leaders.html

Doward, J. (2012, November 4). *Men risk health by failing to seek NHS help, survey finds.* Retrieved April 30, 2018, from The Observer: https://www.theguardian.com/society/2012/nov/04/men-failing-seek-nhs-help

Draper, H. (2007, August). Paternity fraud and compensation for misattributed paternity. *Journal of Medical Ethics, 33*(8), 475-480. doi:10.1136/jme.2005.013268

Dube and Harish. (2017, April). Queens. *The National Bureau of Economic Research.* Retrieved January 20, 2019, from https://www.nber.org/papers/w23337

Dube et al. (2005, June). Long-term consequences of childhood sexual abuse by gender of victim. *Am J Prev Med. , 28*(5), 430-8. Retrieved April 8, 2019, from https://www.ncbi.nlm.nih.gov/pubmed/15894146

Duncker, R. (2017, September 21). *Not drowning, paddling: The English Court's slow row to genital autonomy.* Retrieved March 13, 2019, from Men Do Complain: https://www.mendocomplain.com/2017/09/21/not-drowning-paddling-the-english-courts-slow-row-to-genital-autonomy/

Duterte, B. (2018). *Mogen clamp circumcision video.* Retrieved August 2, 2018, from Stanford medicine: http://med.stanford.edu/newborns/professional-education/circumcision/mogen-clamp-technique.html

Dutta, K. (2015, June 2). *Men are treated fairly when trying to get access to their children in courts, study says.* Retrieved October 11, 2018, from Independent: https://www.independent.co.uk/news/uk/home-news/men-are-treated-fairly-when-trying-to-get-access-to-their-children-in-courts-study-says-10290458.html

Dutton and Corvo. (2006). Transforming a flawed policy: A call to revive psychology and science in domestic violence research and practice. *Agression and Violent Behaviour, 11*, 457-483. Retrieved from http://www.mediaradar.org/docs/Dutton_Corvo-Transforming-flawed-policy.pdf

DVIP Accounts. (2007, March 31). *Home Office Select Committee.* Retrieved October 6, 2018, from https://tinyurl.com/y67n6epx

Earp. (2012, May 22). A fatal irony: Why the "circumcision solution" to the AIDS epidemic in Africa may increase transmission of HIV. *Practical Ethics.* Retrieved August 7, 2018, from http://blog.practicalethics.ox.ac.uk/2012/05/when-bad-science-kills-or-how-to-spread-aids/

Earp. (2016, July/August). Infant circumcision and adult penile sensitivity: implications for sexual experience. *Trends in Urology and Men's Health*, pp. 17-21. Retrieved July 28, 2018, from https://onlinelibrary.wiley.com/doi/epdf/10.1002/tre.531

Earp. (2018a, November 17). Healthcare and Secularism: Gender or genital autonomy? (Video). *Speech at the National Secular Society.* Retrieved March 14, 2019, from https://www.youtube.com/watch?v=I1H2IO8PUNM&feature=youtu.be

Earp. (2018b, November 21). Did a US judge just make FGM legal? An explainer (video). Retrieved March 14, 2019, from https://www.youtube.com/watch?v=qc2-NB9nWt0

Earp et al. (2018c, August 1). Factors Associated with Early Deaths Following Neonatal Male Circumcision in the United States, 20012010. *Clinical Pediatrics, 57*(13), 1532-1540. doi:https://doi.org/10.1177/0009922818790060

Earp, Sardi and Jellison. (2018). False beliefs predict increased circumcision satisfaction in a sample of US American men. *Culture, Health & Sexuality, 20*(8), 945-959. doi:https://doi.org/10.1080/13691058.2017.1400104

Edelson and Joa. (2010, October 9). Differences in Legal Outcomes for Male and Female Children Who Have Been Sexually Abused. *Sexual Abuse, 22*(4), 427-442. doi:https://doi.org/10.1177/1079063210375973

Edsall, T. (2019, January 17). The Fight Over Men Is Shaping Our Political Future. *The New York Times.* Retrieved January 20, 2019, from https://www.nytimes.com/2019/01/17/opinion/apa-guidelines-men-boys.html

EGGSI coordinating team. (2009, October). *Access to Healthcare and Long-Term Care: Equal for Men and Women?* Retrieved April 29, 2018, from http://ec.europa.eu/social/BlobServlet?docId=5590&langId=en

Ehlin. (2018, February 16). Risk Factors of Sexual Assault and Victimization Among Youth in Custody. *Journale of Interpersonal Violence*, 1-24. Retrieved April 11, 2019, from https://doi.org/10.1177/0886260518757226

Ellen. (2009, November 29). This shameful liaison does not deserve prison. *The Guradian.* Retrieved April 8, 2019, from https://www.theguardian.com/commentisfree/2009/nov/29/barbara-ellen-madeleine-martin-comment

Elliott. (1993). *Female Sexual Abuse of Children: The Ultimate Taboo.* Longman. Retrieved from http://tinyurl.com/y6h5jbov

Ellis and Walsh. (2003). Crime, delinquency and intelligence: A review of the worldwide literature. . In H. (ed), *The scientific study of general intelligence: Tribute to Arthur R. Jensen* (pp. 343-366). Pegamon Press, NY.

Ellis et al. (2003, May 16). Does Father Absence Place Daughters at Special Risk for Early Sexual Activity and Teenage Pregnancy? *Child Development, 74*(3), 801-821. doi:https://doi.org/10.1111/1467-8624.00569

Embry and Lyons. (2012, March 19). Sex-Based Sentencing: Sentencing Discrepancies Between Male and Female Sex Offenders. *Feminist Criminology, 7*(2). doi:https://doi.org/10.1177/1557085111430214

Encyclopaedia Britannica. (2018, June). *Britsih Railways.* Retrieved from https://www.britannica.com/topic/British-Railways

Engelhart. (2018, December 15). *Men's rights activists are attacking women's scholarships and programs. The DOE is listening.* Retrieved February 24, 2019, from NBC News: https://www.nbcnews.com/news/us-news/men-s-rights-activists-are-attacking-women-s-scholarships-programs-n947886

Equality and Human Rights Commission. (2018). *Equality and Human Rights Commission.* Retrieved April 14, 2018, from https://www.equalityhumanrights.com/en

Evans, Scourfield and Moore. (2016, December 1). Gender, Relationship Breakdown, and Suicide Risk: A Review of Research in Western Countries. *Journal of Family Issues, 37*(16), 2239-2264. doi:https://doi.org/10.1177/0192513X14562608

Family Law Week. (2014, February 5). *Shared parenting' amendment puts child welfare before presumption of equal access.* Retrieved November 14, 2018, from https://www.familylawweek.co.uk/site.aspx?i=ed127361

Fatherhood Institute. (2013, May 22). *Fatherhood Institute research summary: Fathers' impact on their children's learning and achievement.* Retrieved October 29, 2018, from The Fatherhood Institute: http://www.fatherhoodinstitute.org/2013/fatherhood-institute-research-summary-fathers-and-their-childrens-education/

Fekete. (2005, April 1). Gender Differences in Suicide Attempters in Hungary: Retrospective Epidemiological Study. *Croatian Medical Journal, 46*(2), 288-293. Retrieved February 8, 2019, from https://europepmc.org/abstract/med/15849852

Fenton. (2016, April 28). UK prison system 'in total meltdown' as sexual assaults and violent crimes soar in jails. *Independent.* Retrieved April 11, 2019, from https://www.independent.co.uk/news/uk/home-news/prison-system-in-total-meltdown-as-sexual-assaults-and-violent-crimes-soar-in-jails-a7004926.html

Fernquist. (2003). Does the Level of Divorce or Religiosity Make a Difference? Cross-National Suicide Rates in 21 Developed Countries, 1955-1994. *Archives of Suicide Research, 7*, 265-277. doi:https://doi.org/10.1080/13811110301554

Fiebert. (2012, June). *References Examining Assaults by Women on Their Spouses or Male Partners.* Retrieved September 6, 2018, from Department of Psychology California State University, Long Beach: http://web.csulb.edu/~mfiebert/assault.htm

Fiebert, M. (1997). *Sexuality and Culture, 1*, 273-286.

Fiebert, M. (2004). *Sexuality and Culture, 8*(3-4), 140-177.

Fiebert, M. (2010). *Sexuality and Culture, 14*(1), 49-91.

Finer et al. (2005). Reasons U.S. Women Have Abortions: Quantitative and Qualitative Perspectives. *Perspectives on Sexual and Reproductive Health, 37*(3), 110-118. Retrieved December 21, 2018, from https://www.guttmacher.org/sites/default/files/pdfs/journals/3711005.pdf

Fink, Carson and DeVellis. (2002, May). Adult Circumcision Outcomes Study: Effect on Erectile Function, Penile Sensitivity, Sexual Activity and Satisfaction. *The Journal or Urology, 167*(5), 2113-2116. doi:https://doi.org/10.1016/S0022-5347(05)65098-7

Fisher, A. (2016, December 31). *Tribal circumcision ritual becomes Africa's latest tourist attraction.* Retrieved June 27, 2018, from http://www.abc.net.au/news/2016-12-31/tribal-circumcision-becomes-africas-latest-tourist-attraction/8154314

Fisher, R. (1930). *The Genetical Theory of Natural Selection.* Clarendon Press.

Flood, M. (2004). Backlash: angry men's movements. In S. E. Rossi, *The battle and backlash rage on: why feminism cannot be obsolete* (pp. 261–278). Philadelphia, Pennsylvania. Retrieved 5 18, 2018, from http://xyonline.net/sites/xyonline.net/files/Flood%2C Backlash - Angry men_1.pdf

Flouri. (2005). *Fathering & Child Outcomes.* John Wiley & Sons. Retrieved from https://tinyurl.com/y6euphps

Flouri and Buchanan. (2004, June). Early father's and mother's involvement and child's later educational outcomes. *British Journal of Educational Psychology, 74*(2), 141-153. doi:https://doi.org/10.1348/000709904773839806

Fogg, A. (2012, December 17). *Male circumcision: Let there be no more tragedies like baby Goodluck.* Retrieved August 2, 2018, from The Guardian:

https://www.theguardian.com/commentisfree/2012/dec/17/male-circumcision-baby-goodluck

Ford, R. (2018, June 27). *Two new prisons get go-ahead at Glen Parva and Wellingborough as 'more brutal' sentences on way.* Retrieved July 3, 2018, from The Times: https://www.thetimes.co.uk/edition/news/two-new-prisons-get-go-ahead-at-glen-parva-and-wellingborough-as-more-brutal-sentences-on-way-72r6x79ms

Fox. (2007, December 4). *Circumcision does not affect HIV in US men: study.* Retrieved March 15, 2019, from Reuters: https://www.reuters.com/article/us-aids-circumcision/circumcision-does-not-affect-hiv-in-u-s-men-study-idUSN0345545120071204

Fox. (2018, May 15). *University Superannuation Scheme- What has happened?* Retrieved March 25, 2019, from NW Brwon Group: https://www.nwbrown.co.uk/news/2018/may/15/university-superannuation-scheme-what-has-happened/

Friedan, B. (1963). *The Feminine Mystique.* W.W.Norton.

Frisch. (2012, December 6). Circumcision and Sexual Function Difficulties. Retrieved March 15, 2019, from https://www.youtube.com/watch?v=yfGkZZ-KzpU

Frisch et al. (2013, March). Cultural Bias in the AAP's 2012 Technical Report and Policy Statement on Male Circumcision. *American Academy of Pediatrics*, 796-800. Retrieved August 7, 2018, from http://pediatrics.aappublications.org/content/early/2013/03/12/peds.2012-2896

Frisch, Lindholm and Grønbæk . (2011, October 1). Male circumcision and sexual function in men and women: a survey-based, cross-sectional study in Denmark. *International Journal of Epidemiology, 40*(5), 1367-1381. doi:https://doi.org/10.1093/ije/dyr104

Full Fact. (2012, October). *Were a quarter of prisoners in care as children?* Retrieved October 30, 2018, from https://fullfact.org/crime/were-quarter-prisoners-care-children/

Full Fact. (2015, August 15). *A-levels: from grade inflation to reforms.* Retrieved February 24, 2019, from https://fullfact.org/education/-levels-grade-inflation-reforms/

Furman et al. (2014, January 14). Systems analysis of sex differences reveals an immunosuppressive role for testosterone in the response to influenza vaccination. *111*(2), 869-874. Retrieved April 14, 2018, from http://www.pnas.org/content/111/2/869

Gairdner, D. (1949). The fate of the foreskin: A study of circumcision. *British Medical Journal*, 1433-1437.

Galdas et al. (2005, February 28). Men and health help-seeking behaviour: literature review. *Journal of Advanced, 49*(6), 616-623. Retrieved April 30, 2018, from https://onlinelibrary.wiley.com/doi/epdf/10.1111/j.1365-2648.2004.03331.x

Geater and Jones. (2010, June 20). Support for Suffolk MP who 'fell in front of train'. *East Anglian Daily Times.* Retrieved from https://www.eadt.co.uk/news/support-for-suffolk-mp-who-fell-in-front-of-train-1-464800

George, M. (2002, March 1). Skimmington Revisited. *The Journal of Men's Studies, 10*(2), 111-127. doi:https://doi.org/10.3149/jms.1002.111

Gibb. (2017, November 22). Teacher 'lost two jobs over rape acquittal'. *The Times.* Retrieved March 9, 2019, from https://www.thetimes.co.uk/article/teacher-lost-two-jobs-over-rape-acquittal-v3m038655

Gibb. (2018, November 14). We shouldn't be trawling rape victims' phones, says law chief. *The Times.* Retrieved March 6, 2019, from https://www.thetimes.co.uk/edition/news/we-shouldn-t-be-trawling-rape-victims-phones-says-law-chief-dqkc5gv8c

Gibb, F. (2015, June 2). *Anti father court bias 'is a myth'.* Retrieved October 11, 2015, from The Times: https://www.thetimes.co.uk/article/anti-father-court-bias-is-a-myth-52j30pqmrk7

Gibbons, F. (2001, August 14). *Lay off men, Lessing tells feminists.* Retrieved May 3, 2018, from The Guardian: https://www.theguardian.com/uk/2001/aug/14/edinburghfestival2001.edinburghbookfestival2001

Gibbs. (2007). Identifying Work as a Barrier to Men's Access to Chronic Illness (Arthritis) Self-Management Programs. *International Journal of Men's Health, 6*(2), 143-155. Retrieved April 30, 2018, from https://search.proquest.com/openview/62ab8c2eea2334ebd57d983cfc191924/1?pq-origsite=gscholar&cbl=25645

Gilding. (2005, January). Rampant misattributed paternity: the creation of an urban myth. *People and Place, 13*(2). Retrieved December 17, 2018, from https://www.researchgate.net/publication/241128460_Rampant_misattributed_paternity_The_creation_of_an_urban_myth

Gilding. (2007). *Using Sex Surveys to Calculate the Extent of Paternal Discrepancy.* Retrieved December 17, 2018, from https://tinyurl.com/yxkvtspc

Giolla and Kajonius. (2018, September 11). Sex differences in personality are larger in gender equal countries: Replicating and extending a surprising finding. *International Journal of Psychology.* doi:https://doi.org/10.1002/ijop.12529

girlpowermarketing. (2018). Statistics on the purchasing power of women. Retrieved March 21, 2019, from https://girlpowermarketing.com/statistics-purchasing-power-women/

Glasser et al. (2001, December). Cycle of child sexual abuse: Links between being a victim and becoming a perpetrator. *The British Journal of Psychiatry, 179*(6), 482-494. doi:https://doi.org/10.1192/bjp.179.6.482

Glick. (2005). *Marked in Your Flesh: Circumcision form Ancient Judea to Modern America.* Oxford, UK: Oxford University Press.

Gloucestershire Health and Wellbeing Board. (2018). *Adverse Childhood Experiences (ACEs): Considering an 'ACEs Informed Approach' for Gloucestershire.* Retrieved October 20, 2018, from https://tinyurl.com/y3xp2j8o

Gomella. (2017, October). Where have all the sperm gone? *Canadian Journal of Urology, 24*(5), 8972. Retrieved December 22, 2018, from https://www.canjurol.com/html/free-articles/V24I5_03_Free_Editorial_October17.pdf

Gorman. (2015, April 7). Women now control more than half of US personal wealth, which 'will only increase in years to come'. *Business Insider.* Retrieved March 21, 2019, from https://www.businessinsider.com/women-now-control-more-than-half-of-us-personal-wealth-2015-4?r=US&IR=T

Gotts. (2017, February 13). Women Consumer Power. *GenAnalytics.* Retrieved March 21, 2019, from http://www.genanalytics.co.uk/knowledge/women-consumer-power/

Graham. (2018, July 21). Sex offence fantacists and their police enablers (video). *ICMI18.* Retrieved April 6, 2019, from http://tinyurl.com/yxc3qqqk

Graham, M. (2018, January 24). *Disclosure Failures in Criminal Trials.* Retrieved March 6, 2019, from https://www.mowbraywoodwards.co.uk/mowbray-life/the-source/insight/disclosure-failures-in-criminal-trials

Gray et al. (2007, March 2). Male circumcision for HIV prevention in men in Rakai, Uganda: a randomised trial. *369*(9562), 657-666. doi:https://doi.org/10.1016/S0140-6736(07)60313-4

Gray et al. (2012, March 13). The effectiveness of male circumcision for HIV prevention and effects on risk behaviors in a post-trial follow up study in Rakai, Uganda. *AIDS, 26*(5), 609-615. doi:10.1097/QAD.0b013e3283504a3f

Green and Halliday. (2017, June). *Learning from Cafcass submissions to Serious Case Reviews.* Retrieved from CAFCASS: https://www.cafcass.gov.uk/wp-content/uploads/2017/12/cafcass_learning_from_scr_submissions_-_2017_-_external_version.pdf

Green, C. (2017, December 17). Lawyer Nick Freeman calls for public register to name people who make false rape allegations. *Manchester Evening News.* Retrieved March 6, 2019, from https://www.manchestereveningnews.co.uk/news/greater-manchester-news/lawyer-nick-freeman-calls-public-14050329

Greer. (2000). The Truth behind Legal Dominance Feminism's Two Percent False Rape Claim Figure. *Loyola of Los Angeles Law Review, 33*(947), 947-972.

Gregory Boyle. (2014, September 1). Renowned Psychologist Condemns Child Circumcision. Retrieved March 15, 2019, from https://www.youtube.com/watch?list=UU_YdPMhQXYAJWva_34GAODQ&v=FNgerSYsHEw&feature=player_embedded

Groth. (1979). Sexual Trauma in the Life Histories of Rapists and Child Molesters. *Victimology, 4*(1), 10-16. Retrieved from https://www.ncjrs.gov/App/publications/Abstract.aspx?id=72986

Guido Schmiemann et al. (2010, May). The Diagnosis of Urinary Tract Infection. *Deutsches Arzteblatt International, 107*(21), 361-367. Retrieved August 5, 2018, from https://www.ncbi.nlm.nih.gov/pmc/articles/PMC2883276/

Gulland, A. (2016, June 16). Boys should receive HPV vaccination, doctors urge government. *British Medical Journal, 353*, 3372. Retrieved April22 2018, from https://www.bmj.com/content/353/bmj.i3372.full

Gunnell. (2003, August). Why are suicide rates rising in young men but falling in the elderly?—a time-series analysis of trends in England and Wales 1950–1998. *Social Science & Medicine, 57*(4), 595-612. doi:https://doi.org/10.1016/S0277-9536(02)00408-2

Gwent Partnership Board on VAWDASV. (2016). *Gwent Regional Violence Against Women, Domestic Abuse and Sexual Violence Strategy 2017-2022.* Retrieved from https://democracy.monmouthshire.gov.uk/documents/s13727/Appendix A_Draft VAWDASV Strategy Feb 2018.pdf

Hakim. (2007, August 1). *Who works harder?* Retrieved June 27, 2018, from Prospect: http://www.prospectmagazine.co.uk/magazine/whoworksharder

Hakim. (2011, January). *Feminist Myths and Magic Medicine.* Retrieved March 22, 2019, from Centre for Policy Studies: https://www.cps.org.uk/files/reports/original/111026184004-FeministMythsandMagicMedicine.pdf

Hakim, L. (2018). The not-so-accidental pregnancies. *Essential Baby*. Retrieved from http://www.essentialbaby.com.au/pregnancy/news-views/the-notsoaccidental-pregnancies-20140715-3bz5e#ixzz5aJwYKxQq

Hale, B. (2005, December 5). *Brenda Hale: 'The Sinners and the Sinned Against, Women in the Criminal Justice System'.* Retrieved July 3, 2018, from https://www.longfordtrust.org/longford-lecture/past-lectures/lectures-archive/brenda-hale-the-sinners-and-the-sinned-against-women-in-the-criminal-justice-system/

Hammond. (2012, September 21). *Global Survey of Circumcision Harm.* Retrieved July 29, 2018, from http://circumcisionharm.org/report_GSCH 2012 09 21.pdf

Hammond and Carmack. (2017, February 21). Long-term adverse outcomes from neonatal circumcision reported in a survey of 1,008 men: an overview of health and human rights implications. *The International Journal of Human Rights, 21*(2), 189-218. doi:10.1080/13642987.2016.1260007

Hammond, T. (2015, July 28). Global Survey of Circumcision Harm: Presentation of Results. *Men Do Complain.* Retrieved July 29, 2018, from https://www.mendocomplain.com/2015/07/28/2910/

Hango. (2007). Parental investment in childhood and educational qualifications: Can greater parental involvement mediate the effects of socioeconomic disadvantage? *36*(4), 1371-1390. Retrieved October 29, 2018, from https://www.sciencedirect.com/science/article/pii/S0049089X07000075

Hansard. (1853, April 6). *Aggravated Assaults Bill.* Retrieved from Hansard record of House of Commons proceedings: https://api.parliament.uk/historic-hansard/commons/1853/apr/06/aggravated-assaults-bill

Hansard. (2016, September 15). *Domestic Abuse Victims in Family Law Courts* . Retrieved from https://hansard.parliament.uk/commons/2016-09-15/debates/34FB8AA3-6931-4A38-B1E2-2D5AE13B1F84/DomesticAbuseVictimsInFamilyLawCourts

Hansard. (2018, November 21). Rape Myths and Juries. Retrieved from http://tinyurl.com/y4altxgy

Hansard, House of Lords. (2013a, December 17). *Children and Families Bill.* Retrieved from Hansard, column 1143-4: https://hansard.parliament.uk/Lords/2013-12-17/debates/13121759000785/ChildrenAndFamiliesBill

Hansard, House of Lords. (2013b, December 9). *Children and Families Bill.* Retrieved April 18, 2019, from Hansard (column 593): https://hansard.parliament.uk/Lords/2013-12-09/debates/1312093000345/ChildrenAndFamiliesBill

Hanson and Slater. (1988, December). Sexual victimization in the history of sexual abusers: A review. *Annals of sex research, 1*(4), 485-499. Retrieved April 8, 2019, from https://link.springer.com/article/10.1007/BF00854712

Harding and Newnham. (2015, June). *How do County Courts Share the Care of Children between Parents?* Retrieved October 9, 2018, from http://www.nuffieldfoundation.org/sites/default/files/files/Full%20report.pdf

Harley and Sutton. (2013, Sept/Oct). A Stereotype Threat Account of Boys' Academic Underachievement. *Child Development, 84*(5), 1716-1733. Retrieved May 3, 2018, from https://www.deepdyve.com/lp/wiley/a-stereotype-threat-account-of-boys-academic-underachievement-aZbbwh0u6c

Harman, Kruk and Hines. (2018, December). Parental Alienating Behaviors: An Unacknowledged Form of Family Violence. *Psychological Bulletin, American*

Psychological Association, 144(12), 1275-1299. doi:http://dx.doi.org/10.1037/bul0000175

Harman, Leder-Elder and Biringen. (2016, June). Prevalence of parental alienation drawn from a representative poll. *Prevalence of parental alienation drawn from a representative poll, 66*, 62-66. doi:http://dx.doi.org/10.1016/j.childyouth.2016.04.021

Harretz. (2018, February 25). 500 Icelandic Physicians Back Bill to Outlaw Circumcision. Retrieved March 14, 2019, from https://www.haaretz.com/world-news/europe/500-icelandic-physicians-back-bill-to-outlaw-circumcision-1.5847630

Harrington and Bailey. (2005). *Mental Health Needs and Effectiveness of Provision for Young Offenders in Custody.* Retrieved July 4, 2018, from Youth Justice Board for England and Wales 2005: https://www.researchgate.net/publication/237806818_Mental_Health_Needs_and_Effectiveness_of_Provision_for_Young_Offenders_in_Custody

Hartley-Parkinson, R. (2017, December 15). Student Liam Allan cleared of rape after police 'sat on evidence' casting doubt over case. Retrieved March 5, 2019, from https://metro.co.uk/2017/12/15/student-liam-allan-cleared-rape-police-sat-evidence-casting-doubt-case-7161774/

Haux, McKay, and Cain. (2017, October). Shared Care after Separation in the UK: Limited Data, Limited Practice? *Family Court Review, 55*(4), 572–585. doi:10.1111/fcre.12305

Hawkes et al. (2018, February). *The Global Health 50/50 Report 2018.* Retrieved April 14, 2018, from https://globalhealth5050.org/wp-content/uploads/2018/03/GH5050-Report-2018_Final.pdf

Health and Safety Executive. (2010). *The burden of occupational cancer in Great Britain.* Retrieved June 20, 2018, from http://www.hse.gov.uk/research/rrhtm/rr800.htm

Health and Safety Executive. (2014, December 4). *2013-14 names and details of fatalities.* Retrieved June 27, 2018, from HSE: http://www.hse.gov.uk/foi/fatalities/2013-14.htm

Health and Safety Executive. (2017a, November). *Hand arm vibration in Great Britain.* Retrieved June 21, 2018, from http://www.hse.gov.uk/statistics/causdis/vibration/index.htm

Health and Safety Executive. (2017b, November). *LFS - Labour Force Survey - Self-reported work-related ill health and workplace injuries: Index of LFS tables.* Retrieved from http://www.hse.gov.uk/statistics/lfs/index.htm

Health and Safety Executive. (2017c). *Noise induced hearing loss in Great Britain.* Retrieved June 20, 2018, from http://www.hse.gov.uk/statistics/causdis/deafness/index.htm

Health and Safety Executive. (2017d). *Non-fatal injuries at work in Great Britain.* Retrieved June 27, 2018, from http://www.hse.gov.uk/statistics/causinj/index.htm

Health and Safety Executive. (2017e, November). *Occupational Cancer.* Retrieved June 20, 2017, from http://www.hse.gov.uk/statistics/causdis/cancer/index.htm

Health and Safety Executive. (2017f, November). *Trends in work-related ill health and workplace injury in Great Britain, 2017.* Retrieved June 20, 2018, from http://www.hse.gov.uk/statistics/history/historical-picture.pdf

Health and Safety Executive. (2017g, November). *Working days lost.* Retrieved from http://www.hse.gov.uk/statistics/dayslost.htm

Health and Safety Executive. (2017h). *Work-related ill health and occupational disease in Great Britain.* Retrieved June 21, 2018, from http://www.hse.gov.uk/statistics/causdis/index.htm

Health and Safety Executive. (2017j, November). *Work-related Musculoskeletal Disorders (WRMSDs) Statistics in Great Britain 2017.* Retrieved June 21, 2018, from http://www.hse.gov.uk/statistics/causdis/musculoskeletal/msd.pdf

Health and Safety Executive. (2017k, November). *Work-related Stress, Depression or Anxiety Statistics in Great Britain 2017.* Retrieved June 20, 2018, from http://www.hse.gov.uk/statistics/causdis/stress/stress.pdf

Health and Safety Executive. (2017m, July). *Fatal injuries arising from accidents at work in Great Britain 2017.* Retrieved June 27, 2018, from http://www.hse.gov.uk/statistics/pdf/fatalinjuries.pdf

Health Impact News. (2018, May 10). *Screening Mammography Fails 99% of Women.* Retrieved from Health Impact News: http://healthimpactnews.com/2014/screening-mammography-fails-99-of-women/

Heath and Safety Executive. (2018, November). *Silicosis and coal workers' pneumoconiosis 2017* . Retrieved from http://www.hse.gov.uk/statistics/causdis/pneumoconiosis/pneumoconiosis-and-silicosis.pdf

Heikkinen. (1995, June). Recent Life Events in Elderly Suicide: A Nationwide Study in Finland. *International Psychogeriatrics, 7*(2), 287-300. doi:https://doi.org/10.1017/S1041610295002043

HEqual. (2019, March). *Feminist MP Layla Moran admits to being the latest female perpetrator of domestic violence in Parliament.* Retrieved from https://hequal.wordpress.com/2019/03/24/feminist-mp-layla-moran-admits-to-being-the-latest-female-perpetrator-of-domestic-violence-in-parliament/

Hetherton. (1999, February). The idealization of women: its role in the minimization of child sexual abuse by females. *Child Abuse Negl., 23*(2), 161-174. Retrieved from https://www.ncbi.nlm.nih.gov/pubmed/10075185

Higgins. (2019, February 23). Dunmurry woman Kelly Marie Meighan avoids jail after abusing girls as a teen. *Belfast Telegraph.* Retrieved from https://www.belfasttelegraph.co.uk/news/northern-ireland/dunmurry-woman-kelly-marie-meighan-avoids-jail-after-abusing-girls-as-a-teen-37844191.html

Higher Education Statistics Authority. (2014/15). *Yearly Overviews.* Retrieved April 18, 2018, from Higher Education Statistics Authority (HESA): https://www.hesa.ac.uk/data-and-analysis/staff/overviews?breakdown%5B%5D=583&year=2

Higher Education Statistics Authority. (2016). *Staff numbers and characteristics.* Retrieved from https://www.hesa.ac.uk/data-and-analysis/staff

Hill, A. (2017, June 20). *'Buried alive': the old men stuck in Britain's prisons.* Retrieved from The Guardian: https://www.theguardian.com/news/2017/jun/20/buried-alive-the-old-men-stuck-in-britains-prisons?CMP=share_btn_tw

Hiroyuki Kayaba et al. (1996, November). Analysis of Shape and Retractability of the Prepuce in 603 Japanese Boys. *The Journal of Urology, 156*(5), 1813-1815. Retrieved July 28, 2018, from https://www.sciencedirect.com/science/article/pii/S0022534701655447

HOC Justice Committee. (2018, July 20). *Disclosure of evidence in criminal cases.* Retrieved March 6, 2019, from UK Parliament: https://publications.parliament.uk/pa/cm201719/cmselect/cmjust/859/85902.htm

Hoff Sommers, C. (2000). *The War Against Boys.* Simon & Schuster. Retrieved from https://tinyurl.com/y5nmcuxl

Holley, G. (2008, August 7). *'Quiet conspiracy' of society against male teachers, head of Government body claims.* Retrieved May 21, 2018, from The Telegraph: https://i.telegraph.co.uk/multimedia/archive/00787/Graham_Holley_s_let_787315a.pdf

Home Office. (2018). Freedom of Information Act Enquiry, FOI51514.

Home Office Select Committee. (2008, February 19). *Examination of Witnesses (Questions 220 - 237).* Retrieved October 6, 2018, from https://tinyurl.com/y4zxvdye

Home Office Statistical Bulletin. (2009). *Homicides, Firearm Offences and Intimate Violence 2007/08: Supplementary Volume 2 to Crime in England and Wales 2008/09 (Third Edition).*

Homeless Link. (2018, October). *Severe Weather Responses 2017-18 Survey of winter provision for people sleeping rough.* Retrieved 1 1, 2019, from https://www.homeless.org.uk/sites/default/files/site-attachments/SWEP survey report 2017-18.pdf

Homeless Link. (2018, March). *Support for single homeless people in England Annual Review 2017.* Retrieved 1 1, 2018, from https://www.homeless.org.uk/sites/default/files/site-attachments/Annual Review 2017_0.pdf

Hopkins, Uhrig, and Colahan. (2016, November 24). *Associations between being male or female and being sentenced to prison in England and Wales in 2015.* Retrieved July 1, 2018, from Ministry of Justice Analytical Services: https://assets.publishing.service.gov.uk/government/uploads/system/uploads/attachment_data/file/571737/associations-between-sex-and-sentencing-to-prison.pdf

Horley. (2014, August 3). *Domestic violence refuge provision at crisis point, warn charities.* Retrieved September 3, 2018, from The Guardian: https://www.theguardian.com/society/2014/aug/03/domestic-violence-refuge-crisis-women-closure-safe-houses

Horley. (2018, May 31). *Refuge calls on the Government to put victims at the heart of its once-in-a-generation Domestic Abuse Bill.* Retrieved September 3, 2018, from Refuge: https://www.refuge.org.uk/refuge-calls-government-put-victims-heart-generation-domestic-abuse-bill/

House of Commons. (2017, April 20). *Briefing Paper: UK Prison Population Statistics.* Retrieved July 1, 2018, from http://researchbriefings.files.parliament.uk/documents/SN04334/SN04334.pdf

House of Commons Briefing Paper. (2018, March 9). *Women and the Economy.* Retrieved June 25, 2018, from http://researchbriefings.files.parliament.uk/documents/SN06838/SN06838.pdf

House of Commons Library. (2017, November 21). *UK Defence Personnel Statistics, Briefing Paper Number CBP7930.* Retrieved March 22, 2019, from https://researchbriefings.files.parliament.uk/documents/CDP-2018-0016/CBP-7930.pdf

Howard League. (2014). coercive-sex-in-prison. Retrieved April 11, 2019, from https://howardleague.org/publications/coercive-sex-in-prison/

Hoyle et al. (2017). *The Impact of Being Wrongly Accused of Abuse in Occupations of Trust: Victims' Voices.* University of Oxford Centre for Criminology. Retrieved March 9, 2019, from https://www.law.ox.ac.uk/research-and-subject-groups/impact-being-wrongly-accused-abuse-occupations-trust-victims-voice

Hudson. (2012, June 21). In Uganda, a Male Circumcision Campaign Goes Horribly Wrong. *The Atlantic.* Retrieved March 15, 2019, from https://www.theatlantic.com/international/archive/2012/06/uganda-male-circumcision-campaign-goes-horribly-wrong/326625/

Hughes et al. (2018). *Sources of resilience and their moderating relationships with harms from adverse childhood experiences.* Retrieved October 20, 2018, from Public Health Wales: http://www.wales.nhs.uk/sitesplus/documents/888/ACE & Resilience Report (Eng_final2).pdf

Hughes, K. (2014, May 15). *Gender roles in the 19th century.* Retrieved May 18, 2018, from Discovering Literature: Romantics and Victorians: https://www.bl.uk/romantics-and-victorians/articles/gender-roles-in-the-19th-century

Human Tissue Act. (2004). *Human Tissue Act 2004.* Retrieved December 18, 2018, from Uk Government legislation: http://www.legislation.gov.uk/ukpga/2004/30/contents

Human Tissue Authority. (2018). *DNA Consent Flowcharts.* Retrieved December 19, 2018, from https://www.hta.gov.uk/dna-consent-flowcharts#b

Hunt and MacLeod. (2008, September). *Outcomes of applications to court for contact orders after parental separation or divorce.* Retrieved October 8, 2018, from http://dera.ioe.ac.uk/9145/1/outcomes-applications-contact-orders.pdf

INQUEST. (2018, June 28). *Deaths in prison.* Retrieved July 4, 2018, from https://www.inquest.org.uk/deaths-in-prison

insideMAN. (2016, March 29). *More than 40 advocates for men and boys sign joint letter calling for equal focus on men's health.* Retrieved from insideMAN: http://www.inside-man.co.uk/2016/03/29/40-advocates-men-boys-sign-joint-letter-calling-equal-focus-mens-health/

Ipsos. (2014, September 14). *Majority of Men Say They Would Be Likely to Take Hormone Pill or Injection as a Means of Birth Control, Regardless of Their Relationship Status.* Retrieved December 21, 2018, from https://news.blog.gustavus.edu/files/2017/09/Gustavus_Male_Contraception_Survey_7.17.pdf

Jackson. (2012, October 29). William Hague hails Malala Yousafzai after hospital visit. *The Guardian.* Retrieved April 18, 2019, from https://www.theguardian.com/world/2012/oct/29/hague-visit-yousafzai-hospita

Jaggar, K. (2018, May 10). *How Routine Mammography Screening Leads to Overdiagnosis & Overtreatment.* Retrieved from Breast Cancer Action: https://www.bcaction.org/2016/10/17/how-routine-mammography-screening-fails-women/

Jay. (2014, August 21). *Independent Inquiry into Child Sexual Exploitation in Rotherham (1997 – 2013).* Retrieved April 9, 2019, from Rotherham Metropolitan Borough Council: https://www.rotherham.gov.uk/downloads/file/1407/independent_inquiry_cse_in_rotherham

Jo Blanden. (2006). *'Bucking the trend': What enables those who are disadvantaged in childhood to succeed later in life?* Retrieved October 29, 2018, from Department for Workand Pensions: http://dera.ioe.ac.uk/7729/1/WP31.pdf

John Barry. (2019, January 10). *Is there an alternative to the new APA guidelines for working with men and boys?* Retrieved January 18, 2018, from https://malepsychology.org.uk/2019/01/10/is-there-an-alternative-to-the-new-apa-guidelines-for-working-with-men-and-boys/

Johnson. (2017, April 8). Bono, #GirlsCount Fight Girls' Education Crisis. *BORGEN magazine*. Retrieved March 18, 2019, from https://www.borgenmagazine.com/fight-girls-education-crisis/

Johnson and Scott. (2010, August 4). Association of Sexual Violence and Human Rights Violations With Physical and Mental Health in Territories of the Eastern Democratic Republic of the Congo. *JAMA Network*. doi:10.1001/jama.2010.1086

Jones. (2011, November 3). The craving for a baby that drives women to the ultimate deception. *Mail On Sunday*. Retrieved November 21, 2018, from https://www.dailymail.co.uk/femail/article-2056875/Liz-Jones-baby-craving-drove-steal-husbands-sperm-ultimate-deception.html

Judicial College. (2018, February). *Equal Treatment Bench Book*. Retrieved July 3, 2018, from https://www.judiciary.uk/wp-content/uploads/2018/02/equal-treatment-bench-book-february2018-v5-02mar18.pdf

Kan and Laurie. (2016, January). *Gender, ethnicity and household labour in married and cohabiting couples in the UK*. Retrieved June 27, 2018, from Institute for Social and Economic Research: https://www.iser.essex.ac.uk/research/publications/working-papers/iser/2016-01.pdf

Karmin et al. (2015, April). A recent bottleneck of Y chromosome diversity coincides with a global change in culture. *Genome Research, 25*(4), 459-466. doi:10.1101/gr.186684.114

Kay. (2011, January 24). *Barbara Kay on circumcision: A painless live-saving (sic) surgery*. Retrieved July 27, 2018, from National Post: https://nationalpost.com/full-comment/barbara-kay-on-circumcision-a-painless-live-saving-surgery/

Kay. (2019, January 10). The American Psychological Association goes to war against boys and men. *Signs Of The Times*. Retrieved April 27, 2019, from https://www.sott.net/article/404659-The-American-Psychological-Association-goes-to-war-against-boys-and-men

Kay, B. (2016, October 18). *Barbara Kay: Review puts to bed activist-inspired case on circumcision*. Retrieved July 27, 2018, from National Post: https://nationalpost.com/opinion/barbara-kay-review-puts-to-bed-activist-inspired-case-on-circumcision

Kellogg. (1888). Treatment for Self-Abuse and its Effects. In *Plain Facts for Old and Young* (p. 295). Burlington, Iowa: F.Segner & Co.

Kelly. (2003). Disabusing the Definition of Domestic Violence: How Women Batter Men and the Role of the Feminist State. *Florida State University Law Review, 30*(4). Retrieved September 3, 2018, from https://ir.law.fsu.edu/lr/vol30/iss4/7

Kelly et al. (2013, September). Adverse childhood experiences and premature all-cause mortality. *European Journal of Epidemiology, 28*(9), 721-734. doi:10.1007/s10654-013-9832-9

Kendler et al. (2017, May 1). Divorce and the Onset of Alcohol Use Disorder: A Swedish Population-Based Longitudinal Cohort and Co-Relative Study. *American Journal of Psychiatry, 174*(5), 451-458. doi:https://doi.org/10.1176/appi.ajp.2016.16050589

Keziah. (2013, June 25). *Boys: The Under-mentioned Victims of Child Sex Trafficking and Sexual Exploitation.* Retrieved April 9, 2019, from http://tinyurl.com/yy6xsd3u

Kirkup et al. (2008). Relationships between A level Grades and SAT Scores in a Sample of UK Students. *Annual Meeting of the American Educational Research Association, New York, 24-28 March 2008.* Retrieved February 24, 2019, from https://www.nfer.ac.uk/publications/44412/44412.pdf

Kõlves. (2010, January). Suicidal ideation and behaviour in the aftermath of marital separation: Gender differences. *Journal of Affective Disorders, 120*(1-3), 48-53. doi:https://doi.org/10.1016/j.jad.2009.04.019

Kovess-Masfety. (2011, September). High and low suicidality in Europe: A fine-grained comparison of France and Spain within the ESEMeD surveys. *Journal of Affective Disorders, 133*(1-2), 247-256. doi:https://doi.org/10.1016/j.jad.2011.04.014

Kposowa. (2000). Marital status and suicide in the National Longitudinal Mortality Study. *Journal of Epidemiology and Community Health, 54*(4), 254-261. Retrieved from https://jech.bmj.com/content/54/4/254?ijkey=8fc439c8190e03194d4e6546cace23988f537e7c&keytype2=tf_ipsecsha

Kposowa. (2003). Divorce and suicide risk. *Journal of Epidemiology and Community Health, 57*, 993-995. doi:http://dx.doi.org/10.1136/jech.57.12.993

Kraemer, S. (2000, December 23). The fragile male. *British Medical Journal, 321*, 1609. Retrieved April 14, 2018, from https://www.bmj.com/content/321/7276/1609

Krasny. (2012, February 17). INFOGRAPHIC: Women Control The Money In America. Retrieved March 21, 2019, from https://www.businessinsider.com/infographic-women-control-the-money-in-america-2012-2?IR=T

Kruk. (2018). Parental Alienation as a Form of Emotional Child Abuse: Current State of Knowledge and Future Directions for Research. *Family Science Review, 22*(4), 141-164. Retrieved April 16, 2019, from http://parentalalienationresearch.com/PDF/2018kurk.pdf

Kruk, E. (1992). Psychological and Structural Factors Contributing to the Disengagement of Noncustodial Fathers After Divorce. *Family and Conciliation Courts Review, 29*(2), 81-101. Retrieved from https://www.academia.edu/5034988/Psychological_and_Structural_Factors_Contributing_to_the_Disengagement_of_Noncustodial_Fathers_After_Divorce

Kruk, E. (1993). *Divorce and Disengagement: Patterns of Fatherhood Within and Beyond Marriage.* Retrieved October 17, 2018, from Fathers For Life: http://www.fathersforlife.org/divorce/kruk22.htm

Kuhn, T. (2012). *The Structure of Scientific Revolutions: 50th Anniversary Edition.* University of Chicago Press. Retrieved from https://tinyurl.com/y2fcgemw

Kulze. (2013, October 30). *The Hard Truth About Girl-on-Guy Rape.* Retrieved April 10, 2019, from https://www.vocativ.com/underworld/crime/hard-truth-girl-guy-rape/

Kumar, Deb and Das. (2009, April 16). reputial adhesions — A misunderstood entity. *The Indian Journal of Pediatrics, 76*, 829. doi:https://doi.org/10.1007/s12098-009-0120-3

Kumar, S. (2010, June 15). *Circumcision video.* Retrieved August 2, 2018, from YouTube: https://www.youtube.com/watch?v=ra5t0OsmWf0&has_verified=1

LaBounty et al. (2008, November). Mothers' and Fathers' Use of Internal State Talk with theirYoung Children. *Social Development, 17*(4), 757-775. doi:https://doi.org/10.1111/j.1467-9507.2007.00450.x

Lagat. (2015, April 22). Anxiety in Eldoret after NGO 'forcibly' circumcises 30 boys. *Dily Nation.* Retrieved from https://www.nation.co.ke/counties/eldoret/Uasin-Gishu-NGO-30-boys-cut/-/1954186/2694018/-/4fqerr/-/index.html

Lamb (editor). (2010). *The Role of the Father in Child Development.* John Wiley & Sons, 5th edition. Retrieved from https://tinyurl.com/y3js4pao

Landor and Eisenchlas. (2012, December). "Coming Clean" on Duty of Care: Australian Print Media's Representation of Male Versus Female Sex Offenders in Institutional Contexts. *Sexuality & Culture, 16*(4), 486-502. Retrieved April 9, 2019, from https://link.springer.com/article/10.1007%2Fs12119-012-9134-5

Langford, N. (2015, October 5). *An Exercise in Absolute Futility: How feminism, falsehood and myth changed the landscape of family law.* CreateSpace Independent Publishing Platform. Retrieved from https://tinyurl.com/y6x7aqo8

Larke et al. (2011, June 22). Male circumcision and penile cancer: a systematic review and meta-analysis. *Cancer Causes & Control, 22*(8), 1097-1110. doi:10.1007/s10552-011-9785-9

Laville. (2016, December 22). *Revealed: how family courts allow abusers to torment their victims.* Retrieved October 18, 2018, from The Guardian: https://www.theguardian.com/society/2016/dec/22/revealed-how-family-courts-allow-abusers-to-torment-their-victims

Legal Aid Agency. (2018, June 28). *Legal aid statistics: January to March 2018.* Retrieved October 18, 2018, from Ministry of Justice: https://www.gov.uk/government/statistics/legal-aid-statistics-january-to-march-2018

Legal Aid Agency. (2018, January 8). *The Legal Aid, Sentencing and Punishment of Offenders Act (LASPO) 2012 - Evidence Requirements for Private Family Law Matters.* Retrieved October 17, 2018, from https://assets.publishing.service.gov.uk/government/uploads/system/uploads/attachment_data/file/672143/evidence-requirements-private-family-law-matters-guidance-version-8.pdf

Legislation UK Government. (1983). *Mental Health Act 1983.* Retrieved January 21, 2019, from http://www.legislation.gov.uk/ukpga/1983/20/contents

Legislation UK Government. (2007). *Menatl Health St 2007.* Retrieved January 21, 2019, from https://www.legislation.gov.uk/ukpga/2007/12/contents

Lempert. (2018, November 22). Genital cutting and the laws of unintended consequences. *National Secular Society.* Retrieved March 14, 2019, from https://www.secularism.org.uk/opinion/2018/11/genital-cutting-and-the-laws-of-unintended-consequences

Leone et al. (2016, October 3). Development and Testing of a Conceptual Model Regarding Men's Access to Health Care. *American Journal of Men's Health, 11*(2), 262-274. Retrieved from http://journals.sagepub.com/doi/abs/10.1177/1557988316671637

Lester. (1992, October). Alcohol consumption and rates of personal violence in Australia. *Drug and Alcohol Dependence, 31*(1), 15-17. doi:https://doi.org/10.1016/0376-8716(92)90003-U

Lester. (1995). Remarriage Rates and Suicide and Homicide in the United States. *Journal of Divorce and remarriage, 23*(1-2), 207-210. doi:https://doi.org/10.1300/J087v23n01_14

Levant et al. (2019, February). Moderation and mediation of the relationships between masculinity ideology and health status. *Health Psychology (APA PsychNET), 38*(2), 162-171. doi:http://dx.doi.org/10.1037/hea0000709

Levine et al. (2017, July 25). Temporal trends in sperm count: a systematic review and meta-regression analysis. *Human Reproduction Update, 23*(6), 646-659. doi:https://doi.org/10.1093/humupd/dmx022

Levitt. (2013). *Cases Involving Allegedly False Rape and Domestic Violence Allegations.* Retrieved from Crown Prosecution Service.

Ley. (2018, May 28). Men favoured in NHS pay, minister Caroline Dinenage admits. *The Times.* Retrieved March 12, 2019, from https://www.thetimes.co.uk/article/men-favoured-in-nhs-pay-minister-caroline-dineage-admits-wl0t7h82d

Lightowlers, C. (2018, October 19). Drunk and Doubly Deviant? The Role of Gender and Intoxication in Sentencing Assault Offences. *The British Journal of Criminology,* azy041. doi:https://doi.org/10.1093/bjc/azy041

Lisak et al. (2010). False Allegations of Sexual Assualt: An Analysis of Ten Years of Reported Cases. *Violence Against Women, 16*(12), 1318-1334. doi:10.1177/1077801210387747

Lloyd et al. (2003). *Fathers in Sure Start.* Retrieved October 29, 2018, from Univeristy of Lancashire: http://eprints.lancs.ac.uk/10975/1/3.pdf

London Safeguarding Children Board. (2017). *28. Safeguarding children affected by domestic abuse, 5th edition.* Retrieved October 19, 2018, from London Child Protection Procedures: http://www.londoncp.co.uk/chapters/sg_ch_dom_abuse.html

London Safeguarding Children Board. (2017a). *Male Circumcision.* Retrieved August 3, 2018, from http://www.londoncp.co.uk/chapters/male_circum.html

London Safeguarding Children Board. (2017b). *Section 28. Safeguarding children affected by domestic abuse (5th edition).* Retrieved from London Child Protection Procedures: http://www.londoncp.co.uk/chapters/sg_ch_dom_abuse.html

Longfield. (2018a, March 1). *Growing Up North - Look North: A generation of children await the powerhouse promise.* Retrieved April 15, 2018, from https://www.childrenscommissioner.gov.uk/wp-content/uploads/2018/03/Growing-Up-North-March-2018-1.pdf

Longfield, A. (2017, April). *Children's Commissioner Business Plan 2017-18.* Retrieved July 4, 2018, from https://www.childrenscommissioner.gov.uk/wp-content/uploads/2017/06/Childrens-Commissioner-for-England-Business-Plan-2017-18-1.3-1.pdf

Longfield, A. (2018b, March). *Voices from the Inside: The experiences of girls in Secure Training Centres.* Retrieved July 4, 2018, from https://www.childrenscommissioner.gov.uk/wp-content/uploads/2018/03/CCO-Voices-from-the-Inside-MARCH-2018-1.pdf

Lukianoff and Haidt. (2018). *The Coddling of the American Mind.* Penguin Random House UK. Retrieved from https://www.thecoddling.com/

Luscombe. (2010, September 1). *Workplace Salaries: At Last, Women on Top*. Retrieved March 29, 2019, from TIME magazine: http://content.time.com/time/business/article/0,8599,2015274,00.html

Lyytinen et al. (1998, September). Parental contribution to child's early language and interest in books. *European Journal of Psychology of Education, 13*, 297. Retrieved October 28, 2018, from https://link.springer.com/article/10.1007/BF03172946

MacDermott, R. (2019, January 8). *Addressing Media Misrepresentation of the Men's Guidelines*. Retrieved January 19, 2019, from http://division51.net/homepage-slider/twitter-message-not-reflecting-the-guidelines-for-boys-and-men/

MacFarlane, Sir Andrew. (2019, April). Resolution Conference 2019, Keynote Address. https://www.judiciary.uk/wp-content/uploads/2019/04/Resolution-Key-Note-2019-final.docx-8-April-2019.pdf

Mahrer et al. (2018). Does Shared Parenting Help or Hurt Children in High-Conflict Divorced Families? *Journal of Divorce & Remarraige, 59*(4), 324-347. doi:https://doi.org/10.1080/10502556.2018.1454200

Maimonides, M. (translation 1963). Quotations from Maimonides, The Guide of the Perplexed. In S. P. Hoffman (Ed.), *Covenant of Blood*. University of Chicago Press.

Malawi24. (2015, August 4). *Malawi: Circumcision Disaster - Malawi HIV Infection Rate Doubles*. Retrieved March 15, 2019, from allAfrica: https://allafrica.com/stories/201508040740.html

Malik. (2017, August 27). *Barnardo's: Sexual exploitation of boys 'overlooked'*. Retrieved April 9, 2019, from BBC News: https://www.bbc.com/news/uk-28935733

Mankind Initiative. (2017). *Male victims of domestic and partner abuse 35 key facts*. Retrieved September 6, 2018, from Mankind.org: https://www.mankind.org.uk/wp-content/uploads/2018/04/35-Key-Facts-Male-Victims-March-2018-1.pdf

Marotta, B. (2018). American Circumcision. Retrieved March 15, 2019, from https://circumcisionmovie.com/see-the-film/

Marriage & Religion Research Institute. (2014, October). *Effects of Fatherlessness on Children's Development*. Retrieved from https://downloads.frc.org/EF/EF14K18.pdf

Marriage Foundation. (2018). *Establishing the facts about family breakdown and transforming the debate about marriage*. Retrieved from http://marriagefoundation.org.uk/research/

Martin Seager. (2018, October 3). *The Power Threat Meaning Framework (PTMF) takes a dim view of the male gender*. Retrieved January 18, 2019, from https://malepsychology.org.uk/2018/10/03/the-power-threat-meaning-framework-ptmf-takes-a-dim-view-of-the-male-gender/

Martino, E. (2018, April 12). *Training the Masculinity Out of Children*. Retrieved from Quillette: http://quillette.com/2018/04/12/training-masculinity-children/

Masocco. (2008, December). Suicide and Marital Status in Italy. *Psychiatric Quarterly, 79*(4), 275-285. Retrieved from https://link.springer.com/article/10.1007/s11126-008-9072-4

Masocco. (2010, March). Completed Suicide and Marital Status According to the Italian Region of Origin. *Psychiatric Quarterly, 81*(1), 57-71. Retrieved February 8, 2019, from https://link.springer.com/article/10.1007/s11126-009-9118-2

Mattha Busby agency. (2018, June 3). Danish parliament to consider becoming first country to ban circumcision of boys. *The Independent*. Retrieved March 14, 2019, from https://www.independent.co.uk/news/world/europe/denmark-boyhood-circumcision-petition-danish-parliament-debate-a8381366.html

Matthews. (1996). *TheInvisibleBoy: Revisioning the Victimization of Male Children and Teens.* Minister of Public Works and Government Services Canada . Retrieved April 8, 2019, from https://canadiancrc.com/PDFs/The_Invisible_Boy_Report.pdf

Maugham. (2018, May 4). No, the legal system isn't biased against men – it allows them to rape with near impunity. *The New Statesman.* Retrieved March 4, 2019, from https://www.newstatesman.com/politics/feminism/2018/05/no-legal-system-isn-t-biased-against-men-it-allows-them-rape-near-impunity

Mayhew et al. (2018, March). *Inequalities matter an investigation into the impact of deprivation on demographic inequalities in adults.* Retrieved from http://www.ilcuk.org.uk/images/uploads/publication-pdfs/Inequalities_matter.pdf

McDonagh, M. (2010, October 23). Who's the daddy? Retrieved December 18, 2018, from https://www.spectator.co.uk/2010/10/whos-the-daddy/

McEvoy. (2019, April 25). video address to audience opposite Downing Street on Parental Alienation Awareness Day. Retrieved from https://www.facebook.com/neiljmcevoy/videos/358344378136457/?t=36

McGrath. (2011, October 3). Anatomy of the Penis: Penile and Foreskin Neurology. Retrieved March 15, 2019, from https://www.youtube.com/watch?feature=player_embedded&v=DD2yW7AaZFw

McGrath, K. (2000). The Frenular Delta: A New Preputial Structure. *Ken McGrath is author of The Frenular Delta: A New PUnderstanding Circumcision: A Multi-DiscipProceedings of the Sixth International Symposium on Genital Integrity: Safeguarding Fundamental Human Rights in the 21st Century.* Sydney. Retrieved from https://link.springer.com/chapter/10.1007/978-1-4757-3351-8_11

McGrath, K. (2011, October 3). Anatomy of the Penis: Penile and Foreskin Neurology. Retrieved from https://www.youtube.com/watch?v=DD2yW7AaZFw

McGurran. (2014, July 29). Why Bury St Edmunds MP David Ruffley had to resign. Retrieved April 4, 2019, from https://www.bbc.com/news/uk-england-28553382

McIntosh et al. (2010, May). *Post-separation parenting arrangements and developmental outcomes for infants and children. Collected reports.* Retrieved November 9, 2018, from Family Transitions; Report to the Australian Government Attorney-General's Department: https://tinyurl.com/y3aalabg

McLanahan, Tach and Schneider. (2013). The Causal Effects of Father Absence. *Annual Review of Sociology, 39*, 399-427. doi:0.1146/annurev-soc-071312-145704

McManus et al. (2014). *Suicidal thoughts, suicide attempts, and self-harm.* Retrieved from Adult Psychiatric Morbidity Survey 2014 Chapter 12: https://webarchive.nationalarchives.gov.uk/20180328140249/http://digital.nhs.uk/catalogue/PUB21748

McManus et al. (2016, September 29). *Mental Health and Wellbeing in England: Adult Psychiatric Morbidity Survey 2014.* Retrieved January 14, 2018, from NHS Digital: https://webarchive.nationalarchives.gov.uk/20180328140249/http://digital.nhs.uk/catalogue/PUB21748

Medicalization of Circumcision Timeline. (2014). Retrieved from Involuntary Foreskinectomy Awareness: https://sites.google.com/site/completebaby/medicalization

Medscape. (2017, August 24). *Balanitis Overview.* Retrieved August 5, 2018, from https://emedicine.medscape.com/article/777026-overview

Megan. (2014, June 29). neonatal Gomco Circumcision Live. Retrieved August 2, 2018, from YouTube: https://www.youtube.com/watch?v=J1kSx4TkuRo&sns=fb&has_verified=1

Melendy, M. R. (1915). *The ideal woman for maidens, wives, mothers.* E.E.Miller.

Men and Boys Coalition. (2018, May 1). *Victory for Men and Boys Coalition on bringing the Equalities and Human Rights Commission into the HPV Vaccination for boys campaign.* Retrieved March 10, 2019, from http://www.menandboyscoalition.org.uk/newsevents/victory-for-men-and-boys-on-bringing-the-equalities-and-human-rights-commission-into-the-hpv-vaccination-campaign/

Men's Health Forum. (2014, April 7). *Balanitis FAQs.* Retrieved August 5, 2018, from https://www.menshealthforum.org.uk/balanitis-faqs

Men's Health Forum. (2014, July 17). *More than four in ten of the UK's unpaid carers are male.* Retrieved June 27, 2018, from https://www.menshealthforum.org.uk/news/more-four-ten-uks-unpaid-carers-are-male

Mertz, T. (2014, November 3). *No job for a man? Meet the male midwives.* Retrieved June 19, 2018, from The Telegraph: https://www.telegraph.co.uk/men/thinking-man/11202075/No-job-for-a-man-Meet-the-male-midwives.html

Miller et al. (2017, March). Do Perceptions of Their Partners Affect Young Women's Pregnancy Risk? Further Study of Ambivalent Desires. *Popul Stud (Camb), 71*(1), 101-116. doi:10.1080/00324728.2016.1253858

Miller, Drake & Nafziger. (2013). *What works to reduce recidivism by domestic violence offenders.* Retrieved October 6, 2018, from Olympia: Washington State Institute for Public Policy.: https://tinyurl.com/yx9mtuh6

Mining Institute. (2016, January). *Mining accidents and safety.* Retrieved June 20, 2018, from https://mininginstitute.org.uk/wp-content/uploads/2016/02/Mining-accidents-and-safety-Jan16.pdf

Ministry of Housing, Communities and Local Government. (2018a, December 13). *Statutory Homelessness, April to June (Q2) 2018: England.* Retrieved December 31, 2018, from gov.uk: https://assets.publishing.service.gov.uk/government/uploads/system/uploads/attachment_data/file/764301/Statutory_Homelessness_Statistical_Release_April_-_June_2018.pdf

Ministry of Housing, Communities and Local Government. (2018b, February 16). *Annual statistical release evaluating the extent of rough sleeping.* Retrieved 1 1, 2018, from https://www.gov.uk/government/statistics/rough-sleeping-in-england-autumn-2017

Ministry of Housing, Communities and Local Government. (2018c, February 12). *Rough Sleeping Statistics Autumn 2017, England (Revised).* Retrieved from https://www.gov.uk/government/statistics/rough-sleeping-in-england-autumn-2017

Ministry of Housing, Communities and Local Government. (2018d, December 13). *Acceptances and Decisions live tables.* Retrieved December 31, 2018, from Live tables on homelessness: https://www.gov.uk/government/statistical-data-sets/live-tables-on-homelessness

Ministry of Housing, Communities and Local Government. (2018e, December 13). *Prevention and Relief Tables.* Retrieved December 31, 2018, from Live tables on homelessness: https://www.gov.uk/government/statistical-data-sets/live-tables-on-homelessness

Ministry of Housing, Communities and Local Government. (2018f, December 13). *Initial Decision Tables.* Retrieved December 31, 2018, from https://www.gov.uk/government/statistical-data-sets/live-tables-on-homelessness

Ministry of Justice. (2010a, November). *Providing anonymity to those accused of rape: An assessment of evidence.* Retrieved March 5, 2019, from Ministry of Justice Research Series 20/10: http://www.justice.gov.uk/downloads/publications/research-and-analysis/moj-research/anonymity-rape-research-report.pdf#page=23

Ministry of Justice. (2010b). *Statistics on Women and the Criminal Justice System.* Retrieved July 2, 2018, from https://assets.publishing.service.gov.uk/government/uploads/system/uploads/attachment_data/file/217824/statistics-women-cjs-2010.pdf

Ministry of Justice. (2011, November 3). *Family justice review: final report.* Retrieved November 14, 2018, from gov.uk: https://www.gov.uk/government/publications/family-justice-review-final-report

Ministry of Justice. (2012). *Criminal Justice Statistics, Quarterly Update to March 2012, Ministry of Justice Statistics Bulletin.*

Ministry of Justice. (2013a, January 10). *An Overview of Sexual Offending in England and Wales.* Retrieved February 28, 2019, from Ministry of Justice, Home Office & the Office for National Statistics: https://assets.publishing.service.gov.uk/government/uploads/system/uploads/attachment_data/file/214970/sexual-offending-overview-jan-2013.pdf

Ministry of Justice. (2014). *Transforming Rehabilitation: a summary of evidence on reducing reoffending.* Retrieved October 6, 2018, from Ministry of Justice Analytical Section: https://assets.publishing.service.gov.uk/government/uploads/system/uploads/attachment_data/file/305319/transforming-rehabilitation-evidence-summary-2nd-edition.pdf

Ministry of Justice. (2015, October 8). *Female offenders and child dependents.* Retrieved July 3, 2018, from https://assets.publishing.service.gov.uk/government/uploads/system/uploads/attachment_data/file/465916/female-offenders-child-dependents-statistics.pdf

Ministry of Justice. (2016a, November 24). *Statistics on Women and the Criminal Justice System 2015: A Ministry of Justice publication under Section 95 of the Criminal Justice Act 1991.* Retrieved July 1, 2018, from https://assets.publishing.service.gov.uk/government/uploads/system/uploads/attachment_data/file/572043/women-and-the-criminal-justice-system-statistics-2015.pdf

Ministry of Justice. (2016b, November 24). *Women and the criminal justice system statistics 2015: Chapter 3 – victims tables.* Retrieved August 27, 2018, from UK Gov: https://www.gov.uk/government/statistics/women-and-the-criminal-justice-system-statistics-2015

Ministry of Justice. (2016c, November 24). *Women and the criminal justice system statistics 2015: Chapter 6: offender characteristics tables.* Retrieved April 30, 2019, from https://www.gov.uk/government/statistics/women-and-the-criminal-justice-system-statistics-2015

Ministry of Justice. (2017a, July 27). Offender Management statistics quarterly, England and Wales Quarter: January to March 2017, Prison population: 30 June 2017. Retrieved April 7, 2019, from https://assets.publishing.service.gov.uk/government/uploads/system/uploads/attachment_data/file/633154/offender-managemen-statistics-bulletin_-q1-2017.pdf

Ministry of Justice. (2017b, December 8). *Practice Direction 12J - Child Arrangement and Contact Orders: Domestic Abuse and Harm.* Retrieved October 19, 2018, from UK Government Justice: https://www.justice.gov.uk/courts/procedure-rules/family/practice_directions/pd_part_12j

Ministry of Justice. (2018a, May 17). *Criminal Justice System statistics quarterly: December 2017.* Retrieved July 1, 2018, from https://www.gov.uk/government/statistics/criminal-justice-system-statistics-quarterly-december-2017

Ministry of Justice. (2018b, April 26). *Offender Management Statistics quarterly: October to December 2017: Prison releases 2017.* Retrieved July 2, 2018, from https://www.gov.uk/government/statistics/offender-management-statistics-quarterly-october-to-december-2017

Ministry of Justice. (2018c, June 8). *Youth custody data.* Retrieved July 4, 2018, from https://www.gov.uk/government/statistics/youth-custody-data

Ministry of Justice. (2018d, July 28). *Safety in custody quarterly update to March 2016.* Retrieved July 4, 2018, from https://www.gov.uk/government/statistics/safety-in-custody-quarterly-update-to-june-2016

Ministry of Justice. (2018e, August 16). *Criminal Justice System Statistics publication: Outcomes by Offence 2007 to 2017: Pivot Table Analytical Tool for England and Wales.* Retrieved March 4, 2019, from Criminal Justice System statistics quarterly: December 2017: https://www.gov.uk/government/statistics/criminal-justice-system-statistics-quarterly-december-2017

Ministry of Justice. (2018f, June 28). *Family Court Statistics Quarterly, Jan - March 2018.* Retrieved October 11, 2018, from https://www.gov.uk/government/statistics/family-court-statistics-quarterly-january-to-march-2018

Ministry of Justice. (2019, January 31). Offender Management Statistics Bulletin, England and Wales, Quarterly July to Sept 2018 Prison population: 31 December 2018. Retrieved April 7, 2019, from https://assets.publishing.service.gov.uk/government/uploads/system/uploads/attachment_data/file/775078/offender-management-quarterly-q3-2018.pdf

Morley. (2016, March 13). Pensions apartheid? How public and private systems compare. *The Telegraph.* Retrieved March 25, 2019, from https://www.telegraph.co.uk/pensions-retirement/financial-planning/pensions-apartheid-how-public-and-private-systems-compare/

Morley, L. (2013, June 13). *Gender survey of UK professoriate, 2013.* Retrieved April 18, 2018, from Times Higher Education: https://www.timeshighereducation.com/news/gender-survey-of-uk-professoriate-2013/2004766.article

Morris. (2018). *About the Author - Professor Emeritus Brian J. Morris.* Retrieved August 5, 2018, from circinfo.net: http://www.circinfo.net/about_the_author_professor_brian_j_morris.html

Morris et al. (2016, October). Canadian Pediatrics Society position statement on newborn circumcision: a risk-benefit analysis revisited. *Canadian Journal of Urology, 23*(5), 8495-8502. Retrieved August 5, 2018, from https://www.ncbi.nlm.nih.gov/pubmed/27705739

Morris et al. (2017, February 8). Early infant male circumcision: Systematic review, risk-benefit analysis, and progress in policy. *World Journal of Clinial Pediatrics, 6*(1), 89-102. doi:10.5409/wjcp.v6.i1.89

Moss and Washbrook. (2016, July 18). *Understanding the Gender Gap in Literacy and Language Development.* Retrieved May 8, 2018, from University of Bristol Graduate School of Education: https://tinyurl.com/y288z7zk

Mumsnet. (2014, July). *Chores: who does what in the modern family home?* Retrieved June 27, 2018, from https://www.mumsnet.com/surveys/chores-survey-results

Murphy. (2017, June). Are the hsitories of male prisoners less traumatic than those of female prisoners? (video). Retrieved from https://www.youtube.com/watch?v=ziUmxWW-0ig&t=103s

Murphy. (2019, March 15). Podcast interview with Davinci Mind. Retrieved from https://davincimind.net/2019/03/15/25381/

Murray. (2015, October 16). Disturbing rise of the women child sex predators: How sickening slew of babysitters and teachers are abusing young boys and girls – but would they be punished so leniently if they were men? *Daily Mail.* Retrieved April 8, 2019, from Daily Mail: https://www.dailymail.co.uk/news/article-3274956/Disturbing-rise-women-child-sex-predators-s-punished-leniently-men.html

MWM. (circa 2013). Man Woman & Myth, videos including Michele Elliott. Retrieved from http://tinyurl.com/y5ytywqj, http://tinyurl.com/y36vdrbm, http://tinyurl.com/y2tohv64

Nathanson and Young. (2001). *Spreading Misandry: The Teaching of Contempt for Men in Popular Culture.* McGill-Queen's University Press. Retrieved from https://tinyurl.com/y4n5jxzc

Nathanson and Young. (2006). *Legalising Misandry: From Public Shame to Systemic Discrimination against Men.* McGill-Queen's university press.

National Assembly for Wales, Petitions Committee. (2018, September 25). *Senedd Assembly Wales.* Retrieved from http://www.senedd.assembly.wales/ieListDocuments.aspx?CId=430&MId=5065

National Cancer Institute. (2015, February 19). *HPV and Cancer: What are human papillomaviruses?* Retrieved April 22, 2018, from https://www.cancer.gov/about-cancer/causes-prevention/risk/infectious-agents/hpv-fact-sheet

National Cancer Institute. (2017, October 4). *Prostate-Specific Antigen (PSA) Test.* Retrieved from https://www.cancer.gov/types/prostate/psa-fact-sheet

National Health Service. (2016, January 22). *Circumcision in men.* Retrieved August 2, 2018, from https://www.nhs.uk/conditions/circumcision-in-men/#Risks

National Institutes of Health. (2017). *Report of the Advisory Committee on Women's Health, Fiscal Years 2015/16'.* Retrieved March 10, 2019, from Offce of Research on Women's Health : https://orwh.od.nih.gov/sites/orwh/files/docs/ORWH_Biennial_Report_WEB_508_FY-15-16.pdf

National Literacy Trust. (2012, July 2). *Boys' Reading Commission.* Retrieved May 3, 2018, from National Literacy Trust: https://literacytrust.org.uk/policy-and-campaigns/all-party-parliamentary-group-literacy/boys-reading-commission/

National Survey for Wales. (2016/17). *Population Health - Lifestyle* . Retrieved from https://gov.wales/docs/statistics/2017/170629-national-survey-2016-17-population-health-lifestyle-en.pdf

National Union of Teachers. (2001, March 6). *National Union of Teachers (NUT).* Retrieved April 17, 2018, from Gender and Education: NUT Policy Statement: https://www.teachers.org.uk/sites/default/files2014/genderandeducation.pdf

NationMaster. (2005). *Education > Girls to boys ratio > Tertiary level enrolment: Countries Compared.* Retrieved March 18, 2019, from https://www.nationmaster.com/country-info/stats/Education/Girls-to-boys-ratio/Tertiary-level-enrolment

NationMaster. (2006). *Education > School life expectancy > Primary to tertiary > Male: Countries Compared* . Retrieved from http://www.nationmaster.com/country-info/stats/Education/School-life-expectancy/Primary-to-tertiary/Male# , and similarly for Female#

NCANDS. (2016, July). *Child Maltreatment 2016: Summary of Key Findings.* Retrieved September 7, 2018, from https://www.childwelfare.gov/pubPDFs/canstats.pdf

NCANDS. (2016b, July). *Child Abuse and Neglect Fatalities 2016: Statistics and Interventions.* Retrieved September 7, 2018, from https://www.childwelfare.gov/pubPDFs/fatality.pdf#page=3&view=What groups of children are most vulnerable?

NCANDS. (2017). *Child Maltreatment 2017.* Retrieved April 13, 2019, from https://www.acf.hhs.gov/sites/default/files/cb/cm2017.pdf

Ncayiyana, D. (2011, November). The illusive promise of circumcision to prevent female-to-male HIV infection – not the way to go for South Africa. *South African Medical Journal, 101*(11). Retrieved August 6, 2018, from http://samj.org.za/index.php/samj/article/view/5384/3655

NCVO UK Civil Society Almanac. (2017). *UK Civil Society Almanac 2017 / Workforce.* Retrieved June 20, 2017, from https://data.ncvo.org.uk/a/almanac17/workforce-4/

Nelson, S. (2017, February 21). *The Drug Trial That Went Wrong: What Happened To The Infamous 'Elephant Men' from 2006.* Retrieved from https://www.huffingtonpost.co.uk/entry/the-drug-trial-bbc-examines-what-went-wrong-in-the-infamous-elephant-men-case_uk_58ac3bd1e4b07028b703c926

New Scientist. (2018, April 7). Don't screen out the facts. (3172), 5.

NHS. (2016, March 24). *Urinary Tract Infection in Children.* Retrieved August 5, 2018, from https://patient.info/doctor/urinary-tract-infection-in-children

NHS. (2017, October 31). *HPV vaccine.* Retrieved April 22, 2018, from Vaccinations: https://www.nhs.uk/conditions/vaccinations/hpv-human-papillomavirus-vaccine/

NHS Choices. (2016, April 13). *About the National Health Service (NHS).* Retrieved June 20, 2018, from https://www.nhs.uk/NHSEngland/thenhs/about/Pages/overview.aspx

NHS Digital. (2017, October 10). *Mental Health Act Statistics, Annual Figures: 2016-17, Experimental statistics.* Retrieved January 21, 2019, from https://digital.nhs.uk/data-

and-information/publications/statistical/mental-health-act-statistics-annual-figures/mental-health-act-statistics-annual-figures-2016-17-experimental-statistics

NHS Digital. (2018a, November). *Mental Health of Children and Young People in England, 2017: Summary of Key Findings*. Retrieved January 16, 2019, from https://files.digital.nhs.uk/F6/A5706C/MHCYP%202017%20Summary.pdf

NHS Digital. (2018b, November). *Mental Health of Children and Young People in England, 2017 [PAS]*. Retrieved January 16, 2019, from https://digital.nhs.uk/data-and-information/publications/statistical/mental-health-of-children-and-young-people-in-england/2017/2017

NHS England. (2018, March 3). *NHS launches 'one-stop' service to slash diagnosis times for prostate cancer*. Retrieved April 22, 2018, from http://home.bt.com/news/uk-news/nhs-launches-one-stop-service-to-slash-diagnosis-times-for-prostate-cancer-11364255448347

Nielsen. (2014). Woozles: Their Role in Custody Law Reform, Parenting Plans, and Family Court. *Psychology, Public Policy, and Law, American Psychological Association, 20*(2), 164-180. doi:10.1037/law0000004

Nielsen. (2017). Re-examining the Research on Parental Conflict, Coparenting, and Custody Arrangements. *Psychology, Public Policy, and Law, 23*(2), 211–231. doi: http://dx.doi.org/10.1037/law0000109

Nielsen. (2018). Preface to the Special Issue: Shared Physical Custody: Recent Research, Advances, and Applications. *Journal of Divorce and Remarriage, 59*(4), 237-246. doi:https://doi.org/10.1080/10502556.2018.1455303

Nuffield Foundation. (2015, June 2). *Study finds English courts not discriminating against fathers*. Retrieved October 12, 2018, from http://www.nuffieldfoundation.org/news/study-finds-english-family-courts-not-discriminating-against-fathers

Obama White House. (2014, May 10). Weekly Address: The First Lady Marks Mother's Day and Speaks Out on the Tragic Kidnapping in Nigeria (video). Retrieved March 18, 2019, from https://www.youtube.com/watch?v=PAncJ3nuczI

O'Brien. (1989). *Characteristics of Male Adolescent Sibling Incest Offenders*. Safer Society Press, Orwell VT.

OECD. (2015). *The ABC of Gender Equality in Education: Aptitude, Behaviour, Confidence*. Retrieved April 17, 2018, from Programme for International Student Assessment (PISA): http://www.oecd.org/pisa/keyfindings/pisa-2012-results-gender-eng.pdf

Office for National Statistics. (2011). *Population by Religion Age and Sex*. Retrieved August 2, 2018, from http://www.ons.gov.uk/ons/guide-method/census/2011/census-data/2011-census-ad-hoc-tables/ct0116---religion--detailed--by-sex-by-age---england-and-wales.xls

Office for National Statistics. (2013, May 16). *Full story: The gender gap in unpaid care provision: is there an impact on health and economic position?* Retrieved June 27, 2018, from https://www.ons.gov.uk/peoplepopulationandcommunity/healthandsocialcare/healthandwellbeing/articles/fullstorythegendergapinunpaidcareprovisionisthereanimpactonhealthandeconomicposition/2013-05-16

Office for National Statistics. (2014, June 11). *Marriage summary statistics (Provisional)*. Retrieved November 20, 2018, from https://www.ons.gov.uk/peoplepopulationandcommunity/birthsdeathsandmarria

ges/marriagecohabitationandcivilpartnerships/datasets/marriagesummarystatistics provisional

Office for National Statistics. (2015a, November 18). *Annual Survey of Hours and Earnings: 2015 Provisional Results.* Retrieved June 18, 2018, from https://www.ons.gov.uk/employmentandlabourmarket/peopleinwork/earningsandworkinghours/bulletins/annualsurveyofhoursandearnings/2015provisionalresults#gender-pay-differences

Office for National Statistics. (2015b, November 4). *Life Expectancy at Birth and at Age 65 by Local Areas in England and Wales.* Retrieved April 21, 2018, from https://www.ons.gov.uk/peoplepopulationandcommunity/birthsdeathsandmarriages/lifeexpectancies/datasets/lifeexpectancyatbirthandatage65bylocalareasinenglandandwalesreferencetable1

Office for National Statistics. (2015c, November 23). *Divorces in England and Wales: Children of Divorced Couples.* Retrieved October 14, 2018, from https://www.ons.gov.uk/peoplepopulationandcommunity/birthsdeathsandmarriages/divorce/datasets/divorcesinenglandandwaleschildrenofdivorcedcouples

Office for National Statistics. (2015d, November 23). *Divorces in England and Wales, 2013.* Retrieved November 20, 2018, from https://webarchive.nationalarchives.gov.uk/20160106011921/http:/www.ons.gov.uk/ons/dcp171778_424206.pdf

Office for National Statistics. (2015e, November 5). *Families and Households, 2015.* Retrieved November 20, 2015, from ONS: https://webarchive.nationalarchives.gov.uk/20160106020640/http:/www.ons.gov.uk/ons/dcp171778_422175.pdf

Office for National Statistics. (2015f, August 27). *Births by parents' country of birth, England and Wales: 2014.* Retrieved November 20, 2018, from https://www.ons.gov.uk/peoplepopulationandcommunity/birthsdeathsandmarriages/livebirths/bulletins/parentscountryofbirthenglandandwales/2015-08-27

Office for National Statistics. (2015g, June 17). *Public Sector Employment, UK: March 2015.* Retrieved March 28, 2019, from https://www.ons.gov.uk/employmentandlabourmarket/peopleinwork/publicsectorpersonnel/bulletins/publicsectoremployment/2015-06-17#public-sector-employment-by-industry

Office for National Statistics. (2015h, July 16). *Median Contribution Rates to Workplace Pensions by Age Group and Sector.* Retrieved March 25, 2019, from https://www.ons.gov.uk/peoplepopulationandcommunity/personalandhouseholdfinances/pensionssavingsandinvestments/datasets/mediancontributionratestoworkplacepensionsbyagegroupandsector

Office for National Statistics. (2015j, September 9). *How has life expectancy changed over time?* Retrieved March 25, 2019, from https://www.ons.gov.uk/peoplepopulationandcommunity/birthsdeathsandmarriages/lifeexpectancies/articles/howhaslifeexpectancychangedovertime/2015-09-09

Office for National Statistics. (2016a, December 9). *Find out the gender pay gap for your job.* Retrieved June 19, 2018, from https://www.ons.gov.uk/employmentandlabourmarket/peopleinwork/earningsandworkinghours/articles/findoutthegenderpaygapforyourjob/2016-12-09

Office for National Statistics. (2016b, February 11). *Focus on Violent Crime and Sexual Offences data - Appendix Tables.* Retrieved September 4, 2018, from https://www.ons.gov.uk/peoplepopulationandcommunity/crimeandjustice/compendium/focusonviolentcrimeandsexualoffences/yearendingmarch2015/bulletintablesfocusonviolentcrimeandsexualoffencesyearendingmarch2015

Office for National Statistics. (2016c, February 11). *Findings from analyses based on the Homicide Index recorded by the Home Office covering different aspects of homicide.* Retrieved September 7, 2018, from https://www.ons.gov.uk/peoplepopulationandcommunity/crimeandjustice/compendium/focusonviolentcrimeandsexualoffences/yearendingmarch2015/chapter2homicide

Office for National Statistics. (2017a, June 15). *Adult smoking habits in the UK: 2016.* Retrieved June 13, 2018, from https://www.ons.gov.uk/peoplepopulationandcommunity/healthandsocialcare/healthandlifeexpectancies/bulletins/adultsmokinghabitsingreatbritain/2016

Office for National Statistics. (2017b, October 26). *Annual Survey of Hours and Earnings: 2017 provisional and 2016 revised results.* Retrieved June 18, 2018, from https://www.ons.gov.uk/employmentandlabourmarket/peopleinwork/earningsandworkinghours/bulletins/annualsurveyofhoursandearnings/2017provisionaland2016revisedresults

Office for National Statistics. (2017c, October 26). *Annual Survey of Hours and Earnings: 2017 provisional and 2016 revised results.* Retrieved June 19, 2018, from https://www.ons.gov.uk/employmentandlabourmarket/peopleinwork/earningsandworkinghours/bulletins/annualsurveyofhoursandearnings/2017provisionaland2016revisedresults#regional-earnings

Office for National Statistics. (2017d, October 26). *Annual Survey of Hours and Earnings: Age Group - ASHE: Table 6.* Retrieved June 18, 2018, from https://www.ons.gov.uk/employmentandlabourmarket/peopleinwork/earningsandworkinghours/datasets/agegroupashetable6

Office for National Statistics. (2017e, July 19). *Death registrations summary tables - England and Wales - 2016 dataset.* Retrieved June 20, 2018, from https://www.ons.gov.uk/peoplepopulationandcommunity/birthsdeathsandmarriages/deaths/datasets/deathregistrationssummarytablesenglandandwalesreferencetables

Office for National Statistics. (2017f, August 16). *EMP04: Employment by occupation.* Retrieved June 19, 2018, from https://www.ons.gov.uk/employmentandlabourmarket/peopleinwork/employmentandemployeetypes/datasets/employmentbyoccupationemp04

Office for National Statistics. (2017g, November 8). *Families and Households: 2017.* Retrieved June 18, 2018, from https://www.ons.gov.uk/peoplepopulationandcommunity/birthsdeathsandmarriages/families/bulletins/familiesandhouseholds/2017#how-does-the-number-of-people-who-live-alone-vary-by-age-and-sex

Office for National Statistics. (2017h, July 19). *Deaths by single year of age tables - UK.* Retrieved April 21, 2018, from https://www.ons.gov.uk/peoplepopulationandcommunity/birthsdeathsandmarriages/deaths/datasets/deathregistrationssummarytablesenglandandwalesdeathsbysingleyearofagetables

Office for National Statistics. (2017j, February 9). *Appendix Tables - focus on violent crime and sexual offences.* Retrieved April 21, 2018, from https://www.ons.gov.uk/peoplepopulationandcommunity/crimeandjustice/datasets/appendixtablesfocusonviolentcrimeandsexualoffences

Office for National Statistics. (2017k, November 7). *Alcohol-related deaths by sex, age group and individual cause of death.* Retrieved April 21, 2018, from https://www.ons.gov.uk/peoplepopulationandcommunity/healthandsocialcare/causesofdeath/datasets/alcoholrelateddeathsbysexagegroupandindividualcauseofdeath

Office for National Statistics. (2017m, August 2). *Deaths Related to Drug Poisoning, England and Wales.* Retrieved April 21, 2018, from https://www.ons.gov.uk/peoplepopulationandcommunity/birthsdeathsandmarriages/deaths/datasets/deathsrelatedtodrugpoisoningenglandandwalesreferencetable

Office for National Statistics. (2017n, September 7). *Suicide occurrences England and Wales.* Retrieved from ONS: https://www.ons.gov.uk/peoplepopulationandcommunity/birthsdeathsandmarriages/deaths/datasets/suicideinenglandandwales

Office for National Statistics. (2017p, November 23). *Domestic abuse in England and Wales: year ending March 2017.* Retrieved September 3, 2018, from https://www.ons.gov.uk/releases/domesticabuseinenglandandwalesyearendingmarch2017

Office for National Statistics. (2017q). *Divorces in England and Wales 2017.* Retrieved from https://www.ons.gov.uk/peoplepopulationandcommunity/birthsdeathsandmarriages/divorce

Office for National Statistics. (2017r, November 8). *Families and Households: 2017.* Retrieved November 20, 2018, from ONS: https://www.ons.gov.uk/peoplepopulationandcommunity/birthsdeathsandmarriages/families/bulletins/familiesandhouseholds/2017

Office for National Statistics. (2017s, November 24). *Childbearing for women born in different years.* Retrieved November 20, 2018, from https://www.ons.gov.uk/peoplepopulationandcommunity/birthsdeathsandmarriages/conceptionandfertilityrates/datasets/childbearingforwomenbornindifferentyearsreferencetable

Office for National Statistics. (2017t, February 6). *Focus on violent crime and sexual offences, England and Wales: year ending March 2016 (Appendix Tables).* Retrieved February 28, 2019, from https://www.ons.gov.uk/releases/violentcrimeandsexualoffencesinenglandandwalesfinancialyearendingmar2016

Office for National Statistics. (2017u, February 9). *Bulletin Tables - Focus on violent crime and sexual offences.* Retrieved September 4, 2018, from https://www.ons.gov.uk/peoplepopulationandcommunity/crimeandjustice/datasets/bulletintablesfocusonviolentcrimeandsexualoffences

Office for National Statistics. (2017v, February 9). *Appendix Tables - focus on violent crime and sexual offences, 2016.* Retrieved September 4, 2018, from https://www.ons.gov.uk/peoplepopulationandcommunity/crimeandjustice/datasets/appendixtablesfocusonviolentcrimeandsexualoffences

Office for National Statistics. (2018a, May 18). *Prison population figures: 2018.* Retrieved from Prison population figures: 2018: https://www.gov.uk/government/statistics/prison-population-figures-2018

Office for National Statistics. (2018aa, July 19). *Crime in England and Wales: Appendix Tables, year ending March 2018 (Table A4).* Retrieved August 27, 2018, from https://www.ons.gov.uk/peoplepopulationandcommunity/crimeandjustice/datasets/crimeinenglandandwalesappendixtables

Office for National Statistics. (2018ab, July 19). *Crime in England and Wales: Police Force Area Data Tables, year ending March 2018.* Retrieved August 27, 2018, from https://www.ons.gov.uk/peoplepopulationandcommunity/crimeandjustice/datasets/policeforceareadatatables

Office for National Statistics. (2018ac, July 19). *Crime in England and Wales: Annual Trend and Demographic Tables, Table D1.* Retrieved August 27, 2018, from https://www.ons.gov.uk/peoplepopulationandcommunity/crimeandjustice/datasets/crimeinenglandandwalesannualtrendanddemographictables

Office for National Statistics. (2018ad, July 19). *Crime in England & Wales, year ending March 2018 - Annual trend and demographic tables, Table D3.* Retrieved August 27, 2018, from https://www.ons.gov.uk/peoplepopulationandcommunity/crimeandjustice/datasets/crimeinenglandandwalesannualtrendanddemographictables

Office for National Statistics. (2018ae, August 16). *Criminal Justice System statistics quarterly: December 2017 - Sentencing Data Tool.* Retrieved August 26, 2018, from https://www.gov.uk/government/statistics/criminal-justice-system-statistics-quarterly-december-2017

Office for National Statistics. (2018af, November 22). *Domestic abuse: findings from the Crime Survey for England and Wales: year ending March 2018.* Retrieved from https://www.ons.gov.uk/peoplepopulationandcommunity/crimeandjustice/articles/domesticabusefindingsfromthecrimesurveyforenglandandwales/yearendingmarch2018

Office for National Statistics. (2018ag, April 10). *Loneliness - What characteristics and circumstances are associated with feeling lonely?* Retrieved January 3, 2019, from https://www.ons.gov.uk/peoplepopulationandcommunity/wellbeing/articles/lonelinesswhatcharacteristicsandcircumstancesareassociatedwithfeelinglonely/2018-04-10

Office for National Statistics. (2018ah, December 20). *Deaths of homeless people in England and Wales: 2013 to 2017.* Retrieved January 3, 2018, from https://www.ons.gov.uk/peoplepopulationandcommunity/birthsdeathsandmarriages/deaths/bulletins/deathsofhomelesspeopleinenglandandwales/2013to2017#quality-and-methodology

Office for National Statistics. (2018b). *Crime in England and Wales: year ending September 2017.* Retrieved April 15, 2018, from https://www.ons.gov.uk/peoplepopulationandcommunity/crimeandjustice/bulletins/crimeinenglandandwales/yearendingseptember2017

Office for National Statistics. (2018c, November 22). *Domestic abuse in England and Wales: year ending March 2018.* Retrieved February 6, 2019, from https://www.ons.gov.uk/peoplepopulationandcommunity/crimeandjustice/bulletins/domesticabuseinenglandandwales/yearendingmarch2018

Office for National Statistics. (2018d, Janaury 18). *Family spending in the UK: financial year ending 2017.* Retrieved June 18, 2018, from https://www.ons.gov.uk/peoplepopulationandcommunity/personalandhouseholdfinances/expenditure/bulletins/familyspendingintheuk/financialyearending2017

Office for National Statistics. (2018e, June 12). *HOUR01 NSA: Actual weekly hours worked (not seasonally adjusted)*. Retrieved June 25, 2018, from https://www.ons.gov.uk/employmentandlabourmarket/peopleinwork/earningsandworkinghours/datasets/actualweeklyhoursworkednotseasonallyadjustedhour01nsa

Office for National Statistics. (2018f, February 8). *Appendix tables: homicide in England and Wales*. Retrieved September 7, 2018, from https://www.ons.gov.uk/peoplepopulationandcommunity/crimeandjustice/datasets/appendixtableshomicideinenglandandwales

Office for National Statistics. (2018g, March 1). *NEET statistics quarterly brief: October to December 2017*. Retrieved June 19, 2018, from https://www.gov.uk/government/statistics/neet-statistics-quarterly-brief-october-to-december-2017

Office for National Statistics. (2018h, June 12). *Public sector employment, UK: March 2018*. Retrieved from https://www.ons.gov.uk/employmentandlabourmarket/peopleinwork/publicsectorpersonnel/bulletins/publicsectoremployment/latest

Office for National Statistics. (2018j, June 12). *UK labour market: June 2018*. Retrieved June 19, 2018, from https://www.ons.gov.uk/employmentandlabourmarket/peopleinwork/employmentandemployeetypes/bulletins/uklabourmarket/latest#economic-inactivity

Office for National Statistics. (2018k, June 12). *Unemployment*. Retrieved from https://www.ons.gov.uk/employmentandlabourmarket/peoplenotinwork/unemployment

Office for National Statistics. (2018m, March 14). *Child mortality (death cohort) tables in England and Wales*. Retrieved April 3, 2019, from http://tinyurl.com/y2p76ma9

Office for National Statistics. (2018n, April 26). *Crime in England and Wales: year ending December 2017*. Retrieved July 1, 2018, from https://www.ons.gov.uk/peoplepopulationandcommunity/crimeandjustice/bulletins/crimeinenglandandwales/yearendingdecember2017

Office for National Statistics. (2018p, September 26). *Divorces in England and Wales: 2017*. Retrieved November 20, 2018, from https://www.ons.gov.uk/peoplepopulationandcommunity/birthsdeathsandmarriages/divorce/bulletins/divorcesinenglandandwales/2017

Office for National Statistics. (2018q, July 27). *Population estimates by marital status and living arrangements, England and Wales*. Retrieved November 20, 2018, from https://www.ons.gov.uk/peoplepopulationandcommunity/populationandmigration/populationestimates/datasets/populationestimatesbymaritalstatusandlivingarrangements

Office for National Statistics. (2018r, February 28). *Marriages in England and Wales*. Retrieved November 20, 2018, from https://www.ons.gov.uk/peoplepopulationandcommunity/birthsdeathsandmarriages/marriagecohabitationandcivilpartnerships/datasets/marriagesinenglandandwales2013

Office for National Statistics. (2018s, September 14). *Suicide occurrences, England and Wales*. Retrieved February 9, 2019, from https://www.ons.gov.uk/peoplepopulationandcommunity/birthsdeathsandmarriages/deaths/datasets/suicideinenglandandwales

Office for National Statistics. (2018t, September 4). Suicides in the UK. Retrieved April 28, 2019, from https://www.ons.gov.uk/peoplepopulationandcommunity/birthsdeathsandmarriages/deaths/datasets/suicidesintheunitedkingdomreferencetables

Office for National Statistics. (2018u, February 8). Sexual offences in England and Wales: year ending March 2017. Retrieved April 7, 2019, from https://www.ons.gov.uk/peoplepopulationandcommunity/crimeandjustice/articles/sexualoffencesinenglandandwales/yearendingmarch2017#reporting-of-sexual-assault-by-rape-or-penetration

Office for National Statistics. (2018v, September 6). *Occupational Pensions Schemes Survey, UK: 2017.* Retrieved March 25, 2019, from https://www.ons.gov.uk/peoplepopulationandcommunity/personalandhouseholdfinances/pensionssavingsandinvestments/bulletins/occupationalpensionschemessurvey/uk2017#what-are-the-average-contribution-rates-in-private-sector-occupational-pension-schemes

Office for National Statistics. (2018w, March 2). *Criminal Justice System statistics quarterly: December 2016.* Retrieved from https://www.gov.uk/government/statistics/criminal-justice-system-statistics-quarterly-december-2016

Office for National Statistics. (2018x, July 19). *Crime in England and Wales: Appendix Tables.* Retrieved August 25, 2018, from https://www.ons.gov.uk/peoplepopulationandcommunity/crimeandjustice/datasets/crimeinenglandandwalesappendixtables

Office for National Statistics. (2018y, July 19). *Crime in England and Wales: year ending March 2018.* Retrieved August 26, 2018, from https://www.ons.gov.uk/peoplepopulationandcommunity/crimeandjustice/bulletins/crimeinenglandandwales/yearendingmarch2018

Office for National Statistics. (2018z, February 8). *Homicide in England and Wales: year ending March 2017.* Retrieved August 27, 2018, from https://www.ons.gov.uk/peoplepopulationandcommunity/crimeandjustice/articles/homicideinenglandandwales/yearendingmarch2017

Office for National Statistics. (2019a, March 19). *HOUR01 NSA: Actual weekly hours worked (not seasonally adjusted).* Retrieved from https://www.ons.gov.uk/employmentandlabourmarket/peopleinwork/earningsandworkinghours/datasets/actualweeklyhoursworkednotseasonallyadjustedhour01nsa

Office for National Statistics. (2019b, January 24). *Crime in England and Wales: Appendix tables; year ending September 2018.* Retrieved February 28, 2019, from https://www.ons.gov.uk/peoplepopulationandcommunity/crimeandjustice/datasets/crimeinenglandandwalesappendixtables

Olson, R. (2014, June 25). *Average IQ of students by college major and gender ratio.* Retrieved February 24, 2019, from http://www.randalolson.com/2014/06/25/average-iq-of-students-by-college-major-and-gender-ratio/

O'Pie. (2012). *Exposing Feminism: The Thirty Years' War Against Men.* The Men's Press. Retrieved from https://tinyurl.com/y46qnoty

Oral Health Foundation. (2017, July 19). *Action launched on HPV for boys.* Retrieved April 22, 2018, from https://www.dentalhealth.org/News/unjust-unfair-and-discriminatory-decision-will-cost-lives-charity-slams-jcvi-decision-on-hpv

ORCHID. (2018, April 9). *Report reveals 4 in 10 prostate cancer cases are diagnosed late and an impending crisis in prostate cancer provision.* Retrieved June 14, 2018, from https://orchid-cancer.org.uk/news/new-report-reveals-4-in-10-prostate-cancer-cases-are-diagnosed-late-and-an-impending-crisis-in-prostate-cancer-provision/

Orr. (2013, September 13). Acquittal does not make someone a victim – this is just the system at work. *Guardian.* Retrieved April 6, 2019, from https://www.theguardian.com/commentisfree/2013/sep/13/acquittal-does-not-make-victim

Oryszczuk, S. (2018, February 28). *The Jewish parents cutting out the bris.* Retrieved August 3, 2018, from https://jewishnews.timesofisrael.com/the-jewish-parents-cutting-out-the-bris/

Oster, J. (1968, April). Further fate of the foreskin. Incidence of preputial adhesions, phimosis, and smegma among Danish schoolboys. *Arch.Dis.Child., 43*(228), 200–203. Retrieved from https://www.ncbi.nlm.nih.gov/pmc/articles/PMC2019851/?page=2

Ouazad and Page. (2012, January). *Students' Perceptions of Teacher Biases: Experimental Economics in Schools.* Retrieved May 3, 2018, from Centre for the Economics of Education, London School of Economics: http://cee.lse.ac.uk/ceedps/ceedp133.pdf

Owings and Williams. (2010). *Trends in Circumcision for Male Newborns in U.S. Hospitals: 1979–2010.* Retrieved August 3, 2018, from National Centre for Health Statistics: https://www.cdc.gov/nchs/data/hestat/circumcision_2013/circumcision_2013.pdf

Pabalan et al. (2015, December). Association of male circumcision with risk of prostate cancer: a meta-analysis. *Prostate Cancer Prostatic Dis., 18*(4), 352-357. doi:10.1038/pcan.2015.34

Pahl, J. (2000, January). *The gendering of spending within households.* Retrieved June 18, 2018, from Radical Statistics Group: http://www.radstats.org.uk/no075/pahl.htm

Palmer. (2006, October 22). If two people accuse you, then you are guilty. They get compensation, you get jail. *The Telegraph.* Retrieved March 6, 2019, from https://www.telegraph.co.uk/comment/personal-view/3633405/If-two-people-accuse-you-then-you-are-guilty.-They-get-compensation-you-get-jail.html

Panscofar and Vernon-Feagans. (2006). Mother and father language input to young children: contributions to later language development. *Journal of Applied Developmental Psychology, 27*, 571-587. doi:https://doi.org/10.1016/j.appdev.2006.08.003

Parental Alienation Research Institute. (2019, April 25). *Parental Alienation Research Institute* . Retrieved from http://parentalalienationresearch.com/

Parry and Tolhurst. (2018, May 2). *Screening Scandal 270 women died after NHS IT glitch meant 450,000 missed breast cancer screening – as Jeremy Hunt 'apologises wholeheartedly' to families involved.* Retrieved from The Sun: https://www.thesun.co.uk/news/6193120/breast-cancer-screening-nhs-mistake-jeremy-hunt/

Parson, L. (2016, January 18). Are STEM Syllabi Gendered? A Feminist Critical Discourse Analysis. *The Qualitative Report at NSUWorks, 21*(1), Article 9. Retrieved May 21, 2018, from http://nsuworks.nova.edu/tqr/vol21/iss1/9

PASK. (2013a, May). *About PASK, The Partner Abuse State of Knowledge Project.* Retrieved September 6, 2018, from Journal of Partner Abuse: https://domesticviolenceresearch.org/

PASK. (2013b, May). *The Impact and Consequences of Partner Abuse on Partners.* Retrieved September 6, 2018, from https://domesticviolenceresearch.org/impact-of-abuse-on-partners/

Patai and Koertge. (1994). *Professing Feminism: Cautionary Tales from the Strange World of Women's Studies.* New Republic Books (Harper Collins). Retrieved from https://tinyurl.com/y4zufusk

Patel, Palmer and Sheriff. (2005). Penile Sensitivity and Sexual Satisfaction after Circumcision: Are We Informing Men Correctly? *Urologia Internationalis, 75*, 62-66. doi:https://doi.org/10.1159/000085930

Payne et al. (2007, May). Sensation and Sexual Arousal in Circumcised and Uncircumcised Men. *Journal of Sexual Medicine, 4*(3), 667–674. Retrieved July 27, 2017, from https://www.jsm.jsexmed.org/article/S1743-6095(15)31551-4/fulltext

Peachey. (2018, November 30). Women's state pension changes to get legal review. Retrieved March 28, 2019, from https://www.bbc.com/news/business-46400290

Pemberton, H. (2017, March 10). WASPI's Is (Mostly) a Campaign for Inequality. Retrieved March 28, 2019, from https://onlinelibrary.wiley.com/doi/abs/10.1111/1467-923X.12347

Pence and Paymar. (1993). *Education Groups for Men Who Batter: The Duluth Model.* Springer. Retrieved from http://www.springerpub.com/education-groups-for-men-who-batter-9780826179906.html

Penis Project. (2016, March 9). *Foreskin during sex vs Circumcised.* Retrieved July 27, 2018, from https://tinyurl.com/y2au4mrz

Peter Wright. (2014). *Gynocentrism: From Feudalism to the Modern Disney Princess.* Independent. Retrieved from https://www.amazon.com/Gynocentrism-Feudalism-Modern-Disney-Princess/dp/1520327323/ref=tmm_pap_title_0?_encoding=UTF8&qid=&sr=

Peterson. (2015, March 16). *New 'No Boys Allowed" School Day Aims To Help Girls With Science and Math.* Retrieved February 25, 2019, from The Libertarian Republic: http://thelibertarianrepublic.com/new-no-boys-allowed-school-day-aims-to-help-girls-with-science-and-math/

Petrovic. (2009, March 1). The influence of marital status on epidemiological characteristics of suicides in the southeastern part of Serbia. *Central European Journal of Public Health , 17*(1), 41-46. doi:10.1007/s10389-008-0209-6

Petrovich and Templer. (1984, June 1). Heterosexual Molestation of Children Who Later Became Rapists. *Psychological Reports, 54*(3). doi:https://doi.org/10.2466/pr0.1984.54.3.810

Pew Research. (2008, September 25). *Gender and Power: Women Call the Shots at Home; Public Mixed on Gender Roles in Jobs.* Retrieved March 22, 2019, from https://tinyurl.com/y4so3a93

Phil Rumney. (2018, May 4). Retrieved March 4, 2019, from https://twitter.com/phil_rumney/status/992535693745426433

Phillips, J. (2015, November 19). We need International Men's Day about as much as white history month, or able body action day. *Independent.* Retrieved May 18, 2018, from https://www.independent.co.uk/voices/we-need-international-mens-day-about-as-much-as-a-white-history-month-or-able-body-action-day-a6740646.html

Phipps and Young. (2013). *That's what she said: Women students' experiences of 'lad culture' in higher education.* Retrieved May 21, 2018, from National Union of Students: https://www.nus.org.uk/Global/Campaigns/That's%20what%20she%20said%20full%20report%20Final%20web.pdf

Pinker, S. (1997, November 2). Why They Kill Their Newborns. *New York Times.* Retrieved September 7, 2018, from http://www.gargaro.com/pinker.html

Pinkerton and Abramson. (1997, May). Effectiveness of condoms in preventing HIV transmission. *Social Science & Medicine,* 1303-1312. doi:https://doi.org/10.1016/S0277-9536(96)00258-4

Pizzey, E. (2011). *This Way to the Revolution: A Memoir.* Peter Owen Ltd.

Pleasance. (2017, June 29). Brace yourself, this might sting a bit... Boys scream in pain as they are circumcised with NO anaesthetic in Turkey. *Daily Mail.* Retrieved March 15, 2019, from https://www.dailymail.co.uk/news/article-4650152/Turkish-boys-circumcised-no-anaesthetic.html?login#readerCommentsCommand-message-field

Poole, G. (2017). *You Can Stop Male Suicide.* Retrieved February 11, 2019, from https://stopmalesuicide.com/book/

Poole, G. (2014a, September 18). *Surely everyone carrying out circumcisions should be registered?* Retrieved August 2, 2018, from https://www.telegraph.co.uk/men/active/mens-health/11101320/Surely-everyone-carrying-out-circumcisions-should-be-registered.html

Poole, G. (2014b, September 23). *So much for sex equality, ZERO per cent of Brits think mums should work more than dads.* Retrieved June 25, 2018, from InsideMAN: http://www.inside-man.co.uk/2014/09/23/so-much-for-sex-equality-zero-per-cent-of-brits-think-mums-should-work-more-than-dads/

Powell and Jenkins. (2016, September 25). Ex-husband of Labour's domestic abuse Minister 'still has nightmares about her' after attack during divorce . *Mail Online.* Retrieved April 4, 2019, from https://www.dailymail.co.uk/news/article-3806018/Ex-husband-Labour-s-domestic-abuse-Minister-nightmares-attack-divorce.html

Press Association. (2009, November 9). Children's claims of sex abuse by women double. *The Guardian.* Retrieved April 8, 2019, from https://www.theguardian.com/society/2009/nov/09/sex-abuse-by-women-doubles

Price. (1996, December). *Male Circumcision: A Legal Affront.* Retrieved August 3, 2018, from The Circumcision Reference Library: http://www.cirp.org/library/legal/price-uklc/

Princeton. (2018). *Fragile Families and Child Wellbeing Study.* Retrieved October 28, 2018, from https://fragilefamilies.princeton.edu/sites/fragilefamilies/files/ff_fact_sheet.pdf

Priskorn et al. (2018, April 11). Average sperm count remains unchanged despite reduction in maternal smoking: results from a large cross-sectional study with annual investigations over 21 years . *human reproduction, 33*(6), 998-1008. doi:https://doi.org/10.1093/humrep/dey090

Prison Reform Trust. (2010). *Punishing Disadvantage: a profile of children in custody.* Retrieved July 4, 2018, from

http://www.prisonreformtrust.org.uk/uploads/documents/PunishingDisadvantage.pdf
Prison Reform Trust. (2013). *Prison: the facts Bromley Briefings Summer 2013.* Retrieved July 4, 2018, from http://www.prisonreformtrust.org.uk/Portals/0/Documents/Prisonthefacts.pdf
Prostate Cancer UK. (2016a, March). *Prostate Cancer UK policy position on the PSA test.* Retrieved from https://prostatecanceruk.org/media/2493257/prostate-cancer-uk-policy-position-on-the-psa-test-2016.pdf
Prostate Cancer UK. (2016b, November). *What if my GP won't give me a PSA test?* Retrieved April 22, 2018, from The PSA Test: https://www.prostatecanceruk.org/prostate-information/prostate-tests/psa-test
Prostate Cancer UK. (2018a). *Implementing mpMRI before biopsy: learning from those that have succeeded.* Retrieved March 10, 2019, from https://prostatecanceruk.org/for-health-professionals/best-practice/mpmri-case-studies
Prostate Cancer UK. (2018b, June). *mpMRI before biopsy: Improving diagnosis for men with prostate cancer.* Retrieved March 10, 2019, from https://prostatecanceruk.org/for-health-professionals/our-projects/mpmri-before-biopsy
Public Health Agency of Canada. (2007). *The Maternity Experiences Survey (MES) 2006-2007 - Data Tables.* Retrieved August 3, 2018, from http://www.phac-aspc.gc.ca/rhs-ssg/pdf/tab-eng.pdf
Public Health England. (2014, May 14). *Change in schedule from three to two doses in the HPV vaccination programme* . Retrieved April 22, 2018, from NHS England: https://assets.publishing.service.gov.uk/government/uploads/system/uploads/attachment_data/file/310958/HPV_Joint_Letter_14_May.pdf
Public Health Wales. (2016, January 13). *Adverse Childhood Experiences and their impact on health-harming behaviours in the Welsh adult population.* Retrieved October 20, 2018, from https://tinyurl.com/jzza8lt
Public Health Wales. (2016b, March). *Measuring the health and well-being of a nation.* Retrieved April 22, 2018, from http://gov.wales/docs/phhs/publications/160329frameworken.pdf
Public Health Wales. (2017). *Infographic for prevalence of ACEs in Wales.* Retrieved from http://www.wales.nhs.uk/sitesplus/documents/888/PHW ACEs Resilience infographic (Eng).pdf
Public Health Wales Observatory. (2016, May 23). *Women set to benefit from new cervical screening test.* Retrieved April 22, 2018, from NHS Wales: http://www.publichealthwalesobservatory.wales.nhs.uk/news/41479/
Public Health Wales Observatory. (2017, July 20). *Child profile - key messages chapter 5.* Retrieved April 22, 2018, from http://www.publichealthwalesobservatory.wales.nhs.uk/child-profile-key-messages-5/
Purdy. (2016). *Their Angry Creed: The shocking history of feminism and how it is destroying our way of life.* lps publishing. Retrieved from https://tinyurl.com/y3rtjdg6
Quranic Path. (2018). *Circumcision - Does the Qur'an Approve it? Genital Mutilation.* Retrieved August 3, 2018, from http://www.quranicpath.com/misconceptions/circumcision.html
Radl, Salazar and Cebolla-Boado. (2017). Does Living in a Fatherless Household Compromise Educational Success? A Comparative Study of Cognitive and Non-cognitive Skills. *Eur J Population, 33*, 217-242. doi:DOI 10.1007/s10680-017-9414-

Rantzen. (2009, November 9). Gender-blindness on child sexual abuse. *The Guardian.* Retrieved April 8, 2019, from https://www.theguardian.com/commentisfree/2009/nov/09/boys-sexual-abuse-childline

Ravanos et al. (2018, October). Declining Sperm Counts… or Rather Not? A Mini Review. *Obstetrical & Gynecological Survey, 73*(10), 595-605. doi:10.1097/OGX.0000000000000599

Refuge. (2018). *myths of domestic violence.* Retrieved September 3, 2018, from Refuge: https://www.refuge.org.uk/our-work/forms-of-violence-and-abuse/domestic-violence/myths-of-domestic-violence/

Refugee Law Project. (2012, May 21). Gender Against Men. Retrieved April 11, 2019, from https://www.youtube.com/watch?v=mJSl99HQYXc

Refugee Law Project. (2015, March 30). They Slept With Me. Retrieved April 11, 2019, from https://www.youtube.com/watch?v=xQ2RH8kxCTI

Research Councils UK. (2013). *RCUK Expectations for Equality and Diversity.* Retrieved April 18, 2018, from Research Councils UK: https://www.ukri.org/files/legacy/skills/equalitystatement-pdf/

Resnick, P. (1970). Murder of the newborn: a psychiatric review of neonaticide. *Am J Psychiatry, 126*(10), 1414-1420. doi:10.1176/ajp.126.10.1414

Respect. (2012). *Accreditation Standard.* Retrieved October 6, 2018, from Respect: https://democracy.walthamforest.gov.uk/documents/s47298/Domestic%20Violence%20Appendix%201.pdf

Reynolds. (2015, January 3). *Juveniles Sexually Abused by Staffers at Corrections Facilities: Scandal in Idaho Shines Light on Victimization of Young People by Staff.* Retrieved April 11, 2019, from Instapundit.com: https://pjmedia.com/instapundit/200500/

Richard Warshak. (2014). Social science and parenting plans for young children: A consensus report. *American Psychological Association: Psychology, Public Policy, and Law, 20*(1), 46-67. doi:http://dx.doi.org/10.1037/law0000005

Richters et al. (2006, August 1). Circumcision in Australia: prevalence and effects on sexual health. *International Journale of STD & AIDs, 17*(8), 547-554. doi:https://doi.org/10.1258/095646206778145730

Rijken. (2013a). *Ulwaluko.* Retrieved July 27, 2018, from Dr Dingeman Rijkens site: http://www.ulwaluko.co.za/Photos.html

Rijken. (2013b). *Ulwaluko.* Retrieved July 27, 2018, from Dr Dingeman Rijkens site: http://www.ulwaluko.co.za/Home.html

Robinson, Jefferies and Lacaze. (2017, February). *Letter to the Editor - Re: Canadian Pediatrics Society position statement on newborn circumcision: a risk benefit analysis revisited.* Retrieved August 5, 2018, from http://www.canjurol.com/html/free-articles/V24I1_19_FREE_Letter_Editor_Feb17.pdf

Robinson, N. H. (2016, May). *Boys to Men: The underachievement of young men in higher education – and how to start tackling it .* Retrieved April 17, 2018, from Higher Education Policy Institute: http://www.hepi.ac.uk/wp-content/uploads/2016/05/Boys-to-Men.pdf

Rodríguez-Pulido. (1992, March). Suicide in the Canary Islands: standardized epidemiological study by age, sex, and marital status. *Social Psychiatry and Psychiatric Epidemiology, 27*(2), 69-74. Retrieved from https://link.springer.com/article/10.1007/BF00788508

Roger. (2018, July 24). *HPV vaccine to be offered to boys - but only some.* Retrieved March 10, 2019, from Birmingham Live: https://www.birminghammail.co.uk/news/health/hpv-vaccine-offered-boys-only-14946215

Rose, D. (2018, May 6). *Finally - boys will be given potentially lifesaving HPV vaccine, Health Minister hints.* Retrieved from Daily Mail: http://www.dailymail.co.uk/news/article-5695509/Finally-boys-given-potentially-lifesaving-HPV-vaccine-Health-Minister-hints.html#ixzz5EhVctBPt

Ross, L. F. (1996, April). Disclosing Misattributed Paternity. *bioethics, 10*(2), 114-130. doi:https://doi.org/10.1111/j.1467-8519.1996.tb00111.x

Rossow. (1993, December). Suicide, alcohol, and divorce; aspects of gender and family integration. *88*(12), 1659-1665. doi: https://doi.org/10.1111/j.1360-0443.1993.tb02041.x

Royal Australasian College of Physicians. (2010, September). *CIRCUMCISION OF INFANT MALES.* Retrieved August 3, 2018, from https://www.racp.edu.au/docs/default-source/advocacy-library/circumcision-of-infant-males.pdf

Royal Courts of Justice. (2015, January 14). *In the matter of B and G (Children) (No 2) by Sir James Munby.* Retrieved March 13, 2019, from Family Court sitting at Leeds; Case No: LJ13C00295: https://www.judiciary.uk/wp-content/uploads/2015/01/BandG_2_.pdf

Royal Dutch Medical Society. (2010, May 27). *Non-therapeutic circumcision of male minors.* Retrieved August 3, 2018, from KNMG: https://www.knmg.nl/actualiteit-opinie/nieuws/nieuwsbericht/nieuwsuur-over-jongensbesnijdenis.htm

Rucki, A. (2014, April 11). *Bogus circumcision nurse who almost killed baby jailed.* Retrieved August 2, 2018, from Evening Standard: https://www.standard.co.uk/news/crime/bogus-circumcision-nurse-who-almost-killed-baby-jailed-9255143.html

Rumney. (2006). False allegations of rape. *The Cambridge Law Journal, 65*(1), 125-158. doi:http://dx.doi.org/10.1017/S0008197306007069

Runeson et al. (2010, July 13). Method of attempted suicide as predictor of subsequent successful suicide: national long term cohort study. *341:c3222* . doi:https://doi.org/10.1136/bmj.c3222

Rush. (2014, August 5). A dozen men are ambushed, stripped naked and forced to undergo circumcisions in Kenya after their wives complained that they were not as good in bed as circumcised men. *Mail Online.* Retrieved March 15, 2019, from https://tinyurl.com/y688ckz9

Ryan et al. (2006, May). Is One Good Parent Good Enough? Patterns of Mother and Father Parenting and Child Cognitive Outcomes at 24 and 36 Months. *Parenting, 6*(2/3), 211 - 228. doi:DOI: 10.1080/15295192.2006.9681306

Sally Davies. (2018, December 21). *Chief Medical Officer (CMO): annual reports.* Retrieved December 22, 2018, from gov.uk: https://www.gov.uk/government/collections/chief-medical-officer-annual-reports

Samaritans. (2012, September). *Men, Suicide and Society.* Retrieved February 8, 2019, from https://www.samaritans.org/about-samaritans/research-policy/middle-aged-men-suicide/

Samaritans. (2017). *Samaritans suicide report 2017*. Retrieved July 4, 2018, from https://www.samaritans.org/sites/default/files/kcfinder/files/Suicide_statistics_report_2017_Final.pdf

Sanghani. (2015, June 23). Underage sex conviction: Why older women have sex with young boys. *Telegraph*. Retrieved April 8, 2019, from https://www.telegraph.co.uk/women/womens-life/11694528/female-sex-offenders-Why-older-women-sleep-with-young-boys.html

Sanomat. (2006, August 7). *Court rules circumcision of four-year-old boy illegal*. Retrieved from http://www.cirp.org/news/helsinginsanomat2006-08-07/

Sariola. (2012, March 7). Retrieved August 3, 2018, from The Central Union for Child Welfare, Finland: https://www.lskl.fi/blogi/paluuta-entiseen-ei-ole/

Sarkadi et al. (2008). Fathers' involvement and children's developmental outcomes: a systematic review of longitudinal studies. *Acta Pædiatrica, 97*, 153-158. Retrieved October 29, 2018, from http://www.effeps.it/res/site39917/res630646_fathers-involvement.pdf

Scholz. (2012, December 12). Circumcision remains legal in Germany. *dw.com*. Retrieved March 14, 2019, from https://www.dw.com/en/circumcision-remains-legal-in-germany/a-16399336

Schroder, N. (2009, April). The dilemma of unintentional discovery of misattributed paternity in living kidney donors and recipients. *Current opinion in organ transplantation, 14*(2), 196-200. doi:10.1097/MOT.0b013e328327b21f

Scott. (2018a, June 2). *Rape juries: Jolyon Maugham hits the wrong target*. Retrieved March 4, 2019, from The Barrister Blogger: http://barristerblogger.com/2018/06/02/rape-juries-jolyon-maugham-hits-the-wrong-target/

Scott. (2018b, November 23). Scrapping juries in rape trials would be a mistake. *The Spectator*. Retrieved March 4, 2019, from https://blogs.spectator.co.uk/2018/11/scrapping-juries-in-rape-trials-would-be-a-mistake/

Scott, M. (2017, December 15). *Liam Allan's case shows why our criminal justice system is becoming a matter of national shame*. Retrieved March 6, 2019, from The Barrister Blogger: http://barristerblogger.com/2017/12/15/liam-allans-case-shows-criminal-justice-system-becoming-matter-national-shame/

Scottish Government. (2018, June 19). *Homelessness in Scotland 2017/18; Excel Tables and Charts*. Retrieved 1 1, 2019, from Scottish Homelessness Statistics: https://www2.gov.scot/Topics/Statistics/Browse/Housing-Regeneration/RefTables

Scottish Public Health Network. (2016, May). *'Polishing the Diamonds' Addressing Adverse Childhood Experiences in Scotland*. Retrieved October 20, 2018, from https://www.scotphn.net/wp-content/uploads/2016/06/2016_05_26-ACE-Report-Final-AF.pdf

Scruton. (1999, August). Modern Manhood. *City Journal, NY*. Retrieved April 5, 2019, from https://www.city-journal.org/html/modern-manhood-11823.html

Sengupta et al. (2016, April 19). The Disappearing Sperms: Analysis of Reports Published Between 1980 and 2015 . *American Journal of Men's Health, 11*(4), 1279-1304. doi:https://doi.org/10.1177/1557988316643383

Sengupta, Borges and Dutta. (2018). Decline in sperm count in European men during the past 50 years . *Human & Experimental Toxicology, 37*(3), 247-255. doi:https://doi.org/10.1177/0960327117703690

Senkul et al. (2004, January). Circumcision in adults: effect on sexual function. *Urology, 63*(1), 155-158. doi:https://doi.org/10.1016/j.urology.2003.08.035

Shahid. (2005, March 5). Phimosis in Children. *ISRN Urology*, 707329. doi:10.5402/2012/707329

she-conomy. (2013). Marketing to women quick facts. Retrieved March 21, 2019, from http://she-conomy.com/report/marketing-to-women-quick-facts

Shepherd and Pence. (1999). *Coordinating Community Responses to Domestic Violence: Lessons from Duluth and Beyond (SAGE Series on Violence against Women).* Sage. Retrieved from https://tinyurl.com/y4wbsukk

Sherwood. (2018, February 18). Iceland law to outlaw male circumcision sparks row over religious freedom. *The Guardian.* Retrieved March 14, 2019, from https://www.theguardian.com/society/2018/feb/18/iceland-ban-male-circumcision-first-european-country

Silverstein and Sayre. (2009, September). The Female Economy. *Harvard Business Review.* Retrieved March 21, 2019, from https://hbr.org/2009/09/the-female-economy

Simmons et al. (2004). Human sperm competition: testis size, sperm production and rates of extra pair copulations. *Animal Behaviour, 68*, 297-302. doi:10.1016/j.anbehav.2003.11.013

Slack. (2014, July 31). Eight prisons have only sex offenders: Historic abuse cases fuel rise in prison population. Retrieved April 7, 2019, from https://www.dailymail.co.uk/news/article-2711482/Eight-prisons-sex-offenders-Historic-abuse-cases-fuel-rise-prison-population.html

Smajdor, A. (2016, April 6). *Mike Buchanan and a female ethicist discuss mandatory paternity testing at birth.* Retrieved December 18, 2018, from Shelagh Fogerty's show on LBC Radio: https://www.youtube.com/watch?v=0f3V7tRpSRs&t=238s

Smith. (2012). Uncomfortable Places, Close Spaces: Female Correctional Workers' Sexual Interactions With Men and Boys in Custody. *UCLA LAW Review*, 1690. Retrieved from https://www.uclalawreview.org/uncomfortable-places-close-spaces-female-correctional-workers'-sexual-interactions-with-men-and-boys-in-custody-2/

Smith, C. (2015, June 2). *No anti-father bias in family courts, research finds.* Retrieved October 11, 2018, from The Law Society Gazette: https://www.lawgazette.co.uk/law/no-anti-father-bias-in-family-courts-research-finds/5049142.article

Social Exclusion Unit. (2002). *Reducing re-offending by ex-prisoners.* Retrieved July 4, 2018, from http://webarchive.nationalarchives.gov.uk/+/http:/www.cabinetoffice.gov.uk/media/cabinetoffice/social_exclusion_task_force/assets/publications_1997_to_2006/reducing_summary.pdf

Sorrells, et al. (2007, April). Fine-touch pressure thresholds in the adult penis. *British Journal of Urology International, 99*(4), 864-869. Retrieved July 27, 2018, from https://onlinelibrary.wiley.com/doi/pdf/10.1111/j.1464-410X.2006.06685.x

South African Health News Service. (2014, June 25). *Health-E News.* Retrieved July 27, 2018, from The South African Health News Service: https://www.health-e.org.za/2014/06/25/half-million-initiates-maimed-knife/

Spencer. (2019). Breakthrough in prostate cancer diagnosis as scientists 17 genes that radically increase chance of carriers devloping the disease. Daily Mail 3 May 2019, retrieved from https://www.dailymail.co.uk/health/article-6965065/Scientists-discover-17-genes-increase-chance-carriers-developing-prostate-cancer.html

Spencer and Hargreaves. (2018, July 17). Thousands of men are being left in agony as NHS denies them of hernia operations unless they are in so much pain they can't work. *Daily Mail.* Retrieved March 11, 2019, from https://tinyurl.com/y6ly88hk

Spiegel Online. (2013, September 27). German Court Sets New Circumcision Rules. *Spiegel Online.* Retrieved March 14, 2019, from http://www.spiegel.de/international/germany/new-circumcision-ruling-requires-doctors-to-discuss-procedure-a-924984.html

Starr, S. (2012, August 1). *Estimating Gender Disparities in Federal Criminal Cases.* Retrieved July 3, 2018, from University of Michigan Law School Scholarship Repository: https://tinyurl.com/y6bv28sr

Stats Wales. (2011). *Deaths by cause.* Retrieved April 21, 2018, from Stats Wales: https://statswales.gov.wales/Catalogue/Health-and-Social-Care/Births-Deaths-and-Conceptions/Deaths/Deaths-by-Cause

StatsWales. (2017). *Rough Sleepers by local authority.* Retrieved January 3, 2019, from https://statswales.gov.wales/Catalogue/Housing/Homelessness/Rough-Sleepers/roughsleepers-by-localauthority

StatsWales. (2018, July 26). *Households for which assistance has been provided by outcome, age and gender.* Retrieved September 21, 2018, from https://statswales.gov.wales/Catalogue/Housing/Homelessness/Statutory-Homelessness-Prevention-and-Relief/householdsforwhichassistancehasbeenprovided-by-outcome-age-gender

Steinmetz, S. K. (1977). The Battered Husband Syndrome. *VICTIMOLOGY 2*, 499-509.

Stemple. (2008/9). Male Rape and Human Rights. *Hastings Law Journal, 60*(3), 605. Retrieved April 11, 2019, from http://tinyurl.com/y3exwt5u

Stemple and Meyer. (2014, June). The Sexual Victimization of Men in America: New Data Challenge Old Assumptions. *Am J Public Health., 104*(6), e19-e26. Retrieved April 9, 2019, from https://www.ncbi.nlm.nih.gov/pmc/articles/PMC4062022/

Stemple and Meyer. (2017, October 10). Sexual Victimization by Women Is More Common Than Previously Known. *Scientific American.* Retrieved April 9, 2019, from https://www.scientificamerican.com/article/sexual-victimization-by-women-is-more-common-than-previously-known/

Stemple, Flores and Meyer. (2017, May). Sexual victimization perpetrated by women: Federal data reveal surprising prevalence. *Aggression and Violent Behavior, 34*, 302-311. doi:https://doi.org/10.1016/j.avb.2016.09.007

Stevens and Haidt. (2017, September 4). *The Greater Male Variability Hypothesis – An Addendum to our post on the Google Memo.* Retrieved April 27, 2019, from Heterodoxy Academy: https://heterodoxacademy.org/the-greater-male-variability-hypothesis/

Stockl et al. (2017, August 11). Child homicide perpetrators worldwide: a systematic review. *BMJ Paediatrics Open, 1*(1), e000112. doi:https://www.ncbi.nlm.nih.gov/pmc/articles/PMC5862181/

Stoet and Geary. (2018, February 14). The Gender-Equality Paradox in Science, Technology, Engineering, and Mathematics Education. *Psychological Science, 29*(4), 581-593 . Retrieved March 22, 2019, from https://doi.org/10.1177/0956797617741719

Storr. (2011, July 17). The rape of men: the darkest secret of war. *The Observer.* Retrieved April 11, 2019, from https://www.theguardian.com/society/2011/jul/17/the-rape-of-men

Stowe Family Law. (2017, January 27). *False accusations of domestic violence: what can you do?* Retrieved October 17, 2018, from Stow Family Law Blog: https://www.stowefamilylaw.co.uk/blog/2017/01/27/false-accusations-of-domestic-violence-what-can-you-do/

Stowe, M. (2011, October 26). *Is Paternity Fraud really a "ticking time bomb"?* Retrieved December 18, 2018, from Stowe Family Law Blog: https://www.stowefamilylaw.co.uk/blog/2011/10/26/is-paternity-fraud-really-a-ticking-time-bomb/

Straton, J. C. (1994). The Myth of the "Battered Husband Syndrome". *Masculinities: Interdisciplinary Studies on Gender 2, 4*, 79-83. Retrieved September 3, 2018, from https://tinyurl.com/y6r3xn5h

Stubbs, B. (2017). *National GCSE and A level performance figures.* Retrieved April 16, 2018, from Student Performance Analysis: http://www.bstubbs.co.uk/natfig.htm

Sylvester and Bennett. (2018, June 26). Use of 'chemical cosh' drugs on children doubles in a decade. *The Times.* Retrieved January 16, 2019, from https://www.thetimes.co.uk/edition/news/use-of-chemical-cosh-drugs-on-children-doubles-in-a-decade-2h90r9xgf

Taft et al. (2018, March 13). *Unintended and unwanted pregnancy in Australia: a cross-sectional, national random telephone survey of prevalence and outcomes.* Retrieved December 21, 2018, from https://www.mja.com.au/system/files/issues/209_09/10.5694mja17.01094.pdf

Taxpayers' Alliance. (2018, August 27). *Pension Inequality.* Retrieved March 25, 2019, from https://www.taxpayersalliance.com/pensions_inequality_press_release

Taylor and Lockwood. (1996, February). The prepuce: specialized mucosa of the penis and its loss to circumcision. *British Journal of Urology, 77*(2), 291-295. Retrieved July 27, 2018, from https://onlinelibrary.wiley.com/doi/abs/10.1046/j.1464-410X.1996.85023.x

The Equality Trust. (2016). *The Scale of Economic Inequality in the UK.* Retrieved May 18, 2018, from The Equality Trust: https://www.equalitytrust.org.uk/scale-economic-inequality-uk

The King's Fund. (2018). *Overview of the health and social care workforce.* Retrieved June 20, 2018, from https://www.kingsfund.org.uk/projects/time-think-differently/trends-workforce-overview

The Liz Library. (2018). *Fatherless Children.* Retrieved from http://www.thelizlibrary.org/site-index/site-index-frame.html#soulhttp://www.thelizlibrary.org/fatherless/effects-of-fatherlessness.html

The Male Contraception Initiative. (2018, March). *Contraceptives in active development.* Retrieved December 21, 2018, from https://www.malecontraceptive.org/male-contraception-research/prospective-male-contraceptive-options/

The Male Contraceptive Initiative. (2017, August 31). *Getting male birth control to market.* Retrieved December 21, 2018, from https://www.malecontraceptive.org/2017/08/31/birth-control-for-men-market/

The Marriage Foundation. (2014, June 6). *Nearly half of today's 20 year olds will never marry.* Retrieved November 20, 2018, from The Marriage Foundation: http://marriagefoundation.org.uk/nearly-half-of-todays-20-year-olds-will-never-marry/

The Marriage Foundation. (2016). *Top 10 key facts on marriage.* Retrieved November 20, 2018, from http://marriagefoundation.org.uk/research/

The Marriage Foundation. (2017, July). *Establishing the facts about family breakdown transforming the debate about marriage.* Retrieved November 20, 2018, from http://marriagefoundation.org.uk/wp-content/uploads/2017/07/Establishing-the-facts-about-family-breakdown-1.pdf

The Pensions Regulator. (2019). *Contributions and funding.* Retrieved from https://www.thepensionsregulator.gov.uk/en/employers/managing-a-scheme/contributions-and-funding

The Scotsman. (2005, March 29). *'Hidden' death toll of Forth Bridge revealed.* Retrieved June 20, 2018, from https://www.scotsman.com/news/hidden-death-toll-of-forth-bridge-revealed-1-1006801

This Is Africa. (2015, January 16). WATCH: Kenyan man forcibly circumcised in public. Retrieved March 15, 2019, from https://thisisafrica.me/watch-kenyan-man-forcibly-circumcised-public/

Thomas. (2010, February). *Are juries fair?* Retrieved March 2, 2019, from Ministry of Justice Research Series 1/10: https://www.justice.gov.uk/downloads/publications/research-and-analysis/moj-research/are-juries-fair-research.pdf

Thomas. (2012). *Homelessness kills: An analysis of the mortality of homeless people in early twenty-first century England Summary.* Retrieved January 3, 2019, from Crisis: https://www.crisis.org.uk/media/236799/crisis_homelessness_kills_es2012.pdf

Thomson, A. (2017, May 17). *Caring for the elderly shouldn't be a girl's job.* Retrieved June 27, 2018, from The Times: https://www.thetimes.co.uk/edition/comment/caring-for-the-elderly-shouldn-t-be-a-girl-s-job-hlk0vvtdf

Thurley and McInnes. (2018, November 6). *As women's pension age reaches 65, how equal are pension incomes?* HOC Library.

Tieman. (2011, March 16). *The one good man.* Retrieved April 27, 2019, from AVFM: https://www.avoiceformen.com/feminism/the-one-good-man/

Times Higher Education. (2016, June 28). *Improve gender balance in Irish HE or face fines, says review.* Retrieved April 18, 2018, from Times Higher Education: https://www.timeshighereducation.com/news/improve-gender-balance-irish-he-or-face-fines-says-review

Tobian and Gray. (2011, October 5). The Medical Benefits of Male Circumcision. *JAMA, 306*(13), 1479-1480. doi:10.1001/jama.2011.1431

Topping. (2018, November 21). Scrap juries in rape trials, Labour MP suggests. *The Guardian.* Retrieved March 4, 2019, from https://www.theguardian.com/society/2018/nov/21/scrap-juries-in-rape-trials-labour-mp-ann-coffey

Townsend and Syal. (2009, October 4). Up to 64,000 women in UK 'are child-sex offenders'. *The Guardian.* Retrieved April 8, 2019, from https://www.theguardian.com/society/2009/oct/04/uk-female-child-sex-offenders

Trading Economics. (2018, June). *United Kingdom GDP.* Retrieved from https://tradingeconomics.com/united-kingdom/gdp

Trovato. (1991, December 1). Sex, marital status, and suicide in Canada:. *Sociological Perspectives, 34*(4), 427-445. doi:https://doi.org/10.2307/1389401

Truss. (2017, Fen=bruary 12). *Liz Truss to ban 'humiliating' questioning of women by abusive exes in court.* Retrieved October 18, 2018, from https://www.politicshome.com/news/uk/home-affairs/justice-system/news/83274/liz-truss-ban-humiliating-questioning-women-abusive

Tsirigotis et al. (2011, August 1). *Med Sci Monit., 17*(8), PH65-70. doi:10.12659/MSM.881887

Tsopelas et al. (2012, July-August). Female perpetrators of sexual abuse of minors: What are the consequences for the victims? *International Journal of Law and Psychiatry, 35*(4), 305-310. doi:https://doi.org/10.1016/j.ijlp.2012.04.003

Tucker. (2018, September 12). *Scholarships for Women in Male-Dominated Industries.* Retrieved February 24, 2019, from TopUniversities.com: https://www.topuniversities.com/student-info/scholarship-advice/scholarships-women-male-dominated-industries

Turner. (2017, June 11). Oxford University blasted for 'insulting' decision to allow students to sit exams at home as it implies women are the 'weaker sex'. *The Telegraph.* Retrieved February 24, 2019, from https://www.telegraph.co.uk/education/2017/06/11/oxford-university-blasted-insulting-decision-allow-students/

Turner. (2018, March 15). Oxford University set to feminise curriculum by requesting inclusion of women on reading lists. Retrieved February 24, 2019, from https://www.telegraph.co.uk/education/2018/03/14/oxford-university-set-feminise-curriculum-requesting-inclusion/

Turner. (2019a, February 9). Oxford University's Classics degree to be overhauled in bid to boost number of female students getting Firsts. *The Telegraph.* Retrieved February 24, 2019, from https://www.telegraph.co.uk/education/2019/02/09/oxford-universitys-classics-degree-overhauled-bid-boost-number/

Turner. (2019b, January 11). Oxford ends women-only fellowship after university rules that it breaches equality law. *The Telegraph.* Retrieved February 24, 2019, from https://www.telegraph.co.uk/education/2019/01/11/oxford-ends-women-only-fellowship-university-rules-breaches/

Turner and Kirk. (2017, August 17). *A-level results 2017: Boys beat girls to top grades for first time in 17 years amid tougher exams.* Retrieved April 16, 2018, from The Telegraph: https://www.telegraph.co.uk/education/2017/08/17/a-level-results-2017-first-rise-top-grades-six-years-despite/

U.S. Department of Health and Human Services. (2012, December 20). *Intended and Unintended Births in the United States: 1982 - 2010.* Retrieved December 21, 2018, from National Health Statistics Reports: https://www.cdc.gov/nchs/data/nhsr/nhsr055.pdf

U.S. Preventive Services. (2018, May). *Final Recommendation Statement: Prostate Cancer Screening.* Retrieved June 14, 2018, from https://www.uspreventiveservicestaskforce.org/Page/Document/RecommendationStatementFinal/prostate-cancer-screening1

UCAS. (2017a, July 13). *June Deadline Analysis: Sex and age.* Retrieved April 16, 2018, from University and College Admissions System (UCAS): https://www.ucas.com/file/115911/download?token=EokhytEH

UCAS. (2017b, December). *Applicants and acceptances by groups of applicants 2017.* Retrieved April 16, 2018, from University and Colleges Admissions System:

https://www.ucas.com/corporate/data-and-analysis/ucas-undergraduate-releases/ucas-undergraduate-end-cycle-data-resources/applicants-and-acceptances-groups-applicants-2017

UCAS Analysis & Research. (2017, December 14). *End of Cycle Report 2017 Patterns by Applicant Characteristics.* Retrieved April 17, 2018, from UCAS: https://www.ucas.com/file/140396/download?token=TC7eMH9W

UCL Institute of Health Equity. (2015). *The impact of adverse experiences in the home on the health of children and young people, and inequalities in prevalence and effects.* Retrieved April 16, 2019, from http://www.instituteofhealthequity.org/resources-reports/the-impact-of-adverse-experiences-in-the-home-on-children-and-young-people/impact-of-adverse-experiences-in-the-home.pdf

UK Government. (1989). *Children Act 1989.* Retrieved from http://www.legislation.gov.uk/ukpga/1989/41/contents

UK Government. (2003). *Sexual Offences Act 2003.* Retrieved March 7, 2019, from http://www.legislation.gov.uk/ukpga/2003/42/contents

UK Government. (2010). *Equality Act 2010.* Retrieved April 14, 2018, from http://www.legislation.gov.uk/ukpga/2010/15/contents

UK Government. (2012a). *Legal Aid, Sentencing and Punishment of Offenders Act 2012.* Retrieved from http://www.legislation.gov.uk/ukpga/2012/10/contents/enacted

UK Government. (2012b). *Preventing suicide in England: A cross-government outcomes strategy to save lives.* Mental Health and Disability Division, Department of Health.

UK Government. (2013, November 25). *School workforce in England: November 2012.* Retrieved April 17, 2018, from UK Givernment: https://www.gov.uk/government/statistics/school-workforce-in-england-november-2012

UK Government. (2014). *Children and Families Act 2014.* Retrieved November 14, 2018, from http://www.legislation.gov.uk/ukpga/2014/6/contents/enacted

UK Government. (2015a, August 13). *Sex offender sentences hit record levels.* Retrieved April 7, 2019, from https://www.gov.uk/government/news/sex-offender-sentences-hit-record-levels

UK Government. (2015b). *National curriculum assessments: key stage 2, 2015 (revised).* Retrieved April 15, 2018, from https://www.gov.uk/government/statistics/national-curriculum-assessments-at-key-stage-2-2015-revised

UK Government. (2016a, September 1). *National curriculum assessments: key stage 2, 2016 (provisional).* Retrieved April 15, 2018, from https://www.gov.uk/government/statistics/national-curriculum-assessments-key-stage-2-2016-provisional

UK Government. (2016b, March 29). *Prostate cancer risk management programme: overview.* Retrieved from https://www.gov.uk/guidance/prostate-cancer-risk-management-programme-overview

UK Government. (2017a, January 28). *Gender Pay Gap Reporting.* Retrieved June 18, 2018, from https://www.gov.uk/government/news/gender-pay-gap-reporting

UK Government. (2017b, July 20). *School workforce in England: November 2016.* Retrieved April 17, 2018, from UK Government: https://www.gov.uk/government/statistics/school-workforce-in-england-november-2016

UK Government. (2017c, June 30). *Prison population figures: Population weekly bulletin 30 June 2017*. Retrieved from https://www.gov.uk/government/statistics/prison-population-figures-2017

UK Government. (2017d, November 28). *HIV: annual data tables*. Retrieved August 6, 2018, from https://www.gov.uk/government/statistics/hiv-annual-data-tables

UK Government. (2018a, March 6). *Income and tax, by gender, region and country*. Retrieved June 30, 2018, from https://www.gov.uk/government/statistics/income-and-tax-by-gender-region-and-country-2010-to-2011

UK Government. (2018b, March 8). *Policy paper Spring Budget 2017*. Retrieved June 19, 2018, from https://www.gov.uk/government/publications/spring-budget-2017-documents/spring-budget-2017

UK Government. (2018c, June 18). *Search gender pay gap data*. Retrieved from https://gender-pay-gap.service.gov.uk/

UK Government. (2018d, May). *Minister for Women and Equalities*. Retrieved April 14, 2018, from https://www.gov.uk/government/ministers/minister-for-women-and-equalities--3

UK Government. (2018e, January 25). *Revised GCSE and equivalent results in England: 2016 to 2017*. Retrieved April 15, 2018, from https://www.gov.uk/government/statistics/revised-gcse-and-equivalent-results-in-england-2016-to-2017

UK Government. (2018f, February 5). *HPV vaccination programme for men who have sex with men*. Retrieved April 22, 2018, from https://www.gov.uk/government/news/hpv-vaccination-programme-for-men-who-have-sex-with-men

UK Government. (2018g, June 29). *Prison population figures: 2018*. Retrieved July 1, 2018, from https://www.gov.uk/government/statistics/prison-population-figures-2018

UK Government. (2018h, June 27). *Secretary of State launches dedicated strategy to 'break the cycle' of female offending*. Retrieved July 3, 2018, from https://www.gov.uk/government/news/secretary-of-state-launches-dedicated-strategy-to-break-the-cycle-of-female-offending

UK Government. (2018j). *Child Maintenance Calculator*. Retrieved from https://www.gov.uk/calculate-your-child-maintenance

UK Government. (2018k, April 3). *Homelessness data: notes and definitions*. Retrieved December 31, 2018, from https://www.gov.uk/guidance/homelessness-data-notes-and-definitions

UK Government. (2018m, August 16). *Outcomes by offence data tool 2017*. Retrieved April 8, 2019, from Criminal Justice System statistics quarterly: December 2017: https://www.gov.uk/government/statistics/criminal-justice-system-statistics-quarterly-december-2017

UK Government. (2018n, November 29). *Chapter 5: Defendants tables*. Retrieved April 8, 2019, from Women and the criminal justice system 2017: https://www.gov.uk/government/statistics/women-and-the-criminal-justice-system-2017

UK Government. (2018p, April 20). *Foreign Secretary launches Platform for Girls' Education*. Retrieved March 18, 2019, from https://www.gov.uk/government/news/foreign-secretary-launches-platform-for-girls-education

UK Government. (2018q, July 24). *HPV vaccine to be given to boys in England*. Retrieved March 10, 2019, from https://www.gov.uk/government/news/hpv-vaccine-to-be-given-to-boys-in-england

UK Government. (2018r, September 5). *National HIV surveillance data tables.* Retrieved March 10, 2019, from https://www.gov.uk/government/statistics/hiv-annual-data-tables

UK Government. (2018s, June 28). *Tables: school workforce census 2017.* Retrieved March 28, 2019, from https://www.gov.uk/government/statistics/school-workforce-in-england-november-2017

UK Government. (2018t, September 28). *Personal pensions: estimated number of individuals contributing by gender and age.* Retrieved March 25, 2019, from https://www.gov.uk/government/statistics/personal-pensions-estimated-number-of individuals-contributing-by-gender-and-age

UK Government. (2018u, April). *Guide to Determining Financial Eligibility for Controlled Work and Family Mediation.* Retrieved from https://assets.publishing.service.gov.uk/government/uploads/system/uploads/attachment_data/file/698225/guide-to-determining-controlled-work.pdf

UK Government. (2018v, April 26). *Civil legal aid: means testing.* Retrieved from https://www.gov.uk/guidance/civil-legal-aid-means-testing

UK Government. (2019a, March 6). *Income and tax, by gender, region and country.* Retrieved from https://www.gov.uk/government/statistics/income-and-tax-by-gender-region-and-country-2010-to-2011

UK Government. (2019b, January 21). *Domestic abuse consultation response and draft bill.* Retrieved April 13, 2019, from https://www.gov.uk/government/publications/domestic-abuse-consultation-response-and-draft-bill

UK Government Equalities Office. (2011, June 30). *Equality Act 2010: Public Sector Equality Duty What Do I Need To Know Quick Start Guide for Public Sector Organisations.* Retrieved April 29, 2018, from https://assets.publishing.service.gov.uk/government/uploads/system/uploads/attachment_data/file/85041/equality-duty.pdf

UK Parliament. (2015, March 12). *Impact of changes to civil legal aid under Part 1 of the Legal Aid, Sentencing and Punishment of Offenders Act 2012 - Justice: 4 The domestic violence gateway*. Retrieved October 17, 2018, from https://publications.parliament.uk/pa/cm201415/cmselect/cmjust/311/31107.htm

UK Parliament. (2017a, November 14). *Westminster Hall hosts debate on International Men's Day.* Retrieved May 8, 2018, from https://www.parliament.uk/business/committees/committees-a-z/commons-select/backbench-business-committee/news-parliament-2017/international-mens-day-debate-17-19/

UK Parliament. (2017b, April 20). *Prisons and Courts Bill 2016-17.* Retrieved October 18, 2018, from https://services.parliament.uk/bills/2016-17/prisonsandcourts.html

UK Parliament. (2017c). *Prisons and Courts Bill (HC Bill 170).* Retrieved October 18, 2018, from https://publications.parliament.uk/pa/bills/cbill/2016-2017/0170/cbill_2016-20170170_en_6.htm

UK Parliament. (2018a, May 19). *Women and Equalities Committee.* Retrieved April 14, 2018, from https://www.parliament.uk/womenandequalities

UK Parliament. (2018b, May 2). *HPV Vaccination for Boys.* Retrieved from Hansard.Parliament.UK: https://hansard.parliament.uk/commons/2018-05-

02/debates/234E27F7-7D80-4B93-A72F-8F36A733A504/HPVVaccinationForBoys

UK Parliament. (2018c, June 27). *Canals and Rivers.* Retrieved from https://www.parliament.uk/about/living-heritage/transformingsociety/transportcomms/canalsrivers/overview/canal-acts/

UK Parliament. (2018d, July 6). *Statutory Homelessness in England.* Retrieved December 31, 2018, from https://researchbriefings.parliament.uk/ResearchBriefing/Summary/SN01164

UK Parliament. (2019, February 7). *HPV Vaccination for Boys: Catch-up Programme.* Retrieved March 10, 2019, from https://www.theyworkforyou.com/debates/?id=2019-02-07b.395.3#g395.4

UK Statistics Authority. (2017, November). *Systemic Review of Public Value: Statistics on Housing and Planning in the UK.* Retrieved December 31, 2017, from Office for Statistics Regulation: https://www.statisticsauthority.gov.uk/wp-content/uploads/2017/11/Systemic-Review-of-Statistics-on-Housing-and-Planning-in-the-UK20171110-corrected.pdf

UNAIDS. (2010, April). *Neonatal and child male circumcision: a global review.* Retrieved March 14, 2019, from World Health Orgabisation: https://www.who.int/hiv/pub/malecircumcision/neonatal_child_MC_UNAIDS.pdf

UNdata. (2015). *Youth literacy rate, population 15-24 years (%).* Retrieved March 18, 2019, from http://data.un.org/Data.aspx?d=UNESCO&f=series%3aLR_AG15T24

UNICEF. (2006). *Behind Closed Doors The Impact of Domestic Violence on Children.* Retrieved September 3, 2018, from https://www.unicef.org/media/files/BehindClosedDoors.pdf

University of California Department of Urology. (2018). *Phimosis.* Retrieved August 5, 2018, from https://urology.ucsf.edu/patient-care/children/phimosis

US Department of Education. (2004). *Educator Sexual Misconduct: A Synthesis of Existing Literature.* Retrieved April 8, 2019, from https://www2.ed.gov/rschstat/research/pubs/misconductreview/report.pdf

US Department of Health & Human Services. (2012, December 9). *Information on Poverty and Income Statistics: A Summary of 2012 Current Population Survey Data* . Retrieved November 25, 2018, from https://aspe.hhs.gov/basic-report/information-poverty-and-income-statistics-summary-2012-current-population-survey-data

van Howe. (1997, November). Variability in penile appearance and penile findings: a prospective study. *British Journal of Urology, 80*(5), 776-782. doi:https://doi.org/10.1046/j.1464-410X.1997.00467.x

van Howe. (2006, July 12). *Conservative Treatment of Phimosis:.* Retrieved August 5, 2018, from CIRP: http://www.cirp.org/library/treatment/phimosis/

van Howe. (2013). Sexually Transmitted Infections and Male Circumcision: A Systematic Review and Meta-Analysis. *ISRN Urology*, 109842. doi:http://dx.doi.org/10.1155/2013/109846

Vigil, J. (2007). Asymmetries in the Friendship Preferences and Social. *Human Nature, 18*, 143-161. Retrieved May 7, 2018, from https://www.researchgate.net/publication/226106917_Asymmetries_in_the_Friendship_Preferences_and_Social_Styles_of_Men_and_Women

Voith et al. (2018, June 30). A Paradigm Shift in Batterer Intervention Programming: A Need to Address Unresolved Trauma . *Trauma, Violence & Abuse.* doi:https://doi.org/10.1177/1524838018791268

Voyer and Voyer. (2014, April 28). Gender Differences in Scholastic Achievement: A Meta-Analysis. *Psychological Bulletin, 140*(4), 1174-1204. Retrieved May 21, 2018, from https://www.apa.org/pubs/journals/releases/bul-a0036620.pdf

Walker, P. (2018, January 3). *White working-class boys should be more aspirational, says Labour minister.* Retrieved May 1, 2018, from The Guardian: https://www.theguardian.com/education/2018/jan/03/white-working-class-boys-should-be-more-aspirational-says-labour-minister

Walsh. (2009, November 1). Divergence in Contributing Factors for Suicide among Men and Women in Kentucky: Recommendations to Raise Public Awareness. *Public Health Reports, 124*(6), 861-867. doi:https://doi.org/10.1177/003335490912400614

Walter. (2012, January 24). The top 30 statistics you need to know when marketing to women. Retrieved March 21, 2019, from https://thenextweb.com/socialmedia/2012/01/24/the-top-30-stats-you-need-to-know-when-marketing-to-women/

Ward. (2019, March 24). Lib Dem leadership hopeful Layla Moran admits slapping boyfriend in row over computer cable. *Telegraph.* Retrieved from https://www.telegraph.co.uk/news/2019/03/24/lib-dem-leadership-hopeful-layla-moran-admits-slapping-boyfriend/

Warren. (2011, January 22). Intactivist Doctor - John Warren. Retrieved March 15, 2019, from https://www.youtube.com/watch?v=5TYTBvTWz-M&feature=player_embedded

Watson, L. R. (2014). Unspeakable Mutilations: Circumcised Men Speak Out. Ashburton, New Zealand.

Weare, Porter and Evans. (June 2017). *Forced to Penetrate Cases: Lived Experiences of Men.* Lancaster University Law School. Retrieved April 10, 2019, from http://wp.lancs.ac.uk/forced-to-penetrate-cases/files/2016/11/Project-Report-Final.pdf

Wearmouth. (2019, March 26). Most Women In Prison Are 'There Because Of A Man', Says David Lammy. *Huffington Post.* Retrieved from https://www.huffingtonpost.co.uk/entry/most-bame-women-in-prison-there-because-of-a-man-says-david-lammy_uk_5c9a0912e4b07435554a478c

Weitoft et al. (2003, January 25). Mortality, severe morbidity, and injury in children living with single parents in Sweden: a population-based study. *The Lancet, 361*(9354), 289-295. doi:https://doi.org/10.1016/S0140-6736(03)12324-0

Wellings et al. (2001, December 1). Sexual behaviour in Britain: early heterosexual experience. *The Lancet, 358, Issue 9296*(9296), 1843-1850. doi:https://doi.org/10.1016/S0140-6736(01)06885-4

Wellings et al. (2013, November 30). The prevalence of unplanned pregnancy and associated factors in Britain: findings from the third National Survey of Sexual Attitudes and Lifestyles (Natsal-3). *The Lancet, 382*(9907), 1807-1816. doi:10.1016/S0140-6736(13)62071-1

Welsh Government. (2015a, July 16). *Talk to me 2.* Retrieved February 17, 2019, from Suicide and self harm prevention strategy for Wales 2015-2020: https://gov.wales/topics/health/publications/health/reports/talk2/?lang=en

Welsh Government. (2015b). *Talk to me 2 (Objectives): Suicide and Self Harm Prevention Action Plan for Wales 2015-2020.* Retrieved February 17, 2019, from https://gov.wales/docs/dhss/publications/150716talken.pdf

Welsh Government. (2015c). *Talk to me 2 (main activities): Annexes – Suicide and Self Harm Prevention Strategy and Action Plan for Wales 2015-2020.* Retrieved February 17, 2019, from https://gov.wales/docs/dhss/publications/150716annexesen.pdf

Welsh Government. (2018a, February 1). *National rough sleeping count.* Retrieved 1 3, 2019, from https://gov.wales/statistics-and-research/national-rough-sleeping-count/?lang=en

Welsh Government. (2018b, September 27). *Household estimates.* Retrieved Januar 3, 2018, from https://gov.wales/statistics-and-research/household-estimates/?lang=en

Welsh Government. (2018c, February 13). *National Survey for Wales, 2016-17: Loneliness.* Retrieved January 4, 2019, from https://gov.wales/docs/statistics/2018/180213-national-survey-2016-17-loneliness-en.pdf

Westervelt, A. (2015, April 30). *The medical research gender gap: how excluding women from clinical trials is hurting our health.* Retrieved from https://www.theguardian.com/lifeandstyle/2015/apr/30/fda-clinical-trials-gender-gap-epa-nih-institute-of-medicine-cardiovascular-disease

Whitcombe, S. (2017). Parental alienation: Psychological distress and mental health. *Male Psychology Conference, 4th June 2017 (University College London).* Retrieved October 19, 2018, from https://www.malepsychology.org.uk/wp-content/uploads/2017/08/Male-Psych-slides-edited.pdf

White and Witty. (2009, May 1). Men's under use of health services - finding an alternative approach. *Journal of Men's Health, 6*(2), 95-97. Retrieved April 30, 2018, from https://www.liebertpub.com/doi/full/10.1016/j.jomh.2009.03.001

White, H. (2013, January 17). *Eliminating feminist teacher bias erases boys' falling grades, study finds.* Retrieved June 12, 2018, from https://www.lifesitenews.com/news/eliminating-feminist-teacher-bias-erases-boys-falling-grades-study-finds

Wiedersehn, S. (2017, February 8). *World Journal of Clinical Pediatrics study finds evidence in favour of male infant circumcision.* Retrieved August 5, 2018, from News Corp Australia Network: https://www.news.com.au/lifestyle/parenting/babies/world-journal-of-clinical-pediatrics-study-finds-evidence-in-favour-of-male-infant-circumcision/news-story/c47339e787d393e247777ab3b543ff5c

Wilder, Mobasher and Hammer. (2004, November 1). Genetic Evidence for Unequal Effective Population Sizes of Human Females and Males. *Molecular Biology and Evolution, 21*(11), 2047-2057. doi:https://doi.org/10.1093/molbev/msh214

Wilkins et al. (2008, November). *The Gender and Access to Health Services Study.* Retrieved April 29, 2018, from Ne's Health Forum: https://www.menshealthforum.org.uk/sites/default/files/pdf/gender_and_access_to_health_services_study_2008.pdf

Williams and Ceci. (2015, April 28). National hiring experiments reveal 2:1 faculty preference for women on STEM tenure track. *PNAS (Proceedings of the National Academy of Sciences), 112*(17), 5360-5365. doi:https://doi.org/10.1073/pnas.1418878112

Williams et al. (2006, July 11). The Potential Impact of Male Circumcision on HIV in Sub-Saharan Africa. *PLOS medicine, 3*(7), e262. doi:https://doi.org/10.1371/journal.pmed.0030262

Williams, Papadopoulou and Booth. (2012, March). *Prisoners' childhood and family backgrounds Results from the Surveying Prisoner Crime Reduction (SPCR) longitudinal cohort study of prisoners.* Retrieved July 4, 2018, from Ministry of Justice: https://assets.publishing.service.gov.uk/government/uploads/system/uploads/attachment_data/file/278837/prisoners-childhood-family-backgrounds.pdf

Windisch, K. (2010, July 6). *neonatal circumcision.* Retrieved June 27, 2018, from https://www.youtube.com/watch?v=bXVFFI76ff0&t=3m25s&has_verified=1

Wintour, P. (2008, August 1). DNA testing: One in 500 fathers wrongly identified by mothers in Child Support Agency claims. Retrieved December 18, 2018, from The Guardian: https://www.theguardian.com/politics/2008/aug/01/freedomofinformation.childprotection

Wolford-Clevenger et al. (2015). Prevalence and correlates of suicidal ideation among court-referred male perpetrators of intimate partner violence. *Psychological Services, 12*(1), 9-15. doi:http://dx.doi.org/10.1037/a0037338

Wolford-Clevenger et al. (2017, March). A test of the interpersonal-psychological theory of suicide among arrested domestic violence offenders. *Psychiatry Research, 249*, 195-199. doi:10.1016/j.psychres.2017.01.029

Women's Aid. (2015). Retrieved October 19, 2018, from https://www.womensaid.org.uk/childfirst/

Women's Aid. (2016, January). *Nineteen Child Homicides.* Retrieved October 19, 2018, from https://1q7dqy2unor827bqjls0c4rn-wpengine.netdna-ssl.com/wp-content/uploads/2016/01/Child-First-Nineteen-Child-Homicides-Report.pdf

Women's Aid. (2018a). *What is domestic abuse?* Retrieved September 3, 2018, from women's aid: https://www.womensaid.org.uk/information-support/what-is-domestic-abuse/

Women's Aid. (2018b). *What we believe.* Retrieved September 3, 2018, from women's aid: https://www.womensaid.org.uk/what-we-believe/

Women's Aid. (2018c). *How common is domestic abuse?* Retrieved September 7, 2018, from https://www.womensaid.org.uk/information-support/what-is-domestic-abuse/how-common-is-domestic-abuse/

Woodall. (2019, February 15). *Solving Parental Alienation With The Legal and Mental Health Interlock.* Retrieved from Karen Woodall's blog: https://karenwoodall.blog/2019/02/15/solving-parental-alienation-with-the-legal-and-mental-health-interlock/

Woodall, K. (2018, October 14). *Fogging the Issue: CAFCASS and The High Conflict Pathway.* Retrieved October 20, 2018, from https://karenwoodall.blog/2018/10/14/fogging-the-issue-cafcass-and-the-high-conflict-pathway/

Woodruff, T. (2010, June 10). Putting gender on the agenda. *Nature, 465*(7299). Retrieved June 13, 2018, from https://www.nature.com/articles/465665a.pdf

World Health Organisation. (2008). *Global Burden of Disease: 2004 Update.* Retrieved January 20, 2019, from https://www.who.int/healthinfo/global_burden_disease/2004_report_update/en/

World Health Organisation. (2012). *Non-surgical male circumcision device.* Retrieved August 3, 2018, from http://www.who.int/medical_devices/innovation/compendium_med_dev2012_13.pdf

World Health Organisation. (2017, August). *Voluntary medical male circumcision for HIV prevention in 14 priority countries in eastern and southern Africa: Progess Brief 2017.* Retrieved August 6, 2018, from http://www.who.int/hiv/pub/malecircumcision/vmmc-progress-brief-2017/en/

World Health Organisation. (2018a, June). *Disease burden and mortality estimates: DALY estimates, 2000–2016: Global summary estimates.* Retrieved January 20, 2019, from https://www.who.int/healthinfo/global_burden_disease/estimates/en/index1.html

World Health Organisation. (2018b, July 17). *Prevalence of HIV among adults aged 15 to 49: Estimates by Country.* Retrieved August 6, 2018, from Global Health Observatory data repository: http://apps.who.int/gho/data/node.main.622?lang=en

Wurtele et al. (2013, November 11). Sexual Interest in Children Among an Online Sample of Men and Women: Prevalence and Correlates. *Sexual Abuse, 26*(6), 546-568 . doi:https://doi.org/10.1177/1079063213503688

Wyder. (2009, August). Separation as a suicide risk factor. *J.Affect.Discord, 116*(3), 208-213. doi:10.1016/j.jad.2008.11.007

Yingying Wang et al . (2013, July 19). Do men consult less than women? An analysis of routinely collected UK general practice data. *BMJ Open, 3*, 003320. Retrieved April 29, 2018, from BMJ Open: http://bmjopen.bmj.com/content/bmjopen/3/8/e003320.full.pdf

Yorkshire Dales Trail. (2011, May 19). *Ribblehead Viaduct - The Human Story.* Retrieved June 20, 2018, from http://www.yorkshiredales-trail.co.uk/blog/ribblehead-viaduct-the-human-story/

Your Fertility. (2018). *Age.* Retrieved December 21, 2018, from https://www.yourfertility.org.au/everyone/age

Zeiss. (1981). Sex Differences in Initiation of and Adjustment to Divorce. *Journal of Divorce, 4*(2), 21-33. doi:https://doi.org/10.1300/J279v04n02_02

Zuleyka Zevallos. (2015, Msy 5). *The myth about women in science? Bias at work in the study of gender inequality in STEM.* Retrieved February 25, 2019, from London School of Economics: https://blogs.lse.ac.uk/impactofsocialsciences/2015/05/05/women-in-science-gender-inequality-stem/

Index

CPSIA information can be obtained
at www.ICGtesting.com
Printed in the USA
BVHW011307260620
582322BV00001B/1

9 780957 168886